Operations

Operations Research
Principles and Applications
SECOND EDITION

G. SRINIVASAN

Professor
Department of Management Studies
Indian Institute of Technology Madras

PHI Learning Private Limited

New Delhi-110001
2010

₹ 350.00

OPERATIONS RESEARCH: Principles and Applications, Second Edition
G. Srinivasan

© 2010 by PHI Learning Private Limited, New Delhi. All rights reserved. No part of this book may be reproduced in any form, by mimeograph or any other means, without permission in writing from the publisher.

ISBN-978-81-203-4208-8

The export rights of this book are vested solely with the publisher.

Third Printing (Second Edition) ... ... **October, 2010**

Published by Asoke K. Ghosh, PHI Learning Private Limited, M-97, Connaught Circus, New Delhi-110001 and Printed by Baba Barkha Nath Printers, Bahadurgarh, Haryana-124507.

To

My Parents
and
My Wife and Our Children

Contents

Preface   *xiii*
Acknowledgements   *xv*
About Operations Research   *xvii*

1. Linear Programming Formulations   1–20
    1.1 Terminology   *2*
    1.2 Assumptions in Linear Programming Problem   *7*
    Solved Examples   *8*
    CASE STUDY 1.1 Choosing the Best School   *16*
    Exercises   *17*

2. Linear Programming—Solutions   21–59
    2.1 The Graphical Method   *21*
    2.2 The Algebraic Method   *23*
    2.3 Algebraic Form of the Simplex Algorithm   *24*
    2.4 Tabular Form of the Simplex Algorithm   *26*
       2.4.1 Initialization   *30*
       2.4.2 Iteration   *35*
       2.4.3 Termination   *36*
       2.4.4 Special Examples   *41*
    Solved Examples   *44*
    CASE STUDY 2.1   *53*
    Exercises   *54*

3. Duality and Sensitivity Analysis   60–103
    3.1 Dual to the LP with Mixed Type of Constraints   *61*
    3.2 Primal–Dual Relationships   *63*
    3.3 Mathematical Explanation to the Dual   *68*
    3.4 Economic Interpretation of the Dual   *68*
    3.5 Simplex Method Solves both the Primal and the Dual   *69*
    3.6 The Dual Simplex Algorithm   *71*

viii Contents

    3.7   Solving Problems with Mixed Type of Constraints   73
    3.8   Matrix Representation of the Simplex Method   75
    3.9   Sensitivity Analysis   79
          3.9.1   Changes in Values of Objective Function Coefficients (C_j)   80
          3.9.2   Changes in RHS Values   81
          3.9.3   Changes in Coefficient of Constraint (of a Non-basic Variable)   82
          3.9.4   Adding a New Product   83
          3.9.5   Adding a New Constraint   83
    Solved Examples   84
    CASE STUDY 3.1   The Writewell Pen Company   95
    Exercises   96

4. Transportation Problem   104–144

    4.1   Solving Balanced Transportation Problems   105
          4.1.1   North West Corner Rule   106
          4.1.2   Minimum Cost Method   107
          4.1.3   Vogel's Approximation Method (Penalty Cost Method)   108
    4.2   Basic Feasible Solution to a Transportation Problem   110
          4.2.1   Degenerate Basic Feasible Solutions   111
    4.3   Finding the Optimal Solution to the Transportation Problem   112
          4.3.1   Stepping Stone Method   112
          4.3.2   Modified Distribution (MODI) Method or *u-v* Method   116
          4.3.3   Optimum Solution with a Degenerate Basic Feasible Solution   119
    4.4   Getting Started—Which Method?   123
          4.4.1   Choosing between the Stepping Stone Method and the MODI Method   123
    4.5   Optimality of the MODI Method   124
    4.6   Solving Unbalanced Transportation Problems   125
    4.7   Unimodularity of the Transportation Problem   127
    Solved Examples   128
    CASE STUDY 4.1   Sri Bhima Sweets   138
    Exercises   139

5. Assignment Problem   145–170

    5.1   Assignment Problem, Transportation Problem and Linear Programming   146
    5.2   Properties of the Optimal Solution   146
    5.3   Solving the Assignment Problem—Hungarian Algorithm   147
    5.4   Additional Points   152
    5.5   The Optimality of the Hungarian Algorithm   153
    5.6   The Auction Algorithm for Assignment Problem   154
    Solved Examples   158
    CASE STUDY 5.1   The Fountain Pen Company   165
    Exercises   166

Contents   ix

6. Advanced Linear Programming   **171–237**
- 6.1 How Good is the Simplex Method? *171*
  - 6.1.1 Time Taken Per Iteration *171*
  - 6.1.2 Efficient Ways to Invert the Basis Matrix *172*
- 6.2 Simplex Algorithm for Bounded Variables *180*
  - 6.2.1 Algebraic Method *181*
  - 6.2.2 Simplex Algorithm for Bounded Variables *183*
- 6.3 Solving the One-dimensional Cutting Stock Problem *185*
  - 6.3.1 Column Generation—Cutting Stock Problem *186*
  - 6.3.2 Knapsack Problem *188*
- 6.4 The Decomposition Algorithm *193*
  - 6.4.1 The Master Problem *193*
- 6.5 The Primal Dual Algorithm *199*
- 6.6 Goal Programming *202*
- 6.7 How Fast and Good is the Simplex Method? *210*

Solved Examples   *214*
CASE STUDY 6.1   Allocating Minor Streams   *231*
CASE STUDY 6.2   Western Constructions   *233*
Exercises   *234*

7. Integer Programming   **238–300**
- 7.1 Integer Programming Formulation *239*
- 7.2 How to Solve Integer Programming Problems? *244*
- 7.3 Types of Integer Programming Problems *246*
- 7.4 Zero-One Problems *246*
- 7.5 Solving Zero-One Problems—Implicit Enumeration *248*
  - 7.5.1 The Additive Algorithm *249*
  - 7.5.2 Speeding the Search *252*
  - 7.5.3 Converting a Given Problem to the Standard Form *252*
  - 7.5.4 Zero-One Non-linear Problems *253*
- 7.6 Integer Programming—Gomory's Cutting Plane Algorithm *253*
  - 7.6.1 Explaining the Gomory Cut *256*
  - 7.6.2 Other Issues in the Cutting Plane Algorithm *257*
  - 7.6.3 Efficient Representation of the Simplex Table for Integer Programming *258*
- 7.7 Branch and Bound Algorithm for Integer Programming *259*
  - 7.7.1 Improving the Lower Bound *265*
  - 7.7.2 Implicit Enumeration Algorithm as a Branch and Bound Algorithm *266*
- 7.8 All Integer Algorithms *268*
  - 7.8.1 All Integer Dual Algorithm *268*
  - 7.8.2 All Integer Primal Algorithm *271*
  - 7.8.3 Mixed Constraints, Infeasibility and Unboundedness *274*

7.9 Mixed Integer Programming   276
    7.9.1 A Cutting Plane Algorithm for the MILP   277
    7.9.2 Bender's Partitioning Algorithm for MILP   279
Solved Examples   281
CASE STUDY 7.1   Balaji Auto Garage   294
CASE STUDY 7.2   Purewhite Washing Machines   295
Exercises   296

8. Network Problems   301–349

8.1 Graph Theory—Basic Definitions   301
8.2 Interesting Problems in Graph Theory   303
8.3 Some More Definitions and Problems in Graph Theory   303
8.4 Some Graph Theoretic Problems and Corresponding Optimization Problems   303
    8.4.1 Spanning Trees   303
    8.4.2 Matching Problem   304
    8.4.3 Travelling Salesman Problem and Hamiltonian Circuits   305
    8.4.4 The Chinese Postman Problem and Eulerian Circuits   305
8.5 Network Problems   306
    8.5.1 Capacitated Minimum Cost Flow Problem on a Network   306
8.6 The Minimum Spanning Tree Problem (MST Problem)   308
    8.6.1 Prim's Algorithm   308
    8.6.2 Kruskal's Algorithm   309
    8.6.3 Applications of Minimum Spanning Trees   309
8.7 The Shortest Path Problem   309
    8.7.1 Dijkstra's Algorithm   310
    8.7.2 Other Instances of Shortest Path Problem   312
    8.7.3 Dual of the Shortest Path Problem   313
    8.7.4 Shortest Path between All Pairs of Nodes in a Network   314
    8.7.5 Successive Shortest Path in a Network   316
    8.7.6 Constrained Shortest Path Problems   317
8.8 The Maximum Flow Problem   318
    8.8.1 Flow Augmenting Path   320
    8.8.2 A Labelling Algorithm for Flow Augmenting Path   322
    8.8.3 Maximum Flow and Minimum Cut   324
    8.8.4 The Shortest Augmenting Path Algorithm   326
8.9 Minimum Cost Flow Problem—Transshipment Problem   330
    8.9.1 Optimality of the Network Simplex Method   333
    8.9.2 A Transportation Model for the Problem   334
Solved Examples   335
CASE STUDY 8.1   The Kasi-Yatra Problem   345
Exercises   346

9. Travelling Salesman and Distribution Problems   350–390

- 9.1 The Travelling Salesman Problem (TSP)   *350*
  - 9.1.1 Mathematical Programming Formulation of the Travelling Salesman Problem   *351*
  - 9.1.2 Another Formulation for Subtour Elimination   *352*
  - 9.1.3 The TSP and the Theory of NP-Completeness   *353*
- 9.2 Optimal Solution to TSP Using Branch and Bound Algorithms   *354*
  - 9.2.1 Algorithm 1   *355*
  - 9.2.2 Algorithm 2   *360*
  - 9.2.3 Algorithm 3   *362*
- 9.3 Heuristic Algorithms for the TSP   *365*
  - 9.3.1 Nearest Neighbourhood Algorithm   *365*
  - 9.3.2 Pairwise Interchange Heuristic   *366*
  - 9.3.3 Three-opt Heuristic   *366*
  - 9.3.4 Twice Around the Tree Heuristic   *366*
  - 9.3.5 Heuristic Using Perfect Matching   *368*
- 9.4 Search Algorithms   *370*
- 9.5 Chinese Postman Problem   *371*
  - 9.5.1 An Algorithm Using Shortest Paths and Matching   *372*
- 9.6 Vehicle Routing Problems   *373*
  - 9.6.1 Optimal Solutions   *374*
  - 9.6.2 Heuristic Solutions   *375*
  - 9.6.3 Holmes and Parker Refinement   *376*
  - 9.6.4 Other Forms of Savings Based Method   *377*
- 9.7 Other Forms of Vehicle Routeing Problems   *378*
- *Solved Examples*   *378*
- CASE STUDY 9.1   The Wafer Electronics Company   *386*
- *Exercises*   *387*

10. Dynamic Programming   391–424

- 10.1 Stage Coach Problem   *391*
- 10.2 Reliability Problem   *394*
- 10.3 Equipment Replacement Problem   *396*
- 10.4 Continuous Variables   *398*
- 10.5 Continuous Variables—Higher Degree   *400*
- 10.6 Factorizing the Terms   *401*
- 10.7 Manpower Planning Problem   *402*
- 10.8 Oil Exploration Problem   *404*
- 10.9 Integer Programming   *405*
- 10.10 Linear Programming   *407*
- 10.11 Some Additional Comments   *408*
- *Solved Examples*   *409*
- CASE STUDY 10.1   Nalabagam Foods   *421*
- *Exercises*   *421*

11. Basic Queueing Models   425–441
   11.1 Single Server Infinite Queue Length Model   *426*
   11.2 Single Server Finite Queue Length Model   *429*
   11.3 Multiple Server Infinite Queue Length Model   *430*
   11.4 Multiple Server Finite Queue Length Model   *431*
   Solved Examples   *431*
   CASE STUDY 11.1   The Railway Reservation System   *439*
   Exercises   *440*

12. Non-linear Programming   442–452
   12.1 Unconstrained Extremum Points   *442*
   12.2 Constrained Optimization Problems—Lagrangean Method for Equality Constraints   *443*
   12.3 Constrained Optimization Problems—Kuhn Tucker Conditions for Inequality Constraints   *444*
   12.4 Quadratic Programming   *446*
   Solved Examples   *448*
   CASE STUDY 12.1   An Investment and Gain Company   *450*
   Exercises   *451*

13. Deterministic Inventory Models   453–491
   13.1 Continuous Demand Instantaneous Replenishment Model   *454*
   13.2 Considering Backordering   *456*
   13.3 Production Consumption Model   *459*
   13.4 Production Consumption Model 3 with Backordering   *461*
   13.5 Inventory Model with Discount   *463*
   13.6 Multiple Items Inventory (Constraint on Total Number of Orders)   *464*
   13.7 Multiple Items Inventory (Constraint on Inventory Value)   *467*
   13.8 Multiple Items Inventory (Constraint on Space)   *470*
   13.9 Multiple Items Inventory and Multiple Constraints   *473*
   Solved Examples   *474*
   CASE STUDY 13.1   XYZ Limited   *487*
   Exercises   *488*

Appendix: Solutions to Selected Exercise Problems   493–505

Bibliography   507–510

Index   511–513

Preface

One of the things that one would like to do after teaching a subject for fifteen years is to write a book on the subject. However, two questions have to be answered when we start thinking about writing a book on our favourite subject.

Why another book? What is new in my book that has not been addressed by earlier authors?

To identify a book to teach a first course in Operations Research is not a difficult task. To identify a book for a second level course is difficult considering that the available books may not include all the topics. Ordinarily, most curriculums have only one course in Operations Research at the undergraduate or graduate level unless one specializes in Operations Research. The minor stream courses in Operations Research taught at the undergraduate level at IIT Madras have also created a need for a book with additional topics to meet the requirements of an advanced course.

I have attempted to include chapters on all the topics that I teach in two courses at IIT Madras. Chapters 1 to 5, 10 and 13 are taught as fundamentals of Operations Research and the rest of the chapters are taught as Advanced Operations Research. I have kept the treatment of queueing theory and non-linear optimization to a minimum, though the material can be expanded. I have not included material on Game theory, simulation and probabilistic inventory models that are usually covered in OR books. I have concentrated more on advanced topics in Linear Programming, Integer Programming, Network Models and on the Travelling Salesman Problem. An extended treatment of the cutting stock problem, eta factorization of the basis, improving bounds in the branch and bound algorithm, all integer algorithms, Bender's partitioning, minimum spanning tree based heuristics for TSP and their performance are special to this book. In addition, the examples and situations are from the Indian context, which the Indian reader will be comfortable with.

Throughout the book, I have tried to explain new concepts and algorithms using a numerical illustration first and then explaining the theory wherever necessary. This approach has been appreciated by my students in the class and I have followed the same here. To that extent the book will appear to be simple if the student wishes only to solve problems using the tools of Operations Research. I also believe that the theory and the exercises need to be to together provide the requisite depth of understanding to the reader.

I sincerely hope that this book would prove useful to the reader and be able to motivate youngsters to take up a career in Operations Research—teaching or practice.

G. SRINIVASAN

Acknowledgements

Let me begin by acknowledging the help and support that I have received from IIT Madras, where I have the privilege and honour of serving as a faculty. The opportunity to teach some of the best students in the country is something that I am proud of as a teacher. I also acknowledge the support given by the Centre of Continuing Education, IIT Madras in terms of the financial support and permission for writing this book.

I respectfully remember all the professors who taught me this subject—Professors Amarnath and K.N. Balasubramanian during my undergraduate days, and Professors T.T. Narendran and S. Kalpakam at IIT Madras. Professor Narendran has been a great teacher, a good friend and a valuable colleague. His contribution in shaping my career as a teacher is acknowledged. I thank my colleagues in the Department of Management Studies at IIT Madras and other colleagues from the Department of Humanities and Social Sciences, where I served earlier. The interactions with Professor Panneerselvam of Pondicherry University were useful.

The first thought of writing a book on OR came during my stay at Lehigh University. I should thank Professor E.W. Zimmers (Jr) for the opportunity and the experience. Here I had the opportunity to interact with Professor M.P. Groover, whose useful tips on book writing came in handy when I actually started writing. I also remember the meetings with Professor A. Ravindran both at Penn State and at IIT Madras, from whom I drew motivation to write a book.

It is impossible to acknowledge the names of all the students to whom I have taught this subject. All of them have had a role in my process of learning to be a good teacher. Many other students with whom I have spent hours discussing many things including Operations Research have contributed in their own way to what I am today. Natarajan Gautham and Hari Natarajan, two of my students with whom I discussed 'interesting OR problems' in person and over e-mails have finetuned my thinking and teaching. My doctoral student Viswanath Kumar helped me in converting some of the material into power point slides that have been useful. I take a lot of pleasure in acknowledging the help that I received from my student Srikanth Srinivasan, with whom I have had several coffee sessions that turned out to be OR sessions. We continue our discussions on OR topics over phone, e-mail and over a cup of coffee frequently. The only way I can acknowledge the enormous support that I have received from my students is by including some of their names in the problem situations that are presented in this book. Here again, it is impossible to acknowledge all of them but I do remember all those students who contributed to the discussions I had with them.

My father is one person who certainly deserves a special mention. He believed that his son should write a book and constantly reminded me and encouraged me in this effort. I hope I have made my parents proud through this effort. My wife Lata and kids Sathya and Hari have helped me in their own way and words cannot describe the happiness that they have given me.

Finally, I thank my publisher, PHI Learning for the spontaneous acceptance of my manuscript and all for all the help and support extended to me during the production process of the book. I also wish an enjoyable reading of this book.

About Operations Research

Operations Research (OR) is a discipline that provides a set of analytical models for problem solving and decision making. The results from solving OR problems are used extensively in engineering, management and public systems.

OR models use theories, results and theorems of mathematics, statistics and probability in the problem-solving process. It also has its own theories and algorithms that are being used by academicians and practitioners.

Operations Research is called "Operational Research" in Europe/Britain but the abbreviation OR is used for both throughout the world. This field is also called Management Science (MS) by Americans. Sometimes both OR and MS are combined and called ORMS.

OR as a field is over fifty years old. It started in the late 1930s and the history of OR has been traced to several eminent contributors. In 1936, the early work in the field of attempting to integrate radar data with the ground-based observer data for fighter interception, was the start of OR. In 1938, a team to carry out research into the Operational (as opposed to technical) aspects was created and the term **Operational Research** (Research into Military Operations) was coined by Beasley. In the year 1942, the US Navy and Air Force used Operations Research in their war planning activities.

Today, the OR models include Mathematical Programming, Network Models, Decision Theory, Queueing Theory and Nonlinear Optimization. Some books have included Simulation Models in their chapters while some have included Forecasting, Scheduling and Replacement Models in their chapters. The topics under Mathematical Programming include Linear Programming, Transportation and Assignment Problems, Integer Programming, Dynamic Programming and Nonlinear Programming.

The field of optimization techniques also deals with OR models such as linear, dynamic and nonlinear programming models. Linear and nonlinear optimization is common to both the fields of operations research and optimization techniques.

Another category of OR models is to classify them as deterministic and probabilistic models. Mathematical Programming deals with deterministic models while Stochasting Programming and Queueing theorgy use Probabilistic models. The field of inventory control, also part of OR, has Probabilistic models.

While most of the basic theories have been derived from Mathematics, the applications are from engineering, management and public systems. Most OR models attempt to provide optimal solutions to problems and a lot of efforts have gone into providing or creating polynomially bounded algorithms to several problems. Therefore, there are also inputs from computer science in topics of OR related to algorithms and analysis. Some OR problems have come out of graph theoretic problems and, therefore, there is a strong relationship among mathematics, computer science and graph theory.

The solution to a problem using OR techniques involves three stages or phases. These are:
- Formulation
- Solution
- Implementation

Among these, solution methods have attracted the most attention among theoreticians while the practitioners of OR are interested in the implementation of the results. The formulation part involves both these groups. Most textbooks, research monographs and research publications provide more treatment to solution methods than the other two aspects.

It is difficult to trace the history of OR from the point of view of development of models because several results from mathematics are used in the OR models. Tracing the history of OR, one may be tempted to say that the book Mathematical Methods of Organization and Planning Production, by L.V. Kantorovich in the year 1939 could be termed the starting point of OR. The transportation problem was introduced in 1941 by Hitchcock. Several results and algorithms that are used in OR today such as Königsberg Bridge Problem (by Euler), Bayes Rule (Bayes), Lagrangian multipliers (Lagrange), Solution of inequality systems (Farkas), Pareto Optimality (Pareto), Markov Chains (Markov), Probability theory (Erland) came much earlier in the 18th to the 20th centuries.

One of the significant contributors to the field of OR is G.B. Dantzig who is credited with the Simplex Algorithm (in 1947) and the Linear Programming theory. The Game theory was proposed by John von Neumann in his work *Theory of Games and Economic Behavior*, in 1944 and developments in Game theory and Linear Programming were happening around the same time.

The first OR journal, *Operational Research Quarterly* was started in 1950 and the Simplex method was formally established by Dantzig in 1952. *Operations Research*, first US OR journal was started in 1952 and the Operations Research Society of America (ORSA) was also founded in 1952. The first books on OR started appearing in the 1950s and 1960s while the first course in OR in MIT has been introduced earlier in 1948.

In about six decades since its begining, OR became a well established field in its own right with several universities in the world offering graduate and doctoral programmes. It is learnt as a core subject in various engineering and management programmes all over the world. It is also taught and learnt as an elective in various undergraduate programmes of engineering, science and management.

A first course in OR usually deals with topics such as Linear Programming, Transportation and Assignment problems, Dynamic Programming and Inventory. Sometimes Queueing, Game Theory and CPM are included in the first course. An advanced course would address topics such as Integer Programming, Advanced Topics in Linear Programming, Network Models and Nonlinear Programming.

Linear Programming Formulations

Let us begin our discussion of Linear Programming (LP) with an example.

ILLUSTRATION 1.1

Product Mix Problem

Consider a small manufacturer making two products A and B. Two resources R_1 and R_2 are required to make these products. Each unit of Product A requires 1 unit of R_1 and 3 units of R_2. Each unit of Product B requires 1 unit of R_1 and 2 units of R_2. The manufacturer has 5 units of R_1 and 12 units of R_2 available. The manufacturer also makes a profit of Rs. 6 per unit of Product A sold and Rs. 5 per unit of Product B sold.

Let us address the above problem. The manufacturer has to decide on the number of units of products A and B to produce. It is acceptable that the manufacturer would like to make as much profit as possible and would decide on the production quantities accordingly. The manufacturer has to ensure that the resources needed to make the products are available.

Before we attempt to find out the decision of the manufacturer, let us redefine the problem in an algebraic form. The manufacturer has to decide on the production quantities. Let us call them X and Y which are defined as follows:

$$X = \text{Number of units of Product A made}$$
$$Y = \text{Number of units of Product B made}$$

The profit associated with X units of Product A and Y units of Product B is $6X + 5Y$. The manufacturer would determine X and Y such that this function has a maximum value.

The requirements of the two resources are $X + Y$ for R_1 and $3X + 2Y$ and the manufacturer has to ensure that these are available.

The problem is to find X and Y such that $6X + 5Y$ is maximized and $X + Y \leq 5$ and $3X + 2Y \leq 12$ are satisfied. Also it is necessary that $X, Y \geq 0$ so that only non-negative quantities are produced.

If we redefine the production quantities as X_1 and X_2 (for reasons of uniformity and consistency) then the problem becomes

Maximize $\quad Z = 6X_1 + 5X_2$

Subject to

$$X_1 + X_2 \leq 5$$
$$3X_1 + 2X_2 \leq 12$$
$$X_1, X_2 \geq 0$$

1.1 TERMINOLOGY

The problem variables X_1 and X_2 are called **decision variables** and they represent the solution or the output decision from the problem. The profit function that the manufacturer wishes to increase, represents the objective of making the decisions on the production quantities and is called the **objective function**. The conditions matching the resource availability and resource requirement are called **constraints**. These usually limit (or restrict) the values the decision variables can take.

We have also explicitly stated that the decision variable should take non-negative values. This is true for all linear programming problems. This is called **non-negativity restriction**.

The problem that we have written down in the algebraic form represents the mathematical model of the given system and is called the **problem formulation**. The problem formulation has the following steps:

1. Identifying the decision variables
2. Writing the objective function
3. Writing the constraints
4. Writing the non-negativity restrictions.

In the above formulation, the objective function and the constraints are linear. Therefore, the model that we formulated is a linear programming problem.

A **linear programming problem** has a linear objective function, linear constraints and the non-negativity constraints on all the decision variables.

Let us consider some more examples to understand the linear programming formulations better.

ILLUSTRATION 1.2

Production Planning Problem

Let us consider a company making a single product. The estimated demand for the product for the next four months are 1000, 800, 1200, 900, respectively. The company has a regular time capacity of 800 per month and an overtime capacity of 200 per month. The cost of regular time production is Rs. 20 per unit and the cost of overtime production is Rs. 25 per unit. The company can carry inventory to the next month and the holding cost is Rs. 3 per unit per month. The demand has to be met every month. Formulate a linear programming problem for the above situation.

Decision variables: X_j = Quantity produced using regular time production in month j
                         Y_j = Quantity produced using overtime production in month j
                         I_j = Quantity carried at the end of month j to the next month

Objective function: Minimize $20 \sum_{j=1}^{4} X_i + 25 \sum_{j=1}^{4} Y_j + 3 \sum_{j=1}^{4} I_j$

Constraints:
$$X_1 + Y_1 = 1000 + I_1 \quad \text{(Month 1 requirement)}$$
$$I_1 + X_2 + Y_2 = 800 + I_2$$
$$I_2 + X_3 + Y_3 = 1200 + I_3$$
$$I_3 + X_4 + Y_4 = 900$$
$$X_j \leq 800 \; j = 1,...,4$$
$$Y_j \leq 200 \; j = 1,...,4$$
$$X_j, Y_j, I_j \geq 0$$

The above formulation has 12 decision variables and 12 constraints. Out of these, 4 are equations. We can eliminate the variables I_j by rewriting the constraints as:

$$X_1 + Y_1 \geq 1000 \quad \text{(Month 1 requirement)}$$
$$X_1 + Y_1 + X_2 + Y_2 \geq 1800$$
$$X_1 + X_2 + X_3 + Y_1 + Y_2 + Y_3 \geq 3000$$
$$X_1 + X_2 + X_3 + X_4 + Y_1 + Y_2 + Y_3 + Y_4 \geq 3900$$
$$X_j \leq 800 \; j = 1,...,4$$
$$Y_j \leq 200 \; j = 1,...,4$$
$$X_j, Y_j \geq 0$$

The objective function becomes

Minimize $20 \sum_{j=1}^{4} X_j + 25 \sum_{j=1}^{4} Y_j + 3 \, (X_1 + Y_1 - 1000 + X_1 + Y_1 + X_2 + Y_2 - 1800 + X_1 + X_2 + X_3 + Y_1 + Y_2 + Y_3 - 3000 + X_1 + X_2 + X_3 + X_4 + Y_1 + Y_2 + Y_3 + Y_4 - 3900)$

If the total production exceeds 1000, the excess production is carried as inventory to the second month and so on. This explains the four-demand constraints. It may not be necessary to consider ending inventory at the end of the fourth month. This constraint can be an equation. For reasons of uniformity we have an inequality there. The cost of inventory is included in the objective function. In any case, since the excess inventory is going to add to the cost in the objective function, the minimization function will not allow excess inventory at the end of the fourth period in the solution.

The second formulation has 8 variables and 12 constraints all of which are inequalities. In LP formulations, it is desirable to have inequalities. This is a better formulation than the first for this problem.

Let us consider a third formulation by a new definition of decision variables. Let X_{ijk} represent production in month i to meet the demand of month j using production type k. ($k = 1$ means regular time production and $k = 2$ means over time production). The constraints are

$$X_{111} + X_{112} = 1000$$
$$X_{121} + X_{122} + X_{221} + X_{222} = 800$$
$$X_{131} + X_{132} + X_{231} + X_{232} + X_{331} + X_{332} = 1200$$
$$X_{141} + X_{142} + X_{241} + X_{242} + X_{341} + X_{342} + X_{441} + X_{442} = 900$$
$$X_{111} + X_{121} + X_{131} + X_{141} \leq 800$$
$$X_{221} + X_{231} + X_{241} \leq 800$$
$$X_{331} + X_{341} \leq 800$$
$$X_{441} \leq 800$$
$$X_{112} + X_{122} + X_{132} + X_{142} \leq 200$$
$$X_{222} + X_{232} + X_{242} \leq 200$$
$$X_{332} + X_{342} \leq 200$$
$$X_{442} \leq 200$$

$X_{111}, X_{121}, X_{131}, X_{141}, X_{221}, X_{231}, X_{241}, X_{331}, X_{341}, X_{441}, X_{112}, X_{122}, X_{132}, X_{142}, X_{222}, X_{232}, X_{242}, X_{332}, X_{342}, X_{442} \geq 0$

The objective function is:

Minimize $20(X_{111} + X_{121} + X_{131} + X_{141} + X_{221} + X_{231} + X_{241} + X_{331} + X_{341} + X_{441}) + 25(X_{112} + X_{122} + X_{132} + X_{142} + X_{222} + X_{232} + X_{242} + X_{332} + X_{342} + X_{442}) + 3(X_{121} + X_{122} + X_{231} + X_{232} + X_{341} + X_{342}) + 6(X_{131} + X_{132} + X_{241} + X_{242}) + 9(X_{141} + X_{142})$

This formulation has 20 variables and 12 constraints out of which 4 are equations. This is not efficient as compared to the second formulation. (This formulation introduces us to minimization of the objective function, and also helps us understand that the inequalities are desirable and the formulation with fewer constraints and variables is a better formulation).

ILLUSTRATION 1.3

Cutting Stock Problem (Gilmore and Gomory 1961)

Consider a big steel roll from which steel sheets of the same length but different width have to be cut. Let us assume that the roll is 20-cm wide and the following sizes have to be cut:

9 inch	511 numbers
8 inch	301 numbers
7 inch	263 numbers
6 inch	383 numbers

It is assumed that all the cut sheets have the same length (say, 25 inches). One dimensional cutting is only allowed. The problem is to cut the sheets in such a way as to minimize wastage of material.

From a 20-inch wide sheet, we can cut two 9 inches with a wastage of 2 inch. This is called a cutting pattern and we can represent it is as [2 0 0 0] with a wastage of 2 inches. We write all the possible patterns such that the wastage is less than 6 inches (minimum thickness desired), under the assumption that if the wastage exceeds 6, we can cut a 6-inch sheet out of the wastage. The possible cutting patterns are:

1. [2 0 0 0] wastage = 2
2. [0 2 0 0] wastage = 4
3. [0 0 2 1] wastage = 2
4. [0 0 0 3] wastage = 2
5. [1 1 0 0] wastage = 3
6. [1 0 1 0] wastage = 4
7. [1 0 0 1] wastage = 5
8. [0 1 1 0] wastage = 5
9. [0 1 0 2] wastage = 0
10. [0 0 1 2] wastage = 1

Let X_j be the number of sheets cut using pattern j. We have

$$2X_1 + X_5 + X_6 + X_7 \geq 511 \quad \text{(9 inch sheets)}$$
$$2X_2 + X_5 + X_8 + X_9 \geq 301 \quad \text{(8 inch sheets)}$$
$$2X_3 + X_6 + X_8 + X_{10} \geq 263 \quad \text{(7 inch sheets)}$$
$$X_3 + 3X_4 + X_7 + 2X_9 + 2X_{10} \geq 383 \quad \text{(6 inch sheets)}$$
$$X_j \geq 0$$

The objective function is to minimize wastage. This is given by

Minimize $2X_1 + 4X_2 + 2X_4 + 3X_5 + 4X_6 + 5X_7 + 5X_8 + X_{10}$

However, if we make an assumption that excess sheets produced in every width are included as waste (they are all inequalities because it may not be possible to get the exact number required), the objective function becomes

Minimize $2X_1 + 4X_2 + 2X_4 + 3X_5 + 4X_6 + 5X_7 + 5X_8 + X_{10} + 9(2X_1 + X_5 + X_6 + X_7 - 511) + 8(2X_2 + X_5 + X_8 + X_9 - 301) + 7(2X_3 + X_6 + X_8 + X_{10} - 263) + 6(X_3 + 3X_4 + X_7 + 2X_9 + 2X_{10} - 383)$

This reduces to

Minimize $20X_1 + 20X_2 + 20X_3 + 203X_4 + 20X_5 + 20X_6 + 20X_7 + 20X_8 + 20X_9 + 20X_{10} - 11146$.

The constant term does not alter the solution to the problem and can be left out. Since all the variables in the objective function have the same common factor, this can be left out. The objective function reduces to

Minimize $\sum_{j=1}^{10} X_j$

The problem of minimizing waste reduces to one of minimizing the total number of cuts. The assumption that the excess sheets of a given width contribute to the waste gives us an objective function that minimizes the total number of cuts. In practice, these excess sheets are retained for subsequent use. The final formulation is

Minimize $\sum_{j=1}^{10} X_j$

Subject to

$$2X_1 + X_5 + X_6 + X_7 \geq 511$$
$$2X_2 + X_5 + X_8 + X_9 \geq 301$$
$$2X_3 + X_6 + X_8 + X_{10} \geq 263$$
$$X_3 + 3X_4 + X_7 + 2X_9 + 2X_{10} \geq 383$$
$$X_j \geq 0$$

In the above formulation, can we consider patterns whose waste exceed the minimum required width of 5? For example, can we consider a pattern [1 0 0 0] with waste = 11?

If we consider all such patterns, the number of patterns become large and, therefore, the number of variables is also very large. The number of constraints remain the same. However, it will be possible to have exactly the number of required cuts of each width in this case (the excess have been added to the waste) and the constraints become equations instead of inequalities. In this case also, minimizing the waste reduces to the objective of minimizing the number of cuts. The formulation becomes

Minimize $\sum_{j=1}^{n} X_j$

Subject to

$$\sum_{j=1}^{n} a_{ij} X_j = b_i$$
$$X_j \geq 0$$

(In fact, this formulation with more number of variables can be used if we develop a column generation approach to solve the problem. This will be covered later in Chapter 6).

ILLUSTRATION 1.4

Game Theory Problem

Consider two manufacturers (A and B) who are competitors for the same market segment for the same product. Each wants to maximize the market share and adopts two strategies. The gain (or pay off) for A when A adopts strategy i and B adopts strategy j is given by a_{ij}. 2×2 pay-off matrix is shown in Table 1.1.

Table 1.1 Pay-off Matrix

3	-2
-1	4

During a given time period T, both A and B have to mix their strategies. If A plays only Strategy 1, then B would play Strategy 2 to gain, which A would not want. Each, therefore, wants to mix their strategies so that they gain maximum (or the other loses maximum).

Let us consider A's problem of trying to maximize his return. Assume that A plays Strategy 1 p_1 proportion of times and plays Strategy 2 p_2 proportion of times. We have

$$p_1 + p_2 = 1$$

If B consistently plays Strategy 1, then A's expected gain is $3p_1 - p_2$. If B consistently plays Strategy 2, A's expected gain is $-2p_1 + 4p_2$.

Player A also knows that B will not consistently play a single strategy but would play his (her) strategies in such a way that A gains minimum. So A would like to play his (her) strategies in proportions p_1 and p_2 to maximize this minimum return that B would allow.

A's strategy is called **maximin** strategy and would maximize the minimum of $3p_1 - p_2$ and $-2p_1 + 4p_2$.

Let us define u as minimum of $3p_1 - p_2$ and $-2p_1 + 4p_2$. A's problem is to

Maximize u
Subject to

$$u \leq 3p_1 - p_2$$
$$u \leq -2p_1 + 4p_2$$
$$p_1 + p_2 = 1$$
$$p_1, p_2 \geq 0, u \text{ unrestricted in sign}$$

(This is because A can also end up making an expected loss. Therefore, u can be positive, zero or negative in sign).

Let us consider B's problem. B has to decide on q_1 and q_2, the proportion of times he (she) plays the two strategies. We have

$$q_1 + q_2 = 1$$

If A plays strategy 1 always, B's expected loss is $3q_1 - 2q_2$. If A plays Strategy 2 all the time, B's expected loss would be $-q_1 + 4q_2$.

B knows that A will play his strategies in such a way that B incurs maximum loss. Therefore, B will play his strategies in such a way that he minimizes the maximum loss.

Let the maximum loss be v. B's problem will be

Minimize v

$$v \geq 3q_1 - 2q_2$$
$$v \geq -q_1 + 4q_2$$
$$q_1 + q_2 = 1$$
$$q_1, q_2 \geq 0, v \text{ unrestricted in sign.}$$

(This is because B can end up making either a profit or loss. Hence v is unrestricted in sign).

Since A's gain is B's loss and vice versa, we know that at the optimum, A's problem and B's problem will have the same value of the objective function. It is also not necessary to solve both because it is possible to get the solution of one problem from another. Later, when we learn duality theory we can understand that B's problem is the dual of A's problem and vice versa.

1.2 ASSUMPTIONS IN LINEAR PROGRAMMING PROBLEM

1. *Linearity:* The objective function and constraints are linear. The profit from A and B is the sum of the individual profits.
2. *Proportionality:* If the profit of one item is A, the profit of two items is $2A$.

3. *Divisibility and multiplicity:* Multiplicity is the same as proportionality. Divisibility ensures that profit of ½ item is A/2.
4. *Deterministic:* All parameters and coefficients are deterministic and are known with certainty. They don't change during or after the formulation.

EXAMPLE 1.1 The postal department is considering the purchase of vehicles to pick up and deliver mail from various offices. They are considering three types of vehicles. The cost of each of these are Rs. 5 lakhs, Rs. 10 lakhs and Rs. 8 lakhs per vehicle, respectively. These require a crew of 2, 4 and 4 persons per day considering multiple shifts. They expect these to run for 60, 100 and 80 km per day. They expect that the total distance to be covered by the vehicles per day would be 2000 km. Based on the fuel economy, the operating cost per day for these vehicles are Rs. 200, Rs. 350 and Rs. 300 per day. They have a budget restriction of Rs. 1.6 crore and have 80 people available as crew. Formulate a model to minimize the operating costs.

Solution: Let us define

X_1 = Number of vehicles of Type A being purchased
X_2 = Number of vehicles of Type B being purchased
X_3 = Number of vehicles of Type C being purchased

Objective function: Minimize $Z = 200X_1 + 350X_2 + 300X_3$

Constraint equations: $5X_1 + 10X_2 + 8 \le 160$ (Budget constraint)

$2X_1 + 4X_2 + 4X_3 \le 80$ (Crew constraint)

$60X_1 + 100X_2 + 80X_3 \ge 2000$

$X_1, X_2, X_3 \ge 0$, and integers

EXAMPLE 1.2 A call centre has the following minimal daily requirements for personnel as shown in Table 1.2:

Table 1.2 Minimum Requirements for Personnel

Time of the day (24-hour clock)	Period	Minimum number of people required
2–6	1	20
6–10	2	15
10–14	3	8
14–18	4	6
18–22	5	12
22–24	6	30

Formulate a linear programming model to find an optimal schedule.

Note: Consider Period 1 as following immediately after Period 6.
Each person works eight consecutive hours.

Solution: Let

x_1 = Number of people starting their shift at the beginning of Period 1
x_2 = Number of people starting their shift at the beginning of Period 2
x_3 = Number of people starting their shift at the beginning of Period 3
x_4 = Number of people starting their shift at the beginning of Period 4
x_5 = Number of people starting their shift at the beginning of Period 5
x_6 = Number of people starting their shift at the beginning of Period 6

Each person works for two slots, the one that he or she begins and the next one.

Objective function: Minimize $\quad Z = x_1 + x_2 + x_3 + x_4 + x_5 + x_6$

Constraints:

$\quad x_6 + x_1 \geq 20 \quad$ (First slot)
$\quad x_1 + x_2 \geq 15$
$\quad x_2 + x_3 \geq 8$
$\quad x_3 + x_4 \geq 6$
$\quad x_4 + x_5 \geq 12$
$\quad x_5 + x_6 \geq 30 \quad$ (Last slot of the day)

Also, $\quad x_1, x_2, x_3, x_4, x_5, x_6 \geq 0$

EXAMPLE 1.3 In a transport company, 6 trucks of Type 1, 10 trucks of Type 2 and 8 trucks of Type 3 are available for each day's requirements. The tonnage capacities are 16 for Type 1, 12 for Type 2 and 9 for Type 3.

The company dispatches its trucks to Cities A and B. Tonnage requirements are 20 at City A and 30 at City B; excess tonnage capacity supplied to a city has no value. Considering the distances, it is possible for the trucks to go only once to the destinations everyday. The cost of sending a truck to each city is given in Table 1.3:

Formulate this problem as a linear programming problem.

Table 1.3 Cost of Sending Trucks

	Type 1	Type 2	Type 3
City A	2000	1800	1200
City B	3000	2400	2200

Solution: Let the number of trucks of type i going to City j be X_{ij} (i = 1 to 3, j = 1, 2).

Objective function: Minimize $Z = 2000X_{11} + 1800X_{21} + 1200X_{31} + 3000X_{12} + 2400X_{22} + 2200X_{32}$

Constraints: (Demand constraints)

$$16X_{11} + 12X_{21} + 9X_{31} \geq 20$$
$$16X_{12} + 12X_{22} + 9X_{32} \geq 30$$

(Availability constraints)

$$X_{11} + X_{12} \leq 6$$
$$X_{21} + X_{22} \leq 10$$
$$X_{31} + X_{32} \leq 8$$
$$X_{ij} \geq 0, \text{ and integer}$$

EXAMPLE 1.4 A Media planning company has to optimally allocate its client's advertising budget using linear programming. The eight possible advertising vehicles are television (national and private channels), newspapers (one English, one Hindi and one in Bengali), local magazine and

on its website and on a popular radio channel. The client is also interested in targeting two different types of audience for their products (working women and retired couples). The company estimates that for every rupee spent on vehicle i, the number of people exposed in category j is a_{ij}.
Consider the following additional requirements:
1. There is a budget restriction of Rs. B.
2. The client wants a minimum of d_j people of type j to be exposed to the advertisements.
3. There is an upper limit of Rs. C that can be spent on television advertisements.
4. At least R people should be exposed through radio channel.
   (a) Formulate a linear programming problem for the above situation.
   (b) Will the client end up spending on all the eight possible advertising vehicles?

Solution: Let the money spent on vehicle i be X_i. The objective function is to maximize total exposure.

$$\text{Maximize} \sum_{i=1}^{8} \sum_{j=1}^{2} a_{ij} X_j$$

The constraints are:

$$\sum_{i=1}^{8} X_i \leq B \quad \text{(Budget restriction)}$$

$$\sum_{i=1}^{8} a_{ij} X_i \geq d_j \quad \text{(Required exposure of each type)}$$

$$X_1 + X_2 \leq C \quad \text{(Limit on television advertisement)}$$

$$a_{81} X_1 + a_{82} X_2 \geq R$$

$$X_j \geq 0$$

There are four constraints and, therefore, the client will end up using only four out of the eight advertising vehicles. The number of variables in the solution will be equal to the number of constraints. This aspect will be described in the Chapter 2. If the client wants to use all vehicles, we should either have a minimum desirable exposure for each of the advertising vehicles or define a minimum amount to be spent on each advertising vehicle.

EXAMPLE 1.5 Software Creator has to decide how to hire and train programmers over the next four months to complete an ongoing project. The requirements, expressed in terms of the number of programming hours needed, are 8000 in September, 9000 in October, 10,000 in November and 7000 in December.

It takes one month of training before a newly recruited programmer can be trained and put to the project. A programmer must be hired a month before working on the actual project. A trainee requires 100 hours of training by experienced programmers during the month of training so that 100 hours less are available from existing trained programmers.

Each experienced programmer can work upto 180 hours in a month, and the company has 50 regular programmers at the beginning of September.

If the maximum time available from experienced programmers exceeds a month's requirement, they are paid salary for a month.

By the end of each month, 10% of the experienced programmers quit their jobs to study or for other reasons. The company pays an experienced programmer effectively Rs. 30,000 per month including other benefits and Rs. 15,000 for a trainee.

Formulate the hiring and training as a linear programming problem.

Solution: Let us assume X_1 = Number of trainees hired during the month of September
X_2 = Number of trainess hired during the month of October
X_3 = Number of trainess hired during the month of November.

We do not hire trainees in December because they will be available for January only.
Now

Number of experienced programmers at the beginning of September $e_1 = 50$

Number of experienced programmers at the beginning of October $e_2 = 0.9(50 + X_1)$

Number of experienced programmers at the beginning of the month of November $e_3 = 0.9(e_2 + X_2)$

Number of experienced programmers at the beginning of the month of December $e_4 = 0.9(e_3 + X_3)$

The objective function is:

$$\text{Minimize} \quad Z = 30{,}000 \sum_{i=1}^{4} e_i + 15{,}000 \sum_{i=1}^{3} X_i$$

The constraints are:

$$180e_1 - 100X_1 \geq 8000 \text{ (September)}$$
$$180e_2 - 100X_2 \geq 9000 \text{ (October)}$$
$$150e_3 - 100X_3 \geq 10{,}000 \text{ (November)}$$
$$150e_4 \geq 7000 \text{ Also, } e_2, e_3, e_4, X_1, X_2, X_3 \geq 0$$

(We assume that a programmer becomes trained after one month of training and can leave the organization. We also observe that while the decision variables have to be integers, we are treating them as continuous variables while formulating linear programming problems).

EXAMPLE 1.6 Drink Co., a company manufactures a health drink called "Taste and Strength". They use five ingredients wheat, milk, nuts, spices and other cereals. They are particular about the amount of starch, carbohydrates and fat contents of the drink. The amount of starch, carbohydrates and starch from ingredient i per kg is a_{i1}, a_{i2} and a_{i3}, respectively. They require a lower and upper limit of l_j and u_j of starch, carbohydrates and fat contents. The cost per kg of ingredient i is C_i. Formulate a linear programming problem to minimize the cost of production of the health drink.

Solution: Let the proportion of ingredient i used in 1 kg of the health drink be X_i. The objective function is:

$$\text{Minimize} \quad \sum_{i=1}^{5} C_i X_i$$

The constraints are:

Starch $$l_1 \leq \sum_{i=1}^{5} a_{i1} X_i \leq u_1$$

Carbohydrates $\qquad l_2 \leq \sum_{i=1}^{5} a_{i2} X_i \leq u_2$

Fat $\qquad l_3 \leq \sum_{i=1}^{5} a_{i3} X_i \leq u_3$

$$X_i \geq 0$$

EXAMPLE 1.7 Acid Co., a chemical engineering company manufactures two types of acids A and B. Both of these involve two chemical operations for each. Each unit of Acid A requires 3 hours on Operation 1 and 4 hours on Operation 2. Each unit of Acid B requires 3 hours on Operation 1 and 2 hours on Operation 2. Available time for Operation 1 is 20 hours and for Operation 2, 18 hours. The production of B also results in a by-product C at no extra cost. A part of this by-product can be sold at a profit, but the remainder has to be destroyed.

Acid A sells for P_1 rupees profit per unit while Acid B sells for P_2 rupees profit per unit. The by-product C can be sold at a unit profit of P_3 rupees, but if it cannot be sold it must be destroyed; the destruction cost is P_4 rupees per unit. Forecasts by sales department show that a maximum of K units of C can be sold; n units of C result for every unit of B produced.

Formulate a linear programme to determine the production quantities of A and B, keeping C in mind, so that the total profits will be maximized.

Solution: Let X_1 = Amount of Acid A being produced
X_2 = Amount of Acid B being produced
X_3 = Amount of by-product sold
nX_2 = Amount of C produced
$nX_2 - X_3$ = Amount of by-product not sold

The objective function is

Maximize $\quad Z = P_1 X_1 + P_2 X_2 + P_3 X_3 - P_4(nX_2 - X_3)$

The constraint equations are

First operation: $\qquad 3X_1 + 4X_2 \leq 20$ (Capacity constraint)
Second operation: $\qquad 3X_1 + 2X_2 \leq 18$ (Capacity constraint)
$\qquad X_3 \leq nX_2$ (Relationship between X_3 and X_2)
$\qquad X_3 \leq k$ (Sales limit)

Also $\qquad X_1, X_2, X_3 \geq 0$

EXAMPLE 1.8 M/s. Fertilizer and Co. manufactures two products that give rise to effluents containing two pollutants. The details are tabulated in Table 1.4.

Table 1.4 Data for Example 1.8

Pollutant	Kilogram of pollutant emitted per litres of		Legally permissible limit of pollutant
	Product-1	Product-2	(in kg)
1.	P_{11}	P_{12}	m_1
2.	P_{21}	P_{22}	m_2
Profit per litre	R_1	R_2	
Sales commitment (min)	S_1	S_2	

The production manager can use an anti-pollution device to keep the pollution within the prescribed limits. The device can reduce the two pollutants by $u_1\%$ and by $u_2\%$, respectively when used. It also costs Rs. r to use the device per litre of either of the products.

The percentage reduction is the same for either product. The device can be used to treat part or whole or the production of a product. Formulate this as a linear programming problem to determine the optimal production plan.

Solution: Let us assume that

$$\text{Amount of Product 1 produced} = X_1 \text{ litres}$$
$$\text{Amount of Product 2 produced} = X_2 \text{ litres}$$
$$\text{Amount of Product 1 treated using the device} = Y_1 \text{ litres}$$
$$\text{Amount of Product 1 treated using the device} = Y_2 \text{ litres}$$

The objective function is to maximize profit.

$\therefore$ Maximize $Z = R_1 X_1 + R_2 X_2 - r(Y_1 + Y_2)$

The constraints for the pollutant limit after using the device are

$$P_{11}(X_1 - Y_1) + P_{12}(X_2 - Y_2) + (1 - u_1/100)(P_{11}Y_1 + P_{12}Y_2) \le m_1$$
$$P_{21}(X_1 - Y_1) + P_{22}(X_2 - Y_2) + (1 - u_1/100)(P_{21}Y_1 + P_{22}Y_2) \le m_2$$
$$Y_1 \le X_1$$
$$Y_2 \le X_2$$

These place restrictions on the amount of product can be treated using the device.

Also $\qquad X_{11}, X_{12}, X_{21}, X_{22} \ge 0$

EXAMPLE 1.9 Tool Co., a production company, is to undertake its annual maintenance week starting Monday. Most employees would like to avail vacation of during this period since there is little work due to the maintenance. The company also operates on a reduced production mode to meet the demand during the week. The projected number of people required to work in the two shifts for the five days are given in Table 1.5. The company also decides that the operators work only for four days in the week and decides to have them work for only three consecutive days out of the four days.

Table 1.5 Number of People Required

	AM	PM
Monday	10	8
Tuesday	8	9
Wednesday	7	9
Thursday	8	5
Friday	12	10

How should the available workers be allotted so that the maximum number of people can go on leave on all days of the week? Formulate an LP.

Solution: Since all of them have to work on Mondays and Fridays, we define as:

Number of people on leave on Tuesday (AM shift)   = X_1
Number of people on leave on Wednesday (AM shift) = X_2
Number of people on leave on Thursday (AM shift) = X_3
Number of people on leave on Tuesday (PM shift)   = Y_1
Number of people on leave on Wednesday (PM shift) = Y_2
Number of people on leave on Thursday (PM shift) = Y_3

The constraints are

For AM shift: (Monday through Friday)

$$X_1 + X_2 + X_3 \geq 10$$
$$X_2 + X_3 \geq 8$$
$$X_1 + X_3 \geq 7$$
$$X_2 + X_3 \geq 8$$
$$X_1 + X_2 + X_3 \geq 12$$

For PM shift: (Monday through Friday)

$$Y_1 + Y_2 + Y_3 \geq 8$$
$$Y_2 + Y_3 \geq 9$$
$$Y_1 + Y_3 \geq 6$$
$$Y_2 + Y_3 \geq 5$$
$$Y_1 + Y_2 + Y_3 \geq 10$$

All $X_i, Y_i \geq 0$ and integer

(One can leave out the Monday AM shift constraint and the Friday AM shift constraints because they are weak compared to the Monday PM and Friday PM shift constraints, respectively. This reduces the constraints by two).

We want maximum people to leave the shift and go on leave on all days. This means that we want to minimize the total number of people working in the shift. This leads to an objective function:

Minimize $X_1 + X_2 + X_3 + Y_1 + Y_2 + Y_3$

(The problem reduces to two independent LP problems each with four constraints for the AM and PM shifts, respectively).

EXAMPLE 1.10 Consider the following network (Figure 1.1) where arc weights represent the capacity of flow in the arc represent the capacity of flow in the arc. Formulate an LP to find out the maximum flow from Nodes 1 to 5.

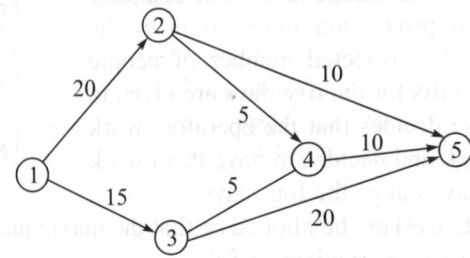

Figure 1.1   Maximum flow problem.

Solution: Let X_{ij} be the quantity of flow in Arc i–j. Flow leaving Node 1 is $X_{12} + X_{13}$. Nodes 2, 3 and 4 are intermediate node and hence flow conservation equations hold for these nodes. We have

$$X_{12} = X_{24} + X_{25}$$
$$X_{13} = X_{34} + X_{35}$$
$$X_{45} = X_{24} + X_{34}$$

Flow that reaches Node 5 (terminal node) is $X_{25} + X_{35} + X_{45}$. By flow conservation this should be equal to $X_{12} + X_{13}$. We also have the flow capacity constraints and the non-negativity constraints. The formulation is

Maximize $Z = X_{12} + X_{13}$

Subject to

$$X_{12} = X_{24} + X_{25}$$
$$X_{13} = X_{34} + X_{35}$$
$$X_{45} = X_{24} + X_{34}$$
$$0 \le X_{ij} \le U_{ij} \quad \text{(the } U_{ij} \text{ values are the arc capacities)}$$

(This formulation is for the maximum flow problem, which we will consider in detail in Chapter 8 in the book. The later formulation will be slightly different from the earlier formulation. The formulation that we have made now is called the **node-arc formulation**. There is also an alternate path-arc formulation where all paths are evaluated and the decision variables are the quantities flowing in each of the paths. The student may try the path-arc formulation as an exercise.)

EXAMPLE 1.11 (The caterer problem). A private caterer has undertaken a contract for a series of dinners to be given by a club for its "Gold card" members. There will be n dinners, one on each of the n successive days. The club has asked the caterer to provide a special type of cloth napkins with the name of the function written on them. The napkins become useless after the dinner series.

During the dinner series, however, soiled napkins can be washed and reused. Two types of laundry service are available to the caterer: Regular service and Express service. Regular service takes p days; so a napkin sent on k^{th} day to the laundry is available again on day $k + p$; this service costs u rupees per napkin. Express service takes q days ($q < p$) and costs v rupees per napkin ($v > u$). New napkin costs s rupees each. Let a_k be the number of napkins needed on the kth day $(1, 2, \ldots, n)$. The caterer wants to minimize the costs associated with purchasing and laundering napkins. Formulate a linear programming model for determining the following daily decisions:

(a) How many napkins to buy?
(b) How many napkins to be sent to Regular laundry service?
(c) How many napkins to be sent to Express Laundry service?

Solution: Let the number of new napkins used on day i be X_i. Assume that the number of napkins sent to Regular laundry on day i be Y_i and the number of napkins sent to Express laundry on the ith day be Z_i.
The objective function is

Minimize $$Z = s\sum_{i=1}^{n} X_i + u\sum_{i=1}^{n} Y_i + v\sum_{i=1}^{n} Z_i$$

The constraint equations are

$$Y_i + Z_i \leq a_i \quad \text{(for all } i\text{)}$$

$$\sum_{i=1}^{n} X_i + \sum_{i=q+1}^{n} X_{i-q} + \sum_{i=p+1}^{n} X_{i-p} \geq \sum_{i=1}^{n} a_i$$

$X_i, Y_i, Z_i \geq 0$ and integer

CASE STUDY 1.1: Choosing the Best School

Mr. Shyam Prasad has been recently transferred to Chennai from Lucknow and has the issue of admitting his two children to a good high school. Being in a senior government position, he can admit them in the centrally funded schools in Chennai. He has three choices of the school and it is likely that his children would be allotted one of them. Mr. Prasad has chosen his best three schools (we call them A, B and C) and wishes to rank them. He would be happy if the children get either the first or second choice.

Some data are available and Mr. Prasad identifies three important parameters that serve as inputs. These are:

1. Number of students enrolled in the twelfth standard,
2. Number of teachers in the high school section,
3. Facilities available (infrastructure, sports, co-curricular and extra curricular).

While data for the first two parameters are directly available from records that the school maintains, Mr. Prasad has his estimate for the points for infrastructure based on availability of buildings, laboratories, computing facility, internet availability, etc.

Among the many parameters that he would evaluate the schools, Mr. Prasad believes that the following three adequately represent the output (performance) of the schools. These are:

1. Number of students who enter professional courses per year (average),
2. Number of sportspersons who have played state level (in the last five years),
3. Number of students (alumni) who have become visible entrepreneurs, CEOs and eminent leaders.

Tables 1.6 and 1.7 provide the data for the input and output parameters respectively. Mr Prasad believes in a linear relationship among the input and output parameters and wishes to rank them based on their relative efficiencies.

Table 1.6 Input Parameters

	Strength	Teachers	Facilities
School A	800	60	32
School B	1000	90	34
School C	600	40	28

Table 1.7 Output Parameters

	Professional courses	Sports	Visible Entrepreneurs
School A	175	36	43
School B	186	37	60
School C	163	40	36

Hints: This case introduces the reader to the concepts of Data Envelopment Analysis (Charnes et al. 1981).

Try and define efficiency for each school as the ratio of weighted output to weighted input. The weights to the inputs and outputs are the decision variables. Each school should assign weights such as to maximize its efficiency subject to the condition that for the defined weights no school has an efficiency exceeding 1. The efficiency is a fraction and by defining the input to 1, we can convert the problem to an LP problem.

EXERCISES

1.1 Three students want to go from their hostel to their department. They have only one bicycle and only one person can ride the bicycle at a time. The three students can walk at speeds a_1, a_2 and a_3, respectively and can ride the bicycle at speeds b_1, b_2 and b_3, respectively. Assume that the slowest cycling speed is more than the fastest walking speed. A person riding the cycle can park it at any point and walk the rest of the journey. He does not wait near the cycle till the next person arrives (the cycle is safe even if it is unlocked and left unattended). A person rides the cycle only once during the travel. Formulate an LP problem that finds out when earliest all three reach the department. Assume the distance between the hostel and the department to be d.

1.2 PBL India makes two types of refrigerators: small (185 litres) and large (300 litres). The monthly demands for these two types are 2000 and 1000, respectively. Both these items require two important parts, compressor and body. The shop producing compressors can make 1200 large compressors per month if it makes only large compressors or 3000 small compressors if it makes only small compressors. It can make a suitable linear combination if it decides to produce both. Similarly, the shop making the body can make 1500 large if it makes only large or 2500 small if it makes only small or a suitable linear combination.

The company makes a profit of Rs. 1500 per large fridge sold and a profit of Rs. 1000 per small fridge sold. The fixed overheads are Rs. 15 lakhs per month. The company wants to draw the production plan for the coming month. Formulate an LP model for the above situation.

The production manager believes in increasing the production and argues that they should produce the maximum possible quantity of 2000 small refrigerators and use the rest of the capacity, if available, to produce the large refrigerators. The marketing manager believes in producing the maximum possible quantity of 1000 of large refrigerators because the profit is higher per fridge and use the rest of the capacity, if available, to produce small refrigerators.

How do you react to the above two views based on your solution to the problem?

1.3 Thick and Drink, a coffee shop, provides three types of coffee (strong, medium and light) to its customers in various outlets. They use three varieties of coffee beans to make the three types of coffee blends from which the types of coffee are provided. Although the recipes for the three types are not fully precise, certain restrictions must be satisfied when combining the three varieties of beans:

Component 1 should constitute not more than 20% of final Blend 1 by weight
Component 2 should constitute at least 30% of Blend 3 by weight.
Components 2 and 3 combined should constitute at least 70% of Blend 2 by weight.

In addition to these restrictions, there is limited availability of the three varieties. The maximum weekly availability is 8000, 10,000 and 9000 kg, respectively. Weekly capacity of the plant is 25,000 kg. To satisfy the needs of a nearby office customer, weekly production of Blend 1 should be at least 5000 kg.

Given that the three varieties cost the manufacturer Rs. 120, Rs. 130 and Rs. 110 per kg and the coffee sold using the blends yield Rs. 300, Rs. 320 and Rs. 280 per kg, find the number of kg of each variety to be used in each type so that it maximizes the final profit.

1.4 A cotton shirt company has introduced a new brand called "Ultimate comfort" that it sells through retail outlets. The company has the capacity to produce P shirts per week. The demand from retail outlet j is D_j. The total demand being higher than the capacity, the company engages a subcontractor who can make the same shirt and sends the subcontractor made shirt to the retail outlet only after it passes the strict quality control of the company. Let us call the two types as Type A shirt and Type B shirt, respectively.

The company wants to be fair to its retail outlets and, therefore, wants to ensure that they get their proportionate share of Type A shirts. They find it difficult to give the exact proportion and, therefore, would like to give to every retailer between 90% and 110% of their proportional share of Type A shirts. The subcontractor can produce only Q amount of Type B shirts every week. The company incurs a penalty of C_j for every unfulfilled demand of retailer j, after taking into account Type B shirts. Each Type A shirts costs Rs. R to produce and each Type B shirt costs Rs. S including for production by the subcontractor and quality check.

Formulate a linear programming problem for the cost minimization for the cotton shirt company.

1.5 M students want to apply for the higher studies in OR. There are n universities available. Each student has a success factor associated with a university. This is a number between 0 and 10 and has zero if the student does not want to apply to that university. Student i wants to apply to not more than u_i and not less than l_i universities. They also do not want more than b_j students to apply to university j. They want to maximize the total success factor. Formulate this as an OR problem.

1.6 A university wishes to give leave during the last week of the year to its non-vacation staff. However, keeping in mind routine jobs and the need to answer the enquiries, they decide to have reduced staff working. The requirement of staff for the five days is 6, 4, 5, 3 and 7 people. The additional requirements are:

(a) Each employee must be on duty exactly for four days.
(b) An employee does not wish to work for more than three consecutive days.

Formulate this problem as a linear programming problem.

1.7 A Trim sheet company requires rectangular sheets of width 8, 11, 13 and 15 inches to be cut from a two different rolls of width 50 and 60, respectively. One dimensional cutting is considered. The requirements are 503, 613, 291 and 407 sheets of the four thicknesses, respectively. Formulate a linear programming problem to minimize waste assuming that the excess sheets cut are treated as waste.

1.8 A manufacturing company produces a final product that is assembled using one each of three different parts. The parts are manufactured within the company by two different departments. Owing to the different set up of the machines, the two departments produce the three parts at different rates. Table 1.8 gives the production rates and the available time per week to manufacture these three parts.

Table 1.8 Production Rates and Available Time per Week

Department	Available hours per week	Production rate (units per hour)		
		Part 1	Part 2	Part 3
1	100	8	5	10
2	80	6	12	4

Formulate a linear programming problem to maximize the number of assembled products.

1.9 Two jobs A and B are manufactured in two dedicated cells I and II separated from each other. Job A requires processing on four machines that are arranged in a line layout. The unit processing times are 3, 4, 5, and 3 minutes, respectively. Job B requires five machines that are arranged in a line and the unit processing times are 3, 2, 5, 3 and 2 minutes, respectively. Exactly 100 pieces of both A and B have to be made and sent to the same customer after both are completed.

There are five operators available and the problem is to find the number of operators allocated to each of the cells. The production system is such that every operator processes the part on all the machines, taking the part individually from one machine to another. The operators follow each other in a "rabbit chasing" mode. Each operator takes a new piece after finishing all the operations on the existing piece.

Neglecting walking times, formulate a linear programming problem to minimize the time taken to completely produce A and B?

1.10 Rohit has Rs. 10 lakhs with him and wishes to invest it for the next ten years. Three schemes are available. The first scheme he can invest in multiples of 1 lakh and gets 5% return at the end of the year. In the second scheme, he can invest in multiples of 2 lakhs for a two-year period and gets 6% per year simple interest. The third scheme he has to invest in multiples of 3 lakhs for a three-year period and gets 7% per year simple interest. How should he invest to maximize his return at the end of ten years?

1.11 One hundred students have taken an examination and three teachers are available for evaluation. They can correct at the rate of 10, 8 and 9 scripts per hour. School wants to announce the marks to the students within four hours. The three evaluators are likely to be total the marks correctly 95%, 97% and 98% of the times. The students can bring the answer books for re-evaluation if the totals are incorrect. Formulate a linear programming problem to allot answer books to teachers to minimize the re-evaluation.

1.12 A Taste Jam Company makes a special type of mixed fruit jam, which uses three types of fruits. There are three growers, each growing all the three types of fruits. These fruits are then transported to two processing plants to be converted into jam.

Plant i requires b_{ik} cartons of fruit of type k. Let a_{jk} be the maximum number of cartons of fruit k that can be grown and supplied by Grower j.

The cost per carton of purchasing fruit k from Grower j is C_{jk} and the cost of transporting one carton of fruit k from Grower j to Plant i is C_{ijk}. Formulate an appropriate linear programme to determine the optimal purchasing and distribution policies.

1.13 Charan has applied to three jobs and wishes to prepare his resume specific to the job applied to. He has eight days available to prepare the resumes. He estimates his probability of success (in percentage) to be $55 + 3X_1$, $51 + 4X_2$ and $48 + 6X_3$, respectively if X_1, X_2 and X_3 days are allotted to the three resumes. He wishes to allot the days in such a way to maximize the minimum expected success estimate. Formulate a linear programming problem for this situation.

2

Linear Programming—
Solutions

Let us consider the following linear programming problem given by

Maximize $Z = 6X_1 + 5X_2$

Subject to

$$X_1 + X_2 \leq 5$$
$$3X_1 + 2X_2 \leq 12$$
$$X_1, X_2 \geq 0$$

The problem has two variables and two constraints. Let us first explain the graphical method to solve the problem.

2.1 THE GRAPHICAL METHOD

The graph corresponding to the constraints is shown in Figure 2.1. There are four corner points given by (0, 0), (4, 0), (0, 5) and (2, 3).

The shaded region has all points satisfying all the constraints. All points in this region satisfy all the constraints and are **feasible solutions**. This region is called the **feasible region**. The region other than the feasible region is the **infeasible region**, in which every point violates at least one constraint. We are interested only in the feasible region since we want to solve the given problem to find the best solution satisfying all the constraints.

Let us consider any point inside the feasible region, say (1, 1). There is always one point to the right or above this point that is feasible and has a higher value of the objective

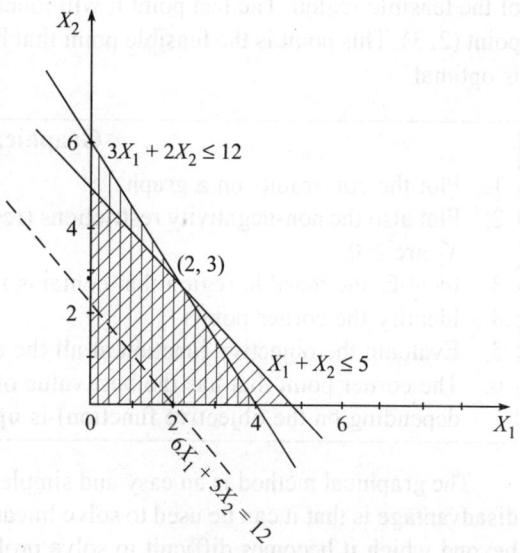

Figure 2.1 Graphical solution.

21

function. For example, points (1, 2) and (2, 1) have better values of the objective function than the point (1, 1). This is because the objective function coefficients are both positive. This means that for every point inside the feasible region, we can move to the right or move above till we come out of the feasible regions and the last point inside the feasible region will have a better value of the objective function. If the objective function had negative coefficients, points to the left or below will be superior. This means that it is enough to consider the boundary of the feasible region to search for the best solution.

Let us consider the objective function $6X_1 + 5X_2$. The slope of the objective function is different from the slope of both of the constraints. In such cases, we can show that for every point on the boundary of the feasible region, one of the corner points (points of intersection of the constraints) will be superior in terms of the objective function. Therefore, it is enough to consider only the corner points to reach the best solution.

In our example, there are four corner points. These are (0, 0), (4, 0), (0, 5) and (2, 3). Let us evaluate the objective function at these points.

At (0, 0), $Z = 0$
At (4, 0), $Z = 24$
At (0, 5), $Z = 25$
At (2, 3), $Z = 27$

We observe that the corner point (2, 3) given by the solution $X_1 = 2, X_2 = 3$ has the maximum objective function value of $Z = 27$. This is the best solution or **optimal solution**.

Another way to reach the optimum solution is to plot the objective function for some arbitrary value $6X_1 + 5X_2 = 12$ (say). This line is shown in Figure 2.1. Since we want to maximize $6X_1 + 5X_2$, we plot another line for $6X_1 + 5X_2 = 20$ (say). This line is parallel to the first line and is moving in the direction of increase of the objective function line. If we want to maximize $6X_1 + 5X_2$, then we move it in the direction of increase. We can move the line until it comes out of the feasible region. The last point it will touch before it leaves the feasible region is the corner point (2, 3). This point is the feasible point that has the highest value of the objective function and is optimal.

Graphical method

1. Plot the constraints on a graph.
2. Plot also the non-negativity restrictions (restrict yourself to the quadrant where both X_1 and X_2 are ≥ 0.
3. Identify the feasible region that contains the set of points satisfying all the constraints.
4. Identify the corner points.
5. Evaluate the objective function at all the corner points.
6. The corner point that has the best value of the objective function (maximum or minimum depending on the objective function) is **optimal**.

The graphical method is an easy and simple approach to get to the optimal solution. The only disadvantage is that it can be used to solve linear programming problems with two variables only, beyond which it becomes difficult to solve problems using this approach.

2.2 THE ALGEBRAIC METHOD

Let us consider the earlier problem again and illustrate the algebraic method.

Maximize $Z = 6X_1 + 5X_2$
Subject to
$$X_1 + X_2 \leq 5$$
$$3X_1 + 2X_2 \leq 12$$

Assuming that we know to solve linear equations, we convert the inequalities into equations by adding slack variables X_3 and X_4, respectively. These two slack variables do not contribute to the objective function. The linear programming problem becomes

Maximize $Z = 6X_1 + 5X_2 + 0X_3 + 0X_4$
Subject to
$$X_1 + X_2 + X_3 = 5$$
$$3X_1 + 2X_2 + X_4 = 12$$

With the addition of the slack variables, we now have four variables and two equations. With two equations, we can solve only for two variables. We have to fix any two variables to some arbitrary value and can solve for the remaining two variables. The two variables that we fix arbitrary values can be chosen in $^4C_2 = 6$ ways. In each of these six combinations, we can actually fix the variables to any arbitrary value resulting in infinite number of solutions. However, we consider fixing the arbitrary value to zero and hence consider only six distinct possible solutions. The variables that we fix to zero are called **non-basic variables** and the variables that we solve are called **basic variables**. These solutions obtained by fixing the non-basic variables to zero are called **basic solutions**. There are as many basic variables as the number of constraints.

The six basic solutions are:

1. Variables X_1 and X_2 are non-basic and set to zero. Substituting, we get $X_3 = 5$, $X_4 = 12$ and the value of the objective function $Z = 0$.
2. Variables X_1 and X_3 are non-basic and set to zero. Substituting, we solve for $X_2 = 5$ and $2X_2 + X_4 = 12$ and get $X_2 = 5$, $X_4 = 2$ and value of objective function $Z = 25$.
3. Variables X_1 and X_4 are non-basic and set to zero. Substituting, we solve for $X_2 + X_3 = 5$ and $2X_2 = 12$ and get $X_2 = 6$, $X_3 = -1$
4. Variables X_2 and X_3 are non-basic and set to zero. Substituting, we solve for $X_1 = 5$ and $3X_1 + X_4 = 12$ and get $X_1 = 5$, $X_4 = -3$.
5. Variables X_2 and X_4 are non-basic and set to zero. Substituting, we solve for $X_1 + X_3 = 5$ and $3X_1 = 12$ and get $X_1 = 4$, $X_3 = 1$ and value of objective function $Z = 24$.
6. Variables X_3 and X_4 are non-basic and set to zero. Substituting, we solve for $X_1 + X_2 = 5$ and $3X_1 + 2X_2 = 12$ and get $X_1 = 2$, $X_2 = 3$ and value of objective function $Z = 27$.

Among these six basic solutions, we observe that four are feasible. Those basic solutions that are feasible (satisfy all constraints) are called **basic feasible solutions**. The remaining two (Solutions 3 and 4) have negative values for some variables and are, therefore, **infeasible**. We are interested only in feasible solutions and, therefore, do not evaluate the objective function for infeasible solutions.

The optimal solution is the basic feasible solution that maximizes the objective function. The optimal solution is $X_1 = 2, X_2 = 3$ and $Z = 27$. It is to be observed that there are as many variables in the solution as the number of constraints.

Let us consider a non-basic solution from the sixth solution. Let us assume that variables X_3 and X_4 are fixed to arbitrary values (other than zero). We have to fix them at non-negative values because otherwise they will become infeasible. Let us fix them as $X_3 = 1$ and $X_4 = 1$. On substitution, we get $X_1 + X_2 = 4$ and $3X_1 + 2X_2 = 11$ and get $X_1 = 3, X_2 = 1$ and value of objective function $Z = 23$. This non-basic feasible solution is clearly inferior to the solution $X_1 = 2, X_2 = 3$ obtained as a basic feasible solution by fixing X_3 and X_4 to zero. The solution (3, 1) is an interior point in the feasible region while the basic feasible solution (2, 3) is a corner point. We have already seen that it is enough to evaluate corner points.

We can observe that the four basic feasible solutions correspond to the four corner points. Every non-basic solution that is feasible corresponds to an interior point in the feasible region and every basic feasible solution corresponds to a corner point solution. Therefore, in the algebraic method it is enough to evaluate the basic solutions, find out the feasible ones and evaluate the objective function to obtain the optimal solution.

Algebraic method

1. Convert the inequalities into equations by adding slack variables.
2. Assuming that there are *m* equations and *n* variables, set *n-m* (non-basic) variables to zero and evaluate the solution for the remaining *m* basic variables. Evaluate the objective function if the basic solution is feasible.
3. Perform Step 2 for all the ^nC_m combinations of basic variables.
4. Identify the optimum solution as the one with the maximum (minimum) value of the objective function.

The following are the limitations of the algebraic method:

1. We have to evaluate all the ^nC_m basic solutions before we obtain the optimum.
2. Some basic solutions can be feasible and we have to evaluate them also.
3. Among the basic feasible solutions, we don't evaluate better and better solutions. Some of the subsequently evaluated basic feasible solutions can have inferior value of the objective function when compared to the best solution.

What we therefore need is a method that

1. Does not evaluate any basic infeasible solution.
2. Progressively obtains better and better feasible solutions.
3. Identifies the optimum solution the moment it is reached so that all basic feasible solutions are not evaluated.

The algorithm that has all the above characteristics is the *simplex algorithm* (Dantzig 1963). We first explain this algorithm in an algebraic form and then in the tabular form.

2.3 ALGEBRAIC FORM OF THE SIMPLEX ALGORITHM

Let us consider the same problem which was discussed earlier to illustrate this algorithm.

Maximize $\quad Z = 6X_1 + 5X_2 + 0X_3 + 0X_4$

Subject to
$$X_1 + X_2 + X_3 = 5$$
$$3X_1 + 2X_2 + X_4 = 12$$
$$X_1, X_2 \geq 0$$

Iteration 1

We start with a basic feasible solution with X_3 and X_4 as basic variables. We write the basic variables in terms of the non-basic variables as:

$$X_3 = 5 - X_1 - X_2$$
$$X_4 = 12 - 3X_1 - 2X_2$$
$$Z = 0 + 6X_1 + 5X_2$$

The present solution has $Z = 0$, since X_1 and X_2 are presently non-basic with value zero. We want to increase Z and this is possible by increasing X_1 or X_2. We choose to increase X_1 by bringing it to the basis because it has the highest rate of increase.

Considering the equation $X_3 = 5 - X_1 - X_2$, X_1 can be increased to 5 beyond which X_3 will be negative and infeasible. Considering the equation $X_4 = 12 - 3X_1 - 2X_2$, X_1 can be increased to 4 beyond which X_4 will become negative. The limiting value of X_1 (or the allowable upper limit on X_1) is 4 from the second equation.

Iteration 2

Since variable X_1 becomes basic based on the following equation:

$$X_4 = 12 - 3X_1 - 2X_2 \tag{2.1}$$

We rewrite Eq. (2.1) as

$$3X_1 = 12 - 2X_2 - X_4 \tag{2.2}$$

from which

$$X_1 = 4 - \frac{2}{3}X_2 - \frac{1}{3}X_4 \tag{2.3}$$

Substituting the value of X_1 from Eq. (2.3) in the following equation

$$X_3 = 5 - X_1 - X_2 \tag{2.4}$$

we get

$$X_3 = 5 - (4 - \frac{2}{3}X_2 - \frac{1}{3}X_4) - X_2$$

which on simplification yields

$$X_3 = 1 - \frac{1}{3}X_2 + \frac{1}{3}X_4 \tag{2.5}$$

Now,

$$Z = 6(4 - \frac{2}{3}X_2 - \frac{1}{3}X_4) + 5X_2 = 24 + X_2 - 2X_4 \tag{2.6}$$

Our objective is to maximize Z and this can be achieved by increasing X_2 or by decreasing X_4. Decreasing X_4 is not possible because X_4 is at zero and decreasing it will make it infeasible. Increasing X_2 is possible since it is at zero.

From Eq. (2.3) we observe that X_2 can be increased to 6 beyond which variable X_1 would become negative and infeasible. From Eq. (2.5) we observe that X_2 can be increased up to 3 beyond which variable X_3 will be negative. The limiting value is 3 and variable X_2 replaces variable X_3 in the basis.

Iteration 3

Rewriting Eq. (2.5) in terms of X_2, we get

$$X_2 = 3 - 3X_3 + X_4 \qquad (2.7)$$

Substituting for X_2 in Eq. (2.3), we have

$$X_1 = 4 - \frac{2}{3} X_2 - \frac{1}{3} X_4 = 4 - \frac{2}{3}(3 - 3X_3 + X_4) - \frac{1}{3} X_4$$

$$X_1 = 2 + 2X_3 - X_4 \qquad (2.8)$$

Now,
$$Z = 24 + 3 - 3X_3 + X_4 - 2X_4 = 27 - 3X_3 - X_4$$

We would still like to increase Z and this is possible only if we can decrease X_3 or X_4 since both have a negative coefficient in Z. Both are non-basic at zero and will only yield infeasible solutions if we decrease them. We observe that the optimum is reached since there is no entering variable. The optimum solution is given by

$$X_1 = 2, \qquad X_2 = 3 \qquad \text{and} \qquad Z = 27$$

We observe that the above method meets all our requirements but does some extra computations in finding out the limiting value of the entering variable for every iteration. Experience has indicated that this method is superior and computationally faster than the algebraic method.

2.4 TABULAR FORM OF THE SIMPLEX ALGORITHM

The simplex method can be represented in a tabular form, where only the numbers are written in a certain easily understandable form. Several forms are available but we present only one version of the simplex method in tabular form. Table 2.1 represents the simplex tableau for the first iteration.

Table 2.1 Simplex Tableau for the First Iteration

C_B	Basic variables	6 X_1	5 X_2	0 X_3	0 X_4	RHS	θ
0	X_3	1	1	1	0	5	5
0	X_4	3	2	0	1	12	4
	$C_j - Z_j$	6	5	0	0		

The second row has all the variables listed. Above them (in the first row) are the objective function coefficients of the variables. Under the basic variables, variables X_3 and X_4 are shown. To their left are the objective function values of the basic variables. To the right of the basic variables are the constraints written in the form of the equations along with the right hand side values of the constraints.

The $C_j - Z_j$ for a variable is C_j minus the dot product of the C_B and the column corresponding to the variable j. For example, $C_1 - Z_1 = 6 - (0 \times 1 + 0 \times 3) = 6$. The variable with maximum positive value of $C_j - Z_j$ enters. In our example, it is variable X_1 shown with an arrow. The θ values are the ratios between the RHS value and the coefficient under the entering variable column. In our example, these are $5/1 = 5$ and $12/3 = 4$, respectively. The minimum θ is 4 and variable X_4 is the leaving variable. Now, variable X_1 replaces X_4 as the basic variable in the next iteration.

In the previous iteration, we were solving for variables X_3 and X_4. They had an identity matrix as their coefficients (or X_3 and X_4 appeared in one equation only with a + 1 coefficient), so that we can directly solve them. In the next iteration, we need to rewrite the constraints (rows) such that X_3 and X_1 have the identity matrix as coefficients. We call the row corresponding to the leaving variable as the *pivot row* and the corresponding element in the entering column as the *pivot element*. The pivot element is shown in bold in Table 2.1. Table 2.2 shows the first two iterations of the simplex algorithm.

Rules for row operations in a simplex table

1. Rewrite the new pivot row by dividing every element in the row by the pivot element.
2. For every non-pivot row i rewrite every element j in this row as new a_{ij} = old $a_{ij} - a_{j1} \times a_{kj}$ where a_{j1} is the element in the entering column 1 and row k is the pivot row.

Table 2.2 First Two Iterations of the Simplex Algorithm

C_B	Basic variables	6 X_1	5 X_2	0 X_3	0 X_4	RHS	θ
0	X_3	1	1	1	0	5	5
0	X_4	**3** ↑	2	0	1	12	4 →
	$C_j - Z_j$	6	5	0	0		
0	X_3	0	1/3	1	−1/3	1	3 →
6	X_1	1	2/3 ↑	0	1/3	4	6
	$C_j - Z_j$	0	1	0	−2	24	

Here variable X_2 with a positive value of $C_j - Z_j$ enters the basis. The θ values are $1 \div 1/3 = 3$ and $4 \div 2/3 = 6$, respectively. Since minimum $\theta = 3$ from first equation, variable X_3 leaves the basis and is replaced by X_2. The row operations resulting in the identity matrix for columns X_2 and X_1 are carried out as explained before. Table 2.3 shows all the three iterations.

Table 2.3 Three Iterations

C_B	Basic variables	6 X_1	5 X_2	0 X_3	0 X_4	RHS	θ
0	X_3	1	1	1	0	5	5
0	X_4	3↑	2	0	1	12	4 →
	$C_j - Z_j$	6	5	0	0	0	
0	X_3	0	1/3	1	−1/3	1	3 →
6	X_1	1	2/3↑	0	1/3	4	6
	$C_j - Z_j$	0	1	0	−2	24	
5	X_2	0	1	3	−1	3	
6	X_1	1	0	−2	1	2	
	$C_j - Z_j$	0	0	−3	−1	27	

The $C_j - Z_j$ values for the non-basic variables are −3 and −1 and are negative. The algorithm terminates with the solution $X_1 = 2$, $X_2 = 3$ with $Z = 27$ as the optimal solution.

We observe that the **increase** in the objective function value in every iteration is the **product** of the $C_j - Z_j$ value of the entering variable and the minimum θ corresponding to the leaving variable.

ILLUSTRATION 2.1

Consider the example:

Maximize $Z = 6X_1 + 8X_2$

Subject to

$$X_1 + X_2 \leq 10$$
$$2X_1 + 3X_2 \leq 25$$
$$X_1 + 5X_2 \leq 35$$
$$X_1, X_2 \geq 0$$

Adding slack variables, we get

Maximize $Z = 6X_1 + 8X_2 + 0X_3 + 0X_4 + 0X_5$

Subject to

$$X_1 + X_2 + X_3 = 10$$
$$2X_1 + 3X_2 + X_4 = 25$$
$$X_1 + 5X_2 + X_5 = 35$$
$$X_1, X_2, X_3, X_4, X_5 \geq 0$$

The iterations of the simplex algorithm for the problem are shown in Table 2.4.

Table 2.4 Simplex iterations for Illustration 2.1

		6	8	0	0	0		
		X_1	X_2	X_3	X_4	X_5	RHS	θ
0	X_3	1	1	1	0	0	10	10
0	X_4	2	3	0	1	0	25	25/3
0	X_5	1	5	0	0	1	35	7
	$C_j - Z_j$	6	8	0	0	0	0	
0	X_3	4/5	0	1	0	–1/5	3	15/4
0	X_4	7/5	0	0	1	–3/5	4	20/7
8	X_2	1/5	1	0	0	1/5	7	35
	$C_j - Z_j$	22/5	0	0	0	–8/5	56	
0	X_3	0	0	1	–4/7	1/7	5/7	5
6	X_1	1	0	0	5/7	–3/7	20/7	---
8	X_2	0	1	0	–1/7	2/7	45/7	45/2
	$C_j - Z_j$	0	0	0	–22/7	2/7	480/7	
0	X_5	0	0	7	–4	1	5	
6	X_1	1	0	3	–1	0	5	
8	X_2	0	1	–2	1	0	5	
	$C_j - Z_j$	0	0	–2	–2	0	70	

The important observations from Table 2.4 are as follows:

1. The variable X_5 leaves the simplex table in the first iteration but enters the table again as a basic variable in the fourth (last) iteration. This can happen frequently in simplex iterations. A variable that leaves the table can enter the basis again in a subsequent iteration. This also indicates that there is no upper limit for the number of iterations. If the condition that a leaving variable does not enter again holds, then it is possible to define an upper limit on the number of iterations. Unfortunately this is not true.
2. Every iteration is characterized by the set of basic variables and not by the presence or absence of a single variable.
3. In the third iteration we have not computed all the values of θ. There is one place where we have to divide the RHS value (20/7) by a negative number (–3/7). We do not compute this value of θ. We have to compute values of θ, only when they are strictly non-negative. This is because a negative value or infinity of θ indicates that for any value of the entering variable, the leaving variable does not become negative.

The **three** important steps (or stages) in the simplex algorithm are:

1. The algorithm starts with a basic feasible solution (Initialization). The Right Hand Side (RHS) values are always non-negative.
2. The algorithm goes through the intermediate iterations where solution with better values of the objective function are found (Iteration).
3. The algorithm terminates when there is no entering variable to provide the optimal solution (Termination).

Are there issues that have to be explicitly considered? Do all linear programming problems have optimal solutions? Does the simplex algorithm always terminate by providing optimal solution? Let us look at these and other issues in initialization, iteration and termination in detail.

2.4.1 Initialization

ILLUSTRATION 2.2

Let us consider the following problem:
Minimize $Z = 3X_1 + 4X_2$
Subject to
$$2X_1 + 3X_2 \geq 8$$
$$5X_1 + 2X_2 \geq 12$$
$$X_1, X_2 \geq 0$$

The first step is to convert the inequalities into equations. We add variables X_3 and X_4, called **negative slack** (or surplus) **variables** that have to be subtracted from the left hand side values to equate to the RHS values. These surplus variables are also defined to be ≥ 0 (non-negative). The problem now becomes
Minimize $Z = 3X_1 + 4X_2 + 0X_3 + 0X_4$
Subject to
$$2X_1 + 3X_2 - X_3 = 8$$
$$5X_1 + 2X_2 - X_4 = 12$$
$$X_1, X_2, X_3, X_4 \geq 0$$

Once again we have four variables and two equations (constraints). We need a starting basic feasible solution to start the simplex algorithm. The easiest among the basic solutions is to fix the surplus variables as basic variables and solve the problem. Such a solution is easily readable because each surplus variable appears only in one constraint and has +1 coefficient. There is an identity coefficient matrix associated with the surplus variables.

Unfortunately this solution is $X_3 = -8$ and $X_4 = -12$ which is infeasible. This is not a basic feasible solution and cannot be used as an initial solution to start the simplex table.

In general, when the constraints are inequalities, starting the simplex algorithm with surplus variables as basic is not possible because we will be starting with an infeasible solution.

We, therefore, have to identify a starting basic feasible solution which has some other set of basic variables. One way to do this is to follow the algebraic method till we get a feasible solution and start with this as the first iteration for the simplex method. We don't follow this approach because it may take many trials in an algebraic method before we get a first feasible solution.

We normally use an indirect approach to get the starting solution for the simplex table. If we introduced two new variables arbitrarily (say, X_5 and X_6) such that
$$2X_1 + 3X_2 - X_3 + X_5 = 8$$
$$5X_1 + 2X_2 - X_4 + X_6 = 12$$

Variables X_5 and X_6 automatically provide us with a starting basic feasible solution with $X_5 = 8$ and $X_6 = 12$. This is basic feasible and we can proceed with the simplex table.

We should understand that variables X_5 and X_6 are not part of the original problem and have been introduced by us to get a starting basic feasible solution. These are called **artificial variables** and have been introduced for the specific purpose of starting the simplex table. These are now denoted by a_1 and a_2. Since they are not part of the original problem, we have to ensure that they should not be in the optimal solution (when we find the optimum). We ensure this by giving a very large and positive value (say, 10,000) to the objective function value.

The problem now becomes

Minimize $Z = 3X_1 + 4X_2 + 0X_3 + 0X_4 + 10,000a_1 + 10,000a_2$
Subject to

$$2X_1 + 3X_2 - X_3 + a_1 = 8$$
$$5X_1 + 2X_2 - X_4 + a_2 = 12$$
$$X_1, X_2, X_3, X_4, a_1, a_2 \geq 0$$

If the given problem has an optimal solution, it will not involve a_1 or a_2 because a_1 and a_2, the artificial variables are not part of the original problem. Every basic feasible solution to the new problem (with the artificial variables) will have an objective function value more than every basic feasible solution without either of the artificial variables, because the artificial variables have a very large and positive contribution to the minimization objective function. Therefore, providing a large positive value to the objective function coefficient of the artificial variable ensures that the artificial variables do not appear in the optimal solution (if it exists).

We define the large and positive value to the objective function coefficient of the artificial variable as M (big M), which is large and positive and tending to infinity. We have

$$M * \text{constant} = M$$
$$M \pm \text{constant} = M$$

Now, we begin the simplex table to start solving the problem. Since our standard problem has a maximization objective function, we multiply the coefficients of the objective function of the minimization problem by -1 and convert it to a maximization problem. The simplex iteration is shown in Table 2.5.

Table 2.5 Simplex Table for Illustration 2.2

		−3	−4	0	0	−M	−M		
		X_1	X_2	X_3	X_4	a_1	a_2	RHS	θ
−M	a_1	2	3	−1	0	1	0	8	4 12/5 →
−M	a_2	5↑	2	0	−1	0	1	12	
	$C_j - Z_j$	5M−3	5M−4	−M	−M	0	0		
−M	a_1	0	11/5 ↑	−1	2/5 − 3/5	1	−2/5	16/5	16/116 →
−3	X_1	1	2/5	0	0	0	1/5	12/5	
	$C_j - Z_j$	0	11/5M + 14/5	−M	2/5M − 3/5	0	−7/5M + 3/5		
−4	X_2	0	1	−5/11	2/11	5/11	−2/11	16/11	
−3	X_1	1	0	2/11	−3/11	−2/11	3/11	20/11	
	$C_j - Z_j$	0	0	−14/11	−1/11	−ve	−ve	−124/11	

The optimum solution is $X_1 = 20/11$, $X_2 = 16/11$ and $Z = 124/11$. The simplex table will show a negative value because we have solved a maximization problem by multiplying the objective function by -1.

The Simplex method involving big M is called the **Big M** method.

Some important observations are

1. It is easier to introduce artificial variables when the problem does not have a visible initial basic feasible solution. We introduce as many artificial variables as the number of constraints. The number of variables increases and not the number of constraints. The big M ensures that the artificial variables do not appear in the optimal solution (if one exists).
2. Since we have two artificial variables as the starting basic variables, we need a minimum of two iterations to find the optimum, since they have to leave the basis.
3. We need not evaluate the $C_j - Z_j$ values corresponding to the artificial variables at all because we don't want the artificial variable to enter the basis. They have been shown as negative in Table 2.5.

There is another method called **two-phase method** from which we can get an initial basic feasible solution for the simplex algorithm using artificial variables. This is explained below for the same example.

Here, the artificial variables have an objective function coefficient of -1 (Maximization). The other variables have an objective function coefficient of zero. The simplex iterations are shown in Table 2.6.

Table 2.6 Phase I of two-phase Method

		0	0	0	0	−1	−1		
		X_1	X_2	X_3	X_4	a_1	a_2	RHS	θ
−1	a_1	2	3	−1	0	1	0	8	4 12/5
−1	a_2	5	2	0	−1	0	1	12	
	$C_j - Z_j$	5	5	−1	−1	0	0		
−1	a_1	0	11/5	−1	2/5 − 1/5	1	−2/5	16/5	16/116
0	X_1	1	2/5	0		0	1/5	12/5	
	$C_j - Z_j$	0	11/5	−1	−2/5	0	−7/5		
0	X_2	0	1	−5/11	2/11	5/11	−2/11	16/11	
0	X_1	1	0	2/11	−3/11	−2/11	3/11	20/11	
	$C_j - Z_j$	0	0	0	0	−1	−1	0	

Having obtained the optimum for the first phase with $X_1 = 20/11$ and $X_2 = 16/11$, we can start the second phase of the simplex algorithm from the first phase by eliminating the artificial variables. The second phase iterations are shown in Table 2.7.

Table 2.7 Phase II of two-phase Method

		−3	−4	0	0	
		X_1	X_2	X_3	X_4	RHS
−4	X_2	0	1	−5/11	2/11	16/11
−3	X_1	1	0	2/11	−3/11	20/11
	$C_j - Z_j$	0	0	−14/11	−1/11	−124/11

For our example, we realize that the starting basic feasible solution without artificial variables at the end of the first phase is optimal. If it is not, then we proceed with the simplex iterations to get the optimal solution.

Initialization deals with getting an initial basic feasible solution for the given problem. Identifying a set of basic variables with an identity coefficient matrix is the outcome of the initialization process. We have to consider the following aspects of initialization (in the same order as stated):

1. Right Hand Side (RHS) values
2. Variables
3. Objective function
4. Constraints.

Let us consider each of them in detail.

The Right Hand Side (RHS) value of every constraint should be non-negative. It is usually a rational number. If it is negative, we have to multiply the constraint by −1 to make the RHS non-negative. The sign of the inequality will change.

The variables can be of three types: ≥ type, ≤ type and unrestricted. Of the three, ≥ type is desirable. If we have ≤ type variable, we replace it with another variable of ≥ type as follows:

If variable X_k is ≤ 0, we replace it with variable $X_p = -X_k$ and $X_p \geq 0$. This change is incorporated in all the constraints as well as in the objective function.

If a variable is unrestricted, then it can take a negative value, positive value or zero. For example, if variable X_k is unrestricted, it is replaced by $X_k = X_p - X_q$ where both X_p and X_q are ≥ 0. This change is incorporated in all the constraints as well as in the objective function.

The objective function can be either maximization or minimization. If it is minimization, we multiply it with −1 and convert it to a maximization problem and solve.

Constraints are of three types: ≥ type, ≤ type and equation. If a constraint is of ≤ type, we add a slack variable and convert it to an equation. If it is of ≤ type, we add a surplus variable (negative slack) and convert it to an equation. If necessary, we add artificial variables to identify a starting basic feasible solution. We illustrate this using some examples.

ILLUSTRATION 2.3

Maximize $Z = 7X_1 + 5X_2$
Subject to

$$2X_1 + 3X_2 = 7$$
$$5X_1 + 2X_2 \geq 11$$
$$X_1, X_2 \geq 0$$

We convert the second constraint into an equation by adding a negative slack variable X_3. The equations are:

$$2X_1 + 3X_2 = 7$$
$$5X_1 + 2X_2 - X_3 = 11$$

The constraint coefficient matrix is

$$C = \begin{bmatrix} 2 & 3 & 0 \\ 5 & 2 & -1 \end{bmatrix}$$

We do not find variables with coefficients as in an identity matrix. We have to add two *artificial variables* a_1 and a_2 to get

$$2X_1 + 3X_2 + a_1 = 7$$
$$5X_1 + 2X_2 - X_3 + a_2 = 11$$

We have to start with a_1 and a_2 as basic variables and use the big M method.

ILLUSTRATION 2.4

Maximize $Z = 7X_1 + 5X_2 + 8X_3 + 6X_4$
Subject to

$$2X_1 + 3X_2 + X_3 = 7$$
$$5X_1 + 2X_2 + X_4 \geq 11$$
$$X_1, X_2, X_3, X_4 \geq 0$$

In this example, we add surplus variable X_5 to the second constraint to convert it to an equation. We get

$$2X_1 + 3X_2 + X_3 = 7$$
$$5X_1 + 2X_2 + X_4 - X_5 = 11$$

We observe that variables X_3 and X_4 have coefficients of the identity matrix and we can start with these as initial basic variables to have a basic feasible solution. We need not use artificial variables in this case.

If the second constraint was $5X_1 + 2X_2 + 2X_4 \geq 11$, we can write it as $5/2X_1 + X_2 + X_4 \geq 11/2$ and then add the surplus variable and choose X_4 as a starting basic variable.

Adding artificial variables

1. Ensure that the RHS value of every constraint is non-negative.
2. If we have a $\leq$ constraint, we add a slack variable. This automatically qualifies to be an initial basic variable.
3. If we have a $\geq$ constraint, we add a negative slack to convert it to an equation. This negative slack *cannot* qualify to be an initial basic variable.
4. In the system of equations identify whether there exist variables with coefficients corresponding to the column of the identity matrix. Such variables qualify to be basic variables. Add minimum artificial variables otherwise to get a starting basic feasible solution.

2.4.2 Iteration

During iteration, only one issue needs to be addressed. Let us explain this with an example.

ILLUSTRATION 2.5

Maximize $Z = 4X_1 + 3X_2$
Subject to
$$2X_1 + 3X_2 \leq 8$$
$$3X_1 + 2X_2 \leq 12$$
$$X_1, X_2 \geq 0$$

Adding slack variables X_3 and X_4, we get
$$2X_1 + 3X_2 + X_3 = 8$$
$$3X_1 + 2X_2 + X_4 = 12$$

We set up the simplex table with X_3 and X_4 as basic variables. The simplex iterations are shown in Table 2.8.

Table 2.8 Simplex Table for Illustration 2.5

C_B	Basic variables	4 X_1	3 X_2	0 X_3	0 X_4	RHS	θ
0	X_3	2	3	1	0	8	4
0	X_4	3↑	2	0	1	12	4→
	$C_j - Z_j$	4	3	0	0	0	
0	X_3	0	5/3	1	−2/3	0	0→
4	X_1	1	2/3↑	0	1/3	4	6
	$C_j - Z_j$	0	1/3	0	−4/3	16	
3	X_2	0	1	3/5	−2/5	0	
4	X_1	1	0	−2/5	3/5	4	
	$C_j - Z_j$	0	0	−1/5	−6/5	16	

In the simplex Table 2.8, there was a tie for the leaving variable. We had a choice between X_3 and X_4. We chose to leave out X_4. This tie resulted in a basic variable getting value zero in the next iteration. Although the optimal solution was found in the second iteration, it was not apparent then. We performed one more iteration without increasing the objective function but to obtain the optimality condition.

Whenever there is a tie for the leaving variable, one of the basic variable takes the value zero in the next iteration. This phenomenon is called **degeneracy**. We could perform some extra iterations that do not increase the value of the objective function. In this example, degeneracy occurs at the optimum.

Degeneracy results in extra iterations that do not improve the objective function value. Since the tie for the leaving variable, leaves a variable with zero value in the next iteration, we do not have an increase in the objective function value (Note that the increase in the objective function is the product of the $C_j - Z_j$ and θ, and the minimum θ takes the value zero).

Sometimes degeneracy can take place in the intermediate iterations. In such cases, if the optimum exists, the simplex algorithm will come out of the degeneracy by itself and terminate at the optimum. In these cases, the entering column will have a zero (or negative) value against the leaving row and hence that θ will not be computed, resulting in a positive value of the minimum θ.

There is no proven way to eliminate degeneracy or to avoid it. Sometimes a different tie breaking rule can result in termination in fewer iterations. In this example, if we had chosen to leave X_3 instead of X_4 in the first iteration, the algorithm terminates and gives the optimum after one iteration.

2.4.3 Termination

There are four aspects to be addressed while discussing termination conditions. These are:

1. Alternate optimum
2. Unboundedness
3. Infeasibility
4. Cycling

Let us consider each through an example.

ILLUSTRATION 2.6

Maximize $Z = 4X_1 + 3X_2$

Subject to

$$8X_1 + 6X_2 \leq 25$$
$$3X_1 + 4X_2 \leq 15$$
$$X_1, X_2 \geq 0$$

Adding slack variables X_3 and X_4, we can start the simplex iteration with X_3 and X_4 as basic variables. This is shown in Table 2.9.

Table 2.9 Simplex Table for Illustration 2.6

C_B	Basic variables	4 X_1	3 X_2	0 X_3	0 X_4	RHS	θ
0	X_3	8	6	1	0	25	25/8
0	X_4	3↑	4	0	1	15	
	$C_j - Z_j$	4	3	0	0	0	
4	X_1	1	3/4↑	1/8	0	25/8	25/6
0	X_4	0	7/4	–3/8	1	45/8	45/14
	$C_j - Z_j$	0	0	–1/2	0	25/2	
4	X_1	1	0	2/7	–3/7	5/7	
3	X_2	0	1	–3/14	4/7	45/14	
	$C_j - Z_j$	0	0	–1/2	0	25/2	

At the end of the first iteration we observe that the non-basic variables (X_2 and X_3) have non-positive values of $C_j - Z_j$, indicating that the optimum solution has been reached. However, one of the non-basic variables X_2 has a $C_j - Z_j$ value of zero. If we enter this, we get another optimum solution with the same value of the objective function. Now, non-basic variable X_3 has $C_3 - Z_3 = 0$ and if we enter X_3 and iterate, we get the table as in Iteration 2.

It looks as though the simplex algorithm seems to be getting into an infinite loop although the optimum has been found. This phenomenon is called **alternate optimum**. This happens when one of the constraints is parallel to the objective function. Actually there are infinite number of alternate optimum solutions for this problem, but the simplex algorithm shows only two of them corresponding to the corner points. Every point on the line joining these two solutions is also optimal.

The advantage of computing the alternate cornet point optima is that one of them may be chosen for implementation after considering other aspects. For example, the solution with $X_1 = 25/8$ can result in usage of lesser resources since resource X_4 is basic. The solution $X_1 = 5/7$, $X_2 = 45/14$ uses all the resources. Sometimes one of the solution may be integer valued resulting in immediate acceptance for implementation.

ILLUSTRATION 2.7

Maximize $Z = 4X_1 + 3X_2$
Subject to
$$X_1 - 6X_2 \leq 5$$
$$3X_1 \leq 11$$
$$X_1, X_2 \geq 0$$

Adding slack variables X_3 and X_4, we can start the simplex iteration with X_3 and X_4 as basic variables. This is shown in Table 2.10.

Table 2.10 Simplex Table for Illustration 2.7

C_B	Basic variables	4 X_1	3 X_2	0 X_3	0 X_4	RHS	θ
0	X_3	1	−6	1	0	5	5
0	X_4	3↑	0	0	1	11	11/3
	$C_j - Z_j$	4	3	0	0	0	
0	X_3	0	−6	1	−1/3	4/3	
4	X_1	1	0↑	0	1/3	11/3	
	$C_j - Z_j$	0	3	0	−4/3	44/3	

At the end of the first iteration, we observe that variable X_2 with $C_2 - Z_2 = 3$ can enter the basis but we are unable to fix the leaving variable because all the coefficients in the entering column are ≤ 0. The algorithm terminates because it is unable to find a leaving variable.

This phenomenon is called **unboundedness**, indicating that the variable X_2 can take any value and still none of the present basic variables would become infeasible. By the nature of the first constraint, we can observe that X_2 can be increased to any value and yet the constraints are feasible. The value of the objective function is infinity.

In all simplex iterations, we enter the variable with the maximum positive value of $C_j - Z_j$. Based on this rule, we entered variable X_1 in the first iteration. Variable X_2 also with a positive value of 3 is a candidate and if we had decided to enter X_2 in the first iteration we would have realized the unboundedness at the first iteration itself.

[Though, most of the times we enter a variable based on the largest coefficient rule (largest $C_j - Z_j$), there is no guarantee that this rule terminates with minimum iterations. Any non-basic variable with a positive value of $C_j - Z_j$ is a candidate to enter. Other rules for entering variable are:

1. *Largest increase rule:* Here for every candidate for entering variable, the corresponding minimum θ is found and the increase in the objective function, i.e. the product of θ and $C_j - Z_j$ is found. The variable with the maximum increase (product) is chosen as entering variable.
2. *First positive $C_j - Z_j$:* The first variable with $C_j - Z_j > 0$ enters.
3. *Random:* A non-basic variable is chosen randomly and the value of $C_j - Z_j$ is computed. It becomes the entering variable if the $C_j - Z_j$ is positive. Otherwise another variable is chosen randomly. This is repeated till an entering variable is found.]

Coming back to unboundedness, we observe that unboundedness is caused when the feasible region is not bounded. Sometimes, the nature of the objective function can be such that even if the feasible region is unbounded, the problem may have an optimum solution. An unbounded LP means that there is no finite optimum solution and the problem is unbounded.

One more aspect to be considered is called **infeasibility**. Can we have a situation where the linear programming problem does not have a solution at all? Let us consider the following example:

ILLUSTRATION 2.8

Maximize $Z = 4X_1 + 3X_2$
Subject to

$$X_1 + 4X_2 \leq 3$$
$$3X_1 + X_2 \geq 12$$
$$X_1, X_2 \geq 0$$

Adding slack variables X_3 and X_4 (surplus) and artificial variable a_1 we can start the simplex algorithm using the big M method with X_3 and a_1 as basic variables. This is shown in Table 2.11.

Table 2.11 Simplex Table for Illustration 2.8

C_B	Basic variables	4 X_1	3 X_2	0 X_3	0 X_4	−M a_1	RHS	θ
0	X_3	1	4	1	0	0	3	3 →
−M	a_1	3	1	0	−1	1	12	4
	$C_j - Z_j$	3M + 4	M + 3	0	−M	0		
4	X_1	1	4	1	0	0	3	
−M	a_1	0	−11	−3	−1	1	3	
	$C_j - Z_j$	0	−11M + 13	−3M − 4	−M	0		

Here the algorithm terminates when all the non-basic variables X_2, X_3 and X_4 have negative values of $C_j - Z_j$. The optimality condition seems to be satisfied but an artificial variable is in the basis. This means that the problem is infeasible and does not have a feasible solution.

Infeasibility is indicated by the presence of at least one artificial variable after the optimum condition is satisfied. In this problem $a_1 = 3$ indicates that the second constraint should have the RHS value reduced by 3 to get a feasible solution with $X_1 = 3$. Simplex algorithm not only is capable of detecting infeasibility but also shows the extent of infeasibility.

Termination conditions (Maximization objective)

1. All non-basic variables have negative values of $C_j - Z_j$. Basic variables are either decision variables or slack variables. Algorithm terminates indicating unique optimum solution.

2. Basic variables are either decision variables or slack variables. All non-basic variables have $C_j - Z_j \leq 0$. At least one non-basic variable has $C_j - Z_j = 0$. It indicates alternate optimum. Proceed to find the other corner point and terminate.

3. Basic variables are either decision variables or slack variables. The algorithm identifies an entering variable but is unable to identify leaving variable because all values in the entering column are ≤ 0. It indicates unboundedness and algorithm terminates.

4. All non-basic variables have $C_j - Z_j \leq 0$. Artificial variable still exists in the basis. It indicates infeasiblity and algorithm terminates.

If the simplex algorithm fails to terminate (based on the above conditions), then it cycles. We describe cycling using the following example (Beale 1955):

ILLUSTRATION 2.9

Maximize $\quad Z = \dfrac{3}{4}X_1 - 20X_2 + \dfrac{1}{2}X_3 - 6X_4$

Subject to

$$\dfrac{1}{4}X_1 - 8X_2 - X_3 + 9X_4 \leq 0$$

$$\dfrac{1}{2}X_1 - 12X_2 - \dfrac{1}{2}X_3 + 3X_4 \leq 0$$

$$X_3 \leq 1$$

$$X_j \leq 0$$

We introduce slack variables X_5, X_6 and X_7 and start the simplex table. We consistently enter the non-basic variable with most positive $C_j - Z_j$ value. When there is a tie, we leave the variable with the smallest subscript. The simplex iterations are shown in Table 2.12.

Table 2.12 Simplex Table for Illustration 2.9

		3/4	−20	1/2	−6	0	0	0	
		X_1	X_2	X_3	X_4	X_5	X_6	X_7	RHS
0	X_5	1/4	−8	−1	9	1	0	0	0 →
0	X_6	1/2	−12	−1/2	3	0	1	0	0
0	X_7	0 ↑	0	1	0	0	0	1	1
	$C_j - Z_j$	3/4 ↑	−20	1/2	−6	0	0	0	0
3/4	X_1	1	−32	−4	36	4	0	0	0
0	X_6	0	4	3/2	−15	−2	1	0	0 →
0	X_7	0	0 ↑	1	0	0	0	1	1
	$C_j - Z_j$	0	4 ↑	7/2	−33	−3	0	0	0
3/4	X_1	1	0	8	−84	−12	8	0	0 →
−20	X_2	0	1	3/8	−15/4	−1/2	1/4	0	0
0	X_7	0	0	1 ↑	0	0	0	1	1
	$C_j - Z_j$	0	0	2 ↑	−18	−1	−1	0	0
1/2	X_3	1/8	0	1	−21/2	−3/2	1	0	0
−20	X_2	−3/64	1	0	3/16	1/16	−1/8	0	0 →
0	X_7	−1/8	0	0	21/2 ↑	3/2	−1	1	1
	$C_j - Z_j$	−1/4	0	0	3 ↑	2	−3	0	0
1/2	X_3	−5/2	5/6	1	0	2	−6	0	0 →
0	X_4	−1/4	16/3	0	1	1/3	−2/3	0	0
0	X_7	5/2	−56	0	0	−2 ↑	6	1	1
	$C_j - Z_j$	1/2	−16	0	0	1 ↑	−1	0	0
0	X_5	−5/4	28	1/2	0	1	−3	0	0
−6	X_4	1/6	−4	−1/6	1	0	1/3	0	0 →
0	X_7	0	0	1	0	0	0 ↑	1	1
	$C_j - Z_j$	7/4	−44	−1/2	0	0	2 ↑	0	0
0	X_5	1/4	−8	−1	9	1	0	0	0 →
0	X_6	1/2	−12	−1/2	3	0	1	0	0
0	X_7	0 ↑	0	1	0	0	0	1	1
	$C_j - Z_j$	3/4 ↑	−20	1/2	6	0	0	0	0

From Table 2.12, we observe that after six iterations, we come back to the starting basis and, therefore, the algorithm cycles. The problem has an optimum solution with $X_1 = X_3 = 1$ with an objective function value of $Z = 5/4$.

Clearly, to get back to the same basis, the objective function should not increase in any iteration. It is also observed that all the iterations have basic variables with zero value as a result of which the value of objective function remains at zero.

The phenomenon of cycling is different from degeneracy because the algorithm gets back to an earlier basis and fails to terminate. In case of degeneracy, it would not get back to an earlier basis and eventually terminate.

Both degeneracy and cycling are limitations of the simplex algorithm and not due to the nature of the LP problem. One of the ways of overcoming cycling is by using the Bland's rule or smallest subscript rule (Bland 1977) where

1. The entering variable is the one with the smallest subscript among those with a positive value of $C_j - Z_j$ (for maximization).
2. In case of a tie, the leaving variable is one with the smallest subscript.

[Another rule to overcome cycling is the lexicographic rule, but we restrict ourselves to the Bland's rule in this chapter].

If we apply Bland's rule to our example, we would enter variable X_1 instead of variable X_5 in the fifth iteration. The simplex iterations are shown in Table 2.13.

Table 2.13 Application of Bland's Rule to Illustration 2.9

		3/4	−20	1/2	−6	0	0	0	
		X_1	X_2	X_3	X_4	X_5	X_6	X_7	RHS
1/2	X_3	−5/2	5/6	1	0	2	−6	0	0
0	X_4	−1/4	16/3	0	1	1/3	−2/3	0	0
0	X_7	5/2	−56	0	0	−2	6	1	1 →
	$C_j - Z_j$	1/2	−16	0	0	1	−1	0	0
1/2	X_3	0	0	1	0	0	0	1	0
−6	X_4	0	−4/15	0	1	2/15	−1/15	−1/10	1/10→
3/4	X_1	1	−112/5	0	0	−4/5	12/5	2/5	2/5
	$C_j - Z_j$	0	−62/5	0	0	7/5	1/20	3/40	1/5
1/2	X_3	0	0	1	0	0	0	1	1
0	X_5	0	−2	0	15/2	1	−1/2	3/4	3/4
3/4	X_1	1	−24	0	6	0	2	1	1
	$C_j - Z_j$	0	−2	0	−21/2	0	−3/2	−5/4	5/4

It is also observed that while Bland's rule guarantees termination of the simplex algorithm, it does not ensure termination within minimum number of iterations. Nevertheless, it is an important result considering that there is no rule that guarantees termination within minimum number of iterations.

2.4.4 Special Examples

Simplex method can be used to solve simultaneous linear equations (if the solution has non-negative values). Let us consider the following example:

ILLUSTRATION 2.10

Solve
$$4X_1 + 3X_2 = 25$$
$$2X_1 + X_2 = 11$$

We add artificial variables a_1 and a_2 and rewrite the equations as

$$4X_1 + 3X_2 + a_1 = 25$$
$$2X_1 + X_2 + a_2 = 11$$

We define an objective function:

Minimize $Z = a_1 + a_2$

If the original equations have a non-negative solution then we should have feasible basis with X_1 and X_2 having $Z = 0$ for the linear programming problem. The simplex iterations are shown in Table 2.14.

Table 2.14 Simplex Table for Illustration 2.10

		0	0	−1	−1		
		X_1	X_2	a_1	a_2	RHS	θ
−1	a_1	4	3	1	0	25	25/4
−1	a_2	2↑	1	0	1	11	11/2 →
	$C_j - Z_j$	6	4	0	0	−36	
−1	a_1	0	1	1	−2	3	3 →
0	X_1	1	1/2	0	1/2	11/2	11
	$C_j - Z_j$	0	1↑	0	−1	−3	
0	X_2	0	1	1	−2	3	
0	X_1	1	0	−1/2	3/2	4	
	$C_j - Z_j$	0	0	−1	−1	0	

The optimum solution $X_1 = 4$, $X_2 = 3$ is the solution to the simultaneous linear equations.

This example assumes that the variables should be strictly ≥ 0 at the optimum. However, if this condition need not be true (they could take negative values), we can define the variables to be unrestricted in sign and solve the resultant system.

Simplex method can also detect linear dependency among equations. Let us consider the following example:

ILLUSTRATION 2.11

Solve

$$2X_1 + 3X_2 = 6$$
$$4X_1 + 6X_2 = 12$$

As in the previous example, we add artificial variables a_1 and a_2. We write an objective function:

Minimize $Z = a_1 + a_2$

and set up the simplex table with a_1 and a_2 as basic variables. The simplex iterations are shown in Table 2.15.

Table 2.15 Simplex Table for Illustration 2.11

		0	0	-1	-1		
		X_1	X_2	a_1	a_2	RHS	θ
-1	a_1	2	3	1	0	6	2 →
-1	a_2	4	6↑	0	1	12	3
	$C_j - Z_j$	6	9	0	0	-21	
0	X_2	2/3	1	1/3	0	2	3 →
-1	a_2	0↑	0	-2	1	0	--
	$C_j - Z_j$	0	0	-3	0	0	
0	X_1	1	3/2	1/2	0	3	
-1	a_2	0	0	-2	1	0	
	$C_j - Z_j$	0	0	-3	0	0	

The simplex algorithm has all $C_j - Z_j \leq 0$ after one iteration. An artificial variable exists in the basis with value zero. This indicates a linearly dependent system. Also variable X_1 can enter the basis (as in alternate optimum) and we will get the solution in the next iteration. Presence of artificial variable with value zero at the optimum indicates a linearly dependent system.

Let us consider another example to illustrate an unrestricted variable.

ILLUSTRATLION 2.12

Maximize $Z = 4X_1 + 5X_2$
Subject to

$$2X_1 + 3X_2 \leq 8$$
$$X_1 + 4X_2 \leq 10$$
$$X_1 \text{ unrestricted}, X_2 \geq 0$$

We replace variable X_1 by $X_3 - X_4$. We add slack variables X_5 and X_6 to get

Maximize $Z = 4X_3 - 4X_4 + 5X_2$
Subject to

$$2X_3 - 2X_4 + 3X_2 + X_5 \leq 8$$
$$X_3 - X_4 + 4X_2 + X_6 \leq 10$$
$$X_3, X_4, X_5, X_6 \geq 0$$

The simplex iterations are shown in Table 2.16.

Table 2.16 Simplex Table for Illustration 2.12

		4	-4	5	0	0		
		X_3	X_4	X_2	X_5	X_6	RHS	θ
0	X_5	2	-2	3	1	0	8	8/3
0	X_6	1	-1	4	0	1	10	5/2
	$C_j - Z_j$	4	-4	5	0	0	0	
0	X_5	5/4	-5/4	0	1	-3/4	1/2	2/5
5	X_2	1/4	-1/4	1	0	1/4	5/2	10
	$C_j - Z_j$	11/4	-11/4	0	0	-5/4	25/2	
4	X_3	1	-1	0	4/5	-3/5	2/5	--
5	X_2	0	0	1	-1/5	2/5	12/5	6
	$C_j - Z_j$	0	0	0	-11/5	2/5	68/5	
4	X_3	1	-1	3/2	1/2	0	4	
0	X_6	0	0	5/2	-1/2	1	6	
		0	0	-1	-2	0	16	

Here the optimum solution is $X_3 = 4$, $Z = 16$, indicating that the original variable $X_1 = 4$ at the optimum. However, we observe that variable X_4 has $C_4 - Z_4 = 0$ and can enter. We also realize that there is no leaving variable. Does this indicate unboundedness?

The answer is No. This is because the original unrestricted variable has been rewritten as two variables. $X_3 = 4$, $X_4 = 0$ indicate that the original variable $X_1 = 4$. Incidentally, $X_1 = 4$ can be represented by any combination of X_3 and X_4 such that $X_3 - X_4 = 4$ and $X_3, X_4 \geq 0$. This is what is implied by variable X_4 trying to enter the basis and indicating that it can take any positive value.

Whenever we have an unrestricted variable in the original problem that has been written as the difference of two variables, this phenomenon will occur. If the original unrestricted variable is in the optimum solution then one of the two will take a positive value at the optimum and the other will try to enter and represent unboundedness because it can take any value and adequately retain the value of the original variable at the optimum.

It is to be noted that both X_3 and X_4 will not be basic at the optimum. Either one of them will be in the basis if the original variable is in the solution. Both will be non-basic if the original unrestricted variable is not in the optimum solution.

SOLVED EXAMPLES

EXAMPLE 2.1 Consider the following linear programming problem:

Minimize $Z = X_1 - X_2$
Subject to
$$X_1 + X_2 \geq 2$$
$$X_1 + 2X_2 \leq 8$$
$$X_1 \geq 0, X_2 \geq 0,$$

Identify the feasible region on a graphical representation of the problem and answer the following questions:

(a) What is the optimal solution
   (i) to the given problem?
   (ii) when the objective function is maximize $Z = X_1 + X_2$?
   (iii) When X_1 and X_2 are unrestricted in sign?
(b) How should the first constraint be altered so that a feasible unbounded solution would exist for condition (iii) above for both cases (i) and (ii)?

Solution: The graph for the problem is shown in Figure 2.2. The corner points are (2, 0), (8, 0), (0, 2) and (0, 4). Substituting in the objective function $X_1 - X_2$, the minimum occurs at the point (0, 4) which is the optimal solution.

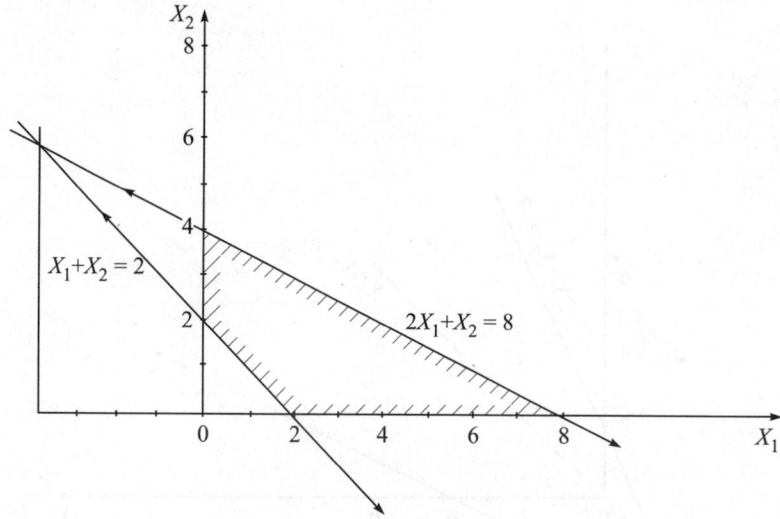

Figure 2.2 Graph for Example 2.1.

If the objective is to maximize $X_1 + X_2$, the optimal solution on substituting the corner points is (8, 0) with $Z = 8$.

When the variables are unrestricted in sign, the optimal solution is (–4, 6) with $Z = -10$. This point is the point of intersection of both the constraints.

In order to get a feasible unbounded solution for the unrestricted variables for both the objective functions, $X_1 + X_2 \geq 2$ should be changed to $X_1 + X_2 \leq 2$ so that we have a unbounded region with objective function $Z = X_1 - X_2$.

For the objective function $Z = X_1 + X_2$, we have the same unbounded region but with alternate optima.

EXAMPLE 2.2 Consider the following linear programming problem:
Maximize $Z = X_1 - X_2$
Subject to
$$X_1 - 2X_2 \leq 4$$
$$2X_1 - X_2 \geq -2$$
$$X_1 \geq 0, X_2 \geq 0$$

Plot the feasible region on a graph and answer the following questions based on the graph. Does a feasible finite optimum exist

(a) to the given problem?
(b) when the objective function is:

Minimize $Z = X_1 + X_2$

(c) when a third constraint $X_1 + X_2 \leq 4$ is added to the problem?

Give reasons for your answers.

Solution: The graph for this problem is shown in Figure 2.3. The feasible region is unbounded. The objective function *Maximize* $Z = X_1 - X_2$ moves in a direction indicating unbounded solution.

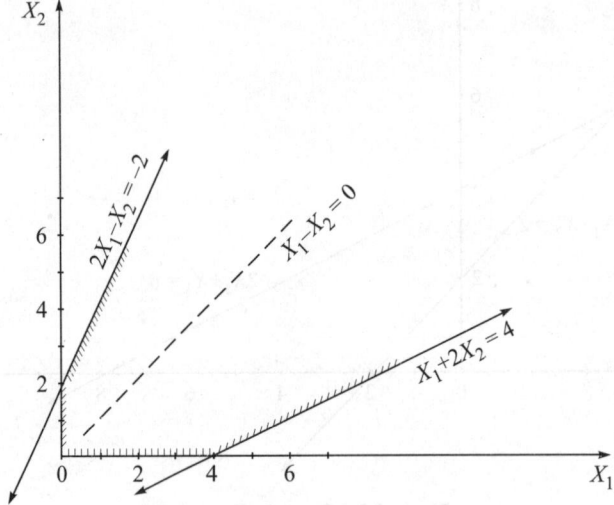

Figure 2.3 Graph for Example 2.2(a).

When the objective *function is Minimize* $Z = X_1 + X_2$, the objective function is moving in a direction such that the *optimum* is (0, 0) with an objective function value 0.

The graph for this problem, when a third constraint $X_1 + X_2 \leq 4$ is added, is shown in Figure 2.4.

When the objective is to *Minimize* $Z = X_1 + X_2$, the optimum is (4, 0) with an objective function value 4. There is alternate optima. When the objective function is to *Minimize* $Z = X_1 - X_2$, we have an unbounded solution.

EXAMPLE 2.3 Consider the following linear programming problem:

Minimize $Z = X_1 + 3X_2$

Subject to

$$5X_1 + 4X_1 \geq 20$$
$$3X_1 + 4X_2 \leq 24$$
$$X_1 \geq 0, X_2 \geq 0$$

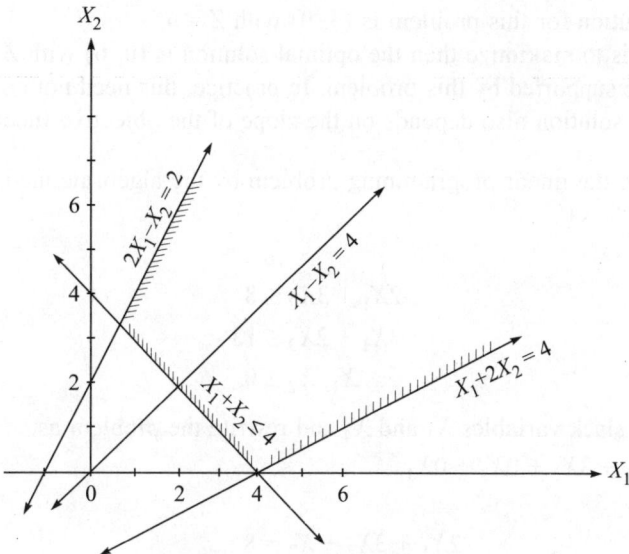

Figure 2.4 Graph for Example 2.2(c).

Identify the feasible region on a graphical representation of the problem. Determine the optimal solution from the graph for this problem. What would be the optimal solution if the objective function were to be maximized?

The optimal solution from a graph by the corner point of the feasible region that is (a) nearest to origin for a minimization problem and (b) farthest from the origin for a maximization problem.

Is the above statement supported by this problem? Is the statement true? Why or why not?

Solution: The feasible region for the given problem is shown in Figure 2.5.

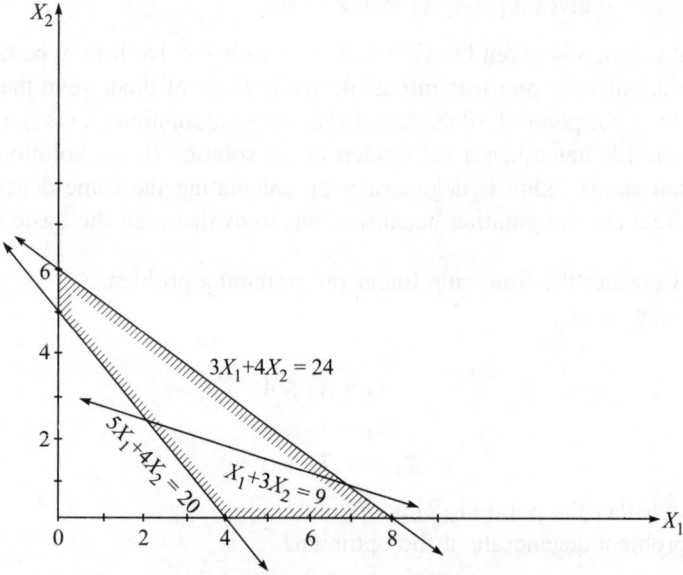

Figure 2.5 Graph for Example 2.3.

The optimal solution for this problem is (4, 0) with Z = 4.
If the objective is to maximize then the optimal solution is (0, 6) with Z = 18.
The statement is supported by this problem. In practice, this need not hold for all situations because the optimal solution also depends on the slope of the objective function.

EXAMPLE 2.4 Solve the linear programming problem by the algebraic method?
Maximize $Z = 4X_1 + 3X_2$
Subject to
$$2X_1 + 3X_2 \leq 8$$
$$3X_1 + 2X_2 \leq 12$$
$$X_1, X_2 \geq 0$$

Solution: We add slack variables X_3 and X_4 and rewrite the problem as:
Maximize $Z = 4X_1 + 3X_2 + 0X_3 + 0X_4$
Subject to
$$2X_1 + 3X_2 + X_3 = 8$$
$$3X_1 + 2X_2 + X_4 = 12$$
$$X_1, X_2, X_3, X_4 \geq 0$$

There are six basic solutions by fixing two out of the four variables to zero. These are

1. $X_1 = X_2 = 0$ gives $X_3 = 8, X_4 = 12, Z = 0$
2. $X_1 = 0, X_3 = 0$ gives $X_2 = 8/3, X_4 = 20/3, Z = 32/3$
3. $X_1 = 0, X_4 = 0$ gives $X_2 = 6, X_3 = -10$ (infeasible solution)
4. $X_2 = 0, X_3 = 0$ gives $X_1 = 4, X_4 = 0, Z = 16$
5. $X_2 = 0, X_4 = 0$ gives $X_1 = 4, X_3 = 0, Z = 16$
6. $X_3 = 0, X_4 = 0$ gives $X_1 = 4, X_2 = 0, Z = 16$

The optimal solution is given by $X_1 = 4, X_2 = 0$ with $Z = 16$. It may be observed that out of the six basic solutions only one was infeasible while three of them gave the optimal solutions. This shows that the same point (4, 0) represented three basic solutions. This is a case of degeneracy where a basic variable has taken a zero value in the solution (basic solutions 4, 5 and 6). The algebraic solution shows exhibits degeneracy by calculating the same degenerate point again. This does not affect the computation because it has to evaluate all the basic solutions.

EXAMPLE 2.5 Consider the following linear programming problem:
Maximize $Z = 6X_1 + 3X_2$
Subject to
$$X_1 + X_2 \leq 4$$
$$2X_1 + X_2 \leq 4$$
$$X_1 \geq 0, X_2 \geq 0$$

(a) Verify whether the point (1, 2) is optimal?
(b) Is the problem degenerate at the optimum?

The simplex iterations are shown in Table 2.17.

Table 2.17 Simplex Table for Example 2.5

		6	3	0	0		
		X_1	X_2	X_3	X_4	RHS	θ
0	X_3	1	1	1	0	4	4
0	X_4	2↑	1	0	1	4	2 →
	$C_j - Z_j$	6	3	0	0	0	
0	X_3	0	1/2	1	−1/2	2	4 →
6	X_1	1	1/2↑	0	1/2	2	4
	$C_j - Z_j$	0	0	0	−3	12	
3	X_2	0	1	2	−1	4	
6	X_1	1	0	−1	1	0	
	$C_j - Z_j$	0	0	−1	0	12	

Simplex table indicates optimum after one iteration with the solution $X_1 = 2$, $X_3 = 2$ and $Z = 12$. However variable X_2 can enter with a zero value of $C_2 - Z_2$ indicating alternate optimum. The alternate optimum solution is $X_1 = 0$, $X_2 = 4$ with $Z = 12$.

(a) The point (1, 2) is not a corner point solution (simplex does not show this solution as either of the alternate optima). However, it has the same value of the objective function and hence is optimal. Also it lies in the line segment joining the alternate optima points (2, 0) and (0, 4) and hence is also optimal.

Only in the case of alternate optima we can find non-basic solutions that are optimal. Therefore, any feasible solution that has the same value of the objective function as an optimal solution is also optimal. There are several non-basic optimal solutions in the alternate optima case. Another non-basic optimum solution is (1/2, 3).

(b) One of the corner point optimal solutions is degenerate. Observe that there was a tie for the leaving variable and we have chosen X_3 to leave. This is also represented by a basic variable taking zero value in the next iteration (alternate optima iteration). If we had chosen to leave X_1 we could have got the solution $X_2 = 4$, $X_3 = 0$ and $Z = 12$. The variable X_1 now would have $C_1 - Z_1 = 0$ and would have provided the alternate optimum solution.

EXAMPLE 2.6 Given the linear programming problem:
Minimize $8X_1 - 6X_2$
Subject to

$$X_1 - X_2 \leq 4$$
$$4X_1 - 3X_2 \leq 8$$
$$X_1, X_2 \geq 0$$

(a) Solve the problem optimally using simplex algorithm.
(b) What happens when the first constraint becomes $X_1 - X_2 \geq 4$?
(c) What happens to the original problem if the function is:
Minimize $Z = 8X_1 + 6X_2$

Solution: (a) We convert the problem into a maximization problem and add an artificial variable to the first constraint. The simplex iterations are shown in Table 2.18.

Table 2.18 Initial Simplex Table for Example 2.6

		−8 X_1	6 X_2	0 X_3	0 X_4	RHS
0	X_3	1	−1	1	0	4
0	X_4	4	−2	0	1	8
	$C_j - Z_j$	−8	6	0	0	0

Variable X_2 enters the basis but there is no leaving variable. The problem has an unbounded solution. This can be seen from the problem itself because variable X_2 has both the constraint coefficients negative (watch out for the ≤ constraints with non-negative RHS values).

(For the problem to have an unbounded solution verify that the feasible region is unbounded. Verify this by drawing the graph corresponding to the constraints).

(b) When the first constraint is $X_1 - X_2 \geq 4$, we introduce an artificial variable in the first constraint which becomes an initial basic variable. The simplex iterations are shown in Table 2.19.

Table 2.19 Simplex Iterations for Example 2.6

		−8 X_1	6 X_2	0 X_3	0 X_4	−M a_1	RHS
−M	a_1	1	−1	−1	0	1	4
0	X_4	4	−2	0	1	0	8
	$C_j - Z_j$	−8 + M	6−M	−M	0	0	0
−M	a_1	0	−1/2	−1	−1/4	1	2
−8	X_1	1	−1/2	0	1/4	0	2
	$C_j - Z_j$	0	2−M/2	−M	2−M/4	0	

All $C_j - Z_j$ values are ≤ 0. The optimum is reached. However, the artificial variable is still in the basis indicating infeasible solution.

(Verify from the graph corresponding to the constraints that there is no feasible region. The simplex table shows variable X_2 having a positive coefficient in the objective function and negative coefficients in the constraints. The problem is infeasible due to the nature of the constraints).

(c) When the objective function is to *Minimize* $Z = 8X_1 + 6X_2$, the initial tableau is optimal because $C_2 - Z_2$ is also ≤ 0. The optimal solution is $X_1 = X_2 = 0$ with $Z = 0$.

(There is a unique optimum in this case even when the feasible region is unbounded. When the feasible region is unbounded, we can have an optimum. This depends on the objective function).

EXAMPLE 2.7 Table 2.20 shows a simplex tableau for a maximization problem after the first iteration. Can you reconstruct the original problem from this? (Assume there are no artificial variables).

Table 2.20 Final Simplex Table for Example 2.7

Basis	X_1	X_2	X_3	X_4	X_5	
$0X_4$	3	−1	0	1	−1	5
$4X_3$	3/5	4/5	1	0	1/5	4
$C_j - Z_j$	31/5	−11/5	0	0	−4/5	

Since there are no artificial variables, we can assume that X_4 and X_5, the slack variables are the initial basic variables. Variable X_3 has replaced X_5 in the first iteration. In order to get back X_4 and X_5 as basic variables, we can enter variable X_5 into the basis (in spite of a negative $C_j - Z_j$) because we are moving backward and leave X_3 from the basis. The iterations are shown in Table 2.21.

Table 2.21 Simplex Iterations for Example 2.7

		X_1	X_2	X_3	X_4	X_5	RHS	θ
0	X_4	3	−1	0	1	−1	5	
4	X_5	3/5	4/5	1	0	1/5	4	
	$C_j - Z_j$	3/5	−11/5	0	0	−4/5	0	
0	X_4	6	3	5	1	0	25	
0	X_5	3	4	5	0	1	20	
	$C_j - Z_j$							

From the table (2.7), we can calculate the C_j values.

$$C_1 - 12/5 = 3/5 \text{ from which } C_1 = 3$$
$$C_2 - 16/5 = -11/5 \text{ from which } C_2 = 1$$

The given problem is
Maximize $Z = 3X_1 + X_2 + 4X_3$
Subject to

$$6X_1 + 3X_2 + 5X_3 \leq 25$$
$$3X_1 + 4X_2 + 5X_3 \leq 20$$
$$X_1, X_2 \geq 0$$

(The above method is a violation of the simplex algorithm—in fact is the reverse of it. It enters a variable with a −ve $C_j - Z_j$ into the basis because we want to go to the previous iteration.)
Aliter
From the given simplex table, we have

$$3X_1 - X_2 + X_4 - X_5 = 5$$

and
$$\frac{3}{5}X_1 + \frac{4}{5}X_2 + X_3 + \frac{1}{5}X_5 = 4$$

Multiplying the second equation by 5, we get

$$3X_1 + 4X_2 + 5X_3 + X_5 = 20$$

Substituting for X_5 in the first equation, we get

$$3X_1 - X_2 + X_4 - (20 - 3X_1 - 4X_2 - 5X_3) = 5$$

or
$$6X_1 + 3X_2 + 5X_3 + X_4 = 25$$

Removing the slack variables, we get the two constraints as inequalities. The objective function can be calculated the same way as in the earlier solution.

EXAMPLE 2.8 A simplex tableau is given below in tabular form (Table 2.22).

Table 2.22 Simplex Tableau

C_B	Basis	3 X_1	2 X_2	0 X_3	0 X_4	0 X_5	b
0	X_3	0	1	1	0	1	7
0	X_4	0	5	0	1	−3	5 →
3	X_1	1	−1 ↑	0	0	1	3
$C_j - Z_j$		0	5	0	0	−3	Z = 9

(a) Perform the next iteration and get the new simplex tableau.
(b) Has the optimal solution been reached?
(c) If so, are there any alternate optimal solutions?

The simplex tableau in the next iteration is shown in Table 2.23.

Table 2.23 Simplex Iteration for Example 2.8

		3 X_1	2 X_2	0 X_3	0 X_4	0 X_5	RHS	θ
0	X_3	0	0	1	−1/5	8/5	6	→
2	X_2	0	1	0	1/5	−3/5	1	
3	X_1	1	0	0	1/5	2/5 ↑	4	
$C_j - Z_j$		0	0	0	−1	0	14	

The optimum solution has been reached. However, variable X_5 with $C_5 - Z_5 = 0$ enters replacing variable X_3 (alternate optimum). This is shown in Table 2.24.

Table 2.24 Alternate Optimum

		3 X_1	2 X_2	0 X_3	0 X_4	0 X_5	RHS	θ
0	X_5	0	0	1	−1/8	1	30/8	
2	X_2	0	1	0	1/8	0	13/4	
3	X_1	1	0	0	1/4	0	5/2	
$C_j - Z_j$		0	0	0	−1	0	14	

EXAMPLE 2.9 In the simplex tableau for the maximization problem given in Table 2.25, the values of constants α, β and δ are unknown. Assume that there are no artificial variables.

$$X_1, X_2, \ldots, X_5 \geq 0$$

Table 2.25 Simplex Table for Example 2.9

		4 X_1	5 X_2	α X_3	0 X_4	0 X_5
4	X_1	1	0	1/2	β	$-1/2$	3
5	X_2	0	1	3/4	$-1/4$	3/4	δ
	$C_j - Z_j$	0	0				39/2

State the restrictions on the unknowns (α, β and δ), which would make the following statements true about the given tableau (Subdivisions are independent of each other):

(a) The current solution is optimal but an alternate optimum exists.
(b) The current solution will yield a degenerate basic feasible solution in the next iteration.
(c) The current solution is feasible but the problem has no finite optimum.
(d) The current solution is feasible but the objective can be improved if X_3 replaces X_2 in the basis. What will be the change in the value of the objective function?

Solution: (a) For the current solution to be optimal, all $C_j - Z_j \leq 0$ and for alternate optimum to exist one of the non-basic variables should have $C_j - Z_j = 0$. We should be able to identify a leaving variable if this variable is entered.

Either $C_3 - Z_3 = 0$ and $C_4 - Z_4 < 0$ or $C_4 - Z_4 = 0$ and $C_3 - Z_3 < 0$
Either $\alpha - 23/4 = 0$ and $5/4 - 4\beta < 0$ or $5/4 - 4\beta = 0$ and $\alpha - 23/4 < 0$
Either $\alpha = 23/4$ and $\beta > 5/16$ or $\beta = 5/16$ and $\alpha < 23/4$

(b) For a degenerate solution, there has to be a tie for the leaving variable. This can happen only if X_3 enters. $\alpha - 23/4 > 0$ which gives $\alpha > 23/4$ and for tie in the leaving variable, we have $6 = 3\delta/4$ from which $\delta = 8$.

(c) $\delta \geq 0$ indicates that the present solution is feasible. For unboundedness, we should have an entering variable and no leaving variable. This can happen when X_4 enters and when $\beta \leq 0$. For X_4 to enter we have $\beta \leq 5/4$. The condition is $\beta \leq 0$.

(d) For X_3 to enter the basis, we should have $\alpha > 23/4$. For X_2 to leave we should have $3\delta/4 < 6$, which gives $\delta < 8$. The change in the objective function is the product of the $C_j - Z_j$ and the corresponding θ value. Here it will be $3\delta(\alpha - 23/4)/4$.

CASE STUDY 2.1

A Machine Co. has set up a small manufacturing plant to make a single product for a nearby automobile manufacturer. The customer has a Just-in-time system in place and hence insists that the Machine Co. also sends the product just-in-time. The Machine Co. has created two cells that feed to an assembly from which the finished product is sent to the customer. The product has two components, each of which is made in a cell. The first cell has five machines and the second cell has three machines.

The Machine Co. uses a rabbit chasing approach in both the cells. For example, if there are two operators allotted to the cell, the first operator will take a piece, machine it in all the machines by moving from one machine to another till it completes the machining. He would take the next piece and start the machining. Meanwhile the second operator would have taken a piece and followed the first operator. The second operator would wait for his turn if the first operator is using a machine. If the cell has three operators, the second operator would follow the first, the third would follow the second and the first would follow the third operator and so on. Each cell could have any number of operators.

The first component requires five operations and the five machines are arranged according to the sequence of operations required. The unit processing times are 20, 15, 20, 10 and 25 seconds for the operations. The second cell has the three machines that take care of the three operations of the second components. The machines are arranged according to the sequence of the operations required and the operation times are 22, 25 and 18 seconds per piece.

The Machine Co. has at present ten trained permanent operators and the company works two shifts a day and five days a week. Five operators are available per shift. Trainees are available when required and are paid Rs. 500 per shift when used. Due to Quality considerations, the Machine Co. would like to minimize the number of trainees used and wishes to use them only when absolutely necessary. The customer requirement for the Machine Co.'s product for the five days in the coming week is 1800, 2500, 2200, 2000 and 1500 respectively. The company is committed to delivering the daily demand. The company estimates the cost of holding inventory as Re. 1/product/day.

Mr. Rahul Singh, the CEO believes that the problem is a linear programming problem and asks Nakul, a summer trainee to formulate it for him. Mr. Singh believes that he can round off the LP solution suitably if required.

EXERCISES

2.1 Solve the following linear programming problem by the simplex method?

Minimize $Z = X_1 + X_2 - 2X_3 + \frac{1}{2} X_4$

Subject to

$$X_2 + X_3 + 2X_4 \leq 12$$

$$2X_1 + 2X_2 - 2X_3 + \frac{1}{2} X_4 \leq 4$$

$$X_1, X_2, X_4 \geq 0$$

X_3 unrestricted in sign

Does the problem have an alternate optimum? Why or why not?

2.2 Solve the following LP problem by the graphical and simplex algorithms.
Maximize $Z = 2X_1 + X_2$
Subject to
$$X_1 + 2X_2 \leq 3$$
$$X_2 \leq 5$$
X_1 unrestricted
$$X_2 \geq 0$$

2.3 Consider the following simplex tableau (Table 2.26) and answer the following questions.

Table 2.26 Simplex Tableau

			3	6	8	0	g	0	
			X_1	X_2	X_3	X_4	X_5	X_6	
6	X_2	e	1	0	−1/2	0	2/3	100
8	X_3	f	0	1	c	0	−1/4	100
g	X_5	0	0	0	−1/2	1	−1/3	A
		b	0	0	d	0	h	

State restrictions on a, b, c, d, e, f, g and h such that
(a) Current solution is optimal but an alternate optimum exists.
(b) Current solution is infeasible.
(c) Current solution will yield a degenerate basic feasible solution in the next iteration.
(d) Current solution is feasible but the problem has no optimum.
(e) Current solution is feasible but the objective function can be improved if X_1 replaces X_3 in the basis. What will be the change in the objective function value?

2.4 Solve the LPP
Maximize $Z = 2X_1 + X_2 + 4X_3$
Subject to
$$2X_1 + X_2 + 4X_3 = 12$$
$$3X_1 + 4X_2 + X_3 = 21$$
$$7X_1 + 6X_2 + 7X_3 = 45$$
$$x_i \geq 0$$

(a) Given X_1, X_2, and X_3 as basic variables, find the basic solution.
(b) How will be the optimum simplex table look like for this problem? Comment.

2.5 Maximize $Z = 2X_1 + X_2$
Subject to
$$X_1 + X_2 \leq -8$$
$$3X_1 + 4X_2 \leq 15$$
X_1 unrestricted, $X_2 \leq 0$

(a) Solve the problem using the graphical method.
(b) How many variables would simplex tableau have for this problem?
(c) How would simplex terminate for this problem?

2.6 Table 2.27 shows a simplex tableau for a maximization problem. Find the values of α, β, γ and δ for the following situations:

Table 2.27 Simplex Tableau

		2 X_1	-2 X_2	α X_3	9 X_4	-1 X_5	0 X_6	RHS
α	X_3	0	0	1	γ	0	-1	δ
2	X_1	1	-1	0	-4	4	2	β

(a) The problem has an unbounded solution.
(b) The present solution is degenerate but comes out of degeneracy in the next iteration.
(c) The problem represents a linearly dependent system of equations.
(d) The problem represents a situation where an unrestricted variable is in the basis at the optimum.

2.7 Solve the linear programming problem
Maximize $Z = 8x_1 + 5x_2$
Subject to
$$x_1 + 2x_2 \leq 8$$
$$3x_1 - x_2 \leq 8$$
$$x_1 \geq 0$$
x_2 unrestricted in sign

2.8 Find all the basic feasible solutions to the following LP problem?
Maximize $Z = 3x_1 + x_2 + 2x_4$
Subject to
$$x_1 + x_2 - 1/2 x_4 = 4$$
$$x_1 - x_2 + 3x_3 = 12$$
$$x_1, x_2, x_3, x_4 \geq 0$$

(**Hint:** Use the algebraic method to solve the problem. Does the simplex algorithm evaluate all the basic solutions?)

2.9 Solve the LPP
Maximize $Z = 2X_1 + X_2 + 4X_3$
Subject to
$$2X_1 + X_2 + 4X_3 = 12$$
$$3X_1 + 4X_2 + X_3 = 21$$
$$7X_1 + 6X_2 + 7X_3 = 20$$
$$X_i \geq 0$$

2.10 Solve the following LP problem:
Maximize $Z = 2X_1 + X_2$
Subject to
$$3X_1 + 4X_2 + X_3 \leq 12$$
$$2X_1 + 3X_2 + X_3 \geq 12$$
$$X_i \geq 0$$

Interpret your solution. If the above problem is from a practical situation, what are your comments about the formulation?

2.11 Formulate a linear programming problem that can determine whether the system $\Sigma a_{ij} X_j \leq 0$, $i = 1,m$, $\Sigma b_j X_j > 0$, $X_j \geq 0$ has a solution.

2.12 Solve the following linear programming problem by the simplex method.

Maximize $Z = X_1 + X_2 - 2X_3 + \dfrac{1}{2} X_4$

Subject to
$$X_2 + X_3 + 2X_4 \leq 12$$
$$2X_1 + 2X_2 - 2X_3 + \dfrac{1}{2} X_4 \leq 4$$
$$X_1, X_2, X_4 \geq 0$$
X_3 unrestricted in sign

Does the problem have an alternate optimum? Why or why not?

2.13 Plot the following constraints of an LP problem on a free hand graph:
$$2x_1 + x_2 \leq 2$$
$$2x_1 - x_2 \leq 2$$
$$2x_1 + x_2 \geq -2$$
$$2x_1 - x_2 \geq -2$$
$$x_1, x_2 \geq 0$$

What is the optimal solution for
(a) Maximize $Z = X_1 + X_2$
(b) Minimize $Z = X_1 + 10X_2$ with X_1, X_2 unrestricted in sign?

2.14 Consider the single constrained LP
Maximize $Z = \Sigma C_j X_j$
Subject to
$$\Sigma a_j X_j = b$$
$$X_j \geq 0$$

(a) Develop a simple test to identify a feasible solution.
(b) Develop a test to detect whether the problem is unbounded.
(c) Find the optimum solution.

2.15 Solve the following LP problem:
Maximize $Z = 2X_1 + 2X_2 + 2X_3 + 2X_4$
Subject to
$$X_1 + X_2 - X_3 - X_4 = 3$$
$$2X_1 - 2X_2 - 2X_3 + 2X_4 = 2$$
$$X_1, X_2, X_3, X_4 \geq 0$$
X_3 unrestricted in sign

2.16 Consider a two-variable linear programming problem. Using the graphical method, the corner points of the feasible region are found to be (1, 0), (2, 0), (1, 2), (2, 3) and (4, 1). Answer the following questions:
(a) Give an objective function such that (2, 3) is optimum.
(b) Give an objective function such that there exist multiple optimum solutions.
(c) Find the optimal solution for the function
  Maximize $Z = 6X_1 + 7X_2$
(d) Change one constraint such that the problem is infeasible.

2.17 Minimize $Z = 2X_1 + X_2 + X_3 + X_5$
Subject to
$$3X_1 + X_2 - X_3 + X_4 - X_5 = 3$$
$$-X_1 + X_2 + 3X_3 - 2X_4 + 2X_5 = 3$$

Observe that $X_i = 1$ is a feasible solution. Obtain a basic feasible solution from this.

2.18 Consider the linear programming problem:
Maximize $Z = 8X_1 + 6X_2 + X_3$
Subject to
$$8X_1 + 6X_2 + 2X_3 \leq 13$$
$$X_1 + X_2 + 2X_3 \leq 4$$
$$X_1, X_2, X_3 \geq 0$$

Find an optimal non-basic solution to the above problem.

2.19 Given a linear programming problem
Maximize $Z = 10X_1 + X_2$
Subject to
$$X_1 \leq 1$$
$$20X_1 + X_2 \leq 100$$
$$X_1, X_2, \geq 0$$

(a) Solve the problem by the simplex method by entering the variable with the largest positive $C_j - Z_j$ in every iteration.
(b) Use the largest increase rule—choose the entering variable that has the largest increase in objective function and solve the LP.
(c) Use $X_1 = 0.01Y_1$ and $X_2 = Y_2$ and solve the resultant LP by the largest coefficient rule (most positive $C_j - Z_j$)
How many iterations does the problem take in the three cases?

2.20 Four boys wish to socialize with four girls on a holiday. The "happiness" that boy i gets per hour of socializing with girl j is given in the matrix in Table 2.28. Formulate a linear programming problem where the decision variable is the proportion of the available time boy i spends with girl j and the objective function is to maximize "total happiness"? What are the optimal X_{ij} values? (We will discuss this problem in more detail in Exercises of Chapter 5.)

Table 2.28 Data for Problem 2.20

6	7	10	3
6	5	4	8
2	9	3	3
8	5	2	4

2.21 Solve the following linear programming problem by the graphical method:

Minimize $\quad Z = 13X_1 + 4X_2$

Subject to

$$8X_1 + X_2 \geq 8$$
$$6X_1 + X_2 \geq 6$$
$$2X_1 + X_2 \leq 1$$
$$X_1, X_2 \geq 0$$

3

Duality and Sensitivity Analysis

Let us consider the following linear programming problem:
Maximize $Z = 6X_1 + 5X_2$
Subject to

$$X_1 + X_2 \leq 5$$
$$3X_1 + 2X_2 \leq 12$$
$$X_1, X_2 \geq 0$$

Let us assume that we do not know the optimum solution. Let Z^* be the optimum value of Z. Let us try to find a value higher than Z^* without solving the problem. We wish to have as small a value as possible but it should be greater than or equal to Z^*.

1. The obvious value is infinity because it is a maximization problem. If we ignore both the constraints, the value will be infinity.
2. Let us multiply the second constraint by 3 to get $9X_1 + 6X_2 \leq 36$. The optimum solution has to be feasible ($X_1, X_2 \geq 0$) and, therefore, should satisfy $9X_1 + 6X_2 \leq 36$. Since $6X_1 + 5X_2 \leq 9X_1 + 6X_2 \leq 36$ for $X_1, X_2 \geq 0$, the upper estimate of Z^* is 36.
3. Let us multiply the first constraint by 6 to get $6X_1 + 6X_2 \leq 30$. The optimum solution has to be feasible ($X_1, X_2 \geq 0$) and, therefore, should satisfy $6X_1 + 6X_2 \leq 30$. Since $6X_1 + 5X_2 \leq 6X_1 + 6X_2 \leq 30$ for $X_1, X_2 \geq 0$, the upper estimate of Z^* is 30.
4. Let us multiply the first constraint by 1 and second constraint by 2 and add them to get $7X_1 + 5X_2 \leq 29$. The optimum solution has to be feasible ($X_1, X_2 \geq 0$) and, therefore, should satisfy $7X_1 + 5X_2 \leq 29$. Since $6X_1 + 5X_2 \leq 7X_1 + 6X_2 \leq 29$ for $X_1, X_2 \geq 0$, the upper estimate of Z^* is 29.

From the above arguments we understand that if we multiply the first constraint by a non-negative quantity a and the second constraint by a non-negative quantity b and add them such that the resultant constraint has all the coefficients more than that in the objective function then the right hand side value is an upper bound to Z^*. This is under the assumption that the constraints are of $\leq$ type.

The lowest value that can be achieved will have a certain value of a and b, if such a value exists. Let such values of a and b be Y_1 and Y_2.

In order to get the upper estimate of Z^*,

$$Y_1 + 3Y_2 \geq 6 \qquad (3.1)$$
$$Y_1 + 2Y_2 \geq 5 \qquad (3.2)$$
$$Y_1, Y_2 \geq 0 \qquad (3.3)$$

For every Y_1 and $3Y_2$, satisfying Eqs. (3.1) to (3.3), $W = 5Y_1 + 12Y_2$ is an upper estimate of Z^*. The lowest value W can take is given by the linear programming problem.

Minimize $W = 5Y_1 + 12Y_2$
Subject to

$$Y_1 + 3Y_2 \geq 6$$
$$Y_1 + 2Y_2 \geq 5$$
$$Y_1, Y_2 \geq 0$$

The above problem is called the **dual** of the given problem. The given problem is called the **primal**.

3.1 DUAL TO THE LP WITH MIXED TYPE OF CONSTRAINTS

From the previous section, we generalize that if the primal is:
Maximize $Z = CX$
Subject to

$$AX \leq b$$
$$X \geq 0$$

The dual is:
Minimize $W = Yb$
Subject to

$$A^T Y \geq C$$
$$Y \geq 0$$

We are aware that we can have two types of objective functions (Maximize and Minimize), three types of constraints ($\geq$ type, equation and $\leq$ type) and three types of variables ($\geq$ type, unrestricted and $\leq$ type). Let us consider a primal that has all these features. Consider Illustration 3.1.

ILLUSTRATION 3.1

Minimize $Z = 8X_1 + 5X_2 + 4X_3$
Subject to

$$4X_1 + 2X_2 + 8X_3 = 12$$
$$7X_1 + 5X_2 + 6X_3 \geq 9$$
$$8X_1 + 5X_2 + 4X_3 \leq 10$$
$$3X_1 + 7X_2 + 9X_3 \geq 7$$
$$X_1 \geq 0, X_2 \text{ unrestricted in sign and } X_3 \leq 0$$

Solution: Let us bring the primal to the standard form:

Maximize $Z = CX$

Subject to
$$AX \leq b$$
$$X \geq 0$$

Variable X_2 is unrestricted in sign. We replace it as the difference of two variables $X_2 = X_4 - X_5$, where both X_4 and $X_5 \geq 0$. Variable $X_3 \leq 0$ is replaced by $-X_6$ where $X_6 \geq 0$. Now, the problem becomes

Minimize $Z = 8X_1 + 5X_4 - 5X_5 - 4X_6$

Subject to
$$4X_1 + 2X_4 - 2X_5 - 8X_6 = 12$$
$$7X_1 + 5X_4 - 5X_5 - 6X_6 \geq 9$$
$$8X_1 + 5X_4 - 5X_5 - 4X_6 \leq 10$$
$$3X_1 + 7X_4 - 7X_5 - 9X_6 \geq 7$$
$$X_1, X_4, X_5, X_6 \geq 0$$

We convert the objective function to maximization by multiplying with −1. The first constraint, which is an equation, is rewritten as two constraints one with a ≤ sign and another with ≥ sign. All the ≥ constraints are written as ≤ constraints by multiplying them with −1. Making the changes, we get

Maximize $Z = -8X_1 - 5X_4 + 5X_5 + 4X_6$

Subject to
$$4X_1 + 2X_4 - 2X_5 - 8X_6 \leq 12$$
$$-4X_1 - 2X_4 + 2X_5 + 8X_6 \leq -12$$
$$-7X_1 - 5X_4 + 5X_5 + 6X_6 \leq -9$$
$$8X_1 + 5X_4 - 5X_5 - 4X_6 \leq 10$$
$$-3X_1 - 7X_4 + 7X_5 + 9X_6 \leq -7$$
$$X_1, X_4, X_5, X_6 \geq 0$$

Now, the primal is converted to the standard form for which we can write the dual. Introducing variables Y_1 to Y_5 for each of the constraints, we write the dual as:

Minimize $Z = 12Y_1 - 12Y_2 - 9Y_3 + 10Y_4 - 7Y_5$

Subject to
$$4Y_1 - 4Y_2 - 7Y_3 + 8Y_4 - 3Y_5 \geq -8$$
$$2Y_1 - 2Y_2 - 5Y_3 + 5Y_4 - 7Y_5 \geq -5$$
$$-2Y_1 + 2Y_2 + 5Y_3 - 5Y_4 + 7Y_5 \geq 5$$
$$-8Y_1 + 8Y_2 + 6Y_3 - 4Y_4 + 9Y_5 \geq 4$$
$$Y_1, Y_2, Y_3, Y_4, Y_5 \geq 0$$

Since the primal is a minimization problem, the dual should be a maximization problem. Multiplying by −1, we get

Maximize $Z = -12Y_1 + 12Y_2 + 9Y_3 - 10Y_4 + 7Y_5$

Subject to
$$4Y_1 - 4Y_2 - 7Y_3 + 8Y_4 - 3Y_5 \geq -8$$
$$2Y_1 - 2Y_2 - 5Y_3 + 5Y_4 - 7Y_5 \geq -5$$
$$-2Y_1 + 2Y_2 + 5Y_3 - 5Y_4 + 7Y_5 \geq 5$$
$$-8Y_1 + 8Y_2 + 6Y_3 - 4Y_4 + 9Y_5 \geq 4$$
$$Y_1, Y_2, Y_3, Y_4, Y_5 \geq 0$$

Defining $Y_6 = Y_2 - Y_1$ and substituting, we get

Maximize $Z = 12Y_6 + 9Y_3 - 10Y_4 + 7Y_5$

Subject to
$$-4Y_6 - 7Y_3 + 8Y_4 - 3Y_5 \geq -8$$
$$-2Y_6 - 5Y_3 + 5Y_4 - 7Y_5 \geq -5$$
$$2Y_6 + 5Y_3 - 5Y_4 + 7Y_5 \geq 5$$
$$8Y_6 + 6Y_3 - 4Y_4 + 9Y_5 \geq 4$$

Y_6 unrestricted in sign, $Y_3, Y_4, Y_5 \geq 0$

Replacing Y_4 by $-Y_7$ such that $Y_7 \leq 0$, we get

Maximize $Z = 12Y_6 + 9Y_3 + 10Y_7 + 7Y_5$

Subject to
$$-4Y_6 - 7Y_3 - 8Y_7 - 3Y_5 \geq -8$$
$$-2Y_6 - 5Y_3 - 5Y_7 - 7Y_5 \geq -5$$
$$2Y_6 + 5Y_3 + 5Y_7 + 7Y_5 \geq 5$$
$$8Y_6 + 6Y_3 + 4Y_7 + 9Y_5 \geq 4$$

Y_6 unrestricted in sign, $Y_3, Y_5 \geq 0, Y_7 \leq 0$

Multiplying the first and second constraints by -1. Writing constraints 2 and 3 as equation, we get the dual as:

Maximize $W = 12Y_6 + 9Y_3 + 10Y_7 + 7Y_5$

Subject to
$$4Y_6 + 7Y_3 + 8Y_7 + 3Y_5 \leq 8$$
$$2Y_6 + 5Y_3 + 5Y_7 + 7Y_5 = 5$$
$$8Y_6 + 6Y_3 + 4Y_7 + 9Y_5 \geq 4$$

Y_6 unrestricted in sign. $Y_3 \geq 0, Y_7 \leq 0, Y_5 \geq 0$

3.2 PRIMAL–DUAL RELATIONSHIPS

We observe that if the above problem was the primal, the original LP would be its dual.

> **Result 3.1**
> In any LPP, the dual of the dual is the primal itself.

We also observe the following based on our examples. Table 3.1 shows some of the relationships between the primal and dual problems.

Table 3.1 Relationships between the Primal and Dual Problems

Primal	Dual
Maximization	Minimization
Minimization	Maximization
Number of variables (*n*)	Number of constraints (*n*)
Number of constraints (*m*)	Number of variables (*m*)
RHS (*b*)	Objective function coefficients (*c*)
Objection function coefficients (*c*)	RHS (*b*)
Constraint coefficients (*A*)	Constraint coefficients (A^T)

If the primal is a maximization problem, the dual is a minimization problem and vice versa. We have as many variables in the dual as the number of constraints in the primal and vice versa. The RHS of the primal becomes the objective function coefficients of the dual and vice versa.

There is also a relationship between the types of variables (of the primal) and the type of constraints (of the dual) and vice versa. This is also shown in Table 3.2

Table 3.2 Primal-Dual Relationships for Constraints and Variables

Primal (Maximization)	Dual (Minimization)
≤ constraint	≥ variable
≥ constraint	≤ variable
equation constraint	unrestricted variable
≥ variable	≥ constraint
≤ variable	≤ constraint
unrestricted variable	equation constraint

We interpret Table 3.2 as follows:

If the first constraint of the primal (maximization) is of ≤ type, the first variable of the dual is of ≥ type and so on.

If the primal is a minimization problem, the table is to be interpreted correspondingly. If the primal is a minimization problem and has third constraint as ≤ type (say) then the third variable of the dual is of the ≤ type.

Result 3.2   Weak Duality Theorem

For a maximization primal, every feasible solution to the dual has a objective function value greater than or equal to every feasible solution to the primal.

Let us apply this result to the following example:
The primal is:
Maximize $Z = 6X_1 + 5X_2$

Subject to
$$X_1 + X_2 \leq 5$$
$$3X_1 + 2X_2 \leq 12$$
$$X_1, X_2 \geq 0$$

The dual is:
Minimize $W = 5Y_1 + 12Y_2$
Subject to
$$Y_1 + 3Y_2 \geq 6$$
$$Y_1 + 2Y_2 \geq 5$$
$$Y_1, Y_2 \geq 0$$

Let W be the objective function value of a solution feasible to the dual.
$$W = 5Y_1 + 12Y_2$$

Since we have a feasible solution X_1, X_2 to the primal, we have $X_1 + X_2 \leq 5$ and $3X_1 + 2X_2 \leq 12$. Substituting, we get
$$W \geq (X_1 + X_2) Y_1 + (3X_1 + 2X_2) Y_2$$

Rearranging the terms, we get
$$W \geq X_1 (Y_1 + 3Y_2) + X_2 (Y_1 + 2Y_2)$$

Since Y_1 and Y_2 are feasible to the dual, we have $Y_1 + 3Y_2 \geq 6$ and $Y_1 + 2Y_2 \geq 5$. Substituting, we get
$$W \geq 6X_1 + 5X_2$$

Since X_1, X_2 are feasible to the primal, $Z = 6X_1 + 5X_2$ and hence $W \geq Z$.

The weak duality theorem also addresses certain other aspects to LP problems. For example, if the primal (maximization) is unbounded, what happens to the dual? Since the primal is unbounded it means that it has a feasible solution. If the dual has a feasible solution then every feasible solution should have an objective function value of infinity, which is not possible. This leads to the conclusion that the dual should be infeasible.

What happens if the primal itself is infeasible? The dual is then unbounded. The dual could also be infeasible (See Solved Example 3.3).

Result 3.3   Optimality Criterion Theorem

If the primal and dual have feasible solution with the same value of the objective function then both have optimal solutions with the same value of the objective function.

The proof of the optimality criterion theorem comes from the weak duality theorem. Since both the primal and dual have feasible solutions with the same value of the objective function, they have to be optimal to the primal and dual, respectively. Otherwise the weak duality theorem will be violated.

> **Result 3.4 Main Duality Theorem**
>
> If primal and dual have feasible solutions then both have optimal solutions with the same value of the objective function.

If the primal and dual have feasible solutions, then they should have optimal solutions. If the primal (maximization) is feasible and unbounded, the dual is infeasible. Weak duality theorem clearly states that the maximization problem cannot have $Z^* > W^*$ (where Z^* and W^* are the objective function values of the primal and dual respectively at the optimum).

We explain later the complimentary slackness conditions, which arise out of the Kuhn Tucker Conditions (described later in Chapter 12) that establish that if the primal and dual are feasible, they have feasible solutions with the same value of the objective function. The optimality criterion theorem also states that if the primal and dual have feasible solution with the same value of the objective function, then both have optimal solutions with the same value of the objective function.

The duality theorems help us generalize the fundamental theorem of linear programming.

> **Result 3.5**
>
> If the primal (maximization) is unbounded, the dual is infeasible.
> If the primal is infeasible, the dual is unbounded or infeasible.

> **Result 3.6 Fundamental Theorem of Linear Programming**
>
> Every linear programming problem is either feasible or unbounded or infeasible. If it has a feasible solution then it has a basic feasible solution. If it has an optimal solution, at least one corner point solution is optimal.

The fundamental theorem defines that three possibilities exist for every LPP. Since the constraints are a linear system of inequalities, there has to be a corner point if a feasible region exists. Also, considering the alternate optima case, if there is an optimal solution, then it has a corner point optimal solution. Unless it is unbounded, it will have at least one corner point solution that is optimal.

> **Result 3.7 Complimentary Slackness Theorem**
>
> If $\mathbf{X}^*$ and $\mathbf{Y}^*$ are the optimal solutions to the primal and dual, respectively and $\mathbf{U}^*$ and $\mathbf{V}^*$ are the values of the primal and dual slack variables at the optimum then
>
> $$\mathbf{X}^* \mathbf{V}^* + \mathbf{Y}^* \mathbf{U}^* = 0$$

Since $\mathbf{X}^* \mathbf{Y}^* \mathbf{U}^* \mathbf{V}^*$ are vectors and all decision and slack variables are greater than or equal to zero, it reduces to every $x_i v_i = y_j u_j = 0$.

Let us apply the complimentary slackness conditions to the earlier example:

ILLUSTRATION 3.2

The primal is:

Maximize $\quad Z = 6X_1 + 5X_2$

Subject to
$$X_1 + X_2 + u_1 = 5$$
$$3X_1 + 2X_2 + u_2 = 12$$
$$X_1, X_2, u_1, u_2 \geq 0 \text{ (where } u_1 \text{ and } u_2 \text{ are slack variables)}$$

The dual is:
Minimize $W = 5Y_1 + 12Y_2$
Subject to
$$Y_1 + 3Y_2 - v_1 = 6$$
$$Y_1 + 2Y_2 - v_2 = 5$$
$$Y_1, Y_2, v_1, v_2 \geq 0$$

The optimal solution to the primal is:
$$X_1^* = 2, \; X_2^* = 3, \; Z^* = 27$$

The optimal solution to the dual is:
$$Y_1^* = 3, \; Y_2^* = 1, \; W^* = 27$$

Applying the complimentary slackness conditions we verify that since X_1 and X_2 are the basic variables at the optimum, v_1 and v_2 are non-basic and take zero value. Similarly, since Y_1 and Y_2 are basic variables of the dual at the optimum, we verify that u_1 and u_2 are non-basic with zero value.

ILLUSTRATION 3.3

Maximize $Z = 3X_1 + 4X_2$
Subject to
$$X_1 + X_2 \leq 12$$
$$2X_1 + 3X_2 \leq 30$$
$$X_1 + 4X_2 \leq 36$$
$$X_1, X_2 \geq 0$$

The dual is:
Minimize $Z = 12Y_1 + 30Y_2 + 36Y_3$
Subject to
$$Y_1 + 2Y_2 + Y_3 \geq 3$$
$$Y_1 + 3Y_2 + 4Y_3 \geq 4$$
$$Y_1, Y_2, Y_3 \geq 0$$

(Variables u_1, u_2 and u_3 are primal slack variables while variables v_1 and v_2 are dual slack variables)
The optimal solution to the primal is:
$$X_1^* = 6, \; X_2^* = 6, \; u_3^* = 6, \; Z^* = 42$$

The optimal solution to the dual is:
$$Y_1^* = 1, \; Y_2^* = 1, \; W^* = 42$$

Since X_1, X_2 are basic variables of the primal at the optimum, dual slack variables v_1 and v_2 are non-basic at the optimum to the dual with zero value. Since variable u_3 is basic at the optimum to the primal, variable Y_3 is non-basic to the dual at the optimum with zero value. Variables Y_1 and Y_2 are basic to the dual at the optimum, slack variables u_1 and u_2 are non-basic at the optimum to the primal.

In fact, we can evaluate the optimum solution to the dual if the optimum solution to the primal is known and vice versa. From the optimum solution, $X_1^* = 6, X_2^* = 6, u_3^* = 6, Z^* = 42$, we observe that variables Y_1 and Y_2 are basic at the optimum to the dual (because slack variables u_1 and u_2 are non-basic at the optimum to the primal). Also variable Y_3 is non-basic at the optimum to the dual because u_3 is basic to the primal at the optimum.

It is enough now to solve for $Y_1 + 2Y_2 = 3$ and $Y_1 + 3Y_2 = 4$. This gives us $Y_1^* = 1$, $Y_2^* = 1, W^* = 42$.

(Using the solution $Y_1^* = 1, Y_2^* = 1, W^* = 42$, we can compute the optimum solution to the primal).

3.3 MATHEMATICAL EXPLANATION TO THE DUAL

Now, we discuss the dual mathematically using the following problem:

Maximize $Z = 6X_1 + 5X_2$

Subject to
$$X_1 + X_2 \leq 5$$
$$3X_1 + 2X_2 \leq 12$$
$$X_1, X_2 \geq 0$$

The optimal solution to the primal is:
$$X_1^* = 2, X_2^* = 1, Z^* = 27$$

The optimal solution to the dual is:
$$Y_1^* = 3, Y_2^* = 1, W^* = 27$$

Let us add a small quantity δ to the first constraint such that the resource available now is $5 + \delta$. Assuming that X_1 and X_2 will remain as basic variables at the optimum and solving for X_1 and X_2 we get $X_1^* = 2 - 2\delta, X_2^* = 3 + 3\delta, Z^* = 27 + 3\delta$.

The increase in objective function value at the optimum for a small increase δ of the first constraint (resource) is 3δ, where 3 is the value of the first dual variable Y_1 at the optimum. The value of the dual variable at the optimum is the rate of change of objective function for a small change in the value of the resource. It can be viewed as the change in the objective function for a unit change of the resource at the optimum (assuming that the change is not significant enough to change the set of basic variable themselves).

3.4 ECONOMIC INTERPRETATION OF THE DUAL

From the previous discussion we know that the objective function increases by 3 for a unit increase in the first resource. If we have to buy the resource we will be willing to pay a maximum of Rs. 3 for the unit increase. Otherwise we will end up making a loss and it will not be profitable considering the purchase of the extra resource.

> **Result 3.8**
> The value of the dual variable is the marginal value of the corresponding resource at the optimum.

We have defined the primal earlier as the problem of the carpenter who makes tables and chairs. Now, the dual is the problem faced by the person who is assumed to be selling the resources to the carpenter. If the person sells the extra resource for a price less than Rs. 3, the carpenter will buy and make more profit than what the problem allows him to make (which the seller would not want). On the other hand, if the seller charges more than Rs. 3, the carpenter will not buy the resource and the seller cannot make money and profit. So both the carpenter and the seller will agree for Rs. 3 (in a competitive environment) and each will make their money and the associated profit.

Consider Illustration 3.4

Maximize $Z = 3X_1 + 4X_2$

Subject to

$$X_1 + X_2 \leq 12$$
$$2X_1 + 3X_2 \leq 30$$
$$X_1 + 4X_2 \leq 36$$
$$X_1, X_2 \geq 0$$

The optimal solution to the primal is:

$$X_1^* = 6, X_2^* = 6, u_3^* = 6, Z^* = 42$$

The optimal solution to the dual is:

$$Y_1^* = 1, Y_2^* = 1, W^* = 42$$

If we add a small δ to the third resource and solve the resultant problem assuming X_1, X_2 and u_3 as basic variables, we realize that the solution does not change and the optimum value of Z remains at 42. This means that the marginal value of the third resource at the optimum is zero. This is because the resource is not completely used at the optimum. The fact that $u_3 = 6$ at the optimum means that only 30 units out of 36 is only consumed and a balance of 6 units is available. Therefore, the person will not want to buy extra resources at extra cost because the resource is already available. Thus, the marginal value of the resource is zero. When a slack variable is in the basis, the corresponding dual decision variable is non-basic indicating that the marginal value of the corresponding dual variable is zero.

3.5 SIMPLEX METHOD SOLVES BOTH THE PRIMAL AND THE DUAL

Let us explain this using the formulation in Illustration 1.1. The simplex table is shown in the usual notation in Table 3.3.

Table 3.3 Simplex Iterations

		6	5	0	0		
		X_1	X_2	u_1	u_2	RHS	θ
0	u_1	1	1	1	0	5	5 →
0	u_2	3	2	0	1	12	4
$C_j - Z_j$		6	5	0	0	0	
0	u_1	0	1/3	1	−1/3	1	3 →
6	X_1	1	2/3	0	1/3	4	6
$C_j - Z_j$		0	1	0	−2	24	
5	X_2	0	1	3	−1	3	
6	X_1	1	0	−2	1	2	
$C_j - Z_j$		0	0	−3	−1	27	

In the optimal tableau, let us observe the $C_j - Z_j$ values. These are 0, 0, −3 and −1 for variables X_1, X_2, u_1 and u_2. We also know (from complimentary slackness conditions) that there is a relationship between X_j and v_j and between u_j and Y_j.

The values of $C_j - Z_j$ corresponding to X_j are the negatives of the values of dual slack variables v_j and the values of $C_j - Z_j$ corresponding to u_j are the negatives of the values of dual decision variables Y_j.

(We will see the algebraic explanation of this subsequently in this chapter).

Therefore, $Y_1^* = 3$, $Y_2^* = 1$, $v_1^* = 0$, $v_2^* = 0$. We also know from the complimentary slackness conditions that if X_j is basic then $v_j = 0$. This is also true because when X_j is basic, $C_j - Z_j$ is zero. When u_j is non-basic and has zero value, its $C_j - Z_j$ is negative at optimum indicating a non-negative value of the basic variable Y_j.

The optimum solution to the dual can be read from the optimum tableau of the primal in the simplex algorithm. We need not solve the dual explicitly.

Let us look at an intermediate iteration (say with basic variable u_1 and X_1). The basic feasible solution is $u_1 = 1$, $X_1 = 4$ with non-basic variables $X_2 = 0$ and $u_2 = 0$. When we apply the above rule (and complimentary slackness conditions), we get the corresponding dual solution to be $Y_1 = 0$, $Y_2 = 2$, $v_1 = 0$, $v_2 = -1$ with $W = 24$ (same value of Z).

This solution is infeasible to the dual because variable v_2 takes a negative value. This means that the second dual constraint $Y_1 + 2Y_2 \geq 5$ is not feasible making $v_2 = -1$. The value of v_2 is the extent of infeasibility of the dual, which is the rate at which the objective function can increase by entering the corresponding primal variable. A non-optimal basic feasible solution to the primal results in an infeasible dual when complimentary slackness conditions are applied. At the optimum, when complimentary slackness conditions are applied, the resultant solution is also feasible and hence optimal.

The simplex algorithm can be seen as one that evaluates basic feasible solutions to the primal (with non-decreasing values of the objective function for maximization problems) and applies complimentary slackness conditions and evaluates the dual. When the primal basic feasible solution is non-optimal, the dual will be infeasible and when the dual becomes feasible, the optimal solution for both primal and dual is known.

3.6 THE DUAL SIMPLEX ALGORITHM

Consider the linear programming problem given by

ILLUSTRATION 3.4

Minimize $Z = 4X_1 + 7X_2$
Subject to
$$2X_1 + 3X_2 \geq 5$$
$$X_1 + 7X_2 \geq 9$$
$$X_1, X_2 \geq 0$$

Normally, we would have added two artificial variables a_1 and a_2 to get an initial basic feasible solution. We do not add these now but write the constraints as equations with slack variables only. The equations are written with a negative RHS (something that the simplex method does not approve). We also convert it as a maximization problem by multiplying the objective function with -1.

The problem becomes

Minimize $Z = 4X_1 + 7X_2 + 0X_3 + 0X_4$
Subject to
$$2X_1 + 3X_2 - X_3 = 5$$
$$X_1 + 7X_2 - X_4 = 9$$
$$X_1, X_2 \geq 0$$

We set up the simplex table as shown in Table 3.4 with slack variables X_3 and X_4 as basic variables and with a negative RHS.

Table 3.4 Simplex Table for Illustration 3.4

		−4	−7	0	0	
		X_1	X_2	X_3	X_4	RHS
0	X_3	−2	−3	1	0	−5
0	X_4	−1	−7	0	1	−9
$C_j - Z_j$		−4	−7	0	0	
q		4	1			

This solution is infeasible because both the basic variables have negative sign. However, it satisfies the optimality condition because all $C_j - Z_j$ are ≤ 0.

To get the optimal solution, we have to make the basic variables feasible. We first decide on the leaving variable (most negative) and choose variable X_4. This row becomes the pivot row. In order that we have feasibility, we should get a non-negative value in the next iteration. This is possible only when the pivot is negative. To find out the entering variable, we divide $C_j - Z_j$ by the corresponding coefficient in the pivot row. We compute the θ row and compute minimum $\theta = 1$ for variable X_2. This variable replaces variable X_4 in the basis. We perform one simplex iteration. The first two iterations are shown in Table 3.5.

Table 3.5 Second Iteration

		−4	−7	0	0	
		X_1	X_2	X_3	X_4	RHS
0	X_3	−2	−3	1	0	−5
0	X_4	−1	−7↑	0	1	−9
	$C_j - Z_j$	−4	−7			
	θ	4	7/4			
0	X_3	−11/7	0	1	−3/7	−8/7
−7	X_2	1/7↑	1	0	−1/7	9/7
	$C_j - Z_j$	−3	0	0	−1	−9
	θ	21/11			7/3	

There is only one candidate for leaving variable because only X_3 has negative value. Variable X_3 leaves the basis and row X_3 is the pivot row. We compute θ. Variables X_1 and X_4 have negative coefficients in the pivot row. The θ value for variable X_1 is −3 ÷ −11/7 = 21/11 and for variable X_4, θ = −1 ÷ −3/7 = 7/3. Variable X_1 has minimum θ and enters the basis replacing variable X_3. We perform iteration. All the iterations are shown in Table 3.6.

Table 3.6 Final Solution

		−4	−7	0	0	
		X_1	X_2	X_3	X_4	RHS
0	X_3	−2	−3	1	0	−5
0	X_4	−1	−7↑	0	1	−9
	$C_j - Z_j$	−4	−7	0	0	
	θ	4	7/4			
0	X_3	**−11/7**	0	1	−3/7	−8/7
−7	X_2	1/7↑	1	0	−1/7	9/7
	$C_j - Z_j$	−3	0	0	−1	−9
	θ	21/11			7/3	
−4	X_1	1	0	−7/11	3/11	8/11
−7	X_2	0	1	1/11	−2/11	13/11
	$C_j - Z_j$	0	0	−21/11	−2/11	123/11

Now, both the basic variables X_1 and X_2 are feasible. In this algorithm, right from the first iteration the optimality condition is satisfied. We do not have a leaving variable. The optimum solution has been reached.

The above algorithm is called the **dual simplex algorithm**. When this is used to solve a minimization problem with all ≥ type constraints, the optimality condition is satisfied all the time. The feasibility condition is not satisfied by the starting solution and after some iterations, when the solution is feasible we say that the optimum solution is reached. This is called **dual simplex** because at any iteration, the dual (of the problem that we are solving) has a feasible solution and the moment we get a primal feasible solution, the optimum is reached.

In fact, for the above example, the moment we get a feasible solution to the primal (RHS ≥ 0) we can terminate even without showing that the optimality condition is satisfied. This is because the dual simplex algorithm maintains the dual feasibility always.

3.7 SOLVING PROBLEMS WITH MIXED TYPE OF CONSTRAINTS

ILLUSTRATION 3.5

Maximize $Z = -X_1 + 5X_2$
Subject to

$$2X_1 - 3X_2 \geq 1$$
$$X_1 + X_2 \leq 3$$
$$X_1, X_2 \geq 0$$

Solution: We solve this problem without introducing artificial variables. We rewrite the constraints as:

$$-2X_1 + 3X_2 + X_3 = 1$$
$$X_1 + X_2 + X_4 = 3$$

The simplex table is set as shown in Table 3.7 with X_3 and X_4 as basic variables. We have a negative value for variable X_3 as well as a positive value for $C_1 - Z_1$. We can do a simplex iteration by entering variable X_1 or do a dual simplex iteration considering variable X_3. We choose the simplex iteration (When both are possible it is better to do the simplex iteration first). Variable X_2 is the entering variable and replaces X_4 (the only candidate for leaving variable). This is also shown in Table 3.7. The simplex iteration (after the first iteration) is shown in Table 3.7.

Table 3.7 Simplex Iteration

		−1	5	0	0		
		X_1	X_2	X_3	X_4	RHS	θ
0	X_3	−2	3	1	0	−1	--
0	X_4	−1	1	0	1	3	2
$C_j - Z_j$		−1	5	0	0		
0	X_3	−5	0	1	−3	−10	
5	X_2	1	1	0	1	3	
$C_j - Z_j$		−6	0	0	−5		
θ		6/5			5/3		

Now, the primal is not feasible but the dual is. We can only do a dual simplex iteration with X_3 as leaving variable. This row becomes the pivot row. We have to find a leaving variable. Variables X_1 and X_4 have negative $C_j - Z_j$ and a negative coefficient in the pivot row. We compute the θ row (dual simplex iteration) and enter X_1 having minimum θ value. We perform a dual simplex iteration leaving variable X_3 from the basis and replacing it with variable X_1. This is shown in Table 3.8.

Table 3.8 Dual Simplex Iteration

		−1	5	0	0		
		X_1	X_2	X_3	X_4	RHS	θ
0	X_3	−2	3	1	0	−1	
0	X_4	1	1	0	1	3	3
$C_j - Z_j$		−1	5	0	0		
0	X_3	0	−3/2	1	2	−10	
5	X_2	1	7/4	0	1	2	
$C_j - Z_j$		0	−76/4	0	−2		
θ							
−1	X_1	1	0	−1/5	3/5	2	
5	X_2	0	1	1/5	2/5	1	
$C_j - Z_j$		0	0	−6/5	−7/5	3	

Here both the primal and dual are feasible. The optimal solution is $X_1 = 2$, $X_2 = 1$, $Z = 5$. The optimal solution to the dual is $Y_1 = 6/5$, $Y_2 = 7/5$, $W = 3$.

ILLUSTRATION 3.6

Maximize $Z = 7X_1 - 3X_2$
Subject to

$$5X_1 - 2X_2 \geq 12$$
$$6X_1 + 3X_2 \leq 10$$
$$X_1, X_2 \geq 0$$

Solution: We solve this problem without introducing artificial variables. We rewrite the constraints as:

$$-5X_1 + 2X_2 + X_3 = -12$$
$$6X_1 + 3X_2 + X_4 = 10$$

The simplex table is set as shown in Table 3.9 with X_3 and X_4 as basic variables. We have a negative value for variable X_3 as well as a positive value for $C_1 - Z_1$. We can do a simplex iteration by entering variable X_1 or do a dual simplex iteration considering variable X_3. We choose the simplex iteration (When both are possible it is better to do the simplex iteration first). Variable X_1 is the entering variable and replaces X_4 (the only candidate for leaving variable). This is also shown in Table 3.9. The simplex iteration (after the first iteration) is shown in Table 3.9.

Table 3.9 Simplex Iteration

		7	−3	0	0		
		X_1	X_2	X_3	X_4	RHS	θ
0	X_3	−5	2	1	0	−12	--
0	X_4	6↑	3	0	1	10	5/3
$C_j - Z_j$		7	−3	0	0		
0	X_3	0	9/2	1	5/6	−11/3	
7	X_1	1	1/2	0	1/6	5/3	
$C_j - Z_j$		0	−13/2	0	−7/6		

Now, the primal is not feasible but the dual is. We can only do a dual simplex iteration first leaving variable X_3. However, we do not find an entering variable because there is variable with a negative coefficient in the pivot row. This indicates **infeasible solution**.

3.8 MATRIX REPRESENTATION OF THE SIMPLEX METHOD

Let us consider a linear programming problem with m constraints and n variables (including slack variables). In the tabular form that we have been using, we compute (or store) a $m \times n$ matrix of the constraint coefficients. We also compute m values of the RHS and a maximum of m values of θ. We also store n values of $C_j - Z_j$ and one value of the objective function. We store $mn + m + n + 1$ values or $(m + 1)(n + 1)$ values.

In a simplex iteration, the first thing that we need is to check whether the optimality condition is satisfied. For this purpose we need $C_j - Z_j$ values of all the $n - m$ non-basic variables. For a maximization problem, we need to either find the variable with the most positive $C_j - Z_j$ or the first variable with a positive value (depending on the rule for the entering variable).

Once the entering variable is known, we need to find the leaving variable. For this purpose we need to compute θ, for which we need the RHS values (m values) and the column corresponding to the entering variable (m values). If the optimal solution is reached, we need to compute the value of the objective function.

Therefore, in iteration, we need only $3m$ values. Can we compute only these values and get to the optimum or can we compute fewer than $(m + 1)(n + 1)$ values per iteration? In the tabular form, we compute the values in iteration from the values of the previous iteration. Can we make these values dependent only on the problem data? We answer these questions using the matrix representation of the simplex method.

The simplex method tries to identify the optimal set of basic variables. Every iteration is characterized by the set of basic variables. Let us call this as X_B. The rest of the variables are non-basic and take zero value. We solve for the set X_B such that

$$BX_B = b$$

where b is the RHS of the given problem and B is the matrix of the values corresponding to the basic variables. If P_j is a column vector corresponding to variable X_j in the constraint matrix A, then B is a sub matrix of A made of the P_j corresponding to X_B.

From $BX_B = b$, we have

$$X_B = B^{-1}b \tag{3.4}$$

Let C_B be the objective function coefficients corresponding to the variables in X_B. Let us assume that in a given iteration P'_j is the column corresponding to variable X_j. Let us assume

$$P'_j = B^{-1}P_j \tag{3.5}$$

We also have

$$C_j - Z_j = C_j - C_B P'_j = C_j - C_B B^{-1} P_j = C_j - yP_j \tag{3.6}$$

where

$$y = C_B B^{-1}$$

Let us explain the matrix form of the simplex algorithm using the following example:

Maximize $Z = 6X_1 + 5X_2$

Subject to

$$X_1 + X_2 \le 5$$
$$3X_1 + 2X_2 \le 12$$
$$X_1, X_2 \ge 0$$

Iteration 1

The initial set of basic variables is given by $X_B = \begin{bmatrix} X_3 \\ X_4 \end{bmatrix}$

RHS values are given by

$$\begin{bmatrix} 5 \\ 12 \end{bmatrix}$$

$$C_B = [0\ 0]$$

$$B = \begin{bmatrix} 1 & 0 \\ 0 & 1 \end{bmatrix} = B^{-1} = I$$

$$y = C_B B^{-1} = [0\ 0]$$

We need to verify whether this is optimal. We compute $C_1 - Z_1 = C_1 - yP_1 = 6$ and $C_2 - Z_2 = 5$. The variable with the most positive value enters. Variable X_1 enters the basis.

To find out the leaving variable we find the entering column corresponding to the entering variable X_1. We have

$$\overline{P}_1 = B^{-1} P_1 = P_1 = \begin{bmatrix} 1 \\ 3 \end{bmatrix}$$

The leaving variable is found by computing θ = minimum of RHS/entering column. θ = Minimum $\{5/1, 12/3\} = 4$. Since the minimum θ happens to be in the second variable, the variable X_4 leaves the basis.

Iteration 2

The set of basic variables is:

$$X_B = \begin{bmatrix} X_3 \\ X_1 \end{bmatrix}$$

$$C_B = [0\ 6]$$

$$B = \begin{bmatrix} 1 & 1 \\ 0 & 3 \end{bmatrix}$$

$$B^{-1} = \begin{bmatrix} 1 & -1/3 \\ 0 & 1/3 \end{bmatrix}$$

RHS values are given by

$$B^{-1}b = \begin{bmatrix} 1 & -1/3 \\ 0 & 1/3 \end{bmatrix} \begin{bmatrix} 5 \\ 12 \end{bmatrix} = \begin{bmatrix} 1 \\ 4 \end{bmatrix}$$

$$y = C_B B^{-1} = [0\ 6] \begin{bmatrix} 1 & -1/3 \\ 0 & 1/3 \end{bmatrix} = [0\ 2]$$

We need to verify whether this is optimal. We compute $C_2 - Z_2 = C_2 - yP_2 = 5 - [0\ 2]\begin{bmatrix}1\\2\end{bmatrix} = 1$ and $C_4 - Z_4 = -2$. The variable with the most positive value enters. Variable X_2 enters the basis.

To find out the leaving variable we find the entering column corresponding to the entering variable X_1. We have

$$\overline{P_2} = B^{-1} P_2 = \begin{bmatrix} 1 & -1/3 \\ 0 & 1/3 \end{bmatrix} \begin{bmatrix} 1 \\ 2 \end{bmatrix} = \begin{bmatrix} 1/3 \\ 2/3 \end{bmatrix}$$

The leaving variable is found by computing θ = minimum of RHS/entering column. θ = Minimum $\{1 \div 1/3, 4 \div 2/3\} = 3$. Since the minimum θ happens to be in the first variable, the variable X_3 leaves the basis.

Iteration 3

The set of basic variables is:

$$X_B = \begin{bmatrix} X_2 \\ X_1 \end{bmatrix}$$

$$C_B = [5\ 6]$$

$$B = \begin{bmatrix} 1 & 1 \\ 2 & 3 \end{bmatrix}$$

$$B^{-1} = \begin{bmatrix} 3 & -1 \\ -2 & 1 \end{bmatrix}$$

RHS values are given by

$$B^{-1}b = \begin{bmatrix} 3 & -1 \\ -2 & 1 \end{bmatrix} \begin{bmatrix} 5 \\ 12 \end{bmatrix} = \begin{bmatrix} 3 \\ 2 \end{bmatrix}$$

$$y = C_B B^{-1} = [5\ 6] \begin{bmatrix} 3 & -1 \\ -2 & 1 \end{bmatrix} = [3\ 1]$$

We need to verify whether this is optimal. We compute $C_3 - Z_3 = C_3 - yP_3 = 0 - [3\ 1]\begin{bmatrix}1\\0\end{bmatrix}$
= –3 and $C_4 - Z_4 = -1$. There is no non-basic variable with positive value of $C_j - Z_j$. The optimal solution has been reached. The optimal solution is $X_1 = 2$, $X_2 = 3$ with $Z = 27$.

What we have carried out is a replica of the simplex algorithm except that we used matrices to represent the constraints, objective function and other parameters. We also calculated B^{-1} explicitly from B.

We observe that B^{-1} is the most important matrix from which the rest of the values can be calculated. A closer look at the simplex table for the problem (Table 2.3) reveals that B^{-1} can be found under the X_3 and X_4 columns (those columns which had the identity matrix in the first iteration). This can be proved in the following way.

In Table 2.1, let us consider the second iteration where X_3 and X_1 were the basic variables. We performed row and columns (based on Gauss Jordan method) to get an identity matrix under X_3 and X_1 so that the solution can be read from the table. This is equivalent to multiplying the entire tableau (every column) by B^{-1} (where B matrix corresponds to X_3 and X_1 in our matrix method) so that there is an identity matrix under X_3 and X_1. The identity matrix (in the first iteration) also gets premultiplied by B^{-1} and the B^{-1} appears under the original identity matrix. This is true for every iteration and, therefore, B^{-1} of the corresponding basis always appears under the original identity matrix.

Since every column is premultiplied by B^{-1} (of the corresponding basis B), the value under the column in an intermediate iteration is the product of B^{-1} and the original column, from which

$$\overline{P}_j = B^{-1} P_j$$

Also, the value of the dual variables y can be seen as the negative of the $C_j - Z_j$ values of the initial slack variables that constituted the identity matrix.

Corresponding to every primal simplex solution, there is a dual solution y.
If the primal is:
Maximize $Z = cX$
Subject to

$$AX \leq b,\ X \geq 0$$

The dual is:
Minimize $Z = yb$
Subject to

$$yA^T \geq c,\ y \geq 0$$

If $X = B^{-1}b$, $y = C_B B^{-1}$. For an initial slack variable $C_j - Z_j = C_j - C_B \overline{P}_j = C_j - C_B B^{-1} P_j = C_j - yP_j = 0 - yI = -y$.

The above results have to be modified slightly when we consider the following two cases:

1. An artificial variable is an initial basic variable.
2. We solve using dual simplex algorithm.

In the first case, the columns under artificial variables have the identity matrix and the slack variables have the negative of the identity matrix. B^{-1} will be seen under the artificial variables and negative of B^{-1} will be under the slack variables.

In the second case, there are no artificial variables but slack variables have an identity matrix but the right hand side values have become negative. This is effectively multiplying the matrix by -1 and the slack variables, therefore, start with the negative of the identity matrix. B^{-1} will be seen under the artificial variables and negative of B^{-1} will be under the slack variables.

3.9 SENSITIVITY ANALYSIS

In sensitivity analysis, we attempt to address issues such as

1. What happens to the solution if the values of the objective function coefficients change?
2. What happens when values of RHS change?
3. What happens when the coefficients in the constraints change?
4. What happens when we add a new variable?
5. What happens when we add a new constraint?

We can address each issue separately or consider a combination of these issues by solving a new problem all over again. However, here we iterate from the given optimal solution and evaluate the effect of these changes.

We illustrate the various aspects of sensitivity analysis using the following example:

ILLUSTRATION 3.7

Consider the linear programming problem:
Maximize $Z = 4X_1 + 3X_2 + 5X_3$
Subject to
$$X_1 + 2X_2 + 3X_3 \leq 9$$
$$2X_1 + 3X_2 + X_3 \leq 12$$
$$X_1, X_2, X_3 \geq 0$$

The simplex solution for this problem is given in Table 3.10.

Table 3.10 Simplex Solution for Illustration 3.7

		4	3	5	0	0		
		X_1	X_2	X_3	X_4	X_5	RHS	θ
0	X_4	1	2	3	1	0	9	3 →
0	X_5	2	3	1	0	1	12	12
$C_j - Z_j$		4	3	5↑	0	0	0	
5	X_3	1/3	2/3	1	1/3	0	3	9
0	X_5	5/3	7/3	0	–1/3	1	9	27/5 →
$C_j - Z_j$		7/3↑	–1/3	0	–5/3	0	15	
5	X_3	0	1/5	1	2/5	–1/5	6/5	
4	X_1	1	7/5	0	–1/5	3/5	27/5	
$C_j - Z_j$		0	–18/5	0	–6/5	–7/5	138/5	

The optimal solution is given by $X_1 = 27/5$, $X_3 = 6/5$, $Z = 138/5$.

3.9.1 Changes in Values of Objective Function Coefficients (C_j)

We consider two cases:

1. Changes in C_j value of a non-basic variable
2. Changes in C_j value of a basic variable

Changes in C_j value of a non-basic variable

In our example, variable X_2 is non-basic at the optimum. Let us consider changes in C_2 values. Let us assume a value C_2 instead of the given value of 3. This will mean that all $C_2 - Z_2$ alone will change. We compute $C_2 - Z_2 = C_2 - 33/5$.

The present value of $C_2 = 3$ results in $C_2 - Z_2$ becoming negative. A value of $C_2 > 33/5$ would make $C_2 - Z_2$ take a positive value resulting in variable X_2 entering the basis.

Let us consider $C_2 = 7$. This would make $C_2 - Z_2 = 2/5$ and the variable X_2 enters the basis. We perform simplex iterations till we reach the optimum. The present optimal table (with the modified values of C_2 and $C_2 - Z_2$ is shown and the subsequent iterations are shown in Table 3.11.

Table 3.11 Simplex Iterations for change in C_2

		4	7	5	0	0		
		X_1	X_2	X_3	X_4	X_5	RHS	θ
5	X_3	0	1/5	1	2/5	–1/5	6/5	6
4	X_1	1	7/5	0	–1/5	3/5	27/5	27/7 →
$C_j - Z_j$		0	2/5↑	0	–6/5	–7/5	138/5	
5	X_3	–1/7	0	1	3/7	–2/7	3/7	
7	X_2	5/7	1	0	–1/7	3/7	27/7	
		–2/7	0	0	–8/7	–11/7	204/7	

The new optimum solution is given by $X_3 = 3/7, X_2 = 27/7$ with $Z = 204/7$. The optimum was found in one iteration starting from the modified optimum table.

Change in C_j value of a basic variable

Let us consider a change in the objective function coefficient of variable X_1. Let us call it C_1. The change will affect all the non-basic $C_j - Z_j$ values. We compute

$$C_2 - Z_2 = 3 - 1 - 7C_1/5$$
$$C_4 - Z_4 = 0 - 2 + C_1/5$$
$$C_5 - Z_5 = 0 + 1 - 3C_1/5$$

For the present value of $C_1 = 4$, the values are $-18/5$, $-6/5$ and $-7/5$. All the values are negative. We also observe that for $C_1 < 10/7$, $C_2 - Z_2$ can become positive. For $C_1 > 10$, $C_4 - Z_4 > 0$ and for $C_1 < 3/5$, $C_5 - Z_5 > 0$.

In the range $6/5 \le C_1 \le 10$, the present set of basic variable will be optimal. Let us consider $C_1 = 12$. $C_2 - Z_2 = C_2 - yP_2 = 3 - [12 \times 7/5 + 1] = -28/5$, $C_4 - Z_4 = -2 + 12/5 = 2/5$ and $C_5 - Z_5 = 1 - 36/5 = -31/5$. Variable X_4 enters the basis and we perform simplex iterations till it reaches the optimum.

The modified optimum (for $C_1 = 12$) and the final solutions are shown in Table 3.12.

Table 3.12 Simplex Iterations for changes in C_1

		12	3	5	0	0		
		X_1	X_2	X_3	X_4	X_5	RHS	θ
5	X_3	0	1/5	1	2/5	–1/5	6/5	3 →
12	X_1	1	7/5	0	–1/5	3/5	27/5	
$C_j - Z_j$		0	–74/5	0	2/5	–31/5	354/5	
0	X_4	0	1/2	5/2	1	–1/2	3	
12	X_1	1	3/2	1/2	0	1/2	6	
$C_j - Z_j$		0	–15	–1	0	–6	72	

Here also, the optimum was found within one iteration. The optimum solution is $X_1 = 12$ and $X_4 = 3$ with $Z = 72$.

3.9.2 Changes in RHS Values

Let us consider change in one of the right hand side values, say b_1. The change results in change of the RHS values.

$$\text{RHS} = B^{-1}b = \begin{bmatrix} 2/5 & -1/5 \\ -1/5 & 3/5 \end{bmatrix} \begin{bmatrix} b_1 \\ 12 \end{bmatrix} = \begin{bmatrix} (2b_1 - 12)/5 \\ (36 - b_1)/5 \end{bmatrix}$$

If b is such that $(2b_1 - 12)/5$ and $(36 - b_1)/5$ are ≥ 0, the current basis will be optimal with the values given by $X_3 = (2b_1 - 12)/5$ and $X_1 = (36 - b_1)/5$. This can happen when $b \le b_1 \le 36$. When b is outside this range, one of the right hand side values will be negative. When $b_1 = 40$, the RHS values become

$$\text{RHS} = B^{-1}b = \begin{bmatrix} 2/5 & -1/5 \\ -1/5 & 3/5 \end{bmatrix} \begin{bmatrix} 40 \\ 12 \end{bmatrix} = \begin{bmatrix} 68/5 \\ -4/5 \end{bmatrix}$$

We carry out dual simplex iterations with the starting solution where one of the right hand side values is negative. These are shown in Table 3.13.

Table 3.13 Dual Simplex Iterations for changes in RHS values

		4	3	5	0	0	
		X_1	X_2	X_3	X_4	X_5	RHS
5	X_3	0	1/5	1	2/5	–1/5	68/5
4	X_1	1	7/5	0	–1/5↑	3/5	–4/5 →
$C_j - Z_j$		0	–18/5	0	–6/5	–7/5	
θ					6		
4	X_3	2	3	1	0	1	12
0	X_4	–5	–7	10	1	–3	4
		–4	–9	0	0	–4	48

The optimum solution is $X_3 = 12$, $X_4 = 4$, $Z = 48$. This was also obtained in one iteration from the modified simplex table.

3.9.3 Changes in Coefficient of Constraint (of a Non-Basic Variable)

We consider change in the constraint coefficient of a non-basic variable X_2. Let us consider that the column vector corresponding to X_2 is $\begin{bmatrix} 2 \\ b \end{bmatrix}$. The corresponding column in the optimum table will be

$$\overline{P}_2 = B^{-1}P_2 \begin{bmatrix} 2/5 & -1/5 \\ -1/5 & 3/5 \end{bmatrix} \begin{bmatrix} 2 \\ b \end{bmatrix} = \begin{bmatrix} (4-b)/5 \\ (3b-2)/5 \end{bmatrix}$$

$$C_2 - Z_2 = 3 - [5\ 4] \begin{bmatrix} (4-b)/5 \\ (3b-2)/5 \end{bmatrix} = (3 - 7b)/5$$

If the change is such that $C_2 - Z_2 \le 0$, the present solution will be optimal. If $b = 1/3$ then $C_2 - Z_2 = 2/15$ and variable X_2 will enter the basis. The value of the entering column will be

$$\overline{P}_2 = B^{-1}P_2 \begin{bmatrix} 2/5 & -1/5 \\ -1/5 & 3/5 \end{bmatrix} \begin{bmatrix} 2 \\ 1/3 \end{bmatrix} = \begin{bmatrix} 11/15 \\ -1/5 \end{bmatrix}$$

The simplex iterations are shown in Table 3.14.

Table 3.14 Simplex Iteration for change in constraint coefficient

		4	3	5	0	0		
		X_1	X_2	X_3	X_4	X_5	RHS	θ
5	X_3	0	11/15	1	2/5	–1/5	6/5	18/11 →
4	X_1	1	–1/5↑	0	–1/5	3/5	27/5	
$C_j - Z_j$		0	2/15	0	–6/5	–7/5	138/5	
3	X_2	0	1	15/11	6/11	–3/11	18/11	
4	X_1	1	0	3/11	–1/11	6/11	63/11	
		0	0	–2/11	–14/11	–15/11	306/11	

The optimum solution is given by $X_2 = 18/11$, $X_1 = 63/11$ with $Z = 306/11$. Here too, the optimum solution is obtained in one iteration.

3.9.4 Adding a New Product

Let us consider adding a new product to the problem. This is incorporated in the formulation by the introduction of a new variable X_6. Let us assume that this product requires 1 unit of resource 1 per product and 3 units of resource 2 per product and fetches a profit of Rs. 6/unit.

This is same as verifying whether $C_6 - Z_6$ can enter the basis. Now,

$$C_6 - Z_6 = C_6 - yP_6. \ P_6 = \begin{bmatrix} 1 \\ 3 \end{bmatrix} \text{ and } C_6 - Z_6 = 6 - 27/5 = 3/5$$

Variable X_6 enters the basis. The modified optimum table is shown and the simplex iterations are shown in Table 3.15.

Table 3.15 Simplex Iterations for adding a variable

		4	3	5	0	0	6		
		X_1	X_2	X_3	X_4	X_5	X_6	RHS	θ
5	X_3	0	1/5	1	2/5	−1/5	−1/5	6/5	
$C_j - Z_j$		0	−18/5	0	−6/5	−7/5	3/5	138/5	
5	X_3	1/8	3/8	1	3/8	−1/8	0	15/8	
6	X_6	5/8	7/8	0	−1/8	3/8	1	27/8	
$C_j - Z_j$		−3/8	−33/8	0	−9/8	−13/8	0	237/8	

The optimum solution is given by $X_3 = 15/8$, $X_6 = 27/8$, $Z = 237/8$.

3.9.5 Adding a New Constraint

It may be possible to add a new constraint to an existing problem. Let the constraint be $X_1 + X_2 + X_3 \leq 8$.

We verify whether the constraint is satisfied by the optimal solution. The solution $X_1 = 27/5$, $X_3 = 6/5$ satisfies this constraint and the present solution continues to be optimal even with the additional constraint.

If the constraint was $X_1 + X_2 + X_3 \leq 6$, the present optimal solution violates the constraint. We rewrite the constraint as an equation by adding a slack variable and write the basic variables in terms of the non-basic variables.

$$X_1 + X_2 + X_3 + X_6 = 8$$

From the optimum simplex table, we have

$$X_1 + \frac{7}{5}X_2 - \frac{1}{5}X_4 + \frac{3}{5}X_5 = \frac{27}{5}$$

and

$$X_3 + \frac{1}{5}X_2 + \frac{2}{5}X_4 - \frac{1}{5}X_5 = \frac{6}{5}$$

Substituting, we get

$$\frac{27}{5} - \frac{7}{5}X_2 + \frac{1}{5}X_4 - \frac{3}{5}X_5 + X_2 + \frac{6}{5} - \frac{1}{5}X_2 - \frac{2}{5}X_4 + \frac{1}{5}X_5 + X_6 = 6$$

or $\qquad -\frac{3}{5}X_2 - \frac{1}{5}X_4 - \frac{2}{5}X_5 + X_6 = -\frac{3}{5}$

(Please observe that if the constraint is binding, as in this case, the final equation after substitution will have a negative value of the right hand side when the slack variable has +1 coefficient). We include this constraint into the optimal table and proceed with dual simplex iterations till the new optimum is reached. This is shown in Table 3.16.

Table 3.16 Dual Simplex Iteration for adding a constraint

		4	3	5	0	0	0	
		X_1	X_2	X_3	X_4	X_5	X_6	RHS
5	X_3	0	1/5	1	2/5	−1/5	0	6/5
4	X_1	1	7/5	0	−1/5	3/5	0	27/5
0	X_6	0	−3/5	0	−1/5	**−2/5**	1	−3/5
$C_j - Z_j$		0	−18/5	0	−6/5	−7/5	0	138/5
5	X_3	0	1/2	1	1/2	0	−1/2	3/2
4	X_1	1	1/2	0	−1/2	0	3/2	9/2
0	X_5	0	3/2	0	1/2	1	−5/2	3/2
$C_j - Z_j$		0	−3/2	0	−1/2	0	−7/2	51/2

The only case we have not considered is when the constraint coefficient of a basic variable changes. Here the basis matrix B changes and hence B^{-1} changes, resulting in the entire optimum table changing. In this case, it is preferable to solve the problem from the beginning and not use sensitivity analysis.

SOLVED EXAMPLES

EXAMPLE 3.1 Maximize $Z = 4X_1 - 3X_2 + 2X_3 - X_4$
Subject to

$$2X_1 + X_2 + 3X_3 + X_4 \leq 3$$
$$X_1 - X_2 + 2X_3 - 3X_4 \leq 7$$
$$X_j > 0$$

(a) Write the dual to the given problem and verify that (2, 0) is a feasible solution to the dual.
(b) Use the information in part (a) to obtain optimal solutions to primal and dual.
(c) Suppose the constraint $X_1 + X_2 + X_3 + X_4 \leq 2$ is imposed on the problem, find the optimal solutions to primal and dual.

Solution: The dual is (a) Minimize $W = 3Y_1 + 7Y_2$
Subject to
$$2Y_1 - Y_2 \geq 4$$
$$Y_1 - Y_2 \geq -3$$
$$3Y_1 + 2Y_2 \geq 2$$
$$Y_1 - 3Y_2 \geq -1$$
$$Y_1, Y_2 \geq 0$$

Substituting (2, 0) in the four dual constraints, we find the constraints are satisfied. Hence it is a feasible solution to the dual.

(b) Minimize $W = 3Y_1 + 7Y_2$
Subject to
$$2Y_1 - Y_2 \geq 4$$
$$Y_1 - Y_2 \geq -3$$
$$3Y_1 + 2Y_2 \geq 2$$
$$Y_1 - 3Y_2 \geq -1$$
$$Y_1, Y_2 > 0$$

Only the first dual constraint is satisfied as an equation. Applying complimentary slackness to the given feasible solution to the dual, we realize that the decision variable X_1 alone is in the basis in the primal. Corresponding primal solution is (3/2, 0, 0, 0) with $Z = 6$.

We have feasible solution to dual and primal satisfying complimentary slackness conditions. They also have the same value of the objective function. They are optimal to primal and dual, respectively.

(c) Suppose the constraint $X_1 + X_2 + X_3 + X_4 \leq 2$ is imposed on the problem, find the optimal solutions to primal and dual.

The constraint $X_1 + X_2 + X_3 + X_4 \leq 2$ is satisfied by the present optimal solution (3/2, 0, 0, 0). Therefore, optimality is intact. Primal slack variable X_7 corresponding to the new constraint will be in the basis with value ½ in the primal. The dual will have one more basic variable Y_3 which will take zero value.

EXAMPLE 3.2 Maximize $Z = 8X_1 + 4X_2 + 9X_3$
Subject to
$$7X_1 + 6X_2 + X_3 \leq 20$$
$$4X_1 + 3X_2 + 2X_3 \leq 29$$
$$X_j \geq 0$$

Write the dual to this problem. Solve the dual optimally and obtain the optimal solution to the primal using complementary slackness conditions.

Solution: The dual is: Minimize $W = 20Y_1 + 29Y_2$
$$7Y_1 + 4Y_2 \geq 8$$
$$6Y_1 + 3Y_2 \geq 4$$
$$Y_1 + 2Y_2 \geq 9$$
$$Y_j \geq 0$$

The optimal solution is (0, 9/2) with $W = 130.5$.
Here we find that Y_2 is in the basis, the slack variable in primal X_5 is zero at the optimum. Since $Y_1 = 0$, slack variable X_4 is in the basis at the optimum.

We observe that the first two dual constraints are satisfied as inequalities at the optimum, indicating that the first two dual slack variables are positive. This means that $X_1 = X_2 = 0$ at the optimum. We also observe that the surplus variable in constraint 3 of dual takes zero value and hence X_3 is basic at the optimum. The primal optimum is $X_3 = 29/2$, $X_4 = 11/2$, $Z = 261/2$.

EXAMPLE 3.3 Construct an LPP such that neither the primal nor the dual has feasible solutions.

Solution: Primal Maximize $Z = 2X_1 - X_2$
Subject to
$$X_1 + X_2 \leq 1$$
$$X_1 + X_2 \geq 2$$

X_i unrestricted in sign

Dual Minimize $W = Y_1 + 2Y_2$
Subject to
$$Y_1 + Y_2 = 2$$
$$Y_1 + Y_2 = -1$$

$Y_1 \geq 0$, $Y_2 \leq 0$ which becomes

Minimize $W = Y_1 - 2Y_2$
Subject to
$$Y_1 - Y_2 = 2$$
$$Y_1 - Y_2 = -1$$
$$Y_1, Y_2 \geq 0$$

Here, both the primal and dual are infeasible.

EXAMPLE 3.4 You are given a linear programming problem:

Maximize $Z = 4X_1 - 3X_2 + 3X_3$
Subject to
$$2X_1 + X_2 + 3X_3 \leq 7$$
$$2X_1 - X_2 + 4X_3 \geq 8$$
$$X_1, X_2, X_3 \geq 0$$

(a) Solve the problem without using artificial variables.
(b) Find the solution to the dual of the given problem.
(c) If the first constraint changes to $2X_1 - 2X_2 + 3X_3 \leq 5$, use sensitivity analysis to find the effect of the change.

Solution: (a) The second constraint would ordinarily have necessitated the use of an artificial variable. Since we are not using the artificial variable, we multiply this constraint by -1 to obtain $-2X_1 + X_2 - 4X_3 \leq -8$. We add slack variables X_4 and X_5 and start the simplex table with $X_4 = 7$ and $X_5 = -8$. The initial simplex table is shown in Table 3.17.

Table 3.17 Simplex Table for Example 3.4

		4	−3	3	0	0	
		X_1	X_2	X_3	X_4	X_5	RHS
0	X_4	2	1	3	1	0	7
0	X_5	−2	1	−4	0	1	−8
$C_j - Z_j$		4	−3	3	0	0	

We have a solution that is non-optimal and infeasible. We can carry out a simplex iteration by entering variable X_1 or we can try performing a dual simplex iteration by leaving variable X_5. In the present table, we cannot identify an entering variable if we choose to do a dual simplex iteration. Since we can perform a simplex iteration, we proceed by entering variable X_1 and leaving out variable X_4 (we have only X_4 as a candidate for leaving variable, since simplex iteration requires a positive pivot). The net iteration is shown in Table 3.18.

Table 3.18 Simplex Iteration

		4	-3	3	0	0	
		X_1	X_2	X_3	X_4	X_5	RHS
4	X_1	1	1/2	3/2	1/2	0	7/2
0	X_5	0	2	-1	1	1	-1
$C_j - Z_j$		0	-5	-3	-2	0	

The solution in Table 3.18 satisfies the optimality conditions but is infeasible. We can perform a dual simplex iteration by leaving variable X_5 and entering X_3 (the only candidate because we require a negative pivot). The next iteration is shown in Table 3.19.

Table 3.19 Simplex Iteration

		4	-3	3	0	0	
		X_1	X_2	X_3	X_4	X_5	RHS
4	X_1	1	7/2	0	2	3/2	2
3	X_3	0	-2	1	-1	-1	1
$C_j - Z_j$		0	-11	0	-5	-3	11

The optimal solution to the given problem is $X_1 = 2, X_3 = 1, Z = 11$.

(b) The optimal solution to the dual can be read from Table 3.19 as $y_1 = 5, y_2 = -3$ and $w = 11$. Ordinarily, the dual value at the optimum is the negative of the $C_j - Z_j$ value. Since we had multiplied the second constrained by -1 to get the identity column, the corresponding value is negative of the $C_5 - Z_5$ value. The value of y_2 is -3. The reason why the dual variable is negative at the optimum is because the second dual variable of the given primal would be of the $\leq$ type.

We also observe that the objective function of the dual at the optimum is $7 \times 5 - 8 \times 3 = 11$

(c) The change $2X_1 - 2X_2 + 3X_3 \leq 5$ would mean two changes in the optimum table, change in RHS value and change in the constraint coefficient of a non-basic variable.

$$\text{New RHS} = B^{-1}b$$

$$B^{-1} = \begin{bmatrix} 2 & -3/2 \\ -1 & 1 \end{bmatrix}$$

From the simplex table, we get the first column directly but we have to multiply the second column (variable X_5 column by -1 because we have multiplied the constraint by -1).

$$\text{RHS} = B^{-1}b = \begin{bmatrix} 2 & -3/2 \\ -1 & 1 \end{bmatrix} \begin{bmatrix} 5 \\ 8 \end{bmatrix} = \begin{bmatrix} -2 \\ 3 \end{bmatrix}$$

$$\overline{P}_2 = B^{-1}P_2 = \begin{bmatrix} 2 & -3/2 \\ -1 & 1 \end{bmatrix} \begin{bmatrix} -2 \\ 1 \end{bmatrix} = \begin{bmatrix} -5/2 \\ 1 \end{bmatrix}$$

$$C_2 - Z_2 = C_2 - yP_2 = -3 - [5\ 3] \begin{bmatrix} -2 \\ 1 \end{bmatrix} = 4$$

Variable X_2 can enter the basis. The modified simplex table is shown in Table 3.20.

Table 3.20 Modified Simplex Table

		4	-3	3	0	0	
		X_1	X_2	X_3	X_4	X_5	RHS
4	X_1	1	-5/2	0	2	3/2	-2
3	X_3	0	1	1	-1	-1	3
	$C_j - Z_j$	0	4	0	-5	-3	

From Table 3.19, we can consider a simplex iteration with X_2 entering or consider a dual simplex iteration with variable X_1 leaving. We are unable to get an entering variable if we choose the dual simplex option while we can identify the leaving variable for the simplex iteration. This is shown in Table 3.21.

Table 3.21 Simplex Iteration

		4	-3	3	0	0	
		X_1	X_2	X_3	X_4	X_5	RHS
4	X_1	1	0	5/2	-1/2	-1	11/2
-3	X_2	0	1	1	-1	-1	3
	$C_j - Z_j$	0	0	-4	-1	1	

We observe that variable X_5 can enter but we are unable to find a leaving variable. Also there is no variable with a negative RHS value. The only possibility is a simplex iteration but we are unable to proceed because there is no leaving variable. Therefore, the problem is unbounded.
(From Table 3.20, we may find that there was no entering variable if we had chosen the dual simplex iteration option. We cannot conclude anything from this because a simplex iteration was possible. If at that stage all $C_j - Z_j$ were non-positive, we could have concluded that the problem was infeasible. In dual simplex, infeasibility is indicated by the presence of a leaving variable with negative RHS and no entering variable while all $C_j - Z_j$ values are non-positive).

EXAMPLE 3.5 A person located in City 1 wants to reach City 5. Figure 3.1 shows the network, connecting the cities along with the time taken to travel. The problem is to determine the path that takes the shortest time to travel from City 1 to City 5.

Duality and Sensitivity Analysis   89

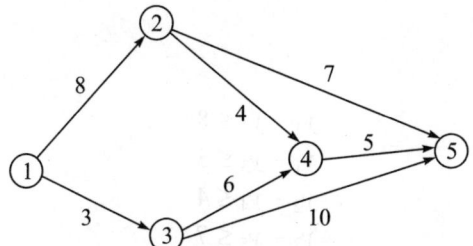

Figure 3.1   Network for Example 3.5.

(a) Formulate the problem as an LPP by considering decision variables $X_{ij} = 1$ if i–j is in the shortest path and zero otherwise.
(b) How many variables and constraints are there in your formulation?
(c) Rewrite your formulation such that every variable has a positive coefficient in one constraint and a negative coefficient in another.
(d) Write the dual to Part (c) considering all $X_{ij} \geq 0$
(e) Initialize $Y_5 = 0$ and solve the dual optimally by inspection.
(f) Obtain the optimal solution to the primal using complementary slackness theorem.

Solution: (a) Minimize $Z = 8X_{12} + 3X_{13} + 4X_{24} + 7X_{25} + 6X_{34} + 10X_{35} + 5X_{45}$
Subject to

$$X_{12} + X_{13} = 1$$
$$X_{13} = X_{34} + X_{35}$$
$$X_{12} = X_{24} + X_{25}$$
$$X_{34} + X_{24} = X_{45}$$
$$X_{25} + X_{45} + X_{35} = 1$$
$$X_{ij} = 0 \text{ or } 1$$

(b) Number of variables = Number of arcs = 7
    Number of constraints = Number of nodes = 5

(c) Minimize $Z = 8X_{12} + 3X_{13} + 4X_{24} + 7X_{25} + 6X_{34} + 10X_{35} + 5X_{45}$
Subject to

$$X_{12} + X_{13} = 1$$
$$-X_{13} + X_{34} + X_{35} = 0$$
$$-X_{12} + X_{24} + X_{25} = 0$$
$$-X_{34} - X_{24} + X_{45} = 0$$
$$-X_{25} - X_{45} - X_{35} = -1$$
$$X_{ij} = 0 \text{ or } 1$$

(d) *Primal*
Minimize $8X_{12} + 3X_{13} + 4X_{24} + 7X_{25} + 6X_{34} + 10X_{35} + 5X_{45}$
Subject to

$$X_{12} + X_{13} = 1$$
$$-X_{12} + X_{24} + X_{25} = 0$$
$$-X_{13} + X_{34} + X_{35} = 0$$
$$-X_{34} - X_{24} + X_{45} = 0$$
$$-X_{25} - X_{45} - X_{35} = -1$$
$$X_{ij} = 0 \text{ or } 1$$

Dual
Maximize $y_1 - y_5$
Subject to
$$y_1 - y_2 \leq 8$$
$$y_1 - y_3 \leq 3$$
$$y_2 - y_4 \leq 4$$
$$y_2 - y_5 \leq 7$$
$$y_3 - y_4 \leq 6$$
$$y_3 - y_5 \leq 10$$
$$y_4 - y_5 \leq 5$$
y_i unrestricted in sign

(e) *Dual*
Maximize $y_1 - y_5$
Subject to
$$y_1 - y_2 \leq 8$$
$$y_1 - y_3 \leq 3$$
$$y_2 - y_4 \leq 4$$
$$y_2 - y_5 \leq 7$$
$$y_3 - y_4 \leq 6$$
$$y_3 - y_5 \leq 10$$
$$y_4 - y_5 \leq 5$$
y_i unrestricted in sign

Given $y_5 = 0$, $y_4 = 5$, $y_3 = 10$, $y_2 = 10$, $y_1 = 13$.
(f) Using complementary slackness theorem, we have
$$X_{24} = 0, X_{25} = 0, X_{45} = 0;$$
So we have
Minimize $8X_{12} + 3X_{13} + 6X_{34} + 10X_{35}$
Subject to
$$X_{12} + X_{13} = 1$$
$$X_{24} - X_{12} = 0$$
$$X_{34} + X_{35} - X_{13} = 0$$
$$X_{34} = 0$$
$$-X_{35} = -1$$
$$x_{ij} = 0 \text{ or } 1$$

which means $X_{13} = 1$ with $Z = 13$.
  We have feasible solutions to primal and dual with the same value of the objective function and satisfying complementary slackness conditions. They have to be optimal to primal and dual respectively.

EXAMPLE 3.6 A factory manufactures three products. Two resources—material and labour—are required to produce these products. Table 3.22 gives the requirements of each of the resources for the three products:

Table 3.22 Requirements of the Resources for Three Products

Product	Resources (Hours) Material	Resources (Hours) Labour	Units Profit (Rs.)
1	1	5	9
2	1	2	7
3	1	3	5

There are 80 units of material and 250 hours of labour available. In order to determine the optimal product mix which maximizes the total profit, the following linear program was solved:

Maximize $Z = 9X_1 + 7X_2 + 5X_3$

Subject to

$$X_1 + X_2 + X_3 \leq 80 \text{ (Material)}$$
$$5X_1 + 2X_2 + 3X_3 \leq 250 \text{ (Labour)}$$
$$X_1, X_2, X_3 > 0$$

X_1, X_2 and X_3 are the quantities of Product 1, Product 2 and Product 3 produced. The optimal solution is given in Table 3.23 where X_4 and X_5 are the slack variables:

Table 3.23 Optimal Solution

Basis	X_1	X_2	X_3	X_4	X_5	b
X_1	1	0	1/3	−2/3	1/3	30
X_2	1	0	2/3	5/3	−1/3	50
$C_j - Z_j$	0	0	−8/3	−20/6	−4/6	Z = 620

Using sensitivity analysis, answer the following with respect to the above optimal tableau:

(a) What should be the profit of Product 3 before it becomes worthwhile to manufacture? Find the most profitable product mix if the profit on Product 3 were increased to Rs. 8.
(b) What is the range on the profit of Product 1 so that the current solution is still optimal?
(c) It is believed that the estimate of the available hours of labour is 250 + α. Find the range of values of α for which the given product mix is still optimal.
(d) Determine the shadow prices of all the resources.
(e) The manufacturing department comes up with a proposal to produce a new product requiring 1 unit of material and ½ hour of labour. The prediction is that the product can be sold at a unit profit of Rs. 6. What should be the management's decision?

Solution: (a) Let the price of Product 3 be C_3. In order for Product 3 to be worthwhile to manufacture (enter the basis), we have $C_3 - Z_3 \geq 0$ which gives $C_3 - 23/3 \geq 0$. When $C_3 \geq 23/3$, variable X_3 enters the basis. When $C_3 = 8$, variable X_3 enters the basis and the simplex iterations are shown in Table 3.24.

Table 3.24 Simplex Iterations

		9	7	8	0	0		
		X_1	X_2	X_3	X_4	X_5	RHS	θ
9	X_1	1	0	1/3	-2/3	1/3	30	90 →
7	X_2	0	1	2/3	5/3	-1/3	50	75
	$C_j - Z_j$	0	0	1/3	-17/3	-2/3	620	
9	X_1	1	-1/2	0	-3/2	1/2	5	
8	X_3	0	3/2	1	5/2	-1/2	75	
		0	-1/2	0	-13/2	-1/2	645	

The optimum value is $X_1 = 5$, $X_3 = 75$ and $Z = 645$.

(b) Range of values of C_1 for which the given solution is optimal, is when for a given C_1, $C_j - Z_j$ for all non-basic variables is non-positive (for a maximization problem).

$$C_3 - Z_3 = 5 - \frac{C_1}{3} - \frac{14}{3} \leq 0 \text{ gives } C_1 \geq 1$$

$$C_4 - Z_4 = 0 + \frac{2C_1}{3} - \frac{35}{3} \leq 0 \text{ gives } C_1 \leq 35/2$$

$$C_5 - Z_5 = 0 + \frac{C_1}{3} - \frac{7}{3} \leq 0 \text{ gives } C_1 \geq 7$$

The range of values of C_1 for which the present solution remains optimal is $7 \leq C_1 \leq 35/2$.

(c) $b = \begin{bmatrix} 80 \\ 250 + \alpha \end{bmatrix}$

$$X_B = B^{-1}b = \begin{bmatrix} -2/3 & 1/3 \\ 5/3 & -1/3 \end{bmatrix} \begin{bmatrix} 80 \\ 250 + \alpha \end{bmatrix} = \begin{bmatrix} (90 + \alpha)/3 \\ (150 - \alpha)/3 \end{bmatrix} \geq 0$$

gives $-90 \leq \alpha \leq 150$ for which the current basis is optimal.

(d) Shadow price of the resource is the value of the dual variables at the optimum. These are available as the $C_j - Z_j$ values of the slack variables (or initial basic variables). For a maximization problem, the $C_j - Z_j$ values are non-positive at the optimum. We take the negative of the $C_j - Z_j$ values of the slack variables X_4 and X_5. The values of the shadow prices of the two resources are 17/3 and 2/3, respectively.

(e) We denote the new product by variable X_6. We have to calculate $C_6 - Z_6 = C_6 - yP_6$. We have $C_6 = 6$, $y = [17/3, 2/3]$ and $P_7 = \begin{bmatrix} 1/2 \\ 1 \end{bmatrix}$. $C_7 - Z_7 = 6 - 21/6 = 5/2$ and the new product (variable X_6) enters the basis. The simplex iteration is shown in Table 3.25.

$$\overline{P_7} = B^{-1}P_7 = \begin{bmatrix} -2/3 & 1/3 \\ 5/3 & -1/3 \end{bmatrix} \begin{bmatrix} 1/2 \\ 1 \end{bmatrix} = \begin{bmatrix} 0 \\ 1/2 \end{bmatrix}$$

Table 3.25 Simplex Iterations

		9	7	5	0	0	6		
9	X_1	1	0	1/3	−2/3	1/3	0	30	400/6
7	X_2	0	1	2/3	5/3	−1/3	1/2	50	--
	$C_j - Z_j$	0	0	−8/3	−17/3	−2/3	5/2	620	
9	X_1	1	0	1/3	−2/3	1/3	0	30	
6	X_6	0	2	4/3	10/3	−2/3	1	100	
	$C_j - Z_j$	0	−5	−6	−14	1	0	870	
0	X_5	3	0	1	−2	1	0	90	
6	X_6	2	2	2	2	0	1	160	
	$C_j - Z_j$	−3	−5	−7	−12	0	0	960	

The new optimal solution is $X_6 = 160$, $Z = 960$.

EXAMPLE 3.7 Chemco Chemicals have to blend three types of raw materials say, P, Q and R, supplied respectively by Pai, Qadar and Ram, in order to obtain their final product. The costs of the raw materials, P, Q and R are Rs. 5, Rs. 3, and Re. 1 per litre, respectively. Each raw material contains two essential ingredients, viz. sulphur and phosphorus, expressed in grams per litre. The final product must contain a specified minimum amount of these ingredients in every barrel. Each barrel contains one or more of the raw materials in sufficient quantities to fulfill the minimum specifications on sulfur and phosphorus. Once the specifications are met, the remaining capacity of the barrel is filled by another liquid at negligible cost.

The following LP problem was formulated to determine the least cost solution.

Minimize $W = 5Y_1 + 3Y_2 + Y_3$

Subject to

$$2Y_1 + 2Y_2 + Y_3 \geq 8 \text{ (Sulphur)}$$
$$3Y_1 + Y_2 + 2Y_3 \geq 6 \text{ (Phosphorus)}$$
$$Y_1, Y_2, Y_3 \geq 0$$

Table 3.26 gives the optimal simplex tableau without the artificial variables columns:

Table 3.26 Optimal Simplex Tableau

	Y_1	Y_2	Y_3	Y_4	Y_5	
Y_3	2	2	1	−1	0	8
Y_5	1	3	0	−2	1	10
	3	1	0	1	0	$W = 8$

Noting that the subdivisions are independent of each other, answer the following questions:

(a) Qadar, who supplies the raw material Q, wants to lower his price so that he can manage to sell some quantity of Q to Chemco Chemicals. What price of Q should be quoted to strike a deal with Chemco?

(b) Pai, the supplier for P tries to convince Ram that he is being exploited by Chemco and so he should raise his price. By how much can the price of R increase without changing the current optimal solution?

(c) Suppose the BIS changes the specification on sulfur content. What extent of change will alter the current basis?

(d) A fourth supplier, Sam, offers to sell a raw material S which contains 3 g of sulfur and 2 g of phosphorus per litre. What price of S would make Chemco think of buying it?

(e) Meanwhile, Pai claims that he has increased the sulphur content in P. What should the new sulfur content in P be, so that Pai can succeed in selling it to Chemco?

(f) The BIS imposes one more specification on the final product with reference to a third ingredient. After some quick laboratory analyses, Chemco frames the third constraint as:

$$0.1Y_1 + 0.2Y_2 + 0.3Y_3 \geq 3$$

What is the new optimal solution?

Solution:

(a) For the supplier of raw material Q to strike a deal, $C_2 - Z_2 \leq 0$. The less than or equal to sign comes because of the minimization objective.

$$C_2 - Z_2 = C_2 - 2 \leq 0$$

which gives $C_2 \leq 2$. If his price is less than or equal to 2 units, he can strike a deal.

(b) Raw material R is represented by variable y_3, which is a basic variable. A change in the objective function coefficient of a basic variable, results in the change in the values of $C_j - Z_j$ values of all the non-basic variables. For the present basis to be optimal, all the $C_j - Z_j$ values have to be non-negative for a minimization problem. We have

$$C_1 - Z_1 = 5 - 2C_3 \geq 0 \quad \text{from which } C_3 \leq 5/2$$
$$C_2 - Z_2 = 3 - 2C_3 \geq 0 \quad \text{from which } C_3 \leq 3/2$$
$$C_4 - Z_4 = 0 + C_3 \geq 0 \quad \text{from which } C_3 \geq 0$$

For the range $0 \leq C_3 \leq 3/2$, the present basis will be optimal. The present basis is optimal till the price of R becomes 1.5.

(c) RHS value becomes $\begin{bmatrix} b \\ 6 \end{bmatrix}$. The effect of this is the change in RHS value of the optimal simplex tableau. This is given by

$$\text{RHS} = B^{-1}b = \begin{bmatrix} 1 & 0 \\ 2 & -1 \end{bmatrix} \begin{bmatrix} b \\ 6 \end{bmatrix} = \begin{bmatrix} b \\ 2b-6 \end{bmatrix}$$

(Here, B^{-1} is the negative of the values under the initial surplus variables).

For the sulphur content change to affect the optimum, we have $2b - 6 \leq 0$ from which $b \leq 3$.

(d) Let us define raw material S by variable y_6. For this to be bought,

$$C_6 - Z_6 = C_6 - yP_6 = C_6 - [1 \ 0]\begin{bmatrix} 3 \\ 2 \end{bmatrix} \leq 0$$

from which $C_6 \leq 3$.

The price has to be Rs. 3 or less for this raw material to be considered.

(e) Let the sulphur content in P be a. For raw material P (variable y_1) to enter,

$$C_1 - Z_1 = C_1 - yP_1 = 5 - [0\ 1]\begin{bmatrix} a \\ 3 \end{bmatrix} \leq 0$$

from which $a \leq 5$. Increase of sulphur content by three units in P will make variable y_1 enter the basis.

(f) The present optimal solution $y_3 = 8$ violates the constraint $0.1y_1 + 0.2y_2 + 0.3y_3 \geq 3$. We have to add another constraint to the table. Substituting for $y_3 = 8 - 2y_1 - 2y_2 + y_4$ in the new constraint, we get

$$5y_1 + 4y_2 - 3y_4 \leq -6$$

We include slack variable y_6 and perform a dual simplex iteration. This is shown in Table 3.27.

Table 3.27 Dual Simplex Iterations

		5	3	1	0	0	0	
		y_1	y_2	y_3	y_4	y_5	y_6	RHS
1	y_3	2	2	1	−1	0	0	8
0	y_1	1	3	0	−2	1	0	10
0	y_6	5	5	0	−3	0	1	−6
	$C_j - Z_j$	3	1	0	1	0	0	---
6	y_3	1/3	2/3	1	0	0	−1/3	10
10	y_5	−7/3	1/3	0	0	1	−2/3	14
50/6	y_4	−5/3	−4/3	0	1	0	−1/3	2
		14/3	7/3	0	0	0	1/3	10

The objective function value increases to 10.

CASE STUDY 3.1: The Writewell Pen Company

The Writewell pen company makes two types of premium fountain pens—the "Blue Boy" and the "Black line". They make these pens using three types of machines, named Blue, Green and Red. The unit processing times (in minutes) for the two pens on the three machines are given in the following table.

	Red Machine	Blue Machine	Green Machine
Pen 1	2.4	2	3
Pen 2	1.6	2.4	1.8

The raw material cost for the pens are Rs. 60 and 72 respectively while the pens are sold at Rs. 80 and 90 respectively. The company works two shifts of eight hours a day for 5 days a week.

Anurag, the marketing manager estimates the present demand for the two pens to be 1000 and 2000 respectively but feels that with more effort and better marketing the demand for "Black Line" can go up to 3000 per week. The company plans to have an advertisement showing a popular cricketer using "Black Line" to autograph on request.

Srivathsan, the production manager wants to find the product mix of the two products. He believes that he can produce more of "Blue Boy" because it gives him more profit margin, while he realizes that "Black Line" has a higher selling price. He also wishes to increase production by considering the possibility of adding a blue machine or a green machine. He can also outsource some hours on blue machine at the rate of Rs. 300/hour. The supplier of Raw material B finds it uneconomical to provide at Rs. 72 per unit. He is bound by an earlier agreement to provide up to 1000 units/week at that cost. He is categorical that he can provide it only at Rs. 74 if the quantity exceeds 1000 units. The purchase department is unable to get another supplier to provide at Rs. 72 but are confident to make the supplier agree for Rs. 72 in the next agreement.

Aniket, the engineering manager has come up with a new variety called "Green and Clean" that requires 1.6 minutes on red machine, 2 minutes on the blue machine and 1.2 minutes on the green machine. It gives a margin of Rs. 16 per pen.

EXERCISES

3.1 You are given the LP problem
Maximize $Z = 7x_1 + 8x_2 + 6x_3$
Subject to
$$x_1 + x_2 + x_3 \leq 6$$
$$2x_1 + 3x_2 + 4x_3 \leq 15$$
$$x_1, x_2, x_3 \geq 0$$

Given that the optimum solution is $x_1 = 3$, $x_2 = 3$, set up the optimum simplex table
(a) Find out the solution to the dual.
(b) If the RHS value of the first constraint changes to 9 and the objective function coefficient of x_3 becomes 10, what happens to the present optimum table?

3.2 Write the dual of the given problem.
Minimize $W = 5X_1 - 9X_2 + 6X_3 - 5X_4$
Subject to
$$4X_1 - 7X_2 + 6X_3 + 7X_4 \leq 8$$
$$5X_1 + 6X_2 + 4X_3 - 5X_4 = 10$$
$$6X_1 - 9X_2 + 8X_3 + 7X_4 \geq 12$$
$$X_1 \leq 0, X_2 \text{ unrestricted and } X_3 \geq 0$$

3.3 Solve the following LP problem by dual simplex algorithm.
Minimize $w = 2y_1 + 3y_2 + y_4$
Subject to
$$y_1 + y_2 - y_3 + y_4 \leq 3$$
$$-2y_1 + y_2 + 2y_3 - y_4 \geq 8$$
$$y_1, y_2, y_4 \geq 0 \ y_3 \text{ unrestricted in sign}$$

Does the problem have an alternate optimum? If so find it and if not, state why not?

3.4 Given a linear programming problem
Maximize $Z = 8X_1 + 6X_2 + X_3$
Subject to
$$8X_1 + 6X_2 + 2X_3 \le 13$$
$$X_1 + X_2 + 2X_3 \le 4$$
$$X_1, X_2, X_3 \ge 0$$

Obtain the value of the objective function at the optimum using the graphical method. (Solve the dual graphically).

3.5 Given a linear programming problem
Maximize $Z = 8X_1 + 9X_2 + X_3$
Subject to
$$8X_1 + 6X_2 + 2X_3 \le 13$$
$$X_1 + 2X_2 + X_3 \le 4$$
$$X_1, X_2, X_3 \ge 0$$

Verify (without solving the problem) that the optimal solution to the problem is $X_1 = 0.2$, $X_2 = 1.9$.

3.6 Consider the linear programming problem
Maximize $Z = 8X_1 + 6X_2 + X_3$
Subject to
$$8X_1 + 6X_2 + 2X_3 \le 13$$
$$X_1 + X_2 + X_3 \le 4$$
$$X_1, X_2, X_3 \ge 0$$

Solve the primal by simplex algorithm and the dual using the dual simplex algorithm. From this example, can you say that if the primal has alternate optimum, dual has a degenerate solution at the optimum.

3.7 Consider the linear programming problem
Maximize $Z = 8X_1 + 6X_2 - X_3$
Subject to
$$8X_1 + 6X_2 - 2X_3 \le 13$$
$$X_1 + X_2 - X_3 \le 4$$
$$X_1, X_2, X_3 \ge 0$$

Solve the primal using simplex and the dual by dual simplex algorithm. From this example, can you say that if the primal has unbounded solution, dual is infeasible.

3.8 You are given a linear programming problem
Maximize $Z = 8X_1 + 5X_2$
Subject to
$$X_1 + X_2 \le 8$$
$$X_1 + 4X_2 \le 12$$
$$X_1, X_2 \ge 0$$

You are given that the optimum solution is $X_1 = 8$ with $Z = 64$. Assuming that the subdivisions are independent of each other, answer the following questions:
(a) What is the solution to the dual of the problem?
(b) If one extra unit of the second resource is available for Re. 1, would you buy it to increase your profit? Explain.
(c) If the cost coefficients change to [6, 7], what happens to the optimum solution?
(d) If the RHS values change to [12, 8], what happens to the optimum solution?
(e) If a constraint of the type $X_1 \leq 4$ is added to the problem, how would you proceed towards the optimum solution? What is the value of X_1 in the optimum solution? (Do not solve this portion optimally)

3.9 Maximize $Z = 3X_1 + 4X_2$
Subject to
$$X_1 + X_2 \leq 12$$
$$2X_1 + 3X_2 \leq 30$$
$$X_1 + 4X_2 \leq 36$$
$$X_1, X_2 \geq 0$$

(a) Perform sensitivity analysis on each of the cost coefficients to determine the extent to which they can be increased/decreased to change the basic variables.
(b) Perform sensitivity analysis on RHS values to determine the extent to which they can be increased/decreased to change the basic variables.

3.10 Consider the linear programming problem
Maximize $Z = 8x_1 + 6x_2$
Subject to
$$4x_1 + 2x_2 \leq 60$$
$$2x_1 + 4x_2 \leq 48$$
$$x_1, x_2 \geq 0$$

(a) Given that Y_1 and Y_2 are the optimal basic variables of the dual, construct the dual optimal table directly.
(b) If in the primal $c_1 = 2$, what is the effect in the primal and dual optimal solutions?
(c) If in the primal $b_1 = 18$, what is the effect in the primal and dual optimal solutions?
(d) If another variable X_3 is added such that it uses 1 unit resource and has a profit of 1, what happens to the solutions?
(e) If a constraint $2x_1 + x_2 \leq 30$ is added to the primal, what happens to the solution?

3.11 The Chemking Chemical Company blends three raw materials A, B and C to obtain their final product. The raw materials cost Rs. 4, Rs. 3 and Rs. 4 per litre, respectively. Each raw material essentially contains two ingredients, Potassium sulphate and Ammonium phosphate, expressed in grams per litre. The least cost solution was obtained from the following LP formulation:
Minimize $w = 4y_1 + 3y_2 + 4y_3$

Subject to
$$2y_1 + y_2 + y_3 \geq 4$$
$$2y_1 + 2y_2 + 3y_3 \geq 6$$
$$y_1, y_2, y_3 \geq 0$$

The optimum simplex tableau is given in Table 3.28.

Table 3.28 Optimum Simplex Tableau

		4	3	4	0	0	
		Y_1	Y_2	Y_3	Y_4	Y_5	
4	Y_1	1	0	–1/2	–1	1/2	1
3	Y_2	0	1	2	1	–1	2
		0	0	0	1	1	$W = 10$

Answer the following questions with reference to the given tableau (Subdivisions are independent of each other):

(a) The price of A has reduced to Rs. 3 per litre. What is the optimal solution?
(b) The specification on ammonium phosphate has changed to 9 grams/litre. What is the optimal solution?
(c) A fourth raw material D is available at Rs. 5 per litre. It contains 3 grams of potassium sulphate and 1.5 grams of ammonium phosphate. What is the optimal solution?
(d) There is a change in the specification on the product with reference to a third ingredient. The corresponding constraint is $y_1 + 1/2\, y_2 + 3/4\, y_3 \geq 3$. What is the optimal solution?

3.12 Pankalal Electric Company manufactures 5 varieties of fans—Thaikan, Lopar, Torien, Ashu and Wisiry. The problem of maximizing the overall profits, given the resource constraints is formulated as a linear programme.

Maximize $Z = 2x_1 + 3x_2 + x_3 + \dfrac{1}{2} x_4 + x_5$

Subject to
$$x_1 + 3x_2 + x_4 \leq 20$$
$$2x_1 + x_2 + 3x_3 + x_5 \leq 15$$
$$x_1, x_2, x_3, x_4, x_5 \geq 0$$

Where x_i represents the number of fans of type i to be made. The optimal table is given in Table 3.29:

Table 3.29 Optimal Table

		2	3	1	1/2	5			
		X_1	X_2	X_3	X_4	X_5	X_6	X_7	
3	X_2	1/3	1	0	1/3	0	1/3	0	20/3
1	X_5	5/3	0	3	–1/3	1	–1/3	1	25/3
		–2/3	0	–2	–5/3	0	–2/3	–1	$W = 85/3$

Noting that the subdivisions are independent of each other, answer the following:
(a) The profit on Thaikan (x_1) increases to Rs. 3 per unit. What is the optimal solution?
(b) Improved methods of working can reduce the time taken by Torien (x_3) at work centre II. By how much should it reduce if Torien is to be manufactured?
(c) A new constraint of the form $x_1 + 3x_2 + x_3 + 2x_4 + 2x_5 \leq 40$ has been identified. What is the new optimal solution?

3.13 Consider the problem
Minimize $W = 5y_1 + 4y_2$
Subject to

$$4y_1 + 3y_2 \geq 4$$
$$2y_1 + y_2 \geq 3$$
$$y_1 + 2y_2 \geq 1$$
$$y_1 + y_2 \geq 2$$
$$y_1, y_2, \geq 0$$

Because the primal has more constraints than variables, the simplex method was applied to the dual. Assume that X_5 and X_6 as dual slack variables. The optimum tableau of the dual is given in Table 3.30.

Table 3.30 Optimum Tableau of the Dual

		4	3	1	2	0	0	
		X_1	X_2	X_3	X_4	X_5	X_6	
3	X_2	1	1	-1	0	1	-1	1
2	X_4	2	0	3	1	-1	2	3
		-3	0	-2	0	-1	-1	$W = 9$

For each of the following independent changes in the original problem, conduct sensitivity analysis by investigating the optimum solution to the dual.
(a) Change objective function to $3y_1 + 5y_2$.
(b) Change RHS to (3, 5, 5, 3)
(c) Change the first constraint to $2y_1 + 4y_2 \geq 7$
(d) Solve the problem

Minimize $W = 5y_1 + 4y_2 + 2y_3$
Subject to

$$4y_1 + 3y_2 \geq 4$$
$$2y_1 + y_2 + y_3 \geq 3$$
$$y_1 + 2y_2 \geq 1$$
$$y_1 + y_2 \geq 2$$
$$y_1, y_2, y_3 \geq 0$$

3.14 Maximize $Z = 8x_1 + 6x_2$
Subject to
$$4x_1 + 2x_2 \leq 60$$
$$2x_1 + 4x_2 \leq 48$$
$$x_1, x_2 \geq 0$$

The optimum solution is $x_1 = 12$, $x_2 = 6$ and $Z = 132$.
(a) If $x_1 \leq 6$ and $x_2 \geq 7$ are added to the problem, what happens to the optimum solution?
(b) If RHS changes to (61, 48), what happens to the optimal solution?
(c) If the cost vector changes to (8, 7), what happens to the optimal solution?

3.15 Pestico Chemicals Ltd. manufactures pesticides by blending three raw materials P, Q and R which cost Rs. 5, Rs. 3 and Rs. 2 per litre, respectively. Each raw material contains two essential ingredients—MIC and PFC expressed in grams per litre. The final product must contain a specified amount of the ingredients in each can (Assume that once the specifications are met, the rest can be made up with a cheap liquid at negligible cost). The following LP problem was formulated:

Minimize $w = 5y_1 + 3y_2 + 2y_3$
Subject to
$$2y_1 + 2y_2 + y_3 \geq 8 \text{ (MIC)}$$
$$3y_1 + y_2 + y_3 \geq 6 \text{ (PFC)}$$
$$y_1, y_2, y_3 \geq 0$$

The optimum simplex tableau is given in Table 3.31.

Table 3.31   Optimum Simplex Tableau

		4	3	4	0	0	
		Y₁	Y₂	Y₃	Y₄	Y₅	
4	Y₂	1/3	1	0	−2/3	1/3	10/3
3	Y₃	4/3	0	1	1/3	−2/3	4/3
		4/3	0	0	4/3	1/3	38/3

Noting that the subdivisions are independent of each other, answer the following questions:
(a) If the price of P decreases to Rs. 3 per litre, find the new minimum cost (without performing a simplex iteration).
(b) Owing to pressure from environmentalists, the specification on MIC is brought down to 2. What is the new optimal solution?

3.16 Consider the linear programming problem given by
Maximize $Z = 2x_1 + x_2$
Subject to
$$x_1 + x_2 \leq 3$$
$$3x_1 + 2x_2 \leq 8$$
$$x_1, x_2 \geq 0$$

The optimal solution is given by
$$x_1 = \frac{8}{3} - \frac{2}{3}x_2 - \frac{1}{3}x_4$$
$$x_3 = \frac{1}{3} - \frac{1}{3}x_2 + \frac{1}{3}x_4$$
$$Z = \frac{16}{3} - \frac{1}{3}x_2 - \frac{2}{3}x_4$$

(a) Find the solution to the dual without solving it.
(b) What happens to the optimal solution to the dual if the primal cost vector changes to [2, 2]?

3.17 You are given an LPP:
Minimize $W = X_2 - X_1$
Subject to
$$X_1 + 4X_2 \geq 4$$
$$2X_1 + X_2 \leq 6$$
$$X_1, X_2 \geq 0$$

(a) Given that the marginal values of both the primal resources at the optimum are non-negative, find the optimum solution to the primal.
(b) If the RHS of the primal changes to $\begin{bmatrix} 4 \\ 1/2 \end{bmatrix}$, use sensitivity analysis to find the optimum to the primal.

3.18 Given a linear programming problem
Maximize $Z = 7X_1 + 6X_2 + X_3$
Subject to
$$2X_1 + 3X_2 + 8X_3 \leq 19$$
$$X_1 + 4X_2 + X_3 \leq 10$$
$$X_1, X_2, X_3 \geq 0$$

(a) Given that the optimal solution is $X_1 = 19/2$, $Z = 133/2$, create the optimal simplex tableau (Do not solve the problem from the beginning!).
(b) Find the optimal solution to the dual of the problem.
(c) If the first constraint changes to $2X_1 + X_2 + 8X_3 \leq 25$, find the optimal solution using sensitivity analysis.
(d) If a constraint $X_3 \geq 2$ is added to the original problem, find the optimal solution.

3.19 Given a project network with the data given in Table 3.32.

Table 3.32 Data for Project Network

Arc	Duration	Activity	Duration
1–3	6	3–6	10
2–4	8	4–6	6
2–5	3	5–6	7

(a) Formulate a problem to find the longest path in the network.
(b) Write the dual of this problem and develop an algorithm (refer Example 3.5) to find the longest path in the network.

4

Transportation Problem

There is a single item that has to be transported from m sources to n destinations. The supply in source i is a_i and the demand in destination j is b_j. The unit cost of transportation from source i to destination j is C_{ij}. The problem is to transport the item at minimum cost from the sources to the destinations. The problem is called **transportation problem** [also called the **Hitchcock problem** based on its origin from Hitchcock (1941)].

Let X_{ij} be the quantity of the item transported from source (supply) i to destination (demand) j. The objective is to

Minimize $\sum_{i=1}^{m} \sum_{j=1}^{n} C_{ij} X_{ij}$

Subject to

$$\sum_{j=1}^{n} X_{ij} \leq a_i \forall i = 1, \ldots, m$$

$$\sum_{i=1}^{m} X_{ij} \geq b_j \forall j = 1, \ldots, n$$

$$X_{ij} \geq 0$$

The first constraint ensures that the quantity transported from every source is less than or equal to the quantity available. The second constraint ensures that the quantity that reaches every destination is greater than or equal to the demand. The decision variables are continuous and are not necessarily integer valued.

In order for the demand at all destination points to be met, it is necessary that $\Sigma a_i \geq \Sigma b_j$. Otherwise, we end up not satisfying the demand of at least one demand point.

We also note that if all $C_{ij} \geq 0$, we will not be transporting more than the minimum required for every destination point. Also if we have $\Sigma a_i = \Sigma b_j$, every source will send exactly all that is available to the various destinations and each destination will get exactly what is required. The transportation problem becomes

Minimize $\sum_{i=1}^{m} \sum_{j=1}^{n} C_{ij} X_{ij}$

Subject to

$$\sum_{j=1}^{n} X_{ij} = a_i \forall i = 1, \ldots, m$$

$$\sum_{i=1}^{m} X_{ij} = b_j \forall j = 1, \ldots, n$$

$$X_{ij} \geq 0$$

This is called a **balanced transportation problem** where total supply is equal to total demand. Here all constraints are equations. The original problem is **called unbalanced transportation problem**, where the total supply is not equal to the total demand.

We solve balanced transportation problems first and then explain a simple way by which every unbalanced transportation problem can be converted to a balanced problem and solved efficiently.

4.1 SOLVING BALANCED TRANSPORTATION PROBLEMS

Though transportation problems are linear programming problems, they are not solved using simplex algorithm for the following two reasons:

1. The balanced transportation problem has all its constraints in equation form and since $\Sigma a_i = \Sigma b_j$, the system of equations (constraints) is linearly dependent. This gives rise to degeneracy and the limitations of the simplex algorithm resulting in more iteration for degenerate problems are well known.
2. The balanced transportation problem by its structure allows the formation of good basic feasible solutions that are close to optimal, while simplex starts with a basic feasible solution that is quite far away from the optimal. Balanced transportation problems are solved by creating an initial basic feasible solution, that is close to optimum and then reaching the optimum in very few iterations.

We discuss three methods to create basic feasible solutions to balanced transportation problems. These are:

1. North West corner rule
2. Minimum cost method
3. Vogel's approximation method (Reinfeld and Vogel 1958)

These are explained in detail using the following numerical example:

ILLUSTRATION 4.1

Consider a transportation problem with three sources (rows) and four demand points (columns). The availability in the supply points are 40, 50 and 60, respectively and the requirements are 20, 30, 30 and 50, respectively. Table 4.1 shows the data including the unit cost of transportation, which is shown in left hand corner of the elements of the matrix.

Table 4.1 Data Including Unit Cost of Transportation

4	6	8	8	40
6	8	6	7	60
5	7	6	8	50
20	30	50	50	

4.1.1 North West Corner Rule

1. Consider the top left hand corner (the North West Corner). The supply available is 40 and the requirement is 20. The maximum possible for allocation is the minimum of the two, which is 20. We allocate 20. The demand of the first point is met and we draw a vertical line indicating this. The available supply in the first supply point now reduces to 40.
2. We now identify first row-second column as the north west corner. The available supply is 20 and the requirement is 30. The maximum possible allocation is 20, and is made. The supply in Row 1 is exhausted and we indicate this with a horizontal line. The demand (unfulfilled) in the second demand point reduces to 10.
3. We now identify second row-second column as the north west corner. The available supply is 60 and the requirement is 10. The maximum possible allocation is 10, and is made. The demand in Row 2 is met completely and we indicate this with a vertical line. The available supply in the second row reduces to 50.
4. We now identify first second row-third column as the north west corner. The available supply is 50 and the requirement is 50. The maximum possible allocation is 50, and is made. The supply in Row 1 is exhausted and the demand in third column is entirely met. We indicate this with a horizontal line and vertical line, respectively.
5. The only available position for allocation is the fourth row-third column. The supply is 50 and the demand is 50. We make the allocation and observe that all allocations have been made. The supplies from all the rows are used and the requirements of all columns have been completely met.
6. We observe that we have made five allocations and the total cost is:

$$20 \times 4 + 20 \times 6 + 10 \times 8 + 50 \times 6 + 50 \times 8 = 980$$

North West corner rule
1. In a balanced transportation problem, identify the north west corner or top left hand corner where allocation can be made. Find the available supply and the required demand. Allocate the maximum possible to this position, which is the minimum of the two values.
2. If the supply in the row is exhausted, mark the row. If the column requirement is entirely met, mark the column update supply/demand.
3. Repeat Steps 1 and 2 till all the supplies are used (all requirements are met).

The starting solution (basic feasible) obtained using the North West Corner Rule is given in Table 4.2

Table 4.2 Starting Solution using North West Corner Rule

	1	2	3	4	Supply
1	4 (20)	6 (20)	8	8	40
2	6	8 (10)	6 (50)	7	60
3	5	7	6	8 (50)	50
Demand	20	30	50	50	

4.1.2 Minimum Cost Method

1. From the cost coefficients, we observe that Row 1-Column 1 has the minimum cost of 4. The supply is 40 and the demand is 20. We allocate the maximum possible, which is the minimum of 40 and 20. The requirement of Column 1 is met and we indicate this with a vertical line. The available supply in Row 1 is now 20.
2. From the cost coefficients of the remaining positions, we observe that Row 1-Column 2 has the minimum cost of 6. The available supply is 20 and the demand is 30. We allocate the maximum possible, which is 20. The supply from Row 1 is used fully and we indicate this with a horizontal line. The unfulfilled demand of Column 2 is now 10.
3. From the cost coefficients of the remaining positions, we observe that Row 2-Column 3 has the minimum cost of 6. The supply is 60 and the demand is 50. We allocate the maximum possible, which is 50. The requirement of Column 3 is met and we indicate this with a vertical line. The available supply in Row 2 is now 10.
4. From the cost coefficients of the remaining positions, we observe that Row 2-Column 4 as well as Row 3-Column 2 have the minimum cost of 7. We break the tie arbitrarily and choose Row 2-Column 4. The available supply is 10 and the demand is 50. We allocate the maximum possible, which is 10. The supply from Row 2 is used fully and we indicate this with a horizontal line. The unfulfilled demand of Column 4 is now 40.
5. Only Row 3 has available supply and the unfulfilled requirements are in Row 3-Column 2 is 10 and Row 3-Column 4 is 40. We make the allocations. Now, all the requirements have been met and we have a basic feasible solution. The cost is:

$$20 \times 4 + 20 \times 6 + 50 \times 6 + 10 \times 7 + 10 \times 7 + 40 \times 8 = 960$$

Minimum cost method

1. From the available positions, find the one with the minimum cost coefficient. Break ties arbitrarily.
2. Find the available supply and the required demand. Allocate the maximum possible to this position, which is the minimum of the two values.
3. If the supply in the row is exhausted, mark the row. If the column requirement is entirely met, mark the column update supply/demand.
4. Repeat Steps 1 to 3 till all the supplies are used (all requirements are met).

The starting solution (basic feasible) obtained using the minimum cost method is given in Table 4.3

Table 4.3 Basic Feasible Solution using Minimum Cost Method

	1	2	3	4	Supply
1	4 (20)	6 (20)	8	8	40
2	6	8	6 (50)	7 (10)	60
3	5	7 (10)	6	8 (40)	50
Demand	20	30	50	50	

4.1.3 Vogel's Approximation Method (Penalty Cost Method)

1. Considering every row or column, we would ideally like to allocate to the position that has the least cost. However, in all situations we may not be able to do so. We define a penalty for not being able to allocate to the least cost position. This is the difference between the second lowest cost and the least cost. This is a non-negative value and can take zero if the minimum cost occurs at two positions in a row or column.

2. The row and column penalties are computed. The row penalties are 2, 0 and 1 and the column penalties are 1, 1, 0, 1, respectively. The maximum penalty is for Row 1 and hence the least cost position in Row 1 is considered first for allocation. The supply is 40 and the demand is 20. The maximum possible, which is the minimum of the two, viz. 20 is allotted. The supply in Row 1 becomes 20 and a vertical line is drawn in Column 1 indicating that the demand has been met.

3. The penalties are now calculated again considering Rows 1 to 3 and Columns 2 to 4. The row penalties are 2, 1 and 1 while the column penalties remain as 1, 0, 1, respectively. The maximum penalty is 2 for Row 1 and hence the least cost position in Row 1 (Column 2) is considered for allocation. The supply is 20 and the demand is 30. The maximum possible, which is the minimum of the two, viz. 20 is allotted. The supply in Row 1 is exhausted and we draw a horizontal line. The unfulfilled demand for Column 2 is 10.

4. The penalties are calculated again considering Rows 2 and 3 and Columns 2 to 4. The row penalties are 1 and 1 while the column penalties are 1, 0, 1, respectively. The maximum penalty is 1 and there is a tie. We break the tie arbitrarily considering Row 3 (say). The least cost position in Row 3 (Column 3) is considered for allocation. The supply is 50 and the demand is 50. The maximum possible, which is the minimum of the two, viz. 50 is allotted. We observe that the demand for Column 3 is completely met and we draw a vertical line. The supply for Row 3 is also consumed and we indicate this with a horizontal line.

5. Since Row 2 is the only available supply, we allocate $X_{22} = 10$ and $X_{24} = 50$. The cost corresponding to this basic feasible solution is:

$$20 \times 4 + 20 \times 6 + 10 \times 8 + 50 \times 7 + 50 \times 6 = 930$$

Vogel's approximation method (Penalty cost method)

1. Calculate penalties for every row and column. This is equal to the difference between the second lowest cost and the least cost. Identify the maximum penalty and the corresponding row or column. Break ties arbitrarily.
2. Find the least cost position in the identified row/column. Find the available supply and the required demand. Allocate the maximum possible to this position, which is the minimum of the two values.
3. If the supply in the row is exhausted, mark the row. If the column requirement is entirely met, mark the column update supply/demand.
4. Repeat Steps 1 to 3 till all the supplies are used (all requirements are met).

The starting solution (basic feasible) obtained using the Vogel's approximation method is given in Table 4.4.

Table 4.4 Basic Feasible Solution using Vogel's Approximation Method (VAM)

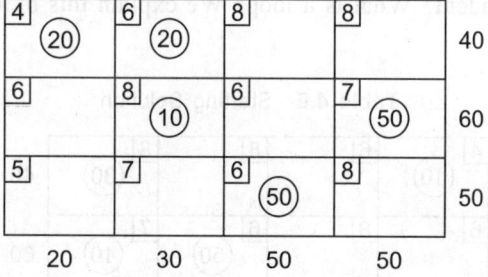

In this case, it is observed that the solution has five allocations as against six obtained using the two earlier methods. We will see more about this solution (with fewer number of allocations) later.

We also note that we will obtain different solutions when the ties are broken differently. For example, if instead of considering Row 3 we had considered Row 2 and proceeded, we would have allotted $X_{224} = 50$. This satisfies the demand for Column 3. Supply in Row 2 becomes 10, and there is only one position for allocation. We allocate $X_{23} = 10$. Row 3 has a supply of 50 which is allotted as $X_{32} = 10$ and $X_{33} = 40$. The solution is $X_{11} = 20, X_{12} = 20, X_{23} = 10, X_{24} = 50, X_{32} = 10$ and $X_{33} = 40$. This basic feasible solution is given in Table 4.5 and the cost is:

$$20 \times 4 + 20 \times 6 + 10 \times 6 + 50 \times 7 + 10 \times 7 + 40 \times 6 = 920$$

We also observe that the solution with Minimum cost method has six allocations while the VAM solution has five. We will see more about the fewer allocations later.

Table 4.5 Another Basic Feasible Solution using VAM

4 (20)	6 (20)	8	8	40
6	8	6 (10)	7 (50)	60
5	7 (10)	6 (40)	8	50
20	30	50	50	

4.2 BASIC FEASIBLE SOLUTION TO A TRANSPORTATION PROBLEM

A basic feasible solution to a transportation problem satisfies the following conditions:

1. The row column (supply-demand) constraints are satisfied.
2. The non-negativity constraints are satisfied.
3. The allocations are independent and do not form a loop.
4. There are exactly $m + n - 1$ allocations.

All the initial solutions listed above satisfy the first and second conditions. Two of the methods result in six allocations while two solutions have five allocations. How do we know that the allocations are independent? What is a loop? We explain this by considering the following solution (Table 4.6):

Table 4.6 Starting Solution

4 (10)	6	8	8 (30)	40
6	8	6 (50)	7 (10)	60
5 (10)	7 (30)	6	8 (10)	50
20	30	50	50	

The above solution satisfies all the supply and demand constraints and the non-negativity constraints. It has seven allocations. These allocations are not independent. The allocations $X_{11} = 10, X_{14} = 30, X_{31} = 10, X_{34} = 10$ form a loop.

Starting from any of the above four allocations, we can move horizontally and vertically alternatively, reach positions that have allocations and can come back to the starting point. This represents a loop and indicates dependency among allocations. In fact, if a feasible solution has more than $m + n - 1$ allocations (as in this case), there is certainly a loop, which has to be broken. Consider any one of the elements forming a loop, say, X_{11}. Let us reduce the allocation X_{11} to 9. This would increase X_{14} to 31, reduce X_{34} to 9 and increase X_{31} to 11. The net change in the cost is $-4 + 8 - 8 + 5 = +1$, which is an increase and is not desirable.

On the other hand, if we consider the exact opposite of what we did earlier and increase X_{11} to 11. This would reduce X_{14} to 29, increase X_{31} to 11 and reduce X_{34} to 9. The net change in the cost is $+4 - 8 + 8 - 5 = -1$, which is a decrease and is desirable. The reduction in total cost for a unit increase of X_{11} is 1. We can try and increase X_{11} to the maximum possible value and reduce the total cost. The maximum possible increase of X_{11} is up to 20, which is limited by X_{34} becoming zero, beyond which X_{34} will become negative and infeasible. The new allocations are $X_{11} = 20$, $X_{14} = 20$ and $X_{31} = 20$. This is shown in Table 4.7.

Table 4.7 Basic Feasible Solution

4 (20)	6	8	8 (20)	40
6	8	6 (50)	7 (10)	60
5 (20)	7 (30)	6	8	50
20	30	50	50	

This solution is basic feasible and does not have a loop. A loop can be broken in two ways, one of which will result in a solution with lesser (non-increasing) cost. It is advisable to break the loop as we did and obtain a better solution with lesser cost.

When a feasible solution has more than $m + n - 1$ allocations (as in our case) there is a loop and we break it to get a basic feasible solution without a loop.

We also observe that the three methods, North west corner rule, Minimum cost method and Vogel's approximation method will not give more than $m + n - 1$ allocations. Since they allocate the maximum possible every time, they will not have solutions with loops.

4.2.1 Degenerate Basic Feasible Solutions

ILLUSTRATION 4.2

Sometimes we can have feasible solutions with $m + n - 1$ allocations that may have a loop. Consider the following feasible solution (Table 4.8).

Table 4.8 Feasible Solution

4 (10)	6	8	8 (30)	40
6 (10)	8 (30)	6	7 (20)	60
5	7	6 (50)	8	50
20	30	50	50	

The solution has six allocations ($m + n - 1$) but has a loop comprising allocations $X_{11} = 10$, $X_{14} = 30$, $X_{21} = 10$ and $X_{24} = 20$. Since a basic feasible solution cannot contain a loop, we break the loop. Let us consider X_{11} and increase the allocation to 11 (increase by 1). This would reduce $X_{14} = 29$, increase X_{24} to 21 and decrease $X_{21} = 9$ so that the resultant solution is feasible. The increase in cost is $+4 - 8 + 7 - 6 = -3$. Since the unit increase in X_{11} decreases the cost, we find out that the maximum decrease possible is 10 (otherwise X_{21} would become negative) and identify the basic feasible solution given in Table 4.9.

Table 4.9 Basic Feasible Solution

4 (20)	6	8 ε	8 (20)	40
6	8 (30)	6	7 (30)	60
5	7	6 (50)	8	50
20	30	50	50	

This solution is basic feasible but has fewer than $m + n - 1$ allocations. This is a **degenerate** basic feasible solution. This means that there is an allocation of zero in one more position. It also means that the sixth allocation is such that it does not form a loop. For example, the sixth allocation could be any of $X_{13}, X_{23}, X_{31}, X_{32}$ or $X_{34} = 0$. This is represented by ε in the solution (X_{13} is shown with ε allocation).

(Note that the three methods to obtain a basic feasible solution, North west corner rule, Minimum cost method and the Vogel's approximation method can give degenerate basic feasible solutions. This can happen when the individual supply quantities are equal to the individual demand quantities).

4.3 FINDING THE OPTIMAL SOLUTION TO THE TRANSPORTATION PROBLEM

In this section we will discuss two methods that provide optimal solutions to the transportation problem. These are:

1. Stepping stone method (Charnes and Cooper 1954)
2. Modified distribution (MODI) method (also called u-v method)

4.3.1 Stepping Stone Method

We start this method with any basic feasible solution. Let us use the solution obtained using the minimum cost method. This solution is given again in Table 4.10.

Table 4.10 Basic Feasible Solution

4 (20)	6 (20)	8	8	40
6	8	6 (50)	7 (10)	60
5	7 (10)	6	8 (40)	50
20	30	50	50	

In the above solution, we have allocations in six positions ($m + n - 1$) allocations and the remaining $[mn - (m + n - 1)]$ allocations have zero allocations. In other words, these unallotted six positions, $X_{13} = X_{14} = X_{21} = X_{22} = X_{31} = X_{33} = 0$. We choose the first position X_{13} and assume that we assign 1 unit to this position. This creates a loop involving $X_{13}, X_{23}, X_{24}, X_{34}, X_{32}$ and X_{12}. Since we add 1 unit to X_{13}, we reduce X_{23} by one, add 1 to X_{24}, remove 1 from X_{34}, add 1 to X_{32} and remove 1 from X_{12} so that the resultant solution is feasible. This is shown in Table 4.11.

Table 4.11 Increasing X_{13}

4 (20)	6 (20−1)	8 (+1)	8	40
6	8	6 (50−1)	7 (10+1)	60
5	7 (10+1)	6	8 (40−1)	50
20	30	50	50	

The increase in cost is $+8 - 6 + 7 - 8 + 10 - 6 = 5$. Since the net increase is positive it is not beneficial to add one unit to X_{13}.

Let us consider the variable X_{14}. This creates a loop involving X_{34}, X_{32} and X_{12}. To maintain feasibility, we subtract 1 unit from X_{34}, add 1 to X_{32} and subtract 1 from X_{12}. This is shown in Table 4.12.

Table 4.12 Increasing X_{14}

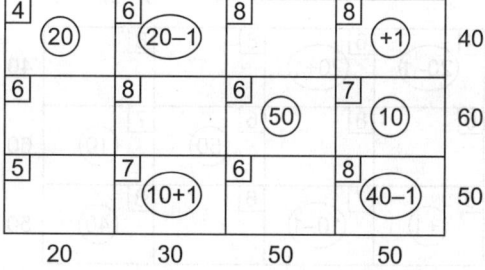

The net increase is $+8 - 8 + 10 - 6 = 4$. Since the net increase is positive it is not beneficial to add one unit to X_{14}.

Let us consider variable X_{21}. This results in a loop involving $X_{24}, X_{34}, X_{32}, X_{12}$ and X_{11}. To maintain feasibility we subtract 1 from X_{24}, add 1 to X_{34}, subtract 1 from X_{32}, add 1 to X_{12} and subtract 1 from X_{11}. This is shown in Table 4.13.

Table 4.13 Increasing X_{21}

4 (20−1)	6 (20+1)	8	8	40
6 (+1)	8	6 (50)	7 (10−1)	60
5	7 (10−1)	6	8 (40+1)	50
20	30	50	50	

The net increase is $+6 - 7 + 8 - 7 + 6 - 4 = 2$. Since the net increase is positive it is not beneficial to add one unit to X_{21}.

Let us consider variable X_{22}. This results in a loop involving X_{24}, X_{34} and X_{32}. To maintain feasibility we subtract 1 from X_{24}, add 1 to X_{34} and subtract 1 from X_{32}. This is shown in Table 4.14.

Table 4.14 Increasing X_{22}

4 (20)	6 (20)	8	8	40
6	8 (+1)	6 (50)	7 (10−1)	60
5	7 (10−1)	6	8 (40+1)	50
20	30	50	50	

The net increase is $+8 - 7 + 8 - 7 = 2$. Since the net increase is positive it is not beneficial to add one unit to X_{22}.

Let us consider variable X_{31}. This results in a loop involving X_{32}, X_{12} and X_{11}. To maintain feasibility we subtract 1 from X_{32}, add 1 to X_{12} and subtract 1 from X_{11}. This is shown in Table 4.15.

Table 4.15 Increasing X_{31}

4 (20−1)	6 (20+1)	8	8	40
6	8	6 (50)	7 (10)	60
5 (+1)	7 (10−1)	6	8 (40)	50
20	30	50	50	

The net increase is $+5 - 7 + 6 - 4 = 0$. Since the net increase is not negative, it is not beneficial to add one unit to X_{41}.

Let us consider variable X_{33}. This results in a loop involving X_{34}, X_{24} and X_{23}. To maintain feasibility we subtract 1 from X_{34}, add 1 to X_{24} and subtract 1 from X_{23}. This is shown in Table 4.16.

Table 4.16 Increasing X_{33}

4	6	8	8	
(20)	(20)			40
6	8	6	7	
		(50–1)	(10+1)	60
5	7	6	8	
	(10)	(+1)	(40–1)	50
20	30	50	50	

The net increase is $+6 - 8 + 7 - 6 = -1$. Since the net increase is negative, it is beneficial to consider adding more units to X_{22}.

In this iteration, we observe that there is only one non-basic variable (X_{33}) when increased has a net effect of decrease in cost. If there is more than one variable that can reduce the cost, we choose the one that results in maximum gain (most negative value).

Considering variable X_{33} and its loop (X_{34}, X_{24} and X_{23}), we realize that the maximum that can be allotted to X_{33} is 40, beyond which X_{34} will become negative. Therefore, the maximum of 40 is allotted to X_{33}. This results in $X_{34} = 0$, $X_{24} = 10 + 40 = 50$, $X_{23} = 50 - 40 = 10$. The updated allocation is shown in Table 4.17.

Table 4.17 Updated Allocation

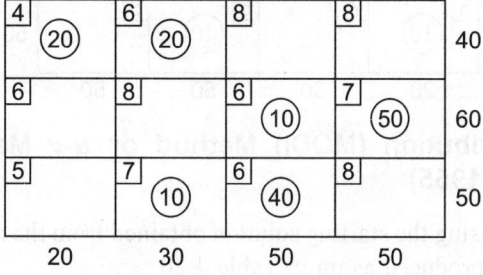

The cost associated with this allocation is:

$$20 \times 4 + 20 \times 6 + 10 \times 6 + 50 \times 7 + 10 \times 7 + 40 \times 6 = 920$$

We repeat the algorithm and try to verify whether the above basic feasible solution is optimal. The non-basic allocations are $X_{13}, X_{14}, X_{21}, X_{22}, X_{31}$ and X_{34}. We try to enter each of these (by allocating $a + 1$ in each, identifying the loop) and evaluate the effect of the allocation. The basic variable, loop and the effect of the allocation are given in Table 4.18.

Table 4.18 Second Iteration of Stepping Stone Method

No.	Entering variable	Loop	Net effect
1.	X_{13}	$X_{13} - X_{33} - X_{32} - X_{12}$	$+8 - 6 + 7 - 6 = 3$
2.	X_{14}	$X_{14} - X_{24} + X_{23} - X_{33} + X_{32} - X_{12}$	$+8 - 7 + 6 - 6 + 7 - 6 = 2$
3.	X_{21}	$X_{21} - X_{23} + X_{33} - X_{32} + X_{12} - X_{11}$	$+6 - 6 + 6 - 7 + 6 - 4 = 1$
4.	X_{22}	$X_{22} - X_{23} + X_{33} - X_{32}$	$+8 - 6 + 6 - 7 = 1$
5.	X_{31}	$X_{31} - X_{32} + X_{12} - X_{11}$	$+5 - 7 + 6 - 4 = 0$
6.	X_{34}	$X_{34} - X_{33} + X_{23} - X_{24}$	$+8 - 6 + 6 - 7 = 1$

Since no entering variable gives us a reduction in the total cost, the optimal solution has been reached. The basic feasible solution $X_{11} = 20$, $X_{12} = 20$, $X_{23} = 10$, $X_{24} = 50$, $X_{32} = 10$, $X_{33} = 40$ is optimal with minimum cost $(Z) = 920$ (Note that the same solution was found when the Vogel's approximation method was applied with arbitrary tie breaks. This solution was shown earlier in Table 4.5. This shows that the Vogel's approximation method can give the optimal solution for some problems).

However, since entering X_{31} gives a net increase of zero at the optimum, we observe that there is an alternate optimum for this example. This can be obtained by entering variable X_{31} through the loop $X_{31} - X_{32} + X_{12} - X_{11}$. X_{32} has an allocation of 10 and X_{11} has an allocation of 20. The maximum allocation possible in X_{31} is 10, which would make $X_{32} = 0$, $X_{12} = 30$ and $X_{11} = 10$. This alternate optimum solution is shown in Table 4.19

Table 4.19 Alternate Optimum Solution

4	6	8	8	
(10)	(30)			40
6	8	6	7	
		(10)	(50)	60
5	7	6	8	
(10)		(40)		50
20	30	50	50	

4.3.2 Modified Distribution (MODI) Method or *u-v* Method (Ferguson and Dantzig, 1955)

We illustrate this method using the starting solution obtained from the minimum cost method. The solution in Table 4.3 is reproduced again in Table 4.20.

Table 4.20 Basic Feasible Solution

4	6	8	8	
(20)	(20)			40
6	8	6	7	
		(50)	(10)	60
5	7	6	8	
	(10)		(40)	50
20	30	50	50	

In this method, we define a set of variables u_i ($i = 1,..., m$) and v_j ($j = 1,..., n$) respectively corresponding to the m rows (supply) and n columns (destinations). We fix $u_1 = 0$.

From the solution in Table 4.20 we observe that $X_{11}, X_{12}, X_{23}, X_{24}, X_{32}$ and X_{34} are basic while $X_{13}, X_{14}, X_{21}, X_{22}, X_{31}$ and X_{33} are non-basic.

We evaluate u_i ($i = 2, ..., m$) and v_j ($j = 1,..., n$) using the relationship $u_i + v_j = C_{ij}$ where X_{ij} is basic. We have

$$u_1 + v_1 = C_{11} = 4$$
$$u_1 + v_2 = C_{12} = 6$$
$$u_2 + v_3 = C_{23} = 6$$
$$u_2 + v_4 = C_{34} = 7$$
$$u_3 + v_2 = C_{32} = 7$$
$$u_3 + v_4 = C_{34} = 8$$

Since $u_1 = 0$, we get $v_1 = 4$ from $u_1 + v_1 = 4$.
From $u_1 + v_2 = 6$, we get $v_2 = 6$
From $u_3 + v_2 = 7$, we get $u_3 = 1$
From $u_3 + v_4 = 8$, we get $v_4 = 7$
From $u_2 + v_4 = 7$, we get $u_2 = 0$
From $u_2 + v_3 = 6$ we get $v_3 = 6$.

Using the values of u_i and v_j, we calculate the values of $C_{ij} - (u_i + v_j)$ for all the non-basic X_{ij}. We compute

$$C_{13} - (u_1 + v_3) = 8 - 0 - 6 = 2$$
$$C_{14} - (u_1 + v_4) = 8 - 0 - 7 = 1$$
$$C_{21} - (u_2 + v_1) = 6 - 0 - 4 = 2$$
$$C_{22} - (u_2 + v_2) = 8 - 0 - 6 = 2$$
$$C_{31} - (u_3 + v_1) = 5 - 1 - 4 = 0$$
$$C_{33} - (u_3 + v_3) = 6 - 1 - 6 = -1$$

Among these we pick that non-basic variable with minimum (most negative) value of $C_{ij} - (u_i + v_j)$. There is only one that has a negative value and we choose variable X_{33}.

We now identify a loop when we enter variable X_{33}. The loop is given by $X_{33} - X_{34} - X_{24} - X_{23} - X_{33}$. Increasing X_{33} by θ will reduce X_{34} by θ, increase X_{24} by θ and decrease X_{23} by θ. The maximum increase in X_{33} is 40 beyond which X_{34} will be negative. This will increase X_{24} to 50 and reduce X_{23} to 10. This solution is given in Table 4.21.

Table 4.21 New Basic Feasible Solution

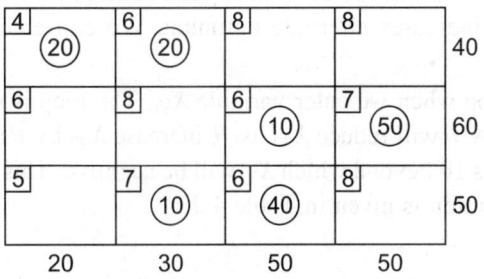

This feasible solution has total cost = $4 \times 20 + 6 \times 20 + 6 \times 10 + 7 \times 50 + 7 \times 10 + 6 \times 40 = 920$. The decrease in cost is 40, which is the product of the unit reduction and the value of θ. We now have to verify if the earlier solution is optimal.

We redefine the set of variables u_i ($i = 1,...,m$) and v_j ($j = 1,...,n$) respectively corresponding to m rows (supply) and n columns (destinations). We fix $u_1 = 0$.

From the solution in Table 4.21 we observe that $X_{11}, X_{12}, X_{23}, X_{24}, X_{32}$ and X_{33} are basic while $X_{13}, X_{14}, X_{21}, X_{22}, X_{31}$ and X_{34} are non-basic.

We evaluate u_i ($i = 2,...,m$) and v_j ($j = 1,...,n$) using the relationship $u_i + v_j = C_{ij}$ where X_{ij} is basic. We have

$$u_1 + v_1 = C_{11} = 4$$
$$u_1 + v_2 = C_{12} = 6$$
$$u_2 + v_3 = C_{23} = 6$$
$$u_2 + v_4 = C_{34} = 7$$
$$u_3 + v_2 = C_{32} = 7$$
$$u_3 + v_3 = C_{33} = 6.$$

Since $u_1 = 0$, we get $v_1 = 4$ from $u_1 + v_1 = 4$.

From $u_1 + v_2 = 6$, we get $v_2 = 6$
From $u_3 + v_2 = 7$, we get $u_3 = 1$
From $u_3 + v_3 = 6$, we get $v_3 = 5$
From $u_2 + v_3 = 6$, we get $u_2 = 1$
From $u_2 + v_4 = 7$ we get $v_4 = 6$

Using the values of u_i and v_j, we calculate the values of $C_{ij} - (u_i + v_j)$ for all the non-basic X_{ij}. We compute

$$C_{13} - (u_1 + v_3) = 8 - 0 - 5 = 3$$
$$C_{14} - (u_1 + v_4) = 8 - 0 - 6 = 2$$
$$C_{21} - (u_2 + v_1) = 6 - 1 - 4 = 1$$
$$C_{22} - (u_2 + v_2) = 8 - 1 - 6 = 1$$
$$C_{31} - (u_3 + v_1) = 5 - 1 - 4 = 0$$
$$C_{34} - (u_3 + v_4) = 8 - 1 - 6 = 1$$

Among these we pick that the non-basic variable with minimum (most negative) value of $C_{ij} - (u_i + v_j)$. There is no variable that has a negative value and the solution is optimal.

After observing that the optimal solution has been reached, we observe that variable X_{31} has a value of zero and this indicates alternate optimum. We can enter X_{31} to get the alternate solution.

We now identify a loop when we enter variable X_{31}. The loop is given by $X_{31} - X_{32} - X_{12} - X_{11} - X_{31}$. Increasing X_{31} by θ will reduce X_{32} by θ, increase X_{22} by θ and decrease X_{11} by θ. The maximum increase in X_{31} is 10 beyond which X_{32} will be negative. This will increase X_{22} to 30 and reduce X_{23} to 10. This solution is given in Table 4.22.

Transportation Problem **119**

Table 4.22 Alternate Optimum

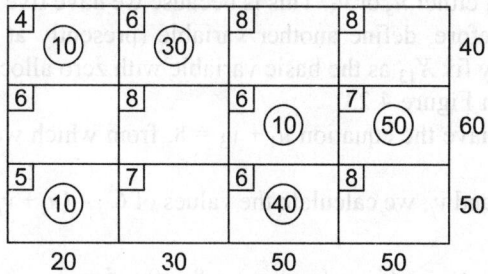

4.3.3 Optimum Solution with a Degenerate Basic Feasible Solution

Let us consider the starting solution given by the Vogel's approximation method. We realize that this basic feasible solution is degenerate. The solution of Table 4.4 is shown again in Table 4.23.

Table 4.23 Degenerate Basic Feasible Solution

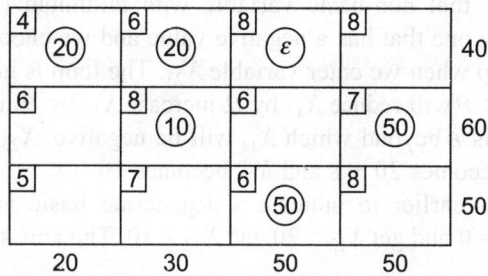

We apply the *u-v* method or MODI method to obtain the optimum solution. We define a set of variables u_i ($i = 1,\ldots,m$) and v_j ($j = 1,\ldots,n$), respectively corresponding to the *m* rows (supply) and *n* columns (destinations). We fix $u_1 = 0$.

From the solution in Table 4.23 we observe that $X_{11}, X_{12}, X_{22}, X_{24}$ and X_{33} are basic while the rest take a zero value.

We evaluate u_i ($i = 2,\ldots,m$) and v_j ($j = 1,\ldots,n$) using the relationship $u_i + v_j = C_{ij}$ where X_{ij} is basic. We have

$$u_1 + v_1 = C_{11} = 4$$
$$u_1 + v_2 = C_{12} = 6$$
$$u_2 + v_2 = C_{22} = 8$$
$$u_2 + v_4 = C_{34} = 7$$
$$u_3 + v_3 = C_{33} = 6$$

(We have five equations as against six in the earlier computations).

Since $u_1 = 0$, we get $v_1 = 4$ from $u_1 + v_1 = 4$.
From $u_1 + v_2 = 6$, we get $v_2 = 6$
From $u_2 + v_2 = 8$, we get $u_2 = 2$
From $u_2 + v_4 = 7$, we get $v_4 = 5$

We are unable to proceed further because the only available equation is $u_3 + v_3 = C_{33} = 6$ and we don't have the values of either u_3 or v_3. This is because we have five basic variables as against the required six. We, therefore, define another variable (presently at zero) as basic with zero allocation. Let us arbitrarily fix X_{13} as the basic variable with zero allocation and we indicate this zero by ε. This is shown in Figure 4.23

Since X_{13} is basic we have the equation $u_1 + v_3 = 8$, from which we get $v_3 = 8$. From $u_3 + v_3 = C_{33} = 6$, we get $u_3 = -2$.

Using the values of u_i and v_j, we calculate the values of $C_{ij} - (u_i + v_j)$ for all the non-basic X_{ij}. We compute

$$C_{14} - (u_1 + v_4) = 8 - 0 - 5 = 3$$
$$C_{21} - (u_2 + v_1) = 6 - 2 - 4 = 0$$
$$C_{23} - (u_2 + v_3) = 6 - 2 - 8 = -4$$
$$C_{31} - (u_3 + v_1) = 5 + 2 - 4 = 3$$
$$C_{32} - (u_3 + v_2) = 7 + 2 - 6 = 3$$
$$C_{34} - (u_3 + v_4) = 8 + 2 - 5 = 5$$

Among these we pick that non-basic variable with minimum (most negative) value of $C_{ij} - (u_i + v_j)$. There is only one that has a negative value and we choose variable X_{23}.

We now identify a loop when we enter variable X_{23}. The loop is given by $X_{23} - X_{13} - X_{12} - X_{22} - X_{23}$. Increasing X_{23} by θ will reduce X_{13} by θ, increase X_{12} by θ and decrease X_{22} by θ. The maximum increase in X_{23} is ε beyond which X_{13} will be negative. X_{23} becomes ε, X_{13} becomes non-basic with zero, X_{12} becomes $20 + \varepsilon$ and X_{22} becomes $10 - \varepsilon$.

We have introduced ε earlier to indicate a degenerate basic variable with value zero. Therefore, we substitute $\varepsilon = 0$ and get $X_{12} = 20$ and $X_{22} = 10$. The new solution is shown in Table 4.24.

Table 4.24 New Degenerate Basic Feasible Solution

4 (20)	6 (20)	8	8	40
6	8 (10)	6 (ε)	7 (50)	60
5	7	6 (50)	8	50
20	30	50	50	

The solution shown in Table 4.24 is the same as that shown in Table 4.23 with the difference in the position of ε. The value of the objective function is the same. This is because of degeneracy, which has resulted in an unnecessary iteration without a decrease in objective function value. If we had chosen variable X_{23} for ε allocation instead of variable X_{13}, we would have started with the solution in Table 4.24. We now proceed further to check if the solution in Table 4.24 is optimal.

From the solution in Table 4.24 we observe that $X_{11}, X_{12}, X_{22}, X_{23}, X_{24}$ and X_{33} are basic while the rest take a zero value.

We evaluate u_i ($i = 2,...,m$) and v_j ($j = 1,...,n$) using the relationship $u_i + v_j = C_{ij}$ where X_{ij} is basic. We have

$$u_1 + v_1 = C_{11} = 4$$
$$u_1 + v_2 = C_{12} = 6$$
$$u_2 + v_2 = C_{22} = 8$$
$$u_2 + v_3 = C_{23} = 6$$
$$u_2 + v_4 = C_{34} = 7$$
$$u_3 + v_3 = C_{33} = 6$$

Since $u_1 = 0$, we get $v_1 = 4$ from $u_1 + v_1 = 4$.
From $u_1 + v_2 = 6$, we get $v_2 = 6$
From $u_2 + v_2 = 8$, we get $u_2 = 2$
From $u_2 + v_3 = 6$, we get $v_3 = 4$
From $u_2 + v_4 = 7$, we get $v_4 = 5$
From $u_3 + v_3 = 6$, we get $u_3 = 2$

Using the values of u_i and v_j, we calculate the values of $C_{ij} - (u_i + v_j)$ for all the non-basic X_{ij}. We compute

$$C_{13} - (u_1 + v_3) = 8 - 0 - 4 = 4$$
$$C_{14} - (u_1 + v_4) = 8 - 0 - 5 = 3$$
$$C_{21} - (u_2 + v_1) = 6 - 2 - 4 = 0$$
$$C_{31} - (u_3 + v_1) = 5 - 2 - 4 = -1$$
$$C_{32} - (u_3 + v_2) = 7 - 2 - 6 = -1$$
$$C_{34} - (u_3 + v_4) = 8 - 2 - 5 = 1$$

Among these we have to pick that non-basic variable with minimum (most negative) value of $C_{ij} - (u_i + v_j)$. There is a tie and let us break the tie arbitrarily. We choose variable X_{31}.

We now identify a loop when we enter variable X_{31}. The loop is given by $X_{31} - X_{33} - X_{23} - X_{22} - X_{12} - X_{11}$. Increasing X_{31} by θ will reduce X_{33} by θ, increase X_{23} by θ, decrease X_{22} by θ, increase X_{12} by θ and decrease X_{11} by θ. The maximum possible increase in X_{31} is 10 beyond which X_{22} will be negative. X_{31} becomes 10, X_{33} becomes 40, X_{23} becomes 10, X_{22} becomes non-basic, X_{12} becomes 30 and X_{11} becomes 10. The new solution is shown in Table 4.25.

Table 4.25 New Degenerate Basic Feasible Solution

	4	6	8	8	
	(10)	(30)			40
	6	8	6	7	
			(10)	(50)	60
	5	7	6	8	
	(10)		(40)		50
	20	30	50	50	

We observe that this solution has six allocations and is not degenerate. This example tells us that a basic feasible solution can come out of degeneracy during the iteration process. There can be situations where it can become degenerate also during the iteration process. You may observe this in some other example.

Now, we have to verify if the solution in Table 4.25 is optimal. From the solution in Table 4.25 we observe that $X_{11}, X_{12}, X_{23}, X_{24}, X_{31}$ and X_{33} are basic while the rest take a zero value.

We evaluate u_i ($i = 2,...,m$) and v_j ($j = 1,...,n$) using the relationship $u_i + v_j = C_{ij}$ where X_{ij} is basic. We have

$$u_1 + v_1 = C_{11} = 4$$
$$u_1 + v_2 = C_{12} = 6$$
$$u_2 + v_3 = C_{23} = 6$$
$$u_2 + v_4 = C_{34} = 7$$
$$u_3 + v_1 = C_{31} = 5$$
$$u_3 + v_3 = C_{33} = 6$$

Since $u_1 = 0$, we get $v_1 = 4$ from $u_1 + v_1 = 4$.

From $u_1 + v_2 = 6$, we get $v_2 = 6$
From $u_3 + v_1 = 5$, we get $u_3 = 1$
From $u_3 + v_3 = 6$, we get $v_3 = 5$
From $u_2 + v_3 = 6$, we get $u_2 = 1$
From $u_2 + v_4 = 7$, we get $v_4 = 6$

Using the values of u_i and v_j, we calculate the values of $C_{ij} - (u_i + v_j)$ for all the non-basic X_{ij}. We compute

$$C_{13} - (u_1 + v_3) = 8 - 0 - 5 = 3$$
$$C_{14} - (u_1 + v_4) = 8 - 0 - 6 = 2$$
$$C_{21} - (u_2 + v_1) = 6 - 1 - 4 = 1$$
$$C_{22} - (u_2 + v_2) = 8 - 1 - 6 = 1$$
$$C_{32} - (u_3 + v_2) = 7 - 1 - 6 = 0$$
$$C_{34} - (u_3 + v_4) = 8 - 1 - 6 = 1$$

Among these we have to pick that non-basic variable with minimum (most negative) value of $C_{ij} - (u_i + v_j)$. All of them are non-negative and hence we understand that the solution is optimal.

However, we observe that at the optimum we have a non-basic variable X_{32} with a zero value of $C_{32} - (u_3 + v_2)$. Entering this variable, identifying the loop, and making changes we get the solution given in Table 4.26. This is the same solution in Table 4.17 and we have already seen the alternate optimum when we discussed the stepping-stone method. If we compute u_i, and v_j for this solution, we get the same values that we obtained for the solution in Table 4.25. You will also observe that $C_{31} - u_3 - v_1 = 0$ indicating alternate optimum.

Table 4.26 Optimum Solution

[4] (20)	[6] (20)	[8]	[8]	40
[6]	[8]	[6] (10)	[7] (50)	60
[5]	[7] (10)	[6] (40)	[8]	50
20	30	50	50	

4.4 GETTING STARTED—WHICH METHOD?

The two optimal approaches, the stepping-stone method and the MODI method require a basic feasible solution to begin with. We have seen three different methods to generate basic feasible solutions. These are:

1. North west corner rule
2. Minimum cost method
3. Vogel's approximation method

All of them have the advantage that the solutions are basic feasible and do not contain a loop. Among the three the Vogel's approximation method is often used as the method for the starting solution because the quality of the feasible solution is superior (on the average) compared to the other two methods. However, the Vogel's approximation method takes more time as compared to the other two. Since this method gives a superior starting basic feasible solution, it is expected to take less number of iterations to reach the optimum and is hence preferred.

It is also advisable that the starting solution is generated using these methods because they don't have loops. We can also begin by any arbitrary feasible solution but we have to first verify if the chosen solution is basic feasible. If it has more than $m + n - 1$ allocations or if it has a loop, the loop must be broken to get a basic feasible solution.

4.4.1 Choosing between the Stepping Stone Method and the MODI Method

We have seen two different methods to obtain the optimum from a given basic feasible solution. Based on the computations that we made, we know that both the methods essentially are the same.

In the stepping stone method, we have to find $C_{ij} - (u_i + v_j)$ values for the $m + n - 1$ non-basic variables by identifying a loop for each and determining the value from the loop. In the MODI method we find the values of u_i and v_j separately and then compute $C_{ij} - (u_i + v_j)$. Once the entering non-basic variable is determined both the methods perform the same set of operations. Both the methods have the same number of iterations.

It may be noted that for small problems where the number of non-basic variables is less, the stepping stone method is used while the MODI method is used when the size of problem is large.

4.5 OPTIMALITY OF THE MODI METHOD

Let us write the primal and dual of the balanced transportation problem. The primal is:
Minimize $\Sigma \Sigma C_{ij} X_{ij}$
Subject to
$$\Sigma X_{ij} = a_i \; \forall i = 1,\ldots,m$$
$$\Sigma X_{ij} = b_j \; \forall j = 1,\ldots,n$$
$$X_{ij} \geq 0$$

Let us introduce dual variables u_i and v_j corresponding to the two sets of constraints. The dual is:

Maximize $\sum_{i=1}^{m} a_i u_i + \sum_{j=1}^{n} b_j v_j$

Subject to
$$u_i + v_j \leq C_{ij}$$

u_i, v_j unrestricted in sign
Since the problem is balanced, we know that

$$\sum_{i=1}^{m} a_i = \sum_{j=1}^{n} b_j$$

Because of this the primal has a set of linearly dependent constraints and hence $m + n - 1$ linearly independent basic variables. Therefore, in the dual also we have $m + n - 1$ linearly independent variables. One dual variable has to be given an arbitrary value. By convention we always put $u_1 = 0$.

The MODI method begins with a basic feasible solution to the primal and also ensures that every solution evaluated for the primal is basic feasible. We find values to the dual variables u_i and v_j by equating $u_i + v_j = c_{ij}$ for every basic X_{ij}. This means that when a primal variable is basic, the corresponding dual variables are such that the corresponding dual constraint is satisfied as an equation. This means that for a basic X_{ij} the corresponding slack is zero. Thus, the complimentary slackness conditions are satisfied.

We evaluate the value of $c_{ij} - (u_i + v_j)$ for all the non-basic X_{ij}. When all the values of $c_{ij} - (u_i + v_j)$ are non-negative, we terminate. A non-negative value of $c_{ij} - (u_i + v_j)$ implies that $u_i + v_j \leq c_{ij}$ (dual feasibility). This means that for a non-basic X_{ij} the corresponding slack variable is non-negative. This also satisfies the complimentary slackness conditions. At any iteration of the MODI method if we have all $c_{ij} - (u_i + v_j)$ non-negative, it means that we have a basic feasible solution to the primal, feasible solution to the dual and complimentary slackness conditions are satisfied. Therefore, the solution is optimal based on the duality theorems.

When we have $c_{ij} - (u_i + v_j)$ negative for a non-basic variable, it means that the dual constraint is not satisfied, when complimentary slackness conditions are applied. This means that the primal is not optimal. The negative dual slack variable represents the corresponding non-basic primal that can yield a better solution. We proceed by entering the non-basic X_{ij} that has a negative $c_{ij} - (u_i + v_j)$.

The balanced transportation problem has the dual variables unrestricted in sign. Therefore, we don't worry even if the values of u_i and v_j become negative when they are computed.

4.6 SOLVING UNBALANCED TRANSPORTATION PROBLEMS

The dual to the unbalanced transportation problem will have variables $u_i \leq 0$ and $v_j \geq 0$. This means that every value of u_i computed should be strictly non-positive and every v_j computed should be non-negative in order to maintain dual feasibility. This will not be easy to achieve.

The easier option is to convert the unbalanced problem to a balanced problem and apply the MODI method as it is to obtain the optimal solution from the starting basic feasible solution.

This is explained by an example. Consider the transportation problem with three supply points and four demand points (in the usual representation) given in Table 4.27.

ILLUSTRATION 4.3

Table 4.27 Unbalanced Transportation Problem

4	6	8	8	30
6	8	6	7	60
5	7	6	8	50
20	30	50	50	

This problem is unbalanced because the total supply (Σa_i) is less than the total requirement (Σb_j). The total supply is 140 and the total demand is 150. In this case, we won't be able to meet a demand of 10 units. We convert this unbalanced problem to a balanced problem by adding an extra supply (row) with 10 units (called **dummy row**). The cost of transportation from this dummy row to all the columns is zero. This is shown in Table 4.28.

Table 4.28 Balanced Transportation Problem

4	6	8	8	30
6	8	6	7	60
5	7	6	8	50
0	0	0	0	10 (Dummy)
20	30	50	50	

We can solve this balanced transportation problem. Whichever demand point (Column) is allotted from the dummy finally will not get the 10 units and will be 10 units short. We have ensured that the existing 140 units have been distributed to the demand points at minimum cost. The dummy is a virtual supply point with non-existent 10 units and has zero cost of transportation from the real demand points.

Consider another transportation problem with three supply points and four demand points (in the usual representation) given in Table 4.29.

ILLUSTRATION 4.4

Table 4.29 Unbalanced Transportation Problem

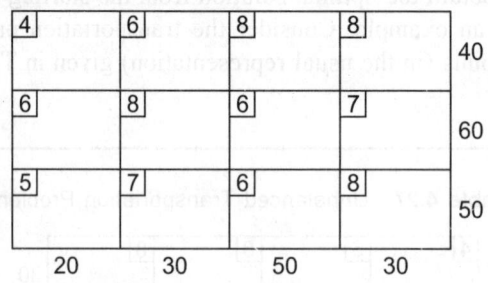

This problem is unbalanced because the total supply (Σa_i) is more than the total requirement (Σb_j). The total supply is 150 and the total demand is 130. In this case, we will have an extra 20 units in one or more supply points after meeting the total demand of 130 units. We convert this unbalanced problem to a balanced problem by adding an extra demand (column) with 20 units (called **dummy column**). The cost of transportation from this dummy column to all the rows is zero. This is shown in Table 4.30.

Table 4.30 Balanced Transportation Problem

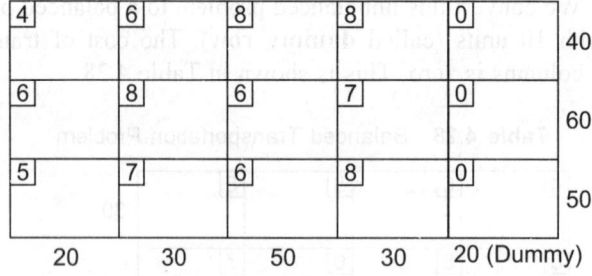

We can solve this balanced transportation problem. Whichever supply point (row) allots to the dummy finally will have that many units not supplied. We have ensured that the required 130 units have been distributed to the demand points at the minimum cost. The dummy is a virtual demand point with non-existent 20 units and has zero cost of transportation from the real demand points.

> **Important points**
> 1. Unless stated otherwise, the transportation problem is a minimization problem. If the objective is to maximize, it is customary to change the sign of the objective function coefficients (make them negative) and solve the resultant problem as a minimization problem (as we did in simplex algorithm). Otherwise we have to modify the rules of North west corner, Minimum cost, VAM and MODI method, which is not desirable.
> 2. If a supply point (row) cannot or should not supply to a demand (column), we assign a M (big M, as in simplex) for the minimization objective. As explained in the simplex algorithm earlier, M is large, positive and tends to infinity. We know that $M \pm$ any constant $= M$.

4.7 UNIMODULARITY OF THE TRANSPORTATION PROBLEM

In a transportation problem, if the demand and supply quantities are integers, the optimal solution is integer valued. This is while identifying the starting basic feasible solution and while getting the optimum we allocate, add or subtract integers.

We can understand that the transportation algorithm is an adaptation of the simplex algorithm. Every simplex algorithm can be seen as obtaining values for a set of basic variable X_B by solving

$$BX_B = b$$

or

$$X_B = B^{-1} b$$

If b has integer values (which is the case assuming that both supply and demand quantities are integers) and B^{-1} is integer valued, then X_B is integer valued.

Now,
$$B^{-1} = \frac{\text{adj } B}{|B|}$$

Also, adj B has integer values if B has integer values. In the transportation problem, the constraint coefficient matrix A is integer valued (has zeros and ones) and, therefore, every B, which is a sub matrix of A is also integer valued. In order for B^{-1} to be integer, $|B|$ should be ± 1.

For the transportation problem, the constraint coefficient matrix A is unimodular. This matrix can be rewritten (by row subtractions) in such a way that every column has two non-zero elements (+1 and $a - 1$) adding to zero, making it unimodular. When the constraint coefficient matrix is unimodular, the IP problem when solved as LPs will give integer values for the decision variables.

There are several conditions for unimodularity Rebman (1974). These are as follows:
1. All entries are 0, +1 or -1.
2. Rows can be partitioned into two disjoint sets S_1 and S_2.
3. Every column contains at most 2 non-zeros.
4. If it has 2 non-zeros of same sign, one is in S_1 and the other in S_2.
5. If it has 2 non-zeros of opposite sign, both are in S_1 or both are in S_2.

It can be verified that the constraint coefficient matrix for the transportation problem satisfies these conditions and hence is unimodular.

SOLVED EXAMPLES

EXAMPLE 4.1 A department store wishes to purchase the following quantities of ladies dresses per month:

Dress type	A	B	C	D
Quantity	100	300	200	100

Tenders are submitted by 3 different manufacturers who undertake to supply not more than the quantities below (all types of dress combined).

Manufacturer	W	X	Y
Quantity	500	600	400

The store estimates that its profit per dress will vary with the manufacturer as shown in Table 4.31. How should orders be placed?

Table 4.31 Profit Data

Dress \ Manufacturer	A	B	C	D
W	2	3	4	2
X	1	3	3	2
Y	3	4	5	4

Solution: The objective function is to maximize profits and hence is a *maximization* transportation problem. We convert it into a minimization problem by negating the C_{ij} values. The problem is unbalanced with the total supply exceeding the total demand. We add a dummy column with a demand of 800 units. The cost coefficients are zero for the dummy column. The transportation matrix is given in Table 4.32.

Table 4.32 Transportation Cost Matrix for a Minimization Problem

	−2	−3	−4	−2	0	500
	−1	−3	−3	−2	0	600
	−3	−4	−5	−4	0	400
	100	300	200	100	800	

We obtain an initial basic feasible solution using penalty cost method (Vogel's approximation method) to the minimization problem (with negative values of the cost coefficients).

The row penalties are 1, 0 and 1, and the column penalties are 1, 1, 1, 2 and 0. We choose Column 4 for allocation. We allocate 100 (demand of D_4) and the supply S_3 becomes 300.

Row penalties for the rows are 1, 0 and 1, and the column penalties are 1, 1, 1 and 0 (We do not calculate for Column 4 since it is fully allocated). There is a tie and we choose Row 1 for allocation. We allocate 200 (demand of D_3) and the supply S_1 becomes 300.

Row penalties for the rows are 1, 2 and 1 and the column penalties are 1, 1 and 0. We choose Row 2 for allocation. We allocate 300 (demand of D_2) and the supply S_2 becomes 300.

Row penalties for the rows are 2, 1 and 3 and the column penalties are 1 and 0. We choose Row 3 for allocation. We allocate 100 (demand of D_1) and the supply S_3 becomes 200.

The rest of the allocations can be carried out to satisfy supply and demand constraints (without calculating the penalties). The basic feasible solution is shown in Table 4.33.

Table 4.33 Basic Feasible Solution

-2	-3	-4 (200)	-2	0 (300)	500
-1	-3 (300)	-3	-2	0 (300)	600
-3 (100)	-4	-5	-4 (100)	0 (200)	400
100	300	200	100	800	

The value of the objective function corresponding to the basic feasible solution is 2400 (maximization). We now follow the MODI method (or the u-v method to get to the optimal solution). We start with $u_1 = 0$ and following the method get $v_3 = -4$. We calculate the values of the u_i and v_js. These are:

$$u_1 = 0, u_2 = 0, u_3 = 0 \text{ and } v_1 = -3, v_2 = -2, v_3 = -4, v_4 = -4, v_5 = 0.$$

We calculate the values of $C_{ij} - u_i - v_j$ for all non-basic positions (where there is no allocation) and observe that $C_{32} - u_3 - v_2$ has the most negative value of -2. We insert a θ allocation here and complete the loop. The value that θ takes is 200. The revised allocation is shown in Table 4.34.

Table 4.34 Revised Allocation

-2	-3	-4 (200)	-2	0 (300)	500
-1	-3 (100)	-3	-2	0 (500)	600
-3 (100)	-4 (200)	-5	-4 (100)	0	400
100	300	200	100	800	

We apply the MODI method to this solution and starting with $u_1 = 0$, we find the rest of the values of the u_i and v_j by considering $C_{ij} = u_i + v_j$ wherever there is an allocation. The values are:

$$u_1 = 0, u_2 = 0, u_3 = -1 \text{ and } v_1 = -2, v_2 = -3, v_3 = -4, v_4 = -3, v_5 = 0.$$

We calculate the values of $C_{ij} - u_i - v_j$ for all non-basic positions (where there is no allocation) and observe that all the computed values are non-negative indicating optimum. However, there are zero values of $C_{ij} - u_i - v_j$ in two positions (X_{11} and X_{12} are non-basic positions that can enter the basis with zero value of $C_{ij} - u_i - v_j$), indicating alternate optima. The value of the objective function at the optimum is 2600 (maximization).

EXAMPLE 4.2 A company has decided to initiate the production of some or all of the four new products at 3 branch plants with excess production capacity. The available capacities in the three plants are 40, 50 and 30 units per week while the demand for the four products are 50, 30, 40, 20 units, respectively. Plant 2 cannot produce Product 2.

The cost per unit of production in the plants is given in Table 4.35:

Table 4.35 Cost per Unit of Production

Plants \ Products	1	2	3	4
1	3	6	5	2
2	4	M	5	4
3	3	4	4	4

Find a basic feasible solution using north west corner rule and obtain the quantities of production at the optimum.

Solution: The problem is a minimization transportation problem where there is a restriction that Plant 2 cannot produce Product 2. We use a large value of $C_{22} = M$ (big M) here so that there is no allocation to that position. The problem is unbalanced and we create a dummy row with supply 20 units to balance it. We apply north west corner rule to obtain an initial basic feasible solution.

We allot $X_{11} = 40$, which meets the demand of first column. $X_{21} = 10$ and since $C_{22} = M$, we do not allot anything to X_{22}. Consequently $X_{23} = 40$ and $X_{32} = 30$. We also get $X_{44} = 20$. The solution is degenerate with four allocations required instead of six and we create two epsilon positions (called ε_1 and ε_2) X_{14} and X_{42} (making sure that there is no loop in the solution). The initial basic feasible solution is shown in Table 4.36.

Table 4.36 Initial Basic Feasible Solution

3 (40)	6	5	2 (ε_1)	40
4 (10)	M	5 (40)	4	50
3	4 (30)	4	4	30
0	0 (ε_2)	0	0 (20)	20
50	30	40	20	

We apply the MODI method to this solution and starting with $u_1 = 0$, we find the rest of the values of the u_i and v_j by considering $C_{ij} = u_i + v_j$ wherever there is an allocation. The values are:

$u_1 = 0$, $u_2 = 1$, $u_3 = 2$, $u_4 = -2$ and $v_1 = 3$, $v_2 = 2$, $v_3 = 4$, $v_4 = 2$.

We calculate the values of $C_{ij} - u_i - v_j$ for all the non-basic positions (where there is no allocation) and observe that $C_{31} - u_3 - v_1$ has the most negative value of –2. We insert a θ allocation here and complete the loop. The revised allocation is shown in Table 4.37.

Table 4.37 Revised Allocation

3 (20)	6	5	2 (20)	40
4 (10)	M	5 (40)	4	50
3 (20)	4 (10)	4	4	30
0	0 (20)	0	0	20
50	30	40	20	

We also observe from Table 4.37 that the present solution is not degenerate and has seven allocations.

We apply the MODI method to this solution and starting with $u_1 = 0$, we find the rest of the values of the u_i and v_j by considering $C_{ij} = u_i + v_j$ wherever there is an allocation. The values are:

$$u_1 = 0, u_2 = 1, u_3 = 0, u_4 = -4 \text{ and } v_1 = 3, v_2 = 4, v_3 = 4, v_4 = 2.$$

We calculate $C_{ij} - (u_i - v_j)$ for all the non-basic positions and observe that there is no non-basic position with a negative value. The optimum is reached. However, there is one position (X_{33}) which has a zero value of $C_{ij} - (u_i - v_j)$ indicating alternate optimum. The value of the objective function at the optimum is 440.

Example 4.3 A manufacturer must produce a certain product in sufficient quantity to meet contracted sales in the next three months. The product may be produced in one month and then held for sale in a later month, but at a storage cost of Re.1 per unit per month. No storage cost is incurred for goods sold in the same month in which they are produced. There is presently no inventory of this product and none is desired at the end of the four months. The production can be in regular time or using overtime. Regular time cost to produce a unit is Rs. 10 while overtime cost is Rs. 15. You cannot meet the demand of a month by producing in a subsequent month. Regular time capacity is 300 units/month and overtime capacity is 100 units/month. The demand for the three months are 200, 400 and 300 units, respectively. Formulate a transportation problem for the above situation to minimize the total cost.

Solution: The transportation table is shown in Table 4.38. A dummy column of 300 units is added to balance the problem. There are six rows indicating two types of production for three months. We use a M where it is not possible to meet the demand of a month by producing in a subsequent month. The cost of producing (including inventory) is shown in Table 4.38.

We obtain the initial basic feasible solution in this case using the north west corner rule. This is shown in Table 4.38.

Table 4.38 Initial Basic Feasible Solution

10 (200)	11 (100)	12	0	300
15	16 (100)	17	0	100
M	10 (200)	11 (100)	0	300
M	15	16 (100)	0	100
M	M	10 (100)	0 (200)	300
M	M	15	0 (100)	100
200	400	300	300	

We apply the stepping stone method to obtain the optimal solution. Let us consider the non-basic (unallocated position) X_{13}. If we add a unit here and complete the loop, the cost incurred is zero. This is true for all the possible non-basic positions except those in the dummy column.

Inserting a unit in the four dummy positions individually, gives us an increase in the cost of 2, –7, –1 and –6, respectively. We enter X_{24} into the basis and complete the allocations. These are shown in Table 4.39.

Table 4.39 Basic Feasible Solution after an Iteration

10 (200)	11 (100)	12	0	300
15	16 (ε_1)	17	0 (100)	100
M	10 (300)	11 (ε_1)	0	300
M	15	16 (100)	0	100
M	M	10 (200)	0 (100)	300
M	M	15	0 (100)	100
200	400	300	300	

The present solution is degenerate and we introduce ε_1 and ε_2 as shown in Table 4.39. We once again use the stepping stone method. Entering in position X_{44} gives the best net gain of –6. We enter X_{44} into the basis and reallocate the values. This is shown in Table 4.40.

Table 4.40 Revised Allocation

10 (200)	11 (100)	12	0	300
15	16 (ε_1)	17	0 (100)	100
M	10 (300)	11 (ε_2)	0	300
M	15	16 (ε_3)	0 (100)	100
M	M	10 (300)	0	300
M	M	15	0 (100)	100
200	400	300	300	

The present solution is degenerate and we introduce two epsilons ε_1 and ε_2 as shown in Table 4.40. We once again use the stepping stone method. We observe that allocating to all non basic positions gives a net positive. Since there is no gain we terminate and the present solution is optimal. The value of the objective function at the optimum is 9100.

EXAMPLE 4.4 Table 4.41 shows a feasible solution to a transportation problem. Is it optimal solution? If not, find an optimal solution using this feasible solution.

Table 4.41 Feasible Solution

2 (10)	3 (30)	3 (40)	4	6 (20)	100
4 (20)	7	6	5 (40)	7	60
5	6	3 (30)	4	3 (20)	50
4	7 (30)	8	4 (50)	8	80
30	60	70	90	40	

Solution: The given solution has 10 allocations, which is more than $m + n - 1$. The solution is feasible but not basic feasible. There are two loops that have to be broken. The existing loops are shown in Table 4.42.

Table 4.42 Loops in the Existing Solution

[2] (10)	[3] (30)	[3] (40)	[4]	[6] (20)	100
[4] (20)	[7]	[6]	[5] (40)	[7]	60
[5]	[6]	[3] (30)	[4]	[3] (20)	50
[4]	[7] (30)	[8]	[4] (50)	[8]	80
30	60	70	90	40	

We add a unit allocation in any position in the loop (say, X_{11}), and balance the rest of the supplies and demands. The additional cost if we add 1 unit to X_{11} is:

$$2 - 3 + 7 - 4 + 5 - 4 = 3$$

Since there is a net loss, we realize that if we subtract 1 unit from X_{11} we can have a net gain. We observe that the maximum possible subtraction to X_{11} is 10 units beyond which X_{11} becomes negative. We add 10 units to X_{11} and the revised allocations are shown in Table 4.43.

(There are always two ways to break a loop. We add 1 unit to any position and evaluate the net gain. If there is a gain, we use that information to add as much as possible. If the net gain is negative, we subtract the maximum possible. This way we always get a solution with less (or equal) cost compared to the starting solution. We could also get a basic feasible solution with a higher cost by directly adding as much possible to the position if there is net loss. However, it is customary to obtain a better solution and proceed to the optimal solution).

There is a second loop which is broken by identifying position X_{13} and adding 20 to it. The basic feasible solution after breaking the loops is shown in Table 4.43.

Table 4.43 Basic Feasible Solution

[2]	[3] (40)	[3] (60)	[4]	[6]	100
[4] (30)	[7]	[6]	[5] (30)	[7]	60
[5]	[6]	[3] (10)	[4]	[3] (40)	50
[4]	[7] (20)	[8]	[4] (60)	[8]	80
30	60	70	90	40	

The present solution is basic feasible (having exactly $m + n - 1$ allocations) and we verify its optimality using the MODI (or u-v method). We set u_1 to zero and evaluate the rest of the u_i and v_j. The values are:

$$u_1 = 0, u_2 = 5, u_3 = 0, u_4 = 4$$
$$v_1 = -1, v_2 = 3, v_3 = 3, v_4 = 0, v_5 = 3$$

We evaluate the values of $C_{ij} - u_i - v_j$ for the non-basic positions (where there is no allocation) and observe that $C_{22} - u_2 - v_2$ is negative. Variable X_{22} enters the basis. We add θ and find that the maximum value that θ can take is 20. The revised allocations are shown in Table 4.44.

Table 4.44 Revised Allocations

2	3 (60)	3 (40)	4	6	100
4 (30)	7	6 (20)	5 (10)	7	60
5	6	3 (10)	4	3 (40)	50
4	7	8	4 (80)	8	80
30	60	70	90	40	

We verify the optimality of the present solution using the MODI (or u-v method). We set u_1 to zero and evaluate the rest of the u_i and v_j. The values are:

$$u_1 = 0, u_2 = 3, u_3 = 0, u_4 = 2$$
$$v_1 = 1, v_2 = 3, v_3 = 3, v_4 = 2, v_5 = 3$$

Since all the values are non-negative, the present solution is optimal.

EXAMPLE 4.5 A company makes a product in three plants with capacities 100, 200 and 150 units. There are four distribution centres to which the product has to be transported. The first centre requires a committed 80 units while the second requires a minimum of 40 and can take an additional 50 units if sent. The third centre requires a maximum of 60 and can accept whatever is sent. The fourth centre requires a minimum of 80 and can take as many as possible as extra. The cost of transportation among the plants and centres are shown in Table 4.45. Formulate a transportation problem to minimize the cost of transportation.

Table 4.45 Cost of Transportation among Plants and Centres

5	4	6	7
8	6	5	7
7	6	8	9

Solution: The total supply is 450 units. The minimum requirement for the centres adds up to 80 + 40 + 0 + 80 = 200. The fourth can, therefore, take an additional 250. The second and fourth centres will now have two columns for the committed and extra items. The demand in the six columns are now 80 + (40 + 50) + 60 + (80 + 250) = 560. We create a dummy supply with 110 units. Wherever there is a definite minimum commitment, this has to go from the regular supplies. We have a cost of *M* in the dummy row for these. The additional columns for Centres 2 and 4 otherwise have the same costs. The formulation is shown in Table 4.46.

Table 4.46 Transportation Formulation

5	4	4	6	7	7	100
8	6	6	5	7	7	200
7	6	6	8	9	9	150
M	M	0	0	M	0	110

80 40 50 60 80 250

EXAMPLE 4.6 Queenpecker Airlines has to periodically remove engines for service. The removed engines are replaced by reconditioned (or new) engines, and the aircraft is used. Each engine removed for maintenance can be serviced by the normal method that requires two months and costs Rs. 15 lakhs and the fast method that takes one month and costs Rs. 20 lakhs. Any number of engines can be handled by either method simultaneously. The airline is planning for a 5-month period and the number to be serviced monthly is 90, 100, 120, 80 and 110, respectively. New engines cost Rs. 60 lakhs each.

Formulate a transportation problem to minimize the total cost of purchase and reconditioning.

Solution: Since 90, 100, 120, 80 and 110 engines are to be sent for service, the demand for good engines for the five months are 90, 100, 120, 80 and 110, respectively. These are shown in the first five columns of Table 4.47. The engines serviced are available for use from the next month onwards and, therefore, we have four supplies of 90, 100, 120 and 80 engines. New engines can be bought and since we require a total of 500 engines (sum of demand), we assume a supply of 500 new engines that can be bought. This creates a dummy of 390 to balance supply and demand. A service engine can meet the demand of the next month onwards. Therefore, some cost values take *M* value indicating that they are not possible. If a service engine meets the next month's demand, it has to be sent to fast service at a cost of 20. It can be sent to normal service at 15 and be used to meet the demand of the months following the next month. Table 4.47 shows the final formulation for the problem.

Table 4.47 Transportation Formulation

M	20	15	15	15	0	90
M	M	20	15	15	0	100
M	M	M	20	15	0	120
M	M	M	M	20	0	80
60	60	60	60	60	0	500

90 100 120 80 110 390

(This problem is similar to the Caterer problem indicated earlier and appeared in the literature about the same time. Similarities between this problem and the Caterer problem is also mentioned in the literature)

EXAMPLE 4.7 The Embeeyeh company, planning to expand, decides to recruit MBAs. Three of the twelve posts advertised require specialized knowledge of finance and carry a salary of Rs. 30,000. A further four need software knowledge and carry a salary of Rs. 40,000 while the remaining require knowledge in human resources management and carry a salary of Rs. 25,000. It is decided that any selected candidate should be paid either one's current salary or the company's minimum salary, whichever is higher.

Of the short-listed applicants, all possess knowledge in human resources management, three in finance and software, five in finance only and four in software only. The present salaries of three groups are Rs. 25,000, Rs. 30,000 and Rs. 35,000, respectively others earn Rs. 20,000 or less.

Formulate a transportation problem to minimize the total salaries paid to the recruited employees.

Solution: A total of 12 people are required and it is assumed that at least twelve people are available with experience in human resources management. A dummy column with 12 people is added to balance the supply and demand. Where candidates do not have special skills, they cannot be given jobs involving these skills. This is indicated by M. Other costs are the maximum of the present salary of the candidate and the salary of the job. Table 4.48 explains the formulation as a minimization transportation problem.

Table 4.48 Transportation Formulation

30	40	25	0	3
30	M	30	0	5
M	40	40	0	4
M	M	25	0	12
3	4	5	12	

EXAMPLE 4.8 Consider the following transportation problem, whose details are given in Table 4.49

Table 4.49 Data for a Transportation Problem

	D1	D2	D3	D4	D5	Supply
S1	4	1	2	6	9	100
S2	6	4	3	5	7	120
S3	5	2	6	4	8	120
Demand	40	50	70	90	90	340

(a) Define row and column penalty cost for every element as the difference between the cost in that element and the minimum row (or column) cost. Create a transportation problem where the unit costs are the sum of row and column penalty costs? Apply VAM to the new matrix and evaluate the cost of the basic feasible solution found?
(b) Use VAM to obtain a basic feasible solution using the given transportation costs and compare the objective function values using the original transportation costs.

Solution: The row penalty for the element is the difference between the cost of transportation of the element and minimum cost in that row. Similarly the column penalty is the difference between the cost of transportation of the element and minimum cost in that column. We illustrate using the first row, first column element.

row penalty = 4 − 1 = 3
column penalty = 4 − 4 = 0. The sum is 3.

A transportation problem where the costs are the sum of row and column penalties as given in Table 4.50.

Table 4.50 Transportation Cost Matrix with Total Opportunity Cost as its Unit Cost

	D1	D2	D3	D4	D5	Supply
S1	3	0	1	7	10	100
S2	5	4	1	3	4	120
S3	4	1	8	2	7	120
Demand	40	50	70	90	90	340

Now the above problem is solved using VAM approach. The final allocation that we get after applying VAM to the cost matrix in Table 4.50 is given in Table 4.51.

Table 4.51 Final Allocation Matrix

	D1		D2		D3		D4		D5		Supply
S1	40	4	20	1	40	2		6		9	100
S2		6		4	30	3		5	90	7	120
S3		5	30	2		6	90	4		8	120
Demand	40		50		70		90		90		340

The total transportation cost = (40 * 4 + 20 * 1 + 40 * 2 + 30 * 3 + 90 * 7 + 30 * 2 + 90 * 4)
= 1400

When we apply VAM to the original cost matrix, the basic feasible solution (based on an arbitrary tie breaking rule) is $X_{11} = 30$, $X_{31} = 70$, $X_{24} = 90$, $X_{25} = 30$, $X_{31} = 10$, $X_{32} = 50$, $X_{35} = 60$, with total cost = 1550

[The above method is called TOC-VAM method (Mathirajan and Meenakshi 2004) and is a well-known extension of the VAM algorithm. We also note that the optimal transportation cost to this problem is 1400 and this method has given the optimal solution for this instance. Improvements such as these have helped in making the basic feasible solutions better so that the optimum can be obtained in lesser iterations of the MODI method.

In solving large transportation problems ties during VAM are broken based on the computation of further penalty which is the difference between the second minimum and the third minimum].

CASE STUDY 4.1: Sri Bhima Sweets

Sri Bhima Sweets is a famous sweet shop in Hastinapur and is particularly famous for its tasty laddus. They have only two outlets where they sell their sweets. The laddus are made in two places in the town and are transported to the retail outlets. Mr. Mithaiwala, the owner is aware of the expected demand for Laddus for Diwali.

Laddus can be made at the rate of 6 kg per hour. The two places that make the laddus have exclusive ovens used to make the laddus. These have four and three ovens respectively. They work for two shifts ordinarily and each shift is for 8 hours. They can work over time if needed and the third shift is for six hours.

The laddus are available for sale on the same day they are produced. Mr. Mithaiwala estimates that the sweets have a life of about one week and therefore uses the daily production to meet the demand of that day and the next day. He also sells some available sweets at half the price on the third day in the name of broken sweets. This way some demand on the third day can be met. The broken sweets are to be sold only in the first shop. Any unfulfilled demand can be met on the next day in either of the shops. As a goodwill gesture the shop undertakes the delivery that costs the shop on an average Rs. 5/kg.

The laddus are sold at Rs. 180/kg in both the shops. The cost of making these (including labour and materials) is Rs. 80 per kg for regular time. The cost of overtime production is Rs. 100/kg. The cost of regular time labour alone is Rs. 40/hour.

To meet the increased demand, Mr. Mithaiwala chooses to use some capacity from Sri Arjun Sweets. He is slightly worried about the quality of the sweets and decides to restrict his daily requirement from them to 50 kg each. He also decides to sell them on the same day and also does not want to use them to meet back ordered demand. The cost price of these sweets are Rs. 100/kg.

The estimated demand for laddus in shop 1 for the three days preceding Diwali are 500, 600 and 670 kg and in shop 2 the estimated demands are 380, 400 and 480 kg respectively. Both the shops are willing to accept additional 10% more sweets on the third day because of a possible further increase in demand.

There is also a transportation cost from the production facilities to the shops. The estimated cost per kg of laddus transported is given in Table 4.52.

Table 4.52 Cost of Transportation

	Manufacturing 1	Manufacturing 2
Sale outlet 1	1.00	1.25
Sale outlet 2	1.30	1.15

Mr. Mithaiwala thinks that the transportation cost can be ignored or can be approximated to an average value of Rs 1.20 per kg transported.

EXERCISES

4.1 Three hostels of Universe College, viz., Jupiter, Venus and Mercury face water shortage and the institution has decided to subcontract from three drinking water suppliers PK & Co., KC & Co. and SKCKSS Bros. The suppliers can provide 3000, 5000 and 5000 litres, respectively while the hostels have different requirements. Jupiter requires exactly 4000 litres, Venus requires at least 3000 litres and is willing to take any excess while Mercury requires not more than 4000 and not less than 3000 litres. The cost of transporting water from supplier (row) to hostel (column) is given in Table 4.53.

Table 4.53 Cost of Transporting Water from Supplier to Hostel

4	8	8
16	24	16
8	16	24

Formulate this problem as a balanced transportation problem clearly indicating the costs of various positions?

At present the management meets the Jupiter requirement by asking PK to supply 2000 litres and KC to supply 2000 litres. It meets Venus requirement by asking SKCKSS to supply 5000 litres. PK supplies 1000 litres to Mercury, while KC supplies 2000 and the extra 1000 to Mercury. Represent this solution in your table.

(a) Is the above solution basic feasible? Why or why not?
(b) Can you get a better basic feasible solution than the given solution?

4.2 Bhojan Prakash is a private caterer who has undertaken a contract for a series of dinners to be given at the Metro club. There will be n dinners on each of the n successive days. The club has asked Bhojan Prakash to provide a special type of cloth napkin (with the club's monogram) for the dinner series. Thus, the napkins become useless after the dinner series. During the series, however, the soiled napkins can be washed and reused. Two types of laundry services are available to the caterer — Regular service and Express service. Regular service takes p days; so that a napkin sent to the laundry on the kth day is available again for use on day $k+p$; this service costs Rs. u per napkin. Express service takes q days; so that a napkin sent to the laundry on the kth day is available again for use on day $k+q$; this service costs Rs. v per napkin ($v > u$ and $p > q$). New napkin costs Rs. s each. Let a_k be the number of napkins needed on k^{th} day ($k = 1, 2,..., n$). Bhojan Prakash wants to minimize the costs associated with purchasing and laundering napkins. Formulate a transportation model for determining the following daily decisions:

(a) How many napkins to buy?
(b) How many napkins to be sent to express laundry?
(c) How many napkins to be sent to ordinary laundry?

4.3 A chemical company has plants at three locations (A to C). The company has been prohibited from disposing of its effluents in these places. Instead the company has to transport the effluents in tankers to their disposal sites at four different places, where they are eventually destroyed. The effluents generated from the three plants are 9000, 8000 and 7000 litres per day, respectively. Sometimes the Plant A generates more than 9000 but never exceeds 12,000 and whatever be the quantity, has to be destroyed. The sites have destruction capacities of 7000, 7500, 8000 and 4000, respectively. The last site, can handle an additional 1500 if required. The costs of transportation per 1000 litres of effluent are given in Table 4.54.

Table 4.54 Costs of Transportation

	Site 1	Site 2	Site 3	Site 4
A	130	110	80	75
B	110	100	95	105
C	90	120	105	115

Formulate a transportation problem in standard form to minimize total cost.

4.4 A company manufactures their product at three different places. The three plants can produce 15, 25 and 30 kg per week, respectively. They have business contacts with four customers—A, B, C and D. Customer A requires exactly 30 kg and the company has committed to supply him this quantity. Similarly, they are also committed to supply

15 kg to Customer B. Customers B and C would like to buy as much of the remaining as possible while Customer D in any case is not interested in buying more than 20 kg for himself. The matrix of profit per kg supplied from i_{th} plant to j_{th} customer is given in Table 4.55.
Formulate and solve a transportation problem for the situation.

Table 4.55 Profit Matrix

	A	B	C	D
Plant 1	8	9	3	2
Plant 2	7	4	4	8
Plant 3	2	1	10	5

4.5 Finn and Co. a finance company has cash-flow problem which will necessitate a bank loan. The loan which will be at a rate of 2% per month, is to be used to balance cash inflow from accounts payable which are shown in Table 4.56

Table 4.56 Accounts Data

Month	Accts. receivable (in lakhs)	Accts. payable (in lakhs)
January	25	40
February	30	50
March	40	30

Assume that both accounts receivable and accounts payable have to be settled by the end of March. In any month, accounts receivable can be used to make payments in the same month. In the first two months, payments can be delayed by almost one month. In such cases, the firm will lose a 1% discount if it had paid in the same month. All bank loans start at the beginning of the month and attract atleast 1 month interest. Any surplus cash can be deposited to the bank and earns 1% interest.
Formulate this problem as transportation problem to determine the optimal borrowing plan for the firm.

4.6 The matrix of transportation costs from Plants A, B, C, D to Warehouses 1, 2, 3, 4 and 5 is given in Table 4.57.
The supplies are 16, 12 15, 12 and the demands are 10, 9 10, 11 15, respectively. Table 4.58 gives a feasible solution to the problem.
Using this as initial feasible solution, proceed to find the optimum solution.

Table 4.57 Transportation Costs from Plants to Warehouses

8	15	9	14	13
17	15	14	14	10
6	9	12	7	12
12	9	10	11	14

Table 4.58 Feasible Solution

4		10	2	
	2			10
6			9	
	7			5

4.7 Consider the transportation problem with the costs shown in Table 4.59.
The supply at three (rows) is 61, 82 and 72, respectively and the demands are 72, 100 and 43, respectively. We also have an additional constraint that $X_{ij} \leq 50$.

(a) Find an initial (basic) feasible solution using the Vogels approximation method.

Table 4.59 Cost Matrix

4	8	8
16	24	16
8	16	24

(b) Try to improve the solution through any of the methods that you know (perform maximum two iterations only).
(c) Comment on the optimality of your method.

4.8 You are given a transportation problem with 4 supply and 5 destination points. The company currently follows the following transportation policy. The allocations and costs are as shown in Table 4.60.
(a) Is the current solution optimal? Why or why not?
(b) If transportation from 1–1 is necessary, what should be the minimum cost that assures this?

Table 4.60 Allocations and Costs

Allocation	Quantity	Cost
1–2	20	8
1–4	20	10
2–2	15	9
2–4	20	7
2–5	15	11
3–3	30	10
4–1	45	12
4–5	15	11

4.9 Table 4.61 shows a feasible solution to a transportation problem (5 rows × 6 columns). However, due to a misunderstanding by the people who collected the data and provided us with the feasible solution, only the costs associated with the allotted cells are known.

Table 4.61 Feasible Solution

Location	Allocation	Unit cost	Location	Allocation	Unit cost
1–1	10	25	3–3	6	20
1–4	6	40	4–2	7	45
1–6	4	30	4–6	8	35
2–2	13	50	5–3	16	30
2–5	9	35	5–5	9	60
3–1	7	40			

Can you find a feasible solution with as small a cost as possible?

4.10 Table 4.62 shows a matrix of transportation costs. A feasible solution is given in Table 4.63. How can you verify if the given solution is optimal?

Table 4.62 Transportation Costs

9	8	15	14	13
12	6	9	7	12
14	17	15	14	10
10	12	9	11	14

Table 4.63 Feasible Solution

Position	Allocation	Position	Allocation
1–1	8	3–5	12
1–2	6	4–1	2
1–5	2	4–3	9
2–2	4	4–5	1
2–4	11		

4.11 Consider a transportation problem with three supply points with supplies 61, 82 and 72, and three demands 72, 100 and 43, respectively. The costs are given in Table 4.64.
(a) Find an initial solution using Vogel's approximation method.
(b) Find the optimum solution.

Table 4.64 Transportation Costs

4	8	8
16	24	16
8	16	24

4.12 You are given a feasible solution to a transportation problem in Table 4.65, where the costs are shown along with the allocation in brackets.

(a) Is the present solution basic feasible? Why or why not?

(b) Can you identify a better solution with the given information? Is it optimal? Why or why not?

(c) Find the range of values of c for which the solution in (b) is optimal.

Table 4.65 Feasible Solution

M	4(40)	M
3(20)	M	5(20)
5(10)	c	6(12)

4.13 XYZ company has three suppliers Rajiv, Puneet and Sanjeev who can supply a single item to its three Factories I, II and III. The unit cost of transportation from supplier i to factory j is given in Table 4.66.
Each supplier can supply a maximum of 100 units while the demands are 50, 10 and 100, respectively.

Table 4.66 Unit Cost of Transportation

10	12	11
8	10	12
8	14	12

(a) Find the minimum cost solution to the transportation problem.

(b) Rajiv is willing to give a discount of Rs. 2/unit if all the units are bought from him. What is the least cost solution now?

(c) Sanjeev is willing to give a discount of Re. 1/unit if at least 50 units are bought from him. What is the least cost solution now?

(d) If Rajiv charges Rs. 10 per unit to transport to Factory II, what happens to the solution?

(e) What happens to the solution if Rajiv can supply 150 instead of 100?

(f) If the condition that all the available items have to be bought from Rajiv, what happens to the solution?

4.14 You are given a minimization transportation problem with the data shown in Table 4.67.

(a) Find the values of α and β such that the given solution is optimal.

(b) If α and β are equal to M (big M), find the optimal solution.

Table 4.67

4 / 20	α	9 / 30
β / 10	7 / 30	8 / 20

4.15 Given a balanced transportation problem with two supply points (50 and 60 units) and three destinations (30, 40 and 40 units), and the following cost matrix shown in Table 4.68:

Table 4.68 Cost Matrix

5	7	8
6	4	7

(a) Verify that the solution using Vogel's approximation method is optimal.

(b) Is it possible to construct a balanced two-supply three-demand transportation problem where Vogel's method does not give the optimum solution?

4.16 The Mathematics department has 120 students who are in three classes (A, B and C) of 40 each. All of them have studied Maths –I and the average class marks for each class is available. These students have to be allotted to three advanced elective courses in their second semester. Each of the elective class should have 40 students. Based on the average marks in the first course, the extra teaching hours required per student to equip the three batches to the advanced courses are given in Table 4.69.

Table 4.69

12	14	10
9	10	6
10	19	18

(a) Solve a transportation problem to determine the number of students who will move from the three Classes A, B and C to each of the advanced electives.

(b) Is it necessary to solve the problem (a) to get the number of students who will move from the three Classes A, B and C to the each of the advanced electives or is it enough to simply allot the entire class to the advanced elective?

(c) What happens to the transportation when we have an equal number of supply and demand points and each of them have the same supply/requirement?

4.17 Five students have to be allotted to three professors for their project work. All the students have to be allotted a guide. The first two professors are willing to take 2 students each while the third professor is willing to take only one student. The preference given by the students (in a scale of 10) is shown in Table 4.70. Solve a transportation problem for the situation.

Table 4.70

6	4	6	5	7
7	5	8	6	5
6	5	8	7	5

5
Assignment Problem

The assignment problem is one of assigning i resources ($i = 1,...,n$) to j tasks ($j = 1,...,n$) to minimize the cost of performing the tasks. The cost associated is C_{ij} when resource i is assigned task j. Each task goes to exactly one resource and each resource gets only one task. Typical examples of assignment problems are the assignment of jobs to machines or assignment of people to tasks.

The mathematical programming formulation of the assignment problem is:

Minimize $\sum_{i=1}^{n} \sum_{j=1}^{n} C_{ij} X_{ij}$

Subject to

$$\sum_{j=1}^{n} X_{ij} = 1 \quad \text{for every } i$$

$$\sum_{i=1}^{n} X_{ij} = 1 \quad \text{for every } j$$

$$X_{ij} = 0, 1$$

The assignment problem is a zero-one problem where variable X_{ij} takes value '1' when resource i is assigned task j and takes value '0' otherwise.

ILLUSTRATION 5.1

Let us consider an example where 4 jobs have to be assigned to 4 persons. The cost of assigning job j to resource i is given in Table 5.1.

A feasible solution to the assignment problem is $X_{11} = X_{22} = X_{33} = X_{44} = 1$ where the first person gets Job 1 and so on. The cost of the assignments is:

5 + 7 + 12 + 6 = 30

The assignment problem of size n (having n tasks and n resources) has $n!$ feasible solutions. The optimal solution is one that is a feasible assignment with least cost. A solution to the assignment problem is feasible when every task is

Table 5.1 Cost of Assigning Job

5	9	3	6
8	7	8	2
6	10	12	7
3	10	8	6

assigned to exactly one resource and every resource gets exactly one task. A feasible solution satisfies to the assignment problem satisfies all the constraints including the 0–1 restriction on the variables.

5.1 ASSIGNMENT PROBLEM, TRANSPORTATION PROBLEM AND LINEAR PROGRAMMING

The assignment problem becomes a linear programming problem when the 0–1 restriction on the variables is relaxed. In fact, the coefficient matrix of the assignment problem is unimodular and, therefore, we can relax the 0–1 restriction and solve it as a linear programming problem to get the optimal solution. But assignment problems are rarely solved using the simplex algorithm but have special algorithms that solve the problem faster and more efficiently.

You may also have observed by now that the assignment problem is similar to the transportation problem since the objective functions are similar and so is the coefficient matrix. The first difference however, is that the assignment problem has a square matrix [equal number of rows (resources) and columns (tasks)] while the transportation problem can have unequal number of supply and demand points. Later in this chapter, we will see what we do if the assignment problem is not square.

The assignment problem is a special case of the transportation problem with $m = n$, all $a_i = 1$ and all $b_j = 1$. We do not solve the assignment problem using the transportation algorithm because it is a degenerate transportation problem. We have already seen that degenerate LP problems and transportation problems may require additional iterations and take long time to reach optimality.

A feasible solution to the $n \times n$ assignment problem has exactly n assignments while the LP formulation has n^2 decision variables and $2n$ constraints. Out of the $2n$ constraints there are $2n - 1$ basic variables because the coefficient matrix represents a linearly dependent system of equations. Since the assignment solution has n allocations out of the $2n - 1$ basic variables, it means that $n - 1$ basic variables take value '0' indicating degeneracy. Hence assignment problem is neither solved as a transportation problem nor as a linear programming problem.

5.2 PROPERTIES OF THE OPTIMAL SOLUTION

> **Property 1**
> If the cost coefficients $C_{ij} \geq 0$, a feasible solution with $Z = 0$ is optimal.

Property 1 is obvious since the assignment problem is a minimization problem. The only important condition is that we should not have a negative value in the cost (objective) coefficient when we are assigning. This property is true of all minimization problems. An important outcome of this property is that we will consider an $i - j$ for assignment only when the corresponding $C_{ij} = 0$ and we can consider any $i - j$ for assignment when the corresponding $C_{ij} = 0$.

Let us consider the same example problem. If resource person 4 changes the cost of performing the tasks to (5, 12, 10, 8), i.e., adds a constant (say, Rs. 2) to all the costs, the optimal solution to the problem will not change because the person has to get exactly one task and he (she) has increased the cost for all the jobs by the same constant. The value of the objective function, however, will change. The same will be true if the person reduced the cost to do all the jobs by the same constant. For example, if the costs were (1, 8, 6, 4), the same result would hold. The same result will also hold if all the persons increase the cost to do a specific job by the same constant. If the cost to do Job 1 becomes (6, 9, 7, 4) instead of (5, 8, 6, 3), the optimal solution does not change. If it becomes (3, 6, 4, 1), the same result will hold.

Property 2

If all the elements of a row or a column is increased or decreased by the same constant, the optimal solution to the assignment problem does not change. Only the value of the objective function changes.

The important outcome of this property is that we can subtract the row minimum and column minimum from every element of row and every column to get a reduced matrix that will be a non-negative coefficient matrix with zeros.

Using the two properties, we can try to solve the assignment problem optimally.

5.3 SOLVING THE ASSIGNMENT PROBLEM—HUNGARIAN ALGORITHM

For the cost matrix in Table 5.1, the row minimum in the four rows are 3, 2, 6 and 3, respectively. Subtracting these from the corresponding elements of the rows, we get the matrix in Table 5.2.

In Table 5.2, $C_{ij} \geq 0$ (since we subtracted the row minimum) and each row has at least one zero. The column minimum of the four columns are 0, 4, 0 and 0, respectively. Subtracting 4 from all the elements of Column 2 and retaining Columns 1, 3 and 4 (subtracting zero from the elements of these columns) results in Table 5.3.

We can make assignments in the zero cost positions in Table 5.3. One feasible solution with $Z = 0$ is $X_{13} = X_{24} = X_{32} = X_{41} = 1$. This solution is optimal with $Z = 3 + 2 + 10 + 3$ (from Table 5.1) = 18.

Table 5.2 Row Minimum Subtraction

2	6	0	3
6	5	6	0
0	4	6	1
0	7	5	3

Table 5.3 Column Minimum Subtraction

2	2	0	3
6	1	6	0
0	0	6	1
0	3	5	3

For a small problem such as our example, it is easy to find out the feasible solution by inspection. For large problems, it may not be easy. It is better to have a step-wise algorithm that is capable of identifying the feasible solution if one exists, and alternately being capable of identifying maximum number of assignments, if a feasible solution (with n assignments) does not exist.

Sometimes, an arbitrary choice may take us away from a feasible solution, even if one exists. For instance, if we had made an arbitrary choice of assigning $X_{31} = 1$, we cannot assign X_{13} and X_{41} (because every row and every column should have only one assignment) and we will get three assignments only (X_{13}, X_{24} and X_{31}) as against four possible assignments.

We proceed to explain a step-wise algorithm that attempts to obtain the maximum number of assignments in the matrix.

Procedure 5.1 Algorithm for allocation

Step 1: If a row or column has exactly one assignable zero, make the assignment. The other zeros in the corresponding column (or row) is not assignable.

Step 2: If a row or column has more than one assignable zero, do not make any assignment. Move to the next row or column and go to Step 1. Terminate when no assignment is possible.

Considering our example, applying Step 1 to Row 1, we assign $X_{13} = 1$ and by applying to Row 2 we assign $X_{24} = 1$. Row 3 has two assignable zeros and we temporarily ignore it. Row 4 has only one zero and we assign $X_{41} = 1$. This makes X_{31} unassignable. We can apply Step 1 to Column 2 or Row 3 and assign $X_{32} = 1$. Now we have obtained four assignments and the algorithm terminates. Since we have obtained a feasible solution

Table 5.4 Feasible Solution

2	2	0	3
6	1	6	0
0	0	6	1
0	3	5	3

with four assignments, we have reached the optimal solution. This is shown in Table 5.4.

The algorithm works similar to the Vogel's approximation method of the transportation problem. When a row or column has only one zero, there is a positive penalty for not assigning that zero, while there is a zero penalty when a row or column has more than one zero. We make the assignment when there is only one zero, because we do not want to incur a positive penalty. We temporarily ignore a row or column with multiple zeros because of zero penalty and the possibility that the corresponding column may incur a positive penalty by having only one zero. The only difference is that we do not quantify the penalty. The penalty is either zero or positive.

ILLUSTRATION 5.2

Let us consider a 5-job 5-machine assignment problem with the cost coefficients shown in Table 5.5.

We subtract the row minimum from every element of each row. The row minima are 6, 6, 4, 9 and 7, respectively. We get the matrix shown in Table 5.6 at the end of this operation.

The column minima for the five columns are 1, 0, 0, 2 and 3, respectively. Subtracting column minimum from every element of the columns, we get the matrix shown in Table 5.7.

Applying Procedure 5.1 to obtain initial set of assignments we assign $X_{12} = 1$ (Row 1 has only one zero). We cross X_{32}, X_{42} and X_{52} and make them unassignable. We assign $X_{23} = 1$ (Row 2 has only one zero). We leave Row 3 because it has two assignable zeros. Rows 4 and 5 do not have assignments because there is no assignable zero. Applying this procedure to the columns, we assign $X_{31} = 1$ and the procedure stops. We have three assignments and, therefore, we do not have a feasible solution. We also observe that every zero in the matrix is either assigned or crossed (not eligible for assignment).

Table 5.5 Data for Illustration 5.2

11	6	9	18	11
13	20	6	12	14
5	4	6	6	7
18	9	12	17	15
12	7	15	20	11

Table 5.6 Row Minimum Subtraction

5	0	3	12	5
7	14	0	6	8
1	0	2	2	3
9	0	3	8	6
5	0	8	13	4

Table 5.7 Column Minimum Subtraction

4	0	3	10	2
6	14	0	4	5
0	0	2	0	0
8	0	3	6	3
4	0	8	11	1

We define Procedure 5.2 that helps us verify whether we have reached the maximum number of assignments possible for the given non-negative cost matrix with at least one zero in every row and column having assignments.

Procedure 5.2 Determining the maximum number of assignments possible

Step 1: Tick all unassigned rows.

Step 2: If a row is ticked and has a zero then tick the corresponding column (if the column is not yet ticked).

Step 3: If a column is ticked and has an assignment then tick the corresponding row (if the row is not yet ticked).

Step 4: Repeat Steps 2 and 3 till no more ticking is possible.

Step 5: Draw lines through unticked rows and ticked columns. The number of lines represent the maximum number of assignments possible.

Applying Procedure 5.2, we tick Rows 4 and 5 (unassigned rows). We tick Column 2 (it has zero) and then tick Row 1 (assignment X_{12}). We draw lines through Rows 2 and 3 and Column 2 to get three ticks and the maximum assignments possible is three. This is shown in Table 5.8.

We now define Procedure 5.3 to create another matrix from Table 5.8 that when solved can yield a better solution (in terms of more assignments). Before we define Procedure 5.3, we realize that all zeros in Table 5.8 have lines passing through them. Some of them have only one line (either horizontal or vertical) while some have two lines (both horizontal and vertical) passing through them. Some non-zero numbers have no lines passing through them; some have one line and some have two lines passing through them.

Table 5.8 Illustration Procedure 5.2

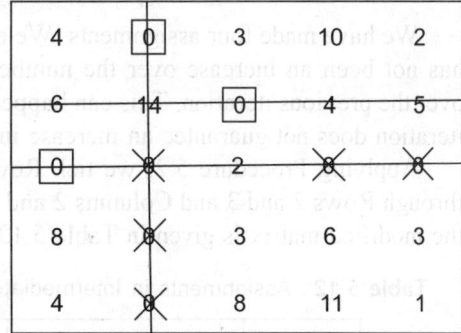

Procedure 5.3 Creating a new assignment matrix

1. Identify the minimum number (say θ) that have no lines passing through them.
2. Update the C_{ij} matrix using the following changes:
   $C_{ij} = C_{ij} - \theta$ if the number has no lines passing through it
   $C_{ij} = C_{ij}$ if the number has one line passing through it (No change)
   $C_{ij} = C_{ij} + \theta$ if the number has two lines passing through it

Identifying $\theta = 1$ and using Procedure 5.3, we obtain a new cost matrix shown in Table 5.9. Using Procedure 5.1, we make the following assignments:

$$X_{12} = X_{23} = X_{55} = X_{31} = 1$$

Using Procedure 5.2, we tick Rows 1 and 4 and Column 2. We draw lines through Rows 2, 3 and 5 and Column 2. We observe that the maximum number of assignments possible is 4 and we have made four assignments. We identify $\theta = 1$. This is shown in Table 5.10.

Table 5.9 Modified Cost Matrix

3	0	2	10	1
6	15	0	4	5
0	1	2	0	0
7	0	2	5	2
3	0	7	10	0

Table 5.10 Assignments in Intermediate Solution

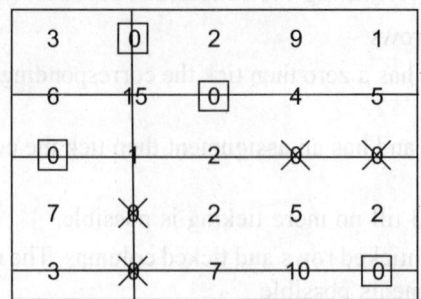

Applying Procedure 5.3, we obtain a new matrix given in Table 5.11.

Table 5.11 Reduced Cost Matrix

2	0	1	8	0
6	16	0	4	5
0	2	2	0	0
6	0	1	4	1
3	1	7	10	0

Applying Procedure 5.1, we obtain the following assignments:

$$X_{23} = X_{55} = X_{31} = X_{42} = 1$$

We have made four assignments. We observe that there has not been an increase over the number of assignments over the previous iteration. This can happen very frequently and we should understand that every iteration does not guarantee an increase in the number of iterations.

Applying Procedure 5.2, we tick Rows 1, 4 and 5 and Columns 2 and 5. We draw lines through Rows 2 and 3 and Columns 2 and 5. We identify $\theta = 1$. This is shown in Table 5.12 and the modified matrix is given in Table 5.13.

Table 5.12 Assignments in Intermediate Solution

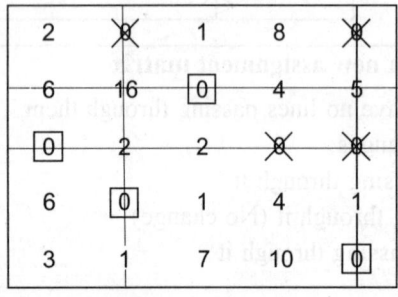

Table 5.13 Modified Matrix

1	0	1	7	0
6	17	0	4	5
0	3	2	0	0
5	0	0	3	0
2	1	6	9	0

Applying Procedure 5.1, we obtain the following assignments shown in Table 5.14.

We have made four assignments.

Applying Procedure 5.2, we tick Rows 4, 1, 2 and 5 and Columns 2, 3 and 5. We draw lines through Row 3 and Columns 2, 3 and 5. We identify $\theta = 1$. This is shown in Table 5.15 and the modified matrix is given in Table 5.16.

Applying Procedure 5.1, we make the following assignments shown in Table 5.16.

$$X_{23} = X_{55} = X_{34} = X_{42} = X_{11} = 1$$

We now have a feasible solution with five assignments and, therefore, the solution is optimal. The value of the objective function is:

$$6 + 11 + 6 + 9 + 11 = 43$$

Table 5.14 Assignments in Intermediate Solution

Table 5.15 Horizontal and Vertical Lines for the Solution in Table 5.14

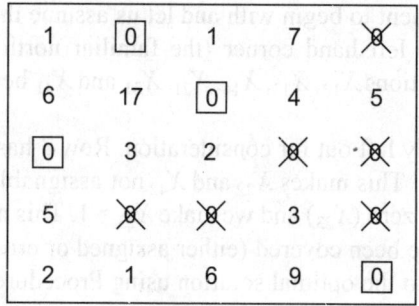
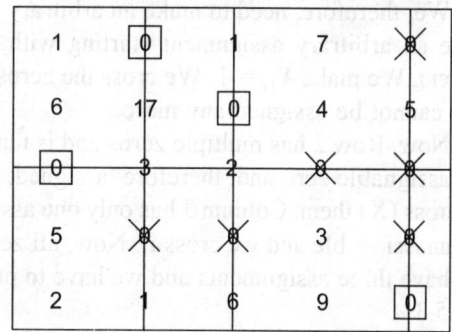

Table 5.16 Optimal Solution

[0]	✗	✗	6	✗
5	17	[0]	3	4
✗	4	2	[0]	✗
✗	[0]	✗	3	✗
1	1	6	8	[0]

The above algorithm is called the **Hungarian Algorithm** (Kuhn, 1954) and is the most widely used algorithm to solve the assignment problem. This algorithm has a polynomial time complexity $O(n^3)$. Better algorithms have been subsequently developed but this algorithm is the most popular and is easy to understand and implement.

ILLUSTRATION 5.3

Let us consider the problem with cost coefficients shown in Table 5.17.

Subtracting the row minimum (1, 2, 3 and 2) from all elements of Rows 1, 2, 3 and 4, respectively, we get Table 5.18. Subtracting the column minimum (2, 0, 0, 3) from all elements of Columns 1, 2, 3 and 4, respectively, we get Table 5.19.

Table 5.17 Cost Matrix

3	1	1	4
4	2	2	5
5	3	4	8
4	2	5	9

Table 5.18 Row Minimum Subtraction

2	0	0	3
2	0	0	3
2	0	1	5
2	0	3	7

Table 5.19 Column Minimum Subtraction

0	0	0	0
0	0	0	0
0	0	1	2
0	0	3	4

Let us apply Procedure 5.1 for allocation. We realize that all the rows and columns have more than one zero and the procedure terminates without making any assignment. In order to apply

Procedure 5.2 to identify the maximum assignments possible, we need a matrix where all zeros are either assigned (□) or covered (X).

We, therefore, need to make an arbitrary assignment to begin with and let us assume that we make an arbitrary assignment starting with the top left hand corner (the familiar north west corner). We make $X_{11} = 1$. We cross the zeros at positions $X_{12}, X_{13}, X_{14}, X_{21}, X_{31}$ and X_{41} because they cannot be assigned any more.

Now, Row 2 has multiple zeros and is temporarily left out for consideration. Row 3 has only one assignable zero and, therefore, assigned; $X_{32} = 1$. This makes X_{22} and X_{42} not assignable and we cross (X) them. Column 3 has only one assignable zero (X_{23}) and we make $X_{23} = 1$. This makes X_{24} unassignable and we cross it. Now, all zeros have been covered (either assigned or crossed). We have three assignments and we have to proceed to the optimal solution using Procedures 5.2 and 5.3.

Let us apply Procedure 5.2 to obtain the minimum number of lines that covers all the zeros (indicating maximum possible assignments).

1. Row 4 is ticked first (unassigned row).
2. Columns 1 and 2 are ticked (they have zeros in positions 4, 1 and 4, 2).
3. Rows 1 and 3 are ticked next because Columns 1 and 2 have assignments (positions 1, 1 and 3, 2)
4. Columns 3 and 4 are ticked because positions 1, 3 and 1, 4 have zeros.
5. Row 2 is ticked because Column 3 has an assignment in position 2, 3.
6. The algorithm terminates since all rows and columns are ticked.
7. Four vertical lines are drawn (through all ticked columns) and there are no horizontal lines (all rows are ticked and there are no unticked rows).

The four lines indicate that four feasible assignments are possible while we have obtained only three using Procedure 5.2. We are unable to continue with Procedure 5.3 towards the feasible solution because we do not have minimum θ. All the numbers in the matrix have lines passing through them and we do not have any number in the matrix that has no lines passing through it.

It is also obvious by inspection that a feasible solution $X_{14} = X_{23} = X_{32} = X_{41} = 1$ exists which is optimal with $Z = 4 + 2 + 3 + 4 = 13$.

It may be noted that in this example, Procedure 5.2 gave us three assignments while a maximum of four was possible. We also observe that once Procedure 5.2 indicates a maximum of n assignments, it is not possible to use Procedure 5.3 to get to the feasible (optimal) solution. In this example, Procedure 5.2 resulted is less than the maximal assignment because we made an arbitrary choice ($X_{11} = 1$). For example, if we had arbitrarily chosen X_{14} instead of X_{11} we would have reached the optimum using Procedure 5.2.

We can encounter situations where we have Procedure 5.3 which indicates a maximum of n lines (n assignments) while Procedure 5.2 has less assignments. We advice that in such situations we try to identify the feasible (optimal solution) by inspection even though procedures exist to find out the extra assignments (Yaspan, 1974).

5.4 ADDITIONAL POINTS

1. Unless otherwise stated, the assignment problem is a minimization problem. However, we can formulate and solve assignment problems with maximization objective. The

easiest way to approach the maximization objective is to convert it to a minimization problem by multiplying the cost coefficients by −1 and by solving the resulting minimization problem.

2. The assignment problem usually has a square matrix with n jobs to be assigned to n resources. Sometimes we may have fewer resources (rows) or fewer jobs (columns). In these cases, we make the matrix square by creating additional dummy rows or dummy columns depending on whether we have fewer rows or columns. For example, if the problem has four rows and six columns, we convert it to a 6 × 6 problem by adding two dummy rows. If it is a 7 × 5 problem, we create two additional dummy columns. The dummies rows and columns have zero cost.

3. Sometimes we may have situations where a particular job j may not be performed by resource i. In such cases, we put $C_{ij} = M$ (where M is large, positive and tends to infinity) in the minimization problem and then proceed.

5.5 THE OPTIMALITY OF THE HUNGARIAN ALGORITHM

Using the two illustrations (5.1 and 5.2) let us show how the Hungarian algorithm yields the optimal solution. To do this, let us define the dual of the assignment problem. Let the dual variables be u_i and v_j for the row and column feasibility constraints. The dual is:

$$\text{Maximize} \sum_{i=1}^{m} a_i u_i + \sum_{j=1}^{n} b_j v_j$$

Subject to

$$u_i + v_j \le C_{ij} \quad i = 1,\ldots,n \text{ and } j = 1,\ldots,n$$

u_i, v_j unrestricted in sign

Let us consider Illustration 5.1 and explain the optimality of the Hungarian algorithm. Assign values $u_1 = 3$, $u_2 = 2$, $u_3 = 6$ and $u_4 = 3$, where 3, 2, 6 and 3, respectively are the row minima that we subtracted from the rows. Let us assign values $v_1 = 0$, $v_2 = 4$, $v_3 = 0$ and $v_4 = 0$, where 0, 4, 0 and 0 are the column minima values that we subtracted from the elements of the columns.

We observe that the values of u and v that we have defined is a feasible solution to the dual. These values satisfy the dual constraints $u_i + v_j \le C_{ij}$ because they are the row and column minima respectively and, therefore, ≥ 0. Assuming that the original C_{ij} matrix has all elements non-negative, the initial values of u_i and $v_j \ge 0$. In any case they are unrestricted in sign and we need not consider their sign at all.

The resultant matrix that we obtain after subtracting the row and column minima has cost coefficients $C'_{ij} = C_{ij} - u_i + v_j \ge 0$. We make assignments where the cost coefficient in the resultant C'_{ij} matrix is zero, which means that wherever we make assignments, $C'_{ij} = C_{ij} - u_i + v_j = 0$. $C_{ij} - u_i + v_j$ represents the dual slack and since we make assignments such that the dual slack is zero, we are satisfying complementary slackness conditions. Therefore, the moment we reach a feasible solution (to the primal) we have reached the optimal solution.

The Hungarian algorithm is an example of a dual algorithm, where the algorithm always has a feasible solution to the dual; satisfies complimentary conditions and reaches optimal when the primal is feasible. Another example of dual algorithm is the dual simplex algorithm.

Let us look at a situation as in Illustration 5.2, where we are not able to get the optimal solution in a single iteration. The row minima and column minima are 6, 6, 4, 9, 7 and 1, 0, 0, 2 and 3, respectively. We now have a feasible solution to the dual with $u_1 = 6$, $u_2 = 6$, $u_3 = 4$, $u_4 = 9$, $u_5 = 7$, $v_1 = 1$, $v_2 = 0$, $v_3 = 0$, $v_4 = 2$ and $v_5 = 3$. In this case, we get only four assignments using Procedure 5.1, which is not optimal, and we use Procedure 5.2 and Procedure 5.3 to obtain a new table after identifying $\theta = 1$. The correct identification of $\theta = 1$ ensures that the resultant table is non-negative.

The steps outlined in Procedure 5.3 to compute C'_{ij} can be explained as follows:

We redefine

$u_i = u_i + \theta$ (if Row i is ticked and, therefore, does not have a line)
$u_i = u_i$ (No change if row has a line)
$v_j = v_j - \theta$ (if Column j is ticked and, therefore, has a line passing through it)
$v_j = v_j$ (No change otherwise)

We can easily show that the new matrix has $C'_{ij} = C_{ij} - u_i + v_j$ where C_{ij} is the original cost coefficient and u_i and v_j are the newly defined values. We also observe that $C'_{ij} \geq 0$ and negative values of u_i and v_j are acceptable because by their definition they are unrestricted in sign.

We also understand that since the new values of u_i and v_j are obtained by adding or subtracting a constant to the old values, we can accept that the new cost matrix is obtained by adding or subtracting a constant consistently from every element of a row and/or column of the original cost coefficient. Therefore, the matrix of C'_{ij} will give the optimal solution to the assignment problem.

5.6 THE AUCTION ALGORITHM FOR ASSIGNMENT PROBLEM

We discuss the auction algorithm for the Assignment Problem (Bertsekas 1990). We explain the concepts for a minimization assignment problem, which we are familiar with. We can modify the Auction Algorithm for a maximization assignment problem suitably.

The Assignment problem is given by

Minimize $\sum_{i=1}^{n} \sum_{j=1}^{n} C_{ij} X_{ij}$

Subject to $\sum_{j=1}^{n} X_{ij} = 1$ for every i

$\sum_{i=1}^{n} X_{ij} = 1$ for every j

$X_{ij} = 0, 1$

The dual of the assignment problem is given by

Maximize $\sum_{i=1}^{m} u_i + \sum_{j=1}^{n} v_j$

Subject to
$$u_i + v_j \leq C_{ij}\ i = 1, n \text{ and } j = 1, n$$

u_i, v_j unrestricted in sign.

Let us consider that n people have given bids for n projects where C_{ij} is the bid or cost of assigning project j to person i. If v_j is the reward or value of project j and is known, the u_i values will be such that

$$u_i = \underset{j}{\text{Minimum}} \{C_{ij} - v_j\}$$

We also know that at the optimum, the complimentary slackness conditions are satisfied. Therefore, if there is an assignment, then

$$u_i + v_j = C_{ij} \text{ from which } v_j - C_{ij} = -u_i = \underset{k}{\text{Maximum}} \{v_k - C_{ik}\}$$

We can now interpret that project k carries a reward v_k and C_{ik} is the cost incurred by person i to do the project. Therefore $v_k - C_{ik}$ indicated the profit for the project and the person should get the most profitable project and bids for it.

Given a starting value for the project, each person will bid for the most profitable project. If a project gets multiple bids, it is given to the lowest bidder. Once a person is allotted a project, the value now becomes the bid price. The unallocated person will now try to bid for a lower price and will try to get a project. The reduction in the bid is logically the difference between the most profitable project and the next most profitable project. The bidding process continues till every person gets the most profitable project (for the current value of the bid prices).

We explain the algorithm using a simple example:

ILLUSTRATION 5.4

Consider the assignment problem with cost coefficients shown in Table 5.20.

Table 5.20 Cost Data

4	6	9
8	2	5
3	4	4

Let the initial prices (v_j) be 9 for each project. We can take the largest among the C_{ij} to be the initial high price (or value).

Let us call the three people as $M_i\ i = 1, 3$ and the projects as jobs $J_j\ j = 1, 3$.

The price and the bid values are shown in Table 5.21.

Table 5.21 Price and Bid Value

	J_1	J_2	J_3	Remarks
Price v_j	9	9	9	
$v_j - C_{ij}$ for M_1	5	3	0	
$v_j - C_{ij}$ for M_2	1	7	4	
$v_j - C_{ij}$ for M_3	6	5	5	
M_1				Bids for J_1 at $9 - (5 - 3) = 7$
M_2				Bids for J_2 at $9 - (7 - 4) = 6$
M_3				Bids for J_1 at $9 - (6 - 5) = 8$

Now J_1 has two bidders and J_1 goes to M_1 (lower bid), while J_2 goes to M_2. The prices (v_j) are now adjusted to 7, 6 and 9 respectively. M_3 is unassigned. We computed the bid values for M_3. These are
$$v_j - C_{3j} = 4, 2, 5.$$
M_3 bids for J_3 at price $9 - (5 - 4) = 8$ and gets it. Now, all persons and projects are assigned. The algorithm terminates with the assignments $M_1 - J_1$, $M_2 - J_2$ and $M_3 - J_3$ with total minimum cost = 10.

The v_j values at the optimum are 7, 6 and 8 while the u_i values are given by $C_{ij} - v_j = -3$, -4 and -4 with total $= 7 + 6 + 8 - 3 - 4 - 4 = 10$.

The auction algorithm described above can have termination issues. We explain this using another example.

ILLUSTRATION 5.5

Consider the assignment problem with cost coefficients shown in **Table 5.22** Cost Data Table 5.22.

Let the initial prices (v_j) be 9 for each project. We can take the largest among the C_{ij} to be the initial high price (or value).

Let us call the four people as M_i $i = 1, 4$ and the projects as jobs J_j $j = 1, 4$.

4	5	2	6
2	2	4	6
3	3	8	7
3	7	9	6

The price and the bid values are shown in Table 5.23.

Table 5.23 Price and Bid Value

	J_1	J_2	J_3	J_4	Remarks
Price v_j	9	9	9	9	
$v_j - C_{ij}$ for M_1	5	4	7	3	
$v_j - C_{ij}$ for M_2	7	7	5	3	
$v_j - C_{ij}$ for M_3	6	6	1	2	
$v_j - C_{ij}$ for M_3	6	2	0	3	
M_1					Bids for J_3 at $9 - (7 - 5) = 7$
M_2					Bids for J_1 at $9 - (7 - 7) = 9$
M_3					Bids for J_1 at $9 - (6 - 6) = 9$
M_4					Bids for J_1 at $9 - (6 - 3) = 6$

Projects J_1 and J_3 have received bids. J_3 is assigned to M_1 and J_1 is assigned to M_4 (lowest bid). The prices (v_j) values become 6, 9, 7, 9 respectively and M_2 and M_3 do not have projects. The computations in the second iteration are shown in Table 5.24.

Table 5.24 Second Iteration

	J_1	J_2	J_3	J_4	Remarks
Price v_j	6	9	7	9	
$v_j - C_{ij}$ for M_2	4	7	3	3	
$v_j - C_{ij}$ for M_3	3	6	-1	2	
M_2					Bids for J_2 at $9 - (7 - 4) = 6$
M_3					Bids for J_2 at $9 - (6 - 3) = 6$

J_2 has received two equal bids and therefore can be given to either of them. We break the tie arbitrarily by assigning J_2 to M_2. The prices (v_j) values become 6, 6, 7, 9 respectively and M_3 does not have a project.

For the new values of v_j, the values of $v_j - C_{3j}$ are computed.

$v_j - C_{3j}$ values are 3, 3, -1, 2. M_3 will bid for J_1 (say) at price $= 6 - (3 - 3) = 6$ and gets it. The prices remain unchanged but M_4 does not have a project.

For the new values of v_j, the values of $v_j - C_{4j}$ are computed.

$v_j - C_{4j}$ values are 3, -1, -2, 3. M_4 will bid for J_1 (say) at price $= 6 - (3 - 3) = 6$ and gets it. The prices remain unchanged but M_3 does not have a project. This can result in a situation where we get into an infinite loop and we are unable to terminate.

(The above assignment problem has a unique solution $X_{13} = X_{22} = X_{31} = X_{44} = 1$ with $Z = 13$. Therefore any arbitrary tie breaking rule should give us the unique optimum).

This is overcome by using an ε-complimentary slackness condition by which the price for which a person bids the most profitable project is reduced further by a small ε. We continue the place where the prices are 6, 6, 7, 9 respectively and M_3 does not have a project.

For the new values of v_j, the values of $v_j - C_{3j}$ are computed.

$v_j - C_{3j}$ values are 3, 3, -1, 2. M_3 will bid for J_1 (say) at price $= 6 - (3 - 3) - \varepsilon = 6 - \varepsilon$ and gets it. The prices now become $6 - \varepsilon$, 6, 7, 9 respectively and M_4 does not have a project. For the new values of v_j, the values of $v_j - C_{4j}$ are computed.

$v_j - C_{4j}$ values are $3 - \varepsilon$, -1, -2, 3. M_4 will bid for J_4 at price $= 6 - (3 - 3) - \varepsilon = 6 - \varepsilon$ and gets it. The allocations are $M_1 - J_3$, $M_2 - J_2$, $M_3 - J_1$ and $M_4 - J_4$ with total value of $u_i + v_j = 13 - 2\varepsilon$.

Therefore the ε-complementary slackness criterion leads to an ε-optimal algorithm. However, if we later approximate ε to zero after the algorithm terminates, we get the same solution.

There can be another interesting situation when we apply the ε-complementary slackness algorithm. We explain this using Example 5.8.

Value of ε and complexity issues (Bertsimas and Tsitsiklis 1997)

- The auction algorithm with the ε-complimentary slackness conditions terminates in a finite number of iterations. The algorithm will terminate when all projects are allotted. For a project not to be allotted there has always to be another project that is more profitable. This would receive an infinite number of bids, which means that its price will tend to $-\infty$. Therefore the unassigned project will be profitable and will be assigned.

- If all the C_{ij} are integer valued and if $0 < \varepsilon < 1$, it can be shown that the auction algorithm with the ε-complimentary slackness conditions terminates with the optimal solution.

The Auction Algorithm for the assignment Problem

1. Set $p_j = \max \{C_{ij}\}$ for each project j.
2. Compute profit $t_{ij} = p_j - C_{ij}$ for all unassigned person i for each project j. Person i bids for project j where $p_j - C_{ij}$ is maximum. The bid value is $p_j - k - \varepsilon$ where k is the difference between the maximum profit and the next highest profit (It is equal to zero when there is more than one value of the maximum profit) and ε is a small value.
3. Assign a project to a bidder if there is only one bidder. If a project has more than one bidder assign to the lowest bidder. If the project has been earlier assigned to another person, make the person unassigned because the project is now given to the new bidder. Replace p_j by the new bid value.
4. Repeat Steps 2 and 3 till all people and all projects are assigned.

SOLVED EXAMPLES

EXAMPLE 5.1 M/s Cow and Calf Dairies makes three types of milk products. They owns three plants, one of which is to be selected for each product. Tables 5.25 and 5.26 give the estimated processing costs and distribution costs per unit of each product processed at each plant:

Table 5.25 Unit Processing Costs (Rs./Litre)

Plant / Product	I	II	III
Standard milk	5.50	5.00	6.00
Flavoured milk	6.00	7.00	6.50
Yogurt	6.50	6.00	7.00

Table 5.26 Unit Distribution Costs (Rs./Litre)

Plant / Product	I	II	III
Standard milk	1.00	2.00	1.00
Flavoured milk	0.50	1.00	1.30
Yogurt	0.60	0.50	0.80

Table 5.27 shows the daily production of each product and the selling prices:

Table 5.27 Daily Production and Selling Price of Products

Product	Planned production (Litres)	Planned price (Rs./Litre)
Standard milk	8000	13.00
Flavoured milk	5000	18.00
Yogurt	2000	20.00

Formulate this problem as an assignment problem to maximize total profit. Find the optimal solution and the profit associated with it.

Solution: There are three products and three plants to produce them. The expected profit if product i is made in plant j is given by

Profit = Planned production × (Planned price$_i$ − Processing cost$_{ij}$ − Distribution cost$_{ij}$)

The profit matrix (in thousands) is as shown in Table 5.23. A sample calculation would look like

$$\text{Profit}_{11} = \text{Volume} \times (\text{Price} - \text{Production cost} - \text{Distribution cost})$$
$$= 8000 \times (13 - 5.5 - 1) = 52,000$$

The problem is to maximize the total profit and, therefore, the negative of the values are taken and a minimization problem is solved. Table 5.28 shows the profit matrix for a maximization problem. Table 5.29 shows data for a minimization problem.

Table 5.28 Profit Matrix

52	48	48
57.5	50	51
25.8	27	24.4

Table 5.29 Data for a Minimization Problem

-52	-48	-48
-57.5	-50	-51
-25.8	-27	-24.4

Subtracting row minimum from every row and column minimum, we get the reduced matrix shown in Table 5.30.

After one iteration we will get the optimal solution. The optimum assignments are: $X_{13} = X_{21} = X_{32} = 1$ with $Z = 1,32,500$.

Table 5.30 Reduced Matrix

0	4	1.4
0	7.5	3.9
1.2	0	0

EXAMPLE 5.2 A parent has to spend on his son's education for the next four years. He has four investments that can be used to meet the requirement for the next four years. These are:

(a) The parent can borrow from his provident fund that would earn 10% interest (compounded annually).
(b) He has a fixed deposit that earns 6% interest per annum compounded semiannually.
(c) He has another deposit that gives him 6.5% interest compounded annually. This is available to meet the third year requirement. It can earn a further 5% for the next year if unutilized.
(d) Investments in post office that earn 8% simple interest that can be used from years 2 onwards.

Formulate an assignment problem to maximize the total return assuming that one investment is used each year. Assume that the amount invested (or available) at the beginning is the same for all the investment alternatives.

Solution: Let us assume that we are at the beginning of year 1, and we have to calculate the amount that Rs. 1000 can get in the remaining three years for the four alternatives. Alternative 1 would get 1.1, 1.1^2 and 1.1^3. Alternative 2 would get 1.03^2, 1.03^4 and 1.03^6 in the next three years. Alternative 3 would get 1.06^2 at the beginning of the third year and $1.06^2 \times 1.05$ at the beginning of the fourth year. It cannot be used for the first two years. Alternative 4 would get 1.08, 1.16 and 1.24 at the beginning of years 2, 3 and 4 and is not available for use at the beginning of year 1.

The profit matrix is shown in Table 5.31.

This is a maximization problem and we take the negative of the values and compute the reduced matrix by subtracting row and column minima. This is given in Table 5.32.

The optimal assignments are $X_{14} = X_{21} = X_{33} = X_{42} = 1$ with $Z = 1331 + 1000 + 1134 + 1080 = 4545$

Table 5.31 Profit Matrix

1000	1100	1210	1331
1000	1061	1125	1267
-M	-M	1134	1191
-M	1080	1160	1240

Table 5.32 Reduced Matrix

64	71	64	0
0	46	85	0
M	M	0	0
M	0	23	0

EXAMPLE 5.3 The official of the Trainpur Railway Station has to decide on assigning diesel locomotives to train services. Investment on diesel locos is heavy. Hence the railways, as a policy, try to keep the idle time of the diesel locos to the barest minimum—a way of maximizing their utilization. The official realizes the implication of this: Allocate locos of arriving trains to departing trains in such a way that the total time spent by the locos at the Trainpur Station is a minimum. This is subject to the constraint that each locomotive should have a gap of at least 2 hours between arrival and departure for refuelling. Timings of the relevant train services are given in Table 5.33.

Table 5.33 Timing of the Train Services

Train number	Departure (Hours)	Arrival (Hours)
2243/2244	09.45	16.45
2429/2430	21.00	06.00
6033/6034	12.00	12.00
5033/5034	22.15	05.15
2651/2652	18.30	08.30
6021/6022	07.30	13.30

Solution: There are six locos to be assigned to six trains. The waiting time when loco i is assigned to train j is the difference between the departure time of train j and the arrival time of loco i. If the difference is less than 2 hours, it is assumed that it leaves the next day and, therefore, 24 hours is added to the waiting time. The assignment cost matrix is given in Table 5.34.

Table 5.34 Assignment Cost Matrix

	1	2	3	4	5	6
1	17	4.25	19.25	5.5	25.75	14.75
2	3.75	15	6	16.25	12.5	25.5
3	21.75	9	24	10.25	6.5	19.5
4	4.5	15.75	6.75	17	13.25	2.25
5	25.25	12.5	3.5	1.75	10	23
6	20.25	7.5	22.5	8.75	5	18

EXAMPLE 5.4 Airking airlines, operates flights on all seven days in a week between two cities (Mumbai and Delhi) according to the schedule shown in Table 5.35. The layover cost per stop is roughly proportional to the square of the layover time. There should be at least one hour difference between an arrival and a departure. How should the planes be assigned (paired) so as to minimize the total layover cost?

Solution: The problem is formulated as a minimization problem. The cost matrix is a 12 × 12 matrix where planes go from Mumbai to Delhi and back to Mumbai. The cost is defined as the square of the layover time (which is the difference between the departure and arrival). When the arrival and departure times are the same it is assumed that there is a gap of 24 hours between the arrival and the departure, because it violates the minimum layover condition. The cost matrix is shown in Table 5.36.

Table 5.35 Schedule of Flights

Flight No.	From	Time of departure	To	Arrival time
1	Mumbai	6.00 am	Delhi	8.00 am
2	Mumbai	7.00 am	Delhi	9.00 am
3	Mumbai	10.00 am	Delhi	12.00 noon
4	Mumbai	2.00 pm	Delhi	4.00 pm
5	Mumbai	6.00 pm	Delhi	8.00 pm
6	Mumbai	8.00 pm	Delhi	10.00 pm
7	Delhi	6.00 am	Mumbai	8.00 am
8	Delhi	8.00 am	Mumbai	10.00 pm
9	Delhi	11.00 am	Mumbai	1.00 pm
10	Delhi	3.00 pm	Mumbai	5.00 pm
11	Delhi	6.00 pm	Mumbai	8.00 pm
12	Delhi	9.00 pm	Mumbai	11.00 pm

Table 5.36 Cost Matrix

	1	2	3	4	5	6	7	8	9	10	11	12
1							484	576	9	49	100	169
2							441	529	4	36	81	144
3							324	400	529	9	36	81
4							196	256	361	529	4	25
5							100	144	225	361	484	1
6							64	100	169	289	400	529
7	484	529	4	36	100	576						
8	400	441	576	16	64	100						
9	289	324	441	1	25	49						
10	169	196	289	441	1	9						
11	100	121	196	324	484	576						
12	49	64	121	225	361	441						

We can solve the 12×12 problem as it is by adding a M for the other undefined cost values. The problem can be solved as two assignment problems of size 6×6 each. We adopt the second approach to solve the problem. The assignments are:

$X_{1,9} = X_{2,10} = X_{3,11} = 1; X_{4,12} = X_{5,7} = 1; X_{6,8} = X_{7,3} = X_{8,4} = X_{9,5} = X_{10,6} = X_{11,1}, X_{12,2} = 1$

From the assignments, the corresponding pairings are made.

EXAMPLE 5.5 Consider the data of Table 5.35. If a crew based in Mumbai arrives at Delhi on a given flight, it must return to Mumbai on a later flight. Assume that for any given pairing, the crew will be based in the city that results in the smaller layover. The problem is to find the pairings so as to minimize the time on ground away from home, subject to a minimum interval of one hour between arrival and departure. Given the pairs of flights, where should the crews be based?

Solution: We construct two 6 × 6 matrices for the layover time, one for layover in Mumbai and the other for Delhi. These are shown in Table 5.37 and Table 5.38, respectively.

Table 5.37 Layoff in Mumbai

	1	2	3	4	5	6
7	22	23	2	6	10	24
8	20	21	24	4	8	10
9	17	18	21	1	5	7
10	13	14	17	21	1	3
11	10	11	14	18	22	24
12	7	8	11	15	19	21

Table 5.38 Layoff in Delhi

	7	8	9	10	11	12
1	22	24	3	7	10	13
2	21	23	2	6	9	12
3	18	20	23	3	6	9
4	14	16	19	23	2	5
5	10	12	15	19	22	1
6	8	10	13	17	20	23

It is to be noted that Table 5.38 is constructed for layoff in Delhi. Here, the difference between the departure time and arrival times of flights at Delhi are computed. We now compute the minimum of the values for the 36 pairs and construct Table 5.39. Here the transpose of the matrix in Table 5.38 have to be included. The values taken from Table 5.38 are shown in italics.

The assignment problem for minimizing the values in Table 5.39 is solved and the solution is to pair 7–3, 8–4, 9–2, 10–5, 11–6, 12–1. The values are 2 (Mumbai), 4 (Mumbai), 2 (Delhi), 1 (Mumbai), 1 (Delhi) and 8 (Delhi). This means that pairs 7–3, 8–4, 9–2, 10–5, 11–6, 12–1 will have layoffs in Mumbai, Mumbai, Delhi, Mumbai, Delhi, Delhi, respectively. They will be based at Delhi, Delhi, Mumbai, Delhi, Mumbai, Mumbai, respectively. The total layoffs is equal to 18 hours.

Table 5.39 Minimum Values from Tables 5.37 and 5.38

	1	2	3	4	5	6
7	22	21	2	6	10	8
8	20	21	20	4	8	10
9	3	2	21	1	5	7
10	7	6	3	21	1	3
11	10	8	5	1	22	1
12	8	10	7	3	20	21

EXAMPLE 5.6 Given the assignment cost matrix shown in Table 5.40, find the maximal assignment.

Solution: Subtracting row and column minima, we get the reduced matrix shown in Table 5.41.

We have two or more zeros in every row and column. We start with an arbitrary assignment X_{12}. We later assign X_{31} and X_{23}. We have made three assignments. When we draw lines, we observe that four lines are possible indicating that four assignments are possible. In fact, an obvious solution $X_{14} = X_{23} = X_{32} = X_{41} = 1$ (by inspection has four assignments and is optimal).

We also realize that fewer assignments than lines happen when we make an arbitrary choice somewhere during the assignments. Also in such cases, when we are able to get a feasible (optimal) solution, we observe that there is alternate optimum. While it is easy to identify one feasible solution by inspection, can we have a procedure (that can be coded) that can get us all the assignments?

Table 5.40 Assignment Matrix

6	2	2	4
6	4	4	6
7	5	6	9
7	5	8	9

Table 5.41 Reduced Matrix

2	0	0	0
0	0	0	0
0	0	1	2
0	0	3	2

Yaspan (1966) developed a procedure that starts with a set of assignments and checks for the maximal assignment and gets it. The procedure is:

(a) Tick an unassigned column.
(b) If there ia a zero in a ticked column, label the row with the designation of the column.
(c) Label the unlabelled columns if there is an assignment in a labelled row. Use the row designation.
(d) Repeat till no more labelling is possible.
(e) Find a row with no assignment having a column with a label.
(f) Make an assignment and remove the existing assignment in the column.
(g) Continue till one extra assignment is made. Repeat the entire procedure.

If we apply this to our example, we start by ticking Column 4. Rows 1 and 2 get label 4. Columns 2 and 3 get labels 1 and 2, respectively. Row 3 gets label 2 and Column 1 gets label 3.

Row 4 has no label but Column 1 has a label. We assign X_{41}. This means that $X_{31} = 0$. Row 3 has label 2 and we assign X_{32}. This means that $X_{12} = 0$. Row 1 has label 4 and we assign $X_{14} = 1$. We have made one extra assignment and now have four assignments. An optimal solution is $X_{14} = X_{23} = X_{32} = X_{41} = 1$.

EXAMPLE 5.7 Four parts have to be assigned to four machines. All the four machines can do all the jobs but one job is to be assigned to one machine and one machine should get one job. The time taken by the machines in minutes is given in Table 5.42. If the parts have to be assembled after machining and assembly takes 10 minutes, find the earliest time the assembly is completed?

Table 5.42 Time Taken by Machines

16	9	8	14
12	8	9	13
12	5	4	10
9	10	12	7

Solution: We solve an assignment problem by the Hungarian algorithm to get the solution $X_{13} = X_{21} = X_{32} = X_{44} = 1$ with $Z = 32$. This is the cheapest solution if we consider the total cost of assignment. This would also mean that the parts can start getting assembled after 12 minutes (the assembly can start only when all parts have been completed). Clearly, we are not interested in minimizing the total time taken to make all the parts but want to minimize the maximum among the assigned times.

We now have to verify whether the maximum time can be brought to less than 12 units. To do this, we replace all costs ≥ 12 with M (big M) indicating that we do not want assignments there and solve the resultant problem. This gives us the solution $X_{13} = X_{22} = X_{34} = X_{41} = 1$ with $Z = 35$. Here, the total time has increased but the maximum has reduced to 10 minutes.

We wish to verify if there can be a solution where the maximum is 9 minutes. Theoretically the possibility exists because such a solution can have a maximum value of 36 which is higher than the present optimum value of 35. The possibility of the maximum being 8 is ruled out (Why?).

We now replace all costs of 10 and 11 in the matrix with a M and solve the resultant assignment problem. This would give us an infeasible solution. The best value, therefore, is a maximum of 10 units with a total time of 35 minutes.

(The problem that we have solved is called **bottleneck assignment problem** or **minimax assignment problem** where by solving a series of assignment problems we try and minimize the maximum among the assigned).

EXAMPLE 5.8 Consider the assignment problem with cost coefficients shown in Table 5.43. Solve using the auction algorithm with the ε complimentary slackness conditions.

Table 5.43 Cost Data

2	2	3
2	2	3
2	2	3

Solution: Let us assume that the prices are 3, 3, and 3 respectively. Let us assume that J_1 has been allotted to M_1 and J_2 has been allotted to M_2. Now M_3 does not have a project allotted.

$v_j - C_{3j}$ values are 1, 1, 0. Person M_3 bids for J_1 with price $3 - \varepsilon$ and gets it. The prices are now $3 - \varepsilon$, 3, 3 and M_1 does not have a project.

$v_j - C_{1i}$ values are $1 - \varepsilon$, 1, 0. Person M_1 bids for J_2 with price $3 - (1 - \varepsilon) - \varepsilon = 3 - 2\varepsilon$ and gets it. The prices are now $3 - \varepsilon$, $3 - 2\varepsilon$, 3 and M_2 does not have a project.

$v_j - C_{2i}$ values are $1 - \varepsilon$, $1 - 2\varepsilon$, 0. Person M_2 bids for J_1 with price $3 - (1 - \varepsilon - 1 + 2\varepsilon) - \varepsilon = 3 - 3\varepsilon$ and gets it. The prices are now $3 - 3\varepsilon$, $3 - 2\varepsilon$, 3 and M_3 does not have a project.

The process is repeated as all the three bids for projects J_1 and J_2 bringing down the price by 2ε in every iteration. If ε tends to zero, we have a situation where we can get into an infinite loop.

We overcome this situation by assuming that as the number of iteration increases, in some kth iteration (k is large), $3 - k\varepsilon < 0$ and hence it will be profitable to one of them to bid for J_3 with a profit of zero than bid for J_1 or J_2 with a negative profit. The algorithm will then terminate with the optimal solution.

EXAMPLE 5.9 Shankar has three positions to fill and has four candidates. He has assessed the suitability of the candidates to the positions (in a scale of 10) and solves an assignment problem (maximization). Here, the rows are the positions and the columns are the people. The fourth row is a dummy row. An intermediate iteration is shown in Table 5.44

Table 5.44 Intermediate Iteration

1	2	0	3
3	5	7	0
0	0	0	1
0	0	1	0

(a) Find the optimal allocation?
His boss now introduces a fourth position and Shankar is asked to consider the same four candidates for the positions. The suitability of the new candidate to the four positions is [6 3 9 5].
(b) Solve the assignment problem with four candidates optimally. Does the allocation change with the introduction of the new candidate?

Solution: The table given is an intermediate table with the fourth row as the dummy row. An optimal solution is $X_{13} = X_{24} = X_{31} = X_{42} = 1$.

Let the dual variables associated with the solution be $[u_1 \; u_2 \; u_3 \; u_4]$ and $[v_1 \; v_2 \; v_3 \; v_4]$ respectively.

In the original problem, the fourth row is a dummy row and should have costs zero. Therefore $u_4 = 0$. The only way C_{43} can be 1 in the optimal table, is if $v_3 = -1$.

One set of possible values for the dual variables are [0 0 0 0] and [0 0 –1 0].

If we replace the dummy row with the row [–6 –3 –9 –5], the equivalent row considering the dual variables would be $C'_{ij} = C_{ij} - (u_i + v_j)$ and is equal to [–6 –3 –8 –5]. Now u_4 becomes –8 and the row becomes [2 5 0 3]. The assignment matrix is shown in Table 5.45.

Table 5.45 Assignment Matrix

1	2	0	3
3	5	7	0
0	0	0	1
2	5	0	3

The optimal solution after one iteration is $X_{11} = X_{24} = X_{32} = X_{43} = 1$ and the allocations are different.

CASE STUDY 5.1: The Fountain Pen Company

The Fountain pen Company makes eight different varieties of gel pens. The manufacture and assembly is a three stage process involving two or three different types of machines depending on the product. There are five machine types that are used to make these products. The requirement in terms of the machines that the eight products visit are given in Table 5.46.

Table 5.46 Machine Requirement for Eight Products

	P1	P2	P3	P4	P5	P6	P7	P8
M1	1	0	1	0	1	0	0	1
M2	0	1	0	1	0	0	0	1
M3	1	1	0	1	0	1	1	0
M4	0	0	1	1	0	1	0	0
M5	1	0	0	0	1	1	1	1

Mr. Ahmed, the production manager, wishes to reorganize the manufacturing system by grouping the products. He wishes to group similar products together to form four groups of two products each. Each product group is to be assigned to a cell that will have the machines required to make both the products. He has five supervisors and wishes to assign four of them to the four cells that are to be formed.

Anil Titus, a newly recruited graduate engineer, is given the task of forming the product groups and allocating supervisors. Anil explains to Mr. Ahmed that the grouping problem is a difficult problem to solve and believes that the assignment method can be used effectively to provide good solutions. He defines a dissimilarity (or distance) index between products i and j as

$$d_{ij} = \sum_{k=1}^{m} |(a_{ik} - a_{jk})|$$

(Based on the above equation $d_{12} = 2$ and $d_{14} = 4$).

Anil computes the dissimilarity matrix (8 × 8 matrix) and solves an assignment problem using the matrix and creates four groups from the assignment solution.

Anil asks the five supervisors to give four choices of the products that they wish to supervise. The data are shown in Table 5.47.

Table 5.47 Choices of Supervisors

	First choice	Second choice	Third choice	Fourth choice
Supervisor 1	1	2	3	4
Supervisor 2	2	5	7	8
Supervisor 3	1	4	5	6
Supervisor 4	2	6	7	8
Supervisor 5	1	3	5	7

Anil decides that after forming the part groups, he would add the corresponding preference for the group for each supervisor and assign them to the manufacturing cells. He wishes to give weights of 4, 3, 2 and 1 to the four preferences. For example, if products 1 and 3 are grouped, the preference of supervisor 1 to this group is $4 + 2 = 6$ out of 10. If there were a group with products 6 and 8, the preference value of supervisor 2 for this group would be $0 + 1 = 1$.

Mr. Ahmed prefers that Supervisor 5 should not be allotted to the manufacturing cell where product 3 is made and also wishes to find out if it really has to be implemented. He is also worried that this decision should not be the reason for the particular supervisor to be left out. He also wishes to allot the supervisors in such a way that the supervisor preferences in the solution are as close to each other as possible. This way he believes that no particular individual would be given a group which was least preferred.

EXERCISES

5.1 The Drinkhot breweries have stocks of five equally sized lots of whisky of different ages buried underground on 1st of January in the years 1986, 1988, 1990, 1991 and 1992, respectively. These five lots have to be taken out for storage for future sales in the next five years starting 1st January 2006. The expected profit function of the distiller is given in Table 5.48.

Assuming that a lot once unearthed has to be taken out in full, formulate an assignment model and solve it to maximize the profit for Drinkhot breweries.

Table 5.48 Expected Profit Function

Age of whisky	Expected profit
1	2000
2	4000
3	7000
4	11,000
5	16,000
6	22,000
7	30,000
8	36,000
9	41,000
10	45,000
11	48,000
12 and above	51,000

5.2 A newly formed greenandblue.com company has recruited two project managers, Ajay and Vijay. This company has five projects each located in different cities. They want to assign them to the five projects such that one gets three projects and the other gets two projects. Since it involves constant travel the company wants to ensure that the

Table 5.49 Distances among the Five Cities

–	7	6	7	8
7	–	10	9	7
6	10	–	11	8
7	9	11	–	9
8	7	8	9	–

distance they travel as they monitor the projects is minimum. The distances among the five cities are given in Table 5.49.

(You may assume that the distance between a city and itself is M)

If Ajay and Vijay have slightly different capabilities and the expected profit when manager i is assigned to project j is as given in Table 5.50, assign the managers to projects. What is the expected profit to the company?

Table 5.50 Capability Matrix

10	8	6	12	10
12	10	8	10	8

5.3 The Turret engineering company has five operators assignable to five lathes. The number of parts that can be produced by operator i (row) on machine j (column) is given in Table 5.51.
Each operator has to be allotted to only one machine and each machine is allotted to only one operator. Each operator gets Rs. 10 per piece produced.

Table 5.51 Number of Parts Produced

18	20	25	30	34
17	21	27	32	38
21	26	33	37	32
19	22	29	35	40
22	26	29	34	39

(a) The operators want to assign themselves to machines and decide to share the maximum possible revenue equally. What is the solution to the problem?

(b) If the company allots operators progressively to machines based on maximum individual profit, what is the solution to the problem? Is it advantageous to the operators? Why?

(c) The company wants to maximize production (quantity) but the operators are not agreeable to share the profits equally. Each operator makes his money but they want to balance the earnings. They want to minimize the difference between the maximum and minimum earnings. Would the total profit increase or decrease? Can you suggest a way to solve this problem?

5.4 Five students reach the railway station in their home town and want to travel to their respective homes in autorickshaws. Each person approaches a rickshaw driver and finds out the charge for the five destinations from him. Table 5.52 denotes the charges.

Table 5.52 Charges for Five Destinations

80	90	40	60	30
40	70	50	80	50
40	90	70	60	60
80	40	60	50	50
70	80	60	60	60

(a) Find out the total charge if the students use the optimal assignment solution?

(b) If the drivers decide not to accept a passenger if he gets less than Rs. 40, what happens to the optimal solution?

5.5 The selling price of wine depends on the age and price as given in Table 5.53.

Table 5.53 Selling Price of Wine

Age	1	2	3	4	5	6	7	8	9	10
price	30	34	37	40	43	45	47	49	51	52

Five bottles of wine have been buried in years 1997, 1999, 2000, 2001 and 2002 for use in years 2003, 2004, 2005, 2006 and 2007. Find the appropriate allocation of wine to time that maximizes profit.

5.6 A company wants to subcontract four subassemblies to four people. The cost matrix for subcontractor i to take subassembly j is given in Table 5.54.

The time taken by subcontractor i to do subassembly j is given in Table 5.55.

Table 5.54 Cost Matrix for Subcontractor

6	5	4	9
8	6	5	9
8	10	13	11
9	8	14	12

(a) What is the least cost assignment?
(b) If the final product can start only after all the subassemblies are completed, when can it start [for solution (a)]?
(c) Is it possible to start the assembly earlier than in (b)? If so when and at what increased cost?

Table 5.55 Time Taken by Subcontractor

9	3	2	4
9	2	1	2
10	7	6	5
11	5	7	6

5.7 Ramesh, Naresh, Suresh and Ganesh, final year students of engineering wish to pursue graduate study in Operations Research in USA. Each of them has chosen to apply four different universities and decided to submit the application forms with the help of four seniors. Four seniors have come down from USA and are going back on 20, 25, 28 and 31 December, respectively. The seniors can take 4, 4, 5 and 5 forms, respectively while each final year student wants to send exactly four forms. The deadlines for the forms of student i to reach his chosen university is given in Table 5.56.

Table 5.56 Deadlines for the Forms

Jan 5	Jan 10	Jan 10	Jan 31
Jan 10	Jan 15	Jan 20	Jan 21
Jan 10	Jan 31	Feb 15	Feb 28
Jan 5	Jan 10	Jan 15	Jan 20

The students want to send the forms through the seniors so that sum of the squares of the earliness is maximized.

(a) A senior can take forms of more than one student and a student can give forms to more than one senior. Formulate a transportation/assignment problem to determine the number of forms taken by each senior.
(b) If all the four forms of a student goes to only one senior, find the optimal solution. (Assume that the forms will reach the university within 3 days of the senior leaving India)

5.8 You are given an intermediate iteration of an assignment problem (Table 5.57).

(a) Starting with the assignment $X_{22} = 1$, complete the rest of the possible assignments.

Proceed with your solution in (a) to get the optimal solution. (Use the algorithm explained in Example 5.6)

Table 5.57 Cost Matrix in an Intermediate Iteration

0	0	3	8
5	0	0	1
3	0	4	0
2	1	3	0

5.9 A political party wants to assign four campaign managers to four constituencies. A matrix of expected number of votes (in tenths of thousands) if manager i is assigned to constituency j is given in Table 5.58.

Provide a solution to the party to maximize the votes.

The party wants to keep up its reputation and, therefore, wants to ensure that each manager gets at least a certain minimum amount in every constituency j. Describe a methodology to solve the problem to maximize the minimum amount.

Table 5.58 Matrix of Expected Number of Votes

8	9	2	10
3	4	10	12
2	4	12	15
12	12	4	3

5.10 Six jobs have to be assigned to four people. All the jobs have to be assigned. A person can get not more than two jobs. The cost matrix of assigning jobs to people is given in Table 5.59. Formulate and solve an assignment problem for the above situation.

Table 5.59 Cost Matrix of Assigning Job

8	7	12	15	9	6
9	7	11	18	11	7
10	9	14	16	12	6
8	10	10	19	10	8

5.11 Let us revisit Problem 2.20 where four boys wish to socialize with four girls on a holiday. The "happiness" that boy i gets per hour of socializing with girl j is given in the matrix in Table 5.60. Formulate a linear programming problem where the decision variable is the proportion of the available time boy i spends with girl j, and the objective function is to maximize "total happiness". Does this problem reduce to an assignment problem (or a marriage problem), where a boy spends all the time with only one girl?

Table 5.60 Matrix of Happiness

6	7	10	3
6	5	4	8
2	9	3	3
8	5	2	4

5.12 Five classes (A to E) have to be assigned to five classrooms (P to T). The class sizes are 40, 60, 50, 50 and 30, respectively, and the classroom capacities are 50, 60, 40, 60 and 50, respectively. Classroom T does not have a projection facility while class E requires a projection facility. It is necessary to meet the capacity requirements. The distance that students of classes A to E have to walk from their earlier class to the rooms (P to T) are shown in Table 5.61. Solve an assignment problem to minimize distance travelled.

Table 5.61 Distance Matrix

10	13	12	14	16
8	10	9	8	7
21	23	22	24	26
14	12	10	16	12
9	6	10	11	8

5.13 Cell and Co. have recently created a new manufacturing cell and have to allot operators to work on the machines in the cells. The requirement is five operators to operate the five machines in the cell, and they have a pool of three experienced operators (A, B and C), and four new operators (D, E, F and G). Operator D cannot operate the first machine in the cell. The cost associated with allotting operators to cells is as shown in Table 5.62.

Table 5.62 Cost Associated with Alloting Operators to Cells

10	21	14	–	17	10	9
12	23	13	22	18	11	7
13	22	12	21	14	12	8
9	26	15	26	19	13	10
11	25	14	25	12	12	6

(a) Solve an assignment problem that allots operators to machines that minimizes total cost.

(b) If at least two experienced operators have to be allocated, what happens to the solution?
(c) If all the experienced operators have to be included, what happens to the assignments?

5.14 A school wishes to train their six top students to get 100% in the Mathematics examination. Three maths teachers are available and the number of hours that teacher i estimates to spend to train student j to get 100% is given in Table 5.63. All the students have to be trained and a professor can take more than one student if required.

Table 5.63 Time Spent to Train Students

15	20	18	14	10	20
18	14	16	15	18	19
21	12	23	14	18	19

5.15 Five students have to be allotted to three professors for their project work. All the students have to be allotted a guide. The first two professors are willing to take two students each while the third professor is willing to take only one student. The preference given by the students (in a scale of 10) is shown in Table 5.64.

Solve an assignment problem for this situation.

Table 5.64 Preferences Given by the Students

6	4	6	5	7
7	5	8	6	5
6	5	8	7	5

Advanced Linear Programming

In this chapter we concentrate on variations that make simplex algorithm run faster. We also address Goal Programming, where we use linear programming tools to handle multiple objectives. We begin by studying the computational aspects of the simplex algorithm.

6.1 HOW GOOD IS THE SIMPLEX METHOD?

We have seen how the simplex method can be used to solve linear programming problems. The next thing to do is to understand how good it is to solve linear programming problems. We expect two attributes from the simplex algorithm. These are:

1. Speed—The algorithm should be able to solve the problem fast.
2. Memory—The storage (memory) requirements (on a computer) should be less.

The speed of the simplex algorithm depends on two aspects:

1. Time taken per iteration
2. Number of iterations

6.1.1 Time Taken Per Iteration

The following are the steps of the simplex algorithm:

1. Solving for a given set of basic variables. This involves inversion of the basis matrix.
2. Verifying whether the computed solution is optimal. This involves calculating the $C_j - Z_j$ values of the non-basic variables.
3. Identifying the entering and leaving variables.
4. Repeating Steps 1–3 until the algorithm terminates.

Among the above steps the matrix inversion is the most time consuming activity. This also depends on the number of constraints. Considerable effort has gone in efficiently inverting the basis matrix. The matrix method that we described earlier is called the **revised simplex algorithm** and is used extensively in practice instead of the tabular form, which is very good only for illustrating the algorithm.

The revised simplex algorithm can be developed with many different forms of matrix inversions and we will learn the product form of the inverse in this chapter.

6.1.2 Efficient Ways to Invert the Basis Matrix

The tabular method of the simplex algorithm uses the Guass Jordan method to invert the basis. Here, the row and column operations are such that the basis matrix is premultiplied by its inverse to get an identity matrix in the columns corresponding to the basic variables.

ILLUSTRATION 6.1

Consider the following example:
Maximize $Z = 6X_1 + 8X_2$
Subject to

$$X_1 + X_2 \leq 10$$
$$2X_1 + 3X_2 \leq 25$$
$$X_1 + 5X_2 \leq 35$$
$$X_1, X_2 \geq 0$$

The final iteration is shown in Table 6.1.

Table 6.1 Final Iteration of the Simplex Algorithm

		6	8	0	0	0		
		X_1	X_2	X_3	X_4	X_5	RHS	θ
0	X_5	0	0	7	–4	1	5	
6	X_1	1	0	3	–1	0	5	
8	X_2	0	1	–2	1	0	5	
	$C_j - Z_j$	0	0	–2	–2	0	70	

The basic variables are X_5, X_1 and X_2 and we are solving for the equations.

$$BX_B = b$$

$$\begin{bmatrix} 0 & 1 & 1 \\ 0 & 2 & 3 \\ 1 & 1 & 5 \end{bmatrix} \begin{bmatrix} X_5 \\ X_1 \\ X_2 \end{bmatrix} = \begin{bmatrix} 10 \\ 25 \\ 35 \end{bmatrix}$$

In the simplex iterations, we perform row and column operations such that the columns under the basic variables are reduced to columns of an identity matrix (in the order of appearance of the variables) from which the solution can be read. In this Gauss Jordan method, we reduce the matrix to an identity matrix so that we can read the solution directly. This method is commonly used in all tabular versions of the simplex algorithm.

Gaussian elimination

Consider solving the set of equations:

$$BX_B = b$$

$$\begin{bmatrix} 0 & 1 & 1 \\ 0 & 2 & 3 \\ 1 & 1 & 5 \end{bmatrix} \begin{bmatrix} X_5 \\ X_1 \\ X_2 \end{bmatrix} = \begin{bmatrix} 10 \\ 25 \\ 35 \end{bmatrix}$$

Here, we perform row operations so as to reduce the matrix to a lower triangular (or upper triangular matrix).
Replace Row 1 by Row 3 − Row 1. We get

$$\begin{bmatrix} 1 & 0 & 4 \\ 0 & 2 & 3 \\ 1 & 1 & 5 \end{bmatrix} \begin{bmatrix} X_5 \\ X_1 \\ X_2 \end{bmatrix} = \begin{bmatrix} 25 \\ 25 \\ 35 \end{bmatrix}$$

Replace Row 3 by Row 1 − Row 3 and divide by −1 to get

$$\begin{bmatrix} 1 & 0 & 4 \\ 0 & 2 & 3 \\ 1 & 1 & 1 \end{bmatrix} \begin{bmatrix} X_5 \\ X_1 \\ X_2 \end{bmatrix} = \begin{bmatrix} 25 \\ 25 \\ 10 \end{bmatrix}$$

Replace Row 3 by Row 2 − 2 Row 3 to get

$$\begin{bmatrix} 1 & 0 & 4 \\ 0 & 2 & 3 \\ 0 & 0 & 1 \end{bmatrix} \begin{bmatrix} X_5 \\ X_1 \\ X_2 \end{bmatrix} = \begin{bmatrix} 25 \\ 25 \\ 5 \end{bmatrix}$$

Replace Row 1 by Row 1 − 4 Row 3 to get

$$\begin{bmatrix} 1 & 0 & 0 \\ 0 & 2 & 3 \\ 0 & 0 & 1 \end{bmatrix} \begin{bmatrix} X_5 \\ X_1 \\ X_2 \end{bmatrix} = \begin{bmatrix} 5 \\ 25 \\ 5 \end{bmatrix}$$

We have an upper triangular matrix. Representing as equations, we get

$$X_5 = 5,\ 2X_1 + 3X_2 = 25 \text{ and } X_2 = 5$$

which by substitution gives us the solution $X_1 = X_2 = X_5 = 5$.

This method called **Gaussian elimination** can be implemented in a faster way than implementing Gauss Jordan method to solve linear equations or to invert a matrix. Let us explain the simplex algorithm using the product form of the inverse.

Product form of inverse

We consider the earlier example and illustrate the matrix method using the product form of the inverse.

Maximize $Z = 6X_1 + 8X_2$
Subject to

$$X_1 + X_2 \leq 10$$
$$2X_1 + 3X_2 \leq 25$$
$$X_1 + 5X_2 \leq 35$$
$$X_1, X_2 \geq 0$$

We add slack variables X_3, X_4 and X_5 to convert the inequalities into equations and start the simplex iterations using the slack variables as the set of basic variables. The set of basic variables

$$X_B = \begin{bmatrix} X_3 \\ X_4 \\ X_5 \end{bmatrix}$$

$$C_B = [0\ 0\ 0]$$

The values that these variables take are 10, 25 and 35, respectively. The basis matrix is given by

$$B_0 = \begin{bmatrix} 1 & 0 & 0 \\ 0 & 1 & 0 \\ 0 & 0 & 1 \end{bmatrix} = I$$

We also have $B_0^{-1} = I$.

We find out y such that $yB_0 = C_B = [0\ 0\ 0]$. This gives us $y = [0\ 0\ 0]$.

To verify whether the present solution is optimal, we find out $C_j - Z_j$ for the non-basic variables X_1 and X_2.

$$C_1 - Z_1 = C_1 - yP_1 = 6 - [0\ 0\ 0]\begin{bmatrix} 1 \\ 2 \\ 1 \end{bmatrix} = 6$$

$$C_2 - Z_2 = 8$$

Variable X_2 enters the basis because it has maximum positive $C_j - Z_j$.

To find the leaving variable, we have to find out minimum θ such that

$$\text{RHS} - \theta P_2' \geq 0$$
$$10 - \theta \geq 0$$
$$25 - 3\theta \geq 0$$
$$35 - 5\theta \geq 0.$$

The minimum value of θ is 7 and the variable X_5 leaves the basis. Variable X_2 replaces X_5 in the basis. The objective function coefficients corresponding to X_B, given by $C_B = [0\ 0\ 8]$. The new set of basic variables is:

$$X_B = \begin{bmatrix} X_3 \\ X_4 \\ X_2 \end{bmatrix} = \begin{bmatrix} 3 \\ 4 \\ 7 \end{bmatrix}$$

The value of the objective function is:

$$C_B X_B = [0\ 0\ 8]\begin{bmatrix} 3 \\ 4 \\ 7 \end{bmatrix} = 56$$

It may be observed that the value of the entering variable in the solution is the value of minimum θ while the existing basic variables will have their values adjusted using the minimum θ.

The basis matrix B corresponding to X_B made from the columns of the variables in X_B from the coefficient matrix A is given by

$$B_1 = \begin{bmatrix} 1 & 0 & 1 \\ 0 & 1 & 3 \\ 0 & 0 & 5 \end{bmatrix}$$

We can show that $B_1 = B_0 E_1$ where E_1 is called **eta matrix**, and is given by

$$E_1 = \begin{bmatrix} 1 & 0 & 1 \\ 0 & 1 & 3 \\ 0 & 0 & 5 \end{bmatrix}$$

The eta matrix is an identity matrix where one column is correspondingly replaced by the entering column of the simplex method. Here variable X_2 enters and variable X_5 leaves. X_5 was occupying the third position as basic variable. Entering column replaced the third column of the identity matrix.

We try to find y such that $yB_1 = C_B = [0 \ 0 \ 8]$

$$yB_0 E_1 = [0 \ 0 \ 8]; \ yE_1 = [0 \ 0 \ 8]$$

$$[y_1 \ y_2 \ y_3] \begin{bmatrix} 1 & 0 & 1 \\ 0 & 1 & 3 \\ 0 & 0 & 5 \end{bmatrix} = [0 \ 0 \ 8]$$

By substitution, we get $y = [0 \ 0 \ 8/5]$

To verify whether the present solution is optimal, we find out $C_j - Z_j$ for the non-basic variables X_1 and X_5.

$$C_1 - Z_1 = C_1 - yP_1 = 6 - [0 \ 0 \ 8/5] \begin{bmatrix} 1 \\ 2 \\ 1 \end{bmatrix} = 6 - 8/5 = 22/5$$

$$C_5 - Z_5 = C_5 - yP_5 = 0 - [0 \ 0 \ 8/5] \begin{bmatrix} 0 \\ 0 \\ 1 \end{bmatrix} = -8/5$$

Variable X_1 enters the basis because it has maximum positive $C_j - Z_j$.

To find the leaving variable, we have to first find the coefficients of the entering column corresponding to the entering variable. We call this as P_1' given by

$$B_1 P_1' = P_1; \ B_0 E_1 P_1' = P_1$$

$$\begin{bmatrix} 1 & 0 & 1 \\ 0 & 1 & 3 \\ 0 & 0 & 5 \end{bmatrix} \begin{bmatrix} a \\ b \\ c \end{bmatrix} = \begin{bmatrix} 1 \\ 2 \\ 1 \end{bmatrix}$$

By substitution, we get

$$P_1 = \begin{bmatrix} 4/5 \\ 7/5 \\ 1/5 \end{bmatrix}$$

We now find out minimum θ such that

$$\text{RHS} - \theta P_1' \geq 0$$

$$3 - \frac{4}{5}\theta \geq 0$$

$$4 - \frac{7}{5}\theta \geq 0$$

$$7 - \frac{1}{5}\theta \geq 0$$

The minimum value of θ is 20/7 and the variable X_4 leaves the basis. Variable X_1 replaces X_4 in the basis. The objective function coefficients corresponding to X_B, given by $C_B = [0\ 6\ 8]$. The new set of basic variables is:

$$X_B = \begin{bmatrix} X_3 \\ X_1 \\ X_2 \end{bmatrix} = \begin{bmatrix} 3 - 4/5 \times 20/7 \\ 20/7 \\ 7 - 1/5 \times 2/7 \end{bmatrix} = \begin{bmatrix} 5/7 \\ 20/7 \\ 45/7 \end{bmatrix}$$

The value of the objective function is:

$$C_B X_B = [0\ 6\ 8] \begin{bmatrix} 5/7 \\ 20/7 \\ 45/7 \end{bmatrix} = \frac{480}{7}$$

It may be observed that the value of the entering variable in the solution is the value of minimum θ while the existing basic variables will have their values adjusted using the minimum θ.

The basis matrix B corresponding to X_B made from the columns of the variables in X_B from the coefficient matrix A is given by

$$B_2 = \begin{bmatrix} 1 & 1 & 1 \\ 0 & 2 & 3 \\ 0 & 1 & 5 \end{bmatrix}$$

Corresponding to the basic variables the objective function coefficients are $C_B = [0\ 6\ 8]$. We find the values of the dual variables y such that $yB_2 = C_B$.
B_2 can be written as $B_1 E_2$ where E_2 is an eta matrix, given by

$$E_2 = \begin{bmatrix} 1 & 4/5 & 0 \\ 0 & 7/5 & 0 \\ 0 & 1/5 & 1 \end{bmatrix}$$

Substituting for B_1, we get

$$B_2 = B_0 E_1 E_2 = E_1 E_2$$

We have
$$yE_1E_2 = [0\ 6\ 8]$$
We write yE_1 as u and find u such that $uE_2 = [0\ 6\ 8]$

$$[u_1\ u_2\ u_3]\begin{bmatrix} 1 & 4/5 & 0 \\ 0 & 7/5 & 0 \\ 0 & 1/5 & 1 \end{bmatrix} = [0\ 6\ 8]$$

By substitution, we get $u = [0\ 22/7\ 8]$. We now find y such that $yE_1 = u = [0\ 22/7\ 8]$.

$$[y_1\ y_2\ y_3]\begin{bmatrix} 1 & 0 & 1 \\ 0 & 1 & 3 \\ 0 & 0 & 5 \end{bmatrix} = [0\ 22/7\ 8]$$

By substitution, we get $y = [0\ 22/7\ -2/7]$. To verify whether the present solution is optimal, we find out $C_j - Z_j$ for the non-basic variables X_4 and X_5.

$$C_4 - Z_4 = C_4 - yP_4 = 0 - [0\ 22/7\ -2/7]\begin{bmatrix} 0 \\ 1 \\ 0 \end{bmatrix} = -22/7$$

$$C_5 - Z_5 = C_5 - yP_5 = 0 - [0\ 22/7\ -2/7]\begin{bmatrix} 0 \\ 0 \\ 1 \end{bmatrix} = 2/7$$

Variable X_5 enters the basis because it has maximum positive $C_j - Z_j$. To find the leaving variable, we have to first find the coefficients of the entering column corresponding to the entering variable. We call this as P_5' given by

$$P_5' = B_2^{-1} P_5 \quad \text{or} \quad B_2 P_5' = P_5$$

Substituting for B_2, we get

$$B_0 E_1 E_2 P_5' = P_5$$

$$E_1 E_2 P_5' = \begin{bmatrix} 0 \\ 0 \\ 1 \end{bmatrix}$$

We call $E_2 P_5'$ as v and find v such that $E_1 v = P_5$

$$\begin{bmatrix} 1 & 0 & 1 \\ 0 & 1 & 3 \\ 0 & 0 & 5 \end{bmatrix}\begin{bmatrix} v_1 \\ v_2 \\ v_3 \end{bmatrix} = \begin{bmatrix} 0 \\ 0 \\ 1 \end{bmatrix}$$

By substitution, we get

$$v = \begin{bmatrix} -1/5 \\ -3/5 \\ 1/5 \end{bmatrix}$$

From $E_2P_5 = v$, we get

$$\begin{bmatrix} 1 & 4/5 & 0 \\ 0 & 7/5 & 0 \\ 0 & 1/5 & 1 \end{bmatrix} \begin{bmatrix} a \\ b \\ c \end{bmatrix} = \begin{bmatrix} -1/5 \\ -3/5 \\ 1/5 \end{bmatrix}$$

Substituting, we get

$$P_5' = \begin{bmatrix} 1/7 \\ -3/7 \\ 2/7 \end{bmatrix}$$

We now find out minimum θ such that

$$\text{RHS} - \theta P_1' \geq 0$$

$$\frac{5}{7} - \frac{1}{7}\theta \geq 0$$

$$\frac{20}{7} + \frac{3}{7}\theta \geq 0$$

$$\frac{45}{7} - \frac{2}{7}\theta \geq 0$$

The minimum value of θ is 5 and the variable X_3 leaves the basis. Variable X_5 replaces X_3 in the basis. The objective function coefficients corresponding to X_B, given by $C_B = [0\ 6\ 8]$. The new set of basic variables is:

$$X_B = \begin{bmatrix} X_5 \\ X_1 \\ X_2 \end{bmatrix} = \begin{bmatrix} \theta \\ 20/7 + 3/7\theta \\ 45/7 - 2/7\theta \end{bmatrix} = \begin{bmatrix} 5 \\ 5 \\ 5 \end{bmatrix}$$

The value of the objective function is:

$$C_B X_B = [0\ 6\ 8] \begin{bmatrix} 5 \\ 5 \\ 5 \end{bmatrix} = 70$$

It may be observed that the value of the entering variable in the solution is the value of minimum θ while the existing basic variables will have their values adjusted using the minimum θ.

The basis matrix B corresponding to X_B made from the columns of the variables in X_B from the coefficient matrix A is given by

$$B_3 = \begin{bmatrix} 0 & 1 & 1 \\ 0 & 2 & 3 \\ 1 & 1 & 5 \end{bmatrix}$$

We have to find y such that $yB_3 = C_B = [0\ 6\ 8]$. We can write $B_3 = B_2 E_3$ where E_3 is an eta matrix given by

$$E_3 = \begin{bmatrix} 1/7 & 0 & 0 \\ -3/7 & 1 & 0 \\ 2/7 & 0 & 1 \end{bmatrix}$$

(The first column is the entering column because the first basic variable leaves. The rest of the columns are as in the identity matrix.)

Substituting, we have

$$yB_0 E_1 E_2 E_3 = [0\ 6\ 8]$$
$$yE_1 E_2 E_3 = [0\ 6\ 8]$$

We write $yE_1 E_2$ as w and find w such that $wE_3 = [0\ 6\ 8]$

$$[w_1\ w_2\ w_3] \begin{bmatrix} 1/7 & 0 & 0 \\ -3/7 & 1 & 0 \\ 2/7 & 0 & 1 \end{bmatrix} = [0\ 6\ 8]$$

By substitution, we get $w = [2\ 6\ 8]$. We write yE_1 as u and find u such that $uE_2 = w$

$$[u_1\ u_2\ u_3] \begin{bmatrix} 1 & 4/5 & 0 \\ 0 & 7/5 & 0 \\ 0 & 1/5 & 1 \end{bmatrix} = [2\ 6\ 8]$$

Substituting, we get $u = [2\ 2\ 8]$. We find y such that $yE_1 = u$

$$[y_1\ y_2\ y_3] \begin{bmatrix} 1 & 0 & 1 \\ 0 & 1 & 3 \\ 0 & 0 & 5 \end{bmatrix} = [2\ 2\ 8]$$

$$y = [2\ 2\ 0]$$

To verify whether the present solution is optimal, we find out $C_j - Z_j$ for the non-basic variables X_3 and X_4.

$$C_3 - Z_3 = C_3 - yP_3 = 0 - [2\ 2\ 0] \begin{bmatrix} 1 \\ 0 \\ 0 \end{bmatrix} = -2$$

$$C_4 - Z_4 = C_4 - yP_4 = 0 - [2\ 2\ 0] \begin{bmatrix} 0 \\ 1 \\ 0 \end{bmatrix} = -2$$

Since both the $C_j - Z_j$ are negative, there is no entering variable and the algorithm terminates. The optimal solution is $X_1 = X_2 = 5$ with $Z = 70$.

We have seen the implementation of the reverse simplex algorithm using the product form of the inverse. It is observed from computational experiments that the time taken per iteration using this method is lesser compared to the simplex tableau (Gauss Jordan implementation) for problems involving more than a few hundred constraints. As the problem size (number of constraints) increases, this method is preferred and widely used in computer implementations. Also, faster methods of matrix inversion are used for different characteristics of bases matrices. Matrix inversion is the most time consuming portion of the iteration and decides the speed per iteration of the simplex algorithm. In fact, the tabular form of simplex is used only for classroom learning, and the computer programmes use the revised simplex algorithm in matrix form using advanced methods for matrix inversion.

6.2 SIMPLEX ALGORITHM FOR BOUNDED VARIABLES

Consider the following linear programming problem:

ILLUSTRATION 6.2

Maximize $Z = 8X_1 + 3X_2$
Subject to

$$3X_1 + X_2 \leq 7$$
$$2X_1 - X_2 \leq 8$$
$$2X_1 + 3X_2 \leq 20$$
$$X_1, X_2 \geq 0$$

Let us solve this problem by the simplex algorithm after introducing slack variables X_3, X_4, X_5, respectively. The simplex iterations are shown in Table 6.2.

Table 6.2 Simplex Iterations

		8	3	0	0	0		
		X_1	X_2	X_3	X_4	X_5	RHS	θ
0	X_3	3	1	1	0	0	7	7/3
0	X_4	2	−1	0	1	0	8	4
0	X_5	2↑	3	0	0	1	20	10
	$C_j - Z_j$	8	3	0	0	0	0	
8	X_1	1	1/3	1/3	0	0	7/3	7
0	X_4	0	−5/3	−2/3	1	0	10/3	--
0	X_2	0	7/3↑	−2/3	0	1	46/3	46/7
	$C_j - Z_j$	0	1/3	−8/3	0	0	56/3	
8	X_1	1	0	3/7	0	−1/7	1/7	
0	X_4	0	0	−8/7	1	5/7	100/7	
3	X_2	0	1	−2/7	0	3/7	46/7	
	$C_j - Z_j$	0	0	−18/7	0	−1/7	146/7	

The optimal solution to the problem is $X_1 = 1/7$, $X_2 = 46/7$ and $Z = 146/7$.

If we choose to add two constraints to the problem $X_1 \leq 2$ and $X_2 \leq 6$ to the above linear programming problem, normally we would be including the two additional constraints and would solve a five constraint linear programming problem.

If we observe the new constraints closely, we observe that they are not explicit constraints but are bounds on the variables. These are upper bound constraints. They need not be explicitly treated as constraints. We can solve the problem as a three-constraint problem by separating the bounds. We first explain an algebraic method to solve the problem, and generalize the simplex algorithm to include bounds.

6.2.1 Algebraic Method

The given problem is:

Maximize $Z = 8X_1 + 3X_2$

Subject to

$$3X_1 + X_2 \leq 7$$
$$2X_1 - X_2 \leq 8$$
$$2X_1 + 3X_2 \leq 20$$

We have the non-negativity restrictions $X_1, X_2 \geq 0$ and the bounds $X_1 \leq 2$ and $X_2 \leq 6$. We add slack variables X_3, X_4 and X_5 to the three constraints and start the solution using the three slack variables. We have

$$X_3 = 7 - 3X_1 - X_2$$
$$X_4 = 8 - 2X_1 + X_2$$
$$X_5 = 20 - 2X_1 - 3X_2$$

and
$$Z = 8X_1 + 3X_2$$

The present solution is $X_3 = 7$, $X_4 = 8$ and $X_5 = 20$ with $Z = 0$. To increase Z we can increase X_1 or X_2 and we choose X_1 because it has a larger coefficient. From the first constraint X_1 can be increased to 7/3 beyond which X_3 will become negative. From the second, X_1 can be increased to 4 beyond which X_4 becomes negative. From the third constraint X_1 can be increased to 10 beyond which X_5 becomes negative.

Normally, we would find the minimum value, which is $X_1 = 7/3$ and X_1 would replace X_3. In this problem, we observe that the minimum value 7/3 exceeds the bound of 2. We, therefore, let X_1 take value 2. Due to this X_3 is forced to take value 1 and is not non-basic anymore. We now have a situation where both X_1 and X_3 are basic but X_1 is at its upper bound value.

We express $X_1 = 2 + X_1^*$ indicating that X_1 is non-basic but at its upper bound value (X_1^* is non-basic with zero value). We rewrite the equations as:

$$X_3 = 7 - 3(2 + X_1^*) - X_2 = 1 - 3X_1^* - X_2$$
$$X_4 = 8 - 2(2 + X_1^*) + X_2 = 4 - 2X_1^* + X_2$$
$$X_5 = 20 - 2(2 + X_1^*) - 3X_2 = 16 - 2X_1^* - 3X_2$$
$$Z = 8(2 + X_1^*) + 3X_2 = 16 + 8X_1^* + 3X_2$$

In order to increase Z further, we can increase X_1^* or X_2. We can't increase X_1^* because increasing X_1^* would mean that X_1 exceeds the upper bound. We enter X_2 into the basis.

From $X_3 = 1 - 3X_1^* - X_2$, we observe that X_2 can be increased to 1 beyond which X_3 would become negative.

From $X_4 = 4 - 2X_1^* + X_2$, we observe that X_2 can be increased to any value and does not affect the feasibility of X_4.

From $X_5 = 16 - 2X_1^* - 3X_2$, we observe that X_2 can be increased to 16/3 beyond which X_5 will become negative.

The maximum value X_2 can take is the minimum of (1, 16/3) = 1. This is within the upper bound value of 2. We enter X_2 and leave variable X_3. The equations become

$$X_2 = 1 - 3X_1^* - X_3$$
$$X_4 = 4 - 2X_1^* + (1 - 3X_1^* - X_3) = 5 - 5X_1^* - X_3$$
$$X_5 = 16 - 2X_1^* - 3(1 - 3X_1^* - X_3) = 13 + 7X_1^* + 3X_3$$
$$Z = 16 + 8X_1^* + 3(1 - 3X_1^* - X_3) = 19 - X_1^* - 3X_3$$

We want to increase Z further if possible. This can be done by either decreasing X_1^* or by decreasing X_3. Decreasing X_3 is not possible because it will become negative. Decreasing X_1^* is possible because this will reduce the value of X_1 from 3 and will not become negative till the decrease is by 3 units. We find out the extent of decrease allowable by the constraints.

From $X_2 = 1 - 3X_1^* - X_3$, we realize that decrease in X_1^* would increase X_2. X_1^* can be decreased by a maximum of 5/3 beyond which X_2 will exceed the upper bound value.

From $X_4 = 5 - 5X_1^* - X_3$, we observe that decreasing X_1^* can increase X_4, and there is no limit. The maximum X_1^* can be decreased is 3 beyond which X_1 will become negative.

From $X_5 = 13 + 7X_1^* + 3X_3$, we observe that X_1^* can be decreased by 13/7 beyond which X_5 will become negative.

The maximum decrease possible is minimum (5/3, 3, 13/7) = 5/3. This decrease brings X_1 back into the basis with a value between 0 and 2. This also makes X_2 reach its upper bound of 6. We substitute $X_2 = 6 + X_2^*$, and rewrite the equations as:

$$X_2 = 1 - 3X_1^* - X_3 \text{ becomes}$$
$$3X_1^* = 1 - X_2 - X_3 = 1 - (6 + X_2^*) - X_3$$
$$3X_1 - 6 = 1 - X_2 - X_3 = 1 - (6 + X_2^*) - X_3$$
$$3X_1 = 1 - X_2^* - X_3$$
$$X_1 = 1/3 - X_2^*/3 - X_3/3$$
$$X_4 = 5 - 5X_1^* - X_3 = 5 - 5X_1 + 10 - X_3$$
$$= 15 - 5X_1 - X_3 = 15 - 5(1/3 - X_2^*/3 - X_3/3) - X_3$$
$$= 40/3 + 5X_2^*/3 + 2X_3/3$$
$$X_5 = 13 + 7X_1^* + 3X_3 = 13 + 7X_1 - 14 + 3X_3$$
$$= 13 - 14 + 7(1/3 - X_2^*/3 - X_3/3) + 3X_3$$
$$= 4/3 - 7X_2^*/3 + 2X_3/3$$
$$Z = 19 - X_1^* - 3X_3 = 19 - X_1 + 2 - 3X_3$$
$$= 21 - (1/3 - X_2^*/3 - X_3/3) - 3X_3 = 62/3 + X_2^*/3 - 8/3X_3$$

We can further increase Z by increasing X_2^* or by decreasing X_3. Increasing X_2^* would increase X_2 beyond its upper bound and decreasing X_3 would make it negative. Both are not possible and the algorithm terminates with the solution:

$$X_1 = \frac{1}{3}, X_2 = 6, Z = \frac{62}{3}$$

6.2.2 Simplex Algorithm for Bounded Variables

Let us represent this in the simplex algorithm. The first iteration, shown in Table 6.3, has variables X_3, X_4 and X_5 as basic variables.

Table 6.3 First Iteration

		8	3	0	0	0			
		X_1	X_2	X_3	X_4	X_5	RHS	θ	α
0	X_3	3	1	1	0	0	7	7/3	–
0	X_4	2	–1	0	1	0	8	4	–
0	X_5	2↑	3	0	0	1	20	10	–
$C_j - Z_j$		8	3	0	0	0	0		

We introduce a new column which finds out the limiting value of the entering variable that can make an existing basic variable reach its upper bound value. The α value will be filled only when the corresponding coefficient in the row is negative. For a variable, we will have either a θ value or an α value. The minimum value is 7/3 which is more than the upper bound. We will have X_1^* in the simplex table. The two iterations are shown in Table 6.4.

Table 6.4 Two Iterations

		8	3	0	0	0			
		X_1	X_2	X_3	X_4	X_5	RHS	θ	α
0	X_3	3	1	1	0	0	7	7/3	–
0	X_4	2	–1	0	1	0	8	4	–
0	X_5	2↑	3	0	0	1	20	10	–
$C_j - Z_j$		8*	3	0	0	0	0		
0	X_3	3	1	1	0	0	1	1	
0	X_4	2	–1	0	1	0	4	–	
0	X_5	2	3↑	0	0	1	16	16/3	
$C_j - Z_j$		8	3	0	0	0	16		

The basic variables remain the same. The RHS values alone change to old RHS – coefficient * UB value of entering variable. The * in the entering variable indicates that the entering variable is at the upper bound value.

At the end of second iteration, the only entering variable is X_2 because X_1^* can enter only with a negative $C_j - Z_j$. X_2 enters and the θ values are found. There are no α values because the existing basic variables do not have an upper bound. Minimum θ is 1, which is less than the upper bound value of 2. We perform a simplex iteration entering variable X_2 and replacing variable X_3. The three iterations are shown in Table 6.5.

(Since X_1^* is entering, we have to use a different formula to compute θ and α. θ is computed when the coefficient is negative and is applicable only for the third row. Here it is 13 divided by the negative of the negative value and is positive. α is computed when a basic variable is a bounded variable, and is at present basic with a valued less than the upper bound. Here, we compute for variable X_2 and is (UB – present value)/coefficient = (6 –1)/3 = 5/3. For the second

Table 6.5 Three Iterations

		8	3	0	0	0			
		X_1	X_2	X_3	X_4	X_5	RHS	θ	α
0	X_3	3	1	1	0	0	7	7/3	–
0	X_4	2	–1	0	1	0	8	4	–
0	X_5	2↑	3	0	0	1	20	10	–
	$C_j - Z_j$	8*	3	0	0	0	0		
0	X_3	3	1	1	0	0	1	1	
0	X_4	2	–1	0	1	0	4	–	
0	X_5	2	3↑	0	0	1	16	16/3	
	$C_j - Z_j$	8	3	0	0	0	0 + 16		
3	X_2	3	1	1	0	0	1	–	5/3
0	X_4	5	0	1	1	0	5	–	0
0	X_5	–7↑	0	–3	0	1	13	13/7	0
	$C_j - Z_j$	–1	0	–3	0	0	3 + 16		

row we compute neither θ nor α because the entering coefficient is positive and the corresponding basic variable is not a bounded variable.

The minimum value is 5/3, which is less than the upper bound for variable X_1. Now, since an α value is the minimum value, the entering variable X_1 replaced X_2 but X_2 is at its upper bound value. We perform a simplex iteration, shown in Table 6.6.

Table 6.6 Simplex Iteration

		8	3	0	0	0			
		X_1	X_2	X_3	X_4	X_5	RHS	θ	α
0	X_3	3	1	1	0	0	7	7/3	–
0	X_4	2	–1	0	1	0	8	4	–
0	X_5	2↑	3	0	0	1	20	10	–
	$C_j - Z_j$	8*	3	0	0	0	0		
0	X_3	3	1	1	0	0	1	1	
0	X_4	2	–1	0	1	0	4	–	
0	X_5	2	3↑	0	0	1	16	16/3	
	$C_j - Z_j$	8	3	0	0	0	0 + 16		
3	X_2	3	1	1	0	0	1	–	5/3*
0	X_4	5	0	1	1	0	5	–	–
0	X_5	–7↑	0	–3	0	1	13	13/7	
	$C_j - Z_j$	–1	0	–3	0	0	3 + 16		
8	X_1	1	1/3	1/3	0	0	1/3		
0	X_4	0	–5/3	–2/3	1	0	10/3 + 10		
0	X_5	0	7/3	–2/3	0	1	46/3 – 7*2		
	$C_j - Z_j$	0	1/3	–8/3	0	0	8/3 + 18		

(The RHS values will have to be further corrected X_4 becomes $10/3 + 5*2 = 40/3$ (5 being the coefficient in the entering column and 2 being the UB value of X_1). Similarly, X_5 becomes $46/3 - 7*2 = 4/3$ by the same rule.

Now, there is no entering variable and the algorithm terminates.

It may be observed that the algebraic method is easier when compared to the simplex method. It is not very difficult to write an algorithm for the simplex algorithm with bounded variables based on the earlier discussions. The reader may attempt to write it in an algorithm form as an exercise.

6.3 SOLVING THE ONE-DIMENSIONAL CUTTING STOCK PROBLEM

So far we have formulated and solved linear programming problems using the simplex algorithm. Many such problems are actually integer programming problems, where the decision variables are constrained to be non-negative integers. In fact, our product mix problem is actually an integer programming problem where the number of tables and chairs have to be integers. It was incidental that the optimal LP solution to the problem gave integer values, and we could accept it. What would have happened if we had non-integer solutions?

Many algorithms are available to solve integer programming problems optimally. In fact, all of these use ideas and principles from LP to solve IP problems. However, it is customary to solve the IP first as an LP and verify if it gives integer solutions. If it does, it is optimal to the IP. If it doesn't, then it is a lower bound to the IP (for a minimization problem), and tells us that the objective function of the IP optimum cannot be lower than the objective function of the LP optimum.

Sometimes the LP optimum can also be used very efficiently to obtain the IP optimum. This happens for the cutting stock problem. The illustration is as follows:

ILLUSTRATION 6.3

Consider a big steel roll from which steel sheets of the same lengths but different width have to be cut. Let us assume that the roll is 20 cm wide and the following sizes have to be cut:

1. 9 inch   511 numbers
2. 8 inch   301 numbers
3. 7 inch   263 numbers
4. 6 inch   383 numbers

The possible patterns are:

1. [2 0 0 0] wastage = 2
2. [0 2 0 0] wastage = 4
3. [0 0 2 1] wastage = 2
4. [0 0 0 3] wastage = 2
5. [1 1 0 0] wastage = 3
6. [1 0 1 0] wastage = 4
7. [1 0 0 1] wastage = 5
8. [0 1 1 0] wastage = 5
9. [0 1 0 2] wastage = 0
10. [0 0 1 2] wastage = 1

The formulation is:

Minimize ΣX_j

Subject to

$$2X_1 + X_5 + X_6 + X_7 \geq 511$$
$$2X_2 + X_5 + X_8 + X_9 \geq 301$$
$$2X_3 + X_6 + X_8 + X_{10} \geq 263$$
$$X_3 + 3X_4 + X_7 + 2X_9 + 2X_{10} \geq 383$$
$$X_j \geq 0$$

The LP optimum for this problem is given by $X_1 = 255.5$, $X_2 = 87.625$, $X_3 = 131.5$, $X_9 = 125.75$ and $Z = 600.375$ cuts (alternate optimum).

The first information that we have is that the minimum number of cuts (lower bound) is 601 since the LP optimum is 600.375 and the variables are integers. We will need 601 or more cuts at the IP optimum.

Let us round off the solution to its higher integer value. $X_1 = 256$, $X_2 = 88$, $X_3 = 132$, $X_4 = 126$. Obviously, this is feasible to the IP problem and has 602 cuts. This feasible solution can have a maximum possible increase of the number of constraints. In this case, the feasible solution (upper bound) has 602 cuts and has 1 more of 9 inch, 1 more of 8 inch, 1 more of 7 inch and 1 more of 6 inch width sheet.

If we are happy with this feasible solution, we have a gap between the upper and lower bounds of (UB − LB)/LB × 100% = 1/601 × 100% = 0.166%

Since we have a lower bound of 601, we need to check if there is a feasible solution with 601 cuts. Let us round off the solution to its lower integer value. $X_1 = 255$, $X_2 = 87$, $X_3 = 131$, $X_9 = 125$ and $Z = 598$ cuts. This solution is infeasible, and we are short of 9 inch by 1, short of 8 inch by 2, short of 7 inch by 1 and short of 6 inch by 2 sheets.

The solution [2 0 0 0] = 255, [0 2 0 0] = 87, [0 0 2 1] = 131 and [0 1 0 2] = 125 equals 598 cuts and we need 1 nine inch, 2 eight inch, 1 seven inch and 2 six inch sheets.

If we cut one sheet with the pattern [0 0 1 2], we get 1 sheet of 7 inch and 2 sheets of 6 inch. If we cut 1 sheet with the pattern [1 1 0 0], we get 1 sheet of 9 inch and 1 sheet of 8 inch. If we cut 1 sheet with the pattern [0 1 0 0], we get 1 eight inch sheet. We now have cut an additional 1 sheet of 9 inch, 2 sheets of 8 inch, 1 sheet of 7 inch and 2 sheets of 6 inches. We have met all the deficit with three additional cuts. We, therefore, have a feasible solution with 601 cuts, which is optimal because we have a lower bound of 601.

Therefore, we realize that by solving a LP, we can get either the optimal solution to IP (with some additional intuition) or a good UB to the IP. Hence, we solve the one-dimensional cutting stock problem as an LP and not as an IP.

6.3.1 Column Generation—Cutting Stock Problem

One of the most popular ways of solving linear programming problems is through column generation. When the number of variables is large, it may be difficult to store the entire coefficient matrix, which is a common practice in the simplex iterations. Even in the revised simplex algorithm, every iteration is represented in terms of the initial coefficients of the matrix. In column generation procedures, we generate the entering column in an iteration by solving a sub problem or by any suitable means. We incur some more computational effort but we save by not storing the entire coefficient matrix in the memory.

We illustrate the column generation by considering the cutting stock problem (Gilmore and Gomory, 1963) discussed earlier.

Consider a big steel roll from which steel sheets of the same lengths but different width have to be cut. Let us assume that the roll is 20 cm wide and the following sizes have to be cut:

1. 9 inch   511 numbers
2. 8 inch   301 numbers
3. 7 inch   263 numbers
4. 6 inch   383 numbers

The formulation is of the form:

Minimize ΣX_j

Subject to

$$\Sigma a_{ij} X_j = b_i$$
$$X_j \geq 0$$

where X_j is the number of sheets cut using pattern j. A pattern is of the form $[a\ b\ c\ d]$ and any a, b, c, or d that satisfies $9a + 8b + 7c + 6d \leq 20$ and $a, b, c, d \geq 0$ is a feasible pattern.

While formulating the cutting stock problem we had enumerated all the possible patterns. While solving the problem, we do not enumerate the patterns. Since we need widths 9, 8, 7, 6 with a sheet width of 20, we assume the first four feasible patterns to be [2 0 0 0], [0 2 0 0], [0 0 2 0] and [0 0 0 3]. We need to cut 255.5 sheets with the first pattern, 150.5 sheets with the second pattern, 131.5 sheets with the third pattern and 127.666 sheets with the fourth pattern to have an initial feasible solution with 665.166 sheets. The feasible solution is:

$$\begin{bmatrix} 205.5 \\ 150.5 \\ 131.5 \\ 127.66 \end{bmatrix}$$

There are four constraints and there are four basic variables in the solution. Each basic variable represents a pattern. The dual to the problem has four variables, which we call y_1 to y_4. The basic matrix for the solution is made of the columns corresponding to the basic variables and is given by

$$B = \begin{bmatrix} 2 & 0 & 0 & 0 \\ 0 & 2 & 0 & 0 \\ 0 & 0 & 2 & 0 \\ 0 & 0 & 0 & 3 \end{bmatrix}$$

The solution to the dual is given by $yB = C_B$. Since all the objective function coefficients are 1, the dual solution is [1/2, 1/2, 1/2, 1/3]. To verify whether the present solution is optimal, we need to verify whether the dual solution is feasible. This dual solution is feasible if for all possible patterns $[a\ b\ c\ d]$ $a/2 + b/2 + c/2 + d/3 \leq 1$.

Alternately, if for any pattern [a b c d] the constraint is violated then the dual is infeasible and the pattern enters the basis. We need to find out a pattern [a b c d] such that

$$\frac{a}{2} + \frac{b}{2} + \frac{c}{2} + \frac{d}{3} > 1$$

and

$$9a + 8b + 7c + 6d \leq 20$$
$$a, b, c, d \geq 0 \text{ and integer}$$

We model this problem as a knapsack problem with one constraint and solve it using a branch and bound method.

6.3.2 Knapsack Problem

The problem that we try to solve is:

Maximize $Z = \dfrac{a}{2} + \dfrac{b}{2} + \dfrac{c}{2} + \dfrac{d}{3}$

Subject to
$$9a + 8b + 7c + 6d \leq 20$$
$$a, b, c, d \geq 0 \text{ and integer}$$

This is rewritten as:

Maximize $Z = \dfrac{1}{2}X_1 + \dfrac{1}{2}X_2 + \dfrac{1}{2}X_3 + \dfrac{1}{3}X_4$

$$9X_1 + 8X_2 + 7X_3 + 6X_4 \leq 20$$
$$X_1, X_2, X_3, X_4 \geq 0 \text{ and integer}$$

We renumber the variables in the decreasing order of c_j/a_j. The values of the ratios are 1/18, 1/16, 1/14 and 1/18. The problem becomes

Maximize $Z = \dfrac{1}{2}X_1 + \dfrac{1}{2}X_2 + \dfrac{1}{2}X_3 + \dfrac{1}{3}X_4$

Subject to
$$7X_1 + 8X_2 + 9X_3 + 6X_4 \leq 20$$
$$X_1, X_2, X_3, X_4 \geq 0 \text{ and integer}$$

We make the objective coefficients integers by taking the LCM and the problem becomes

Maximize $Z = 3X_1 + 3X_2 + 3X_3 + 2X_4$

Subject to
$$7X_1 + 8X_2 + 9X_3 + 6X_4 \leq 20$$
$$X_1, X_2, X_3, X_4 \geq 0 \text{ and integer}$$

The LP optimum to this problem is $X_1 = 20/7$ with $Z = 60/7 = 8.57$.

For a maximization problem the LP optimum is an upper bound to the IP optimum. The upper bound to the IP optimum is $Z = 8$.

Variable X_1 can take either of the values 0, 1 or 2. Fixing $X_1 = 0$ gives us an LP solution of $X_2 = 2.5$ with $Z = 7.5$.

Fixing $X_1 = 1$ gives us an LP solution with $X_2 = 1.75$ and $Z = 3 + 3 \times 1.75 = 8.25$.
Fixing $X_1 = 2$ gives us an LP solution $X_2 = 0.75$ and $Z = 6 + 3 \times 0.75 = 8.25$

We branch from $X_1 = 2$. Now X_2 can take only zero value. X_3 can also take only zero value but X_4 can take value 1 which is a feasible solution to the IP with $Z = 8$. This is optimal because the upper bound is 8. The optimal solution is $X_1 = 2$ and $X_4 = 1$ with $Z = 8$ and to the original problem two 7 inch sheets and 1 six inch sheet with $Z = 4/3$ which is greater than 1. Therefore, the pattern [0 0 2 1] enters the basis.

We have to find out the leaving variable corresponding to the entering variable (pattern) [0 0 2 1]. The entering column is given by

$$\overline{P}_j = B^{-1} P_j$$

We need to find A such that

$$[a\ b\ c\ d]^T \begin{bmatrix} 2 & 0 & 0 & 0 \\ 0 & 2 & 0 & 0 \\ 0 & 0 & 2 & 0 \\ 0 & 0 & 0 & 3 \end{bmatrix} = [0\ 0\ 2\ 1]^T$$

We have $A = [0\ 0\ 1\ 1/3]^T$. We have to find out minimum θ such that

$$131.5 - \theta \geq 0$$

and

$$127.666 - \frac{1}{3}\theta \geq 0$$

The minimum value of θ is 131.5. The leaving column (variable) is [0 0 2 0] and is replaced by [0 0 2 1]. The solution is pattern [2 0 0 0] with 205.5 cuts, pattern [0 2 0 0] with 150.5 cuts, pattern [0 0 2 1] with 131.5 cuts and pattern [0 0 0 3] with 83.833 cuts with a total of 621.333 cuts.

To verify whether this solution is optimal, we compute the dual and check whether it is feasible. The dual is given by $[y_1\ y_2\ y_3\ y_4]$ such that $yB = 1$

$$[y_1\ y_2\ y_3\ y_4] \begin{bmatrix} 2 & 0 & 0 & 0 \\ 0 & 2 & 0 & 0 \\ 0 & 0 & 2 & 0 \\ 0 & 0 & 1 & 3 \end{bmatrix} = [1\ 1\ 1\ 1]$$

$$y = [1/2,\ 1/2,\ 1/3,\ 1/3]$$

We need to find an entering pattern $[a\ b\ c\ d]$ such that

$$\frac{a}{2} + \frac{b}{2} + \frac{c}{3} + \frac{d}{3} > 1$$

and
$$9a + 8b + 7c + 6d \leq 20$$
We solve a knapsack problem as we did earlier. The problem is:

Maximize $Z = \dfrac{a}{2} + \dfrac{b}{2} + \dfrac{c}{3} + \dfrac{d}{3}$

Subject to
$$9a + 8b + 7c + 6d \leq 20$$
$$a, b, c, d \geq 0 \text{ and integer}$$

This is rewritten as:

Maximize $Z = \dfrac{1}{2}X_1 + \dfrac{1}{2}X_2 + \dfrac{1}{3}X_3 + \dfrac{1}{3}X_4$

Subject to
$$9X_1 + 8X_2 + 7X_3 + 6X_4 \leq 20$$
$$X_1, X_2, X_3, X_4 \geq 0 \text{ and integer}$$

We renumber the variables in the decreasing order of c_j/a_j. The values of the ratios are 1/18, 1/16, 1/21 and 1/18. The problem becomes

Maximize $Z = \dfrac{1}{2}X_1 + \dfrac{1}{2}X_2 + \dfrac{1}{3}X_3 + \dfrac{1}{3}X_4$

Subject to
$$8X_1 + 9X_2 + 6X_3 + 7X_4 \leq 20$$
$$X_1, X_2, X_3, X_4 \geq 0 \text{ and integer}$$

We make the objective coefficients integers by taking the LCM and the problem becomes

Maximize $Z = 3X_1 + 3X_2 + 2X_3 + 2X_4$

Subject to
$$8X_1 + 9X_2 + 6X_3 + 7X_4 \leq 20$$
$$X_1, X_2, X_3, X_4 \geq 0 \text{ and integer.}$$

The LP optimum to this problem is $X_1 = 2.5$ with $Z = 7.5$.

For a maximization problem the LP optimum is an upper bound to the IP optimum. The upper bound to the IP optimum is $Z = 7$.

Variable X_1 can take either of the values 0, 1 or 2. Fixing $X_1 = 0$ gives us an LP solution of $X_2 = 20/9$ with $Z = 20/3$. Fixing $X_1 = 1$ gives us an LP solution with $X_2 = 4/3$ and $Z = 3 + 3 \times 4/3 = 7$ and fixing $X_1 = 2$ gives us an LP solution $X_2 = 4/9$ and $Z = 6 + 3 \times 4/9 = 7.333$.

We branch from $X_1 = 2$. Now, X_2 can take only zero value. X_3 and X_4 can also take only zero resulting in a feasible solution to the IP with $Z = 6$.

We branch from $X_1 = 1$. Now, X_2 can take 0 or 1. $X_2 = 1$ gives a solution with $Z = 6$ but $X_2 = 0$ and $X_3 = 2$ gives a feasible solution with $Z = 7$ which is optimal. $X_1 = 1$ and $X_3 = 2$ with $Z = 7$ to the original problem is one 8 inch sheet and 2 six inch sheets with $Z = 7/6$ which is greater than 1. Therefore, the pattern [0 1 0 2] enters the basis.

We have to find out the leaving variable corresponding to the entering variable (pattern) [0 1 0 2]. The entering column is given by

$$\overline{P}_j = B^{-1} P_j$$

We need to find A such that

$$[a\ b\ c\ d]^T \begin{bmatrix} 2 & 0 & 0 & 0 \\ 0 & 2 & 0 & 0 \\ 0 & 0 & 2 & 0 \\ 0 & 0 & 1 & 3 \end{bmatrix} = [0\ 1\ 0\ 2]^T$$

We have $A = [0\ \frac{1}{2}\ -1/3\ 2/3]^T$. We have to find out minimum θ such that

$$150.5 - \frac{1}{2}\theta \geq 0$$

and

$$83.33 - \frac{2}{3}\theta \geq 0$$

The minimum value of θ is 125.75. The leaving column (variable) is [0 0 0 3] and is replaced by [0 1 0 2]. The solution is pattern [2 0 0 0] with 255.5 cuts, pattern [0 2 0 0] with 150.5 − 125.75/2 = 87.625 cuts, pattern [0 0 2 1] with 131.5 cuts and pattern [0 1 0 2] with 125.75 cuts with a total of 600.375 cuts.

To verify whether this solution is optimal, we compute the dual and check whether it is feasible. The dual is given by $[y_1\ y_2\ y_3\ y_4]$ such that $yB = 1$

$$[y_1\ y_2\ y_3\ y_4] \begin{bmatrix} 2 & 0 & 0 & 0 \\ 0 & 2 & 0 & 1 \\ 0 & 0 & 2 & 0 \\ 0 & 0 & 1 & 2 \end{bmatrix} = [1\ 1\ 1\ 1]$$

$$y = [1/2,\ 1/2,\ 3/8,\ 1/4]$$

We need to find an entering pattern $[a\ b\ c\ d]$ such that

$$\frac{a}{2} + \frac{b}{2} + \frac{3c}{8} + \frac{d}{4} > 1$$

and

$$9a + 8b + 7c + 6d \leq 20$$

We solve a knapsack problem as we did earlier. The problem is:

Maximize $\quad Z = \dfrac{a}{2} + \dfrac{b}{2} + \dfrac{3c}{8} + \dfrac{d}{4}$

Subject to

$$9a + 8b + 7c + 6d \leq 20$$
$$a,\ b,\ c,\ d \geq 0 \text{ and integer}$$

This is rewritten as:

Maximize $Z = 1/2X_1 + 1/2X_2 + 3/8X_3 + 1/4X_4$

Subject to

$$9X_1 + 8X_2 + 7X_3 + 6X_4 \leq 20$$
$$X_1, X_2, X_3, X_4 \geq 0 \text{ and integer}$$

We renumber the variables in the decreasing order of c_j/a_j. The values of the ratios are 1/18, 1/16, 3/56 and 1/24. The problem becomes

Maximize $Z = 1/2X_1 + 1/2X_2 + 3/8X_3 + 1/4X_4$

Subject to

$$8X_1 + 9X_2 + 7X_3 + 6X_4 \leq 20$$
$$X_1, X_2, X_3, X_4 \geq 0 \text{ and integer}$$

We make the objective coefficients integers by taking the LCM and the problem becomes

Maximize $Z = 4X_1 + 4X_2 + 3X_3 + 2X_4$

Subject to

$$8X_1 + 9X_2 + 7X_3 + 6X_4 \leq 20$$
$$X_1, X_2, X_3, X_4 \geq 0 \text{ and integer}$$

The LP optimum to this problem is $X_1 = 2.5$ with $Z = 10$. For a maximization problem the LP optimum is an upper bound to the IP optimum. The upper bound to the IP optimum is $Z = 10$.

Variable X_1 can take either of the values 0, 1 or 2. Fixing $X_1 = 0$ gives us an LP solution of $X_2 = 20/9$ with $Z = 80/9 = 8.88$. Fixing $X_1 = 1$ gives us an LP solution with $X_2 = 4/3$ and $Z = 4 + 4 \times 4/3 = 9.33$ and fixing $X_1 = 2$ gives us an LP solution $X_2 = 4/9$ and $Z = 8 + 4 \times 4/9 = 88/9 = 9.77$.

We branch from $X_1 = 2$. Now, X_2 can take only zero value. X_3 and X_4 can also take only zero resulting in a feasible solution to the IP with $Z = 8$.

We branch from $X_1 = 1$. Now, X_2 can take 0 or 1. $X_2 = 1$ gives a solution with $Z = 8$ and $X_2 = 0$, and $X_3 = 1$ gives a feasible solution with $Z = 7$.

Branching from $X_1 = 0$, we can have $X_2 = 0$, 1 or 2. The corresponding solution is $X_2 = 2$, $Z = 8$. The optimum solution is $X_1 = 2$ and $Z = 8$ or $X_1 = X_2 = 1$ with $Z = 8$ and $X_2 = 2$ and $Z = 8$.

All these solutions would mean an objective function of 1 for the original problem. We are unable to find an entering pattern with $a/2 + b/2 + 3c/8 + d/4 > 1$.

The algorithm terminates but has alternate optima because there are patterns [2 0 0 0], [0 2 0 0] and [1 1 0 0] that have objective function value of zero. The patterns [2 0 0 0] and [0 2 0 0] already exist in the solution but entering [1 1 0 0] can give an alternate optimum.

The optimum solution to the cutting stock problem is pattern [2 0 0 0] with 255.5 cuts, pattern [0 2 0 0] with 150.5 − 125.75/2 = 87.625 cuts, pattern [0 0 2 1] with 131.5 cuts and pattern [0 1 0 2] with 125.75 cuts with a total of **600.375 cuts**.

In the above column generation, we don't explicitly store all the possible patterns. We enter them by solving a sub problem. This is called **column generation**. We study column generation again in the decomposition algorithm.

6.4 THE DECOMPOSITION ALGORITHM (DANTZIG AND WOLFE, 1960)

Let us consider the following linear programming problem:

ILLUSTRATION **6.4**

Maximize $Z = 6X_1 + 5X_2 + 3X_3 + 4X_4$
Subject to

$$X_1 + X_2 \leq 5 \quad (6.1)$$
$$3X_1 + 2X_2 \leq 12 \quad (6.2)$$
$$X_3 + 2X_4 \leq 8 \quad (6.3)$$
$$2X_3 + X_4 \leq 10 \quad (6.4)$$
$$X_1 + X_2 + X_3 + X_4 \leq 7 \quad (6.5)$$
$$2X_1 + X_2 + X_3 + 3X_4 \leq 17 \quad (6.6)$$
$$X_1, X_2, X_3, X_4 \geq 0$$

The above problem has four variables and six constraints. We can solve this directly by the simplex algorithm. However, if we observe the problem carefully, we can create two problems if we leave out (relax) the last two constraints. The resultant two problems, each having two variables and two constraints, are independent.

In this case, we create the following two problems and a master problem discussed in Section 6.4.1.

Maximize $Z = 6X_1 + 5X_2$
Subject to

$$X_1 + X_2 \leq 5$$
$$3X_1 + 2X_2 \leq 12$$
$$X_1, X_2 \geq 0$$

Maximize $Z = 3X_3 + 4X_4$
Subject to

$$X_3 + 2X_4 \leq 8$$
$$2X_3 + X_4 \leq 10$$
$$X_3, X_4 \geq 0$$

6.4.1 The Master Problem

$$X_1 + X_2 + X_3 + X_4 \leq 7$$
$$2X_1 + X_2 + X_3 + 3X_4 \leq 17$$

Problems P1 and P2 are called **sub problems** and can be solved separately to give the following solutions:

P1 : Corner points are (0, 0), (4, 0), (0, 5) and (2, 3). Optimal solution is $X_1 = 2, X_2 = 3, Z = 27$.
P2 : Corner points are (0, 0), (5, 0), (0, 4) and (4, 2). Optimal solution is $X_3 = 4, X_4 = 2, Z = 20$.

If we solve the original problem by relaxing constraints (6.5) and (6.6), we get the optimal solution $X_1 = 2, X_2 = 3, X_3 = 4, X_4 = 2, Z = 47$.

If we now include the two constraints (6.5) and (6.6), we realize that the new optimal solution will be lesser than or equal to 47, and the relaxed problem gives an upper bound to the original problem. Also the optimum solution point can be written as a convex combination of the corner points associated with the relaxed problem.

Any point (X_1, X_2, X_3, X_4) such that (X_1, X_2) is a corner point of P1 and (X_3, X_4) is a corner point of P2 is a corner point to the relaxed problem. The optimum solution to the original problem is a convex combination of the points in the set (X_1, X_2, X_3, X_4).

Let us consider the original problem in the form:

Minimize cx

Subject to

$$Ax = b$$
$$x \in X$$

x can be written as $x = \Sigma \lambda_j X_j$ where $\Sigma \lambda_j = 1$ and $\lambda_j \geq 0$ (for a set of corner points $j = 1,...,n$)

The master problem becomes

Minimize $\Sigma c X_j \lambda_j$

Subject to

$$\Sigma A X_j \lambda_j = b$$
$$\Sigma \lambda_j = 1$$
$$\lambda_j \geq 0$$

The number of corner points X_j becomes large if there are many sub problems. It also depends on the problem size. We don't explicitly store all the corner points but use column generation to identify an entering corner point (variable).

Let us assume that we have a basic feasible solution and B^{-1} is known. Let the dual variables be $(w, \alpha) = C_B B^{-1}$.

Revised simplex finds out $Z_k - C_k =$ Maximum $Z_j - C_j$ and enters a variable with the maximum positive value (for minimization).

$$Z_k - C_k = \text{maximum } (w\ \alpha) \begin{bmatrix} AX_j - cX_j \\ 1 \end{bmatrix}$$

Maximize $wAX_j - cX_j + \alpha$

If $Z_k - C_k \geq 0$, then λ_k enters the basis. The leaving variable is found as in simplex and the iterations are continued.

Constraints (6.5) and (6.6) represent $AX \leq b$.

X is the set of corner points representing equations (6.1) to (6.4)

$$A = \begin{bmatrix} 1 & 1 & 1 & 1 \\ 2 & 1 & 1 & 3 \end{bmatrix}$$

$$b = \begin{bmatrix} 7 \\ 17 \end{bmatrix}$$

The initial basis is made of two slack variables corresponding to (6.5) and (6.6) namely, S_1 and S_2 and the variable λ_1 corresponding to the feasible solution (0, 0, 0, 0) $B = I$. The simplex table is shown in Table 6.7.

$(w\ \alpha) = (0\ 0\ 0)$

Maximize $wAX_j - cX_j + \alpha$ = Maximize $6X_1 + 5X_2 + 3X_3 + 4X_4$

(Here $c = [-6, -5, -3, -4]$ because the equations are for minimization problem and we convert our maximization problem into a minimization problem)

Table 6.7 Simplex Table

	B^{-1}			RHS
S_1	1	0	0	7
S_2	0	1	0	17
λ_1	0	0	1	1
Z	0	0	0	0

This is partitioned into two independent sub problems (P1 and P2) that are solved separately.

The first problem has optimal solution $X_1 = 2$, $X_2 = 3$, $Z = 27$ and the second problem has optimal solution $X_3 = 4$, $X_4 = 2$ and $Z = 20$.

The optimal solution is (2, 3, 4, 2) with $Z = 47 > 0$. The corner point (2, 3, 4, 2) enters the basis as variable λ_2. The entering column is given by

$$AX_2 = \begin{bmatrix} 1 & 1 & 1 & 1 \\ 2 & 1 & 1 & 3 \end{bmatrix} \begin{bmatrix} 2 \\ 3 \\ 4 \\ 2 \end{bmatrix} = \begin{bmatrix} 11 \\ 17 \end{bmatrix}$$

The entering column is added to the simplex table and shown in Table 6.8.

Table 6.8 Entering Column

	B^{-1}			RHS	Entering column λ_2	θ
S_1	1	0	0	7	11	7/11
S_2	0	1	0	17	17	1
λ_1	0	0	1	1	1	1
Z	0	0	0	0	47	

Now, λ_2 enters the basis and replaces S_2. The simplex iteration is shown in Table 6.9.

The feasible solution at the end of this iteration is $X = 4/11\ [(0\ 0\ 0\ 0)] + 7/11\ [2\ 3\ 4\ 2] = [14/11, 21/11, 28/11, 14/11]$ with $Z = 329/11$. We need to verify whether this is optimal. From the simplex table, we find $(w, \alpha) = (-47/11, 0, 0)$. We now have to maximize $wAX_j - cX_j + \alpha$. We compute

$$wA - c\ [-47/11\ 0] \begin{bmatrix} 1 & 1 & 1 & 1 \\ 2 & 1 & 1 & 3 \end{bmatrix} - [-6\ -5\ -3\ -4]$$

$$= [19/11\ 8/11\ -14/11\ -3/11]$$

Table 6.9 Simplex Iteration

	B^{-1}			RHS	Entering column λ_2	θ
S_1	1	0	0	7	11	7/11 →
S_2	0	1	0	17	17	1
λ_2	0	0	1	1	1	1
Z	0	0	0	0	47	
λ_2	1/11	0	0	7/11	0	
S_2	−17/11	1	0	68/11	1	
λ_1	−1/11	0	1	4/11	0	
Z	−47/11	0	0	−329/11		

Maximize $\dfrac{19}{11}X_1 + \dfrac{8}{11}X_2 + \dfrac{-14}{11}X_3 + \dfrac{-3}{11}X_4 + 0$

Subject to

(6.1) to (6.4) and $X \geq 0$

This is partitioned into two independent sub problems (P1 and P2) that are solved separately.

The first problem has optimal solution $X_1 = 4, X_2 = 0, Z = 76/11$ and the second problem has optimal solution $X_3 = 0, X_4 = 0$ and $Z = 0$.

The optimal solution is (4 0 0 0) given by $X_1 = 4$, $X_2 = 0$, $X_3 = 0$ and $X_4 = 0$ with $Z = 76/11 + 0 = 76/11$.

Since the maximum $Z_k - C_k$ is positive, variable λ_3 (corner point [4 0 0 0]) enters the basis. The column corresponding to this variable in the original problem is given by

$$AX_3 = \begin{bmatrix} 1 & 1 & 1 & 1 \\ 2 & 1 & 1 & 3 \end{bmatrix} \begin{bmatrix} 4 \\ 0 \\ 0 \\ 0 \end{bmatrix} = \begin{bmatrix} 4 \\ 8 \end{bmatrix}$$

$$P_j = \begin{bmatrix} AX_j \\ 1 \end{bmatrix} = \begin{bmatrix} 4 \\ 8 \\ 1 \end{bmatrix}$$

The corresponding column in the simplex iteration is given by

$$\overline{P}_j = B^{-1} P_j = \begin{bmatrix} 1/11 & 0 & 0 \\ -17/11 & 1 & 0 \\ -1/11 & 0 & 1 \end{bmatrix} \begin{bmatrix} 4 \\ 8 \\ 1 \end{bmatrix} = \begin{bmatrix} 4/11 \\ 20/11 \\ 7/11 \end{bmatrix}$$

The simplex iterations are shown in Table 6.10.

Table 6.10 Simplex Iteration

	B^{-1}			RHS	Entering column λ_3	θ
λ_2	1/11	0	0	7/11	4/11	7/4
S_2	–17/11	1	0	68/11	20/11	68/20
λ_1	–1/11	0	1	4/11	7/11 ↑	4/7 →
Z	–47/11	0	0	–329/11	76/11	
λ_2	1/7	0	–4/7	3/7		
S_2	–9/7	1	20/7	36/7		
λ_3	–1/11	0	11/7	4/7		
Z	–23/7	0	–76/7	–237/7		

The feasible solution to the original problem is 3/7 (2 3 4 2) + 4/7 (4 0 0 0) = (22/7, 9/7, 12/7, 6/7) with Z = 237/7. We need to verify whether this is optimal. From the simplex table, we find $(w, \alpha) = (-23/7, 0, -76/7)$.

We now have to maximize $wAX_j - cX_j + \alpha$. We compute

$$wA - c = [-23/7 \; 0] \begin{bmatrix} 1 & 1 & 1 & 1 \\ 2 & 1 & 1 & 3 \end{bmatrix} - [-6 \; -5 \; -3 \; -4]$$

$$= [19/7 \; 12/7 \; -2/7 \; 5/7]$$

Maximize $\quad \dfrac{19}{7}X_1 + \dfrac{12}{7}X_2 \dfrac{-2}{7}X_3 + \dfrac{5}{7}X_4 - 76/7$

Subject to

(6.1) to (6.4) and $X \geq 0$

This is partitioned into two independent sub problems (P1 and P2) that are solved separately.

The first problem has optimal solution $X_1 = 4$, $X_2 = 0$, $Z = 76/7$ and the second problem has optimal solution $X_3 = 0$, $X_4 = 4$ and $Z = 20/7$.

The optimal solution is (4 0 0 4) given by $X_1 = 4$, $X_2 = 0$, $X_3 = 0$ and $X_4 = 4$ with $Z = 96/7 - 76/7 = 20/7 > 0$. Since the maximum $Z_k - C_k$ is positive, variable λ_4 (corner point [4 0 0 4]) enters the basis. The column corresponding to this variable in the original problem is given by

$$AX_3 = \begin{bmatrix} 1 & 1 & 1 & 1 \\ 2 & 1 & 1 & 3 \end{bmatrix} \begin{bmatrix} 4 \\ 0 \\ 0 \\ 4 \end{bmatrix} = \begin{bmatrix} 8 \\ 20 \end{bmatrix}$$

$$P_j = \begin{bmatrix} AX_j \\ 1 \end{bmatrix} = \begin{bmatrix} 8 \\ 20 \\ 1 \end{bmatrix}$$

The corresponding column in the simplex iteration is given by

$$\overline{P}_j = B^{-1} P_j = \begin{bmatrix} 1/7 & 0 & -4/7 \\ -9/7 & 1 & -20/7 \\ -1/7 & 0 & 11/7 \end{bmatrix} \begin{bmatrix} 8 \\ 20 \\ 1 \end{bmatrix} = \begin{bmatrix} 4/7 \\ 48/7 \\ 3/7 \end{bmatrix}$$

The simplex iterations are shown in Table 6.11.

Table 6.11 Simplex Iteration

	B^{-1}			RHS	Entering column λ_4	θ
λ_2	1/7	0	−4/7	3/7	**4/7**	3/4
S_2	−9/7	1	20/7	36/7	48/7	3/4
λ_3	−1/7	0	11/7	4/7	3/7	4/3
Z	−23/7	0	−76/7	−237/7	20/7	
λ_4	1/4	0	−1	3/4		
S_2	−3	1	68/7	0		
λ_3	−1/4	0	2	1/4		
Z	−4	0	−8	−36		

The feasible solution to the original problem is 1/4 (4 0 0 0) + 3/4 (4 0 0 4) = (4, 0, 0, 1) with $Z = 36$. We need to verify whether this is optimal. From the simplex table, we find $(w, \alpha) = (-4, 0, -8)$. We now have to maximize $wAX_j - cX_j + \alpha$. We compute

$$wA - c \ [-4 \ 0] \begin{bmatrix} 1 & 1 & 1 & 1 \\ 2 & 1 & 1 & 3 \end{bmatrix} - [-6 \ -5 \ -3 \ -4]$$

$$= [2 \ 1 \ -1 \ 0]$$

Maximize $\quad 2X_1 + X_2 - X_3 + 0X_4 - 36$
Subject to
(6.1) to (6.4) and $X \geq 0$

This is partitioned into two independent sub problems (P1 and P2) that are solved separately.

The first problem has optimal solution $X_1 = 4$, $X_2 = 0$, $Z = 8$ and the second problem has optimal solution $X_3 = 0$, $X_4 = 0$ and $Z = 0$.

The optimal solution is (4 0 0 0) given by $X_1 = 4$, $X_2 = 0$, $X_3 = 0$ and $X_4 = 0$ with $Z = 8 - 8 = 0$. Since the maximum $Z_k - C_k$ is not positive, we do not have an entering variable. The algorithm terminates. The solution to the given problem is given by $X_1 = 4$, $X_2 = 0$, $X_3 = 0$, $X_4 = 3$ with $Z = 36$.

6.5 THE PRIMAL DUAL ALGORITHM

Consider the Linear Programming illustration given below

ILLUSTRATION 6.5

Minimize $Z = 3X_1 + 4X_2$
Subject to
$$2X_1 + 3X_2 \geq 8$$
$$5X_1 + 2X_2 \geq 12$$
$$X_1, X_2 \geq 0$$

This can be solved using the two phase method or the Big-M method. We have already seen that both these would require two iterations to get to the optimal solution for this instance. Both the methods would require at least as many iterations as the number of artificial variables to replace them in the basis.

We have also solved this problem using the dual simplex algorithm and this would also require as many iterations as the number of infeasible basic variables in the initial basis. We solve this problem using a new method called the Primal Dual Algorithm.

We add slack variables X_3 and X_4 and rewrite the problem as
Minimize $Z = 3X_1 + 4X_2$
Subject to
$$2X_1 + 3X_2 - X_3 = 8$$
$$5X_1 + 2X_2 - X_4 = 12$$
$$X_1, X_2, X_3, X_4 \geq 0$$

The dual of this problem is
Maximize $8y_1 + 12y_2$
Subject to
$$2y_1 + 5y_2 \leq 3$$
$$3y_1 + 2y_2 \leq 4$$
$$-y_1 \leq 0$$
$$-y_2 \leq 0$$

y_1, y_2 unrestricted in sign

The dual solution $y = [0\ 0]$ is feasible to the dual. Also, this satisfies the third and fourth constraint of the dual as an equation.

If we apply complementary slackness conditions based on the above dual solution, variables X_3 and X_4 become the basic variables. We therefore have to solve for
$$-X_3 = 8$$
$$-X_4 = 12$$

We know that the solution is $X_3 = -8$, $X_4 = -12$ which is infeasible to the primal. However, we can solve $-X_3 = 8$, $-X_4 = 12$ by introducing two artificial variables a_1 and a_2 and solving

Minimize $a_1 + a_2$
Subject to

$$-X_3 + a_1 = 8,$$
$$-X_4 + a_2 = 12$$
$$X_1, X_2, a_1, a_2 \geq 0$$

This is equivalent to the two phase method where $Z = 0$ indicates that there is a basic feasible solution that does not involve the artificial variables. This problem is called the restricted primal.

The optimal solution to our problem is given by $a_1 = 8$, $a_2 = 12$ with $W = 20$. This shows that the restricted primal is infeasible.

We now find another dual feasible solution and repeat this procedure of applying complimentary slackness condition and finding whether the corresponding primal is feasible. The new dual feasible solution should have at least one new constraint satisfied as an equation so that a new basic variable appears in the restricted primal.

Let us consider the dual of the restricted primal. This becomes

Maximize $8v_1 + 12v_2$

Subject to $-v_1 \leq 0$, $-v_2 \leq 0$, $v_1 \leq 1$, $v_2 \leq 1$, v_1, v_2 unrestricted in sign.

The optimum solution to the dual of the restricted primal is $v^* = [1\ 1]$ with $Z = 20$ (please note that the value of the objective function is equal to that of the restricted primal).

We require a new dual feasible solution that would bring another basic variable into the restricted primal. One of the ways to do this is to consider a dual feasible solution $y' = y + \theta v^*$. Substituting,

$$y'a_j - c_j = (y + \theta v^*)\, a_j - c_j = (ya_j - c_j) + \theta v^* a_j$$

Here, a_j is the column corresponding to variable X_j in the given problem (primal). For those constraints in the dual that are satisfied as equations by y, $(y + \theta v^*)a_j - c_j = 0$ and $v^*a_j \leq 0$ (from the restricted primal). For these constraints, $(ya_j - c_j) + \theta v^* a_j \leq 0$.

For those constraints in the dual satisfied as inequalities by y, if $v^*a_j \leq 0$, $(ya_j - c_j) + \theta v^* a_j \leq 0$ because $ya_j - c_j \leq 0$.

We consider those constraints in the dual that are satisfied as inequalities and having $v^*a_j > 0$. For these constraints it is possible to find $\theta > 0$, where

$$\theta = \frac{-(ya_j - c_j)}{v^* a_j} \text{ where } v^* a_j > 0$$

The minimum of such θ can be found so that θ is redefined as

$$\theta = \underset{j}{\text{Minimum}} \frac{-(ya_j - c_j)}{v^* a_j}; \ v^* a_j > 0$$

Now if we define a new set of dual variables $y' = y + \theta v^*$, then at least one new constraint will be satisfied as an equation and this will create a different restricted primal.

For our example, constraints 1 and 2 of the dual are satisfied as inequalities by the solution $y = [0\ 0]$.

We compute $ya_1 - c_1 = -3$, $ya_2 - c_2 = -4$, $v^*a_1 = 7$, $v^*a_2 = 5$. $\theta = $ Minimum $\{3/7, 4/5\} = 3/7$. $y' = y + \theta v^* = [0\ 0] + 3/7\ [1\ 1] = [3/7\ 3/7]$.

For $y = [3/7\ 3/7]$, the first dual constraint is satisfied as an equation. The restricted primal therefore becomes

Minimize $a_1 + a_2$
Subject to
$$2X_1 + a_1 = 8,$$
$$5X_1 + a_2 = 12$$
$$X_1, a_1, a_2 \geq 0$$

The optimal solution is $X_1 = 12/5$, $a_1 = 16/5$. Since the artificial variable is in the basis, the optimal solution to the original problem has not been obtained. The restricted primal is infeasible to the original problem. Also note that the objective function value of the restricted primal has reduced.

The dual of the restricted primal is Maximize $8v_1 + 12v_2$
Subject to $2v_1 + 5v_2 \leq 0$, $v_1 \leq 1$, $v_2 \leq 1$, v_1, v_2 unrestricted in sign.
The optimal solution is $v^* = [1 - 2/5]$ with $Z = 16/5$.
We compute

$$ya_2 - c_2 = [3/7\ 3/7]\begin{bmatrix}3\\2\end{bmatrix} - 4 = -13/7$$

$$v^*a_2 = [1\ -2/5]\begin{bmatrix}3\\2\end{bmatrix} = 11/5$$

V^*a_3 and V^*a_4 are negative. $\theta = $ Minimum $\{13/7 \div 11/5\} = 65/77$. $y' = y + \theta v^* = [3/7\ 3/7] + 65/77\ [1\ -2/5] = [14/11\ 1/11]$.

Now, constraints 1 and 2 are satisfied as equations. The restricted primal is given by

Minimize $a_1 + a_2$
Subject to
$$2X_1 + 3X_2 + a_1 = 8,$$
$$5X_1 + 2X_2 + a_2 = 12$$
$$X_1, X_2, a_1, a_2 \geq 0.$$

The optimum solution to the restricted primal is $X_1 = 20/11$, $X_2 = 16/11$ with $W = 0$. Now, the optimum solution to the restricted primal is feasible to the given problem and hence it is optimal. The optimal solution to the given problem is $X_1 = 20/11$, $X_2 = 16/11$ with $W = 124/11$. The optimum solution to its dual is $y_1 = 14/11$, $y_2 = 1/11$ with $Z = 124/11$.

The Primal-Dual Algorithm

1. Given (P) Minimize cX; subject to $AX \geq b$, $X \geq 0$, convert the constraints to $AX = b$ by adding slack variables. Write the dual to P. $y = [0\ 0]$ is dual feasible.
2. Create the restricted primal and solve it optimally. If $Z = 0$, the given dual solution is optimal.
3. Write the dual of the restricted primal and solve it optimally to get v^*.
4. Compute $\theta = $ Minimum $\dfrac{-(ya_j - c_j)}{v^*a_j}$; $v^*a_j > 0$
5. Update $y = y + \theta v^*$ and find the dual constraints satisfied as equation.
6. Repeat Steps 2 to 5 till $Z = 0$ for the restricted primal. The optimum solution is obtained.

6.6 GOAL PROGRAMMING

So far, in all our problems encountered in linear programming, we considered a single linear objective function and a set of well defined and rigid linear constraints. When even one of the constraints is violated, we encountered an infeasible solution to the problem.

In practice, we could have multiple objectives when addressing real-life situations. Some constraints may be rigid while some may be flexible and would have targets or goals rather than rigid constraints. We model such situations using a technique called **goal programming** (Charnes et al., 1960).

Goal programming is one of the ways to address multiple objectives. The easier way is to convert a multiple objective problem into a single objective problem by considering weights for each of the objectives. Another way is to rank the objectives and solve it as a sequence of single objective problems, considering the ranked objectives one at a time. This method should ensure that the solution obtained for a particular objective does not worsen the solution (objective function) of an earlier solved higher ranked objective. This is called **lexicographic minimization** (optimization) and when applied to goal programming, it is called **lexicographic goal programming**.

In this section, we illustrate some aspects of lexicographic goal programming through few examples and solve them using graphical and simplex algorithms.

ILLUSTRATION 6.6

Consider two products A and B made out of three chemicals (I, II and III). Product A requires 3 of I and 5 of II and 1 of III while product B requires 4 of I, 6 of II. The profit associated with A and B are 70 and 80, respectively. The daily availability of chemicals I and II are 50 and 60, respectively and cannot be changed. It is desirable to maintain profit of over Rs. 800. The daily ordering of resource III should be kept under 8 units. It is also desired to minimize the production quantity so that the transportation is easy.

Let X_1 and X_2 be the daily production quantities of the products A and B, respectively. A linear programming formulation would be as follows:

Minimize $Z = X_1 + X_2$

Subject to

$$3X_1 + 4X_2 \leq 50$$
$$5X_1 + 6X_2 \leq 60$$
$$70X_1 + 80X_2 \geq 800$$
$$X_1 \leq 8$$
$$X_1, X_2 \geq 0$$

The optimal solution to the LP problem is $X_1 = 0$, $X_2 = 10$, $Z = 10$.

Let us consider the formulation from a goal programming point of view. Let us assume that the order in which the statements were made reflect the importance given to each. The statements, in the order of appearance are:

1. The daily availability of chemicals I and II are 50 and 60, respectively and cannot be changed.
2. It is desirable to maintain profit of over Rs. 800.
3. The daily ordering of resource III should be kept under 8 units.
4. It is also desired to minimize the production quantity so that the transportation is easy.

These get reflected as:

1. $3X_1 + 4X_2 \leq 50$ and $5X_1 + 6X_2 \leq 60$
2. $70X_1 + 80X_2 \geq 800$
3. $X_1 \leq 8$
4. $X_1 + X_2$ to be minimized

In goal programming, every constraint (or condition or aspiration or goal) is written as an equation. A closer look at the statements reveals that $3X_1 + 4X_2 \leq 50$ and $5X_1 + 6X_2 \leq 60$ are rigid and cannot be violated, while it is desirable to have $70X_1 + 80X_2$ greater than 800. This is not a rigid condition (constraint) but an aspiration (or goal) that we attempt to attain or satisfy. We can provide a solution where the goal is not entirely met.

Let us write the four constraints/goals as equations. If we consider $70X_1 + 80X_2$ we may obtain a value higher than 800 or lower than 800. We add a positive deviation and a negative deviation to the left hand side and write the goal as $70X_1 + 80X_2 + \eta - \rho = 800$. The first three statements are inequalities with a clearly defined RHS value while the fourth goal (to minimize $X_1 + X_2$ does not have a goal or aspiration. We assume an arbitrary value, say, 8 and write the four statements in the form of equations by adding positive and negative deviations for each.

1. $3X_1 + 4X_2 + \eta_1 - \rho_1 = 50$ and $5X_1 + 6X_2 + \eta_2 - \rho_2 = 60$
2. $70X_1 + 80X_2 + \eta_3 - \rho_3 = 800$
3. $X_1 + \eta_4 - \rho_4 = 8$
4. $X_1 + X_2 + \eta_5 - \rho_5 = 8$

We also have all η and $\rho \geq 0$.

[Here the corresponding η represents the positive deviation from the RHS value (target or goal) and ρ represents the negative deviation from the RHS value (target or goal)].

We first combine all the rigid constraints together and we don't want them to be violated. If we consider the constraint $3X_1 + 4X_2 \leq 50$, which is written as $3X_1 + 4X_2 + \eta_1 - \rho_1 = 50$, we don't want ρ_1 to be positive because it indicates that the constraint is violated. We would ideally want $\rho_1 = 0$ and state this as minimizing ρ_1. If this rigid constraint is satisfied then the minimum value of ρ_1 is zero and if this constraint is violated then the minimum value of ρ_1 is strictly positive.

All $\leq$ constraints will have the goal of minimizing the corresponding ρ and similarly, all $\geq$ constraints will minimize the corresponding η. All the equations will minimize the sum of η and ρ because we want neither to be positive.

Considering both the rigid constraints together, our objective (goal) would be to minimize $\rho_1 + \rho_2$. The profit condition is a $\geq$ constraint and, therefore, we minimize η_3. The condition

$X_1 \leq 8$ would mean minimize ρ_4 and the condition $X_1 + X_2 + \eta_5 - \rho_5 = 8$ would minimize ρ_5. We assume that we would like the total production to be less than 8 (which is a $\leq$ constraint). We could also model it as wanting to be equal to 8 and minimize η_5 and ρ_5.

The goal programming formulation would be minimize $[(\rho_1 + \rho_2), \eta_3, \rho_4, \rho_5]$. Subject to

$$3X_1 + 4X_2 + \eta_1 - \rho_1 = 50$$
$$5X_1 + 6X_2 + \eta_2 - \rho_2 = 60$$
$$70X_1 + 80X_2 + \eta_3 - \rho_3 = 800$$
$$X_1 + \eta_4 - \rho_4 = 8$$
$$X_1 + X_2 + \eta_5 - \rho_5 = 8$$
$$X_j, \eta_5, \rho_5 \geq 0$$

In all goal programming formulations, the objective function has only the deviation variables and not the decision variables. Also the objective function has the deviation variables according to the rank or importance given to each goal/target. The same goals, arranged according to a different order (priority) would give a different goal programming formulation.

*In lexicographic goal programming, the objective function terms are considered according to the order of appearance and solved.

The linear programming solution is $X_1 = 0$, $X_2 = 10$, $Z = 800$. If we evaluate the objective function terms of our goal programming formulation for this formulation, we get $(\rho_1 + \rho_2) = 0$ (The solution $X_1 = 0$, $X_2 = 10$ would mean that $\eta_1 - \rho_1 = 10$. This would force $\eta_1 = 10$ and $\rho_1 = 0$. The deviation variables together are similar to unrestricted variables and only one of them will be in the basis and not both).

$$\eta_3 = 0$$
$$\rho_4 = 0$$
and $$\rho_5 = 2$$

The goal programming objective function would be [0, 0, 0, 2]. The same solution is optimal to the goal programming problem. The value of $\rho_5 = 2$ indicates that the goal of keeping the total production to 8 cannot be achieved but a deviation of 2 units is needed. In this example, the target for the total production was not given in the problem statement, but was chosen by us.

In our example, it is defined as the last among the priorities and we don't have to redefine the target and solve the problem again. If for an intermediate goal, we get a positive value, we may have to revise the target or goal value. We consider this aspect in Illustration 6.7.

ILLUSTRATION 6.7

Consider two products A and B that are assembled. Product A requires 4 hours in assembly and Product B requires 3 hours in assembly. The total time available in assembly as regular time is 90 hours. The profits associated with A and B are 7 and 8, respectively. The daily demand for the products are 20 and 20, respectively. Overtime is possible but reduces the profit by Re. 1. The targets/goals are:

1. The daily requirements have to be met and regular time available is 90.
2. Minimize over time.
3. Maximize the profits.

We are not given targets to overtime and profit and let us assume them to be 20 and 600, respectively. Let us consider formulating an LP of maximizing profit with an overtime restriction of 20 hours.

Suppose X_1 and X_2 represent the units of Products A and B produced using regular time and Y_1 and Y_2 represent the units of Products A and B produced using over time.

Maximize $Z = 7X_1 + 8X_2 + 6Y_1 + 7Y_2$
Subject to

$$X_1 + Y_1 \geq 20$$
$$X_2 + Y_2 \geq 20$$
$$4X_1 + 3X_2 \leq 90$$
$$4Y_1 + 3Y_2 \leq 20$$
$$X_1, X_2, Y_1, Y_2 \geq 0$$

The LP problem when solved will yield an infeasible solution. This is because of a total requirement of 140 hours to make 20 of each assembly. We have 90 hours of regular time and 20 hours of OT.

Let us formulate this problem as a goal programming problem under the following order of targets/goals:

1. Minimum requirement should be satisfied and regular time capacity is exactly 90 hours.
2. Overtime requirement is minimized.
3. Profit is maximized.

The equations, after adding the deviation variables are:

$$X_1 + Y_1 + \eta_1 - \rho_1 = 20$$
$$X_2 + Y_2 + \eta_2 - \rho_2 = 20$$
$$4X_1 + 3X_2 + \eta_3 - \rho_3 = 90$$
$$4Y_1 + 3Y_2 + \eta_4 - \rho_4 = 20$$
$$7X_1 + 8X_2 + 6Y_1 + 7Y_2 + \eta_5 - \rho_5 = 200$$

(The estimates of over time and profit are not available and are assumed to be 20 and 200, respectively).

The first three equations are rigid constraints and the objective function would be to minimize $\eta_1 + \eta_2 + \rho_3$. The OT target would give us an objective function minimize ρ_4 and the profit goal would give us an objective to minimize η_5. The objective function is minimize $[(\eta_1 + \eta_2 + \rho_3), \rho_4, \eta_5]$.

1. When solved as a goal programming problem, we would have a solution with objective function values [0, 30, 0]. $\rho_4 = 30$ indicates that 30 more hours of OT are required. Once the second objective is not satisfied, the algorithm will not optimize η_5 but evaluate. The profit exceeds 200 and it will show η_5 as zero.
2. If for the same situation, the profit estimate were 300, it would evaluate η_5 to 12.5 (since a profit of 187.5 is only possible)

3. If we include the OT as a rigid constraint we would have had $\rho_4 = 30$ in the first objective itself. The first term taking a non-zero value indicates infeasibility.
4. If OT restriction was fixed at 50 or more then ρ_4 will be equal to zero and η_5 will take a value depending on the goal for profit. If profit was set as 200, we would have $\eta_5 = 0$ and for any value more than 287.5, we will have a positive η_5.
5. If more than one objective other than the rigid constraint (be it a target or goal) takes a zero value, it also means that we could change the target value depending on the priority and change the solution to the problem. OT = 50 would give us $\rho_4 = 0$ and a profit of 187.5 and OT = 60 would also give us $\rho_4 = 0$ but a profit of 311.667.

Let us solve the two examples. The first will be solved using the graphical method and the second by the simplex algorithm.

ILLUSTRATION 6.8

Minimize $[(\rho_1 + \rho_2), \eta_3, \rho_4, \rho_5]$
Subject to

$$3X_1 + 4X_2 + \eta_1 - \rho_1 = 50$$
$$5X_1 + 6X_2 + \eta_2 - \rho_2 = 60$$
$$70X_1 + 80X_2 + \eta_3 - \rho_3 = 800$$
$$X_1 + \eta_4 - \rho_4 = 8$$
$$X_1 + X_2 + \eta_5 - \rho_5 = 8$$
$$X_j, \eta_5, \rho_5 \geq 0$$

The lines are shown in Figure 6.1 along with the direction of the objective function (the deviation variable). The rigid conditions imply first the minimization of $\rho_1 + \rho_2$. The arrow marks show the direction of increase of ρ_1 and ρ_2, respectively. The rigid constraints give us the region below line 2 as having both ρ_1 and ρ_2 to zero. The first goal is to have a profit of 800 or more. This is indicated in line 3 and the direction of increasing η_3 is shown. The triangular region between lines 2 and 3 satisfy all the objectives. The vertical line $X_1 = 8$ represents the second goal and the area to the left would give us points with $\rho_4 = 0$. We

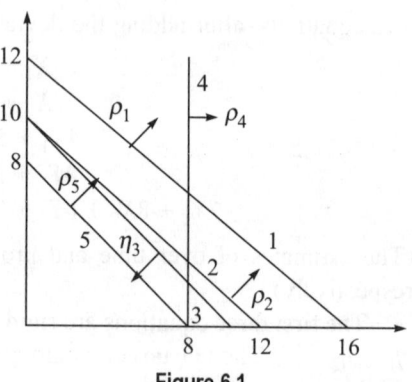

Figure 6.1

still have a feasible region indicating that there are multiple points satisfying all targets/goals. We have set the total production to eight units. This is given by line 5 and the direction of increase of ρ_5 is also shown. Here the area to the left of the line has $\rho_5 = 0$ and we have increase ρ_5 to meet the feasible region. The region $\rho_5 = 0$ and the present feasible region do not have any common area and we have to increase ρ_5 by moving the line in the direction of increase of ρ_5. When $\rho_5 = 2$, the line touches the feasible region giving the solution $X_1 = 0$ and $X_2 = 10$.

The solution is $X_1 = 0$ and $X_2 = 10$ with profit = 800 and minimum production quantity = 10 (away from the target by 2).

If we had fixed the production target at 12 (say) the line $\rho_5 = 0$ would give a feasible region and any point in the region would satisfy all targets and goals. Both the solutions $X_1 = 0$, $X_2 = 10$ with profit = 800 and quantity = 10 as well as $X_1 = 8$, $X_2 = 3.33$ profit = 816.66 and quantity = 11.33 will be acceptable. The objective function for the GP would be [0, 0, 0]. When we have an objective function [0, 0, 0], it means that we have a feasible region that satisfies all targets/goals and we can alter these targets and evaluate changes.

If we fix the profit target to 840, even when we draw the profit line, we will have a single point (12,0) as the feasible region. We will still have $\eta_3 = 0$. When we draw the next line $(X_1 + \eta_4 - \rho_4 = 8)$, we realize that there is no feasible region and we have to move this line to $\rho_4 = 4$ to reach the previous feasible point. So ρ_4 becomes 4 and when we draw the production quantity line we have to move it to $\rho_5 = 4$ to get a production target of 12. The objective function would be [0, 4, 4] with profit = 840 and quantity = 12.

ILLUSTRATION 6.9

Minimize $[(\eta_1 + \eta_2 + \rho_3), \rho_4, \eta_5]$
Subject to

$$X_1 + Y_1 + \eta_1 - \rho_1 = 20$$
$$X_2 + Y_2 + \eta_2 - \rho_2 = 20$$
$$4X_1 + 3X_2 + \eta_3 - \rho_3 = 90$$
$$4Y_1 + 3Y_2 + \eta_4 - \rho_4 = 20$$
$$7X_1 + 8X_2 + 6Y_1 + 7Y_2 + \eta_5 - \rho_5 = 200$$

Since the first term of the objective function has η_1, η_2 and ρ_3 we include the constraints (equations) that have these and create the initial simplex table. This is shown in Table 6.12.

Table 6.12 Initial Simplex Table

		0	0	0	0	1	0	1	0	0	1		
		X_1	Y_1	X_2	Y_2	η_1	ρ_1	η_2	ρ_2	η_3	ρ_3	RHS	θ
1	η_1	1	1	0	0	1	−1	0	0	0	0	20	20
1	η_2	0	0	1	1	0	0	1	−1	0	0	20	−
0	η_3	4	0	3	0	0	0	0	0	1	−1	90	45/2
	$C_j - Z_j$	−1	−1	−1	−1	0	1	0	1	0	1	40	

(In all these problems the variable η automatically qualifies to be a basic variable and the simplex table is started with the η as staring variables. Being a minimization problem, negative values of $C_j - Z_j$ will enter. We enter variable X_1 and variable η_1 leaves. The simplex iterations are shown in Table 6.13.

Table 6.13 Simplex Iterations

		0	0	0	0	1	0	1	0	0	1		
		X_1	Y_1	X_2	Y_2	η_1	ρ_1	η_2	ρ_2	η_3	ρ_3	RHS	θ
1	η_1	1	1	0	0	1	−1	0	0	0	0	20	20 →
1	η_2	0	0	1	1	0	0	1	−1	0	0	20	−
0	η_3	4↑	0	3	0	0	0	0	0	1	−1	90	45/2
	$C_j − Z_j$	−1	−1	−1	−1	0	1	0	1	0	1	40	
0	X_1	1	1	0	0	1	−1	0	0	0	0	20	−
1	η_2	0	0	1	1	0	0	1	−1	0	0	20	20
0	η_3	0	−4	3↑	0	−4	4	0	0	1	−1	10	10/3
	$C_j − Z_j$	0	0	−1	−1	1	0	0	1	0	1	20	

We enter variable X_2 having a negative value of $C_j − Z_j$ (minimization) and variable η_3 leaves. The simplex iterations are shown in Table 6.14.

Table 6.14 Simplex Iterations

		0	0	0	0	1	0	1	0	0	1		
		X_1	Y_1	X_2	Y_2	η_1	ρ_1	η_2	ρ_2	η_3	ρ_3	RHS	θ
1	η_1	1	1	0	0	1	−1	0	0	0	0	20	20 →
1	η_2	0	0	1	1	0	0	1	−1	0	0	20	−
0	η_3	4↑	0	3	0	0	0	0	0	1	−1	90	45/2
	$C_j − Z_j$	−1	−1	−1	−1	0	1	0	1	0	1	40	
0	X_1	1	1	0	0	1	−1	0	0	0	0	20	−
1	η_2	0	0	1	1	0	0	1	−1	0	0	20	20
0	η_3	0	−4	3↑	0	−4	4	0	0	1	−1	10	10/3 →
	$C_j − Z_j$	0	0	−1	−1	1	0	0	1	0	1	20	
0	X_1	1	1	0	0	1	−1	0	0	0	0	20	20
1	η_2	0	4/3	0	1	4/3	−4/3	1	−1	−1/3	1/3	50/3	25/2 →
0	X_2	0	−4/3↑	1	0	−4/3	4/3	0	0	1/3	−1/3	10/3	−
	$C_j − Z_j$	0	−4/3	0	−1	−1/3	4/3	0	1	1/3	2/3	20/3	

Variable Y_1 with the most negative $C_j − Z_j$ enters and variable η_2 leaves. The simplex iterations are shown in Table 6.15.

We have reached the optimum solution with $X_1 = 15/2$, $Y_1 = 25/2$, $X_2 = 20$ with $Z = 0$. Alternate optima exists with Y_1 entering the basis.

Table 6.15 Simplex Iterations

		0	0	0	0	1	0	1	0	0	1		
		X_1	Y_1	X_2	Y_2	η_1	ρ_1	η_2	ρ_2	η_3	ρ_3	RHS	θ
0	X_1	1	1	0	0	1	−1	0	0	0	0	20	20
1	η_2	0	4/3	0	1	4/3	−4/3	1	−1	−1/3	1/3	50/3	5 →
0	X_2	0	−4/3	1	0	−4/3	4/3	0	0	1/3	−1/3	10/3	−
	$C_j - Z_j$	0	−4/3	0	−1	−1/3	4/3	0	1	1/3	2/3	20/3	
0	X_1	1	0	0	−3/4	0	0	−3/4	3/4	1/4	−1/4	15/2	
0	Y_1	0	1	0	3/4	1	−1	3/4	−3/4	−1/4	1/4	25/2	
0	X_2	0	0	1	1	0	0	1	−1	0	0	20	
	$C_j - Z_j$	0	0	0	0	1	0	1	0	0	1	0	

From the first table we could have identified $Y_1 = 20$, $Y_2 = 20$ and $\eta_3 = 90$ as optimum with $Z = 0$. We proceed from our optimum table, from which we find that $\eta_1 = \eta_2 = \eta_3 = \rho_1 = \rho_2 = \rho_3 = 0$. These are all non-basic and do not figure in the remaining constraints of the problem. We remove all of them from the simplex table and introduce the fourth constraint. The simplex table is shown in Table 6.16.

Table 6.16 Simplex Table

		0	0	0	0	0	1		
		X_1	Y_1	X_2	Y_2	η_4	ρ_4	RHS	θ
0	X_1	1	0	0	−3/4	0	0	15/2	
0	Y_1	0	1	0	3/4	0	0	25/2	
0	X_2	0	0	1	1	0	0	20	
0	η_4	0	0	0	0	1	−1	−30 →	
	$C_j - Z_j$	0	0	0	0	0	1	0	

From the simplex table we have $Y_1 = 25/2 - 3/4\ Y_2$. Substituting in $4Y_1 + 3Y_2 + \eta_4 - \rho_4 = 20$, we get $50 - 3Y_2 + 3Y_2 + \eta_4 - \rho_4 = 20$, from which $\eta_4 - \rho_4 = -30$. This is written in Table 6.16 and it is found that the present table is infeasible. A dual simplex iteration is carried out with η_4 as leaving variable and ρ_4 as entering variable. This is shown in Table 6.17.

The present solution is optimal with $\rho_4 = 30$. Now, that we have an optimal solution with a non-zero value of the objective function, we evaluate the fifth goal, which is:

$$7X_1 + 8X_2 + 6Y_1 + 7Y_2 + \eta_5 - \rho_5 = 200.$$

Substituting for X_1, X_2 and Y_1, we get $\rho_5 = 87.5$. The objective function is [0, 30, 0].

Table 6.17 Dual Simplex Iteration

		0	0	0	0	0	1		
		X_1	Y_1	X_2	Y_2	η_4	P_4	RHS	θ
0	X_1	1	0	0	−3/4	0	0	15/2	
0	Y_1	0	1	0	3/4	0	0	25/2	
0	X_2	0	0	1	1	0	0	20	
0	η_4	0	0	0	0	1	−1	−30	→
	$C_j - Z_j$	0	0	0	0	0	1	0	
0	X_1	1	0	0	−3/4	0	0	15/2	
0	Y_1	0	1	0	3/4	0	0	25/2	
0	X_2	0	0	1	1	0	0	20	
1	P_4	0	0	0	0	−1	1	30	
	$C_j - Z_j$	0	0	0	0	1	0	30	

6.7 HOW FAST AND GOOD IS THE SIMPLEX METHOD?

So far, all our discussions on linear programming have involved simplex method as the solution methodology for linear programming problems. We also addressed the issue of the need to solve the linear programming problems quickly and realized that the speed of the simplex algorithm depended on the number of iterations taken and the time taken per iteration. We also studied the revised simplex algorithm as a method to solve an iteration quickly because the matrix inversion method (eta factorization of the basis) is an efficient way to invert large matrices. Let us consider now the other dimension, namely, number of iterations.

Two other factors that have to be considered when we wish to analyze the number of iterations are degeneracy and cycling. We have seen both of them in Chapter 2 where we studied the simplex algorithm. We also saw that the smallest subscript rule (called **Bland's rule**) can be used to prevent cycling. We know that while degeneracy results in more than the minimum number of iterations to solve the problem, cyclic is more serious that the algorithm would not terminate if it cycles. We also mentioned that both the lexicographic rule and the Bland's rule (Bland, 1977, Avis and Chvatal, 1978) will ensure that simplex terminates in a finite number of iterations. Though both the rules guarantee termination, they do not guarantee termination in minimum number of iterations. We will see more of the lexicographic method in Example 6.8.

The number of iterations taken to solve a linear programming problem depends on the rule for entering variable. By now, it is obvious that any variable with a positive value of $C_j - Z_j$ qualifies to be an entering variable. There are at least four popular rules to identify the entering variable in a simplex iteration:
1. Largest coefficient rule
2. Largest increase rule
3. First positive rule
4. Random rule

The largest coefficient rule chooses that the non-basic variable with the most positive value of $C_j - Z_j$ as the entering variable (for a maximization problem). This value represents the maximum rate of increase of the objective function. The $C_j - Z_j$ represents the rate of increase of the objective function for a unit increase in the entering variable. It also represents the extent of infeasibility of the dual and entering the variable with maximum $C_j - Z_j$ represents satisfying the dual constraint that is most violated.

The largest increase rule could be termed as the most *greedy* among the methods. Here we find all the entering variables with a positive value of $C_j - Z_j$ and for each, find the maximum value that the entering variable can take (minimum θ value) and finds the increase in the objective function given by the product of $C_j - Z_j$ and θ. We enter that variable which results in maximum increase in the value of the objective function. This is computationally more intensive compared to the largest coefficient rule.

In first positive rule, we evaluate $C_j - Z_j$ for all non-basic variables and the moment we find a non-basic variable with a positive $C_j - Z_j$, we enter it.

In the random rule, we randomly pick a non-basic variable and if the value of its $C_j - Z_j$ is positive, we enter it. We repeat this procedure till we find the first randomly considered variable with a positive $C_j - Z_j$.

Among these the largest coefficient rule is the most popular and is used extensively. Computational experiments conducted on randomly generated problems have also indicated that this rule has the best average case performance. Though the largest increase rule results in less number of iterations (on an average), the largest coefficient rule is superior in terms of time taken to solve the problem (Chvatal, 1983). No method is distinctly superior to another and outperforms another. However, the first positive rule is often applied in software packages for the simplex algorithm.

The Klee and Minty (1972) problems, however, gave a new perspective to the entering variable rule. These are problems that are of the form:

Maximize $\sum_{j=1}^{n} 10^{n-j} X_j$

Subject to

$$2 \sum_{j=1}^{i-1} 10^{i-j} X_j + X_i \leq 100^{i-1} \quad \forall i$$

$$X_j \geq 0$$

ILLUSTRATION 6.10

Maximize $Z = 100X_1 + 10X_2 + X_3$

Subject to

$$X_1 \leq 1$$
$$20X_1 + X_2 \leq 100$$
$$200X_1 + 20X_2 + X_3 \leq 10000$$
$$X_1, X_2, X_3 \geq 0$$

The simplex tables based on the largest coefficient rule as the entering rule and slack variables as initial basic variables for Illustration 6.9 is shown in Table 6.18.

Table 6.18 Simplex Table

		100	10	1	0	0	0		
		X_1	X_2	X_3	X_4	X_5	X_6	RHS	θ
0	X_4	1	0	0	1	0	0	1	1 →
0	X_5	20	1	0	0	1	0	100	5
0	X_6	200	20	1	0	0	1	10000	50
	$C_j - Z_j$	100	10	1	0	0	0	0	
100	X_1	1	0	0	1	0	0	1	—
0	X_5	0	1	0	−20	1	1	80	80
0	X_6	0	20	1	−200	0	1	9800	490
	$C_j - Z_j$	0	10	1	−100	0	0	100	
100	X_1	1	0	0	1	0	0	1	1 →
10	X_2	0	1	0	−20	1	1	80	—
0	X_6	0	0	1	200	−20	1	8200	41
	$C_j - Z_j$	0	0	0	100	−10	0	900	
0	X_4	1	0	0	1	0	0	1	
10	X_2	20	1	0	0	1	0	100	
0	X_6	−200	0	1	0	−20	1	8000	8000 →
	$C_j - Z_j$	−100	0	1	0	−10	0	1000	
0	X_4	1	0	0	1	0	0	1	1 →
10	X_2	20	1	0	0	1	0	100	5
1	X_3	−200	0	1	0	−20	1	8000	
	$C_j - Z_j$	100	0	0	0	10	−1	9000	
100	X_1	1	0	0	1	0	0	1	→
10	X_2	0	1	0	−20	1	0	80	
1	X_3	0	0	1	200	−20	1	8200	
	$C_j - Z_j$	0	0	0	−100	10	0	9100	
100	X_1	1	0	0	1	0	0	1	→
0	X_5	0	1	0	−20	1	0	80	
1	X_3	0	20	1	−200	10	1	9800	
	$C_j - Z_j$	0	−10	0	100	0	0	9900	
0	X_4	1	0	0	1	0	0	1	
0	X_5	20	1	0	0	1	0	100	
1	X_3	200	20	1	0	0	1	10000	
	$C_j - Z_j$	−100	−10	0	0	0	−1	10000	

The Klee and Minty problems are found to take $2^n - 1$ iterations (where n is the number of variables) to reach the optimum if the entering variable is chosen based on the largest coefficient rule. Our example took seven iterations to terminate. Based on this example, it is accepted that the simplex algorithm is a theoretically a worst case exponential algorithm and, therefore, is not an efficient algorithm.

(In the same example if we had chosen X_3 as a basic variable instead of X_6, the starting solution itself is optimal. Also if we had chosen the largest increase rule in the present table, X_3 would have replaced X_6 and the optimum would have been reached in one iteration. Also if we had scaled the variables as $Y_1 = X_1$, $Y_2 = 0.01X_2$ and $Y_3 = 0.0001X_3$, and used the largest coefficient rule, the optimum would be found in one iteration).

While the three-variable example took seven iterations when we used the largest coefficient rule, it is also possible to create examples that take exponential number of iterations for any given rule. Whether there exists a rule for which it is not possible to create such an example is an open question.

Because the simplex algorithm is a worst case exponential algorithm, there was a need to develop algorithms for linear programming that run in polynomial time. The first effort was to use Kachian's ellipsoid algorithm for this purpose.

Kachian (1979) developed the ellipsoid algorithm to solve inequalities. Solving inequalities means identifying at least one point that satisfies all the given inequalities. Till then, there was no polynomially bounded algorithm for solving inequalities. This algorithm can be applied to solve LP problems.

Consider the primal
Maximize cX
Subject to
$$AX \leq b$$
$$X \geq 0$$

Its dual is
Minimize Yb
Subject to
$$YA^T \geq c^T$$
$$Y \geq 0$$

We also know that the primal and dual have the same values of the objective function at the optimum. Also from the weak duality theorem, the only feasible solution where the primal has an objective function equal to the dual, is the optimal solution. The set of following inequalities
$$AX \leq b$$
$$X \geq 0$$
$$YA^T \geq c^T$$
$$Y \geq 0$$
$$cX \geq Yb$$

can solve both the primal and dual, respectively. Kachian's algorithm can be applied to solve the set of inequalities in polynomial time and hence used to solve LP problems optimally in polynomial time.

There were two issues: One was that the LP problem when converted as a set of inequalities had only one feasible point (if both primal and dual had optimal solutions). There was some difficulty in adapting the ellipsoid algorithm to situations where there was only one feasible point. This was resolved subsequently.

The second issue was that though it was theoretically possible to obtain the optimum in polynomial time using the ellipsoid algorithm, the average case performance of the ellipsoid algorithm was very poor when compared to the simplex algorithm (even for small sized problems). Therefore, simplex continues to be the most widely used algorithm to solve linear programming problems.

The other effort towards solving the linear programming problem in polynomial time was the development of the Karmarkar's algorithm (1984). Here, a polynomially bounded algorithm to solve a specific form of LP problems was developed. A method to convert every LP problem into Karmarkar form in polynomial time was also developed. This algorithm is able to perform better than the simplex algorithm in the average case only for very large sized problems. For the normal sizes that we encounter, simplex still seems to be doing better in average case performance. Simplex algorithm continues to be the most widely used algorithm to solve linear programming problems because of its superior average case performance and ease of understanding and application.

SOLVED EXAMPLES

EXAMPLE 6.1 Consider the linear programming problem:

Maximize $7X_1 + 9X_2$

Subject to
$$X_1 + 3X_2 \leq 12;\ 4X_1 + 2X_2 \leq 15;\ X_1, X_2 \geq 0$$

Assume that you are solving this problem by the product form of inverse (Eta matrices). Given that X_1 and X_2 are the basic variables at the optimum,

(a) Find the E_1 and E_2 matrices.
(b) Find the optimum solution to the dual.
(c) Find the optimum solution to the primal and the objective function value.
(d) If an additional constraint $X_2 \leq 3$ is added, apply an upper bounded simplex algorithm (do not add a constraint) at this stage and get the new optimum.
(e) Explain the reduction in terms of $C_j - Z_j$ and θ.

Solution: (a) X_2 enters the basis and X_3 leaves.

$$E_1 = \begin{bmatrix} 3 & 0 \\ 2 & 1 \end{bmatrix}$$

In second iteration, X_1 enters and X_4 leaves.

$$E_2 = \begin{bmatrix} 0 & a \\ 1 & b \end{bmatrix}$$

Since $E_1 = \begin{bmatrix} 3 & 0 \\ 2 & 1 \end{bmatrix}$, we get

$$E_2 = \begin{bmatrix} 1 & 1/3 \\ 0 & 10/3 \end{bmatrix}$$

(b) $yB = C_B$

$$[y_1 \ y_2] \begin{bmatrix} 3 & 1 \\ 2 & 4 \end{bmatrix} = [9 \ 7]$$

Since $B = E_1 E_2$, we can use these to get the value of y.

$$y = [11/5 \ 6/5]$$

(c) $BX = b$. We can use $B = E_1 E_2$ to get

$$X = \begin{bmatrix} 33/10 \\ 21/10 \end{bmatrix} \text{ and } Z = 222/5$$

(d) $B^{-1} = \begin{bmatrix} 2/5 & -1/10 \\ -1/5 & 3/10 \end{bmatrix}$

$$X_2 = \frac{33}{10} - \frac{2}{5} X_3 + \frac{1}{10} X_4$$

$$X_1 = \frac{21}{10} + \frac{1}{5} X_3 - \frac{3}{10} X_4$$

The upper bound $X_2 \leq 3$ is not satisfied by the LP optimum. We replace $X_2 = 3 + X_2^*$ in the first equation and let X_3 replace X_2 in the basis. The equations are:

$$X_3 = 3/4 - \frac{5}{2} X_2^* + 1/4 \ X_4$$

and

$$X_1 = \frac{9}{4} - \frac{1}{2} X_2^* - \frac{1}{4} X_4$$

$$Z = \frac{171}{4} + \frac{11}{2} X_2^* - \frac{7}{4} X_4$$

This is the optimum solution.

EXAMPLE 6.2 Given a LP

Maximize $3X_1' + 2X_2'$

$$8X_1' + 5X_2' \leq 40$$
$$5X_1' + 9X_2' \leq 45$$
$$1 \leq X_1' \leq 6$$
$$0 \leq X_2' \leq 4$$

(a) Solve the problem using simplex method for bounded variables.
(b) Write an algorithm for the procedure followed by you.
(c) If instead of the second constraint if you had $X_1 + X_2 \geq 5$, what happens to your solution?

Solution: We define a new variable $X_1 = X'_1 - 1$

$$X_2 = X'_2$$

The new problem becomes

Maximize $3X_1 + 2X_2$

Subject to

$$8X_1 + 5X_2 \leq 32$$
$$5X_1 + 9X_2 \leq 40$$
$$0 \leq X_1 \leq 5$$
$$0 \leq X_2 \leq 4$$

Table 6.19 shows the solution using simplex algorithm for bounded variables. We obtain $X_1 = 88/47$ and $X_2 = 160/47$. Thus, $X'_1 = 135/47$ and $X'_2 = 160/47$ and $Z = 725/47$.

Table 6.19 Solution Using Simplex Algorithm

C_J		3	2	0	0			
		X_1	X_2	X_3	X_4	RHS	θ	α
0	X_3	8	5	1	0	32	4	→
0	X_4	5↑	9	0	1	40	8	
	$C_j - Z_j$	3	2	0	0	Z = 0		
	X_1	1	5/8	1/8	0	4	32/5	
	X_4	0	47/8↑	−5/8	1	20	160/47	
	$C_j - Z_j$	0	1/8	−3/8	0	Z = 12		
	X_1	1	0	9/47	−5/47	88/47		
	X_2	0	1	−5/47	8/47	160/47		
	$C_j - Z_j$	0	0	−17/47	−1/47	Z = 584/47		

(b) The linear programming algorithm using simplex method with bounded variables may be summarized as:
- A new column which finds out the limiting value of the entering variable that can make an existing variable reach its upper bound is introduced. This is the alpha column.
- When the entering variable enters with a value higher than its upper bound, we make it reach its upper bound. But it doesn't enter the simplex as basic variable.
- The table remains the same, but the RHS values change.

$$\text{New RHS} = \text{Old RHS} - \text{Coefficient} * \text{UB value of bounded variable}$$

- The variable with the next highest $C_j - Z_j$ enters and the simplex iterations continue.
- In a later iteration, if the variable at the upper bound enters, it need not have a positive $C_j - Z_j$. The leaving variable has a positive alpha. In that case, theta is computed when the coefficient in that row is negative.
- The algorithm terminates when a $C_j - Z_j$ for the variable at its upper bound is positive and remaining $C_j - Z_j s$ are positive or zero.

In our case (c), there was no alpha and the algorithm terminated as there was no entering variable after trying to enter X_2.

(c) The second constraint is replaced by a new constraint. The new problem is:

Maximize $3X'_1 + 2X'_2$

Subject to

$$8X'_1 + 5X'_2 \leq 40$$
$$X'_1 + X'_2 \geq 5$$
$$1 \leq X'_1 \leq 6$$
$$0 \leq X'_2 \leq 4$$

We define a new variable
$$X_1 = X'_1 - 1$$
$$X_2 = X'_2$$

The new problem becomes

Maximize $3X_1 + 2X_2$

Subject to

$$8X_1 + 5X_2 \leq 32$$
$$X_1 + X_2 \leq 4$$
$$0 \leq X_1 \leq 5$$
$$0 \leq X_2 \leq 4$$

The simplex iterations are shown in Table 6.20.

Table 6.20 Simplex Iterations

C_J		3	2	0	0	0		
		X_1	X_2	X_3	X_4	X_5	RHS	θ
0	X_3	8	5	1	0	0	32	4
0	X_5	1	1	0	−1	1	4	4
	$C_J - Z_J$	3	2	0	0	0	Z = 0	
0	X_3	0	−3	1	8	−8	0	0
3	X_1	1	1	0	−1	1	4	—
	$C_J - Z_J$	0	−1	0	3	−3		
0	X_4	0	−3/8	1/8	1	−1	0	
3	X_1	1	5/8	1/8	0	0	4	32/5
	$C_J - Z_J$	0	1/16	−3/8	0	0		
0	X_4	0	−3/8	1/8	1	−1	3/2	
3	X_1	1	5/8	1/8	0	0	3/2	
	$C_J - Z_J$	0	1/16*	−3/8	0	0	Z = 9/2 + 8	

We obtain $X_1 = 3/2$ and $X_2 = X_2^* = 4$. Thus, $X_1' = 5/2$, $X_2' = 4$ and $Z = 31/2$.

EXAMPLE 6.3 Maximize $3X_1 + 5Y + 2X_3$,
Subject to
$$X_1 + Y + 2X_3 \leq 14,$$
$$2X_1 + 4Y + 3X_3 \leq 43,$$
$$0 \leq X_1 \leq 4, \ 7 \leq Y \leq 10, \ 0 \leq X_3 \leq 3$$

Starting with a solution $X_4 = 5/2$, $X_1 = 3/2$, $Z = 109/2$ proceed to get the optimum solution.

Solution: As the current starting solution is $X_1 = 3/2$, $X_4 = 5/2$, $Z = 109/2$, we realize that $Y = 10$. Let us define $Y = Y^* + 10$. Then the problem becomes

Maximize $50 + 3X_1 + 5Y^* + 2X_3$
Subject to
$$X_1 + Y^* + 2X_3 + X_4 = 4,$$
$$2X_1 + Y^* + 3X_3 + X_5 = 3$$

Writing the basic variables X_4 and X_1 in terms of the non-basic variables, we have

$$X_4 = \frac{5}{2} + \frac{X_5}{2} - \frac{X_3}{2} + Y^* \quad \theta = -5/2$$

$$X_1 = \frac{3}{2} - \frac{X_5}{2} - \frac{3X_3}{2} - 2Y^* \quad \alpha = 5/4$$

Advanced Linear Programming   219

$$Z = \frac{109}{2} - \frac{3X_5}{2} - \frac{5X_3}{2} - Y^*$$

Y^* enters the basis, X_1 leaving the basis at its upper bound of 4. Hence, we define $X_1 = 4 + X_1^*$.
We have

$$Y = \frac{35}{4} - \frac{X_1^*}{2} - \frac{X_5}{4} - \frac{3X_3}{4}$$

$$X_4 = \frac{5}{4} + \frac{X_5}{4} - \frac{5X_3}{4} - \frac{X_1^*}{2}$$

$$Z = \frac{223}{4} + \frac{X_1^*}{2} - \frac{7X_4}{5} - \frac{13X_3}{4}$$

The objective function cannot be increased further, since all the dual variables are positive and hence feasible. The optimal solution therefore is:

$$X_1 = 4, X_4 = \frac{5}{4}, Z = 223/4$$

EXAMPLE 6.4 Consider the one-dimensional cutting stock problem to cut 201 sheets of 8 inch 167 sheets of 7 inch and 189 sheets of 6 inch from 20 inch wide sheets. An LP formulation was made using patterns $X_1 = [2\ 0\ 0]$, $X_2 = [0\ 2\ 1]$, $X_3 = [0\ 1\ 2]$, $X_4 = [1\ 0\ 2]$ and $X_5 = [1\ 1\ 0]$. The simplex solution (not using column generation) was $X_1 = 74.125$, $X_2 = 83.5$ and $X_4 = 52.75$.

(a) It was realized that the pattern $[0\ 0\ 3]$ was left out of the formulation by mistake. Is the given solution optimum even if it were considered? If not, find the new optimum.
(b) Find the IP optimum from the LP optimum.
(c) If only 22 inch sheets were available instead of 20 inch sheets, is the solution optimal? If not, find an entering pattern.

$$X_1 = [2\ 0\ 0] = 74.125, X_2 = [0\ 2\ 1] = 83.5 \text{ and } X_4 = [1\ 0\ 2] = 52.75$$

Solution: We find the dual variables using $yB = 1$

$$y = [y_1\ y_2\ y_3] \begin{bmatrix} 2 & 0 & 1 \\ 0 & 2 & 0 \\ 0 & 1 & 2 \end{bmatrix} = [1\ 1\ 1]$$

$$y = \begin{bmatrix} \frac{1}{2} & \frac{3}{8} & \frac{1}{4} \end{bmatrix}$$

(a) Considering the pattern $[0\ 0\ 3]$, we compute

$$[1/2\ 3/8\ 1/4] \begin{bmatrix} 0 \\ 0 \\ 3 \end{bmatrix} = 3/4$$

This is less than 1 and the optimum is not changed.

(b) The higher integer value of the LP optimum provides a lower bound to the IP. LB = 211. The lower integer value of the values taken by the variables at the optimum gives an infeasible solution.

74 of [2 0 0] and 83 of [0 2 1] and 52 of [1 0 2] give us 200 out of 201 8 inch sheets, 166 out of 167 required 7 inch sheets and 187 out of 189 required 6 inch sheets. With 209 sheets we get the above break up. We can introduce a sheet with cut [1 0 2] and another with [0 1 0] to get a total of 211 sheets and a feasible solution. Since 211 is a lower bound, it is optimum to the IP.

(c) If 22 inch sheets are available, we consider a pattern $[y_1\ y_2\ y_3]$ to maximize $1/2\ y_1 + 3/8\ y_2 + 1/4\ y_3$ subject to $8y_1 + 7y_2 + 6y_3 \leq 22$. A feasible pattern [2 0 1] with an objective function value 1.25 (>1) can enter.

EXAMPLE 6.5 Given a cutting stock problem where 97 pieces of 45 inches are required, 610 pieces of 36 inches, 395 of 31 inches and 211 of 14 inches are required; you are given a feasible solution to the LP:

[2 0 0 0] = 48.5, [0 2 0 2] = 105.5, [0 2 0 0] = 100.75 and [0 1 2 0] = 197.5

Verify whether the solution is optimal.

Solution: Since the size of the stock is not given, we shall assume it to be P. From the given patterns of the feasible solution, $P \geq$ max (45*2, 36*2 + 14*2, 36*2, 36*1 + 31*2) = max (90, 100, 72, 98). So, the minimum size of the stock P is 100 inches.

Formulation: The formulation is of the form:

Minimize ΣX_j

Subject to

$$\Sigma a_{ij} X_j = b_i$$
$$X_j \geq 0$$

where X_j is the number of sheets cut using pattern j. A pattern is of the form [a b c d] and any a, b, c, d that satisfies $45a + 36b + 31c + 14d \leq P$ and a, b, c, d ≥ 0 is a feasible pattern.

The given solution is basic as well as feasible as there are 4 constraints and 4 patterns (variables). We take the initial solution to the problem as the patterns in the given feasible solution. Each basic variable represents a pattern. So, the dual to the problem has four variables, which we call y_1 to y_4. The basis matrix for the solution is made of the columns corresponding to the basic variables and is given by

$$B = \begin{bmatrix} 2 & 0 & 0 & 0 \\ 0 & 2 & 2 & 1 \\ 0 & 0 & 0 & 2 \\ 0 & 2 & 0 & 0 \end{bmatrix}$$

The solution to the dual is given by $yB = C_B$. Since all the objective function coefficients are 1, the dual solution is [1/2, 1/2, 1/4, 0]. To verify whether the present solution is optimal, we need to verify whether the dual solution is feasible. This dual solution is feasible if for all possible patterns [a b c d] $a/2 + b/2 + c/4 \leq 1$.

Alternately, if for any pattern [a b c d] the constraint is violated then the dual is infeasible and the pattern enters the basis. We need to find out a pattern [a b c d] such that

$$\frac{a}{2} + \frac{b}{2} + \frac{c}{4} > 1 \text{ and}$$

$$45a + 36b + 31c + 14d \le P$$

$$a, b, c, d \ge 0 \text{ and integer}$$

We model this problem as a knapsack problem with one constraint and solve it using a branch and bound method.

Knapsack problem: The problem that we try to solve now is:

Maximize $\frac{a}{2} + \frac{b}{2} + \frac{c}{4}$ (This should be greater than 1 for the pattern to enter!)

Subject to

$$45a + 36b + 31c + 14d \le P$$

$a, b, c, d \ge 0$ and integer

Arranging the terms in the decreasing order of the (c_j/a_j):

$$\text{Max } \frac{b}{2} + \frac{a}{2} + \frac{c}{4}$$

$$36b + 45a + 31c + 14d \le P$$

So, we have

$$b = \frac{P}{36}$$

Assuming $P < 108$ (and we know that $P > 100$), the integral part of $P/36$ is 2. So, $b = 2$. Substituting $b = 2$ in the constraint, we get

$$45a + 31c + 14d \le P - 72$$

Then we have

$a = \frac{(P-72)}{45} = 0$ since $(P - 72)$ is less than 45 for $P < 108$. Substituting $a = 0$ in the inequality gives:

$$31c + 14d \le P - 72$$

$$\therefore \quad c = \frac{(P-72)}{31} = 0 \text{ for } P < 103$$

For $100 \le P \le 102$, we have $c = 0$. Substituting this gives

$$14d \le P - 72$$

or

$$d = 2$$

But the solution [0 2 0 2] cannot enter since $1/2a + 1/2b + 1/4c = 1$ for this pattern. Moreover, this pattern is already in the given feasible solution!
Now, let's consider the case $103 \le P \le 107$,

Then we have,

$$c = \frac{(P-72)}{31} = 1$$

Substituting $c = 1$ in the inequality gives

$$14d \leq P - 103$$

which gives $d = 0$ for $103 \leq P \leq 107$. So, the new pattern can be [0 2 1 0] if it satisfies the condition $1/2 a + 1/2\ b + 1/4 c > 1$. Substitution in LHS gives

$$\frac{1}{2}*0 + \frac{1}{2}*2 + \frac{1}{4}*0 = \frac{5}{4} > 1$$

The pattern [0 2 1 0] enters if $P > 102$, i.e., the minimum stock size required to have a new optimal is 103 inches.

Conclusion: The given feasible solution is the optimal solution to the problem for a stock size of value less than 103 inches.

EXAMPLE **6.6** Solve the following LPP using the decomposition algorithm by treating the second and third constraint as a sub problem and treating the first constraint as the master problem.

Minimize $8x_1 + 6x_2 + 4x_3$
Subject to

$$3x_1 + x_2 + x_3 \leq 12$$
$$x_1 + x_2 \geq 2$$
$$2x_1 + 3x_2 \geq 8$$
$$x_1, x_2, x_3 \geq 0$$

Solution: Minimize $8X_1 + 6X_2 + 4X_3$
Subject to

$$3X_1 + X_2 + X_3 \leq 12$$
$$X_1 + X_2 \geq 2$$
$$2X_1 + 3X_2 \geq 8$$
$$X_1, X_2 \geq 0$$

The problem has 3 variables and 3 constraints. We treat the first constraint as the master problem, treating the second and third constraints as the subproblem.

Subproblem constraints:

$$X_1 + X_2 \geq 2$$
$$2X_1 + 3X_2 \geq 8$$
$$X_1, X_2, X_3 \geq 0.$$

Master problem constraint:

$$3X_1 + X_2 + X_3 \leq 12$$

Corner points: Corner points for subproblem 1 are (0, 8/3), (4, 0). The optimum solution to the original problem is a convex combination of the corner points. Let us consider the original problem in the form:

Minimize cx

Subject to
$$Ax = b$$
$$x \in X$$

x can be written as:
$$x = \Sigma \lambda_j X_j$$

where $\Sigma \lambda_j = 1$ and $\lambda_j \geq 0$.

The master problem becomes

Minimize $\Sigma c X_j \lambda_j$

Subject to
$$\Sigma A X_j \lambda_j = b$$
$$\Sigma \lambda_j = 1$$
$$\lambda_j \geq 0$$

Let the dual variables be
$$(w, \alpha) = C_B B^{-1}.$$
$$Z_k - C_k = \text{Maximum } (w, \alpha)[AX_j - cX_j + 1]$$

Maximum $wAX_j - cX_j + \alpha$

Constraint of the master problem represent $AX \leq b$. Then
$$A = [3\ 1\ 1]\ b = [1\ 2]$$

The initial basis is made of one slack variable, namely, S_1, the variable λ_1 corresponding to the feasible solution $X_1 = (4, 0, 0)$. $B = I$. The simplex iteration is shown in Table 6.21.

$$(w\ \alpha) = (0\ 0)$$

Maximum $wAX_j - cX_j + \alpha$

i.e., Maximize $-8X_1 - 6X_2 - 4X_3$

Here $c = [8, 6, 4]$

Table 6.21 Simplex Iteration

	B^{-1}		RHS
S_1	1	0	12
λ_1	0	1	1
Z	0	0	−32

Subproblem is solved to get the optimal solution which is (0, 8/3) and $X_3 = 0$ with $Z = -16$. The corner point (0, 8/3, 0) enters the basis as variable λ_2. The entering column is given by

$$A = [3\ 1\ 1]\ b = [1\ 2]$$

$$AX_2 = [3\ 1\ 1] \begin{bmatrix} 0 \\ 8/3 \\ 0 \end{bmatrix} = 8/3$$

The entering column is:

$$\begin{bmatrix} 8/3 \\ 1 \end{bmatrix}$$

The simplex iteration is shown in Table 6.22.

Table 6.22 Simplex Iteration

	B^{-1}		RHS	Entering column λ_2	θ
S_1	1	0	12	8/3	9/2
λ_1	0	1	1	1	1
Z	0	0	−32	16	

Now, λ_2 enters the basis and replaces λ_1. The simplex iteration is shown in Table 6.23.

Table 6.23 Two Iterations

	B^{-1}		RHS	Entering column λ_2	θ
S_1	1	0	12	8/3	12/(8/3)
λ_1	0	1	1	1	1
Z	0	0	−32	−16	
S_1	1	−8/3	12 −8/3	0	
λ_1	0	1	1	1	
Z	0	16	−16		

The feasible solution at the end of this iteration is $X = (0, 8/3, 0)$.
We need to verify whether this is optimal. From the simplex table, we find

$$(w, \alpha) = (0, 16)$$

Now, Maximize $\qquad wAX_j - cX_j + \alpha$
Compute $\qquad wA - c = (-8, -6, -4)$
Maximize $\;\; -8X_1 - 6X_2 - 4X_3$

The sub problem is solved to get the optimal solution which is (0, 8/3, 0).

Since the maximum $Z_k - C_k = 0$, we do not have an entering variable. The algorithm terminates. The solution to the given problem is given by $X_1 = 0$, $X_2 = 8/3$, $X_3 = 0$ with $Z = 16$

EXAMPLE 6.7 Given the linear programming problem:
Maximize $\;\; 4X_1 + 7X_2$
Subject to

$$X_1 + 2X_2 \leq 5$$
$$2X_1 + 3X_2 \leq 9$$
$$X_1, X_2 \geq 0$$

Write the LP as a system of inequalities.
The dual to the given problem is:
Minimize $5Y_1 + 9Y_2$
Subject to

$$Y_1 + 2Y_2 \geq 4$$
$$2Y_1 + 3Y_2 \geq 7$$
$$Y_1, Y_2 \geq 0$$

From weak duality theorem, we know that every feasible solution to the dual has an objective function value higher than every feasible solution to the primal and the only solution (if it exists) is where both the values are equal. We can add a condition $4X_1 + 7X_2 \geq 5Y_1 + 9Y_2$ and write the set of inequalities

$$X_1 + 2X_2 \leq 5$$
$$2X_1 + 3X_2 \leq 9$$
$$X_1, X_2 \geq 0$$
$$Y_1 + 2Y_2 \geq 4$$
$$2Y_1 + 3Y_2 \geq 7$$
$$Y_1, Y_2 \geq 0$$
$$4X_1 + 7X_2 \geq 5Y_1 + 9Y_2$$

The solution to the above inequalities will give us the optimum solution to both primal and dual if they exist. There is also only one point that satisfies all the above inequalities (why?).

EXAMPLE 6.8 You are given a transportation problem in the usual notation in Table 6.24. There is an additional restriction that a maximum of 40 units can be transported from any source to any destination. Apply principles from simplex method for bounded variables and solve the capacitated transportation problem.

Table 6.24 Transportation Problem

8	6	7	6	80
5	8	5	6	100
50	40	40	50	

Solution: The solution using North west corner rule (using upper bounds during allocation) is given in Table 6.25.

Table 6.25 Feasible Solution

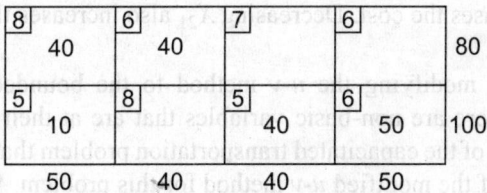

This violates the upper bounds. We allocate $X_{14} = 10$ so that $X_{44} = 40$. The feasible solution to the capacitated problem thus obtained is shown in Table 6.26.

Table 6.26 Feasible Solution to the Capacitated Problem

[8] 30	[6] 40	[7]	[6] 10	80
[5] 20	[8]	[5] 40	[6] 40	100
50	40	40	50	

This feasible solution has $Z = 1080$.

There are three non-basic positions, X_{13} and X_{22} at zero and X_{44} at its upper bound. We consider adding 1 unit to X_{13} and observe that the net cost is decreasing by 1 Re. Adding 1 unit to X_{22} increases the cost while subtracting from X_{24} increases the cost.

If we add θ to X_{13}, the loop is completed by making $X_{23} = 40 - \theta$, $X_{21} = 20 + \theta$ and $X_{11} = 30 - \theta$. The maximum value θ can take is 20 beyond which X_{21} will exceed the upper bound. We update the solution as shown in Table 6.27.

Table 6.27 Updated Solution

[8] 10	[6] 40	[7] 20	[6] 10	80
[5] 40	[8]	[5] 20	[6] 40	100
50	40	40	50	

In the solution shown in Table 6.27, we have three non-basic positions $X_{22} = 0$ and $X_{21} = X_{24} = 40$ (upper bound). Inserting 1 unit at X_{22} will increase the cost while decreasing X_{24} can decrease the cost. The maximum decrease is 20 units beyond which X_{23} will exceed the upper bound and X_{13} will become negative. The new solution is shown in Table 6.28 with a cost of 1020.

Table 6.28 New Solution

[8] 10	[6] 40	[7]	[6] 30	80
[5] 40	[8]	[5] 40	[6] 20	100
50	40	40	50	

We observe that increasing X_{13} can only increase the cost considering the upper bound. Increasing X_{22} also increases the cost. Decreasing X_{21} also increases the cost. The solution given in Table 6.28 is optimal.

(The reader can try modifying the u-v method to the bounded variables transportation problem. Observe that there are non-basic variables that are at their upper bounds. The reader should also write the dual of the capacitated transportation problem that we have tried to solve and establish the optimality of the modified u-v method for this problem. We ask the reader to do all these in Exercise problem 6.19).

EXAMPLE 6.9 Consider the linear programming problem:

Maximize $\frac{3}{4}X_1 - 20X_2 + \frac{1}{2}X_3 - 6X_4$

Subject to

$$\frac{1}{4}X_1 - 8X_2 - X_3 + 9X_4 \leq 0$$

$$\frac{1}{2}X_1 - 12X_2 - \frac{1}{2}X_3 + 3X_4 \leq 0$$

$$X_3 \leq 1$$

$$X_j \leq 0$$

Apply the lexicographic rule to solve this degenerate problem.

Solution: The simplex iterations is shown in Table 6.29. Variable X_1 enters the basis with the largest value of $C_j - Z_j$. There is a tie for leaving table resulting in degeneracy. Applying the lexicographic rule, we choose variable X_6 to leave the basis.

When we apply the lexicographic rule, we divide every element of the row by the element in the entering column. We do this only for the rows that have a tie.

In our example, if we started the table with the identity matrix (X_5, X_6 and X_7 and the rest of the variables in the order X_1 to X_4 — all the rows are lexicographically positive) and applied the lexicographic rule, we get 4, 0, 0, 1, −32, −4, 36, and 0, 2, 0, 1, −24, −1, 6. Considering the positive terms, we observe that the second row is lexicographically smaller (the value 0 is less than 4). We choose X_6 to leave. The rest of the computations have only one entering and leaving variables. The simplex iterations are shown in Table 6.29.

Table 6.29 Simplex Iterations

			3/4	−20	1/2	−6	0	0	0	
			X_1	X_2	X_3	X_4	X_5	X_6	X_7	RHS
0	X_5		1/4	−8	−1	9	1	0	0	0
0	X_6		1/2	−12	−1/2	3	0	1	0	0
0	X_7		0	0	1	0	0	0	1	1
	$C_j - Z_j$		3/4	−20	1/2	−6	0	0	0	0
0	X_5		0	−2	−3/4	−15/2	1	−1/2	0	0
3/4	X_1		1	−24	−1	6	0	2	0	0
0	X_7		0	0	1	0	0	0	1	1
	$C_j - Z_j$		0	−2	5/4	−21/2	0	−3/2	0	0
0	X_5		0	−2	0	15/2	1	−1/2	3/4	3/4
3/4	X_1		1	−24	0	6	0	2	1	1
1/2	X_3		0	0	1	0	0	0	1	1
	$C_j - Z_j$		0	−2	0	−21/2	0	−3/2	−5/4	5/4

The problem that cycled based on the largest coefficient rule terminates in two iterations using the lexicographic rule.

EXAMPLE 6.10 Solve the following linear programming problem by goal programming:

Maximize $Z = 4X_1 + 3X_2$

Subject to

$$X_1 + 4X_2 \leq 3$$
$$3X_1 + X_2 \geq 12$$
$$X_1, X_2 \geq 0$$

A convenient thing to do is to fix that the objective function to be greater than zero. Both the constraints are rigid.

Solution: The goal programming formulation is:

Minimize $[(\rho_1 + \eta_2), \eta_3]$

$$X_1 + 4X_2 + \eta_1 - \rho_1 = 3$$
$$3X_1 + X_2 + \eta_2 - \rho_2 = 12$$
$$4X_1 + 3X_2 + \eta_3 - \rho_3 = 0$$
$$X_j, \eta_i, \rho_i \geq 0$$

We start the simplex table with η_1 and η_2 as basic variables. This is shown in Table 6.30.

Table 6.30 Simplex Iterations

		0	0	0	1	1	0		
		X_1	X_2	η_1	ρ_1	η_2	ρ_2	RHS	θ
0	η_1	1	4	1	−1	0	0	3	3
1	η_2	3	1	0	0	1	−1	12	--
	$C_j - Z_j$	−3	−1	0	1	0	0	12	
0	X_1	1	4	1	−1	0	0	3	
1	η_2	0	−11	−3	3	1	−1	3	
	$C_j - Z_j$	0	11	3	−2	0	1	3	
0	X_1	1	1/3	0	0	1/3	−1/3	4	
1	ρ_1	0	−11/3	−1	1	1/3	−1/3	1	
	$C_j - Z_j$	0	11/3	1	0	2/3	1/3	1	

The algorithm terminates but we have $\rho_1 = 1$ at the optimum giving an objective function value of 1. This means that we do not have a solution not involving η and ρ that satisfies the rigid constraints. This indicates that the given problem is infeasible. We do not proceed to evaluate the objective function at $X_1 = 4$ because the given problem is infeasible. There is no infeasibility to the goal programming problem because it terminates with $X_1 = 4$, $\rho_1 = 1$ but the given LP is infeasible.

EXAMPLE 6.11 The MBA department has to offer electives in the Finance and Marketing specializations. There are twenty students and each student takes five electives with at least two electives in one of the specializations. There are ten electives listed in the syllabus with five each in the two specializations. Each student has been asked to give his/her first and second choices for finance and marketing electives. Formulate a goal programming problem to allot students to the electives under the following constraints/goals:

1. Each student registers for exactly five electives.
2. Each student takes two electives in one stream and three in the other.
3. Each student gets at least one first choice course (either finance or marketing) and at least one three out of his four choices (goal).
4. Each selected course should have atleast five students (constraint) and maximum of fifteen students (goal).
5. Minimize the number of courses that are selected (goal).

Solution: Let

$X_j = 1$ if finance course j is offered and Y_j if marketing course j is offered.
$X_{ij} = 1$ if student i is allotted to finance course j and $Y_{ij} = 1$ if student i is allotted to marketing course j.
$a_{ij} = 1$ if finance course j is the first choice for student i
$b_{ij} = 1$ if finance course j is the second choice for student i
$c_{ij} = 1$ if marketing course j is the first choice for student i
$d_{ij} = 1$ if marketing course j is the second choice for student i

Then,

$$\sum_{j=1}^{5} (X_{ij} + Y_{ij}) = 5 \qquad \text{(i)}$$

$$X_{ij} \leq X_j \qquad \text{(ii)}$$

$$Y_{ij} \leq Y_j \qquad \text{(iii)}$$

$$\sum_{j=1}^{5} X_{ij} \geq 2 \qquad \text{(iv)}$$

$$\sum_{j=1}^{5} Y_{ij} \geq 2 \qquad \text{(v)}$$

$$\sum_{j=1}^{5} a_{ij}X_{ij} + \sum_{j=1}^{5} c_{ij}Y_{ij} \geq 1 \qquad \text{(vi)}$$

$$\sum_{j=1}^{5} a_{ij}X_{ij} + \sum_{j=1}^{5} c_{ij}Y_{ij} + \sum_{j=1}^{5} b_{ij}X_{ij} + \sum_{j=1}^{5} d_{ij}Y_{ij} \geq 3 \qquad \text{(vii)}$$

$$\sum_{i=1}^{20} X_{ij} \geq 5 \qquad \text{(viii)}$$

$$\sum_{i=1}^{20} Y_{ij} \geq 5 \qquad (ix)$$

$$\sum_{i=1}^{20} X_{ij} \leq 20 \qquad (x)$$

$$\sum_{i=1}^{20} Y_{ij} \geq 20 \qquad (xi)$$

Minimize $\sum_{j=1}^{5} X_j + Y_j$ (xii)

We add the slacks η and ρ for every constraint set. Constraint set (i) has as many constraints as the number of students. We define the slacks as η_{1i} and ρ_{1i} for this constraint set and so on. We will have up to $\eta_{12,j}$ and $\rho_{12,j}$, respectively. Constraints (i) to (vi), (viii) and (ix) are rigid constraints and sets (viii), (x) to (xii) are goals. We assume a target of 8 courses considering that there are 20 students taking five courses each and an upper limit goal of 20 students per selected course.

The objective function is:

Minimize $\left[\left(\sum_{i=1}^{20} \eta_{1i} + \rho_{1i} + \sum_{i=1}^{20} \sum_{j=1}^{5} \rho_{2ij} + \rho_{3ij} + \sum_{i=1}^{20} \eta_{4i} + \eta_{5i} + \eta_{6i} + \sum_{j=1}^{5} \eta_{8j} + \eta_{9j} \right) \right]$

Minimize $\left[\left(\sum_{i=1}^{20} \eta_{7i} \right), \left(\sum_{j=1}^{5} \eta_{10,j} + \eta_{11,j} \right), (\rho_{12}) \right]$

The lexicographic order is to minimize the rigid constraints followed by the expression for the goals. The constraints and goals are rewritten as follows:

$$\sum_{j=1}^{5} (X_{ij} + Y_{ij}) + \eta_{1i} - \rho_{1i} = 5$$

$$X_{ij} - X_j + \eta_{2ij} - \rho_{2ij} = 0$$

$$Y_{ij} - Y_j + \eta_{3ij} - \rho_{3ij} = 0$$

$$\sum_{j=1}^{5} X_{ij} + \eta_{4i} - \rho_{4i} = 2$$

$$\sum_{j=1}^{5} Y_{ij} + \eta_{5i} - \rho_{5i} = 2$$

$$\sum_{j=1}^{5} a_{ij} X_{ij} + \sum_{j=1}^{5} c_{ij} Y_{ij} + \eta_{6i} - \rho_{6i} = 1$$

Advanced Linear Programming **231**

$$\sum_{j=1}^{5} a_{ij}X_{ij} + \sum_{j=1}^{5} c_{ij}Y_{ij} + \sum_{j=1}^{5} b_{ij}X_{ij} + \sum_{j=1}^{5} d_{ij}Y_{ij} + \eta_{7i} - \rho_{7i} = 3$$

$$\sum_{i=1}^{20} X_{ij} + \eta_{8j} - \rho_{8j} = 5$$

$$\sum_{i=1}^{20} Y_{ij} + \eta_{9j} - \rho_{9j} = 5$$

$$\sum_{i=1}^{20} Y_{ij} + \eta_{10,j} - \rho_{10,j} = 20$$

$$\sum_{i=1}^{20} Y_{ij} + \eta_{11,j} - \rho_{11,j} = 20$$

$$\sum_{j=1}^{5} X_j + Y_j + \eta_{12} - \rho_{12} = 8$$

$$X_j, X_{ij}, Y_j, Y_{ij} = 0, 1$$

(The above is a zero-one formulation involving decision variables that take either zero or one. We will discuss methods to solve zero-one problems with a single objective in Chapter 7)

CASE STUDY 6.1: Allocating Minor Streams

The undergraduate and dual degree curriculum of a university requires that every student registers for a minor stream specialization. The student credits four courses in a minor stream specialization one course each in semesters five through eight. About 550 students have to be allotted a minor stream at the end of their second year and the Dean, Professor Kumar believes that no academic criterion such as CGPA (Cumulative Grade Point Average) should be used in the allocation. He believes that every student should get his/her first choice.

The administrative officer, Mr. Rajan, however faces difficulty in giving the first choice to each student. About fifteen minor streams are offered and each has an upper limit on the number of students that it can accommodate. These upper limits vary from 25 to 60. There are additional restrictions where students who major in some subjects cannot choose some minors due to overlap.

Mr. Rajan asks each student to write the preference and insists that every student should give 15 preferences. Otherwise some students give only one or very few preferences. Mr. Rajan also informs the students that if they do not fill all the preferences, they will be allotted a stream randomly which may not have been indicated by the student. Mr. Rajan uses the following algorithm to allocate students to minor streams:

1. For a particular stream, if the number of first choices is less than the capacity, all the students get this stream.

2. If the number of first choices is more than the capacity, students are chosen randomly and given their first choice.
3. Rest of the students are randomly allotted to meet the unfilled capacity of the rest of the available streams.

Ravi, the student secretary thinks that the random allocation has to be replaced by an optimization algorithm that can give every student within some k choices and wishes to minimize k. Mr Rajan agrees to this but thinks that if a k is chosen (say, $k = 3$), he would start filling the third choice before he fills the second choices. Ravi wants a progressive allocation of choices.

He conducts a sample survey of 100 students and four specializations (A to D). Each student is asked to give four choices. Table 6.31 gives the summary of the number of choices.

Table 6.31 Summary of Choices

	A	B	C	D
I choice	2	3	56	39
II choice	10	20	35	35
III choice	18	50	7	25
IV choice	70	27	2	1

The maximum number of students that can be accommodated in the minor streams are 30, 30, 20 and 20 respectively.

Mr Rajan's algorithm gives the allocation shown in Table 6.32 to the data

Table 6.32 Allocations

	A	B	C	D
I choice	2	3	20	20
II choice	5	10		
III choice	10	10		
IV choice	13	7		

Ravi's solution however to the same data is shown in Table 6.33.

Table 6.33 Solution

	A	B	C	D
I choice	2	3	20	20
II choice	10	20		
III choice	18	7		
IV choice				

Ravi believes that the objective is to minimize the number of students who get their fourth choice. Prof Kumar believes that it is a multiple objective problem and also informs Ravi that it would become difficult to solve the actual problem with 550 students and fifteen specializations in a single formulation.

Mr. Rajan, after discussions with Prof Kumar and faculty who offer these courses is ready to increase the maximum number of students that can be accommodated in the minor streams to 40, 40, 30 and 30 respectively. In this situation he would want all the streams to get students. Prof Kumar would like an equal distribution of students to the various minor streams.

CASE STUDY 6.2: Western Constructions

The Western Construction Company has to solve a cutting stock problem every time a new job order is taken for processing. They require steel rods of different lengths and different cross sections. Their supplier is willing to supply rods of given cross section but can supply only 3 m long rods because of the limitation of the transporting truck. The requirements for the current job order is given in Table 6.34.

Table 6.34 Requirements

Length	Requirement
45	382
55	410
65	296

The planning department headed by Mr. Pinaki Basu works manually by preparing a table of all feasible cutting patterns and provide with the best possible combination. This usually takes three to four hours of their time. Mr. Basu is aware of an integer programming formulation of the problem but does not have software that can solve integer programming problems. He has a linear programming solver but does not use it because the number of feasible patterns has to be generated for every order and this takes as much time as the manual solution. The planning department has to provide feasible cutting pattern solutions at least two to three times a week and the required lengths can vary from 30 cm to 80 cm.

Mr. Basu was wondering if someone would provide him a computer program that can provide the feasible cutting patterns. He requests Sumant Jain, a newly recruited graduate trainee specialized in Operations Research and computer programming to address this issue.

Sumant formulates a linear programming problem and shows Mr. Basu that the formulation that minimizes the waste reduces to minimizing the number of cuts. Mr. Basu is unable to accept that the excess material is treated as a waste while it is possible to use it in the future.

Sumant also looks at the eighteen patterns generated by Mr. Basu's team and chooses the best three in terms of minimum wastage as feasible patterns and evaluates a basic feasible solution using these. He also shows that the remaining patterns can be evaluated using the dual of the present basic feasible solution and may suitably enter the basis. He provides a computer program that enumerates all the feasible patterns and uses the above algorithm to solve the problem and wishes to compare his algorithm with the column generation based LP solution.

Sumant also impresses upon Mr. Basu the need for an increased length of the raw material and shows that for the same demand, a longer raw material length would reduce the number of rods to be cut. He recommends 4 m rods instead of the present practice of using 3 m rods. Mr. Basu is hesitant because he thinks that the actual cuts required may increase with increase in the length. He finally agrees with Sumant and finally convinces the supplier to send them 4 m long rods transporting them using a different truck.

EXERCISES

6.1 You are solving a LP problem and realize that the solution is infeasible. You have to increase or decrease one of the RHS values to obtain feasibility. How will you do this (a) without solving the problem again (b) by solving a different LP. Illustrate with an example.

6.2 Assume that you are in the middle of a simplex iteration for a maximization problem with bounded variables. Every variable in the problem has a constraint $X_j \le u_j$. At present a non-basic variable X_k enters the basis. The values in the entering column are a_1 to a_m and the values of the basic variables are b_1 to b_m. Clearly state the rules to identify the leaving variable.

6.3 Solve the following LP by bounded variables method:

Maximize $5X_1 + 4X_2$

Subject to

$X_1 - X_2 \le 5$, $2X_1 + 3X_2 \le 15$ $0 \le X_1 \le 6$ $0 \le X_2 \le 2$

6.4 Solve the LP problem:

Maximize $8x_1 + 6x_2 + 4x_3 + 5x_4$

Subject to

$3x_1 + x_2 + x_3 + 2x_4 \le 12$, $x_1 \le 2$, $x_2 \le 3$ all $x_j \ge 0$

6.5 You are given an LP problem:

Minimize $8X_1 + 4X_2 + 3X_3$

Subject to

$4X_1 + 6X_2 + 2X_3 \ge 12$, $3X_1 + 2X_2 + 5X_3 \ge 15$, $X_1, X_2, X_3 \ge 0$

(a) Given that X_2 and X_3 are the basic variables at the optimum, find the solutions to the primal and dual using the Eta matrices.

(b) If a bounded variable $X_3 \le 2$ is added to the problem, use a bounded variables algorithm from the solution in (a) to reach the optimum.

6.6 Given the linear programming problem:

Maximize $6X_1 + 4X_2$

Subject to $X_1 - X_2 \le 5$, $2X_1 + 3X_2 \le 12$, $X_1, X_2 \ge 0$

Convert this problem into a system of inequalities such that solving this set would give the optimal solution to the given problem. How many feasible solutions should the system of inequalities have?

6.7 Consider the following LP problem:

Maximize $8X_1 + 7X_2 + 4X_3 + 9X_4$

Subject to

$2X_1 + X_2 + 3X_3 + 2X_4 \le 10$

$X_1 + X_2 + X_3 + X_4 \le 6$

$X_1 + X_2 \le 4$; $X_1 + 3X_2 \le 8$ (sub problem 1 with 2 constraints)
$X_3 + X_4 \le 6$; $2X_3 + X_4 \le 8$ (sub problem 1 with 2 constraints)
$X_j \ge 0$

The corner points for subproblem 1 are (0, 0), (4, 0), (0, 8/3) and (2, 2). The corner points for subproblem 2 are (0, 0), (4, 0), (0, 6) and (2, 4). The optimum solution to the given LP problem (original problem) is $X_2 = 2$, $X_4 = 4$ with $Z = 50$.
If you were to represent the optimum solution to the original problem as a linear combination of the corner points of the subproblems, which corner points would you choose and with what weights?

6.8 Given the LPP:
Minimize $Z = 8X_1 + 3X_2 + 4X_3 + 6X_4 + X_5$

$X_1 + 4X_2 + X_3 \ge 6$, $-2X_1 + 4X_2 + X_3 \ge 4$, $3X_1 + X_4 + 2X_5 \ge 3$, $X_1 + 2X_4 - Y_5 \ge 10$, $X_1, X_2, X_3, X_4, X_5 \ge 0$

Solve the dual of the above problem using the decomposition algorithm.

6.9 Minimize $12X_1 + 12X_2 + 9X_3 - 15X_4 - 80X_5 - 26X_6 + 2X_7$
Subject to $3X_1 + 4X_2 + 3X_3 + 3X_4 + 15$, $X_5 + 13X_6 + 16X_7 \le 35$, $0 \le X_j \le 1$
If constraints $X_1 + X_2 \le 3$ and $X_5 + X_6 \le 12$ are added, perform one iteration of the decomposition algorithm.

6.10 Given an LP problem:
Maximize $3X_1 + 5X_2 + X_3 + X_4$
Subject to $X_1 + X_2 + X_3 + X_4 \le 40$, $5X_1 + X_2 \le 12$, $X_3 + X_4 \ge 5$, $X_3 + 5X_4 \le 50$, $X_j \ge 0$

(a) Identify the master problem and the subproblems.
(b) Solved by the Dantzig-Wolfe decomposition algorithm.

6.11 Consider the one-dimensional cutting stock problem to cut 389 sheets of 5 inches, 189 sheets of 7 inches and 201 sheets of 9 inches from 20 inches wide sheets. The patterns in the given solution are [1 2 0], [0 0 2] and [2 0 1].
(a) Verify if the given solution is optimum.
(b) What happens if we want to enter the pattern [4 0 0] in the basis.

6.12 You are given a one-dimensional cutting stock problem where widths of 5, 6 and 7 inches are required. You are given two widths of 16 inches and 18 inches, respectively. Give a general formulation and indicate whether the same column generation based on a knapsack problem can be used to solve the problem.

6.13 The Super Selector problem is as follows:
There is a pool of cricket players who are opening batsmen, middle order batsmen, fast bowlers, spin bowlers, wicket keepers and all rounders. These players are from six different countries and each player belongs to only one of the above six categories. You have to choose five teams on behalf of the organizers. Each player i in the pool has a present score a_i and an expected score b_i. The team has to be chosen to maximize the expected score. Each team should have exactly eleven players with exactly two opening

batsmen, exactly one wicket keeper, between three and four middle order batsmen, between three and four fast bowlers. The rest could be all rounders and/or spin bowlers. The total of the present scores of the players in the teams should be close to 1000. You have to select five teams and the conditions are as follows:

(a) If the score of a team exceeds 1000, minimize the deviation.
(b) Team 1 should maximize the number of Indian players and should include Sachin (as opener).
(c) Team 2 should have at least five English players and should have Sourav (as opener).
(d) Team 3 should have as many Australian players as possible and should minimize South African players.
(e) Team 4 need not have a spinner and has at least two west Indian players.
(f) Maximize the total number of players (the union set) in all the teams put together.
(g) Select teams in such a way that the equal number of players from the six countries figure in the selected pool.

Formulate a goal programming model choosing your own order of the above priorities. Assume that Sachin and Sourav are in the pool of Indian players.

6.14 Jimmy wants to do the following things (not necessarily in the same order) in the next two days. He has 12 hours available in each day. The activities, preferred day and the normal time taken are given in Table 6.35:

Table 6.35 Data for Exercise 6.14

No.	Activity	Preferred day	Normal time
1.	Prepare for an exam	More effort on second day	6 hours
2.	Meet sponsors for a cultural event	More effort on first day	4 hours
3.	Meet an old schoolmate	Second day	6 hours
4.	Project work	First day	6 hours
5.	Meet a friend who is unwell	First day	2 hours
6.	Go to a movie with hostel friends	Any day preferred	4 hours

Jimmy knows that for the first three activities effectiveness is directly proportional to the time spent and wishes to spend more time than normal. For activities that have preferred days, he wishes to complete them within the day. Jimmy has not yet finalized his order of priorities for these activities. Formulate a goal programming problem clearly stating the priorities and goals.

6.15 Eight students have to be divided into two groups of four each. Each group is to be assigned a project. Student j has a CGPA of S_j (less than 10) and each project has a toughness T_i (on a scale from 1 to 10). The student groups are to be formed to balance the overall CGPAs while the projects have to be assigned to balance the gap between the toughness and the average CGPA of the group. Formulate a goal programming problem for the above situation.

6.16 Murali has three OR textbooks and can read four topics in each of the books to prepare for his exams. His expected marks in the exam if he reads chapter i from book j per hour are given in Table 6.36.

He has 7, 6 and 4 hours that he can distribute to the books (as and when he gets them). His primary goal is to maximize his marks. He expects that out of 100 marks, the marks for the topics in the exam are 20, 30, 25 and 15, respectively. His primary objective is to maximize his total marks based on his time allotment and his secondary objective is to close the gap between the expected marks and the computed marks based on his allotment of time. Formulate a goal programming problem for this situation.

Table 6.36 Data for Exercise 6.16

	Book 1	Book 2	Book 3
Topic 1	6	7	0
Topic 2	4	5	6
Topic 3	3	6	7
Topic 4	1	0	0

6.17 Vijay has eight hours to prepare on the night prior to the OR exam. He has three books to read and estimates the expected marks to marks per hour as 5, 3 and 4 and wishes to maximize the total marks. Solve the problem for Vijay. If he places additional bounds such as $X_1 \leq 3$ and $X_2 \leq 3$, use a bounded variables method or otherwise to find the optimal solution.

6.18 You are given a linear programming problem:

Maximize $10X_1 + 10X_2$

Subject to

$$X_1 + 3X_2 \leq 4, \; 2X_1 + 5X_2 \leq 8, \; X_1, X_2 \geq 0$$

Use minimum subscript rule and solve the problem optimally.

6.19 You are given a transportation problem with two supply and three demand points. The supplies are 40 and 60 while the demands are 30, 30 and 40, respectively. The transportation costs are given in Table 6.37.

Table 6.37 Transportation Cost

4	6	7
5	8	7

An additional condition is that a maximum of 20 can be supplied from the first supply point to the first demand point. Introduce bounded variables into the transportation algorithm and solve the problem optimally. Show the optimality by modifying the u-v method for bounded (or capacitated) transportation problem.

(**Hint:** See Example 6.8)

6.20 Write the dual of the capacitated transportation problem and show that the optimality conditions to the dual are:

$(C_{ij} - u_i - v_j) \geq 0$ for non-basic variables $X_{ij} = 0$

$(C_{ij} - u_i - v_j) \leq 0$ for non-basic variables $X_{ij} = U_{ij}$

Integer Programming

We have learnt how to model and formulate real-life situations as linear programming problems. Let us consider a few problems that we encounter in real-life and attempt to model them as linear programming problems:

1. The problem is to assign N jobs to N people. The cost of performing job j using person i is given by C_{ij}. Each person gets exactly one job and each job goes to exactly one person. The problem is to find the least cost assignment of jobs to people.
2. Given N cities, a person has to travel each city once and only once and should return to the starting point. The distance matrix among the cities is given. The problem is to find the tour that has least distance travelled.
3. Given N points and the distance matrix, the problem is to group into p groups such that points within the group are close to each other.
4. Given that the assembly of a product requires N components, each having an assembly time t_j. There are also some precedence relationships that have to be met. The problem is to assign them to minimum number of workstations such that the precedence relationships are satisfied and the cycle time of each workstation does not exceed a given value.
5. N jobs are to be carried out in M machines. Each job has a specific order of visiting the machines. Job i has a processing time p_{ij} on machine j. Each machine can process only one job at a time and vice versa. The problem is to schedule the jobs on machines to minimize the total time at which all jobs have are completed.

All the above problems cannot be formulated entirely as linear programming problems. There are variables that have to take either a zero or one (whenever there is an allocation as in the first four examples) or sometimes we have different types of variables (both zero-one as well as continuous; which we call mixed variables) in our formulations. We will also have variables that take only integer values. If we have a product mix problems where we make say, tables and chairs, the decision variables have to take only integer values (though we formulated and solved these as linear programming problems).

Therefore, we need to study separately the problems that cannot be solved entirely as linear programming problems and those problems that have integer variables, zero-one variables and mixed variables. This part of operations research is called **integer programming**, where the variables take either integer values, or zero-one values or mixed.

7.1 INTEGER PROGRAMMING FORMULATION

Let us first formulate some problem instances (the five examples that we have mentioned in the beginning of this chapter) as integer programming problems.

ILLUSTRATION 7.1

The problem is to assign N jobs to N people. The cost of performing job j using person i is given by C_{ij}. Each person gets exactly one job and each job goes to exactly one person. The problem is to find the least cost assignment of jobs to people.

This example is the well known assignment problem, which we have formulated already. Let $X_{ij} = 1$ if job i goes to person j.

Minimize $\sum_{i=1}^{n} \sum_{j=1}^{n} C_{ij} X_{ij}$ (i)

Subject to

$$\sum_{j=1}^{n} X_{ij} = 1 \ \forall \ i$$ (ii)

$$\sum_{i=1}^{n} X_{ij} = 1 \ \forall \ j$$ (iii)

$$X_{ij} = 0, 1$$ (iv)

The objective function minimizes the total cost of assignment. The constraints (ii) and (iii) ensure that each job goes to only one person and that each person gets only one job. There is a zero-one restriction on the variables, given by Eq. (iv)

We also know that though the assignment problem is a zero-one problem, due to unimodularity of the coefficient matrix, LP solutions will satisfy the zero-one restriction. We solve the assignment problem using the Hungarian algorithm that uses principles from linear programming.

ILLUSTRATION 7.2

Given N cities, a person has to travel each city once and only once and should return to the starting point. The distance matrix among the cities is given. The problem is to find the tour that has least distance travelled.

This problem is the well known Travelling Salesman Problem (TSP) (Flood 1956). The decision variables are:

$X_{ij} = 1$, if the person visits city j immediately after visiting city i. $X_{ij} = 0$, otherwise.
The objective function is to

Minimize $\sum_{i=1}^{n} \sum_{j=1}^{n} d_{ij} X_{ij}$ (i)

Subject to

$$\sum_{j=1}^{n} X_{ij} = 1 \ \forall \ i \qquad (ii)$$

$$\sum_{i=1}^{n} X_{ij} = 1 \ \forall \ j \qquad (iii)$$

The objective function minimizes the total distance travelled. Constraints (ii) and (iii) ensure that we go to only one city from a given city and we reach any city from only one city. However, this formulation is not complete because it fails to eliminate subtours.

For example, in a 5-city TSP, a solution $X_{12} = X_{21} = X_{34} = X_{45} = X_{52} = 1$ satisfies constraints (ii) and (iii) but has a subtour. If this solution is to be explained, the travelling salesman goes from city 1 to 2 and back and goes from 3 to 4, 4 to 5 and comes back to city 2 from 5. This solution is infeasible to the TSP. There are two sub tours 1–2–1 and 3–4–5–3. A feasible solution to the TSP is a tour and, therefore, the formulation should have constraints to eliminate all the sub tours.

For a 5-city TSP, we could have subtours of size 1 (say, $X_{11} = 1$), size 2, 3 or 4. Every subtour will create at least one more subtour. The subtours are eliminated as follows using the following constraints:

If there is a subtour of length 4, there has to be a subtour of length 1. If we eliminate all subtours of length 1, we have eliminated all subtours of length 4. For every TSP, we set $d_{jj} = \infty$ so that X_{ij} does not figure in the solution. By eliminating subtours of size 1, we have eliminated subtours of size 4 and, therefore, subtours of size 4 need not be eliminated explicitly.

Let us consider subtours of length 3. If there is a subtour of size 3, there has to be either a subtour of size 2 or two subtours of size 1. We have already eliminated subtours of size 1. If we now eliminate subtours of size 2, we have eliminated subtours of sizes 2 and 3. This is carried out by inserting a constraint of the form:

$$X_{ij} + X_{ji} \leq 1 \qquad (iv)$$

This constraint would ensure that if $X_{ij} = 1$, X_{ji} has to be zero so that all subtours of size 2 are eliminated. It can happen that a particular X_{ij} need not be in the solution.

We have now eliminated all subtours of lengths 1, 2, 3 and 4 for a 5-city problem. Only tours are permissible. Hence the formulation is complete after we add the zero-one restriction on the variables.

$$X_{ij} = 0, 1 \qquad (v)$$

For a 6-city TSP, eliminating all singleton subtours would eliminate all 5-city subtours and eliminating all 2-city subtours also eliminates all 4-city subtours. We have to write the constraints to eliminate all subtours of length 3. This will be of the form:

$$X_{ij} + X_{jk} + X_{ki} \leq 2 \qquad (vi)$$

Here two of the three can be in the solution but the third cannot be. In general for a n city TSP, where n is odd, we have to eliminate subtours of lengths 1 to $(n-1)/2$ and when n is even we eliminate all subtours of length 1 to $n/2$. There are $^nC_2$ 2-city elimination constraints, $^nC_3$ 3-city elimination constraints and so on.

(There is a slightly better formulation of subtour elimination constraints, which we will see later when we study TSP in detail).

ILLUSTRATION 7.3

Given N points and the distance matrix, the problem is to group into p groups such that points within the group are close to each other.

This is called the **k-median problem** and has extensive applications in grouping and facilities location. We first address the grouping application and then formulate the application to location problems.

Let d_{ij} denote the known distance between points i and j. The decision variables are as follows:

Let $X_{jj} = 1$ if point j is chosen as a median point and let $X_{ij} = 1$ if point i is grouped with median j.

The objective function is:

Minimize $\sum_{i=1}^{n} \sum_{j=1}^{n} d_{ij} X_{ij}$ \hfill (i)

Subject to

$$\sum_{j=1}^{n} X_{ij} = 1 \ \forall \ i \qquad (ii)$$

$$\sum_{j=1}^{n} X_{jj} = p \qquad (iii)$$

$$X_{ij} \leq X_{jj} \qquad (iv)$$

$$X_{ij} = 0, 1 \qquad (v)$$

The objective function minimizes the distance ensuring that points within a group are compact. Constraint (ii) allocates one point to only one median. Constraint (iii) chooses exactly p points as medians thereby making exactly p groups. Constraint (iv) ensures that every point is grouped around a median point. A point i can join the group j (with median j) only when point j is chosen as a median. The zero-one constraints are given in (v).

Let us expand this problem to choose p among m points as locations where plants can be located. Let there be n demand points each having demand b_j. Plant i can produce a_i quantity of the product. There is a transportation cost of d_{ij} between plant i and destination j. There is a fixed cost f_i of setting a plant in location i.

Let $Y_i = 1$ if point i is chosen as a location and X_{ij} be the quantity transported from plant at i to demand point j. The formulation is:

Minimize $\sum_{i=1}^{m} f_i Y_i + \sum_{i=1}^{m} \sum_{j=1}^{n} d_{ij} X_{ij}$ \hfill (vi)

Subject to

$$\sum_{i=1}^{m} Y_i = p \qquad \text{(vii)}$$

$$\sum_{j=1}^{n} X_{ij} \leq Y_i a_i \qquad \text{(viii)}$$

$$\sum_{i=1}^{m} X_{ij} \geq b_j \qquad \text{(ix)}$$

$$X_{ij}, Y_i = 0, 1 \qquad \text{(x)}$$

This problem is called the **fixed charge problem** (Balinski, 1961). The objective function minimizes the sum of the fixed costs of setting up the facilities and the costs of transporting the items. Constraint (vii) ensures that exactly p facilities are chosen. Constraint (viii) ensures that supply is possible only from a point chosen for setting up the facility and that the total amount transported from a chosen facility is less than the capacity. Constraint (ix) ensures that the demand constraints are met and the zero-one constraints are modelled in constraint (x).

ILLUSTRATION 7.4

Given that the assembly of a product requires N components, each having an assembly time t_i. There are also some precedence relationships that have to be met. The problem is to assign them to minimum number of workstations such that the precedence relationships are satisfied and the cycle time of each workstation does not exceed a given value T.

This is the line balancing problem. It is obvious that $T \geq t_i$. It is also assumed that it is possible to set up N workstations each where station i carries out assembly of operation i. We assume that the sequence 1–2–3–...–N is feasible and satisfies the precedence relationships.

Let $S_j = 1$ ($j = 1,..., N$) if workstation number j is chosen. Let $X_{ij} = 1$ if operation i is assigned to workstation j. The objective function is:

Minimize $\sum_{j=1}^{n} S_j$ \qquad (i)

Subject to

$$\sum_{j=1}^{n} X_{ij} = 1 \text{ for every operation } i \qquad \text{(ii)}$$

$$\sum_{i=1}^{n} X_{ij} \leq n S_j \text{ for every workstation } j \qquad \text{(iii)}$$

$$\sum_{i=1}^{n} t_i X_{ij} \leq T \text{ for every workstation } j \qquad \text{(iv)}$$

The objective function minimizes the number of workstations. Constraint (ii) ensures that each operation is assigned to only one workstation. Constraint (iii) ensures that an operation can be assigned to a workstation only if it is chosen and a maximum of N operations can be assigned to a chosen workstation. Constraint (iv) ensures that for every chosen workstation, the time taken is less than the cycle time T.

Now, we have to model the precedence constraints. Let us assume that activity k can be assembled only after operation i is assembled. Let us also assume that we are solving a problem with three maximum workstations. If operation i is assigned to workstation 1, operation k can be assigned to workstations 1, 2 or 3. If operation i is assigned to workstation 2, operation k can be assigned to workstations 2 or 3 (it cannot be allotted to workstation 1). If operation i is assigned to workstation 3, operation k should go to workstation 3. This is modelled as follows:

$$X_{i1} \leq X_{k1} + X_{k2} + X_{k3} \tag{v}$$
$$X_{i2} \leq X_{k2} + X_{k3} \tag{vi}$$
$$X_{i3} \leq X_{k3} \tag{vii}$$

Constraints (v) to (vii) ensure that operation i is assigned to either workstation 1 or 2 or 3. The only difficulty is that we have to write N constraints for each precedence relationship. Finally, we have the zero-one restriction given by

$$X_{ij}, S_j = 0, 1 \tag{viii}$$

ILLUSTRATION 7.5

N jobs are to be carried out in M machines. Each job has a specific order of visiting the machines. Job i has a processing time p_{ij} on machine j. Each machine can process only one job at a time and vice versa. The problem is to schedule the jobs on machines to minimize the total time at which all jobs will be completed.

This is an example of the static job shop scheduling problem. Let us formulate a specific problem where there are three jobs and three machines. The routes of the jobs are:

Job 1 ($J1$) — $M1$, $M3$ and $M2$
Job 2 ($J2$) — $M2$, $M1$ and $M3$
Job 3 ($J3$) — $M2$, $M3$ and $M1$

Let T_{ij} be the start time of processing of job i on machine j. Job 1 finishes all its operations at $T_{12} + p_{12}$. Job 2 finishes all the operations at $T_{23} + p_{23}$ and Job 3 finishes all the operations at $T_{31} + p_{31}$.

We want to schedule the jobs in such a way that all jobs are over at the earliest. This means that we want to minimize the maximum of $(T_{12} + p_{12}, T_{23} + p_{23}, T_{31} + p_{31})$. The objective function is:

Minimize U (i)
Subject to
$$U \geq T_{12} + p_{12} \tag{ii}$$
$$U \geq T_{23} + p_{23} \tag{iii}$$
$$U \geq T_{31} + p_{31} \tag{iv}$$

Since Job 1 follows the sequence $M1$, $M3$ and $M2$, it can start processing on $M3$ after it finishes processing on $M1$ and so on. These are modelled for Job 1 as:

$$T_{13} \geq T_{11} + p_{11} \text{ and } T_{12} \geq T_{13} + p_{13} \tag{v}$$

Similarly for Jobs $J2$ and $J3$, the constraints are:

$$T_{21} \geq T_{22} + p_{22} \text{ and } T_{32} \geq T_{21} + p_{21} \tag{vi}$$

$$T_{33} \geq T_{32} + p_{23} \text{ and } T_{31} \geq T_{33} + p_{33} \tag{vii}$$

If we consider machine $M1$, this processes all jobs $J1$, $J2$ and $J3$. It can however process only one job at a time. If we consider jobs $J1$ and $J2$, either $J1$ should start after $J2$ is completed or $J1$ starts after $J2$ is completed. This means that either $T_{21} \geq T_{11} + p_{11}$ or $T_{11} \geq T_{21} + p_{21}$. This is modelled as:

$$T_{11} + p_{11} - T_{21} \leq M\delta_{121} \tag{viii}$$

$$T_{21} + p_{21} - T_{11} \leq M(1 - \delta_{121}) \tag{ix}$$

Here M is large and positive and tends to infinity. The pair will ensure that only one of them is valid. The value of δ_{121} will be zero or one and will make one of the constraints binding and the other redundant.

For $M1$, we have four more constraints, two each for the pair $J2$–$J3$ and two for the pair $J1$–$J3$. We have six constraints considering $M2$ and six more constraints considering $M3$. We have decision variables $T_{ij} \geq 0$ and $\delta_{ijk} = 0, 1$ (x)

Some inferences from the above formulations are:

Inferences from integer programming formulations

1. Most real-life problems are formulated as integer programming problems in addition to being formulated as linear programming problems.
2. Most allocation problems are formulated as zero-one problems.
3. Some formulations are also of the mixed type involving combinations if zero-one, continuous and integer variables.
4. Problem characteristics such as precedence can give rise to a large number of constraints.

7.2 HOW TO SOLVE INTEGER PROGRAMMING PROBLEMS?

Having formulated integer programming problems, the next issue is to try and solve them. Since we are familiar with solving LP problems, we will be tempted to begin our solution procedure by solving the corresponding LP after relaxing (leaving out) the integer restriction. We will be tempted to believe that the IP optimum should be near the LP optimum and that it may be possible to get the IP optimum by suitably rounding off the LP solution to the nearest integer value.

Let us consider a few examples to illustrate the issues in solving IP problems.

ILLUSTRATION 7.6

Maximize $3X_1 + 4X_2$
Subject to
$$X_1 + X_2 \leq 9$$
$$X_1 + 3X_2 \leq 20$$
$$X_1, X_2 \geq 0 \text{ and integer}$$

The LP solution after relaxing the integer restrictions is $X_1 = 7/2, X_2 = 11/2, Z = 65/2$. The IP problem has more constraints (restriction) than the corresponding LP and for a maximization problem, the LP optimum will have a higher value than the corresponding IP optimum. The LP optimum is an upper bound to the IP problem for a maximization objective (and is a lower bound to the IP optimum for a minimization problem). Also if the optimum to the relaxed LP problem has integer valued solution then the solution is optimum to the IP problem.

From the point (7/2, 11/2), four rounded integer solutions are possible. These are (4, 6), (4, 5), (3, 6) and (3, 5). Before we evaluate the objective function for these rounded solutions, we need to verify whether they are feasible. The point (4, 6) violates both the constraints and the point (3, 6) violates the second constraint. These are infeasible. Points (4, 5) and (3, 5) are feasible and the best rounded solution is (4, 5) with $Z = 32$.

We also observe that the IP optimum to this problem (we will learn how to solve IPs later in this chapter) is $X_1 = 4, X_2 = 5$ with $Z = 32$ which is the same as the best rounded LP solution.

We also observe that for a two variable-two constraint problem, we can have a maximum of four rounded solutions and for a general n variable m constraint problem we can have m basic variables and hence a maximum of 2^m rounded solutions. This is a worst case exponential number of rounded solutions and can result in a combinatorial explosion, and hence not theoretically acceptable.

ILLUSTRATION 7.7

Maximize $X_1 + 4X_2$
Subject to
$$X_1 + X_2 \leq 9$$
$$X_1 + 3X_2 \leq 20$$
$$X_1, X_2 \geq 0 \text{ and integer}$$

The LP solution after relaxing the integer restrictions is $X_1 = 0, X_2 = 20/3, Z = 80/3$.

Two rounded solutions are possible. These are (0, 6) and (0, 7). Out of this (0, 7) is infeasible as it violates the second constraint. The best rounded solution is $X_1 = 0, X_2 = 6$ (which is feasible) with $Z = 24$.

The optimum solution to the IP problem is $X_1 = 2, X_2 = 6$ with $Z = 26$. In this example, the best rounded integer solution is **not** the IP optimum. Our assumption that seemed to be satisfied by the earlier example does not hold for this example. It is possible that when we round off a variable to a lower integer value, the other variable can take a value more than its upper integer value. Finding all such values consumes a lot of time and effort and is not generally followed.

ILLUSTRATION 7.8

Maximize $X_1 + X_2$
Subject to
$$7X_1 - 5X_2 \le 7$$
$$-12X_1 + 15X_2 \le 7$$
$$X_1, X_2 \ge 0 \text{ and integer}$$

The LP solution after relaxing the integer restrictions is $X_1 = 28/9$, $X_2 = 133/45$, $Z = 273/45$. There are four rounded integer solutions given by (4, 3), (3, 3), (4, 2) and (3, 2). Points (4, 3) and (4, 2) violate the first constraint while points (3, 3) and (3, 2) violate the second constraint. All the rounded integer solutions are infeasible. The IP optimum to this problem is (2, 2) with $Z = 4$.

From the examples we understand that we can have situations where all rounded integer solutions can be infeasible but the problem may have an IP optimum.

Therefore, rounding off is not a good strategy both theoretically and in practice. We need to study solving IP problems separately.

Rounding LP optimum to nearest integer values

- Can give the optimum in some cases but will involve an exponential number of evaluations.
- Can give feasible integer solutions but the optimum may be different.
- Can have all solutions infeasible but the IP problem may have an optimum.

7.3 TYPES OF INTEGER PROGRAMMING PROBLEMS

Integer programming problems can be classified into two types:

1. Linear integer programming problem—Here both the objective function and the constraints are linear.
2. Non-linear integer programming problem—Here either the objective function or one or more constraints or both are non-linear.

Based on the type of variables, we can classify integer programming problems as:

1. Zero-one problems—Here all the decision variables take the value of zero or one.
2. Pure integer problems—Here all the variables take integer values.
3. Mixed problems—Here the variables can be zero-one, integer or continuous.

We start with understanding and solving zero-one problems.

7.4 ZERO-ONE PROBLEMS

Let us consider the zero-one knapsack problem defined as follows:

A person going for a trek has the problem of identifying items to take along with him. There are, say, six items and each has a weight and a utility value. The person wishes to take items such that the sum of the utility is maximized and also satisfying a weight restriction. The problem is:

Maximize $\sum_{j=1}^{n} C_j X_j$

Subject to

$$\sum_{j=1}^{n} A_j X_j \leq B$$

$$X_j = 0, 1$$

where C_j represents the utility of item j and A_j represents the weight of item j. If we want to restrict the number of items to N, we can write

$$\sum_{j=1}^{n} X_j \leq N$$

If item 1 represents a torch and item 2 represents battery, the situation that the person takes the battery if he takes the torch is modelled as:

$$X_2 \geq X_1$$

If item 3 represents candle and the person takes either the candle or the torch, we can model it as:

$$X_1 + X_3 \leq 1 \text{ or } (= 1)$$

if the person decides to take one of the two.

Thus, the binary variables are very useful to model allocation problems and to model specific conditions such as either/or k out of n.

In fact, pure integer programming problems can be modelled as zero-one problems. Consider Illustration 7.9.

ILLUSTRATION 7.9

Maximize $\quad 3X_1 + 2X_2$
Subject to

$$X_1 + 2X_2 \leq 6$$
$$3X_1 + 4X_2 \leq 12$$
$$X_1, X_2 \geq 0 \text{ and integer}$$

From the constraints we understand that X_1 can take a maximum value of 4 and X_2 can take a maximum value of 3. We write

$X_1 = Y_1 + 2Y_2 + 3Y_3 \quad \text{and} \quad X_2 = Y_4 + 2Y_5 \quad \text{where} \quad Y_j = 0, 1$. The problem becomes

Maximize $\quad 3Y_1 + 6Y_2 + 9Y_3 + 2Y_4 + 4Y_5$
Subject to

$$Y_1 + 2Y_2 + 3Y_3 + 2Y_4 + 4Y_5 \leq 6$$
$$3Y_1 + 6Y_2 + 9Y_3 + 4Y_4 + 8Y_5 \leq 12$$
$$Y_j = 0, 1$$

7.5 SOLVING ZERO-ONE PROBLEMS—IMPLICIT ENUMERATION

We solve zero-one problems using the method of implicit enumeration (Balas, 1965). Let us illustrate the concepts behind implicit enumeration using an example.

ILLUSTRATION 7.10

Minimize $Z = 5X_1 + 6X_2 + 10X_3 + 7X_4 + 19X_5$
Subject to

$$5X_1 + X_2 + 3X_3 - 4X_4 + 3X_5 \geq 2$$
$$-2X_1 + 5X_2 - 2X_3 - 3X_4 + 4X_5 \geq 0$$
$$X_1 - 2X_2 - 5X_3 + 3X_4 + 4X_5 \geq 2$$
$$X_j = 0, 1$$

There are five decision variables and each is a binary variable. There are 32 possible solutions. These can be represented in the form of a vector (binary number) as follows. For example, the binary number [01011] represents the solution $X_1 = 0$, $X_2 = 1$, $X_3 = 0$, $X_4 = 1$ and $X_5 = 1$. (From the left, the values could represent variables $X_1, X_2, \ldots, X_5$. The value of the objective function for this solution is $Z = 6 + 7 + 9 = 22$.

We define the standard problem to have a minimization objective function with non-negative objective function coefficients. The constraints are all of the $\geq$ type. Later we will explain how to convert every problem to the standard form.

Let us consider the solution $X_5 = 1$. This is feasible and has $Z = 19$. The rest of the variables are at zero and we have evaluated the solution [0 0 0 0 1]. Now, each of the remaining variables can take either zero or one resulting in 15 more solutions. Every one of the fifteen solutions will have an objective function value not lesser than 19 (because all the objective function coefficients are non-negative). Even if some of them are feasible they cannot be optimal because the present solution has a lesser value of the objective function (minimization problem). Therefore, it is unnecessary to evaluate the 15 solutions and by not evaluating them we can conclude that we have implicitly evaluated the 15 solutions. This is called **implicit enumeration** by feasibility.

Rule 1

Whenever we evaluate a feasible solution where some variables are at zero, we do not evaluate solutions where they can be fixed at a value of one. These are implicitly evaluated. This is called **implicit enumeration** by feasibility.

Let us consider a solution $X_2 = 1$, $X_3 = 1$ and the rest of them are at zero. The remaining variables can be fixed at zero or one resulting in seven possible solutions. It is found that the given solution violates the third constraint. In order to make it feasible, we have to fix those variables with positive coefficients in constraint 3 to one so that the left hand side increases. Variables X_1, X_4 and X_5 have positive coefficients in constraint 3. These are called **helpful variables** (Any variable that has a positive coefficient in a violated constraint is a helpful variable). We observe that even if we put all the helpful variable to 1, constraint 3 is violated. Therefore, we do not proceed to get a feasible solution in this case by trying one helpful variable at a time. We do not evaluate the remaining seven solutions because they are all infeasible. This is called **implicit enumeration** by infeasibility.

Rule 2
When putting all the helpful variables in a violated constraint does not give feasibility, we implicitly evaluate solutions through infeasibility.

7.5.1 The Additive Algorithm

We explain the additive algorithm by considering Illustration 7.10, which is given below:
Minimize $Z = 5X_1 + 6X_2 + 10X_3 + 7X_4 + 19X_5$
Subject to

$$5X_1 + X_2 + 3X_3 - 4X_4 + 3X_5 \geq 2$$
$$-2X_1 + 5X_2 - 2X_3 - 3X_4 + 4X_5 \geq 0$$
$$X_1 - 2X_2 - 5X_3 + 3X_4 + 4X_5 \geq 2$$
$$X_j = 0, 1$$

We define a helpfulness index for each variable as the sum of the coefficients in the constraints. These are:

Variable $X_1 = 5 - 2 + 1 = 4$
Variable $X_2 = 1 + 5 - 2 = 4$
Variable $X_3 = 3 - 2 - 5 = -4$
Variable $X_4 = -4 - 3 + 3 = -4$
Variable $X_5 = 3 + 4 + 4 = 10$

We define three vectors S, V and H, where S is a vector of variables in the solution, V is the set of violated constraints and H is the set of helpful variables.
Step 0

$S_0 = \{\ \}$ (No variable is fixed to any value)
$V_0 = \{1, 3\}$—Constraints 1 and 3 are violated. Constraint 2 is satisfied as LHS = 0.
$T_0 = \{1, 2, 3, 4, 5\}$—Variables X_1 to X_3 and X_5 are helpful with respect to constraint 1 and variables X_1, X_4 and X_5 are helpful with respect to constraint 3.

We identify the most helpful variable (variable X_5 has the highest helpfulness index) and fix it to 1.
Step 1

$S_1 = \{5\}$—Variable X_5 is fixed at 1.
$V_1 = \{\ \}$—All constraints are satisfied and we have a feasible solution.

We update the feasible solution as $X_5 = 1$, $Z = 19$. When we have a feasible solution we backtrack.

> **Backtrack**
>
> When we backtrack, we consider vector **S** and the first variable fixed at 1, from the right side is now fixed at zero (indicated with a negative sign). The variables to the right of the chosen variable (that are fixed at zero) and left out of the set S.

In our example, there is only one variable. X_5 is fixed at zero, indicated by -5.

Step 2

$S_2 = \{-5\}$

$V_2 = \{1, 3\}$

$T_2 = \{1, 2, 3, 4\}$—Variable X_5 cannot be included in the helpful list because it is fixed at a value.

We choose the most helpful variable, in this case variable X_1 (we could have chosen X_2 also). A helpful variable is one that is not fixed at a value and has a positive coefficient in at least one violated constraint. We fix X_1 to 1.

Step 3

$S_3 = \{-5, 1\}$

$V_3 = \{2, 3\}$

$T_3 = \{2, 4\}$

The most helpful variable is X_2. We fix this to 1.

Step 4

$S_4 = \{-5, 1, 2\}$

$V_4 = \{3\}$

$T_4 = \{4\}$

We fix variable X_4 to 1.

Step 5

$S_5 = \{-5, 1, 2, 4\}$

$V_5 = \{\ \}$

Since no constraint is violated, we have a feasible solution with $X_1 = X_2 = X_4 = 1$. The value of the objective function is 18. This solution is better than the earlier feasible solution and we update the solution.

Since we have a feasible solution, we backtrack.

Step 6

$S_6 = \{-5, 1, 2, -4\}$

$V_6 = \{2, 3\}$

$T_6 = \{\ \}$

Constraints 2 and 3 are violated. Variable X_3 is the only variable available and not fixed to any value. It is not a helpful variable considering both the violated constraints. We, therefore, evaluate

by infeasibility and backtrack. The first variable from the right fixed at 1 is X_2. This is now fixed at zero. Variable X_4 is left out of the allocation now.
Step 7

$$S_7 = \{-5, 1, -2\}$$
$$V_7 = \{2, 3\}$$
$$T_7 = \{4\}$$

Constraint 2 is violated and does not have a helpful variable. We, therefore, backtrack.
Step 8

$$S_8 = \{-5, -1\}$$
$$V_8 = \{1, 3\}$$
$$T_8 = \{2, 3, 4\}$$

Most helpful variable is X_2. We fix this to 1.
Step 9

$$S_9 = \{-5, -1, 2\}$$
$$V_9 = \{1, 3\}$$
$$T_9 = \{3, 4\}$$

Constraint 3 is violated and the only helpful variable for constraint X_4 cannot bring feasibility. We backtrack.
Step 10

$$S_{10} = \{-5, -1, -2\}$$
$$V_{10} = \{1, 3\}$$
$$T_{10} = \{3, 4\}$$

We choose variable X_3 and fix it to 1.
Step 11

$$S_{11} = \{-5, -1, -2, 3\}$$
$$V_{11} = \{1, 3\}$$
$$T_{11} = \{4\}$$

The only helpful variable X_4 cannot make constraint 3 feasible. We backtrack.
Step 12

$$S_{12} = \{-5, -1, -2, -3\}$$
$$V_{12} = \{1, 3\}$$
$$T_{12} = \{4\}$$

The only helpful variable X_4 cannot make constraint 1 feasible. We try to backtrack and realize that no backtracking is possible. We, therefore, terminate.

The optimum solution (is the current best solution) given by $X_1 = X_2 = X_4 = 1$ and $Z = 18$.

> **When do we backtrack?**
> - When we have a feasible solution.
> - When there is a violated constraint and putting all helpful variables in that constraint cannot bring feasibility.
> - When there is a violated constraint and there is no helpful variable in the set T.

7.5.2 Speeding the Search

It is possible to reduce the number of iterations and make the algorithm faster. For instance, $X_3 = 1$ would make $X_4 = X_5 = 1$ (from the third constraint). When $X_5 = 0$, X_3 has to be zero (constraint 3). $X_5 = 0$ would make $X_4 = 1$ (to satisfy the third constraint). This also means that X_2 should be equal to 1 (from constraints 2 and 3).

With these included, the backtracking algorithm becomes a lot quicker. Let us assume that we have a solution $S_1 = \{5\}$ with $Z = 19$.

We backtrack and make $X_5 = 0$. This would make $X_2 = X_4 = 1$ and $X_3 = 0$. Therefore $S_2 = \{-5, 2, -3, 4\}$ which would make $X_1 = 1$ and give us a feasible solution with $Z = 18$.

We quickly backtrack to $S_3 = \{-5, -2\}$ which can be fathomed by infeasibility (all helpful variables cannot bring feasibility). The algorithm terminates with the solution $X_1 = X_2 = X_4 = 1$ and $Z = 18$.

These can also be generalized and used to increase the speed of the backtracking algorithm. These become useful when we solve large sized problems particularly when the interdependencies of the constraints are significant. Implementing these ideas involves additional computations at the beginning but can reduce the number of iterations. The reader can refer to Garfinkel and Nemhauser (1972) for some more ways of speeding the search in zero-one problems.

7.5.3 Converting a Given Problem to the Standard Form

We use the following rules to convert any given zero-one problem into the standard form:

1. If the objective function is maximization, we convert it to a minimization by multiplying with -1.
2. If we have a $\leq$ constraint, we multiply the constraint with -1 and convert it to $\geq$ type. The RHS value can become negative in the process.
3. If we have a variable with a negative coefficient in the objective function, we define the variable as $Y_j = 1 - X_j$ and substitute in the objective function and in all the constraints. The new variable will also be a zero-one variable, since all existing variables are zero-one.

We illustrate this with the following example.

ILLUSTRATION 7.11

Maximize $4X_1 - 7X_2 + 3X_3$
Subject to
$$2X_1 - 5X_2 + 3X_3 \leq 7$$
$$3X_1 + 2X_2 - 4X_3 \geq 8$$
$$X_j = 0, 1$$

We multiply the objective function by -1 and have

Minimize $-4X_1 + 7X_2 - 3X_3$
Subject to
$$-2X_1 + 5X_2 - 3X_3 \geq -7$$
$$3X_1 + 2X_2 - 4X_3 \geq 8$$
$$X_j = 0, 1$$

Now, variables X_1 and X_3 have negative coefficients in the objective function. We redefine the variables as $Y_1 = 1 - X_1$ and $Y_3 = 1 - X_3$.

Minimize $4Y_1 + 7X_2 + 3Y_3 - 7$
Subject to
$$2Y_1 + 5X_2 + 3Y_3 \geq -2$$
$$-3Y_1 + 2X_2 + 4Y_3 \geq 9$$
$$Y_1, X_2, Y_3 = 0, 1$$

(If a constraint is an equation we can replace it by two constraints one with a $\geq$ sign and the other with a $\leq$ sign. We can also consider eliminating a variable by substitution).

7.5.4 Zero-One Non-linear Problems

When we model practical situations using zero-one variables, sometimes we may formulate problems with non-linear objective function or non-linear constraints or both. We can convert every non-linear zero-one problem into a linear zero-one problem and solve it.

If X_j is a zero-one variable, any power of X_j is also a zero-one variable. Therefore, any power term of the type X_j^n, can be written as X_j and solved.

If we have an $X_1 X_2$ term, we replace it with Y_{12} and add

$$X_1 + X_2 - 2Y_{12} \geq 0$$
$$X_1 + X_2 - Y_{12} \leq 1$$
$$Y_{12} = 0, 1$$

7.6 INTEGER PROGRAMMING—GOMORY'S CUTTING PLANE ALGORITHM

We explain the Gomory's cutting plane algorithm that first appeared in the late 1950s and early 1960s (Ref: Gomory's 1991 article that appeared again in 2002) to solve a pure integer programming problem (all variables are integers) using an example. We consider Illustration 7.8 to illustrate the algorithm.

Maximize $X_1 + X_2$
Subject to
$$7X_1 - 5X_2 \leq 7$$
$$-12X_1 + 15X_2 \leq 7$$
$$X_1, X_2 \geq 0 \text{ and integer}$$

We first solve the LP problem using the simplex algorithm. This is because, if the LP optimum is integer valued, it is optimum to the integer programming problem (IP). We start the simplex algorithm using X_3 and X_4 as slack variables. The simplex iterations are shown in Table 7.1.

Table 7.1 Simplex Iterations

C_B	Basic variables	1 X_1	1 X_2	0 X_3	0 X_4	RHS	θ
0	X_3	7	−5	1	0	7	1
0	X_4	−12	15	0	1	7	--
	$C_j - Z_j$	1	1	0	0	0	
1	X_1	1	−5/7	1/7	0	1	--
0	X_4	0	45/7	12/7	1	19	133/45
	$C_j - Z_j$	0	12/7	−1/7	0	1	
u1	X_1	1	0	1/3	1/9	28/9	
1	X_2	0	1	4/15	7/45	133/45	
	$C_j - Z_j$	0	0	−9/15	−4/15	273/45	

The optimum solution to the LP relaxation is $X_1 = 28/9, X_2 = 133/45, Z = 273/45$. We observe that both the basic variables are not integers at the optimum. We select one among the non-integer values at the optimum (It is customary that the variable with the largest fractional portion is picked under the assumption that it will get rounded to the highest integer). We pick X_2 and write the constraint as:

$$X_2 + \frac{4}{15}X_3 + \frac{7}{45}X_4 = 133/45 \tag{7.1}$$

We write every coefficient in the LHS as the sum of an integer and a positive fraction. We also write the RHS as the sum of a non-negative integer and a fraction. In Eq. (7.1), we do not have any LHS variable with a negative coefficient. Equation 7.1 is rewritten as:

$$X_2 + \frac{4}{15}X_3 + \frac{7}{45}X_4 = 2 + \frac{43}{45}$$

Since X_2, X_3 and X_4 are integers and the coefficients of the fraction terms in LHS are positive and the fraction term in the RHS is a positive fraction less than 1, we can write

$$\frac{4}{15}X_3 + \frac{7}{45}X_4 \geq \frac{43}{45} \tag{7.2}$$

(This is called a **Gomory cut** and this constraint is added to the simplex table as follows:) Constraint (7.2) is rewritten as:

$$-\frac{4}{15}X_3 - \frac{7}{45}X_4 + X_5 = -\frac{43}{45}$$

This is included as a constraint in the simplex table and we proceed with a dual simplex iteration, shown in Table 7.2.

Table 7.2 Dual Simplex Iterations

C_B	Basic variables	X_1	X_2	X_3	X_4	X_5	RHS	θ
		1	1	0	0			
0	X_3	7	−5	1	0		7	1
0	X_4	−12	15	0	1		7	− −
	$C_j - Z_j$	1	1	0	0		0	
1	X_1	1	−5/7	1/7	0		1	− −
0	X_4	0	45/7	12/7	1		19	133/45
	$C_j - Z_j$	0	12/7	−1/7	0			
1	X_1	1	0	1/3	1/9	0	28/9	
1	X_2	0	1	4/15	7/45	0	133/45	
0	X_5	0	0	−4/15	**−7/45**	1	−43/45	
	$C_j - Z_j$	0	0	−9/15	−4/15		273/45	
	θ			9/4	12/7			
1	X_1	1	0	1/7	0	5/7	17/7	
1	X_2	0	1	0	0	1	2	
0	X_4	0	0	12/7	1	−45/7	43/7	
	$C_j - Z_j$	0	0	−1/7	0	−12/7	31/7	

Once again variables X_1 and X_4 that are to be integer valued are continuous. We consider variable X_1 to generate another Gomory cut. We write the equation as:

$$X_1 + \frac{1}{7}X_3 + \frac{5}{7}X_5 = 2 + \frac{3}{7}$$

from which we write

$$\frac{1}{7}X_3 + \frac{5}{7}X_5 \geq \frac{3}{7} \qquad (7.3)$$

We include a slack variable X_6 (≥ 0 and integer) and write the cut equation as:

$$-\frac{1}{7}X_3 - \frac{5}{7}X_5 + X_6 = -\frac{3}{7}$$

and include this as an additional constraint in the simplex table. We also perform a dual simplex iteration. This is shown in Table 7.3.

Table 7.3 Dual Simplex Iteration

C_B	Basic variables	1 X_1	1 X_2	0 X_3	0 X_4	0 X_5	0 X_6	RHS	θ
1	X_1	1	0	1/7	0	5/7	0	17/7	
1	X_2	0	1	0	0	1	0	2	
0	X_4	0	0	12/7	1	−45/7	0	43/7	
0	X_6	0	0	−1/7 ↑	0	−5/7	1	−3/7	→
	$C_j - Z_j$	0	0	−1/7	0	−12/7	0	31/7	
	θ			1		12/5			
1	X_1	1	0	0	0	0	1	2	
1	X_2	0	1	0	0	1	0	2	
0	X_4	0	0	0	1	−10	12	1	
0	X_3	0	0	1	0	5	−7	3	
		0	0	0	0	−1	−1	4	

We have reached the optimal solution to the LP problem. We also observe that it is integer valued. Hence it is optimal to the IP.

7.6.1 Explaining the Gomory Cut

The first Gomory cut was given by the constraint:

$$\frac{4}{15}X_3 + \frac{7}{45}X_4 \geq \frac{43}{45}$$

Let us write the variables X_3 and X_4 in terms of the decision variables X_1 and X_2.

$$4/15\,(7 - 7X_1 + 5X_2) + 7/45\,(7 + 12X_1 - 15X_2) \geq 43/45$$
$$12\,(7 - 7X_1 + 5X_2) + 7\,(7 + 12X_1 - 15X_2) \geq 43$$
$$84 - 84X_1 + 60X_2 + 49 + 84X_1 - 105X_2 \geq 43$$
$$-45X_2 \geq 43 - 84 - 49$$
$$X_2 \leq 2$$

This cut is shown in Figure 7.1 along with the original constraints.

We observe that the point (3, 3) violates the first constraint. The first Gomory cut is $X_2 \leq 2$ and is shown in the graph. Please note that the two integer points in the feasible region are shown as small circles and that the cut does not eliminate any integer point.

The second cut is given by

$$\frac{1}{7}X_3 + \frac{5}{7}X_5 \geq \frac{3}{7}$$

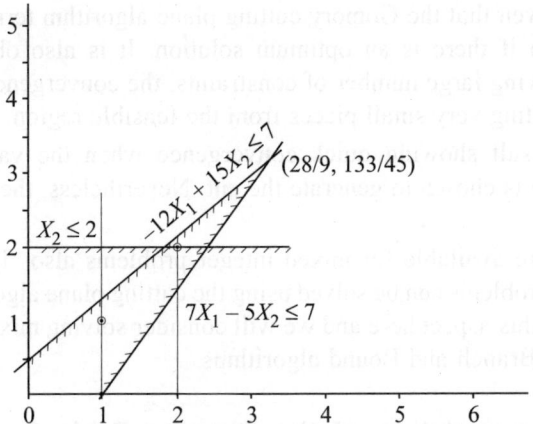

Figure 7.1 Gomory cutting plane algorithm.

We substitute for X_3 and X_5 in terms of the decision variables.

$X_3 = 7 - 7X_1 + 5X_2$ and X_5 is obtained from $4/15 X_3 + 7/45 X_4 - X_5 = 43/45$.

$$X_5 = 4/15 X_3 + 7/45 X_4 - 43/45 (7 + 12X_1 - 15X_2)$$

Substituting, we get

$$\frac{1}{7}X_3 + \frac{5}{7}\left(\frac{4}{15}X_3 + \frac{7}{45}X_4 - \frac{43}{45}\right) \geq 3/7$$

Simplifying, we get

$$\frac{1}{7}X_3 + \frac{4}{21}X_3 + \frac{1}{9}X_4 - \frac{43}{63} \geq 3/7$$

$$\frac{1}{3}X_3 + \frac{1}{9}X_4 \geq 10/9$$

Substituting for $X_3 = 7 - 7X_1 + 5X_2$ and $X_4 = 7 + 12X_1 - 15X_2$ and simplifying, we get

$$\frac{1}{3}(7 - 7X_1 + 5X_2) + \frac{1}{9}(7 + 12X_1 - 15X_2) \geq 10/9$$

$$\frac{7}{3} - \frac{7}{3}X_1 + \frac{5}{3}X_2 + \frac{7}{9} + \frac{4}{3}X_1 - \frac{5}{3}X_2 \geq 10/9$$

from which, $X_1 \leq 2$.

This cut is also shown in Figure 7.1. This gives us the optimum point (2, 2) to the IP.

Each Gomory cut removes a portion of the feasible region (including the existing optimum point). It also ensures that no integer solution is eliminated in the process. When the feasible solution is integer valued, the optimum is reached.

7.6.2 Other Issues in the Cutting Plane Algorithm

1. We can generate a Gomory cut using any variable that has a non-integer value in the solution. There is no strict rule to choose the variable though by practice there is a tendency to generate cuts from variables that have the largest fractional value.

2. It has been proven that the Gomory cutting plane algorithm terminates (and converges) to the optimum if there is an optimum solution. It is also observed that for certain problems involving large number of constraints, the convergence may be slow. The cut may be eliminating very small pieces from the feasible region.
3. There is no result showing quick convergence when the variable with the largest fractional value is chosen to generate the cut. Nevertheless, the algorithm terminates to the solution.
4. Gomory cuts are available for mixed integer problems also. Therefore, mixed integer programming problems can be solved using the cutting plane algorithm. However, we are not addressing this aspect here and we will consider solving mixed integer programming problem using Branch and Bound algorithms.

7.6.3 Efficient Representation of the Simplex Table for Integer Programming

Let us consider the same example to illustrate an efficient way of representing the simplex table for linear and integer programming problems.

Maximize $X_1 + X_2$

Subject to

$$7X_1 - 5X_2 \leq 7$$
$$-12X_1 + 15X_2 \leq 7$$
$$X_1, X_2 \geq 0$$

The initial basic variables are X_3 and X_4 and the non-basic variables are X_1 and X_2. The simplex table is shown in Table 7.4.

Table 7.4 Initial Simplex Table

	RHS	$-X_1$	$-X_2$
$Z_j - C_j$	0	-1	-1
X_3	7	7	-5
X_4	7	-12	15

From the problem constraints, we have $X_3 = 7 - 7X_1 + 5X_2$. Because we have $-X_1$ and $-X_2$, the entries are 7 and -5, respectively. Similarly, the entries in the $Z_j - C_j$ row are also -1 and -1 for maximizing $X_1 + X_2$.

The $Z_j - C_j$ values represent the dual variables and the variable with the most negative dual enters (for a maximization problem). The negative value also represents dual infeasibility and we wish to iterate till the dual is feasible. Variable X_1 enters and the leaving variable is X_3 (there is only one candidate; θ is computed by dividing the RHS value by the positive coefficient in the entering column).

The simplex iterations are carried out using the following rules:
1. The pivot element becomes 1/(pivot).
2. The rest of the pivot row elements are divided by the pivot element.
3. The rest of the elements of the pivot column are divided by the negative of the pivot.
4. For a non-pivot column j, for element in row i,
   New a_{ij} = Old a_{ij} − Old$_{i,\text{pivot}}$ * New$_{\text{pivot},j}$

The next simplex iteration is shown in Table 7.5.

Variable X_2 with a negative dual $(Z_j - C_j)$ enters the basis and the only candidate X_4 leaves the basis. The next simplex iteration is shown in Table 7.6.

The above solution is optimal to the LP problem. Let us introduce the Gomory cut as performed in the earlier tabular method.

We pick variable X_2 for the Gomory cut and the cut becomes $4/15 X_3 + 7/45 X_4 \geq 43/45$. This is written as an additional row in the simplex table shown in Table 7.7.

Variable X_5, is the negative slack variable and leaves the basis (dual simplex iteration) and variable X_4 enters the basis.

Every Gomory cut introduces an additional row in the simplex table. This procedure can be used till the optimal solution to the integer programming problem can be obtained.

The efficient representation (available in Garfinkel and Nemhauser, 1972 and Hu, 1969) makes the simplex table look smaller and simpler. Also, when we introduce the cuts, we observe that the pivot row is always the last row in the table making it easy to carry out the subsequent iterations.

Table 7.5 Simplex Iteration

	RHS	$-X_3$	$-X_2$ ↓
$Z_j - C_j$	1	1/7	−12/7
X_1	1	1/7	−5/7
← X_4	19	12/7	**45/7**

Table 7.6 Simplex Iteration

	RHS	$-X_3$	$-X_4$ ↓
$Z_j - C_j$	273/45	9/15	4/15
X_1	28/9	1/3	1/9
← X_2	133/45	4/15	7/45

Table 7.7 Simplex Iteration

	RHS	$-X_3$	$-X_4$ ↓
$Z_j - C_j$	273/45	9/15	4/15
X_1	28/9	1/3	1/9
← X_2	133/45	4/15	7/45
X_5	−43/45	−4/45	−7/45

7.7 Branch and Bound Algorithm for Integer Programming

We explain the branch and bound algorithm (Land and Doig, 1960) using Illustration 7.8. The problem is:

Maximize $X_1 + X_2$

Subject to

$$7X_1 - 5X_2 \leq 7$$

$$-12X_1 + 15X_2 \leq 7$$

$$X_1, X_2 \geq 0 \text{ and integer}$$

The LP optimum is given by $X_1 = 28/9$, $X_2 = 133/45$ and $Z = 273/45$. Here both the variables have non-integer values. Any one can be taken to branch and we choose variable X_2 having the larger fractional value. Because X_2 should be integer value, we introduce two constraints $X_2 \leq 2$ and $X_2 \geq 3$. Clearly introducing both these to the problem makes the problem infeasible. We add each constraint to the original problem (called P1) and create two Problems P2 and P3 with one constraint added to each. Also the optimal solution to P1 is infeasible to both P2 and P3. Since the additional constraints are integer bounded, no integer feasible solution to the original problem is eliminated by the addition of these. Problems P2 and P3 and their optimal solutions are shown in Tables 7.8 and 7.9, respectively.

Table 7.8 Optimal Solution to P2

> *Problem P2*
> Maximize $X_1 + X_2$
> Subject to
> $$7X_1 - 5X_2 \leq 7$$
> $$-12X_1 + 15X_2 \leq 7$$
> $$X_2 \leq 2$$
> $$X_1, X_2 \geq 0 \text{ and integer}$$
> The optimal solution is $X_1 = 17/7$, $X_2 = 2$, $Z = 31/7$.

Table 7.9 Solution to P3

> *Problem P3*
> Maximize $X_1 + X_2$
> Subject to
> $$7X_1 - 5X_2 \leq 7$$
> $$-12X_1 + 15X_2 \leq 7$$
> $$X_2 \geq 3$$
> $$X_1, X_2 \geq 0 \text{ and integer}$$

The problem has an infeasible solution.

Since Problem P3 is infeasible, we cannot proceed from P3 (because every additional constraint will only continue to make it infeasible) and this is called **fathoming** by infeasibility. We have to proceed from Problem P2.

The optimum solution has X_1 having a non-integer value and by the same argument earlier, we create two problems P4 and P5 by adding constraints $X_1 \leq 2$ and $X_1 \geq 3$, respectively. Problems P4 and P5 and their optimum solutions are shown in Tables 7.10 and 7.11, respectively.

Table 7.10 Optimum Solution to P4

Problem P4
Maximize $X_1 + X_2$
Subject to

$$7X_1 - 5X_2 \le 7$$
$$-12X_1 + 15X_2 \le 7$$
$$X_2 \le 2$$
$$X_1 \le 2$$
$$X_1, X_2 \ge 0 \text{ and integer}$$

The optimal solution is $X_1 = 2, X_2 = 2, Z = 4$.

P4 has a feasible solution and we update this to be the best solution. This solution provides a lower bound to the optimum.

Table 7.11 Solution to P5

Problem P5
Maximize $X_1 + X_2$
Subject to

$$7X_1 - 5X_2 \le 7$$
$$-12X_1 + 15X_2 \le 7$$
$$X_2 \le 2$$
$$X_1 \ge 3$$
$$X_1, X_2 \ge 0 \text{ and integer}$$

The problem has infeasible solution.

Since P5 has an infeasible solution, we fathom again by infeasibility. There are no more problems to be solved and we terminate indicating that the solution $X_1 = X_2 = 2$ is the optimum solution.

We show the branch and bound algorithm using a Branch and Bound tree shown in Figure 7.2.

The original LP solution is non-integer valued and provides an upper bound (UB) to the IP optimum. We can branch from a variable by creating two subproblems: one with an additional $\ge$ constraint and another with a $\le$ constraint. These are called **nodes** that branch from a node that has not been fathomed. We fathom a node by feasibility (Node 4 – Problem P4), when we have a feasible solution to the IP at that node. This also becomes a lower bound to the optimum (for a maximization problem, every feasible represents a lower bound to the IP). We also fathom a node when the node has an infeasible solution to the LP. This is called **fathoming a node by infeasibility**. Every node created two child nodes. Every unfathomed node has a feasible solution to the LP but not a feasible solution to the LP. It provides an upper estimate to the IP optimum

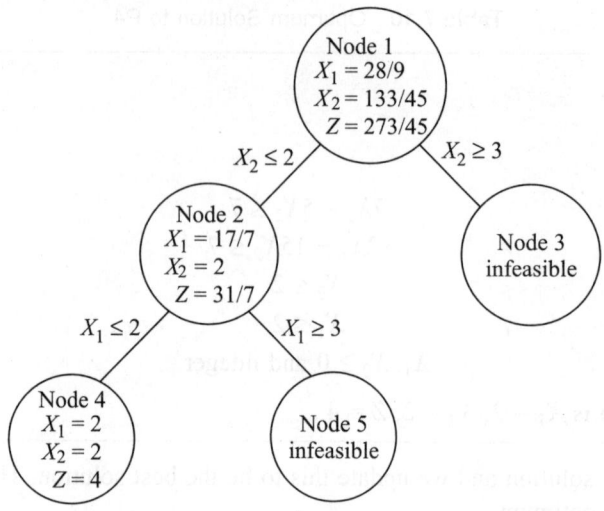

Figure 7.2 Branch and bound tree for Illustration 7.8.

and is clearly infeasible to the IP. It provides an upper bound to the IP (maximization problem). Every unfathomed node can branch to two children nodes. At any stage, we choose one node from among those that are not fathomed. We choose the one that has the highest value of the upper bound. When we encounter a feasible solution to the IP, we update if the new feasible solution is better than the existing best. We terminate the algorithm when all nodes are fathomed. The best solution is the optimum solution.

Branch and bound algorithm for all integer programming (Maximization)

1. Solve the LP. If it is integer valued, then optimum.
2. Otherwise LP optimum is an upper bound to the IP. Identify a non-integer variable X with a value between k and $k + 1$. Create two problems (nodes) with constraints $X_j \leq k$ and $X_j \geq k + 1$.
3. Select the unfathomed node with the highest value of the UB. Solve the LP problem. If LP is infeasible, fathom the node by feasibility.
4. If the LP problem gives an integer valued solution, update the solution if found better. Fathom the node by feasibility.
5. Go to Step 3 till all nodes are fathomed and there is no node for evaluation.
6. The best solution obtained is the optimal solution.

Let us explain the branch and bound algorithm using Illustration 7.6.

Maximize $\quad 3X_1 + 4X_2$

Subject to

$$X_1 + X_2 \leq 9$$

$$X_1 + 3X_2 \leq 20$$

$$X_1, X_2 \geq 0 \text{ and integer}$$

Node 1: The LP optimum is $X_1 = 7/2$, $X_2 = 11/2$, $Z = 65/2$. This is not feasible to IP. Set $UB = 65/2$. Choose node with the highest value of UB. In our case there is only one node. Branch on variable X_1 (in this case both non-integer variables have the same fractional value. Create two nodes: Node 2 and Node 3 with additional constraints $X_1 \le 3$ and $X_1 \ge 4$, respectively.

Node 2: The LP optimum is $X_1 = 3$, $X_2 = 17/3$, $Z = 95/3$. This is not feasible to IP. Set $UB = 95/3$.

Node 3: The LP optimum is $X_1 = 4$, $X_2 = 5$, $Z = 32$. Update the feasible solution. Fathom this node by feasibility.

Branching node: Choose the unfathomed node with the highest UB. Here only Node 2 is available. Variable X_2 has non-integer value. Create two nodes with additional constraints $X_2 \le 5$ and $X_2 \ge 6$, respectively. Solve Nodes 4 and 5.

Node 4: The LP optimum is $X_1 = 3$, $X_2 = 5$, $Z = 29$. This is feasible to IP. This solution is not updated because the existing solution is better. Fathom the node by feasibility.

Node 5: The LP optimum is $X_1 = 2$, $X_2 = 6$, $Z = 30$. This is feasible to IP. This solution is not updated because the existing solution is better. Fathom the node by feasibility.

Branching node: There is no available node for branching. The algorithm terminates. $X_1 = 4$, $X_2 = 5$, $Z = 32$ is the optimum solution. The branch and bound tree is shown in Figure 7.3.

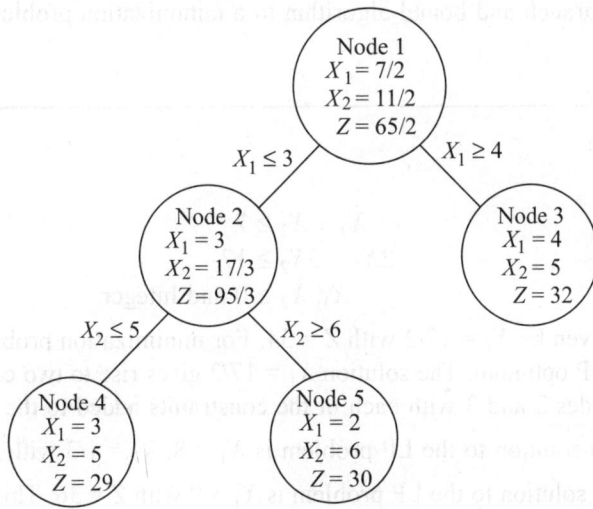

Figure 7.3 Branch and bound tree for Illustration 7.7.

Let us start solving the problem from the beginning. Node 1 gives an upper bound value of 65/2. Since the objective function coefficients are integers and the variables are integers, the value of the objective function to the IP at the optimum has to be an integer. The upper bound can, therefore, be reduced to 32.

At Node 3, we have a feasible solution to the IP with objective function value 32. Before we branch on variable X_2 from Node 2, we observe that the UB value of Node 2 is 95/3 and can be reduced to 31 (integer value of objective function). Branching from that node can only produce solutions with objective function value less than (or equal to) 31 or IP and less than or equal to 95/3 for LPs because we add constraints at every stage, and constraints only reduce the value of the objective function for maximization problems.

When a feasible solution to the IP is evaluated, we also find out whether there are nodes with *UB* value less than the objective function value of the IP. Such nodes can be fathomed by *LB*. Similarly, when the *UB* for a node is evaluated (LP optimum), we can fathom that node if the *UB* is less than the best *LB* (objective function value of the best IP). This is an important aspect of IP and considerably reduces both the computations as well as the storage requirements of branch and bound algorithms.

Rules for fathoming nodes

1. When a node has a feasible solution fathom that node by feasibility.
2. When a feasible solution is evaluated and is updated, fathom all active nodes that have *UB* less than or equal to the *LB*.
3. When a node has an infeasible solution to the LP (fathom by infeasibility).
4. When a node has a feasible solution to LP but non-integer valued, fathom that node if the *UB* is less than the best *LB*.

In our earlier example, at Node 4, we have $LB = 4$ and at Node 3 $UB = 31/7$ (reducible to 4). We need not evaluate Node 5 because it was created from Node 3.

Let us apply the branch and bound algorithm to a minimization problem:

ILLUSTRATION 7.12

Minimize $\quad 4X_1 + 9X_2$

Subject to

$$X_1 + X_2 \geq 7$$
$$2X_1 + 3X_2 \geq 17,$$
$$X_1, X_2 \geq 0 \text{ and Integer}$$

The LP optimum is given by $X_1 = 17/2$ with $Z = 34$. For minimization problems, LP optimum is a lower bound to the IP optimum. The solution $X_1 = 17/2$ gives rise to two constraints $X_1 \leq 8$ and $X_1 \geq 9$. We create Nodes 2 and 3 with each of the constraints added to the original problem.

Node 2: The optimum solution to the LP problem is $X_1 = 8$, $X_2 = 1/3$ with $Z = 35$.

Node 3: The optimum solution to the LP problem is $X_1 = 9$ with $Z = 36$. This is feasible to the IP and acts as an upper bound to the IP. Node 3 is fathomed by feasibility. Since the lower bound of 35 (Node 2) is lesser than 36, we branch from Node 2 creating two nodes with the additional constraints $X_2 \leq 0$ and $X_2 \geq 1$.

Node 4: The LP problem is infeasible and hence the node is fathomed by infeasibility.

Node 5: The LP optimum is $X_1 = 7$, $X_2 = 1$, $Z = 37$ which is feasible to the IP. The node is fathomed by feasibility. Since the IP solution is higher than the best value of 36, the new value is ignored. There are no nodes to branch and the algorithms terminates with the optimum solution $X_1 = 9$ and $Z = 36$. Figure 7.4 shows the branch and bound tree.

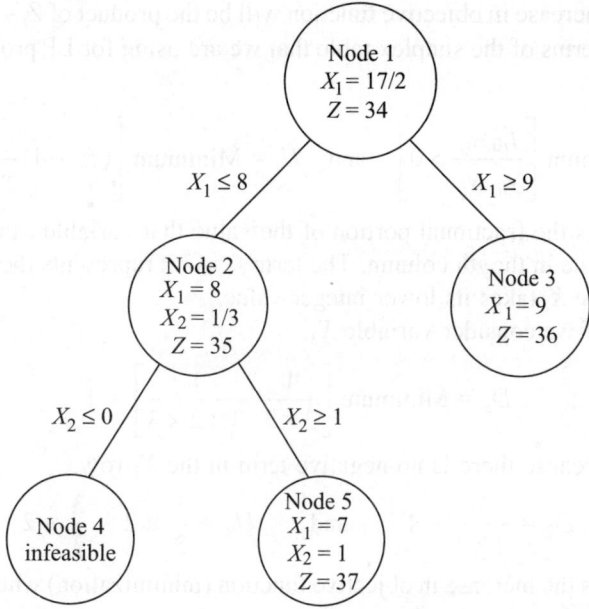

Figure 7.4 Branch and bound tree for Illustration 7.12.

7.7.1 Improving the Lower Bound

Let us consider Node 2 of the branch and bound tree. The LP optimum is $X_1 = 8$, $X_2 = 1.3$ and $Z = 35$. The simplex table is given in Table 7.12.

This is not optimal to the IP since variables X_2 and X_3 have fractional (non-integer values). The simplex algorithm has terminated with a unique optimum since there is no $Z_j - C_j$ with zero value at the optimum. Also the solution is non-degenerate (all basic variables have strictly positive value). This means that the best integer solution from this node will have a value strictly greater than 35.

Table 7.12 Simplex Table for Node 3

	RHS	$-X_4$	$-X_5$
$Z_j - C_j$	–35	1	2
X_3	4/3	1/3	1/3
X_1	8	–1	1
X_2	1/3	1/3	–2/3

If the simplex algorithm had terminated with an alternate optimum, there is a possibility that there could be an integer solution with the objective function value same as that of the LP problem. Since there is no alternate optimum, the additional constraint will increase the value of the objective function and hence the best IP optimum from this node can have an objective function value greater than 35.

Since both the objective function coefficients and decision variables are integers, the IP optimum has to have an integer valued objective function and hence the lower bound at Node 3 can be increased to 36.

If the objective function coefficients were not integers, this increase may not hold but it is possible to evaluate the possible increase (lower estimate) using some ideas from branching.

In any iteration, increase in objective function will be the product of $Z_j - C_j$ and θ. We can also write the increase in terms of the simplex table that we are using for LP problems. The equations are:

$$D_i = \text{minimum} \left[\frac{f_{i0} y_{0j}}{y_{ij}, y_{ij}} > 0 \right] \quad \text{and} \quad U_i = \text{Minimum} \left[(f_{i0} - 1) \frac{y_{0j}}{y_{ij}, y_{ij}} < 0 \right]$$

Here, f_{i0} represents the fractional portion of the value that variable i takes. Y_{0j} is the $Z_j - C_j$ value and y_{ij} is the value in the jth column. The term $f_{i0} y_{0j} / y_{ij}$ represents the increase in objective function when variable X_i takes its lower integer value.

In our example, if we consider variable X_3,

$$D_3 = \text{Minimum} \left[\frac{1}{3 \times 3}, \frac{1}{3 \times 2 \times 3} \right] = 1$$

There is no U_3 because there is no negative term in the X_3 row.

$$D_2 = \frac{1}{3 \times 3} = 1 \quad \text{and} \quad U_2 = \frac{2}{3} \times 2 \times \frac{3}{2} = 2$$

Here U_j represents the increase in objective function (minimization) when variable X_j takes its higher integer value.

$$P_2 = \text{Minimum} (D_2, U_2) = 1$$

We can also use ideas from cutting plane algorithm to find the increase in the objective function when Gomory cuts are created from decision variables with non-integer values. These are given by

$$P'_i = \text{Minimum} \left\{ \frac{f_{i0} y_{0j}}{y_{ij}} \right\} \text{ where } y_{ij} \neq 0$$

Using

$$P'_3 = \text{Minimum} \left\{ \frac{1}{3} \times 1 \times 3, \frac{1}{3} \times 2 \times 3 \right\} = 1$$

$$P'_2 = \text{Minimum} \left\{ \frac{1}{3} \times 1 \times 3, \frac{1}{3} \times 2 \times 3 \right\} = 1$$

Then   Increase = Maximum $\{P_1, P_2, \text{Minimum} (P'_i, P'_2)\} = 1$

The lower bound actually increases to 36.

With the increased lower bound of 36, when we get a feasible solution at Node 4 with $Z = 36$, we can also fathom Node 3 by lower bound and terminate the algorithm. The tightening of the lower bound can fathom some nodes quicker, resulting in faster termination of the branch and bound algorithm. (Additional reading material on the topic can be had from Garfinkel and Nemhauser, 1972 and Nemhauser and Wolsey, 1988)

7.7.2 Implicit Enumeration Algorithm as a Branch and Bound Algorithm

Let us consider the implicit enumeration algorithm (for all binary variables) again, for example,

Minimize $Z = 5X_1 + 6X_2 + 10X_3 + 7X_4 + 19X_5$

Subject to
$$5X_1 + X_2 + 3X_3 - 4X_4 + 3X_5 \geq 2$$
$$-2X_1 + 5X_2 - 2X_3 - 3X_4 + 4X_5 \geq 0$$
$$X_1 - 2X_2 - 5X_3 + 3X_4 + 4X_5 \geq 2$$
$$X_j = 0, 1$$

The solutions evaluated are:

$$S_0 = \{\ \}$$
$$S_1 = \{5\}$$
$$S_2 = \{-5\}$$
$$S_3 = \{-5, 1\}$$
$$S_4 = \{-5, 1, 2\}$$
$$S_5 = \{-5, 1, 2, 4\}$$
$$S_6 = \{-5, 1, 2, -4\}$$
$$S_7 = \{-5, 1, -2\}$$
$$S_8 = \{-5, -1\}$$
$$S_9 = \{-5, -1, 2\}$$
$$S_{10} = \{-5, -1, -2\}$$
$$S_{11} = \{-5, -1, -2, 3\}$$
$$S_{12} = \{-5, -1, -2, -3\}$$

The optimum solution is given by $X_1 = X_2 = X_4 = 1$ and $Z = 18$. The branch and bound tree for this example is shown in Figure 7.5.

Whenever we fix a variable to 1, we branch and create one node (in our numbering system it becomes the next node) and evaluate it. At this point, we do not explicitly create the other node (by fixing the variable to zero).

When we backtrack due to the reasons explained in the earlier section, we go backward (upward) in the tree, identify the first upward node that can branch and create a new node by making the first positive variable equal to zero.

Let us assume that we have evaluated Node 5 and obtained a feasible solution $\{-5, 1, 2, 4\}$. We backtrack, move to Node 4 and realize that variable X_2 presently at 1 can be fixed at zero. We create the next node (Node 6) with $X_5 = X_4 = 0$ and $X_1 = X_2 = 1$. This is done in the implicit enumeration algorithm as $S_6 = \{-5, 1, -2, 4\}$. The implicit enumeration algorithm efficiently represents the node of the branch and bound algorithm.

Let us consider Node 6 with $S_6 = \{-5, 1, 2, -4\}$. We observe that this node is fathomed by infeasibility and we backtrack. Node 7 created by the implicit enumeration algorithm would read $S_7 = \{-5, 1, -2\}$. In the branch and bound algorithm, we move one step above Node 6 and reach Node 4. Now, we cannot further branch from Node 4. We go one level above and reach Node 3 and realize that we can branch from Node 3 ($X_5 = 0$, $X_1 = 1$) to create Node 7 with ($X_5 = 0$, $X_1 = 1, X_2 = 0$). Node 4 had been created from Node 3 by additionally fixing $X_2 = 1$. Thus, we can reach the correct node to branch next using the backtracking idea of the implicit enumeration algorithm.

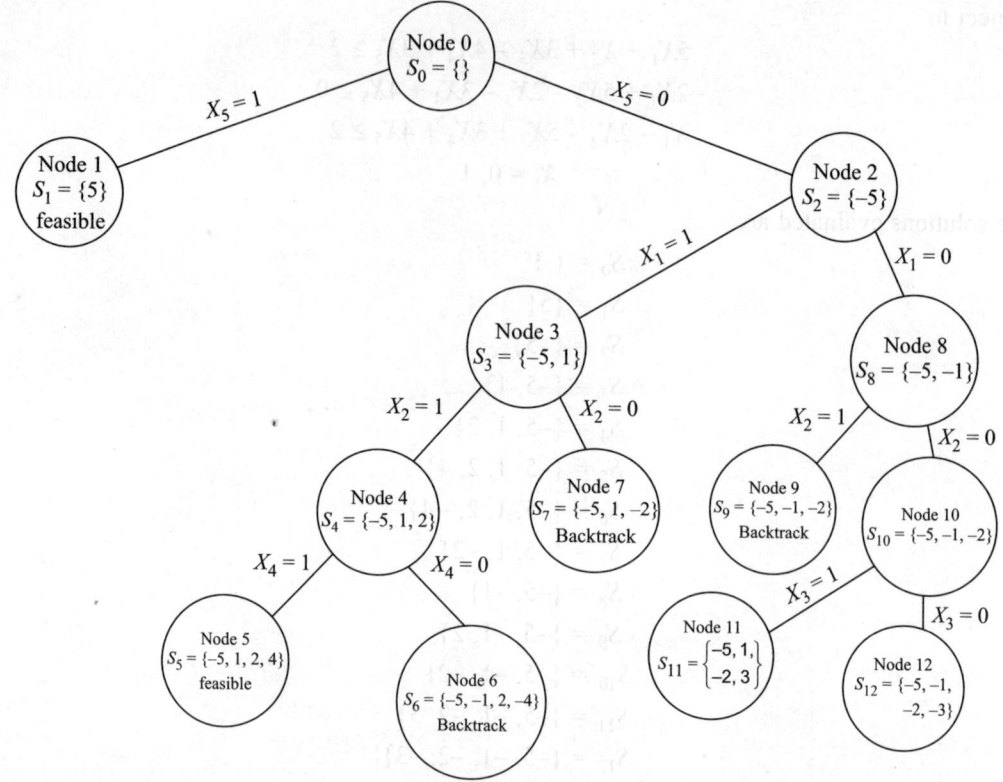

Figure 7.5 Branch and bound tree.

We observe that the implicit enumeration algorithm is actually a branch and bound algorithm to solve zero-one problems but thanks to the zero-one nature of the variable, the backtracking scheme helps in a very efficient and elegant implementation, which is called the **additive algorithm** or the **implicit enumeration algorithm**.

7.8 ALL INTEGER ALGORITHMS (GOMORY, 1963)

In this section, we introduce two all integer algorithms, called the **all integer dual algorithm** and the **all integer primal algorithm**.

7.8.1 All Integer Dual Algorithm

ILLUSTRATION **7.13**

Consider the following example:
Minimize $\quad 8X_1 + 4X_2 + 6X_3$
Subject to
$$4X_1 + 5X_2 + 6X_3 \geq 18$$
$$2X_1 + 3X_2 + 5X_3 \geq 15$$

$$4X_1 + 6X_2 + 3X_3 \geq 20$$
$$X_j \geq 0 \text{ and integer}$$

The problem has all integer coefficients in the objective function and in the constraints. We introduce negative slack variables (X_4 to X_6) and create the simplex table (efficient representation) shown in Table 7.13.

Table 7.13 Simplex Table

	RHS	$-X_1$	$-X_2$	$-X_3$
$Z_j - C_j$	0	8	4	6
X_4	-18	-4	-5	-6
X_5	-15	-2	-3	-5
X_6	-20	-4	-6	-3

It is observed that the solution is dual feasible but primal infeasible (like in dual simplex algorithm). The most negative variable (X_6) is chosen to create the cut. The cut is created using the following steps:

Steps in creating the all integer dual cut
1. Choose the row with the most negative value of the RHS value. This row is called the **source row**.
2. Identify the variables with negative coefficients in the chosen row.
3. Find out the corresponding dual values.
4. Divide the dual values by the smallest value and find the lower integer value. The smallest value gets a corresponding value of 1.
5. Divide the lower integer value by the negative of the corresponding value in the chosen row. These values are positive since the values used in the chosen rows are negative.
6. Find the minimum positive value among those in Step 4.
7. Create a cut by multiplying every element of the source row with the minimum positive value found in Step 6 and take the lower integer values. This introduces a new row and a slack variable S, denoted by a suitable subscript.

Illustration:

1. Step 1 gives us Row 4 with basic variable X_6 as the source row.
2. All values have strictly negative values.
3. The corresponding dual values are 8, 4, 6.
4. The corresponding values are 2, 1, 1.
5. The values are 1/2, 1/6 and 1/3.
6. The minimum value is 1/6.
7. The values are −4, −1, −1 and −1. Slack variable S_1 is introduced.

The simplex table with the cut is shown in Table 7.14.

Table 7.14 Simplex with the All Integer Dual Cut

	RHS	$-X_1$	$-X_2$↓	$-X_3$
$Z_j - C_j$	0	8	4	6
X_4	-18	-4	-5	-6
X_5	-15	-2	-3	-5
X_6	-20	-4	-6	-3
←S_1	-4	-1	-1	-1

Features of the all integer dual cut:

1. We introduce a new row and a new slack variable for every cut. This variable becomes the leaving variable. This is also the pivot row.
2. The entering variable is always the variable with −1 in the pivot row. If there is a tie, we choose the variable with the least dual value $(z_j - c_j)$.
3. The pivot element is always −1 which maintains integer values in the subsequent iterations.
4. The choice of the pivot position also ensures that the dual is feasible in the next iteration (as in dual simplex algorithm). Therefore, this algorithm is called **dual algorithm**.
5. The value of −1 in the pivot element also ensures that the entering variable has a non-negative value of RHS in the next iteration.

The dual simplex iteration is shown in Table 7.15 (the last row represents the cut).

Table 7.15 Dual Simplex Iteration

	RHS	$-X_1$	$-S_1$	$-X_3$↓
$Z_j - C_j$	-16	4	4	2
X_4	2	1	-5	-1
X_5	-3	1	-3	-2
X_6	4	2	-6	3
X_2	4	1	-1	1
←S_2	-2	0	-2	-1

Before introducing the cut, we observe that *variable X_5* has a negative value and becomes the source row. Variables S_1 and X_3 have negative terms. At the end of Step 4, the corresponding values are 2 and 1. The minimum value at the end of Step 6 is ½. Variable S_2 leaves and variable X_3 enters. The next iteration along with the cut is shown in Table 7.16.

Before introducing the cut, we observe that variable X_6 has a negative value and becomes the source row. Variable S_1 alone has negative terms. At the end of Step 4, the corresponding value is 1. The minimum value at the end of Step 6 is 1/12. Variable S_2 leaves and variable X_3 enters. The next iteration is shown in Table. 7.17.

Table 7.16 Dual Simplex Iteration

	RHS	$-X_1$	$-S_1$	$-S_2$
$Z_j - C_j$	-20	4	0	2
X_4	4	1	-3	-1
X_5	1	1	1	-2
X_6	-2	2	-12	3
X_2	2	1	-3	1
X_3	2	0	2	-1
← S_3	-1	0	-1	0

Table 7.17 Optimum Solution

	RHS	$-X_1$	$-S_3$	$-S_2$
$Z_j - C_j$	20	4	0	2
X_4	7	1	-3	-1
X_5	0	1	1	-2
X_6	10	2	-12	3
X_2	5	1	-3	1
X_3	0	0	2	-1
S_1	1	0	-1	0

It is observed that the present solution is both primal and dual feasible and hence is optimal. The optimal solution is $X_2 = 5$ and $Z = 20$. In this example it is observed that there was no improvement in the objective function in the last iteration but the primal became feasible (Does this indicate primal degeneracy?).

All integer algorithms are useful in hand solution of all integer problems. Their uniqueness lies in their ability to exploit the integer coefficients in the problem. Otherwise they do not seem to have better performance compared to cutting plane algorithms when it comes to solving large sized problems.

7.8.2 All Integer Primal Algorithm

Let us consider the same example that we used to explain the Gomory's cutting plane algorithm to illustrate the all integer primal algorithm.

Maximize $X_1 + X_2$

Subject to

$$7X_1 - 5X_2 \leq 7$$

$$-12X_1 + 15X_2 \leq 7$$

$$X_1, X_2 \geq 0 \text{ and integer}$$

We introduce slack variables X_3 and X_4 and start the simplex table with the slack variables. This is shown in Table 7.18.

The solution is feasible to the primal but the dual is infeasible. Variable X_1 enters the basis. The steps in generating the cut are:

Table 7.18 Initial Table

	RHS	$-X_1$	$-X_2$
$Z_j - C_j$	0	-1	-1
X_3	7	7	-5
X_4	7	-12	15

Steps in generating a primal cut

1. Identify a dual variable that is most negative from the $Z_j - C_j$ row.
2. Find the minimum θ and the corresponding pivot element as in simplex. Ensure that the pivot element is positive and θ is non-negative.
3. Create a new row by dividing every element of the source row by the pivot element and reducing it to the lower integer value.

Illustration:

1. There is a tie for entering variable. We choose variable X_1.
2. There is only one value of $\theta = 7/7 = 1$.
3. The values in the new row are the lower integer values of 7/7, 7/7 and -15/7, respectively. The simplex table along with the cut is shown in Table 7.19. A new row and a slack variable S_1 are added. This is shown in Table 7.19.

The simplex iteration is carried out and the table along with the new cut is shown in Table 7.20.

Table 7.19 Primal Cut

	RHS	$-X_1$	$-X_2$
$Z_j - C_j$	0	-1	-1
X_3	7	7	-5
X_4	7	-12	15
S_1	1	1	-1

Table 7.20 Simplex Iteration

	RHS	$-S_1$	$-X_2$
$Z_j - C_j$	1	1	-2
X_3	0	-7	2
X_4	19	12	3
X_1	1	1	-1
S_2	0	-4	1

The cut is based on variable X_2 entering the basis. The cut introduces a new slack variable S_2. The simplex iteration and the new cut are shown in Table 7.21.

The cut is based on variable S_1 entering the basis. The cut introduces a new slack variable S_3. The simplex iteration and the new cut are shown in Table 7.22.

Table 7.21 Simplex Iteration

	RHS	$-S_1$↓	$-S_2$
$Z_j - C_j$	1	−7	2
X_3	0	1	−2
X_4	19	24	−3
X_1	1	−3	1
X_2	0	−4	1
← S_3	0	1	−2

Table 7.22 Simplex Iteration

	RHS	$-S_3$	$-S_2$↓
$Z_j - C_j$	1	7	−12
X_3	0	−1	0
X_4	19	−24	45
X_1	1	3	−5
X_2	0	4	−7
S_1	0	1	−2
← S_4	0	−2	1

The cut is based on variable S_2 entering the basis. The cut introduces a new slack variable S_4. The simplex iteration and the new cut are shown in Table 7.23.

The cut is based on variable S_3 entering the basis. The cut introduces a new slack variable S_5. The simplex iteration and the new cut are shown in Table 7.24.

Table 7.23 Simplex Iteration

	RHS	$-S_3$↓	$-S_4$
$Z_j - C_j$	1	−5	12
X_3	0	−1	0
X_4	19	21	−45
X_1	1	−2	5
X_2	0	−3	7
S_1	0	−1	2
S_2	0	−1	1
← S_5	1	1	−3

Table 7.24 Simplex Iteration

	RHS	$-S_5$	$-S_4$↓
$Z_j - C_j$	1	5	−3
X_3	0	1	−3
X_4	19	−21	18
X_1	1	2	−1
X_2	0	3	−2
S_1	0	1	−1
S_2	0	1	−2
S_3	0	1	−3
← S_6	1	−2	1

The cut is based on variable S_4 entering the basis. The cut introduces a new slack variable S_6. The simplex iteration and the new cut are shown in Table 7.25.

The cut is based on variable S_5 entering the basis. The cut introduces a new slack variable S_7. The simplex iteration and the new cut are shown in Table 7.26.

The present table has both primal and dual which are feasible and hence optimal. The optimal solution is $X_1 = X_2 = 2$ and $Z = 4$.

Features of the all integer primal algorithm

1. The method of generating the cut ensures that the pivot element is +1, making sure that the next table comprises all integer values.
2. The primal will continue to be feasible while the dual variable (that was infeasible) becomes feasible in the next iteration.
3. However, it appears that the primal cuts are weak and usually requires many iterations to converge.

Table 7.25 Simplex Iteration

	RHS	$-S_5$ ↓	$-S_6$
$Z_j - C_j$	4	−1	3
X_3	3	−5	3
X_4	1	15	−18
X_1	2	0	1
X_2	2	−1	2
S_1	1	−1	1
S_2	2	−3	2
S_3	3	−5	3
S_4	1	−2	1
← S_7	0	1	−2

Table 7.26 Simplex Iteration

	RHS	$-S_7$	$-S_6$
$Z_j - C_j$	4	1	1
X_3	3	5	−7
X_4	1	−15	12
X_1	2	0	1
X_2	2	1	0
S_1	1	1	−1

4. The cuts result in degenerate solutions increasing the number of iterations (as it happenned in our example).

7.8.3 Mixed Constraints, Infeasibility and Unboundedness

We provide three problems as exercises to understand how the all integer primal and dual algorithms can be used in tandem to understand solving IP problems with mixed type of constraints, unboundedness and infeasibility.

ILLUSTRATION 7.14

Maximize $-X_1 + 5X_2$

Subject to

$$2X_1 - 3X_2 \geq 1$$
$$X_1 + X_2 \leq 3$$
$$X_1, X_2 \geq 0 \text{ and integer}$$

Here, we have one constraint of the ≥ type and another of the ≤ type. Also one of the variables has a negative coefficient in the objective function. Table 7.27 shows the initial simplex table.

Table 7.27 Initial Simplex Table

	RHS	$-X_1$	$-X_2$
$Z_j - C_j$	0	1	−5
X_3	−1	−2	3
X_4	3	1	1

Here, both the primal and dual are infeasible. We can apply the primal algorithm by entering variable X_2 first or apply the dual algorithm (dual cut) by considering X_3 as the leaving variable. We start by applying the primal cut based on X_2 as the entering variable. There is only one candidate for the leaving variable, which is X_4. Table 7.28 shows the initial table along with the primal cut.

Table 7.28 Initial Simplex Table and the Primal Cut

	RHS	$-X_1$	$-X_2$
$Z_j - C_j$	0	1	−5
X_3	−1	−2	3
X_4	3	1	1
S_1	3	1	1

Table 7.29 shows the solution after a simplex iteration.

Table 7.29 Solution After One Simplex Iteration

	RHS	$-X_1$	$-X_2$
$Z_j - C_j$	15	6	5
X_3	−10	−5	−3
X_4	0	0	−1
X_2	3	1	1
S_2	−2	−1	−1

Table 7.29 shows the solution after a simplex iteration. Here, the dual is feasible but the primal is infeasible. We can proceed as in the dual algorithm. Variable X_3 leaves and both X_1 and S_1 have negative coefficients. The minimum is 5 and the minimum is Min {1/5, 1/3} which is 1/5. The cut is added in Table 7.29.

The solution after one dual simplex iteration with S_2 as leaving variable and X_1 as entering variable is shown in Table 7.30.

Table 7.30 Solution After One Dual Simplex Iteration

	RHS	$-S_2$	$-S_1$
$Z_j - C_j$	3	6	−1
X_3	0	5	2
X_4	0	0	−1
X_2	1	1	0
X_1	2	−1	1
S_3	0	2	1

The primal is feasible but the dual is infeasible. We apply the primal algorithm. Variable S_1 is the entering variable and the cut is based on variable X_3. The cut is added as the last row in Table 7.30. We perform a simplex iteration and the solution is shown in Table 7.31

Table 7.31 Solution After Simplex Iteration

	RHS	$-S_2$	$-S_3$
$Z_j - C_j$	3	0	1
X_3	0	1	−2
X_4	0	2	1
X_2	1	1	0
X_1	2	−3	−1
S_1	0	2	1

The solution is both primal and dual feasible and is optimal. The optimal solution is $X_1 = 3$ with $Z = 3$.

Illustration 7.14 explained how a combination of the all integer dual algorithm and the all integer primal algorithm can be used to solve problems with mixed type of constraints. Here, both the primal and the dual are infeasible in the initial solution. In such cases we can proceed either with a dual cut or the primal cut.

When the dual is feasible and the primal is infeasible, the only alternative is a dual cut. When we can use only the dual cut where the leaving variable is identified first and then the entering variable is identified. If we are unable to find an entering variable after we identify the leaving variable, the problem is infeasible.

When the primal is feasible and the dual is infeasible, the only alternative is a primal cut. When we can use only the primal cut where the entering variable is identified first and then the leaving variable is identified. If we are unable to find a leaving variable after we identify the entering variable, the problem is unbounded.

(Refer to Solved Examples 7.7 and 7.8 and Exercise Problem 7.23).

Some points and observations

1. When considering both types of constraints, depending on the objective function, both simplex and dual simplex iterations (and cuts) may be possible. It is preferable to do a simplex iteration (primal cut) first and then try dual simplex iteration (dual cut) later after all primal cuts are exhausted.
2. In a dual cut, if we find a leaving variable and we don't have an entering variable (all values in the source row are non-negative) it indicates infeasibility (as in dual simplex algorithm).
3. In a primal cut, if we identify an entering variable and we are unable to identify a leaving variable, it indicates unboundedness (as in simplex algorithm).

7.9 MIXED INTEGER PROGRAMMING

We can have integer programming problems where some variables are restricted to be integers while some can be continuous variables. Consider the following IP problem

ILLUSTRATION 7.15

Maximize $3X_1 + 2Y_1$
Subject to
$$X_1 + Y_1 \leq 6$$
$$5X_1 + 2Y_1 \leq 20$$

$X_1 \geq 0$, $Y_1 \geq 0$ and integer.

We first solve the problem as an LP problem by relaxing the integer restriction on Y_1. The *LP* optimum is given by $Y_1 = 10/3$, $X_1 = 8/3$ with $Z = 44/3$. The computations are shown in Table 7.32.

Table 7.32 Optimum Simplex Table

	RHS	$-X_3$	$-X_4$
$Z_j - C_j$	44/3	4/3	1/3
Y_1	10/3	5/3	$-1/3$
X_1	8/3	$-2/3$	1/3

The LP optimum is shown as Node 1 in Figure 7.6.

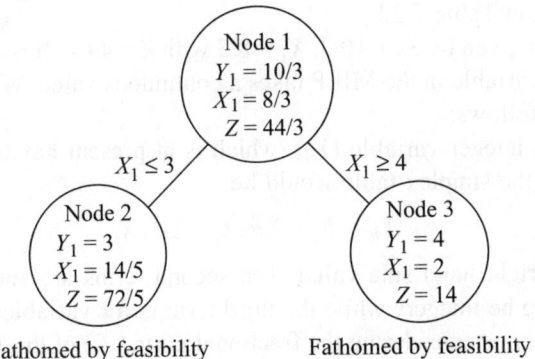

Figure 7.6 Branch and bound tree for Illustration 7.15.

We observe that the LP optimum value 44/3 is an upper bound to the MILP because the given problem is a maximization problem. We also observe that variable Y_1 which should be integer valued, now takes a continuous value of 10/3 which is between 3 and 4.

We create two nodes with $X_1 \leq 3$ and $X_1 \geq 4$ respectively and solve the corresponding LP problems. The optimum solution to the LP in node 2 is given by $Y_1 = 3$, $X_1 = 14/5$ with $Z = 72/5$. This is feasible to the MILP because variable Y_1 takes an integer value. The value 72/5 is a lower bound to the MILP optimum because it represents a feasible solution. This node is fathomed by feasibility.

The LP optimum for the problem in node 3 is given by $Y_1 = 4$, $X_1 = 2$ and $Z = 14$. This is also feasible to the MILP and is a lower bound to the MILP optimum. This node is fathomed by feasibility.

Since there are no more nodes available, the best value of 72/5 is taken as the optimum value of the objective function with the solution $Y_1 = 3$, $X_1 = 14/5$ and $Z = 72/5$. The branch and bound tree is shown in Figure 7.6.
(The reader may refer to Example 7.11 to understand the application of branch and bound algorithm to a minimization MILP.)

7.9.1 A Cutting Plane Algorithm for the MILP

Here we present a cutting plane algorithm for solving a MILP. We explain the algorithm using Illustration 7.15.

Maximize $3X_1 + 2Y_1$
Subject to

$$X_1 + Y_1 \le 6$$
$$5X_1 + 2Y_1 \le 20$$

$X_1 \ge 0$, $Y_1 \ge 0$ and integer.

We first solve the problem as a linear programming problem by treating Y_1 as a continuous variable. The LP optimum is obtained after two iterations of the simplex method. The optimum simples table is shown in Table 7.32.

The LP optimum is given by $Y_1 = 10/3$, $X_1 = 8/3$ with $Z = 44/3$. It is observed that the variable Y_1 which is an integer variable in the MILP takes a continuous value. We have to add a MILP cut which is generated as follows:

Let us consider an integer variable (Y_B), which is at present having a non integer value. A general equation from the simplex table would be

$$Y_B = b_0 - \Sigma a_{ij} Y_j - \Sigma a_{ij} X_j$$

(The first term is the right hand side value. The second terms are summed over all non basic variables constrained to be integers while the third term is for variables that are continuous)

We rearrange the terms considering the fractional parts (f_{ij}) of the coefficients of the integer variables and get

$$\Sigma f_{ij} Y_j + \Sigma a_{ij} X_j - f_0 = [b_0] - \Sigma [a_{ij}] Y_j - Y_B$$

The right hand side of the above equation must be an integer. Hence, the left hand sides are integers and we write that either

$$\Sigma f_{ij} Y_j + \Sigma a_{ij} X_j - f_0 \ge 0 \text{ or } \Sigma f_{ij} Y_j + \Sigma a_{ij} X_j - f_0 \le -1$$

If we divide the continuous variables into two sets R^+ and R^- that have positive and negative a_{ij} values, then

$$\sum_j f_{ij} Y_j + \sum_{j \in R^+} a_{ij} X_j \ge f_0$$

and

$$\sum_{j \in R^-} a_{ij} X_j \le -1 + f_0$$

Multiplying the previous equation by $f_0/(-1 + f_0)$ yields

$$-\sum_{j \in R^-} f_0 a_{ij} X_j / (1 - f_0) \ge f_0$$

Combining equations, we get

$$\sum_j f_{ij} Y_j + \sum_{j \in R^+} a_{ij} X_j - \sum_{j \in R^-} f_0 a_{ij} X_j / (1 - f_0) \ge f_0$$

This is a cut for MILP problems. We apply this equation to our example considering variable Y_1. We have $f_0 = 1/3$. The cut becomes

$$\frac{5}{3}X_3 - \frac{1}{3} \times \left(\frac{-1}{3}\right)\frac{1}{1-(1/3)}X_4 \geq \frac{1}{3}$$

This reduces to

$$\frac{5}{3}X_3 + \frac{1}{6}X_4 \geq \frac{1}{3}$$

This cut is added to the simplex table and we get Table 7.33.

Table 7.33 Simplex Table with the MILP Cut

	RHS	$-X_3$	$-X_4$
$Z_j - C_j$	44/3	4/3	1/3
Y_1	10/3	5/3	-1/3
X_1	8/3	-2/3	1/3
S_1	-1/3	-5/3	-1/6

(Variable S_1 leaves the basis and variable X_3 enters the basis and after a dual simplex iteration we get Table 7.34).

Table 7.34 Optimum Table

	RHS	$-S_1$	$-X_4$
$Z_j - C_j$	72/5	4/5	1/5
Y_1	3	1	-1/2
X_1	14/5	-2/5	2/5
X_3	1/5	-3/5	1/10

This solution is feasible to the MILP and hence is optimal. The optimal solution is $Y_1 = 3$, $X_1 = 14/5$ and $Z = 72/5$.

7.9.2 Bender's Partitioning Algorithm for MILP (Benders 1962)

The Bender's partitioning algorithm is a popular method used to solve MILP problems by partitioning the variables into two sets each one containing the integer variables and the other comprising the continuous variables. We apply the Bender's algorithm to illustration 7.15.

Maximize $3X_1 + 2Y_1$
Subject to
$$X_1 + Y_1 \leq 6$$
$$5X_1 + 2Y_1 \leq 20$$

$X_1 \geq 0$, $Y_1 \geq 0$ and integer

We rewrite the problem as

Maximize $3X_1$
Subject to
$$X_1 \leq 6 - Y_1$$
$$5X_1 \leq 20 - 2Y_1$$
$$X_1 \geq 0$$

The dual to the above problem is

Minimize $(u_1 \quad u_2) \begin{bmatrix} 6-Y_1 \\ 20-2Y_1 \end{bmatrix}$

Subject to $u_1 + 5u_2 = 3$, $u_1, u_2 = 0$.
One feasible solution to the above dual is $u_1 = 3$, $u_2 = 0$.

Since we are using only a feasible solution to the dual, the value becomes an upper bound to the dual (minimization problem). We substitute $u_1 = 3$ and the original problem reduces to
Minimize Z

$$Z \leq 2Y_1 + 3(6 - Y_1)$$

$Z \geq 0$, $Y_1 \geq 0$ and integer. This would reduce solving a MILP within a MILP, which we avoid by treating Z as integer and solving an ILP. The value found is called $\bar{Z}$ and is an upper estimate of the actual optimum.
This gives the optimum solution; $\bar{Z} = 18$ and $Y_1 = 0$
The dual becomes
Minimize $6u_1 + 20u_2$
Subject to $u_1 + 5u_2 \geq 3$; $u_1, u_2 \geq 0$.
This gives a solution $u_1 = 0$, $u_2 = 3/5$ with $Z = 12$
We compute $\bar{Z} - CY = 18 - 2 \times 0 = 18$ with Z and since it is more, we continue.
The primal problem becomes
Minimize Z

$$Z \leq 2Y_1 + 3(6 - Y_1)$$

$$Z \leq 2Y_1 + \frac{3}{5}(20 - 2Y_1)$$

$Z \geq 0$, $Y_1 \geq 0$ and integer.; Z, Y_1, $Y_2 \geq 0$ and integer.

The ILP when we restrict Z to an integer gives an optimal solution $\bar{Z} = 14$ with $Y_1 = 3$. (Actually there is alternate optima with Y_1 taking values 0, 1, 2 or 3 and all of them have the same $\bar{Z} = 14$). However, $Y_1 = 2$ gives the maximum value when Z is treated as a continuous variable $Z = 72/5$.
We substitute these values and solve for u_1 and u_2
Minimize $3u_1 + 14u_2$
Subject to $u_1 + 5u_2 \geq 3$; $u_1, u_2 \geq 0$.
This gives an optimum solution with $u_1 = 0$, $u_2 = 3/5$ with $Z = 42/5$.
Since $\bar{Z} - CY = 14 - 6 < (42/5)$ the solution to the integer variables is found. In order to get the solution to the continuous variables, we substitute to get
Maximize $3X$

$$X_1 \leq 3$$

$$X_1 \leq 14/5$$

$$X_1 \geq 0$$

This gives the solution $X_1 = 14/5$ and the optimum solution to the MILP is $X_1 = 14/5$, $Y_1 = 3$ and $Z = 72/5$.

(The reader may refer to Example 7.4 to understand the application of Bender's partitioning algorithm to a minimization problem)

SOLVED EXAMPLES

EXAMPLE 7.1 Solve the following IP problem:

Maximize $4X_1 - X_2 + 3X_3$

Subject to

$$2X_1 + X_2 + X_3 \leq 8$$
$$X_1 + X_2 + X_3 \geq 2$$
$$4X_1 + 3X_2 + 2X_3 \leq 15$$
$$X_1, X_2, X_3 \geq 0 \text{ and integer}$$

Solution: Changing the second constraint in the general form to apply primal integer algorithm, we get

Maximize $4X_1 - X_2 + 3X_3$

Subject to

$$2X_1 + X_2 + X_3 \leq 8$$
$$-(X_1 + X_2 + X_3) \leq -2$$
$$4X_1 + 3X_2 + 2X_3 \leq 15$$

We introduce slack variables X_4, X_5 and X_6 and start the simplex table with the slack variables. The simplex table is shown in Table 7.35.

Table 7.35 Simplex Table

	RHS	$-X_1$	$-X_2$	$-X_3$
$Z_j - C_j$	0	-4	1	-3
X_4	8	2	1	1
X_5	-2	-1	-1	-1
X_6	15	4	3	2

The solution is infeasible to both primal and dual. Proceeding in the integer primal method, variable X_1 enters the basis. The steps in generating the cut are:
We choose variable X_1.

$$\theta \min = 15/4$$

The values in the new row are the lower integer values of 4/4, 3/4 and 2/4, respectively. A new row and a slack variable S_1 are added. This is shown in Table 7.36.

The simplex iteration is carried out and the table along with the new cut is shown in Table 7.37.

Table 7.36 Simplex Iteration

	RHS	$-X_1\downarrow$	$-X_2$	$-X_3$
$Z_j - C_j$	0	−4	1	−3
X_4	8	2	1	1
X_5	−2	−1	−1	−1
X_6	15	4	3	2
← S_1	3	1	0	0

Table 7.37 Simplex Iteration

	RHS	$-S_1$	$-X_2$	$-X_3\downarrow$
$Z_j - C_j$	12	4	1	−3
X_4	2	−2	1	1
X_5	1	1	−1	−1
X_6	3	−4	3	2
X_1	3	1	0	0
← S_2	1	−2	1	1

The cut is based on variable X_3 entering the basis. The cut introduces a new slack variable S_2. The simplex iteration and the new cut are shown in Table 7.38.

The cut is based on variable S_1 entering the basis. The cut introduces a new slack variable S_3. The simplex iteration and the new cut are shown in Table 7.39.

Table 7.38 Simplex Iteration

	RHS	$-S_1\downarrow$	$-X_2$	$-S_2$
$Z_j - C_j$	15	−2	4	3
X_4	1	0	0	−1
X_5	2	−1	0	1
X_6	1	0	1	−2
X_1	3	1	0	0
X_3	1	−2	1	1
← S_3	3	1	0	0

Table 7.39 Simplex Iteration

	RHS	$-S_3\downarrow$	$-X_2$	$-S_2$
$Z_j - C_j$	21	2	4	3
X_4	1	0	0	−1
X_5	5	1	0	1
X_6	1	0	1	−2
X_1	0	−1	0	0
X_3	7	2	1	1
← S_3	3	1	0	0

In the present table, both primal and dual are feasible and hence optimal. The optimal solution is $X_1 = 0$, $X_2 = 0$, $X_3 = 7$ and $Z = 21$.

EXAMPLE 7.2 Solve the following zero-one problem using implicit-enumeration algorithm.

Maximize $\quad 4X_1 + 3X_2 - 2X_3$

Subject to

$$X_1 + X_2 + X_3 \leq 8$$
$$2X_1 - X_2 - X_3 \leq 4$$
$$X_1, X_2, X_3 = 0, 1$$

Solution: We convert the above problem into the standard problem with a minimization objective and all $\geq$ constraints with all objective function coefficients non-negative. The objective function becomes

Minimize $\quad -4X_1 - 3X_2 + 2X_3$

We define

$$Y_1 = 1 - X_1$$
$$Y_2 = 1 - X_2$$
$$Y_3 = X_3$$

Objective function: Min $-4(1 - Y_1) - 3(1 - Y_2) + 2(Y_3)$
$$= 4Y_1 + 3Y_2 + 2Y_3 - 7$$

Constraints:
$$1 - Y_1 + 1 - Y_2 + Y_3 \le 8$$
$$Y_1 + Y_2 - Y_3 \ge -6$$
$$2(1 - Y_1) - (1 - Y_2) - Y_3 \le 4$$
$$2Y_1 - Y_2 + Y_3 \ge -3$$

Thus, the problem in the standard format is:
Minimize: $4Y_1 + 3Y_2 + 2Y_3$
Subject to
$$Y_1 + Y_2 - Y_3 \ge -6$$
$$2Y_1 - Y_2 + Y_3 \ge -3$$

We use implicit enumeration technique to solve the above zero-one problem.

Step 0
$S_0 = \{ \}$
$V_0 = \{ \}$

As there are no violated constraints, we get one feasible solution with $Y_1 = Y_2 = Y_3 = 0$.

To update the solution we wish to backtrack, but we can't backtrack as the solution variable set is empty. So, we've reached the optimum with
$$X_1 = X_2 = 1, X_3 = 0 \text{ and}$$
$$Z = 7.$$

EXAMPLE 7.3 Solve:
Minimize $10X_1 + 11X_2 + 13X_3$
Subject to
$$3X_1 + X_2 + 3X_3 \ge 4$$
$$2X_1 + 4X_2 + 3X_3 \ge 5$$
$$X_3 \le 1$$
$$X_1, X_2, X_3 \ge 0 \text{ and integer}$$

Solution: We will solve this using the standard *Gomory cutting plane* algorithm. The iterations of the algorithm are shown in Tables 7.40 to 7.45.

Step 1

Table 7.40 Dual Simplex Iteration

	RHS	$-X_1$	$-X_2$	$-X_3$
$Z_j - C_j$	0	10	11	13
X_4	-4	-3	-1	-3
X_5	-5	-2	-4	-3
X_6	1	0	0	1

Step 2

Table 7.41 Dual Simplex Iteration

	RHS	$-X_1$	$-X_5$	$-X_3$
$Z_j - C_j$	−55/4	9/2	11/4	19/4
← X_4	−11/4	**−5/2**	−1/4	−9/4
X_2	5/4	1/2	−1/4	3/4
X_6	1	0	0	1

Step 3 (An asterisk in the row next to a variable name denotes a cut)

Table 7.42 Dual Simplex Iteration

	RHS	$-X_4$	$-X_5$	$-X_3$
$Z_j - C_j$	−187/10	9/5	23/10	7/10
X_1	11/10	−2/5	1/10	9/10
*X_2	7/10	1/5	−3/10	3/10
X_6	1	0	0	1
← S_1	−7/10	−1/5	−7/10	**−3/10**

Step 4

Table 7.43 Dual Simplex Iteration

	RHS	$-X_4$	$-X_5$	$-S_1$
$Z_j - C_j$	−61/3	4/3	2/3	7/3
X_1	−1	−1	−2	3
X_2	0	0	−1	1
← X_6	−4/3	−2/3	**−7/3**	10/3
X_3	7/3	2/3	7/3	−10/3

Step 5

Table 7.44 Dual Simplex Iteration

	RHS	$-X_4$	$-X_6$	$-S_1$
$Z_j - C_j$	−145/7	8/7	2/7	23/7
X_1	1/7	−3/7	−6/7	1/7
*X_2	4/7	2/7	−3/7	−3/7
X_5	4/7	2/7	−3/7	−10/7
X_3	1	0	1	0
← S_2	−4/7	−2/7	**−4/7**	−4/7

Step 6

Table 7.45 Dual Simplex Iteration

	RHS	$-X_4$	$-S_2$	$-S_1$
$Z_j - C_j$	-21	1	1/2	3
X_1	1	0	$-3/2$	1
X_2	1	1/2	$-3/4$	0
X_5	1	1/2	$-3/4$	-1
X_3	0	$-1/2$	7/4	-1
X_6	1	1/2	$-7/4$	1

The algorithm terminates here as both the primal and the dual are feasible and the primal is integer-valued. The solution is given by

$$X_1 = X_2 = 1, X_3 = 0 \text{ and } Z = 21$$

EXAMPLE 7.4 Solve the following MILP using Bender's partitioning algorithm.

Minimize $8X + 4Y_1 + 3Y_2$

Subject to
$$4X + 6Y_1 + 2Y_2 \geq 13$$
$$3X + 2Y_1 + 5Y_2 \geq 15$$

$X \geq 0, Y_1, Y_2 \geq 0$ and integer.

We rewrite the problem as

Minimize $8X$

Subject to

$$\begin{bmatrix} 4 \\ 3 \end{bmatrix} X \geq \begin{bmatrix} 13 - 6Y_1 - 2Y_2 \\ 15 - 2Y_1 - 5Y_2 \end{bmatrix}; X \geq 0$$

The dual to the above problem is

$$\text{Maximize } \begin{bmatrix} u_1 & u_2 \end{bmatrix} \begin{bmatrix} 13 - 6Y_1 - 2Y_2 \\ 15 - 2Y_1 - 5Y_2 \end{bmatrix}$$

subject to $4u_1 + 3u_2 \leq 8, u_1, u_2 \geq 0$.
One feasible solution to the above dual is $u_1 = 2, u_2 = 0$.

Since we are using only a feasible solution to the dual, the value becomes a lower bound to the dual. Hence the original problem reduces to

Minimize Z

$$Z \geq 4Y_1 + 3Y_2 + \max \begin{bmatrix} u_1 & u_2 \end{bmatrix} \begin{bmatrix} 13 - 6Y_1 - 2Y_2 \\ 15 - 2Y_1 - 5Y_2 \end{bmatrix}$$

substituting $(2,0)$ for (u_1, u_2), we have

Minimize Z

$$Z \geq 4Y_1 + 3Y_2 + 2(13 - 6Y_1 - 2Y_2)$$

$Z, Y_1, Y_2 \geq 0$ and integer.

Actually Z need not be an integer and can be fractional. This would mean solving an MILP within an MILP, which is to be avoided. We therefore restrict Z to be an integer. The value found is called $\bar{Z}$ and is an upper estimate of the actual optimum.
This gives a solution $\bar{Z} = 0$; $Y_1 = 4$, $Y_2 = 0$.
The dual becomes
Maximize $-11u_1 + 7u_2$
Subject to $4u_1 + 3u_2 \leq 8$; $u_1, u_2 \geq 0$.
This gives a solution $u_1 = 0$, $u_2 = 8/3$ with $Z = 56/3$
We compare $\bar{Z} - CY$ with Z and since it is less, we continue.
The problem becomes
Minimize Z

$$Z \geq 4Y_1 + 3Y_2 + 2(13 - 6Y_1 - 2Y_2)$$

$$Z \geq 4Y_1 + 3Y_2 + [0 \quad 8/3] \begin{bmatrix} 13 - 6Y_1 - 2Y_2 \\ 15 - 2Y_1 - 5Y_2 \end{bmatrix}; Z, Y_1, Y_2 \geq 0 \text{ and integer.}$$

This gives a solution $Y_1 = 3$, $Y_2 = 4$ with $\bar{Z} = 0$
We substitute these values and solve for u_1 and u_2
Maximize $-13u_1 - 11u_2$
Subject to $4u_1 + 3u_2 \leq 8$; $u_1, u_2 \geq 0$.
This gives a solution with $u_1 = u_2 = 0$ with $Z = 0$
Since $\bar{Z} - CY < Z$, we proceed further.
We Minimize Z

$$Z \geq 4Y_1 + 3Y_2 + 2(13 - 6Y_1 - 5Y_2)$$
$$Z \geq 4Y_1 + 3Y_2 + 8/3(15 - 2Y_1 - 5Y_2)$$
$$Z \geq 4Y_1 + 3Y_2$$

$Z, Y_1, Y_2 \geq 0$ and integer.
This gives a solution $Y_1 = 1$, $Y_2 = 3$ with $\bar{Z} = 15$
Substituting we get
Maximize $u_1 - 2u_2$

$$4u_1 + 3u_2 \leq 8$$
$$u_1, u_2 \geq 0.$$

We have $u_1 = 2$, $u_2 = 0$ and $Z = 2$

Since $\bar{Z} - CY = 15 - [4 \quad 3] \begin{bmatrix} 1 \\ 3 \end{bmatrix} = 2 = Z$, the solution to the integer variables is found. In order to get the solution to the continuous variables, we substitute to get
Minimize $8X$

$$\begin{bmatrix} 4 \\ 3 \end{bmatrix} X \geq \begin{bmatrix} 1 \\ -2 \end{bmatrix}; X \geq 0$$

This gives the solution $X = 1/4$ and the optimum solution to the MILP is $X = 1/4$, $Y_1 = 1$, $Y_2 = 3$ and $Z = 15$.

In this example, the value of the objective function at the optimum is an integer. Therefore we found that $\bar{Z} - CY$ was equal to Z, indicating that the optimum values of the integer variables has been found.

EXAMPLE 7.5 Consider the problem:

Maximize $\quad 4X_1 + 6X_2 + 4X_3 + 6X_4 + 13X_5$

Subject to

$$-3X_1 - 6X_2 + 6X_3 + 12X_4 + 7X_5 \leq 7$$
$$6X_1 + 12X_2 - 3X_3 - 6X_4 + 7X_5 = 7$$
$$X_i = 0, 1$$

Perform two iterations of additive algorithm. Comment on the complexity of the additive algorithm for this problem.

Solution: In the standard form, objective function is a minimization with all its coefficients non-negative and the constraints are all $\geq$ constraints. To convert the given problem to a standard one, substitute $Y_i = (1 - X_i)$

Now, the objective function is:

Minimize $\quad 4Y_1 + 6Y_2 + 4Y_3 + 6Y_4 + 13Y_5 - 33$

Subject to

$$-3Y_1 - 6Y_2 + 6Y_3 + 12Y_4 + 7Y_5 \geq 9$$
$$-6Y_1 - 12Y_2 + 3Y_3 + 6Y_4 - 7Y_5 = 9$$

The second constraint is an equal to constraint. This can be written as two constraints:

$$-6Y_1 - 12Y_2 + 3Y_3 + 6Y_4 - 7Y_5 \geq -9$$
$$-6Y_1 - 12Y_2 + 3Y_3 + 6Y_4 - 7Y_5 \leq -9$$

To change the last constraint to standard form, multiply the inequality by -1 throughout, which gives

$$6Y_1 + 12Y_2 - 3Y_3 - 6Y_4 + 7Y_5 \geq 9$$

So, we have the IP problem in the standard form with three constraints numbered 1, 2 and 3. Defining a helpfulness index for each variable as the sum of the coefficients in the constraints:

Variable $Y_1 = -3$
Variable $Y_2 = -6$
Variable $Y_3 = 6$
Variable $Y_4 = 12$
Variable $Y_5 = 7$

We define three vectors **S**, **V**, **H**, where **S** is a vector of variables in the solution, **V** is the set of violated constraints and **H** is the set of helpful variables.

Step 0:
$$S_0 = \{\ \}$$
$$V_0 = \{1, 3\}$$
$$T_0 = \{1, 2, 3, 4, 5\}$$

Since no variable is fixed to any value. Constraint 2 is satisfied. Variables Y_3, Y_4, Y_5 are helpful with respect to Constraint 1 and variables Y_1, Y_2 and Y_5 are helpful with respect to Constraint 3. We identify the most helpful variable (Y_4) and fix this variable to 1.

Step 1 (*Iteration* 1):
$$S_1 = \{4\}$$
$$V_1 = \{3\}$$
$$T_1 = \{1, 2, 5\}$$

We identify the most helpful variables (among Y_1, Y_2 and Y_5) and fix this to 1.

Step 2 (*Iteration* 2):
$$S_2 = \{4, 5\}$$
$$V_2 = \{3\}$$
$$T_2 = \{1, 2\}$$

The most helpful variable among Y_1 and Y_2 is Y_1. So, Y_1 is fixed to 1. This cannot satisfy the violated Constraint 3. So, the other helpful variable Y_2 has to be set to 1 in the which would satisfy Constraint 3, but this makes Constraint 2 violated. This keeps on repeating. So, we end up checking almost all the possibilities.

So, using additive algorithm in this case (when a constraint is an equation) leads to the addition of an extra constraint. We cannot guarantee towards reaching optimality or feasibility in a minimum number of iterations.

For instance, the given problem has the optimal solution as $X = [0\ 0\ 0\ 0\ 1]$. This is the only feasible solution. Almost all the possibilities are to be performed if the additive algorithm is used to solve this.

EXAMPLE 7.6 Solve the following IP problem:

Maximize $X_1 + X_2$

Subject to
$$30X_1 + 5X_2 \le 24$$
$$-10X_1 + 15X_2 \le 12$$
$$X_1, X_2 \ge 0 \text{ and integer}$$

Solution: We solve the problem using the all integer primal algorithm. The first iteration is shown in Table 7.46. We start with X_3 and X_4 (slack) as basic variables. We enter variable X_1 and the cut is also shown in Table 7.46.

Table 7.46 First Iteration

	RHS	$-X_1$↓	$-X_2$
$Z_j - C_j$	0	-1	-1
X_3	24	30	5
X_4	12	-10	15
← S_1	0	1	0

The first iteration is shown in Table 7.46. Variable X_2 enters the basis. The cut is based on basic variable X_4. The cut is added and shown in Table 7.47. The next iteration is shown in Table 7.48. The solution is optimal with $X_1 = X_2 = 0$ and $Z = 0$.

The LP optimum is shown in Table 7.49. In this example, the only feasible integer solution $X_1 = X_2 = 0$ is optimal.

Table 7.47 Simplex Iteration

	RHS	$-S_1$	$-X_2\downarrow$
$Z_j - C_j$	0	1	-1
X_3	24	-30	5
X_4	12	10	15
X_1	0	1	0
S_2	0	0	1

Table 7.48 Optimum Solution

	RHS	$-S_1$	$-S_2$
$Z_L - C_j$	0	1	1
X_3	24	-30	-5
X_4	12	10	-15
X_1	0	1	0
X_2	0	0	0

Table 7.49 LP Optimum

	RHS	$-X_3$	$-X_4$
$Z_j - C_j$	9/5	1/20	1/20
X_1	3/5	3/100	-1/100
X_2	6/5	1/50	3/50

(It is possible to obtain the IP optimum from the solution in Table 7.49 using the Gomory cutting plane algorithm. The reader may take it as an exercise. Based on the number of additional iterations, the reader may verify that the all integer primal algorithm solved this example problem efficiently. Is this true for all problems where the only feasible solution is the origin?)

EXAMPLE 7.7 Solve the following IP problem:

Maximize $X_1 + X_2$

Subject to

$$30X_1 + 5X_2 \le 24$$
$$-10X_1 + 15X_2 \le 12$$
$$X_1 + X_2 \ge 1/2$$
$$X_1, X_2 \ge 0 \text{ and integer}$$

Solution: We solve this problem again by the all integer algorithm. The first iteration is shown in Table 7.50. We perform a primal iteration whereby variable X_1 enters and the primal cut is based on variable X_3. The cut is also shown in the table.

Table 7.50 First Iteration

	RHS	$-X_1\downarrow$	$-X_2$
$Z_j - C_j$	0	-1	-1
X_3	24	30	5
X_4	12	-10	15
X_5	-1	-2	-2
S_1	0	1	0

The next iteration is shown in Table 7.51. Variable X_2 now enters and the primal cut is based on variable X_4. The cut is also shown in Table 7.51.

The next iteration is shown in Table 7.52. The solution is dual feasible but primal infeasible. Only a dual cut is possible. This is based on the basic variable X_5 that has a negative value. We do not find a negative pivot for this variable and the algorithm terminates indicating **infeasibility** of the IP.

Table 7.51 Simplex Iteration

	RHS	$-S_1$	$-X_2$
$Z_j - C_j$	0	1	-1
X_3	24	-30	5
X_4	12	10	15
X_5	-1	2	-2
X_1	0	1	0
S_2	0	0	1

Table 7.52 Termination of the Algorithm

	RHS	$-S_1$	$-S_2$
$Z_j - C_j$	0	1	1
X_3	24	-30	-5
X_4	12	10	-15
X_5	-1	2	2
X_1	0	1	0
X_2	0	0	1

Infeasibility of IP is indicated in all integer algorithms when only a dual cut is possible and we are unable to find a negative pivot for a basic variable that has a negative value. The LP optimum for this problem is shown in Table 7.53.

Table 7.53 LP Optimum

	RHS	$-X_3$	$-X_4$
$Z_j - C_j$	9/5	1/20	1/20
X_1	3/5	3/100	-1/100
X_2	6/5	1/50	3/50
X_5	13/5	1/10	-1/10

This is an example where the LP has a unique optimum but the IP is infeasible. The reader may also solve the problem using the LP optimum and continuing with Gomory cuts. Here the infeasibility will be indicated (as in dual simplex algorithm) where we may find a leaving variable but no possible entering variable. In fact the same thing happenned in our all integer algorithm.

EXAMPLE 7.8 Solve the following IP:

Maximize $Z = 4X_1 + 3X_2$

Subject to

$$X_1 - 6X_2 \leq 5$$
$$3X_1 \leq 11$$
$$X_1, X_2 \geq 0 \text{ and integer}$$

Solution: We solve the problem using an all integer primal algorithm. The initial tableau is shown in Table 7.54. Variable X_1 enters the basis. The cut is based on variable X_4. The cut is also shown in Table 7.54.

The next iteration is shown in Table 7.55.

From Table 7.55, we observe that variable X_2 can enter but we are unable to identify a basic variable from which we can make a cut. The algorithm terminates giving an ***unbounded*** solution.

Table 7.54 Initial Table

	RHS	$-X_1$	$-X_2$
$Z_j - C_j$	0	-4	-3
X_3	5	1	-6
X_4	11	3	0
S_1	3	1	0

Table 7.55 Termination

	RHS	$-s_1$	$-X_2$
$Z_j - C_j$	12	4	-3
X_3	2	-1	-6
X_4	2	-3	0
X_1	3	1	0

As in simplex, unboundedness is indicated by the presence of an entering variable and the absence of a leaving variable. It is also to be noted that the corresponding LP is unbounded (We have used Illustration 2.7 from Chapter 2 here).

It is necessary for the LP problem to be unbounded if the corresponding IP is unbounded. The IP problem is a restricted LP problem and if the restricted problem is unbounded, the relaxed problem has to be unbounded.

EXAMPLE 7.9   Solve the MILP:

Maximize $2X_1 + 3X_2$

Subject to

$$3X_1 + 4X_2 \leq 10$$
$$X_1 + 3X_2 \leq 7$$
$$X_1 \geq 0, X_2 \geq 0 \text{ and integer}$$

Solution: We first solve this problem using the cutting plane algorithm for MILP. The LP is solved and the optimum table using simplex algorithm is shown in Table 7.56. Here variable X_2 is not integer. Applying the MILP cut equation, we get the cut

$$\frac{3}{5}X_4 - \frac{1}{5} \times \frac{1}{5} \div \frac{4}{5}X_3 \geq \frac{1}{5}$$

This is simplified and the resultant cut is added to Table 7.56. The dual simplex iteration is shown in Table 7.57.

Table 7.56 LP Optimum

	RHS	$-X_3$	$-X_4$
$Z_j - C_j$	37/5	3/5	1/5
X_1	2/5	3/5	-4/5
X_2	11/5	-1/5	3/5
s_1	-1/5	1/20	-3/5

Table 7.57 Optimum Solution

	RHS	$-X_3$	$-s_1$
$Z_j - C_j$	22/3	37/60	1/3
X_1	2/3	2/3	-4/3
X_2	2	-3/20	1
X_4	1/3	-1/12	-5/3

The present solution is optimal with $X_1 = 2/3$, $X_2 = 2$ and $Z = 22/3$.

We can solve the same problem by the branch and bound algorithm. The LP optimum is $X_1 = 2/5, X_2 = 11/5$ with $Z = 37/5$. We would branch on X_2 and create problems. The first problem would have the additional constraint $X_2 \le 2$ and the second problem would have the additional constraint $X_2 \ge 2$.

The first would give an optimum solution of $X_1 = 2/3, X_2 = 2, Z = 22/3$, which is feasible to the MILP. The other problem is infeasible. Hence the optimum to the MILP is $X_1 = 2/3$, $X_2 = 2, Z = 22/3$.

(This example is to show that both the cutting plane algorithm and the branch and bound algorithm can be applied directly to the maximization MILP. The objective function value at the optimum for the MILP will be less than that of the LP optimum because of the maximization objective. The same MILP can be solved using the Bender's decomposition algorithm, which the reader can take it as an exercise).

EXAMPLE 7.10 Given the integer programming problem:

Maximize $X_1 + 3X_2$

Subject to

$$3X_1 + 4X_2 \le 10$$
$$X_1 + 3X_2 \le 7$$
$$X_1, X_2 \ge 0 \text{ and integer}$$

(a) Solve it using an all integer algorithm
(b) Obtain an upper bound using the LP optimum. Can you improve the bound?

Solution: The initial tableau for the all integer primal algorithm is given in Table 7.58. Variable X_2 enters and the primal cut is based on variable X_4. The cut is shown in Table 7.58.

The next iteration is shown in Table 7.59.

Variable X_1 enters and the primal cut is based on variable X_3. The cut is shown in Table 7.59.

Table 7.58 Initial Table

	RHS	$-X_1$	$-X_2$
$Z_j - C_j$	0	-1	-3
X_3	10	3	4
X_4	7	1	3
S_1	2	0	1

Table 7.59 Simplex Iteration

	RHS	$-X_1$	$-S_1$
$Z_j - C_j$	-6	-1	3
X_3	2	3	-4
X_4	1	1	-3
X_2	2	0	1
S_2	0	1	-2

The next iteration is shown in Table 7.60.

Table 7.60 Optimum Solution

	RHS	$-X_3$	$-X_4$
$Z_j - C_j$	-6	1	1
X_3	2	-3	2
X_4	1	-1	-1
X_2	2	0	1
S_1	0	-1	-2

The solution is optimal with $X_1 = 0$, $X_2 = 2$, $Z = 6$. It is to be noted that the soluion is degenerate at the optimum (which happens most of the times in all integer primal algorithm).

(b) The LP optimum is given in Table 7.61.

From Table 7.61 it is observed that the LP has alternate optima. The lower bound cannot be improved using the procedures described earlier because the minimum will become zero due to alternate optima.

However, it is also observed (in this example) that the objective function line is parallel to the line $X_1 + 3X_2$ = 7. The feasible integer points for the inequality are (1, 2), (4, 1), (7, 0). They are all infeasible to the LP considering the first constraint. Therefore, the IP optimum has to be less than or equal to six (considering the integer coefficients in the objective function). One of the rounded LP solutions (0, 2) is feasible with $Z = 6$ and hence is optimal to the IP.

Table 7.61 LP Optimum

	RHS	$-X_1$	$-X_4$
$Z_j - C_j$	−7	0	1
X_3	2/3	5/3	−4/3
X_2	7/3	1/3	1/3

EXAMPLE 7.11 Solve the following MILP problem using the branch and bound algorithm.

Minimize $8X + 4Y_1 + 3Y_2$

Subject to
$$4X + 6Y_1 + 2Y_2 \geq 13$$
$$3X + 2Y_1 + 5Y_2 \geq 15$$

$X \geq 0$, $Y_1, Y_2 \geq 0$ and integer.

For convenience, we have denoted the continuous variables as X and the integer variables as Y.

We call this problem as a Mixed Integer Linear Programming (MILP) problem. We can apply the branch and bound algorithm to solve the problem. The LP optimum is $Y_1 = 35/26$, $Y_2 = 32/13$ with $Z = 166/13$.

We create two nodes with the additional constraints $Y_1 \leq 1$ and $Y_1 \geq 2$. Node 2 has an optimum LP solution with $Y_1 = 1$, $Y_2 = 3.5$ and $Z = 14.5$. Node 3 has an LP optimum with $Y_1 = 2$, $Y_2 = 2.2$ and $Z = 14.6$.

We branch from node 2 because it has the smallest value of the lower bound (LP optimum) to the MILP. We create nodes 4 and 5 by adding constraints $Y_2 \leq 3$ and $Y_2 \geq 4$.

Node 4 has an LP optimum with $X = 0.25$, $Y_1 = 1$, $Y_2 = 3$ with $Z = 15$. This is feasible to the MILP (here X can be continuous) and we obtain a feasible solution to the MILP (upper bound) with $Z = 15$. Node 5 has an LP optimum with $Y_1 = 0.833$, $Y_2 = 4$ and $Z = 15.33$. This is infeasible to the MILP but the node is fathomed because the LP optimum exceeds the existing best upper bound of 15.

We branch from node 3 and create nodes 6 and 7 by adding $Y_2 \leq 2$ and $Y_2 \geq 3$. Node 6 has an LP optimum with $Y_1 = 2.5$, $Y_2 = 2$ with $Z = 16$. This is fathomed by lower bound. Node 7 has an LP optimum with $Y_1 = 2$, $Y_2 = 3$ and $Z = 17$. This is feasible to the MILP and fathomed. The algorithm terminates with the optimum solution $X = 0.25$, $Y_1 = 1$, $Y_2 = 3$ with $Z = 15$. The branch and bound tree for this example is shown in Figure 7.7.

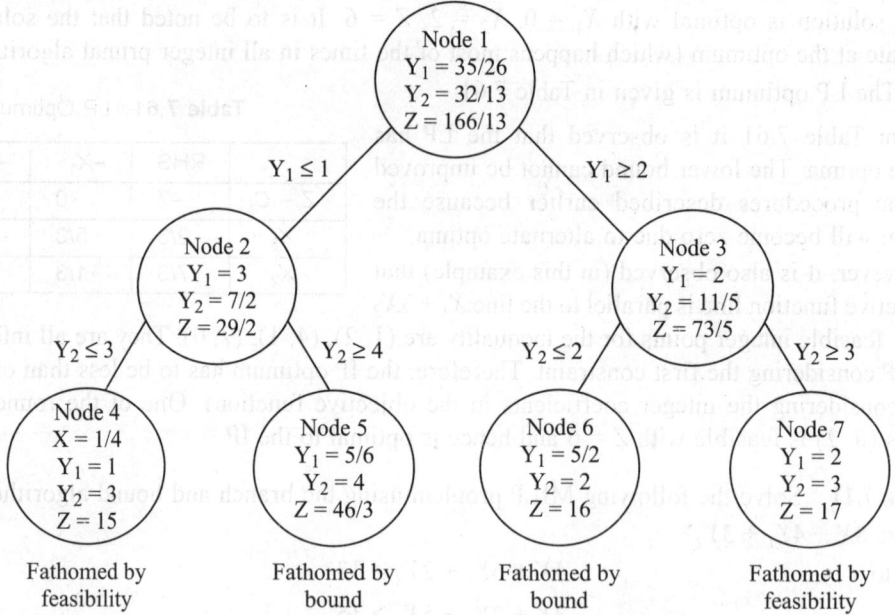

Figure 7.7 Branch and bound tree for Example 7.11.

CASE STUDY 7.1: Balaji Auto Garage

Balaji Auto Garage is a single mechanic auto garage where cars are serviced. The shop opens at eight in the morning and the job orders for the day are taken as cars arrive. One of the biggest advantages with Balaji garage is that the owners can pick up the vehicle the same day. However, if the estimated repair times are large, say, eight hours or more, the owners are told that their vehicle will be delivered the next day. The due time is told to the customer when the job order is taken and this time is calculated based on the estimated time to repair and service the vehicle and on the present status of orders. Usually customer specified due dates are accepted if the repair times are small and if there are major repairs, the garage decides the due date. A buffer is usually added to the processing times to take care of unexpected events.

It happens almost always that some unexpected and unaccounted factor results in the actual servicing times having to be reassessed. This results in delays and the garage is usually behind the due time given to the customer.

Balaji always takes enough jobs such that all the work is expected to be completed by 9.0 p.m. in the evening and continued working only when the jobs are delayed. In such cases, he informs the customers the revised due time and sticks to it. The regular customers are willing to accept the revised delivery time as long as it is completed in time.

Balaji would like to sequence the job using the FIFO (First-in-First Out) rule such that the customer who came first would get the delivery first but realizes that since the processing times are different, such a sequence would result in cascading the delays particularly when an early arrival has considerable time to repair. He chooses to sequence in such a way to minimize the total lateness (tardiness). This would minimize the total number of hours they are behind schedule and think that in the long run this would be a better measure than minimizing the number of late orders or minimizing maximum lateness.

On a Monday morning, there are four orders whose estimated service times are 2, 3, 8 and 10 hours and the revised due times are 6, 3, 14 and 12 hours from the start of the day (8 a.m.). Balaji is aware that the sequencing problem is difficult and may involve evaluating n! sequences in the worst case. He formulates an integer programming problem and evaluates the LP relaxation as a lower bound.

He also develops a branch and bound algorithm to solve his problem of minimizing the total tardiness.

CASE STUDY 7.2: Purewhite Washing Machines

The Purewhite Washing Company manufactures and sells washing machines. They are interested in locating warehouses in South India and have identified Mysore, Kochi, Namakkal and Vijayawada as possible locations for their warehouses. In Mysore and Namakkal they have identified two locations with capacities six lakhs and four lakhs respectively while in Kochi and Vijayawada the capacities are six lakhs.

Anita Krishnan, the logistics manager has been assigned the job of finding the best locations. She divides her market in South India into four regions—north, south, east and west. The demands in the four regions have been stable at 4.6, 4.2, 2.4 and 3.8 lakhs per year. Even though it is unlikely that the entire annual demand is stocked in the warehouse and distributed, she wishes to have capacity enough to hold the annual requirement. This, in her opinion can also take care of future increases in demand.

The average transportation cost per machine from the potential warehouse locations to the four regions has been estimated and are given in Table 7.62.

Table 7.62 Cost in Potential Locations

	North	East	South	West
Mysore	5	5	3	1
Kochi	8	4	1	2
Namakkal	7	3	3	5
Vijayawada	2	10	15	8

The adjusted annual fixed costs of the facilities (in lakhs) are given in Table 7.63.

Table 7.63 Fixed costs

	6l capacity	4l capacity
Mysore	10	6
Kochi	9	
Namakkal	7	5
Vijayawada	8	

The warehouses also incur an inventory cost which is a function of the maximum inventory held in the warehouse. The cost (in lakhs), based on regression is estimated to be

$$C = 0.2 \times (I + \sqrt{I})$$

where I is the maximum inventory (in lakhs) stored in the warehouse.

Anita wishes to solve the problem in four ways

1. Formulate and solve an integer programming problem that minimizes the total fixed costs and transportation costs
2. Solve an LP relaxation of the above problem, round off the integer variables and solve the resulting transportation problem
3. Determine the cheapest location that has enough capacity and solve the resultant transportation problem
4. Solve a transportation problem considering all the facilities and choose those facilities that are in the transportation solution

She is aware that while the first guarantees an optimal solution, the remaining methods provide heuristic solutions that may be quicker in terms of solution time. Consider that the problem is "hard" she is interested in evaluating the goodness of the heuristic methods for this problem.

EXERCISES

7.1 Ten jobs are to be processed and three machines are available. A job is assigned to only one machine. The processing times are different on different machines. Each job requires a fixed number of tools. Each machine has a tool drum that can accommodate 25 tools. The relevant data are given in Table 7.64.

Table 7.64 Data for Exercise 7.1

Jobs	1	2	3	4	5	6	7	8	9	10
1	5	6	5	7	9	9	7	7	6	6
2	4	5	6	5	10	12	4	8	5	8
3	6	3	9	8	10	8	6	9	8	9
Slots	8	5	6	6	7	8	9	8	7	8

The problem is to assign jobs to machines such that the tool constraints are satisfied. The objective is to balance workload among the machines. Formulate the problem as an integer programming problem. Develop a branch and bound algorithm to solve this problem. Discuss the lower bound, branching and bounding strategies.

7.2 You are given a flow shop with four jobs and three machines. In a flowshop, all the jobs visit all the machines in the same sequence or order. They visit Machine 1 first and then Machine 2 and then Machine 3. Job 1 has processing times 4, 9, 6 units, Job 2 has 6, 2, 5 units, Job 3 has 7, 8, 4 units and Job 4 has 4, 6 and 7 units. The flow shop is a special type called *no wait flow shop* where once it starts processing in Machine 1, it has to finish without any interruptions (it can't wait before a machine). The start time on Machine 1 can be suitably adjusted to obtain the no wait condition. Formulate an integer programming problem to find a sequence that minimizes the completion time of the last job in the sequence.

7.3 The course instructor for O R has three books (authors) from which he is likely to pick problems for the exam. The students want to refer the books before the exam. The instructor is willing to give the books subject to the condition that students should go through Book 1 first and then Book 2 and then Book 3 (Book 3 has tougher problems than Book 2). He wants the books to be returned together at the earliest. He is aware of the time at which he will get the books if the students follow the order.

Assume that three groups of students want to refer the books. The estimated available times (in hours) are shown in Table 7.65.

The students realize that the best way to utilize the books is to ensure that one group has one book at a time. They decide to do away with the order but decide to return the books at the earliest. Formulate an O R model to

Table 7.65 Estimated Available Time

	Book 1	Book 2	Book 3
Group 1	40	70	60
Group 2	60	50	50
Group 3	55	65	70

(a) estimate the time at which the instructor expects to get the books.
(b) Derive an expression for the extra time that they can have since the students do away with the order.

7.4 Piyush uses four books that he has borrowed from the library. The time he can spend reading the books are 6, 4, 5 and 8 days. The due dates are 8, 4, 12 and 16 days. There is a penalty of Rs. 10 per book per day of late return. Calculate a lower bound for the delays. Also develop a branch and bound algorithm to solve the problem. (**Hint:** Start with book job as the last book in the sequence)

7.5 Sathya is aware that material from the same four textbooks (Problem 7.4) are available at payment from the internet. She formulates an LP problem where he could maximize the expected marks. The decision variables are the hours to be spent on each book and the coefficients are the per hour viewing (downloading) charges. She decides to spend a maximum of Rs. 11 on this effort, and since reading from the same book can at times be uninteresting, she decides to limit her time per book to a maximum of two hours. Find Sathya's solution to maximize her expected marks.

Maximize $15X_1 + 8X_2 + 16X_3 + 12X_4$

Subject to $2X_1 + 3X_2 + 3X_3 + 4X_4 \leq 11, 0 \leq X_j \leq 2$

She realizes that she is wasting money if the solution turns out to be a fraction of an hour because internet payments are hourwise. She decides to restrict his variables to integers and does not place any upper limit on the hours per book. Obtain the LP optimum and use Gomory cutting plane algorithm to get the IP optimum.

7.6 Hari wishes to buy the same four textbooks to prepare for his exams. He formulates a problem where his decision variables are whether to buy the book or not. He would like to minimize the money spent subject to an expected mark of 80%. He is also short of time and decides not to buy more than two books. Solve Hari's problem using the implicit enumeration algorithm.

Minimize $1000X_1 + 600X_2 + 400X_3 + 500X_4$

Subject to $30X_1 + 40X_2 + 50X_3 + 40X_4 \geq 80$, $X_1 + X_2 + X_3 + X_4 \leq 2$, $X_j = 0, 1$

7.7 Solve the following IP problem:

Maximize $3X_1 + 3X_2 + 13X_3$

Subject to $-3X_1 + 6X_2 + 7X_3 \leq 8$, $6X_1 - 3X_2 + 7X_3 \leq 8$, $X_i \geq 0$ and integer using the cutting plane algorithm.

7.8 Solve Problem 7.7 using an all integer algorithm.

7.9 Solve Problem 7.7 by considering X_3 as a continuous variable using

(a) Branch and bound algorithm
(b) Cutting plane algorithm for MILP
(c) Bender's decomposition algorithm

7.10 Consider the knapsack problem:

Maximize $60X_1 + 60X_2 + 40X_3 + 10X_4 + 20X_5 + 10X_6 + 3X_7$

Subject to $3X_1 + 5X_2 + 4X_3 + 1X_4 + 4X_5 + 3X_6 + 1X_7 \leq 10$, $X_i \geq 0$ and integer

(a) Find the optimum solution using a cutting plane algorithm.
(b) Treat $X_i = 0, 1$ and solve optimally.

7.11 Gautam had four important things to do. Relevant data is given in Table 7.66. Gautam wants to determine the sequence of the activities that minimizes the total delay. He can do only one activity at a time and there is no activity splitting.

Table 7.66 Data for Exercise 7.11

Activity	Duration (days)	Due date (days)
1.	5	9
2.	4	4
3.	5	12
4.	8	11

(a) Formulate an OR problem for the scenario.
(b) Develop a branch and bound algorithm and solve.
(Use $X_{ij} = 1$ if Activity i takes jth position. Also if Activity 4 is scheduled last, the lower bound on total delay is 7)
(c) Develop a quick heuristic for the problem.

7.12 A company is considering investing in five different projects. Each requires a cash outflow at time zero and yields Net Present Value (NPV) as described in Table 7.67.

Table 7.67 Net Present Value

Project	1	2	3	4	5
Cash outflow	4	6	5	4	3
NPV	5	8	7	3	2

Projects 1 and 2 are mutually exclusive (the company cannot undertake both) and so are Projects 3 and 4. Also Project 2 cannot be undertaken unless Project 5 is undertaken. Use implicit enumeration algorithm to determine which projects have to be undertaken. Formulate a relevant zero-one problem.

7.13 Solve the following zero-one problem using implicit enumeration algorithm:

Maximize $4x_1 + 6x_2 + 4x_3 + 6x_4 + 13x_5$

Subject to $-3x_1 - 6x_2 + 6x_3 + 12x_4 + 7x_5 + x_3 \le 8$, $6x_1 + 12x_2 - 3x_3 - 6x_4 + 7x_5 + x_3 \le 8$, $X_i = 0, 1$ $i = 1,5$

7.14 Solve the following zero-one problem:

Minimize $4X_1 + 6X_2 + 8X_3 + 3X_4$

Subject to $2X_1 + 3X_2 + 4X_3 + 4X_4 \ge 6$, $7X_1 - 5X_2 + 2X_3 - X_4 \ge 7$

7.15 Solve the following IP problem using all integer algorithm(s):

Maximize $8X_1 - 6X_2$

Subject to $-X_1 + 3X_2 \le 7$, $2X_1 + 6X_2 \ge 10$, $X_i \ge 0$ and integer

7.16 Consider the following IP problem:

Minimize $4X_1 + 5X_2$

Subject to $2X_1 + 3X_2 \ge 10$, $X_1 + 5X_2 \ge 16$, $X_i \ge 0$ and integer

The LP optimum is given in the standard format in Table 7.68.

Table 7.68 LP Optimum

		$-X_1$	$-X_3$
	$-50/3$	$2/3$	$5/3$
X_4	$2/3$	$7/3$	$-5/3$
X_2	$10/3$	$2/3$	$-1/3$

(a) Formulate a Gomory cut from Table 7.68.
(b) Tighten the lower bound using the Gomory cut.
(c) Solve the problem using a branch and bound algorithm using the above lower bound.

7.17 A machine shop contains M machine types that are used to make P parts. There are m_i machines of Type i available. It is proposed to group them into k groups such that the maximum operations are performed within the groups. A machine-part incidence matrix is available. In this matrix, $a_{ij} = 1$ if part j requires operation on Machine i and is zero otherwise. Each machine goes to only one group and each part goes to only one group. A machine group can have a maximum of B machines (including multiple copies of the same machine). If a part requires operation on a machine and if that machine is not available in the group, there is an intercell move. The objective is to minimize intercell moves. Assume that each machine of type i has time T_i available. Each part j requires volume V_j and the processing time is t_{ij} (ignore set up times). Formulate an integer programming problem to minimize intercell moves.

7.18 One hundred undergraduate students have given their preferences for their "minor stream specialization". There are five minor streams available (A to E) and each student has to give his/her first to fifth preference of the minor streams. Each minor should have a minimum of 10 students and can have a maximum of 30 students.

(a) Formulate a zero-one goal programming problem to verify whether all can get minor streams within their first k choices.
(b) Formulate a zero-one goal programming problem to minimize k.

7.19 Given the linear integer programming problem:

Maximize $8X_1 + 6X_2 - X_3$

Subject to $8X_1 + 6X_2 - 2X_3 \le 13$, $X_1 + X_2 - X_3 \le 4$, $X_1, X_2, X_3 \ge 0$ and integer

(a) Gomory cutting plane algorithm
(b) Branch and bound algorithm

7.20 Eight songs from an artist are available to be recorded on a CD. The songs take 10, 8, 12, 9, 14, 13, 6 and 11 minutes and the maximum time in a CD is 60 minutes. The odd numbered songs are solo while the even numbered songs are duets. The first four songs are old while the next four are new songs. The expected demand for the songs (in lakhs) are 4, 5, 3, 6, 3, 4, 2 and 7, respectively. Formulate a zero-one problem to maximize the expected demand met. Other conditions are that they do not want more than 5 old songs and also require at least two duets.

7.21 Consider the integer programming problem:

Maximize $4X_1 + 3X_2$

Subject to $3X_1 + X_2 \leq 12$, $X_1 + 4X_2 \leq 8$, $X_1, X_2 \geq 0$ and integer

You are given an additional restriction that the variables can take only one of the values 1, 2, or 4. Formulate a zero-one problem for this situation.

7.22 Given a project network with the data shown in Table 7.69.
(a) Formulate a zero-one problem to find the earliest completion of the project (longest path in the network).
(b) If each activity requires one person to execute and two people are available, formulate the problem to find the earliest completion of the project under the additional constraints.

Table 7.69 Data for Project Network

Arc	Duration	Activity	Duration
1–2	8	3–5	9
1–3	6	3–6	10
2–4	8	4–6	6
2–5	3	5–6	7

7.23 Solve the following IP using all integer algorithms?

Maximize $6X_1 + 8X_2$
Subject to $3X_1 + 4X_2 \geq 12$,
$X_1 + 2X_2 \leq 3$,
$X_1, X_2 \geq 0$ and integer

8

Network Problems

We begin this chapter by introducing the reader to basics of graph theory, relevant to this book and study the linkages between graph theory and operations research. The concepts from graph theory are necessary to understand the topics on network problems and to study the travelling salesman problem and its variants (Chapter 9).

8.1 GRAPH THEORY—BASIC DEFINITIONS

A *graph G* is a collection of *nodes* (*vertices*) and *arcs* (*edges*). It usually represents a relationship (connectivity) among the vertices. The extent of connectivity is indicated by a number called **weight**. A graph may be *weighted* or *unweighted*. Usually weighted graphs are called **networks**.

A graph is directed if the direction of the arcs is specified through an arrow. An arc *i-j* can be directed from *i* to *j* or from *j* to *i*. Between two vertices, we can have both the arcs directed in different ways.

In any graph, the nodes are connected through arcs. An arc (or edge) always connects two vertices (or nodes). It is *adjacent* to both the nodes that it connects.

A *path* is a collection of arcs connecting a given vertex to another. If a path exists, it is possible to reach one vertex from another passing through a set of arcs that may go through intermediate vertices.

A graph may be *connected* or *unconnected*. A connected graph has a path from every vertex to every other vertex.

A graph *H* is a *subgraph* of a graph *G* when the edges and vertices of *H* are a subset of those of *G*. A graph is a subset of itself. The *null graph* (containing no edges and vertices) is a subset of every graph.

The *degree* of a vertex is the number of arcs adjacent to it.

Result 1

The sum of the degrees of the vertices of a graph is an even number.

This is because every arc is attached to two vertices. The sum of the degrees is twice the number of arcs and hence an even number.

> **Result 2**
> The number of vertices in a graph with odd degree is even.

This follows from Result 1.

> **Result 3**
> A connected graph with n vertices should have at least $n-1$ edges.

This follows from the definition of connectivity.

As already seen, a path is a collection of edges passing through vertices that connects a given vertex to another given vertex. If we come back to the starting vertex, then it is called a **cycle**.

A connected graph (with n vertices) is a tree if it has exactly $n-1$ edges, and there exists a path from every vertex to every other vertex. We can also show that a tree will have exactly $n-1$ edges and having a path from every vertex to every other vertex.

> **Result 4**
> If an undirected connected graph has n edges or more then there is at least one cycle.

This comes from the definition of a tree.

A tree is a *spanning tree* if it has all the vertices of a given graph. In a graph having n vertices, a spanning tree will have all the vertices and $n-1$ edges which have been picked from the original graph. All trees need not be spanning trees. For a graph having n vertices, a tree from this graph may have m vertices ($m < n$) and having $m-1$ edges.

A matching is a set of edges taken from a graph such that there is no common vertex. A *maximum matching* is the matching with maximum possible edges. For a given graph, many matchings are possible. In fact, a null graph (with no edges and vertices) is also a matching. Therefore, the emphasis is always on finding the maximum matching.

A cover is a set of vertices such that all edges are adjacent to at least one vertex in the cover. Obviously, the set of all vertices is a cover to any graph. Therefore, the emphasis is on finding the *minimum cover,* which is the minimum number of vertices such that all edges are adjacent to the set.

It is also possible to show that the maximum matching problem is the dual to the minimum cover problem and *vice versa.*

A graph is said to be *complete* if there is an edge from every vertex to every other vertex in the graph. A complete graph with n vertices has $^nC_2$ edges. A complete graph with five vertices called K_5 has 10 edges.

A graph is said to be *bipartite,* if the vertices can be divided into two sets such that there is no edge connecting vertices in the same set. There are only edges connecting vertices from one set to another. A connected bipartite graph with m and n vertices, respectively will have at least $m + n - 1$ edges. A *complete bipartite graph* with m and n vertices, respectively in the two parts has exactly mn edges (with only one edge connecting a given pair of vertices).

8.2 INTERESTING PROBLEMS IN GRAPH THEORY

Let us consider a few interesting problems that have attracted the attention of researchers:

1. The Koenigsberg bridge problem dates from 1736 and deals with a puzzle problem requiring creation of a walking route which would cross each of seven bridges on the Pregel river connecting four different land segments exactly once and returns to the starting point. The configuration involves a fork in the river and an island in the river and would not be easy to reproduce here. The graph for the problem is shown in Figure 8.1.

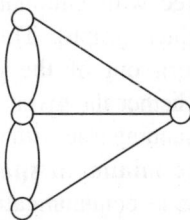

Figure 8.1 Graph for Koenigsberg bridge problem.

2. Given n cities and the distance matrix among the cities, the problem is to find the minimum distance tour of a salesman who wants to start from a city visit every other city once and only once and return to the starting point.
3. Given a graph, it is required to find the minimum number of colours such that every vertex has a colour and two vertices having an edge adjacent to them have different colours.

8.3 SOME MORE DEFINITIONS AND PROBLEMS IN GRAPH THEORY

A graph is said to be *Hamiltonian*, if it is possible to start at a vertex, move along edges to vertex once and only once and return to the starting point. This circuit is called a **Hamiltonian circuit**. If the start and finish vertices are defined then the problem reduces to one of finding a path passing through all vertices once and only once and reaching the destination. This is called the **Hamiltonian path problem.** A graph may or may not have a Hamiltonian circuit and if it has one, it need not be unique. A graph may have multiple Hamiltonian circuits but all of them will have n edges (for a graph with n vertices).

A graph is said to be *Eulerian* if it is possible to return to the same starting vertex by passing through every edge once and only once. Such a circuit is called an **Eulerian circuit.** A graph may or may not be Eulerian, but if it has an Eulerian circuit, the length of the Eulerian circuit is the sum of the weight of the edges.

Two important problems from graph theory are to verify whether a given graph is Hamiltonian or to verify whether the given graph is Eulerian.

8.4 SOME GRAPH THEORETIC PROBLEMS AND CORRESPONDING OPTIMIZATION PROBLEMS

8.4.1 Spanning Trees

We have already defined a spanning tree of a given graph. It is also obvious that every connected graph has a spanning tree. Figure 8.2 shows a graph and a spanning tree. For a corrected graph, the decision problem of finding whether there is a spanning tree is a trivial one. Therefore, the focus is on finding the number of different spanning trees that exist in a given connected graph.

Another important problem is to find the spanning tree with minimum total weight (in a given weighted graph). This is an optimization problem born out of the decision problem of verifying whether the given graph has a spanning tree. The spanning tree with minimum total weight is called the **minimum spanning** tree. This has applications in communication systems where we find the minimum length of wire needed to connect a given set of points.

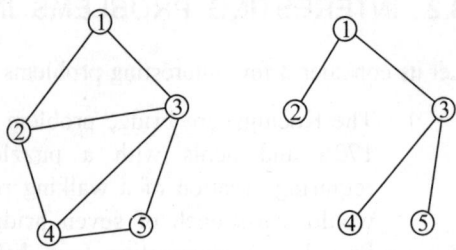

Figure 8.2 A graph and a spanning tree for the graph.

Decision problem: Does the given graph have a spanning tree?

Graph theoretic problem: How many spanning trees does the given unweighted graph have?

Optimization problem: Find the minimum spanning tree in a given weighted graph.

8.4.2 Matching Problem

We have defined a matching problem in a given graph. The first problem is to find whether the given graph has a matching. This is a trivial problem since the null graph is a matching. The next problem is to find out the maximum matching in a given unweighted graph. This problem is also important for bipartite graphs. When we consider a complete bipartite graph with m and n vertices in the two sets, the maximum matching is the minimum of m and n. If we consider a complete bipartite graph with equal number of vertices in each set (n), the maximum matching is n. In this case, if we consider weighted graphs, the problem shifts to the optimization problem of finding the matching (maximum matching) that has minimum weight. This problem is the well known assignment problem in operations research that has several practical applications. Figure 8.3 shows a bipartite graph and matchings.

Decision problem: To find a matching in a given graph.

Graph theoretic problem: To find the maximum matching in a given unweighted graph.

Optimization problem: Find the minimum weighted perfect matching in a given weighted bipartite graph.

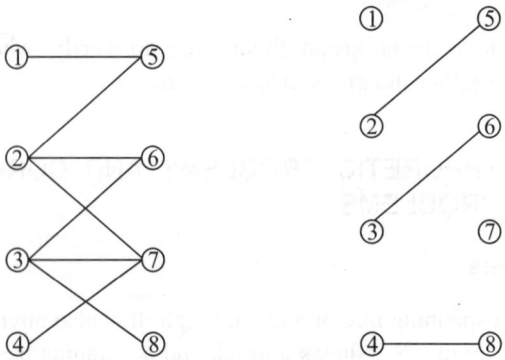

Figure 8.3 A bipartite graph and a matching.

8.4.3 Travelling Salesman Problem and Hamiltonian Circuits

We have defined the Hamiltonian circuit and path problems. The decision problem is to find out whether the given graph is Hamiltonian. However, if the given graph is a complete graph, the problem of finding whether a Hamiltonian circuit exists is trivial. In fact the number of Hamiltonian circuits is also known to be $n!$ for a complete graph with n vertices. If a graph is not complete, the problem is also one of finding all the Hamiltonian circuits. If the graph is complete, the focus then shifts to finding the Hamiltonian with the smallest total weight (or cost) for a weighted graph. This is the well known travelling salesman problem. Figure 8.4 shows a Hamiltonian circuit from a given complete graph.

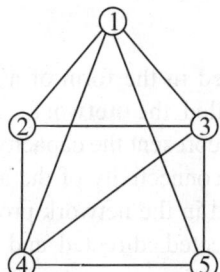 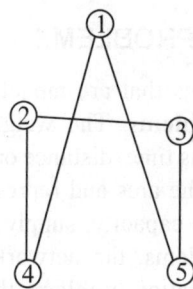

Figure 8.4 A complete graph and a Hamiltonian circuit from the graph.

Decision problem: To find a Hamiltonian circuit in a given graph.

Graph theoretic problem: To find the number of unique Hamiltonian circuits in a given unweighted graph.

Optimization problem: Find the minimum weighted Hamiltonian circuit in a given weighted graph.

8.4.4 The Chinese Postman Problem and Eulerian Circuits

We have defined the Eulerian circuit problem. The important problem is to verify whether the given graph is Eulerian. There are some results available using which we can find out whether the given graph is Eulerian or not. We also know that if a given graph is Eulerian, there is only one Eulerian circuit and, therefore, it does not matter whether the given graph is weighted or not. However, if the given graph is not Eulerian then the optimization problem is to find the minimum additional arcs (in terms of weights) to be added to make the given graph Eulerian. This is called the **Chinese Postman problem** where we find out arcs with minimum total weight to be added to make the given graph Eulerian. Figure 8.5 shows the Eulerian circuit from a graph.

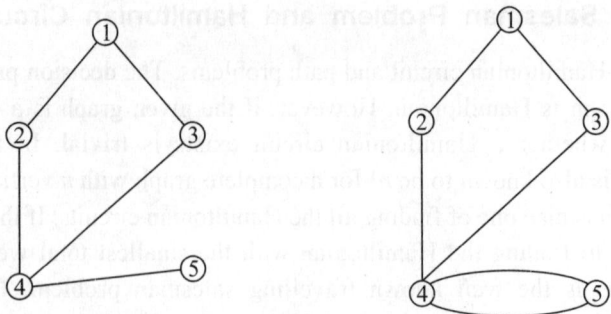

Figure 8.5 A graph (non-Eulerian) and an edge duplicated to get an Eulerian circuit.

8.5 NETWORK PROBLEMS

Optimization problems that are modelled and represented in the form of a weighted graph are called **network problems**. The weighted graph is called the **network**. The weight usually represents data such as time, distance or cost. It can also represent the capacity of the arc. Weights are usually given to the arcs and represent the extent of connectivity of the arc. Sometimes node weights such as node capacity, supply, etc. are also used in the network problems.

In network problems, the network is usually connected, directed and weighted. Network problems are optimization problems that are normally cost minimization problems. Sometimes capacity maximization problems are also modelled as network problems.

8.5.1 Capacitated Minimum Cost Flow Problem on a Network

Let us consider the general network shown in Figure 8.6.

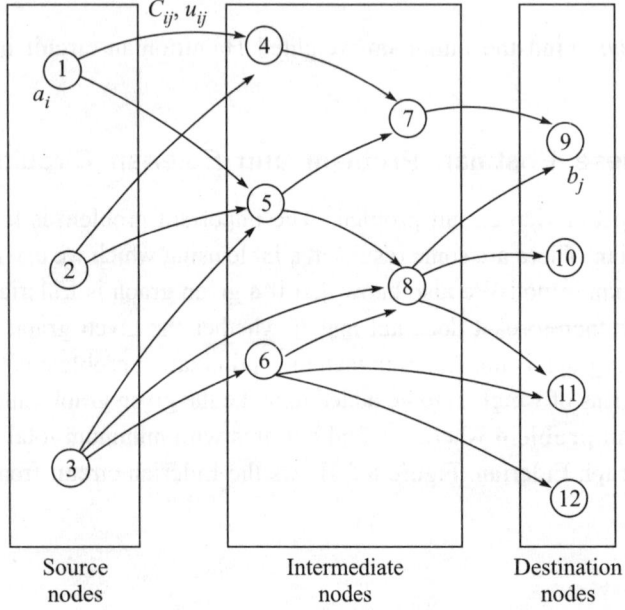

Figure 8.6 Network for minimum cost flow problem (capacitated).

The generalized network problem has a set of origin points M called **source points**. The supply at source i is a_i. There are N destination points each with requirement b_j. There are K intermediate points. The problem is to transport a given commodity from the supply points to destination points such as to minimize the total cost. Such a problem would assume that

$$\underset{\text{supply}}{\sum a_i} \geq \underset{\text{demand}}{\sum b_j}$$

when all the demand is to be met. This is also called the **transshipment problem**. The formulation is as follows:

Minimize $\sum_{i=1}^{m}\sum_{j=1}^{n} C_{ij} X_{ij}$ (over all arcs) \hfill (8.1)

Subject to

$$\sum_{j=1}^{n} X_{ij} \leq a_i \text{ for all } j \in M \; i = \text{supply} \hfill (8.2)$$

$$\sum_{i}^{n} X_{ij} - \sum_{k}^{n} X_{jk} = 0 \text{ for all intermediate nodes } k \hfill (8.3)$$

$$\sum_{i} X_{ij} \geq b_j \text{ for } j = \text{demand node} \hfill (8.4)$$

$$X_{ij} \leq u_{ij} \text{ for all } i,j \hfill (8.5)$$
$$X_{ij} \geq 0 \hfill (8.6)$$

The above minimum cost capacitated network flow problem can be reduced to a few well known problems.

Case 1: When the set of intermediate nodes is zero, which means that there are only supply and destination points and when $u_{ij} = \infty$ the problem reduces to the *transportation problem*.

Case 2: When the set of intermediate nodes is zero, which means that there are only supply and destination points and when $u_{ij} = \infty$, $M = N$ and $a_i = 1$, and $b_j = 1$ the problem reduces to the *assignment problem*.

Case 3: When $M = N = 1$ and $u_{ij} = 1$, $a_1 = b_1 = 1$, the problem reduces to the *shortest path problem*.

Case 4: When $M = N = 1$, $a_1 = b_1 = \infty$, $C_{ij} = -1$, the problem reduces to the *maximum flow problem*.

In this chapter we concentrate on the shortest path problem, the maximum flow problem, the minimum cost flow problem and the minimum spanning tree problem. We have already addressed the transportation and the assignment problem in the earlier chapters.

8.6 THE MINIMUM SPANNING TREE PROBLEM (MST PROBLEM)

ILLUSTRATION 8.1

Consider the graph given in Figure 8.7 with the weight (cost) shown.

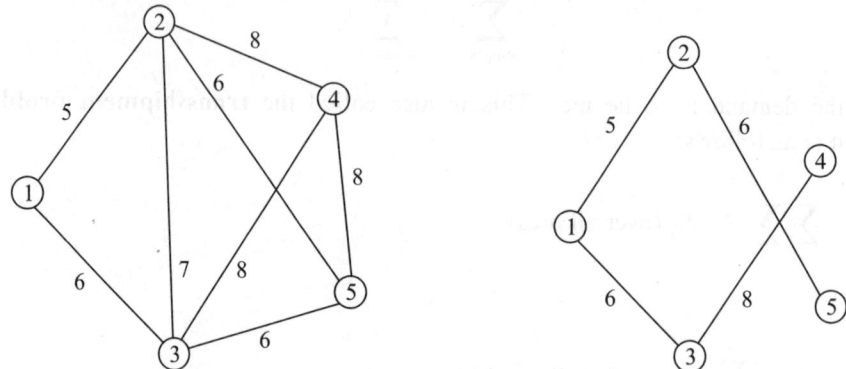

Figure 8.7 A graph and a minimum spanning tree.

The minimum spanning tree is the spanning tree with the minimum total cost (weight).

8.6.1 Prim's Algorithm

The edge with the smallest weight is the starting edge. In our example, it is the edge 1–2 with weight 5. Now edge 1–2 is in the minimum spanning tree. The set of vertices in the spanning tree is $S = \{1-2\}$. The edge with least weight from 1 is 1–3 with 6 and from 2 it is 2–5 with weight equal to 6. We choose the minimum. In this case there is a tie, which can be broken arbitrarily. We choose 1–3 with weight 6. We add this edge to the spanning tree and set $S = \{1, 2, 3\}$. We pick the edge with the smallest weight from every member of S to the set $N - S$. For vertex 1 there is no edge. For Vertex 2 it is edge 2–5 with weight = 6 and for Vertex 3 it is 3–5 with 6. Once again there is a tie and we choose 2–5. This edge goes into the spanning tree and $S = \{1, 2, 3, 5\}$. The set $N - S = \{4\}$. The edge with smallest distance from 1, 2, 3 and 5 to 4 is 2–4, 5–4 and 3–4 all with weight = 8. We can choose any one and we pick 3–4 with weight = 8. Now, all vertices are in S and the algorithm terminates. The minimum spanning tree has edges 1–2, 1–3, 2–5 and 3–4 with total weight = 5 + 6 + 6 + 8 = 25. The minimum spanning tree is also shown in Figure 8.7.

We have more than one minimum spanning tree because we had a tie for the last entering edge.

The Prim's algorithm (Prim, 1957)

1. Initialize $S = \{\}$.
2. Pick the edge with smallest weight and enter this to the MST. Add the vertices in S.
3. For every vertex in S find the edge with minimum weight connecting i in S to j in $N - S$. Let i–j be the minimum weight edge among these. Add vertex j to the set S. Include edge i–j in the MST.
4. Repeat Step 3 till all vertices are in $\{S\}$

8.6.2 Kruskal's Algorithm (Kruskal, 1956)

Here, we arrange the edges according to increasing weights. In our example, the order is 1–2, 1–3, 2–5, 3–5, 2–3, 2–4, 3–4, 4–5. The first edge is added to the spanning tree. We consider the next edge 1–3 and verify whether it forms a loop. It doesn't and we add it to the spanning tree. There are now two edges. The next edge 2–5 does not form a loop and we add it. There are three edges. The next edge 3–5 forms a loop and is not added. The next edge 2–3 also forms a loop and hence is not added. The next edge 2–4 does not form a loop and is added. Now, there are four edges and the algorithm stops because we have $N - 1$ edges in the spanning tree. The minimum spanning tree has edges 1–2, 1–3, 2–5 and 2–4 with a total weight of 25.

The Kruskal's algorithm

1. Initialize n edge = 0. Arrange edges i–j in increasing (nondecreasing) order of weights.
2. Pick the first edge and ignore it if it forms a loop with the existing edges in the MST. Enter this to the MST if it does not form a loop. n edge = n edge + 1. Remove edge i–j and Repeat 2.
3. If n edge = $N - 1$ STOP. Else go to Step 2.

8.6.3 Applications of Minimum Spanning Trees

1. The minimum spanning tree has extensive applications in connectivity problems. The minimum length of wire needed to connect a set of points so that the power supply can be provided, is a minimum spanning tree.
2. This problem also has application in communication networks.
3. More practical problems in the application areas include degree constrained spanning trees (with a limit on the number of edges incident to a vertex). These are difficult problems to solve.
4. In theory, we can show that every feasible solution to a network problem is a spanning tree.
5. The MST can be shown to be a lower bound to the travelling salesman problem and can be used to develop optimal and heuristic algorithms to the TSP. This has a wide range of applications in Distribution planning and in Supply chain management.

8.7 THE SHORTEST PATH PROBLEM

The shortest path problem finds the shortest route on a network from a given source to a given destination.

ILLUSTRATION 8.2

Find the shortest path between vertices 1 and 7 shown in Figure 8.8.

Let us assume that Vertex 1 is the origin (source) and Vertex 7 is the destination. We need to find the path from 1–7 with the shortest length (distance). The formulation is as follows:

Let X_{ij} = 1 if edge (arc) i–j is in the shortest path
= 0 otherwise

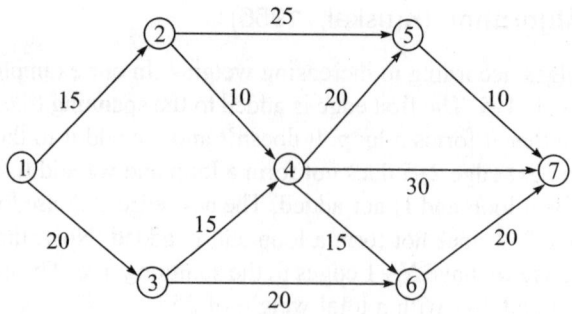

Figure 8.8 Network for shortest path problem.

The objective function is to

Minimize $\sum_{i=1}^{n}\sum_{j=1}^{n} C_{ij} X_{ij}$ (8.7)

Subject to

$$X_{12} + X_{13} = 1 \quad (8.8)$$
$$-X_{12} + X_{24} + X_{25} = 0 \quad (8.9)$$
$$-X_{13} + X_{34} + X_{36} = 0 \quad (8.10)$$
$$-X_{24} - X_{34} + X_{45} + X_{46} + X_{47} = 0 \quad (8.11)$$
$$-X_{25} - X_{45} + X_{57} = 0 \quad (8.12)$$
$$-X_{36} - X_{46} + X_{67} = 0 \quad (8.13)$$
$$-X_{47} - X_{57} - X_{67} = -1 \quad (8.14)$$
$$X_{ij} = 0,1 \quad (8.15)$$

The objective function (8.7) minimizes the total cost (or distance) of travelling from the origin to destination. Constraint (8.8) ensures that we leave the origin by taking 1–2 or 1–3. Constraints 8.9 to 8.14 ensure that if we enter a node then we leave the node. It is also important to note that we need not enter and leave all nodes. Constraint (8.15) ensures that we reach the destination. It should normally read

$$X_{47} + X_{57} + X_{67} = 1 \quad (8.16)$$

This has been written specifically in such a way (Eqs. 8.8 to 8.14) that we can see every variable appears only in two constraints and the column sum of the constraint coefficients is zero. We will use this representation subsequently. The variables are also constrained to be zero-one so that either we take an edge or we don't.

The formulation has as many constraints as the number of nodes and as many variables as the number of arcs.

8.7.1 Dijkstra's Algorithm (Dijkstra, 1959)

Let us explain the algorithm for the network shown in Figure 8.8.

Define $L(1) = 0$ where $L(j)$ is a label corresponding to Node j. From Node 1, we can go to Nodes 2 or 3. Node 2 being the shorter, we choose 1–2 and label $L(2) = L(1) + C_{12} = 15$. From

Node 1 the shortest distance is to go to Node 3 with a distance of 0 + 20 = 20. From 2, the nearest destination is Node 4 with a distance 15 + 10 = 25. We choose the smaller of the two and permanently label $L(3) = 20$.
We repeat the process.

From Node 1, we have no label.
From Node 2, the next destination could be 4 with 15 + 10 = 25.
From Node 3, it could be 4 with distance = 20 + 15 = 35.
We label $L(4) = 25$.
From Node 2, it can be 5 with distance = 40.
From Node 3 it can be 6 with distance = 20 + 20 = 40.
From Node 4, it can be 35 + 15 = 50.

We can label Node 5 or Node 6 as $L(5) = 40$. Additionally from Node 5, the next destination can be 7 with distance = 40 + 10 = 50. We label Node 6 with $L(6) = 40$ because of lesser distance.

From Node 6, the destination will be 7 with distance = 40 + 20 = 60. We label $L(7) = 50$. Since the destination node is labelled, the algorithm stops with the shortest distance = 70. The shortest path is 1–2–5–7.

Dijkstra's algorithm

1. Initialize $L(1) = 0$
2. For all labelled Node i, calculate $d_{ij} = L(i) + c_{ij}$ if there is an arc i–j in the network. Find minimum d_{ij} and label the corresponding node $L(j) = d_{ij}$.
3. Repeat Step 2 till the destination node is labelled.

Table 8.1 sequentially lists the computations using the labelling algorithm for illustration 8.2.

Table 8.1 Computations in the labelling algorithm

Node / Iteration	2	3	4	5	6	7
1	15*	20	∞	∞	∞	∞
2	15	20*	25	40	∞	∞
3	15	20	25*	40	40	∞
4	15	20	25	40	40*	55
5	15	20	25	40*	40	55
6	15	20	25	40	40	50*

***Iteration* 1**

Source Node 1 is connected to 2 and 3. The distances are shown and the rest are taken to be infinity. The smallest distance is 15 and Node 2 is labelled $L(2) = 15$ (shown with a *).

Iteration 2

The labelled nodes retain their labels. $L(2)$ remains as 15. The most recently labelled Node 2 is connected to 4 and 5. We check whether $L(2) + d_{24} <$ existing value of infinity. Now, Node 4 has a value of 25. Similarly, Node 5 has a value of 40. Other unlabelled Nodes 3 and 7 retain their old values of 20 and infinity, respectively. The smallest value is 20 and is for Node 3. Now, Node 3 is labelled as $L(3) = 20$ shown with a*.

Iteration 3

Labelled nodes $L(2) = 15$, $L(3) = 20$. Node 3 is connected to 4 and 6. We check if $L(3) + d_{34} < 25$. It is not and hence Node 4 has the old value of 25. We verify for Node 6 and change the value to 40. The other unlabelled Node 7 is not connected to 3 and hence retains the value of infinity. The minimum value is for Node 4 and $L(4) = 25$.

Iteration 4

$L(2) = 15$, $L(3) = 20$, $L(4) = 25$. Node 4 is connected to 5, 6, 7. We verify $25 + 20 < 40$. Node 5 retains its old value of 40. Similarly, Node 6 also retains the value of 40 but for Node 7, we have $25 + 30 < \infty$. So Node 7 gets the value 55. There is a tie between nodes 5 and 6 for the lowest value among unlabelled nodes. We can choose Node 6 (arbitrarily), $L(6) = 40$.

Iteration 5

$L(2) = 15$, $L(3) = 20$, $L(4) = 25$, $L(6) = 40$. Node 6 is connected to Node 7 and we find that $L(6) + d_{67} > 40$. Node 7 retains its value of 55. Now, Node 5 is labelled with $L(5) = 40$.

Iteration 6

$L(2) = 15$, $L(3) = 20$, $L(4) = 25$, $L(6) = 40$, $L(5) = 40$. Node 5 is connected to Node 7 and we observe that $L(5) + d_{57} < 55$. We update Node 7 value to 50. This is the only unlabelled node and we label $L(7) = 50$.

The destination node has been labelled and hence the algorithm stops with value = 50. The shortest distance between Nodes 1 (source) and 7 (destination) is 50. To determine the path we use the following procedure:

1. Move vertically from the value of 50. The iteration above has 55. The node labelled there was Node 5.
2. Now, move vertically in Node 5 from the present position. The value has changed from ∞ to 40 due to labelling Node 2.
3. Node 2 has been labelled from Node 1.

The path, therefore, is 1–2–5–7.

8.7.2 Other Instances of Shortest Path Problem

We have solved one instance of the shortest path problem—between a given origin and destination. Other instances of the problem are:

1. Between a given origin and all points on the network
2. Between all origins and a single destination on a network
3. Between a given origin and a given destination passing through a certain node

4. Between every point and every other point in the network
5. Second, third and successive shortest paths between a given origin and given destination
6. Constrained shortest path problems

The Dijsktra's algorithm explained earlier to find the shortest path from a given origin and a given destination is a polynomially bounded algorithm and the optimality can be proved easily. It can also be easily shown that it also solves the shortest path between the given origin and all destinations in the network if we extend the algorithm up to the point when all points are labelled. Therefore, the first instance that we have indicated is solved by the Dijkstra's algorithm directly.

To solve the problem of finding the shortest path from all points to a given destination, we have to treat the destination as origin and obtain the shortest distance between the new origin (the original destination) and every point on the network. We have to reverse the directions if the network is directed.

To find the shortest path from a given source (origin) to a given destination passing through a given intermediate node, we find the shortest path from the origin to the intermediate node using an iteration of Dijkstra's algorithm and find the shortest path from the destination to the intermediate node. We use the algorithm twice in this case.

Before we move on to the last three cases, we prove the optimality of the Dijkstra's algorithm and the explanation of the labels.

8.7.3 Dual of the Shortest Path Problem

The primal has as many variables as the number of arcs and as many constraints as the number of nodes. The primal has been written in such a way that each variable appears exactly in two constraints with a $+1$ coefficient in one and -1 coefficient in another. The dual will have as many variables as the number of constraints as the number of arcs and as many variables as the number of nodes.

The primal is a zero-one problem with a minimization objective. The constraints are such that each variable appears in two constraints with $+1$ sign in one and -1 sign in another. We can show that the coefficient matrix corresponding to such a system is unimodular. Therefore, relaxing the zero-one variables to continuous variables will still result in a solution where the decision variables will take zero-one values. We, therefore, have a linear formulation of the primal with all variables ≥ 0.

Let us denote the dual variables to be y_1 to y_m. The dual will be

Maximize $y_1 - y_m$
Subject to
$$y_i - y_j \leq c_{ij}$$
y_j unrestricted in sign

Since the dual variables are unrestricted in sign, the dual can be rewritten as

Maximize $y_m - y_1$
Subject to $y_j - y_i \leq c_{ij}$
y_j unrestricted in sign

Let us write the dual for our numerical illustration based on the rewritten formulation:

Maximize $y_7 - y_1$

Subject to

$$y_2 - y_1 \leq 15$$
$$y_3 - y_1 \leq 20$$
$$y_4 - y_2 \leq 10$$
$$y_5 - y_2 \leq 25$$
$$y_4 - y_3 \leq 15$$
$$y_6 - y_3 \leq 20$$
$$y_5 - y_4 \leq 20$$
$$y_6 - y_4 \leq 15$$
$$y_7 - y_4 \leq 30$$
$$y_7 - y_5 \leq 10$$
$$y_7 - y_6 \leq 20$$

y_j unrestricted in sign.

The primal has exactly as many constraints as the number of nodes. The primal has seven constraints. We also observe that from the way the primal was written, it represents a linearly dependent system. Therefore there can be only six independent basic variables. The dual will therefore have one variable assigned to an arbitrary value, which we fix to be zero.

We start with $y_1 = 0$. This would make $y_2 \leq 15$ and $y_3 \leq 20$. We fix $y_2 = 15$ and $y_3 = 20$ (the maximum possible value). This would make $y_4 \leq 35$, $y_4 \leq 25$. We fix $y_4 = 25$ (the maximum possible value).

Using the values of y_2, y_3 and y_4, we get $y_5 \leq 40$ and $y_5 \leq 45$. We fix $y_5 = 40$. We also get $y_6 \leq 40$ and $y_5 \leq 40$. We fix $y_6 = 40$. From the fixed values we have $y_7 \leq 50$ and $y_7 \leq 55$ and $y_7 \leq 60$. We fix $y_7 = 50$ (maximum possible value).

The dual values are feasible with an objective function value of 50. We can apply complimentary slackness conditions and identify a solution to the primal with $X_{12}, X_{25}, X_{36}, X_{45}, X_{47}, X_{57}$ and X_{67} basic. The values will be $X_{12} = X_{25} = X_{57} = 1$, $X_{36} = X_{45} = X_{47} = X_{67} = 0$. The above solution is a degenerate basic feasible solution to the primal with objective function value 50. Hence it is optimal to the primal. The shortest path is 1-2, 2-5 and 5-7 indicated by the set of basic variables that take value = 1.

The values computed by the Dijkstra's algorithm are exactly the values of the dual at the optimum.

8.7.4 Shortest Path between all Pairs of Nodes in a Network

We address the problems of finding the shortest path from every vertex to every other vertex in the network. Since the Dijkstra's algorithm can be used to find the shortest path from a given source to every other point in the network, it is enough to apply the Dijkstra's algorithm n times, if the network has n nodes, by considering every node as a source. We also have another algorithm that solves this problem.

ILLUSTRATION 8.3

Find the shortest path among all nodes in the network shown in Figure 8.9.
Let the distances be represented by the following matrix:

$$D = \begin{bmatrix} - & 5 & - & 15 \\ 10 & - & 20 & 5 \\ 5 & 15 & - & - \\ - & 10 & 10 & - \end{bmatrix}$$

Let us assume that we travel from every point to every other point passing through Point 1. Therefore $d_{ij} = d_{i1} + d_{1j}$. If this is less than d_{ij}, we update the distance. We now create a matrix D^1 given by

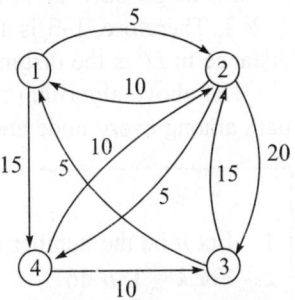

Figure 8.9 Network for shortest path between all pairs.

$$D^1 = \begin{bmatrix} - & 5 & - & 15 \\ 10 & - & 20 & 5 \\ 5 & 10 & - & 15 \\ - & 10 & 10 & - \end{bmatrix}$$

Suppose that we travel from every point to every other point passing through Point 2. Therefore, $d_{ij} = d_{i2} + d_{2j}$. If this is less than d_{ij}, we update the distance. We now create a matrix D^2 given by

$$D^2 = \begin{bmatrix} - & 5 & 25 & 10 \\ 10 & - & 10 & 5 \\ 5 & 10 & - & 15 \\ - & 10 & 10 & - \end{bmatrix}$$

Let us assume that we travel from every point to every other point passing through Point 3. Therefore, $d_{ij} = d_{i3} + d_{3j}$. If this is less than d_{ij}, we update the distance. We now create a matrix D^3 given by

$$D^3 = \begin{bmatrix} - & 5 & 25 & 10 \\ 10 & - & 10 & 5 \\ 5 & 10 & - & 15 \\ 15 & 10 & 10 & - \end{bmatrix}$$

If we travel from every point to every other point passing through Point 4, then $d_{ij} = d_{i4} + d_{4j}$. If this is less than d_{ij}, we update the distance. We now create a matrix D^4 given by

$$D^4 = \begin{bmatrix} - & 5 & 20 & 10 \\ 10 & - & 10 & 5 \\ 5 & 10 & - & 15 \\ 15 & 10 & 10 & - \end{bmatrix}$$

Now, we have defined D^4. This matrix gives the shortest distance from any vertex to any other vertex. For example, the shortest distance between 1 and 3 is 20. To find the path we find in which matrix the value has reduced. Here, it is reduced in D^4. This means that $d_{13} = d_{14} + d_{43}$ and 1–3 is 1–4–3.

Let us go back to 1–4. We find that this reduces from 15 to 10 in D^2. Therefore, 1–4 is 1–2–4. Therefore, 1–3 is 1–2–4–3. For all the three arcs 1–2, 2–4 and 4–3, we realize that the distance in D^4 is the distance given in D. Hence the path is 1–2–4–3.

The above algorithm is called **Floyd's algorithm** and determines the shortest distance and path among every node and every other node in the network.

Floyd's algorithm (Floyd 1962)

1. Let n be the number of nodes and D^0 be the given distance matrix.
2. For $k = 1, n$ do
   For $i = 1, n\; j = 1, n$ do
   $D^k(i, j)$ = Minimum $(D^{k-1}(i, j), D^{k-1}(i, k) + D^{k-1}(k, j))$
3. The matrix D^n gives the shortest distance between any given pair of nodes.
4. The shortest path is as follows:
   For an arc in the path i–j, find k such that d_{ij} in D^k is less than in D^{k-1}. Replace i–j by i–k–j. Repeat this for every arc in the path. Stop when no change in the path takes place.

8.7.5 Successive Shortest Path in a Network

Many times we may be interested in finding the second, third shortest path in a network. Here we describe a procedure to compute successive shortest paths in a network.

ILLUSTRATION 8.4

We describe the algorithm by Yen by considering the same example considered earlier. Figure 8.8 is reproduced as Figure 8.10.

The shortest path is given by 1–2–5–7 with shortest distance = 50. There are three arcs in the shortest path. In order to find the second shortest path we set each of the arcs to ∞ and generate three problems.

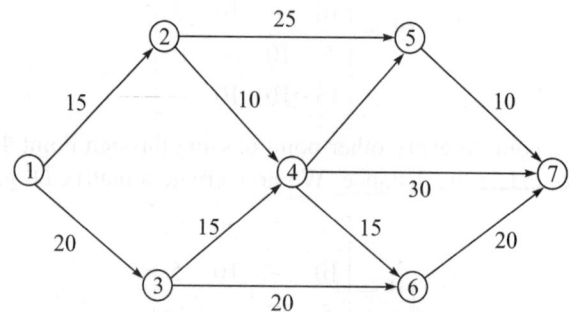

Figure 8.10 Network for successive shortest path.

Problem 1 with $d_{12} = \infty$ gives us the shortest path (using Dijkstra's algorithm) 1–3–6–7 with distance = 60. Problem 2 with $d_{25} = \infty$ gives us the shortest path 1–2–4–5–7 with distance = 55. Problem 3 with $d_{57} = \infty$ gives us the shortest path 1–2–4–7 with distance = 55. We have three paths and we create a list of them in increasing order of distance. We observe that the least distance path has a tie. We can choose one of them (say, 1–2–4–5–7) as the second shortest path. The remaining two paths 1–2–4–7 and 1–3–6–7 in the list.

In order to find the third shortest path, we take the second shortest path 1–2–4–5–7 and create four problems by setting 1–2, 2–4, 4–5, 5–7 to ∞. We should remember that in all these problems 2–5 is already set to ∞. We apply Dijkstra's algorithm and obtain the shortest path for each of the cases. We now have a list of six paths (including the existing two paths). We arrange all the six of them in increasing order of distances and find the one with shortest distance. This becomes the third shortest path. In our example, the path 1–2–4–7 will become the third shortest path (because of the tie).

For our example, we can also say that the path 1–3–6–7 with distance = 60 will become the fourth shortest path.

Successive shortest path algorithm (Yen, 1971)

1. Find the shortest path using the Dijkstra's algorithm.
2. Make the individual arcs of the shortest path to ∞ and solve as many problems as the number of arcs using the Dijkstra's algorithm.
3. Arrange the paths in increasing order of path lengths. The first path in the list is the second shortest path.
4. To identify the kth shortest path, take the $(k-1)$th shortest path and carry out Step 2. Add these paths to the list and arrange them in the increasing order of path lengths. The first in the list is the kth shortest path.

8.7.6 Constrained Shortest Path Problems

The shortest path problem is usually formulated as one of finding the minimum distance path between a given start node and a given destination node. Sometimes, we also solve to minimize cost or time. Sometimes we wish to optimize all the three parameters or two out of them if they are not proportional to each other. These type of applications occur in the airline industry. Here, we solve either a multiobjective problem of say, minimizing distance and time or solve a constrained shortest path problem where time of travel is treated as a constraint. The formulation is as follows:

Minimize $\sum_{i=1}^{n}\sum_{j=1}^{n} C_{ij} X_{ij}$ (8.29)

Subject to

$X_{12} + X_{13} = 1$ (8.30)

$-X_{12} + X_{24} + X_{25} = 0$ (8.31)

$-X_{13} + X_{34} + X_{36} = 0$ (8.32)

$-X_{24} - X_{34} + X_{45} + X_{46} + X_{47} = 0$ (8.33)

$-X_{25} - X_{45} + X_{57} = 0$ (8.34)

$-X_{36} - X_{46} + X_{67} = 0$ (8.35)

$-X_{47} - X_{57} - X_{67} = -1$ (8.36)

$$\sum\sum t_{ij} X_{ij} \le T \qquad (8.37)$$

$$X_{ij} = 0, 1 \qquad (8.38)$$

One of the ways to solve this problem is to relax the time constraint and solve the rest of the problem using the Dijkstra's algorithm. If the solution satisfies the time constraint, it is optimal to the constrained shortest path problems. If it does not then we have to use special algorithms because the constrained shortest path problem does not possess the structure of a network problem where the Dijkstra's algorithm can directly be used.

We use the method of Lagrangean Relaxation (Fisher, 1991), where we introduce a multiplier λ and take the time constraint into the objective function. The problem becomes

Minimize $\sum_{i=1}^{n}\sum_{j=1}^{n} C_{ij} X_{ij} + \lambda \sum_{i=1}^{n}\sum_{j=1}^{n} (t_{ij} X_{ij} - T)$

Subject to Eq. (8.30) to Eq. (8.36) and Eq. (8.38)
The objective function can be rewritten as:

Minimize $\sum_{i=1}^{n}\sum_{j=1}^{n} C'_{ij} X_{ij}$

where $C'_{ij} = C_{ij} + \lambda t_{ij}$ for a chosen value of λ. The problem is solved using Dijkstra's algorithm for chosen values of λ till the optimum or a lower bound is found.

While solving the problem for a chosen value of λ is easy, finding the correct value of λ that provides the best objective is not so straightforward. It is also possible to show that the objective function for a chosen value of λ (≥ 0) is a lower bound to the optimum since we are dualizing the constraint by taking it to the objective function. Methods such as subgradient optimization are used to search for the best value of λ. These aspects are not covered in this book. Ahuja et al. (1993) provide a comprehensive treatment of solving the constrained shortest path problem using Lagrangean Relaxation.

8.8 THE MAXIMUM FLOW PROBLEM

The Maximum flow problem is stated as follows:

ILLUSTRATION 8.5

Given a capacitated directed network with a source and a sink, the problem is to find the maximum flow that is possible. The arc weights denote the arc capacities. We illustrate this problem with an example (Figure 8.11).

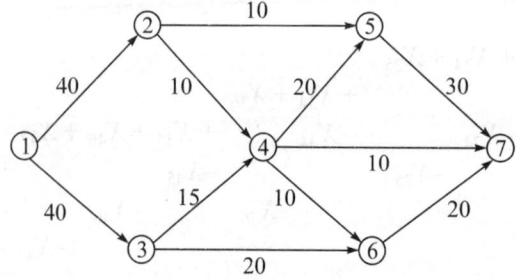

Figure 8.11 Network for maximum flow problem.

Since we are interested in finding the maximum flow in the network, we first find a path from the source to sink. The following paths are available:

1–2–5–7; 1–2–4–7; 1–2–4–5–7; 1–3–6–7; 1–3–4–7; 1–3–4–5–7 and 1–3–4–6–7

We consider the path 1–2–4–5–7. The arc with minimum capacity is 2–4 with 10. This is the maximum flow possible in the path and we augment the flow in each of the arcs to 10. This is given by

$$X_{12} = 10, X_{24} = 10, X_{45} = 10 \text{ and } X_{57} = 10 \text{ with flow} = 10$$

Now, consider the path 1–2–5–7. Arc 1–2 has a remaining capacity of 20, arc 2–4 has a remaining capacity of 10 and 5–7 has a remaining capacity of 20. The maximum possible flow is the minimum of the capacities and we update

$$X_{12} = 20, X_{2-5} = 10 \quad \text{and} \quad X_{57} = 10, \text{Flow} = 10$$

Let us consider the path 1–2–4–7.

Arc 1–2 has a remaining capacity of 20, 2–4 has no remaining capacity and hence we cannot have any flow in this path.

We next consider the path 1–2–4–6–7. Here also we observe that arc 2–4 does not have remaining capacity and, therefore, we cannot increase the flow.

Consider 1–3–4–6–7. 1–3 has a capacity of 40, 3–4 has 15, 4–6 has 10 and 6–7 has 20. We can increase the flow by 10. The solution becomes

$$X_{13} = 10, X_{34} = 10, X_{46} = 10 \quad \text{and} \quad X_{67} = 10, \text{Flow} = 10$$

We consider 1–3–6–7. 1–3 has a remaining capacity of 30, 3–6 has 20 and 6–7 has remaining capacity of 10. This gives us an additional flow = 10 and the solution is:

$$X_{13} = 20, X_{36} = 10 \quad \text{and} \quad X_{67} = 20, \text{Flow} = 10$$

Now, consider 1–3–4–7. Arc 1–3 has a remaining capacity of 20, 3–4 has a remaining capacity of 5 and 4–7 has capacity of 10. We can increase the flow by 5 in this path. The solution is:

$$X_{13} = 25, X_{34} = 15 \quad \text{and} \quad X_{47} = 5, \text{Flow} = 5$$

We have exhausted all the paths and the total flow in the network is given by 45.

Let us repeat the procedure but with a different order of choosing the paths. If we consider paths, 1–3–6–7, 1–2–5–7, 1–2–4–7 and 1–3–4–5–7 in that order, we get a flow of 20 + 10 + 10 + 15 = 55 units. The corresponding flows in the arcs are:

$$X_{12} = 20, X_{13} = 35, X_{25} = 10, X_{24} = 10, X_{34} = 15, X_{36} = 20, X_{45} = 15, X_{46} = 0,$$
$$X_{47} = 10, X_{57} = 25 \text{ and } X_{67} = 20$$

From the above, we conclude that

1. The order in which the paths are chosen is important and different choices can result in different flows.
2. If we need a good method to solve the problem, it should get the maximum flow, independent of the order in which the paths are chosen.

3. Finding all paths in a network may be difficult and we should consider those paths that can increase (or augment) the flow. Such paths are called **flow augmenting paths.** The algorithm should identify flow augmenting paths in polynomial time.

8.8.1 Flow Augmenting Path

A path is flow augmenting if it can increase the flow in the network. Let us consider the same example network with the flows given as follows Figure (8.12):

$$X_{12} = 20, X_{13} = 20, X_{24} = 10, X_{25} = 10, X_{34} = 10, X_{36} = 10, X_{45} = 10, X_{46} = 10,$$
$$X_{57} = 20, X_{67} = 20.$$

The flows and capacities are shown for every arc as (a, b) in the figure.

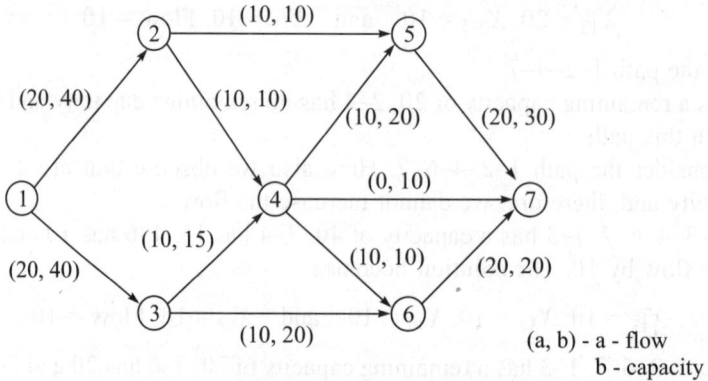

Figure 8.12 Network with flows.

From Figure 8.12 we can identify a path 1–3–4–7. Here all the arcs in the paths have additional capacity. Arc 1–3 can take an additional flow of 20, Arc 3–4 can take an additional 5 and Arc 4–7 can take a flow of 10 units. The additional flow in the path is the minimum of these flows, i.e., 5 units. The flows are updated and shown in Figure 8.13.

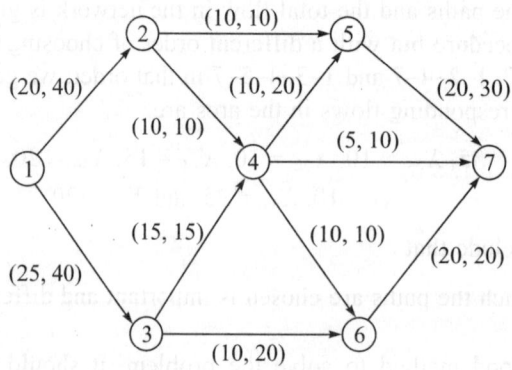

Figure 8.13 Updated flows.

We call the path 1–3–4–7 as a flow augmenting path because we can increase the flow by considering the path. Here all arcs have additional capacity and the flow can be augmented by an amount equal to the minimum of the additional capacities.

Flow augmenting path

A path is flow augmenting if its all arcs have additional (spare) capacity. The augmented flow is the minimum of the spare capacities of the arcs.

We also observe that we cannot identify any more flow augmenting path of the type we have just defined because all the paths have at least one arc whose flow cannot be increased.

Let us consider the path 1–3–6–4–7. This is not a valid path because flow from 6–4 is not allowed. However, in the chosen path we observe that in the arcs where flow is allowed, i.e., 1–3, 3–6, 4–7 flow can be increased in the direction allowed and in the arc 6–4 where flow is not allowed, there is a flow in the allowed direction 4–6, which can be decreased (or shifted). We call this path also as a **flow augmenting path**.

We observe that the minimum flow that can be increased by considering 1–3, 3–6, and 4–7 is 10 and the flow that can be taken from 4–6 is 5. The net increase will be the minimum of these, which is 5. The flow in the network increases by 5 and the individual flows are:

$$X_{13} = 30, X_{36} = 15, X_{46} = 5, X_{47} = 10$$

We have reduced the flow 4–6 from 10 to 5. This is called **backward flow** and since we are introducing flow in the direction 6–4, we remove that the amount of flow in the allowed direction 4–6 (where there is a flow).

The flows in the network are shown below in Figure 8.14.

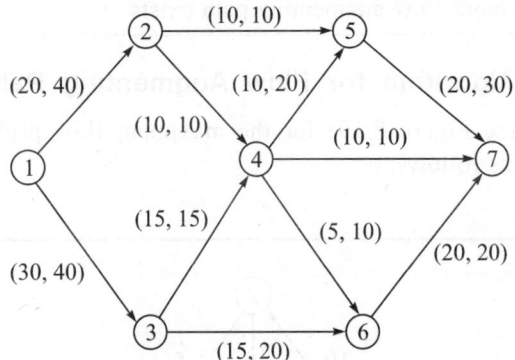

Figure 8.14 Updated flows.

This is equivalent to redistributing a flow of 5 from 4–6 and 6–7 to 4–7 (previous figure) and creating a capacity of 5 in 6–7 so that an additional 5 can be sent in the path 1–2–6–7. Every flow augmenting path involving a backward arc is actually equivalent to redistributing existing flows to create a path that can accommodate additional flow.

In a similar manner we can identify another flow augmenting path with a backward arc 1–3–6–4–5–7 with arc 4–6 being a backward arc. A flow of 5 is possible through this path and the flow in the network increases to 55. The final flows are shown in Figure 8.15.

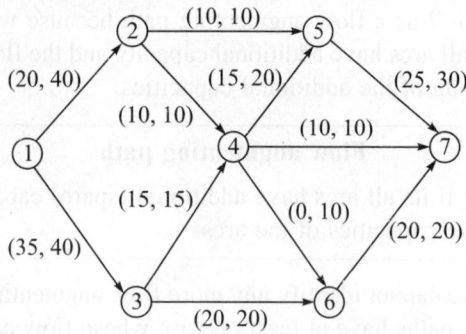

Figure 8.15 Final solution to the maximum flow problem.

Flow augmenting path

A path is flow augmenting when
1. All its arcs allow flow in the forward direction and have additional (spare) capacity. The augmented flow is the minimum of the spare capacities of the arcs.
2. Arcs are forward or backward. A backward arc means that we are considering flow in the direction opposite to the allowed direction. All forward arcs should have spare capacity while all backward arcs should have flows in the allowed direction. The augmented flow is the minimum of the spare capacities of the arcs (in forward direction) and the minimum of the flows of the backward arcs.

Flow augmenting path algorithm

1. Identify a flow augmenting path and increase the flow in the network.
2. Terminate when no more flow augmenting path exists.

8.8.2 A Labelling Algorithm for Flow Augmenting Path

A labelling algorithm (see Figure 8.16) for the maximum flow problem based on the flow augmenting algorithm is as follows:

ILLUSTRATION 8.6

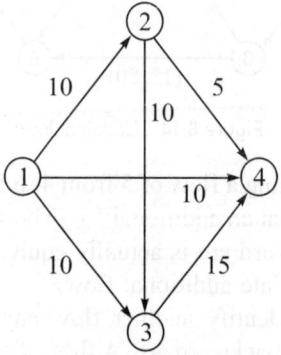

Figure 8.16 Network for maximum flow problem.

> **Flow augmenting path—A labelling algorithm**
>
> Initialize $X_{ij} = 0$ for all arcs.
> 1. Set $L(1) = [-, \infty]$
> 2. If node i is labelled and node j is not and $X_{ij} < U_{ij}$, set $L(j) = [+i, \Delta_j]$ where Δ_j is Minimum $\{\Delta_i, U_{ij} - X_{ij}\}$. If node i is labelled and node j is not and $X_{ji} > 0$, set $L(j) = [-i, \Delta_j]$ where Δ_j is Minimum $\{\Delta_i, X_{ji}\}$. Repeat Step 2 till node m is labelled or no more node can be labelled.
> 3. If node m is not labelled, STOP. The solution has been found. If node m is labelled, update the solution as follows:
>
> Set $\Delta = \Delta_m$. If the first entry of node m is $+k$, add Δ_m to the flow X_{km}. If the first entry is $-k$, subtract Δ_m from X_{mk}. Backtrack and repeat till Node 1 is reached. Go to Step 1.

In the above algorithm, U_{ij} represents the maximum allowable flow in Arc i–j and there are m nodes in the network with Node 1 as source and node m as sink.

We illustrate the labelling algorithm (Bazaara et al., 1990) using the example in Figure 8.16.

Iteration 1

All $X_{ij} = 0$

$L(1) = [-, \infty]$. $L(2)$ is not labelled and $X_{12} < U_{12}$. We label $L(2) = [+1, 10]$. Label $L(3)$ is not labelled and $X_{23} < U_{23}$. We label $L(3) = [+2, 10]$. Node $L(4)$ is not labelled and $X_{34} < U_{34}$. We label Node $L(4) = [+3, 10]$. Though $U_{34} - X_{34} = 15$, we choose the minimum of $[15, L(3)]$ and label $L(4)$ with 10. Node m is labelled. We update the flows.

Now, $$X_{34} = X_{23} = X_{12} = \Delta_4 = 10$$

Iteration 2

$L(1) = [-, \infty]$. $L(2)$ is not labelled but $X_{12} = U_{12}$. We, therefore, do not consider Node 2. Node 3 is not labelled and $X_{13} < U_{13}$. We label $L(3) = [+1, 10]$. Node $L(4)$ is not labelled and X_{34} ($=10$) $< U_{34}$ ($=15$). We label $L(4) = [+3, 5]$ because $U_{34} - X_{34} = 5$, which is smaller than Label 3. Node is labelled now. We update the flows.

$$X_{13} = \Delta_4 = 5, X_{34} = 10 + \Delta_4 = 15$$

Iteration 3

$L(1) = [-, \infty]$. $L(2)$ cannot be labelled because $X_{12} = U_{12}$. Node 3 is not labelled and $X_{13} < U_{13}$. We label $L(3) = [+1, 5]$, which is the value of $U_{13} - X_{13}$. Node $L(4)$ cannot be from 3 because $X_{34} = U_{34}$. We can label Node 2 from 3 because X_{23} has a positive flow. We label Node 3 as $L(3) = [-2, 5]$ considering that the backward flow of 10 is less than the value of Node 3. Node 4 can be labelled from 2 since $X_{24} < U_{24}$. $L(4) = [+2, 5]$.

$$X_{13} = 5 + \Delta_4 = 10, X_{23} = 10 - \Delta_4 = 5, X_{24} = \Delta_4 = 5$$

Iteration 4

$L(1) = [-, \infty]$. We cannot label Node 2 because $X_{12} = U_{12}$. We cannot label Node 3 because $X_{13} = U_{13}$. We can label Node 4 from Node 1 because $X_{14} < U_{14}$. $L(4) = [+1, 10]$. We update the flows

$$X_{14} = \Delta_4 = 10$$
$$\text{Total flow} = 10 + 5 + 5 + 10 = 30$$

Iteration 5

$L(1) = [-, \infty]$. We cannot label Nodes 2, 3 and 4 because they have $X_{ij} = U_{ij}$. The algorithm terminate with a maximum flow of 30.

8.8.3 Maximum Flow and Minimum Cut

There exists a relationship between the maximum flow in the network and the minimum cut (or cut set). We explain this relationship in this section and validate it using primal-dual relationship. Let us take the same example and explain the concept of a cut.

The network, shown in Figure 8.17, has seven nodes. A cut represents two sets into which the seven nodes are separated. Node 1 (source) is always in the first set and Node 7 (sink) is always in the second set.

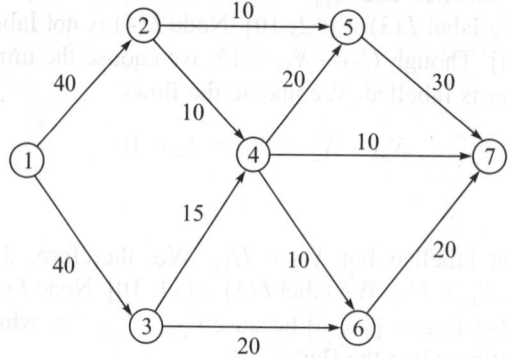

Figure 8.17 Example for maximum flow problem to explain a "cut".

For example, a cut set could be $S_1 = \{1, 2, 3, 4\}$ and $S_2 = \{5, 6, 7\}$. This means that the edges connecting the sets 2–5, 3–6, 4–5, 4–6, and 4–7 are removed from the network so that there is no flow possible between the two sets. The sum of the arc capacities is $10 + 20 + 20 + 10 + 10 = 70$ and represents the value of the cut.

For example, a cut $S_1 = \{1\}$ and $S_2 = \{2, 3, 4, 5, 6, 7\}$ have a capacity of the weights of arcs 1–2 and 1–3 = 80. A cut $S_1 = \{1, 2, 3, 4, 5, 6\}$ and $S_2 = \{7\}$ has a value of $30 + 10 + 20 = 55$.

A cut $S_1 = \{1, 3, 5\}$ and $S_2 = \{2, 4, 6, 7\}$ means that arcs 1–2, 3–4, 3–6, and 5–7 are removed. The capacity is $40 + 15 + 20 + 30 = 105$.

There exist many cuts for a given network. The capacity of each can be found. The relationship between the maximum flow and the cut is as follows:

Maximum flow minimum cut theorem (Ford and Fulkerson, 1962)
In any network the value of the maximum flow is equal to the cut with minimum value.

In our example network, the maximum flow was 55 and the arcs that had flows equal to their capacities were 2–4, 2–5, 3–4, 3–6 with a capacity of 55 (see Figure 8.18).

This gives us a corresponding cut set with $S_1 = \{1, 2, 3\}$ and $S_2 = \{4, 5, 6, 7\}$. Though arcs 4–7 and 6–7 also have flow equal to their capacity, their capacities are not included because Nodes 4, 6, and 7 belong to set S_2.

Therefore, the cut set $S_1 = \{1, 2, 3\}$ and $S_2 = \{4, 5, 6, 7\}$ is the optimal cut set.

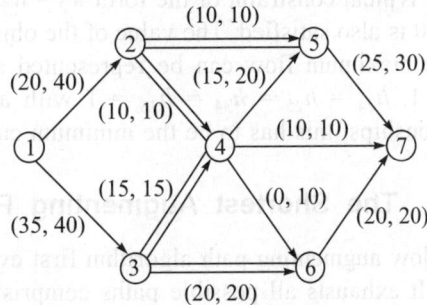

Figure 8.18   Minimum cut corresponding to maximum flow.

The maximum flow minimum cut theorem can also be explained using primal dual relationships. Let us write the primal to the maximum flow example.

Maximize f
Such that
$$X_{12} + X_{13} - f = 0$$
$$-X_{12} + X_{24} + X_{25} = 0$$
$$-X_{13} + X_{34} + X_{36} = 0$$
$$-X_{24} - X_{34} + X_{45} + X_{46} + X_{47} = 0$$
$$-X_{25} - X_{45} + X_{57} = 0$$
$$-X_{36} - X_{46} + X_{67} = 0$$
$$-X_{47} - X_{57} - X_{67} + f = 0$$
$$X_{ij} \le U_{ij}$$

$X_{ij} \ge 0$ and f is unrestricted in sign
(In the above formulation we assume f as unrestricted in sign, although $f \ge 0$ when $X_{ij} \ge 0$.)

We now write the dual to the above formulation assuming w_1 to w_7 to be the dual variables corresponding to the nodes and h_{ij} as variables corresponding to the arcs (upper bound constraints). The dual is:

Minimize $\sum_{i=1}^{n} \sum_{j=1}^{n} u_{ij} h_{ij}$

Subject to
$$w_i - w_j + h_{ij} \ge 0$$
$$w_7 - w_1 = 1$$

w_i unrestricted in sign, $h_{ij} \ge 0$

We can show that every cut is a feasible solution to the dual of the maximum flow problem. For example, the cut set $S_1 = \{1, 2, 3, 4\}$ and $S_2 = \{5, 6, 7\}$ with a capacity of 70 (given by the capacities of the arcs 2–5, 3–6, 4–5, 4–6 and 4–7) can be represented by the dual feasible solution.

$w_7 = 1$, $w_1 = 0$, $h_{25} = h_{36} = h_{45} = h_{46} = h_{47} = 1$, $w_2 = w_3 = w_4 = 0$ and $w_5 = w_6 = 1$

A typical constraint of the form $w_2 - w_5 + h_{25} \geq 0$ is satisfied. Another constraint $w_1 - w_2 + h_{12} \geq 0$ is also satisfied. The value of the objective function is 70. Similarly, the optimal solution to the maximum flow can be represented as a solution $w_1 = w_2 = w_3 = 0$, $w_4 = w_5 = w_6 = w_7 = 1$. $h_{24} = h_{25} = h_{34} = h_{36} = 1$ with an objective function value of 55. By primal dual relationships, this has to be the minimum cut. Hence the maximum flow equals minimum cut.

8.8.4 The Shortest Augmenting Path Algorithm

The flow augmenting path algorithm first evaluates all the paths in the network in a systematic way. It exhausts all possible paths comprising entirely forward arcs and then tries to identify whether an augmenting path comprising a backward arc can further increase the flow. It terminates when no more flow augmenting path can be identified.

It is also true that whenever a flow augmenting path considers a backward arc, it should have used at least one flow augmenting path that did not have a backward arc. This is true because any path involving backward arcs can increase flow by diverting some existing flow. The first flow augmenting path will always have only forward arcs. It is also true that there exists a correct order of paths such that the optimal solution can be found without evaluating any backward arc path. Therefore it is possible to improve the flow augmenting path algorithm to provide the optimum solution without evaluating any path with backward arcs.

It is not absolutely necessary that flow augmenting paths with backward flow arcs should be considered only after exhausting all augmenting paths with only forward arcs. It is possible to consider backward arc flows immediately after the first path is augmented.

There is yet another limitation of the flow augmenting path algorithm. This is explained through Illustration 8.7.

ILLUSTRATION 8.7

Find the maximum flow in the network given in Figure 8.19.

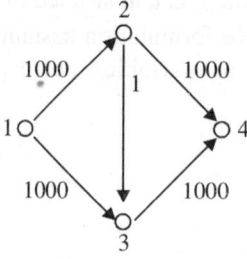

Figure 8.19 Network for maximum flow problem.

Arc 2–3 has a capacity of one while 1–2, 1–3, 2–4 and 3–4 have capacity of 1000. We can start with a flow augmenting path 1–2–3–4 and send 1 unit of flow. We can use the flow augmenting path 1–3–2–4 and send 1 extra unit to 4. These can be repeated 1000 times to finally send 2000 units from 1 to 4. On the other hand, two paths 1–2–4 and 1–3–4 can each send 1000 units and in two evaluations we can send the same 2000 units. The flow augmenting path algorithm can compute a large number of iterations running into pseudo polynomial complexity of $O(nC)$ where n is the number of nodes and C is the maximum capacity of any arc.

Some important points to be noted from the above example are

1. We can first evaluate all flow augmenting paths containing only forward path arcs and then consider paths with backward arcs.
2. Evaluating all the paths in a network can be non polynomial. There is a need to develop an algorithm that runs in polynomial time. We do have an LP formulation for the maximum flow problem and hence can have an algorithm that runs in polynomial time
3. Whenever a backward arc path augments the flow, it means that either there exists a path made up of entirely forward arcs that can at present augment the flow or there was a wrong choice of order of the paths where a path with more number of forward arcs was considered ahead of a path with lesser number of forward arcs. This is because the backward arc path effectively diverts flow from the longer path to the shorter path (in terms of number of edges).

This motivation led to the development of the shortest augmenting path algorithm where a path with least number of arcs is considered among the candidates. A polynomial time algorithm was developed for the same. The algorithm is explained using Illustration 8.8.

ILLUSTRATION 8.8

Compute the maximum flow in the network shown in Figure 8.20.

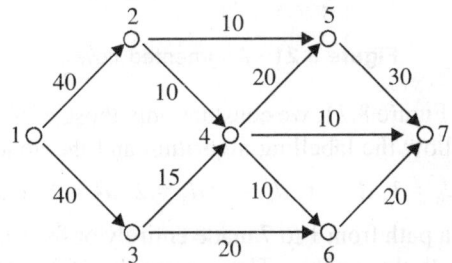

Figure 8.20 Network for maximum flow problem.

We first label the nodes 1 to 7 with labels d_1 to d_7. The relationships among the labels are

Node Labels
$d_{\text{sink}} = 0$
$d_i \le d_j + 1$ for all arcs in G that have $r_{ij} > 0$

Iteration 1

G represents the given network. The residual flow r_{ij} represents the flow that can be increased in arc i–j. To begin with, all arcs in G have $r_{ij} > 0$. The initial labels are

$d_7 = 0$, $d_6 = 1$, $d_5 = 1$, $d_4 = 1$, $d_3 = 2$, $d_2 = 2$ and $d_1 = 3$.

Nodes 5 and 6 get a label of 1 because there are arcs 5–7 and 6–7. Considering node 4, we have arcs 4–5, 4–6 and 4–7. Therefore $d_4 \leq 2$ (considering node 5), $d_4 \leq 1$ (considering node 6) and $d_4 \leq 1$ (considering node 7). The smallest value d_4 can take is 1 and therefore it is labelled as 1.

Node 1 gets a label $d_1 = 3$. This shows that there is a path from 1 to 7 containing 3 forward arcs that can augment the flow. We have to find that path. In our example it could be any one of 1–2–4–7, 1–2–5–7, 1–3–4–7 and 1–3–6–7.

(Even though we have a path 1–2–4–5–7 that can augment the flow, we do not consider this path at this stage because it contains 4 arcs. The label $d_1 = 3$ tells us about the existence of a path with three edges. It also gives us the shortest length path in terms of number of arcs travelled).

Let us consider the path 1–2–4–7 and augment the flow. Now, flow = minimum {40, 10, 10} = 10. We have $X_{12} = X_{24} = X_{47} = 10$.

Iteration 2

The network given in Figure 8.21 shows the flows augmented.

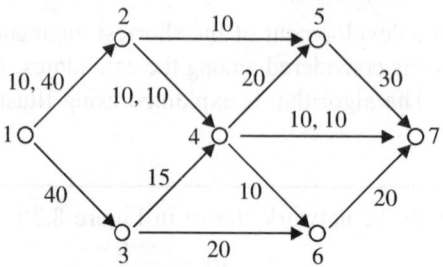

Figure 8.21 Augmented flows.

In the network shown in Figure 8.21, we consider only those arcs (and all the nodes) that have forward arc residues. We follow the labelling algorithm and the node labels are

$$d_7 = 0, d_6 = 1, d_5 = 1, d_4 = 2, d_3 = 2, d_2 = 2 \text{ and } d_1 = 3.$$

This shows that there is a path from 1 to 7 made entirely of forward arcs. This can be the path 1–2–5–7 or 1–3–6–7 both with three edges. These paths do not have any backward arcs because the backward arc residues are not included in Figure 8.21. Also every augmenting path with backward arcs would have length equal to four or more in our illustration (example 1–3–4–2–5–7 in Figure 8.21).

We update the flows considering the path 1–3–6–7 and the total flow becomes 30. The solution is $X_{12} = X_{24} = X_{47} = 10$ and $X_{13} = X_{36} = X_{67} = 20$.

Iteration 3

We again follow the labeling procedure to obtain the labels. The network with the augmented flows is shown in Figure 8.22.

$$d_7 = 0, d_5 = 1, d_4 = 2, d_3 = 3, d_2 = 2 \text{ and } d_1 = 3.$$

We identify a path 1–2–5–7 from Figure 8.22 with flow = 10 made of entirely forward arcs. The total flow is now 40. The solution is $X_{12} = 20$, $X_{24} = X_{47} = X_{25} = X_{57} = 10$ and $X_{13} = X_{36} = X_{67} = 20$.

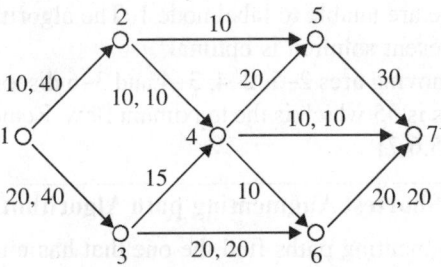

Figure 8.22 Augmented flows.

Iteration 4

We again follow the labelling procedure to obtain the labels. The network with augmented flows is shown in Figure 8.23.

$$d_7 = 0, d_5 = 1, d_4 = 2, d_3 = 3, \text{ and } d_1 = 4.$$

We identify a path 1–3–4–5–7 from Figure 8.23 with flow = 15 made of entirely forward arcs. The total flow is now 55. The solution is $X_{12} = 20, X_{24} = X_{47} = X_{25} = 10$ and $X_{13} = 35, X_{34} = 15, X_{45} = 15, X_{57} = 25, X_{36} = X_{67} = 20$.

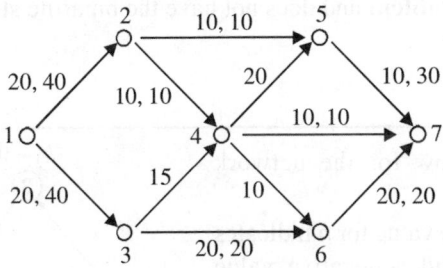

Figure 8.23 Augmented flows.

Iteration 5

We again follow the labeling scheme to obtain the labels. The network with only forward arcs and augmented flows is shown in Figure 8.24.

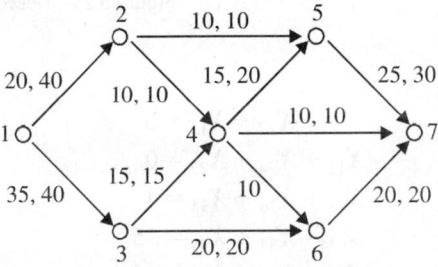

Figure 8.24 Augmented flows and optimal solution.

$d_7 = 0$, $d_5 = 1$, $d_4 = 2$. We are unable to label node 1. The algorithm terminates because node 1 cannot be labelled. The present solution is optimal.

We also observe that removing arcs 2–5, 2–4, 3–4 and 3–6 disconnects the network. The sum of the capacities of these arcs is 55 which is the maximum flow. Removing these arcs gives us the optimum cut set {1,2,3} {4,5,6,7}.

Shortest Augmenting path Algorithm

1. Among the flow augmenting paths find the one that has minimum number of arcs.
2. Augment the flow using the above shortest augmenting path.
3. Repeat steps 1 and 2 till no more augmenting path exists.

8.9 MINIMUM COST FLOW PROBLEM—TRANSSHIPMENT PROBLEM

The minimum cost flow in a network is defined as follows:

Given a network with *m* nodes, each acting as a source or sink or intermediate node, the problem is to find the least cost transportation of a single commodity such that the demands of the sinks are met. The difference between this problem and the transportation problem is that here transportation between two source points is also allowed if it is cheaper. This problem is also called the **transshipment problem** and does not have the bipartite structure of the transportation problem.

ILLUSTRATION 8.9

Find the minimum cost flow for the network shown in Figure 8.25.

In Figure 8.25, a positive value for *b* indicates that it is a supply point and a negative value indicates that the point is a demand point. The problem is balanced such that the total supply and total demand are equal to 10 units. For the given example, the minimum cost flow problem can be formulated as:

Figure 8.25 Network for minimum cost flow problem.

Minimize $\sum_{i=1}^{n} \sum_{j=1}^{n} C_{ij} X_{ij}$

Subject to

$$X_{12} + X_{13} = 6$$
$$-X_{12} + X_{24} + X_{25} = 0$$
$$-X_{13} + X_{34} + X_{35} = 4$$
$$-X_{24} - X_{34} + X_{45} = -5$$
$$-X_{25} - X_{35} - X_{45} = -5$$
$$X_{ij} \geq 0$$

X_{ij} represents the quantity transported from Node *i* to Node *j*.

Let us consider a feasible solution given by $X_{12} = 6$, $X_{24} = 6$, $X_{34} = 4$ and $X_{45} = 5$ with $Z = 122$. Let us verify whether this is optimal. We define values for w_1 to w_5. The value of w_5 is fixed at zero and w_i is written such that

$$w_i - w_j = C_{ij}$$

where

$$X_{ij} \geq 0.$$

We have $w_4 = 4$, $w_3 = 10$, $w_2 = 9$ and $w_1 = 17$. We calculate $w_i - w_j - C_{ij}$ where $X_{ij} = 0$.

For $X_{13} = 0$, $w_1 - w_3 - C_{13} = 17 - 10 - 6 = 1$
For $X_{25} = 0$, $w_2 - w_5 - C_{25} = 9 - 0 - 7 = 2$
For $X_{35} = 0$, $w_3 - w_5 - C_{35} = 10 - 0 - 3 = 7$

The maximum positive value is for variable X_{35}. This enters the basis and is indicated by θ. The solution is given in Figure 8.26.

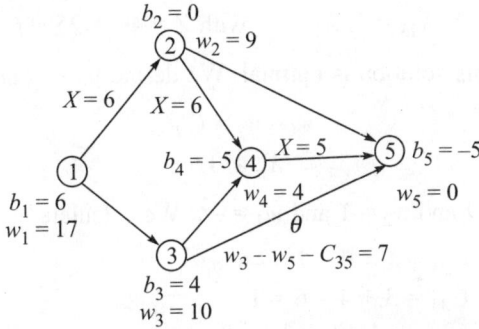

Figure 8.26 A basic feasible solution and improvement.

Entering variable X_{35} into the solution with flow $= \theta$ would make $X_{34} = 4 - \theta$ and $X_{45} = 5 - \theta$ for flow balance. The maximum value that θ can take is 4 and the solution becomes

$$X_{12} = 6, X_{24} = 6, X_{45} = 1 \quad \text{and} \quad X_{35} = 4 \text{ with } Z = 48 + 30 + 4 + 12 = 94$$

We wish to verify if this solution is optimal. We define $w_5 = 0$ and w_i is written such that

$$w_i - w_j = C_{ij}$$

where

$$X_{ij} \geq 0.$$

We have $w_4 = 4$, $w_3 = 3$, $w_2 = 9$ and $w_1 = 17$. We calculate $w_i - w_j - C_{ij}$ where $X_{ij} = 0$.

For $X_{13} = 0$, $w_1 - w_3 - C_{13} = 17 - 3 - 6 = 8$
For $X_{25} = 0$, $w_2 - w_5 - C_{25} = 9 - 0 - 7 = 2$
For $X_{34} = 0$, $w_3 - w_4 - C_{34} = 3 - 4 - 6 = -7$

The maximum positive value is for variable X_{13}. This enters the basis and is indicated by θ. The solution is given in Figure 8.27.

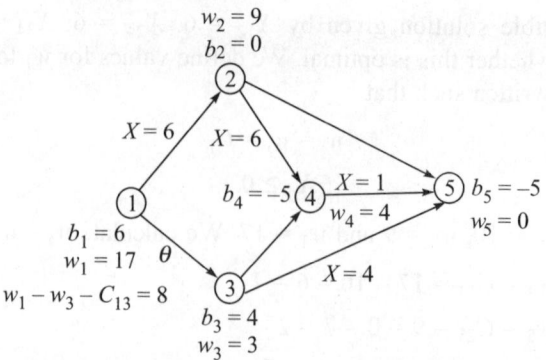

Figure 8.27 Improved solution. X_{13} enters the basis.

Entering variable X_{13} with θ would make $X_{35} = 4 + \theta$, $X_{12} = 6 - \theta$, $X_{24} = 6 - \theta$ and $X_{45} = 1 - \theta$. The minimum value that θ can take is 1 and the solution becomes

$$X_{12} = X_{24} = 5, X_{13} = 1, X_{35} = 5 \text{ with } Z = 40 + 25 + 6 + 15 = 86$$

We wish to verify if this solution is optimal. We define $w_5 = 0$ and w_i is written such that

$$w_i - w_j = C_{ij}$$

where
$$X_{ij} \geq 0$$

We have $w_3 = 3$, $w_1 = 9$ and $w_2 = 1$ and $w_4 = -4$. We calculate $w_i - w_j - C_{ij}$ where $X_{ij} = 0$.

For $X_{25} = 0$, $w_2 - w_5 - C_{25} = 1 - 0 - 7 = -6$
For $X_{34} = 0$, $w_3 - w_4 - C_{34} = 3 + 4 - 6 = 1$
For $X_{45} = 0$, $w_4 - w_5 - C_{45} = -4 - 0 - 4 = -8$

The maximum positive value is for variable X_{34}. This enters the basis and is indicated by θ. The solution is given in Figure 8.28.

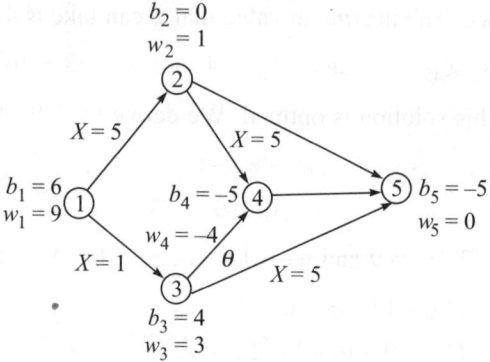

Figure 8.28 Further improvement in the solution.

Entering variable X_{35} with θ would make $X_{25} = 5 - \theta$, $X_{12} = 5 - \theta$, $X_{24} = 5 - \theta$ and $X_{13} = 1 + \theta$. The minimum value that θ can take is 5 and the solution becomes

$$X_{13} = 6, X_{34} = 5, X_{35} = 5 \text{ with } Z = 36 + 30 + 15 = 81$$

We wish to verify if this solution is optimal. We define $w_5 = 0$ and w_i is written such that

$$w_i - w_j = C_{ij}$$

where

$$X_{ij} \geq 0.$$

We have $w_3 = 3$, $w_4 = -3$, $w_1 = 9$. We have only three basic variables and, therefore, have a degenerate solution. We assume that X_{24} is basic with $X_{24} = 0$. This gives $w_2 = 2$. We calculate $w_i - w_j - C_{ij}$ where $X_{ij} = 0$.

For $X_{12} = 0$, $w_1 - w_2 - C_{12} = 9 - 2 - 8 = -1$
For $X_{25} = 0$, $w_2 - w_5 - C_{25} = 2 - 0 - 7 = -5$
For $X_{45} = 0$, $w_4 - w_5 - C_{45} = -3 - 0 - 4 = -7$

All the values are negative and the solution $X_{13} = 6$, $X_{34} = 5$, $X_{35} = 5$ with $Z = 36 + 30 + 15 = 81$ is optimal. We also observe that the optimal solution is degenerate since we have three basic variables with positive values at the optimum against four variables in the earlier iterations.

The above algorithm is called the **network simplex algorithm.** It is able to capture the steps of the simplex algorithm in the network itself.

(In our example, we started with a given basic feasible solution. One of the ways of getting a starting basic feasible solution is to create a dummy node to which all supply and demand nodes are connected. The new dummy arcs can have a cost M. A starting basic feasible solution would be to transport all the supplies to the dummy node and to meet all the demand from the dummy node. The network simplex algorithm is applied in a manner similar to the two-phase method of linear programming to get a basic feasible solution not involving the dummy arcs. Once this solution is obtained, the dummy node and all dummy arcs can be deleted and the network simplex algorithm can be applied to get the optimal solution.)

8.9.1 Optimality of the Network Simplex Method

We introduce dual variables w_i, $i = 1, n$ for the nodes. The dual constraints are of the form.

$$w_i - w_j \leq C_{ij}, w_i \text{ unrestricted in sign}$$

We also have a linearly dependent system as in the transportation problem, if the given minimum cost flow is balanced (total supply equals total demand). Therefore, one of the dual variables (w_n) is fixed to an arbitrary value of zero. Wherever there is a transportation ($X_{ij} > 0$ and basic), we compute the value of w_j using the relation $w_i - w_j = C_{ij}$. This satisfies complimentary slackness conditions because the dual slack variables are forced to be zero (the constraint is treated as an equation) when the corresponding primal variables are basic. For all the non-basic X_{ij} (where there is no flow), we calculate the dual feasibility by evaluation of the dual slack (calculate $w_i - w_j - C_{ij}$). If the dual slack is negative, it implies dual feasibility because $w_i - w_j < C_{ij}$. If the value of $w_i - w_j - C_{ij} > 0$, it means that the dual constraint is violated by the values of w_j and that the corresponding primal can enter the basis. The value of the entering variable is given by θ as in the transportation problem.

Finally for the computed values of w_j, if all $w_i - w_j - C_{ij} < 0$, the dual is feasible and, therefore, the primal basic feasible solution is optimal.

8.9.2 A Transportation Model for the Problem

We illustrate the transportation model for our example problem (see Figure 8.29).

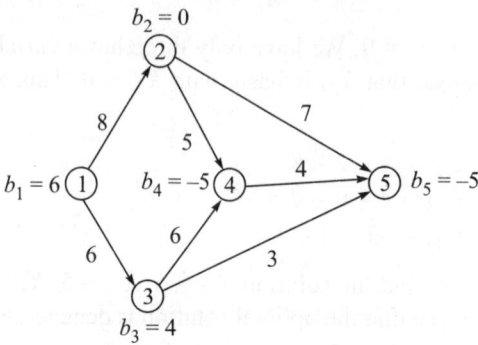

Figure 8.29 Network for transportation model of minimum cost flow problem.

There are five nodes out of which two are supply nodes and two are demand points. Since we can transport from one supply point to another and from one demand point to another, each point can become a supply and demand. We, therefore, create a 5 × 5 transportation problem with each capable of supplying an additional 10 units (the total supply and total demand). We also define the cost of transporting from a point to itself is zero. Where transportation is not possible (if there is no arc in the network), we have a large transportation cost (=M). The transportation table is shown in Table 8.2.

Table 8.2 Transportation Table

0	8	6	M	M	16
M	0	M	5	7	10
M	M	0	6	3	14
M	M	M	0	4	10
M	M	M	M	0	10
10	10	10	15	15	

Node 1 with an original supply of 6 has a supply of 16 while Node 3 now has a supply of 15. Node 4 with an original demand of 5 now has a demand of 15 and so on. All the points get a total of 10 units added to their actual supplies and demands.

The above transportation problem is solved and the optimal solution is $X_{11} = X_{22} = X_{44} = X_{55} = 10$, $X_{13} = 6$, $X_{33} = 4$, $X_{34} = 5$, $X_{35} = 5$ with an objective function value of 81. The solution to the transportation problem is degenerate (as in the network simplex algorithm).

The solution to the minimum cost flow problem (Transshipment problem) is $X_{13} = 6$, $X_{34} = 5$ and $X_{45} = 5$ with $Z = 81$. We leave out all self assignments (X_{jj}) that have zero cost and the rest forms the solution. This is the same solution obtained using the network simplex algorithm.

SOLVED EXAMPLES

EXAMPLE 8.1 A person wants to travel from City 1 to City 6. The network arcs are given in Table 8.3 along with the cost data.

Table 8.3 Network Arcs with Cost

Arc	Cost	Arc	Cost	Arc	Cost	Arc	Cost
1–2	1	2–4	1	3–5	12	5–6	2
1–3	10	2–5	2	4–5	10		
3–2	1	3–4	5	4–6	1		

(a) Find the least cost path from 1 to 6?
(b) Find the second shortest path for the problem?

Solution: (a) The shortest cost path from 1 to 6 by Dijkstra's algorithm is 1–2–4–6 with cost = 3. The time taken is 10 + 1 + 1 = 12 > 10. Figure 8.24 shows the network and the computations.

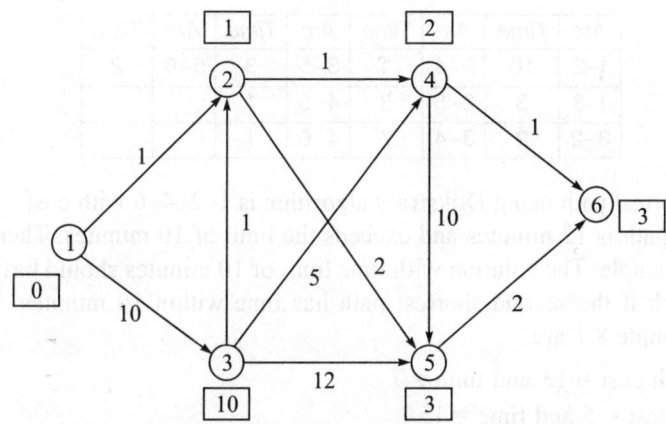

Figure 8.30 Network for shortest path problem and computations.

(b) We find the second shortest path by fixing 1–2, 2–4 and 4–6 to ∞. The first of the three where $C_{12} = \infty$ is shown in Figure 8.31.
Applying Dijkstra's algorithm, we get three solutions

1–3–2–4–6 with cost = 13
1–2–5–6 with cost = 5
1–2–5–6 with cost = 5

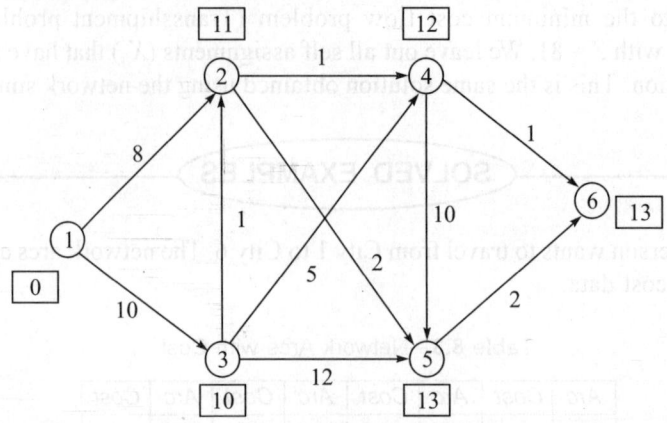

Figure 8.31 Shortest path not involving 1–2.

The second shortest path is the one with minimum cost among these solutions. It is the path 1–2–5–6 with cost = 13.

EXAMPLE 8.2 Consider the same data in Table 8.3. The time taken (in minutes) to travel the arcs are given in Table 8.4. If there is an additional restriction that the time taken should not exceed 10 minutes, find the solution to the Shortest path problem.

Table 8.4 Time Taken to Travel the Arcs

Arc	Time	Arc	Time	Arc	Time	Arc	Time
1–2	10	2–4	1	3–5	3	5–6	2
1–3	3	2–5	3	4–5	1		
3–2	2	3–4	7	4–6	1		

Solution: The shortest path using Dijkstra's algorithm is 1–2–4–6 with cost = 3. However, the time taken for this path is 12 minutes and exceeds the limit of 10 minutes. There is no alternate optimum for this example. The solution with time limit of 10 minutes should have cost more than three. We can check if the second shortest path has time within 10 minutes. The two distinct solutions from Example 8.1 are:

1–3–2–4–6 with cost = 13 and time = 7
1–2–5–6 with cost = 5 and time = 15

We observe that any solution having 1–2 has a cost more than 10. The only other arc from 1 being 3, the solution 1–3–2–4–6 with cost = 13 and time = 7 is the best solution with time ≤ 10.

The above method of solving the constrained shortest path problem may not be the most efficient way particularly if it leads us to some *k*th shortest path. We also observe that we cannot directly solve the problem including the constraints by the Dijkstra's algorithm. Let us formulate the constrained shortest path problem for this example as follows:

Minimize $\sum_{i=1}^{n}\sum_{j=1}^{n} C_{ij} X_{ij}$

Subject to

$$X_{12} + X_{13} = 1$$
$$-X_{12} - X_{32} + X_{24} + X_{25} = 0$$
$$-X_{13} + X_{32} + X_{34} + X_{35} = 0$$
$$-X_{24} - X_{34} + X_{45} + X_{46} = 0$$
$$-X_{25} - X_{35} - X_{45} + X_{56} = 0$$
$$-X_{46} - X_{56} = -1$$
$$\sum_{i=1}^{n}\sum_{j=1}^{n} t_{ij} X_{ij} \leq 10$$
$$X_{ij} = 0, 1$$

If we introduce a multiplier λ and take the time constraint into the objective function, our formulation becomes

Minimize $\sum_{i=1}^{n}\sum_{j=1}^{n} C_{ij} X_{ij} + \lambda \left(\sum_{i=1}^{n}\sum_{j=1}^{n} t_{ij} x_{ij} - 10 \right)$

subject to the same constraints. Here λ is another variable that has been used to dualize the constraint (move it into the objective function). While the new objective function becomes non-linear considering X_{ij} and λ, it becomes easier to solve for a chosen value of λ. For a chosen value of λ, the objective function becomes

Minimize $\sum_{i=1}^{n}\sum_{j=1}^{n} (C_{ij} + \lambda t_{ij}) X_{ij}$

For a chosen λ, we can solve the problem using the Dijkstra's algorithm. We observe that for $\lambda = 4$, we get the solution 1–3–2–4–6 with cost = 13 and time = 7, which we know is the optimal solution to the constrained shortest path problem.

(The method that we have outlined here is called **Lagrangean relaxation**. The reader should observe that we have not outlined a procedure to determine the optimal value of λ here. We have only attempted to introduce the concept. Methods such as subgradient optimization are available to solve the Lagrangean problem. These are not covered in this book).

EXAMPLE 8.3 A machine shop contains an expensive drill press that must be replaced periodically. The replacement plan for seven years is to be considered. The cost, salvage value and maintenance expenditure are given in Table 8.5.

Table 8.5 Cost, Salvage Value and Maintenance Expenditure

	1	2	3	4	5	6	7
New	100	105	110	115	120	125	130
Salvage	50	25	10	5	2	1	–
Operating Expense	30	40	50	50	60	70	100

Formulate a shortest path problem for the above situation and solve.

Solution: Figure 8.32 shows the network and the node labels when Dijkstra's algorithm is applied to solve the problem. Table 8.6 shows the distances among the nodes of the network.

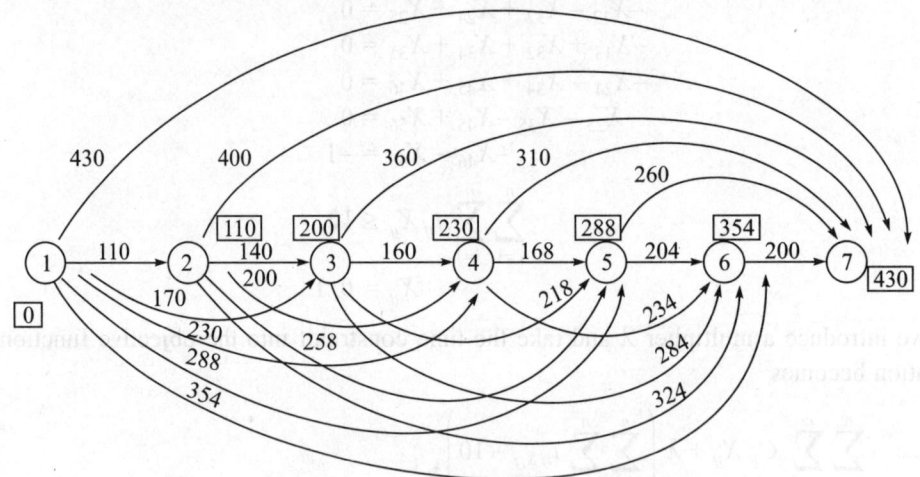

Figure 8.32 Shortest path formulation of equipment replacement problem.

Table 8.6 Distances among the Nodes of the Network

	2	3	4	5	6	7
1	110	170	230	288	354	430
2		140	200	258	324	400
3			160	218	284	360
4				168	234	310
5					204	260
6						200

Shortest path from 1 to 7 computed using Dijkstara's algorithm is 1–7 with cost = **430.**

EXAMPLE 8.4 Consider the shortest path problem with eight vertices. The arcs and the costs are given in Table 8.7.

Table 8.7 Arcs and Costs

Arc	Cost	Arc	Cost	Arc	Cost	Arc	Cost
1–2	1	2–7	1	5–4	1	6–7	3
1–3	4	7–2	1	4–8	4	7–6	3
1–4	6	3–4	3	5–6	1	6–8	4
2–3	3	3–5	5	6–5	1	7–8	7
2–6	5	4–5	1	5–8	2		

Find the shortest path from every node to the terminal node using Dijkstra's algorithm.

Solution: We rewrite the network with 8 as starting Node (1) and 1 as finish Node (8).
Given arc 1–2 becomes 8–7 and our network is reversed to 7–8 with distance = 1.
Distances from 1 to every node is calculated using a single pass of Dijkstra's algorithm.
Figure 8.33 shows the network and the node labels when Dijkstra's algorithm is applied to solve the problem.

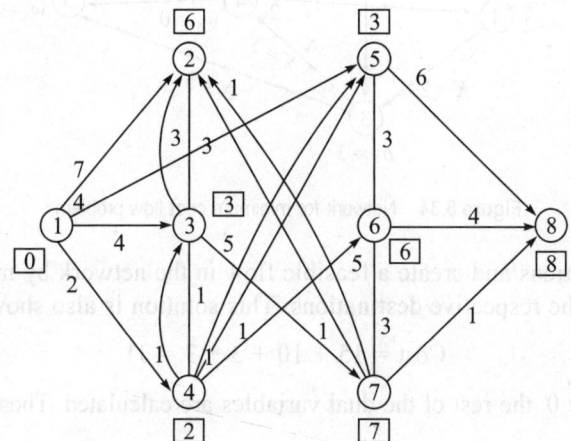

Figure 8.33 Network with nodes and arcs reversed.

1–4–3–2 with $Z = 6$ is 7–6–5–8 with $Z = 6$
1–4–3 with $Z = 3$ is 6–5–8 with $Z = 3$
1–4 with $Z = 2$ is 5–8 with $Z = 5$
1–4–5 with $Z = 3$ is 4–5–8 with $Z = 3$
1–4–5–6 with $Z = 6$ is 3–4–5–8 with $Z = 6$
1–4–3–2–7 with $Z = 7$ is 2–7–6–5–8 with $Z = 7$
1–4–3–2–7–8 with $Z = 8$ is 1–2–7–6–5–8 with $Z = 8$

Shortest distance from all nodes to 8 has been found using a single pass of the algorithm.

EXAMPLE 8.5 Use principles of shortest path problem to find a feasible solution to the minimum cost flow problem given in Table 8.8. Capacities of Nodes 1 to 5 are –2, 5, 3, –3, –3.

Check whether the feasible solution is optimal. If not, perform an iteration of network simplex algorithm to determine a better solution.

Table 8.8 Arcs and Costs

Arc	Cost	Arc	Cost
1–2	2	4–1	2
2–3	3	5–2	4
3–4	1	1–3	5
4–5	2	3–5	1

Solution: Figure 8.34 shows the network for the problem. The problem is a minimum cost flow problem. We first find the shortest path from Node 2 to all the nodes.

The shortest path from Node 2 to other nodes are as follows:

2–3, 2–3–4, 2–3–4–1 and 2–3–5

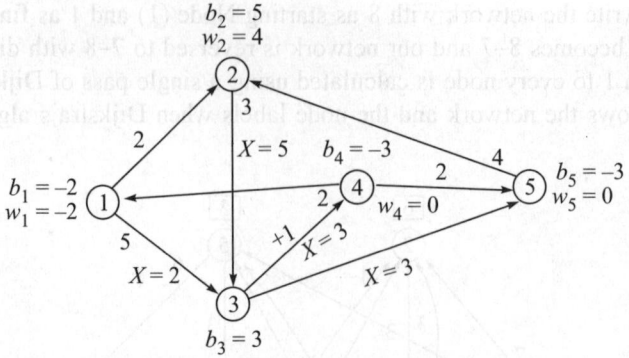

Figure 8.34 Network for minimum cost flow problem.

We use these solutions and create a feasible flow in the network by moving all 5 units from 2 to 3 and from 3 to the respective destinations. This solution is also shown in Figure 8.34.

$$\text{Cost} = 15 + 10 + 3 + 3 = 31$$

Starting with $w_5 = 0$, the rest of the dual variables are calculated. These are $w_1 = -2$, $w_2 = 4$, $w_3 = 1$, $w_4 = 2$.

The values of $w_i - w_j - C_{ij}$ are calculated for the non-basic arcs and these are found to be negative. The present basic feasible solution is optimal.

EXAMPLE 8.6 Consider the maximum flow problem for which the arcs and capacities are given in Table 8.9.

Write the dual to the maximum flow problem. Verify that the capacity of the maximum flow is equal to that of the minimum cut.

Table 8.9 Arcs and Capacities

Arc	Capacity
1–2	10
2–3	5
1–3	7
2–4	4
3–4	10

Solution: Figure 8.35 shows the network corresponding to the problem. The flow augmenting paths are:

1–2–4 with flow $Z = 4$
1–2–3–4 with flow $Z = 5$
1–3–4 with flow $Z = 5$
Total flow = 14

The dual of the given maximum flow problem is:

Minimize $\sum_{i=1}^{n} \sum_{j=1}^{n} u_{ij} h_{ij}$

Subject to

$$w_4 - w_1 = 1$$
$$w_1 - w_2 + h_{12} = 0$$
$$w_1 - w_3 + h_{13} = 0$$

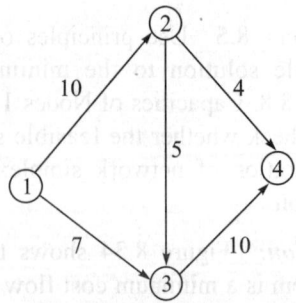

Figure 8.35 Network for maximum flow problem.

$$w_2 - w_3 + h_{23} = 0$$
$$w_2 - w_4 + h_{24} = 0$$
$$w_3 - w_4 + h_{34} = 0$$
$$w_j \text{ unrestricted}, h_{ij} \geq 0$$

Optimum solution to the dual is $w_4 = 1$, $w_1 = w_2 = w_3 = 0$, $h_{12} = h_{13} = h_{23} = 0$, $h_{24} = h_{34} = 1$, $W = 14$.

Therefore, max flow is equal to the min cut (optimum to dual of maximum flow problem)

$$Z = W = 14$$

EXAMPLE 8.7 Table 8.10 gives the distance matrix among five points. Identify the relevant OR model and determine the minimum length of wire required connecting all points.

Solution: The minimum spanning tree gives the minimum length of wire needed to connect the five points. The arcs in increasing order of lengths are 2–3(4), 1–5(5), 2–4(5), 4–5(5), 3–5(6), 3–5(6), 1–4(7), 3–4(7), 1–3(8) and 1–2(10). Figure 8.36 shows the minimum spanning tree.

The minimum spanning tree is 1–5, 2–3, 2–4 and 4–5 with length = 19.

Table 8.10 Distance Matrix among Five Points

–	10	8	7	5
10	–	4	5	6
8	4	–	7	6
7	5	7	–	5
5	6	6	5	–

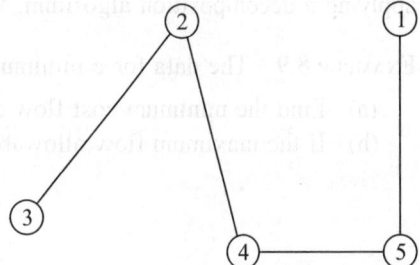

Figure 8.36 Minimum spanning tree.

EXAMPLE 8.8 Consider a network with four nodes and five arcs. Two types of commodities can flow in the arcs and the arcs have different capacities for each of the commodities (items). The unit cost for the flow is also different for the two commodities. The data is given in Table 8.11.

Table 8.11 Arcs and Costs

Arc	U_{ij}(1st item)	U_{ij}(2nd item)	C_{ij}(1st item)	C_{ij}(2nd item)
1–2	5	3	4	2
1–3	5	3	1	1
2–4	2	2	2	2
1–4	3	3	5	4
3–4	7	2	1	2

The node demands/supplies are (5, 3), (0, 2), (2, –2) and (7, –3), respectively.

(a) Find the minimum cost solution to the flow problem.
(b) If each arc also has a total capacity restriction given by 8, 6, 2, 5, 7, respectively for the arcs given in Table 8.11, find a feasible solution to the problem and the associated cost.

Solution: (a) The network is shown in Figure 8.37. We assume that each arc has individual upper bounds for the two items given in Table 8.11 and also a total capacity which is the sum of the two capacities. We consider Item 1 and the minimum cost flow solution is $X_{13} = 5$, $X_{34} = 7$ with cost = 12. The minimum cost flow solution for Item 2 is $X_{13} = 3$, $X_{34} = 1$, $X_{24} = 2$ with cost = 9. The total cost is 21.

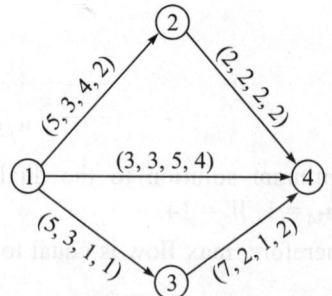

Figure 8.37 Network for multicommodity flow problem.

(b) Here there is a capacity restriction on the total and this is different from the sum of the two capacities. The solution to (a) violates the total capacity for arc 1–3 which has a total capacity of 6. We are forced to send 3 units of Item 1 through arc 1–4 and the feasible solution would be $X_{13} = 3, X_{34} = 3, X_{14} = 2$ for Item 1 with cost = 15 and the same for Item 2 as in (a). The total cost is now 24.

(The problem that we addressed in (b) is called **multicommodity flow problem**. In this problem, we have costs and bounds for multiple commodities as well as total capacity restriction for each arc. The optimal solution to the multicommodity flow problem can be obtained by applying a decomposition algorithm. We are not addressing this algorithm in this book).

EXAMPLE 8.9 The data for a minimum cost flow problem is shown in Figure 8.38.
   (a) Find the minimum cost flow and the associated cost.
   (b) If the maximum flow allowable in any arc is 60, find the optimal solution.

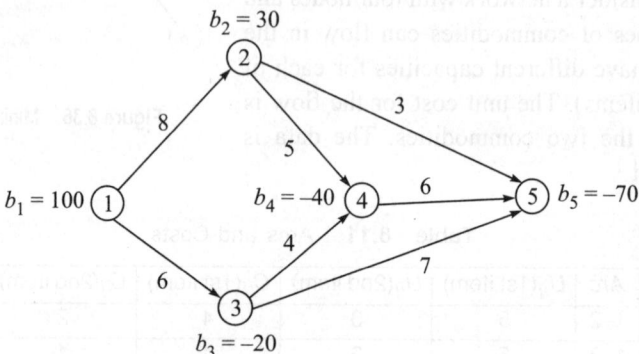

Figure 8.38 Network for capacitated minimum cost flow problem.

Solution: We start with a feasible solution $X_{13} = 100, X_{25} = 30, X_{34} = 40$ and $X_{35} = 40$ with cost = 1130. We fix $w_5 = 0$ and evaluate the other dual variables using the condition:

$$w_i - w_j = C_{ij}$$

where X_{ij} is basic. The values are $w_3 = 7, w_2 = 3, w_4 = 3$ and $w_1 = 13$. The values of $w_i - w_j - C_{ij}$ for the non-basic arcs are 2 for X_{12}, –3 for X_{45} and –5 for X_{24}. Since $w_1 - w_2 - C_{12}$ is positive, variable X_{12} enters the basis. Figure 8.39 explains these computations.

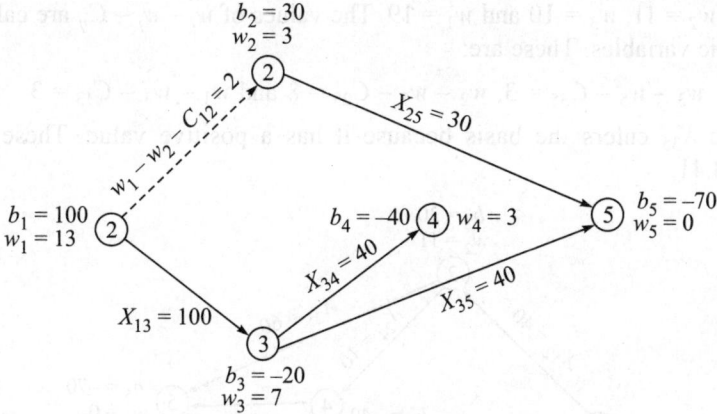

Figure 8.39 Basic feasible solution and computations.

The revised allocations are shown in Figure 8.40. The allocations are $X_{12} = 40$, $X_{25} = 70$, $X_{13} = 60$, $X_{34} = 40$.

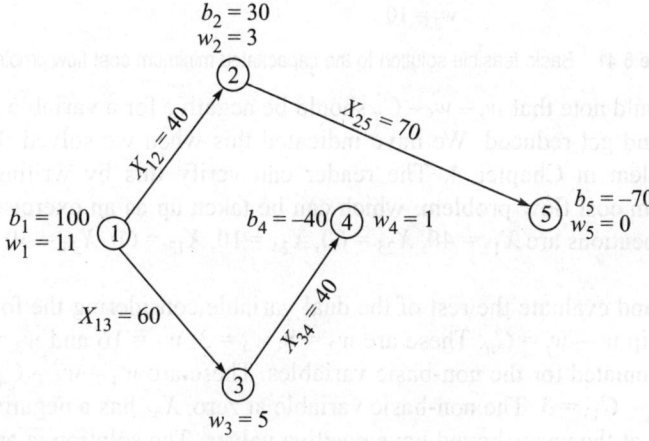

Figure 8.40 Optimal solution.

We fix $w_5 = 0$ and evaluate the other dual variables using the condition:

$$w_i - w_j = C_{ij}$$

where X_{ij} is basic. The values are $w_3 = 5$, $w_2 = 3$, $w_4 = 1$ and $w_1 = 11$. The values of $w_i - w_j - C_{ij}$ for the non-basic arcs are -2 for X_{35}, -5 for X_{45} and -3 for X_{24}. Since all the values are negative, the solution is optimal with cost = 105.

(b) The solution evaluated in (a) violates the upper bound of 60 for variable X_{25}. Using the solution in (a), we create a feasible solution to the bounded (capacitated) min cost flow problem. This is given by $X_{12} = 40$, $X_{25} = 60$, $X_{24} = 10$, $X_{13} = 60$, $X_{34} = 40$ and $X_{45} = 10$ with cost = 1130. Four out of the six are basic while two of the arcs X_{13} and X_{25} are non-basic at their upper bound value. We fix $w_5 = 0$ and evaluate the rest of the dual variable considering the four basic variables using the relationship $w_i - w_j = C_{ij}$. These are

$w_4 = 5$, $w_2 = 11$, $w_3 = 10$ and $w_1 = 19$. The values of $w_i - w_j - C_{ij}$ are calculated for the non-basic variables. These are:

$$w_3 - w_5 - C_{35} = 3, \quad w_2 - w_5 - C_{25} = 8 \text{ and } w_1 - w_3 - C_{13} = 3$$

Variable X_{35} enters the basis because it has a positive value. These are shown in Figure 8.41.

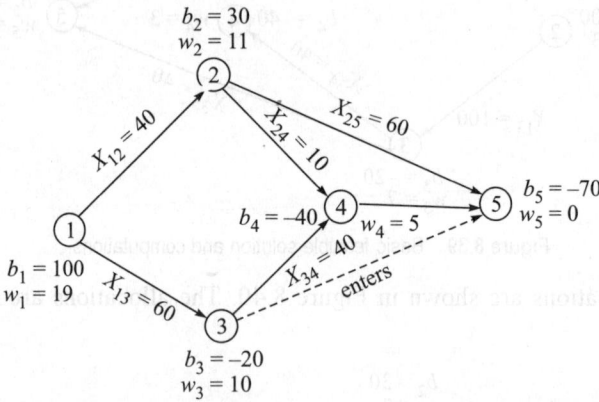

Figure 8.41 Basic feasible solution to the capacitated minimum cost flow problem.

(The reader should note that $w_i - w_j - C_{ij}$ should be negative for a variable at its upper bound to enter the basis and get reduced. We have indicated this when we solved the upper bounded transportation problem in Chapter 4. The reader can verify this by writing the dual of the capacitated minimum cost flow problem, which can be taken up as an exercise).

The revised allocations are $X_{12} = 40$, $X_{25} = 60$, $X_{24} = 10$, $X_{13} = 60$, $X_{34} = 30$ and $X_{35} = 10$ with cost = 1100.

We fix $w_5 = 0$ and evaluate the rest of the dual variable considering the four basic variables using the relationship $w_i - w_j = C_{ij}$. These are $w_2 = 8$, $w_4 = 3$, $w_1 = 16$ and $w_3 = 7$. The values of $w_i - w_j - C_{ij}$ are calculated for the non-basic variables. These are $w_4 - w_5 - C_{45} = -3$, $w_2 - w_5 - C_{25} = 5$ and $w_1 - w_3 - C_{13} = 3$. The non-basic variable at zero, X_{45} has a negative value while the non-basic variables at the upper bound have positive values. The solution is optimal with cost = 1100. Figure 8.42 shows the optimal solution.

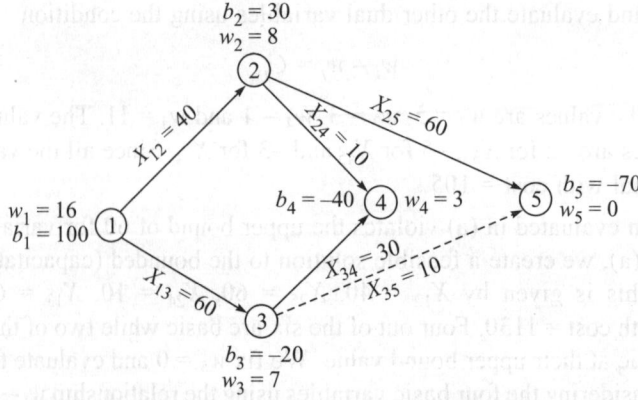

Figure 8.42 Optimal solution to the capacitated minimum cost flow problem.

EXAMPLE 8.10 Table 8.12 gives the distance matrix among five points. Find the minimum spanning tree for the network and identify two groups of points from the minimum spanning tree.

Solution: The edges forming the minimum spanning tree using Prim's algorithm are 4–5 (distance = 3), 1–5 (distance = 4), 4–3 (distance = 5) and 3–2 (distance = 4) with a total distance of 16. This is shown in Figure 8.43.

The spanning tree represents all the points in one group. Removal of edges from the minimum spanning tree results in spanning forest (a collection of spanning trees). We remove the edge with maximum distance (edge 4–3) and obtain two spanning trees from which two groups can be identified. The groups are {1, 5, 4} and {3, 2}.

The above solution need not be exact. The exact solution can be obtained by solving a 2-median problem optimally for the above data using integer programming or otherwise. The above method provides a frequently used heuristic solution to the grouping or clustering problem.

If we had obtained the minimum spanning tree using the Kruskal's algorithm, the edges chosen would have been 4–5 (distance = 3), 1–5 (distance = 4), 2–3 (distance = 4). We need not find the fourth edge because our heuristic solution to two groups has three edges only to include all the vertices. We have obtained the same solution that we obtained by deleting an edge from the minimum spanning tree obtained using Prim's algorithm. The solution is shown in Figure 8.44.

Table 8.12 Distance Matrix among Five Points

Point	1	2	3	4	5
1	–	8	9	7	4
2	8	–	5	6	7
3	9	5	–	4	5
4	7	6	4	–	3
5	4	7	5	3	–

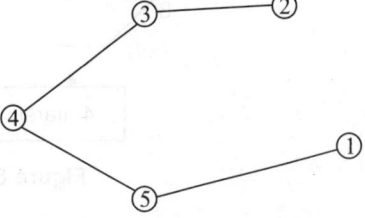

Figure 8.43 Minimum spanning tree.

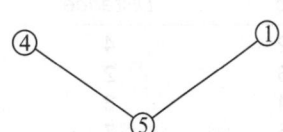

Figure 8.44 Two groups from the minimum spanning tree.

CASE STUDY 8.1: The Kasi-Yatra Problem

There lived an old couple in Ujjain during the 18th century. They wanted to migrate to Kasi to spend their last days at this holy city. To die at Kasi was the desire of every Hindu those days!

Between Ujjain and Kasi lay a vast dacoit-infested area. So a journey from Ujjain to Kasi was fraught with the danger of attack by dacoits and consequent loss of life. The old couple, understandably, was keen on reaching Kasi alive! Horse-carriages and bullock-carts plied between some of the intermediate towns between Kasi and Ujjain. These were the only modes of transport available. The charges levied for travel by the cart-owners were proportional to the risk of dacoits in the route. The couple realized that the route of lowest total cost minimizes risk to life.

A schematic diagram indicating the possible routes and the associated distances is given in Figure 8.45.

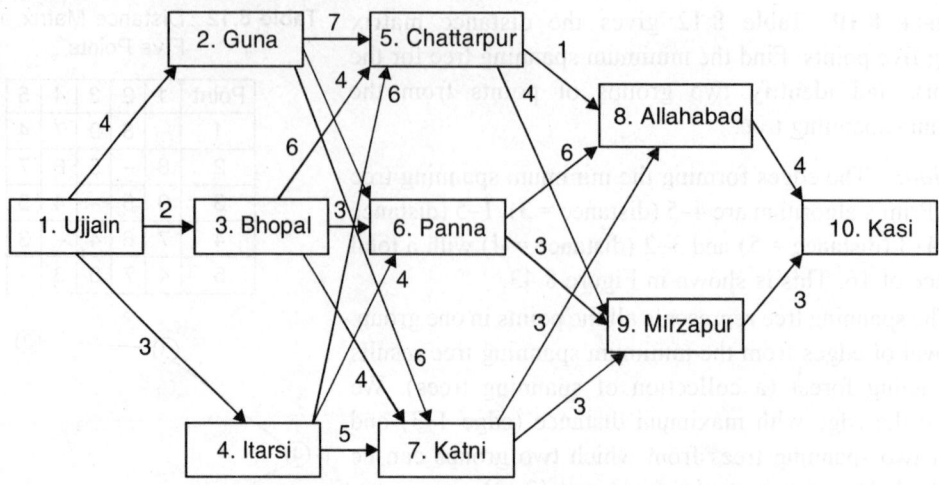

Figure 8.45 Network for Kasi yatra problem.

The cities (1 to 10) are Ujjain, Guna, Bhopal, Itarsi, Chattarpur, Panna, Katni, Allahabad, Mirzapur and Kasi. The distances among the nodes and the number of temples that they can visit in each arc are given in Table 8.13.

Table 8.13 Arc Distances and Temples in the Route

Arc	Distance	Temples	Arc	Distance	Temples
1-2	4	2	4-6	4	3
1-3	2	2	4-7	5	3
1-4	3	3	5-8	1	2
2-5	7	4	5-9	4	5
2-6	4	2	6-8	6	4
2-7	6	3	6-9	3	2
3-5	6	3	7-8	3	4
3-6	3	1	7-9	3	2
3-7	4	1	8-10	4	2
4-5	6	4	9-10	3	3

The couple was also interested in visiting temples that are in their route. The number of temples that are available in the route is also given. They wish to visit at least 10 temples before they reach Kasi. They were not going to pray in these temples later.

EXERCISES

8.1 The daily requirements of napkins in a hotel is d_k. Each new napkin costs s paise. The napkins can be sent to laundry and used again. There are two types of laundry—fast service costs q paise and taking v days and ordinary service costing p paise and taking u days ($u > v$ and $p < q < s$). Formulate this problem as an integer programming problem assuming that demands for the next ten days are known. Show that it is a transshipment/ minimum cost flow problem by drawing the network.

8.2 Solve the following transshipment problem of Table 8.14 using network simplex method.

Table 8.14 Transshipment Problem

Arc	Cost	Arc	Cost
1-2	8	2-6	6
1-3	3	5-4	2
1-5	4	5-6	4
2-3	6	4-6	3
3-4	5	2-4	1
3-5	2		

8.3 Consider eleven cities (named 1 to 11). The arcs are shown in Table 8.15.
The arcs are assumed to be unidirectional.
 (a) Compute the shortest path and distance between 1 and 11.
 (b) If the user decides to pass through Node 4, find the shortest path. Is it the same as the second shortest path?
 (c) Find the third shortest path from 1 to 11.

Describe an algorithm to find the shortest path from a source to a destination passing through a given node.

Table 8.15 Arcs and Distances

Arc	Distance	Arc	Distance
1-2	20	4-10	60
1-3	35	5-6	30
1-4	66	5-7	45
2-3	33	6-9	35
2-5	55	7-9	30
3-4	55	7-10	35
3-5	42	8-10	60
3-6	60	9-10	35
3-7	45	9-11	15
4-8	25	10-11	30

8.4 The edges and the weights of a graph are given in Table 8.16. Find the maximum spanning tree from the graph. (Modify Prim's or Kruskal's algorithm to choose maximum weight edge. Is the solution optimal?)

Table 8.16 Edges and Weights of a Graph

Edge	Weight	Edge (i-j)	Weight	Edge (i-j)	Weight
1-1	7	2-1	8	3-3	9
1-2	5	2-3	6	4-1	6
1-3	6	3-2	7	4-3	10

8.5 The circulatory flow problem is as follows: Given a network with arc weights l_{ij}, u_{ij} and c_{ij}, where these represent the lower and upper bounds on the flow and the cost, respectively. The problem is to minimize the total cost while maintaining that the actual flows are within the bounds. Formulate the problem for a network whose arcs are 1-2, 1-3, 1-4, 2-3 and 3-4. Write the dual to this problem.

8.6 Explain the "flow augmenting path using a backward arc" in the context of a maximum flow problem using an illustration. How are we justified in subtracting a flow from an arc but increasing the total flow in the network?

8.7 Ten people have to be grouped into four groups. A similarity matrix among them is given in Table 8.17.

Table 8.17 Similarity Matrix

-	6	7	6	9	2	3	4	8	9
6	-	6	6	5	8	4	9	1	6
7	6	-	6	6	5	5	6	8	9
6	6	6	-	4	4	9	5	3	6
9	5	6	4	-	7	6	6	2	0
2	8	5	4	7	-	6	8	3	0
3	4	5	9	6	6	-	6	0	0
4	9	6	5	6	8	6	-	1	0
8	1	8	3	2	3	0	1	-	0
9	6	9	6	0	0	0	0	0	-

Obtain a maximum spanning tree and create groups from the tree. Assume that removal of edges from a spanning tree can create groups.

8.8 Consider the reduced cost matrix from an intermediate iteration of the assignment problem (Table 8.18) where we draw lines that cover all the zeros of the matrix after the assignments have been made. Formulate a maximum flow problem to identify the minimum number of lines.

(**Hint:** Draw a bipartite graph with equal number of points representing the rows and columns. Connect them if there is a zero and allow a maximum flow of 1 in the arc. Create a source and sink with equal capacities and proceed)

Table 8.18 Reduced Cost Matrix

1	0	1	8	0
6	17	0	4	5
0	3	2	0	0
5	0	0	3	0
2	1	6	9	0

8.9 Consider a zero-one matrix with 3 rows and 4 columns. The row and column sums are given. Formulate a maximum flow problem to verify, if exists, such a matrix for the given row and column sums.

8.10 Given a project network with the data given in Table 8.19.

Find the longest path in the network and the duration.

(**Hint:** To find the longest path, modify Dijkstra's algorithm to label the node using the largest of the distances. Try and show that it is optimal).

Table 8.19 Data for a Project Network

Activity	Duration	Activity	Duration
1–2	9	3–5	8
1–3	6	3–6	10
2–4	8	4–6	6
2–5	3	5–6	7

8.11 Table 8.20 provides the data for a minimum cost flow problem on a network.

The capacities of Nodes 1 to 5 are 5, 4, –2, –2, –3, respectively.

(**Hint:** This is an unbalanced minimum cost flow problem. Create a dummy requirement of 2 units and connect it from all the other nodes. What should be the dummy cost that you will use?)

Table 8.20 Data for a Minimum Cost Flow Problem

Arc	Cost	Arc	Cost
1–2	2	4–1	3
2–3	3	5–2	4
3–4	6	1–3	5
4–5	2	3–5	1

8.12 You are given a network with 5 nodes and 11 arcs. The data is shown in Table 8.21.

Table 8.21 Arcs and Distances

Arc	Distance	Arc	Distance	Arc	Distance
1–2	5	3–2	5	5–3	5
2–1	10	4–3	20	3–5	10
1–4	10	4–5	10	4–2	10
2–3	10	5–4	10		

(a) Find the shortest path from 1 to 5 using Dijkstra's algorithm.
(b) Find the shortest distance from every node to every other node using Floyd's algorithm.

8.13 You are given a network with 9 nodes and 16 arcs. The data is shown in Table 8.22.

Table 8.22 Arcs and Distances

Arc	Distance	Arc	Distance	Arc	Distance	Arc	Distance
1–2	10	2–6	6	4–7	10	6–7	9
1–3	8	3–4	10	4–8	8	6–8	5
2–4	12	3–5	6	5–7	10	7–9	8
2–5	8	3–6	8	5–8	8	8–9	9

Find the first three shortest paths using Yen's algorithm. What happens if there are two first shortest paths in a network?

8.14 You are given a network with 6 nodes and 9 arcs. The data is shown in Table 8.23.

Table 8.23 Arcs and Capacities

Arc	Capacity	Arc	Capacity	Arc	Capacity
1–2	40	1–4	30	4–6	20
1–3	60	1–5	40	3–6	30
2–4	20	3–5	20	5–6	30

Find the maximum flow in the network from source 1 to sink 6.

8.15 Table 8.24 gives the distance matrix among six points.
(a) Find the minimum spanning tree using Kruskal's algorithm.
(b) If there is an additional restriction that the maximum degree of a vertex is less than or equal to three, find a feasible solution by adding the constraint into the algorithm.

Table 8.24 Distance Matrix

Points	1	2	3	4	5	6
1	–	8	6	4	5	3
2	8	–	7	10	5	8
3	6	7	–	12	8	7
4	4	10	12	–	6	5
5	5	5	8	6	–	8
6	3	8	5	7	8	–

9

Travelling Salesman and Distribution Problems

In this chapter we address the following problems related to distribution:

1. Travelling salesman problem
2. Chinese postman problem
3. Vehicle routeing problem

We explain the formulations, concepts and algorithms to solve these problems. These problems have application in various aspects of Management including Supply Chain Management and Logistics.

9.1 THE TRAVELLING SALESMAN PROBLEM (TSP)

This is the most interesting and perhaps the most researched problem in the field of operations research. This problem was posed, in 1934, by a scholar, Hassler Whitney in a seminar talk at Princeton University. This "easy to state" and "difficult to solve" problem has attracted the attention of both academicians and practitioners who have been attempting to solve and use the results in practice.

The problem is stated as follows:

A salesman has to visit n cities and return to the starting point. How should he (she) visit the cities such that the total distance travelled is minimum?

It is assumed that the starting city is included in the n cities (or points) to be visited. Since the person comes back to the starting point, any of the n cities can be a starting point. Therefore, for a given solution there are $n - 1$ other solutions that are same. The starting city is usually not specified at all. Any city can be the starting city. For a n city TSP, the person travels exactly n arcs (or n distances).

There is also a *travelling salesman path problem* where the start and end points are specified. Here the person travels $n - 1$ arcs and reaches the destination.

Usually in the TSP statement there is also a mention that the person visits each city *once and only once* and returns to the starting point. If the distance matrix is made of Euclidean distances, it satisfies *triangle inequality* (Given three points i, j, k, $d_{ik} \leq d_{ij} + d_{jk}$), which would force the salesman to visit each city once and only once (Bellmore and Nemhauser, 1968). If the distances do not satisfy triangle inequality or if we are considering cost or time instead of distances, these may not satisfy triangle inequality and we have to mention explicitly that the person visits each city once and only once.

9.1.1 Mathematical Programming Formulation of the Travelling Salesman Problem

Consider a n city TSP with a known distance matrix D. We consider a 5 city TSP for explaining the formulation, whose distance matrix is given in Table 9.1.

Let $X_{ij} = 1$ if the salesman visits city j immediately after visiting city i. The formulation is:

Table 9.1 Distance Matrix

–	10	8	9	7
10	–	10	5	6
8	10	–	8	9
9	5	8	–	6
7	6	9	6	–

Minimize $\sum_{i=1}^{n} \sum_{j=1}^{n} d_{ij} X_{ij}$ (9.1)

Subject to

$$\sum_{j=1}^{n} X_{ij} = 1 \quad \forall \ i \quad (9.2)$$

$$\sum_{i=1}^{n} X_{ij} = 1 \quad \forall \ j \quad (9.3)$$

Let us verify whether the formulation is adequate and satisfies all the requirements of a TSP. The objective function minimizes the total distance travelled. The constraints ensure that every city is visited only once. This formulation is clearly inadequate since it is the formulation of the assignment problem. For example, a feasible solution to a 5 × 5 assignment problem can be $X_{12} = X_{23} = X_{31} = X_{45} = X_{54} = 1$. This is not feasible to the TSP because this says that the person leaves City 1 goes to City 2 from there goes to City 3 and comes back to City 1. He also goes to City 4 (from 5?) and comes back from 5. This is infeasible to the TSP because this contains subtours. For example, $X_{12} = X_{23} = X_{31} = 1$ is a subtour of cities 1–2–3–1. It is also obvious that if there is a subtour there is always one more in the solution. We have the other subtour given by $X_{45} = X_{54} = 1$ where $X_{12} = X_{24} = X_{45} = X_{53} = X_{31} = 1$ represents the solution 1–2–4–5–3–1 and is not a subtour. It represents a full tour and is feasible to the TSP. The formulation should results in solutions not having subtours. We need to add subtour elimination constraints.

For a 5-city TSP we can have subtours of length 1, 2, 3 or 4. For example, $X_{jj} = 1$ is a subtour of length 1. We indirectly eliminate subtours of length 1 by considering $d_{jj} = \infty$ (shown as (–) in the distance matrix). Fixing $d_{jj} = \infty$ will not allow $X_{jj} = 1$. This will also indirectly not allow a 4-city subtour because if there is a 4-city subtour in a 5 city TSP, there has to be a 1-city subtour.

A constraint of the form $X_{ij} + X_{ji} \leq 1$ will eliminate all 2-city subtours. This has to be added to the formulation. This will also eliminate all 3-city subtours because a 3-city subtour should result in a 2-city subtour in a 5-city TSP. Therefore, addition of the 2-city subtour elimination constraint will complete our formulation of the 5-city TSP.

The complete formulation is:

Minimize $\sum_{i=1}^{n}\sum_{j=1}^{n} d_{ij}X_{ij}$

Subject to

$$\sum_{j=1}^{n} X_{ij} = 1 \quad \forall\ i$$

$$\sum_{i=1}^{n} X_{ij} = 1 \quad \forall\ j$$

$$X_{ij} + X_{ji} \le 1 \quad \forall\ i, j$$

$$X_{ij} = 0, 1$$

If we consider a 6-city TSP, we have to add 2-city subtour elimination constraints and also add a 3-city subtour elimination constraint of the form:

$$X_{ij} + X_{jk} + X_{ki} \le 2 \quad \forall\ i, j, k$$

This increases the number of constraints significantly.

In general for a n city TSP, where n is odd we have to add subtour elimination constraints for eliminating subtours of length 2 to $n-1$ and when n is even, we have to add subtour elimination constraints for eliminating subtours of length 2 to n.

For $n = 6$, the number of 2-city subtour elimination constraints is $^6C_2 = 15$ and the number of 3-city subtours is $^6C_3 = 20$.

9.1.2 Another Formulation for Subtour Elimination

Let us consider another type of subtour elimination constraint of the form:

$$U_i - U_j + nX_{ij} \le n - 1 \quad \text{for } i = 1, 2, \ldots, n-1 \text{ and } j = 2, 3, \ldots, n$$
$$U_j \ge 0 \quad \text{(Bellmore and Nemhauser, 1968)}$$

For our 5-city example we will have $(n-1)^2$ constraints. Let us consider an infeasible solution having a subtour (not involving City 1) $X_{45} = X_{54} = 1$. The two relevant constraints are:

$$U_4 - U_5 + 5X_{45} \le 4$$

and
$$U_5 - U_4 + 5X_{54} \le 4$$

This is clearly infeasible because the two constraints when added together gives

$$5X_{45} + 5X_{54} \le 8$$

which is infeasible for $X_{45} = X_{54} = 1$. Therefore, every subtour not involving City 1 will violate the relevant set of constraints.

Let us consider a subtour involving City 1 given by

$$X_{12} = X_{23} = X_{31} = 1$$

We have two constraints:

$$U_1 - U_2 + 5X_{12} \leq 4$$
$$U_2 - U_3 + 5X_{23} \leq 4$$

The constraint $U_3 - U_1 + 5X_{31} \leq 4$ does not exist for $U_j = 1$.

Adding the two constraints, we get

$$U_1 - U_3 + 10 \leq 8 \quad \text{for } X_{12} = X_{23} = 1$$

It is possible to have values U_1 and U_3 that satisfy the constraints and, therefore, the constraint $U_i - U_j + nX_{ij} \leq n - 1$ is unable to prevent subtours involving City 1 from occurring. However, we realize that for every subtour involving City 1 there has to be a subtour that does not involve City 1 (the subtour $X_{45} = X_{54} = 1$ in our example) and the constraints are able to prevent them from happenning. Therefore, the constraints eliminate all subtours. The only requirement is that we define $d_{jj} = \infty$ (or M) so that singleton subtours are indirectly eliminated.

Let us consider a feasible solution $X_{12} = X_{24} = X_{45} = X_{53} = X_{31}$. The relevant constraints are:

$$U_1 - U_2 + 5X_{12} \leq 4$$
$$U_2 - U_4 + 5X_{24} \leq 4$$
$$U_4 - U_5 + 5X_{45} \leq 4$$
$$U_5 - U_3 + 5X_{53} \leq 4$$

The constraint $U_3 - U_1 + 5X_{31} \leq 4$ does not exist for $U_j = 1$.

Adding the constraints, we get $U_1 - U_3 + 20 \leq 16$ for the given feasible solution. Clearly, we can define values for U_1 and U_3 to satisfy the constraint. Therefore, the constraint does not eliminate any feasible solution. This can effectively replace the earlier set of constraints.

9.1.3 The TSP and the Theory of NP-Completeness

The TSP is important from the point of view of NP-completeness theory. To understand the theory of NP-completeness, we first define the complexity of algorithms. The complexity theory deals with the study of resources (time and memory) required to solve a problem.

Any algorithm that solves a problem carries out various steps that can be reduced to additions, subtraction, multiplication and division and other basic operations. Assuming that each of these operations take unit processing time, it is possible to represent the time taken to implement an algorithm in terms parameters such as problem, size, etc. This function can be a polynomial function or an exponential function. If it is a polynomial function, we say that the algorithm has a complexity of $O(N^k)$ where N is a problem parameter (say, size) and k is the order of the polynomial. The order is the power corresponding to the highest degree in the polynomial and is used because the rate of increase of the polynomial depends on the order of the polynomial. If the function is exponential, we say that the algorithm is exponential. Examples of exponential functions could be $n!$, e^n, etc.

An algorithm is polynomial if the order of complexity is of the form $O(N^k)$ and the problem is in the category of "easy" problems. Examples of easy problems are matrix inversion, solving linear equations, assignment problem, etc.

For a problem, if so far no polynomial algorithm has been developed then it belongs to the "NP hard" category. The word NP stands for non-deterministic polynomial and may include problems that have pseudopolynomial algorithms.

Among the "hard" problems, we have a set of problems that possess additional features. These set of problems constitute the NP complete set. For example, every problem in this set is reducible to every other problem in this set. Two problems are reducible if it is possible to develop a polynomial algorithm that can show that the problems are equivalent. When two problems are equivalent it means that if we are able to solve one of them, it is possible to solve the other, the additional effort being polynomial. The TSP is an important problem in the class of NP complete problems.

A given problem is NP complete if it can be transformed into zero-one integer programming problem in polynomial time and if zero-one integer programming problem can be transformed to it in polynomial time (Bertsimas and Tsitsiklis, 1997). To show that a given problem is NP complete, it is customary to reduce it to a known NP complete problem. There are several instances where a given problem has been shown to be NP complete by showing that it is reducible to the TSP. (For further reading on the theory of NP-completeness, the reader is referred to Garey and Johnson, 1979, Papadimitriou and Steiglitz, 1982 and Wilf, 1975).

NP complete problems

1. So far no polynomial algorithm has been developed to solve any one of the NP complete problems.
2. So far no one has shown that it is impossible to develop a polynomial algorithm to solve any one of the NP complete problems
3. It is possible to solve every one of the NP complete problems in polynomial time if a polynomial algorithm is developed to solve one of the NP complete problems
4. It is possible to show that it is impossible to solve any of the problems using polynomial algorithms if it is shown that it is impossible to develop a polynomial algorithm for one of the NP complete problems.

We have exact algorithms to solve the TSP but these are worst case exponential and enumerate all possible solutions. We have branch and bound algorithms that perform implicit enumeration of some of the solutions. We also have heuristic algorithms that run in polynomial time but do not guarantee optimal solutions. We first study the branch and bound algorithms for solving the TSP and later study heuristics.

9.2 OPTIMAL SOLUTION TO TSP USING BRANCH AND BOUND ALGORITHMS

We study three different types of branch and bound algorithms to solve the TSP optimally. These are explained in Sections 9.2.1 to 9.2.3, respectively.

9.2.1 Algorithm 1

ILLUSTRATION 9.1

We explain the branch and bound algorithm using the 5-city example shown again in Table 9.2.

Since we have to leave each city once, the minimum distance that will have to be travelled is the minimum in each row and the sum of the five row minimum values gives us a lower bound for the value of the minimum length tour.

Table 9.2 Distance Matrix

–	10	8	9	7
10	–	10	5	6
8	10	–	8	9
9	5	8	–	6
7	6	9	6	–

Lower bound $(LB) = 7 + 5 + 8 + 5 + 6 = 31$

We create the branch and bound tree by defining four ways of leaving City 1. We can have $X_{12} = 1$, $X_{13} = 1$, $X_{14} = 1$ and $X_{15} = 1$. We can compute a lower bound corresponding to each assignment.

We illustrate the computation of the lower bound for $X_{12} = 1$. The assignment gives a fixed value of 10. In addition, we need to have the minimum distance travelled from 2, 3, 4 and 5 without going to City 2 again. We leave out row 1 and column 2 from the original matrix and have a 4 × 4 matrix shown in Table 9.3. The from-to cities are shown in bold.

Table 9.3 Reduced Distance Matrix

	1	3	4	5
2	–	10	5	6
3	8	–	8	9
4	9	8	–	6
5	7	9	6	–

We observe that we have written d_{21} in the new matrix as – (infinity). This is because we cannot have $X_{21} = 1$ since this will result in a subtour. The sum of the minimum in every row in Table 9.3 is $5 + 8 + 6 + 6 = 25$. We add the distance of the fixed allocation $d_{12} = 10$ and get a lower bound of 35.

(Realizing that d_{21} can be set to ∞ and using it at every lower bound can actually increase the lower bound and make it tighter. In this example, we could have used $d_{12} = 10$ and would still have got the same LB. Generally it is to our advantage to use the additional information and tighten the bound if possible).

The lower bound corresponding to $X_{13} = 1$ is computed by creating a similar table with row 1 and column 3 left out and by fixing $d_{31} = ∞$. The value of the LB is $8 + 5 + 8 + 5 + 6 = 32$.

For $X_{14} = 1$, the lower bound is $9 + 6 + 8 + 5 + 6 = 34$ and for $X_{15} = 1$ it is $7 + 5 + 8 + 5 + 6 = 31$. All these are shown in the branch and bound tree in Figure 9.1.

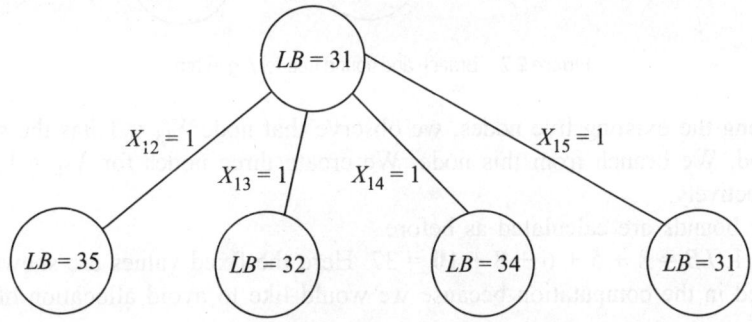

Figure 9.1 Branch and bound tree for Algorithm 1.

We branch further from the node that has the smallest value of the lower bound. This is because there is still a possibility of getting an optimum of 31 while branching from Node 1 can give us LBs and solutions with values greater than or equal to 35. Since we want to minimize the total distance we branch from node X_{15}.

At the second level of fixing the variables, we decide to fix the three possible ways from branching from Node 2 even though we have not reached Node 2. Since X_{15} is fixed we don't consider branching from X_{25}. At the second level we realize that the branches are $X_{21} = 1$, $X_{23} = 1$ and $X_{24} = 1$. We illustrate the lower bound computation for the node where $X_{15} = X_{21} = 1$. We write the table leaving out rows 1 and 2 and columns 1 and 5 (Table 9.4).

Table 9.4 Reduced Distance Matrix

	2	3	4
3	10	–	8
4	5	8	–
5	6	9	6

The sum of the row minimum elements is $8 + 5 + 6 = 19$. We add the distances corresponding to the fixed allocations $d_{15} + d_{21} = 17$. The lower bound is 36.

The lower bound for the other node created by fixing $X_{23} = 1$ is $8 + 5 + 6 + 7 + 10 = 36$ (The allocated distances d_{15} and d_{23} are shown in bold).

The lower bound for the other node created by fixing $X_{24} = 1$ is $8 + 8 + 6 + 7 + 5 = 34$ (The allocated distances d_{15} and d_{24} are shown in bold). Since X_{24} is fixed as 1, we make $d_{42} = \infty$ in computing this lower bound. The branch and bound tree is shown in Figure 9.2.

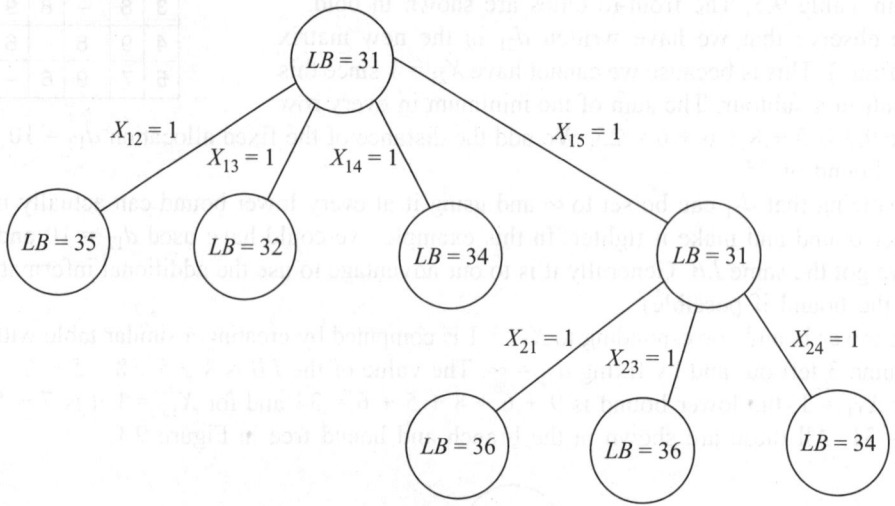

Figure 9.2 Branch and bound tree for Algorithm.

From among the existing live nodes, we observe that node $X_{13} = 1$ has the smallest value of lower bound. We branch from this node. We create three nodes for $X_{21} = 1$, $X_{24} = 1$ and $X_{25} = 1$, respectively.

The lower bounds are calculated as before.

For $X_{21} = 1$, $LB = 8 + 5 + 6 + \mathbf{8} + \mathbf{10} = 37$. Here the fixed values are shown in bold and $d_{32} = \infty$ is used in the computation because we would like to avoid allocation of X_{32}.

For $X_{24} = 1$, $LB = 9 + 6 + 6 + 8 + 5 = 34$. Here the fixed values are shown in bold and $d_{31} = d_{42} = \infty$ is used in the computation because we would like to avoid allocations of X_{31} and X_{42}.

For $X_{25} = 1$, $LB = 8 + 5 + 6 + 8 + 6 = 33$. Here the fixed values are shown in bold and $d_{31} = d_{52} = \infty$ is used in the computation because we would like to avoid allocations of X_{31} and X_{52}. This is shown in the tree in Figure 9.3.

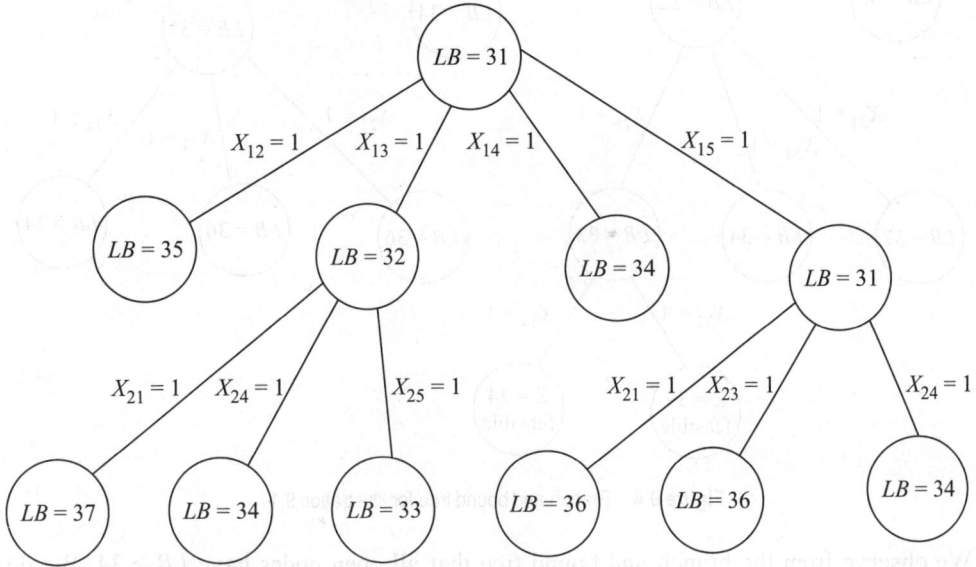

Figure 9.3 Branch and bound tree for Illustration 9.1.

We observe that node $X_{13} = X_{25} = 1$ has the lowest value of $LB = 33$. We branch from here and create two nodes with $X_{32} = 1$ and $X_{34} = 1$.

Let us consider the node $X_{13} = X_{25} = X_{32} = 1$. We can compute the lower bound as we did before but since only two more cities have to be assigned (and this can be done in two ways), we create two possible solutions considering the two possibilities. These are:

1. $X_{13} = X_{25} = X_{32} = 1$, $X_{41} = X_{54} = 1$ with $Z = 39$ (feasible)
2. $X_{13} = X_{25} = X_{32} = 1$, $X_{44} = X_{51} = 1$ (infeasible and hence not evaluated)

Let us consider the node $X_{13} = X_{25} = X_{34} = 1$. Only two more cities have to be assigned (and this can be done in two ways), we create two possible solutions considering the two possibilities. These are:

1. $X_{13} = X_{25} = X_{34} = 1$, $X_{42} = X_{51} = 1$ with $Z = 34$ (feasible)
2. $X_{13} = X_{25} = X_{34} = 1$, $X_{41} = X_{52} = 1$ (infeasible and hence not evaluated)

(It also turns out that only one of the two solutions is feasible.)

The best between the feasible solutions has $Z = 34$ and is an upper bound to the objective function.

The branch and bound tree is updated as shown in Figure 9.4.

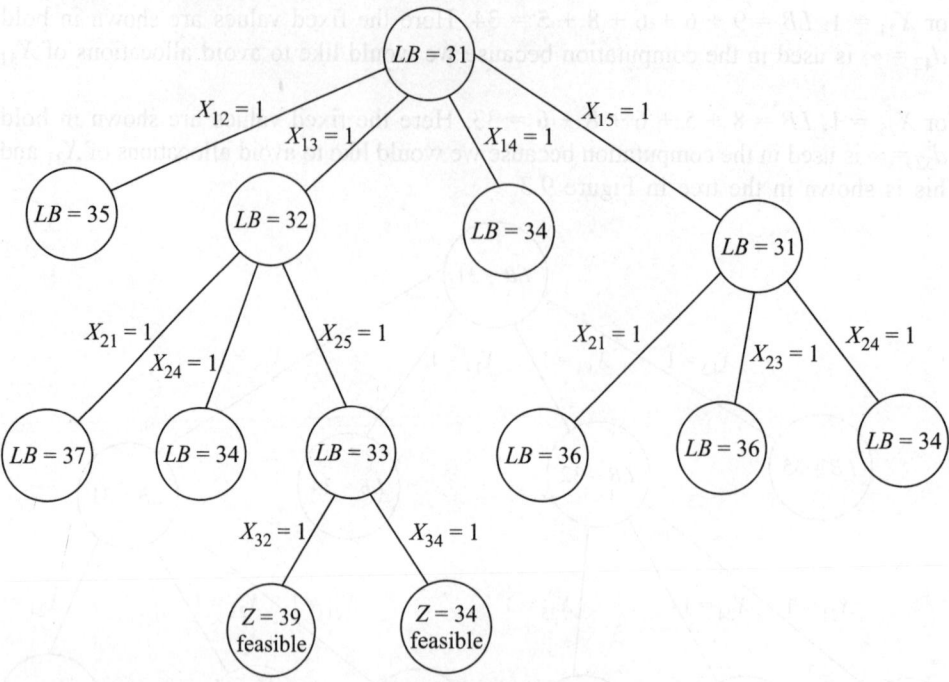

Figure 9.4 Branch and bound tree for Illustration 9.1.

We observe from the branch and bound tree that all open nodes have $LB \geq 34$. We do not proceed from nodes having $LB > 34$ because these can result in solutions with $Z > 34$. These nodes are fathomed by $LB > UB$. Those nodes with $LB = 34$ can in the best case lead to solutions with $Z = 34$ and these are also evaluated because we are interested in one optimal solutions and not multiple (if they exist). All the nodes are fathomed and since there is no active node, the algorithm terminates. The optimum solution is:

$$X_{13} = X_{25} = X_{34} = 1, X_{42} = X_{51} = 1 \text{ with } Z = 34$$

Branch and bound algorithm
1. Compute a lower bound to the objective function. Set upper bound $= \infty$
2. Construct the branching tree and branch on possible values one of the variables can take.
3. Evaluate the lower bound for every node. If the node (solution up to that point) is infeasible or if the lower bound is greater than the best upper bound, fathom the node.
4. If at Step 3, the allocation results in a feasible solution, evaluate the feasible solution. Update the upper bound if the new solution is better. Fathom all nodes where the lower bound is greater than the present upper bound.
5. The algorithm stops when there is no open node. The present best feasible solution is the optimal solution.

We should understand that any branch and bound algorithm is a worst case complete enumeration algorithm. We may end up evaluating all the $(n-1)!$ feasible solutions and the optimum may be found in the last solution. The branch and bound algorithm, therefore, is a worst case exponential algorithm.

It is also an implicit enumeration algorithm as it fathoms certain nodes after proving that it is unnecessary to evaluate them because they are either infeasible or cannot give feasible solutions that are better than the existing best. Therefore, all feasible solutions are not explicitly evaluated and some are implicitly evaluated.

A node is fathomed if we do not branch from it further. A node can be fathomed in two ways:

1. By infeasibility when the present node is infeasible after the branching.
2. By upper bound. We branch and compute the lower bound. If the value is more than that of the existing best feasible solution, we fathom that node because branching further can only increase the lower bound (for minimization problems).

There are three aspects in branch and bound algorithms. They are:

1. Branching strategy
2. Bounding strategy
3. Node selection strategy

In the above algorithm we branch by fixing the next variable to all possible (feasible) values. For example, if we have selected a node X_{15} for branching, we branch on the next variable, namely, variable 2 and create three nodes X_{21}, X_{23}, X_{24}. In our example, there are five cities and if we are branching at the second stage, there will be three branches. We have excluded X_{22} because it creates an infeasible branch. We have also excluded X_{25} because we already fixed X_{15} and there can be only one way of reaching City 5.

We can also branch on the variable that represents the city just reached. We can branch on City 5 and create three nodes by fixing X_{52}, X_{53} and X_{54} to 1. Here we leave out X_{55} because of infeasibility and X_{51} because it will create a subtour with the fixed X_{15}.

The bounding strategy computes the lower bound for a partial assignment. Any feasible solution has five distances added and the lower bound has the sum of the fixed distances and the lower estimate of the unfixed distances. If we consider the branch $X_{15} = X_{21} = 1$, we have a fixed distance of travel of $d_{15} + d_{21} = 7 + 10 = 17$. We need three more estimates. We now ignore the assigned rows and columns and get a matrix with rows 3, 4 and 5 and columns 2, 3 and 4. This is given in Table 9.5.

Table 9.5 Reduced Distance Matrix

	2	3	4
3	10	–	8
4	5	8	–
5	6	9	6

We observe that we have to leave the remaining three cities and add the minimum additional distance which is the row minimum. The values are 8 (row 3), 5 (row 4) and 6 (row 5). The lower bound is $17 + 8 + 5 + 6 = 36$. We have fixed X_{15} and X_{21} to 1. We cannot have $X_{52} = 1$ because it will create a subtour. We can, therefore, treat $d_{52} = \infty$ and take row minimum for row 5. In this example, we still get 6 but there is a possibility that the value may become higher and better.

In all the minimization problems, the higher the value of lower bound, the better it is. Therefore, the effort is always towards making the lower bounds higher and higher so that the node can be fathomed based on upper bound.

The node selection strategy usually followed is to branch from the unfathomed node that has the least value of the lower bound. This assumes that we would like to move towards feasible solutions with smaller values of the objective function so that when a feasible solution is found, it fathoms many existing nodes. The node selection strategy should also be such that we get a feasible solution quickly so that fathoming by upper bound starts happening. Otherwise there can be many unfathomed nodes in the consuming memory. If the node selection strategy generate feasible solutions later, it is customary to evaluate some feasible solutions and use the best as the current best upper bound.

9.2.2 Algorithm 2 (Using the Assignment Problem)

ILLUSTRATION 9.2

We have earlier seen that the Travelling salesman problem when formulated is an assignment problem with additional subtour elimination constraints. This branch and bound algorithm is based on the assignment problem (Eastman, 1958 referred in Boffey, 1982). Since the TSP is a restricted version (having additional constraints) of the assignment problem, we relax it by temporarily removing the additional constraints and solving it as an assignment problem (minimization). The solution to the assignment matrix of given distances (Table 9.6) is $X_{13} = X_{25} = X_{31} = X_{42} = X_{54} = 1$ with objective function value $Z = 33$.

Table 9.6 Distance Matrix

–	10	8	9	7
10	–	10	5	6
8	10	–	8	9
9	5	8	–	6
7	6	9	6	–

The optimal solution to the relaxed assignment problem is infeasible to the TSP because it has two subtours 1–3–1 and 2–5–4–2. If the optimal assignment solution is feasible to the TSP then it would have been optimal to the TSP. Since it is infeasible, the optimal assignment value is a lower bound to the optimal TSP value. This is because if the optimal solution of a relaxed problem is infeasible to the original problem then the value becomes a lower bound to the optimal value of the original minimization problem.

Therefore,

$$\text{LB (TSP)} = 33$$

The table (Hungarian algorithm) from which we obtained the optimal solution to the assignment problem is given in Table 9.7 (the assignments are shown in bold).

The two subtours are shown in Figure 9.5.

Table 9.7 Reduced Matrix

–	4	**0**	3	**0**
4	–	3	**0**	0
0	3	–	1	1
3	**0**	1	–	0
0	0	1	**0**	–

In order to get a tour (feasible solution) we have to remove edges from the subtours and add edges that can create a tour. From Table 9.7 all assignments have been made with zero costs and removing edges from subtours will not decrease the cost (distance). If we add edges from one subtour to another, we would like to add minimum lengths. We have to leave City 1 or City 3 and reach either 2 or 4 or 5. The minimum among 1–2, 1–4, 1–5, 3–2, 3–4, 3–5 is chosen. This turns out to be zero. Since we have to reach 1 or 3 from 2, 4 or 5, the minimum among 2–1, 4–1, 5–1, 2–3, 4–2, 5–2 is chosen. This turns out to be zero. Therefore, the net addition is zero. Sometimes, we may get a positive value here and the lower bound can be increased. This method of improving the lower bound to TSP is from Christofides (1972).

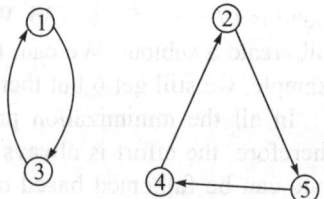

Figure 9.5 Two subtours in the assignment solution to Example 9.1.

Since the assignment solution has subtours, we break them. Considering subtour $X_{13} = X_{31} = 1$, we can break it by creating two assignment problems one with $X_{13} = 1$ and the other with $X_{13} = 0$. The first assignment problem is a 4×4 problem considering rows 2, 3, 4 and 5 and columns 1, 2, 4 and 5. Here the value of d_{31} is set to infinity since $X_{31} = 1$. The second assignment matrix is a 5×5 matrix with d_{13} set to infinity. The two assignment matrices are shown in Tables 9.8 and 9.9, respectively.

Table 9.8 Assignment Matrix

10	–	5	6
–	10	8	9
9	5	–	6
7	6	6	–

Table 9.9 Assignment Matrix

–	10	–	9	7
10	–	10	5	6
8	10	–	8	9
9	5	8	–	6
7	6	9	6	–

The solutions to the two assignment problems are:
Problem 2 (with $X_{13} = 1$) is $X_{13} = X_{24} = X_{35} = X_{42} = X_{51} = 1$ with $Z = 34$
Problem 3 (with $X_{13} = 0$) is $X_{15} = X_{24} = X_{31} = X_{42} = X_{53} = 1$ with $Z = 34$

The branch and bound tree is shown in Figure 9.6.

We consider the solution to problem P2 and observe that there is a subtour 2–4–2. We create two new problems the same way as we did before, with $X_{24} = 1$ and $X_{42} = 0$. When we solve the assignment problems we have to include the earlier branch (fixed variables). Wherever a variable is set to 1, the size of the assignment problem reduces. Also one of the distance elements that could create a subtour is set to infinity. Wherever we set a variable to zero, the corresponding d_{ij} is set to infinity. We call these as problems P4 and P5.

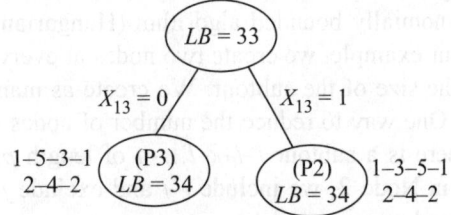

Figure 9.6 Branch and bound tree using assignment problem.

We consider the solution to problem P3 and observe that there is a subtour 2–4–2. We create two new problems the same way as we did before, with $X_{24} = 1$ and $X_{24} = 0$. We call these as problems P6 and P7.

The assignment solution to problem P7 (having $X_{13} = 0$ and $X_{24} = 0$) is $X_{15} = X_{23} = X_{31} = X_{42} = X_{54} = 1$ with $Z = 36$. This is a feasible solution to TSP (with no subtour) and hence represents an upper bound to the optimum. We update the upper bound (the current best objective function to 36). We fathom this node by feasibility.

The assignment solution to problem P5 (where $X_{13} = 1$ and $X_{24} = 0$) is $X_{13} = X_{25} = X_{34} = X_{42} = X_{51} = 1$ with $Z = 34$. This is a feasible solution to TSP (with no subtour) and hence represents an upper bound to the optimum. We update the upper bound (the current best objective function to 34). We fathom this node by feasibility.

We observe that the other nodes corresponding to problems P4 and P6 (unfathomed) should have a lower bound value of at least 34 because they branch from nodes with lower bound = 34. We fathom these node using the principle that $LB \geq UB$. There is no unfathomed node and the algorithm stops. The optimal solution is the best upper bound obtained till now. The solution $X_{13} = X_{25} = X_{34} = X_{42} = X_{51} = 1$ with $Z = 34$ is optimal.

The branch and bound tree is shown in Figure 9.7.

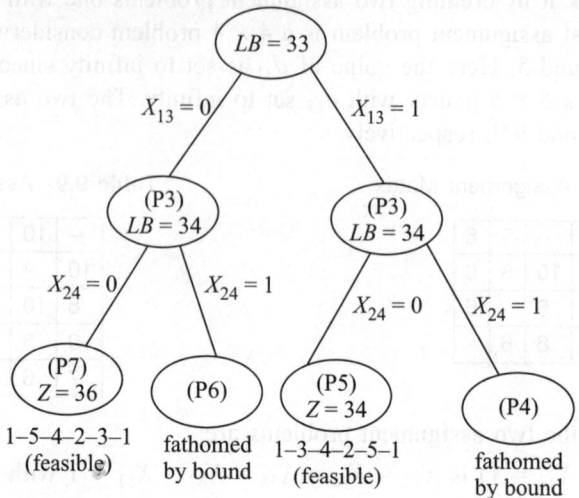

Figure 9.7 Branch and bound tree using assignment algorithm.

This branch and bound algorithm that used the assignment problem is called the **Eastman's method**. Here the lower bound is calculated by solving another optimization problem (the assignment problem) at every node. It is to be noted that the assignment algorithm has a polynomially bounded algorithm (Hungarian algorithm) that can be used to solve the problem. In our example, we create two nodes at every stage. Again the number of nodes created depends on the size of the subtour. We create as many nodes as the size of the smallest length subtour.

One way to reduce the number of nodes is to use results from Held and Karp (1970). Here, if there is a subtour i–j–k–l…–i of length p, we create p nodes where in Node 1, we exclude i–j, in Node 2, we include i–j and exclude j–k, in Node 3 we include i–j and j–k and exclude k–l and so on.

9.2.3 Algorithm 3

ILLUSTRATION 9.3

We explain the algorithm using the same example given again in Table 9.10.

Since we have to leave every city once in the optimal tour, we add the row minimum of each row to get a lower bound. The matrix after subtracting the row minima is given in Table 9.11 and the lower bound is $7 + 5 + 8 + 5 + 6 = 31$.

We also observe that every column has to be reached once and subtract the column minima. The third column has a non-zero minimum and the reduced matrix after subtraction is given in Table 9.12. The lower bound increases to $LB = 31 + 1 = 32$.

The reduced matrix has a zero in every row and every column. We also have to make assignments in zero positions. We try to compute the penalty for not assigning at every zero position. This is the sum of the next highest number in the *corresponding row and column*. The penalties are shown in Table 9.13.

Table 9.10 Distance Matrix

-	10	8	9	7
10	-	10	5	6
8	10	-	8	9
9	5	8	-	6
7	6	9	6	-

Table 9.11 Row Minimum Subtraction

-	3	1	2	0
5	-	5	0	1
0	2	-	0	1
4	0	3	-	1
1	0	3	0	-

Table 9.12 Column Minimum Subtraction

-	3	0	2	0
5	-	4	0	1
0	2	-	0	1
4	0	2	-	1
1	0	2	0	-

Table 9.13 Computing the Penalties

Zero position	Penalty
1–3	0 + 2 = 2
1–5	0 + 1 = 1
2–4	0 + 1 = 1
3–1	1 + 0 = 1
3–4	0 + 0 = 0
4–2	0 + 1 = 1
5–2	0 + 0 = 0
5–4	0 + 0 = 0

Among the penalties Position 1–3 has the maximum penalty of not assigning to that position. We have to start assigning with this position. We create two nodes one by assigning to Position 1–3 ($X_{13} = 1$) and the other with $X_{13} = 0$. For the node with $X_{13} = 0$, the lower bound increases by 2 (the penalty) and becomes 34. For the node with $X_{13} = 1$, we have a resultant matrix with row 1 and column 3 left out. This is given in Table 9.14.

We have changed d_{31} to ∞ (shown as dash) because we cannot have $X_{31} = 1$ because we have fixed X_{13} to 1. This makes column 1 and column 5 without a zero. We subtract 1 from every element. The resultant matrix is shown in Table 9.15 and the lower bound for the node $X_{13} = 1$ increases by 2 to 34. The branch and bound tree is shown in Figure 9.8.

Table 9.14 Reduced Matrix

	1	2	4	5
2	5	-	0	1
3	-	2	0	1
4	4	0	-	1
5	1	0	0	-

Table 9.15 Reduced Matrix

	1	2	4	5
2	4	-	0	0
3	-	2	0	0
4	3	0	-	0
5	0	0	0	-

```
        LB = 32
       /        \
   X₁₃ = 0    X₁₃ = 1
     /            \
  LB = 34      LB = 34
```

Figure 9.8 Branch and bound algorithm (Little's algorithm) for Problem 9.1.

The node with $X_{31} = 1$ has the same lower bound value as the other node. We branch from the right side node always. We calculate penalties for the matrix shown in Table 9.15. These are shown in Table 9.16.

Position 5–1 is chosen for branching and we create two nodes, one with $X_{51} = 1$ and the other with $X_{51} = 0$. The node with $X_{51} = 0$ will have the lower bound increased by the penalty of three to $34 + 3 = 37$. The node $X_{51} = 1$ has a reduced distance matrix with row 5 and column 1 left out from Table 9.14. This is shown in Table 9.17.

Table 9.16 Computing Penalties

Zero position	Penalty
2–4	0 + 0 = 0
2–5	0 + 0 = 0
3–4	0 + 0 = 0
3–5	0 + 0 = 0
4–2	0 + 0 = 0
4–5	0 + 0 = 0
5–1	3 + 0 = 3
5–2	0 + 0 = 0
5–3	0 + 0 = 0

Table 9.17 Reduced Matrix

	2	4	5
2	–	0	0
3	2	0	–
4	0	–	0

Table 9.17 has $d_{35} = \infty$ because $X_{51} = X_{13} = 1$ should not have an assignment $X_{35} = 1$ (this can create a subtour). The lower bound for the node $X_{51} = 1$ remains as 34 because every row and column has a zero. The branch and bound tree is shown in Figure 9.9.

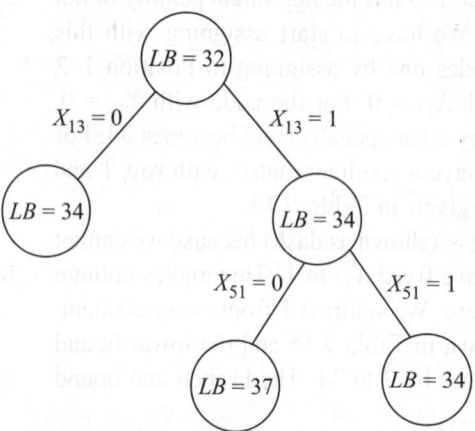

Figure 9.9 Little's algorithm for Illustration 9.3.

We branch from the node $X_{13} = X_{51} = 1$. We compute the penalties for all the zero positions. These are shown in Table 9.18.

The maximum penalty is for both 3–4 and 4–2. We break the tie arbitrarily and choose variable X_{34} to branch further. We create two nodes $X_{34} = 1$ and $X_{34} = 0$. The node $X_{34} = 0$ has its lower bound increased by the penalty of 2 to 36. The node with $X_{34} = 1$ has now three assignments and we have a 2 × 2 resultant matrix given in Table 9.19.

Table 9.18 Computing Penalties

Zero position	Penalty
2–4	0 + 0 = 0
2–5	0 + 0 = 0
3–4	2 + 0 = 2
4–2	0 + 2 = 2
4–5	0 + 0 = 0

Since we have assignments $X_{51} = X_{13} = X_{34} = 1$, we cannot have $X_{45} = 1$. The only feasible assignment from the matrix is $X_{42} = X_{25} = 1$ giving us a feasible solution $X_{51} = X_{13} = X_{34} = X_{42} = X_{25} = 1$. This feasible solution has $Z = 7 + 8 + 8 + 5 + 6 = 34$.

Table 9.19 Reduced Matrix

	2	5
2	–	0
4	0	0

We have an upper bound (feasible solution) with $Z = 34$. We update this solution and fathom this node by feasibility. We observe that all unfathomed nodes have lower bounds ≥ 34. All of them are fathomed by lower bound $\geq UB$. The algorithm terminates giving us the optimal solution (best feasible solution) $X_{51} = X_{13} = X_{34} = X_{42} = X_{25} = 1$ with $Z = 7 + 8 + 8 + 5 + 6 = 34$.

This branch and bound algorithm was developed by Little et al. (1963). Here we always branch from the rightmost node so that we get a feasible solution (UB) first. Usually this upper bound is very good and can fathom all the left nodes (with $X_{ij} = 0$). The left nodes have a higher value of lower bound because the maximum penalty is added to the previous bound. On an average this algorithm is found to work faster and better than the other two.

9.3 HEURISTIC ALGORITHMS FOR THE TSP

We have seen that the TSP is an NP complete problem and that branch and bound algorithms (worst case enumerative algorithm) can be used to solve them optimally. We do not have polynomially bounded algorithms to get the optimal solutions. The branch and bound algorithms can solve the problem optimally up to a certain size. For large sized problems, we have to develop approximate algorithms or heuristic algorithms. In this section, we explain a few heuristic algorithms for the TSP.

9.3.1 Nearest Neighbourhood Algorithm (Rosenkrantz et al., 1974 Referred in Golden et al., 1980)

ILLUSTRATION 9.4

In this algorithm, we start from a city and proceed towards the nearest city from there. We illustrate this algorithm using the example given in Table 9.20.

Table 9.20 Distance Matrix

–	10	8	9	7
10	–	10	5	6
8	10	–	8	9
9	5	8	–	6
7	6	9	6	–

If we start from City 1, we can go to the nearest city, which is City 5. From 5 we can reach City 2 (there is a tie between 2 and 4) and from 2 we can reach 4 from which we reach City 3. The solution is 1–5–2–4–3–1 with $Z = 34$.

Starting from City 2 and moving to the nearest neighbour, we get the solution 2–4–5–1–3–2 with $Z = 36$.

Starting with City 3, the solution is 3–1–5–2–4–3 with $Z = 34$
Starting with City 4, the solution is 4–2–5–1–3–4 with $Z = 34$
Starting with City 5, the solution is 5–2–4–3–1–5 with $Z = 34$

The best solution is 1–5–2–4–3–1 with $Z = 34$. This also happens to be the optimal solution. The nearest neighbourhood search heuristic is a "greedy" search heuristic where the last city to be added to the list is not optimized. Therefore, this can give poor results. The worst case performance bound for the nearest neighbourhood search for a symmetric TSP is given by

$$\frac{L_h}{L_o} \le \frac{(1+\log_2 n)}{2}$$

This shows that in the worst case, the heuristic will be away from the optimum by a factor of $(1 + \log_{10} n)/2$. For a 128 city problem, the worst case bound is 4 indicating that the heuristic can be four times the optimum in the worst case.

9.3.2 Pairwise Interchange Heuristic

ILLUSTRATION 9.5

We start with a feasible solution and try to improve it by exchanging the cities pairwise. In an n-city problem, $^nC_2$ interchanges are possible and the best is chosen.

We can start with any sequence, say, 1–2–3–4–5–1 with $Z = 41$. The sequence is represented by 1–2–3–4–5 indicating that we will come back to the first from the last city. Interchanging Positions 1 and 2, we get the sequence 2–1–3–4–5 with $Z = 38$. This is better and we accept this solution.

We start the algorithm all over again with the starting solution 2–1–3–4–5 with $Z = 38$. On interchanging 2 and 5, we get 5–1–3–4–2 with $Z = 34$. Further exchanges do not improve the solution and the best solution after evaluating $^nC_2$ interchanges is 5–1–3–4–2–5 with $Z = 34$.

The pairwise interchange heuristic evaluates $^nC_2$ interchanges and can take a considerable amount of CPU time. Sometimes we use an adjacent pairwise interchange where we exchange $(n - 1)$ sequences, take the best and proceed till no more improvement is possible.

9.3.3 Three-opt Heuristic

ILLUSTRATION 9.6

This very popular heuristic is by Lin (1965). This is an improvement heuristic where three arcs are considered at a time for improvement. Let us assume that we have three distinct arcs a–b, p–q and u–v taken from a feasible solution. We can create seven more feasible solutions by changing the arcs such that at least one new edge is created in the solution. The seven possibilities are:

a–b, p–u, q–v
a–p, b–q, u–v
a–p, b–u, q–v
a–q, u–b, p–v
a–q, u–p, b–v
a–u, q–b, p–v
a–u, q–p, b–v

If the three arcs have common nodes, some of the seven new solutions will repeat. We can choose three arcs in $^nC_3$ ways. Each iteration has $7\ ^nC_3$ solutions out of which some can repeat.

In our example, let us start with a feasible solution 1–2–3–4–5 with $Z = 41$. We consider edges 1–2, 2–3 and 4–5 as a–b, p–q and u–v. We retain edges 3–4 and 5–1. One out of the seven new solutions gives us 1–3, 4–2 and 2–5, which along with the fixed edges 3–4 and 5–1 gives us the TSP solution 1–3–4–2–5–1 with $Z = 34$, which is the optimal. After this solution is reached, and the three-opt method would show no improvement. This is shown in Figure 9.10.

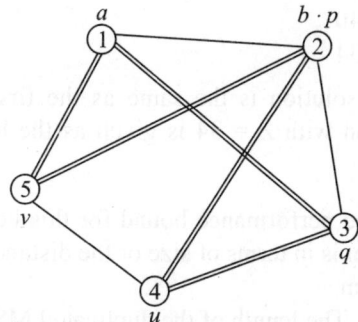

Figure 9.10 One out of the seven solutions using three-opt heuristic for Illustration 9.6.

9.3.4 Twice Around the Tree Heuristic
(Kim, 1975 referred in Golden, 1980)

ILLUSTRATION 9.7

This heuristic uses the minimum spanning tree and constructs a feasible solution to the TSP. Considering the data in Table 9.20, the minimum spanning tree is constructed and shown in Figure 9.11.

The length of the minimum spanning tree is 5 + 8 + 6 + 7 = 26. This is a lower bound to the optimum TSP. This is because the TSP has 5 edges and removal of an edge from the optimum circuit will give a spanning tree. This will be greater in length than the MST. As long as all the distances are ncn-negative, the length of the minimum spanning tree $L_{MST} \leq L_o$ where L_o is the length of the optimum TSP.

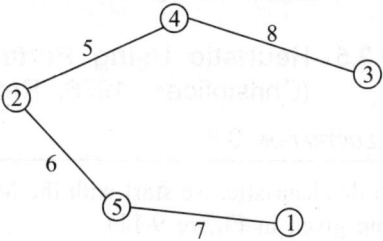

Figure 9.11 A minimum spanning tree for Illustration 9.7.

In this heuristic, we duplicate the edges of the MST. This gives us a length of 52. The graph is given in Figure 9.12.

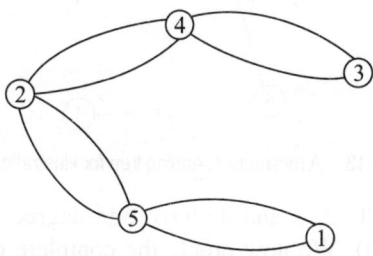

Figure 9.12 Duplicating the edges of the MST shown in Figure 9.11.

From the duplicated graph, we can create an Eulerian circuit. This is given by 1–5–2–4–3–4–2–5–1 with a length of 52. From this Eulerian, we can create feasible solutions by suitably deleting repeated edges. We get the following feasible solutions to TSP:

1. 1–5–2–4–3–1 with Z = 34
2. 1–2–4–3–5–1 with Z = 39

3. 1–4–3–2–5–1 with $Z = 40$
4. 1–3–4–2–5–1 with $Z = 34$

We observe that the fourth solution is the same as the first due to the symmetry of the distance matrix. The best solution with $Z = 34$ is given as the heuristic solution to the TSP.

Performance of the heuristic

It is possible to have a worst case performance bound for this heuristic. This bound would tell us that no matter what the problem is in terms of size or the distances, the heuristic will be within a certain multiple of the optimum.

We have seen that $L_{MST} \leq L_o$. The length of the duplicated MST is the length of the Eulerian graph which is $2L_{MST}$. If the distance matrix follows triangle inequality then the length of every feasible solution is $\leq 2L_{MST}$. This is because every feasible solution has been created from the Eulerian circuit in a certain order in which the vertices appear.

For example, when we create 1–5–2–4–3–1 from 1–5–2–4–3–4–2–5–1, from triangle inequality we can show that 3–1 has a length (distance) $\leq$ 3–4–2–5–1.

The best heuristic solution has a length (distance) L_h. Then $L_h \leq 2L_{MST}$. Since $L_{MST} \leq L_o$, $L_h \leq 2L_o$. The solution obtained using this heuristic will always be less than or equal to twice the optimum. This heuristic is called **twice around the tree heuristic**.

9.3.5 Heuristic Using Perfect Matching
(Christofides, 1976, Referred in Golden 1980)

ILLUSTRATION 9.8

In this heuristic, we start with the MST solution given in Figure 9.13 (This is different from the one given in Figure 9.11).

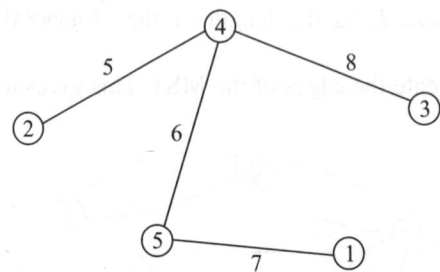

Figure 9.13 A minimum spanning tree for Illustration 9.8.

In the MST, four vertices (1, 2, 3 and 4) have odd degree (in any graph, the number of vertices with odd degree is even). We now create the complete graph with these four vertices and find out the minimum weighted perfect matching. The possible matchings are:

1–2, 3–4 with weight 18
1–3, 2–4 with weight 13
1–4, 2–3 with weight 19

(In practice, the minimum weighted matching has polynomially bounded algorithms. Here we have used enumeration because of the small size of the problem). The minimum weighted matching is 1–3, 2–4 with weight 18. We superimpose these edges on the MST to get a graph that is Eulerian. This is shown in Figure 9.14.

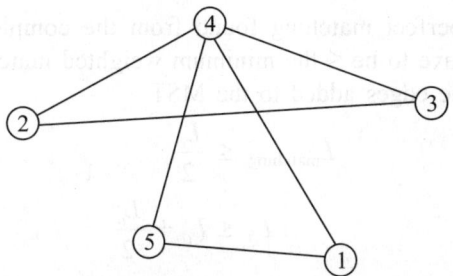

Figure 9.14 Minimum spanning tree + minimum weighted matching.

We have added two edges with a weight of 13 which when added to the MST would give us an Eulerian 1–4–2–3–4–5–1 (or 1–4–3–2–4–5–1). From this Eulerian, we obtain feasible solutions to TSP as we did in the earlier algorithm. The TSP solutions are:

1–4–2–3–5–1 with $Z = 40$
1–2–3–4–5–1 with $Z = 41$
1–4–3–2–5–1 with $Z = 40$
1–3–2–4–5–1 with $Z = 36$

The best solution is given as the heuristic solution with $Z = 36$.

Performance of the heuristic

In this heuristic, we obtain feasible solutions to the TSP from the Eulerian circuit. Assuming that the distance matrix satisfies triangle inequality, we know that every feasible solution obtained from the Eulerian has a length less than or equal to the Eulerian. Therefore,

$$L_h \leq L_e$$

(where L_e is the length of the Eulerian. We also know that the Eulerian is formed by adding the minimum weighted perfect matching to the MST. Therefore,

$$L_e = L_{\text{MST}} + L_{\text{matching}}$$

Hence $L_h \leq L_{\text{MST}} + L_{\text{matching}}$

Knowing that $L_{\text{MST}} \leq L_o$, we have

$$L_h \leq L_o + L_{\text{matching}}$$

Let us derive the relationship between L_o and L_{matching}. The matching is obtained from a perfect graph formed out of the vertices of the MST with odd degree. Since any graph has an even number of vertices with odd degree, the number of edges in the matching is $\leq n/2$ or $(n-1)/2$ depending on whether n is even or odd.

The optimum L_o has n vertices. In our example, there are five vertices. Four out of them have odd degree in the MST. In L_o, if we leave out vertex 5 and join the two vertices that are incident to vertex 5, the length of such a tour will be $\leq L_o$ (by triangle inequality). We can always find the weight of the minimum perfect matching from the resultant tour and the length of such a matching will be $\leq L_o/2$. This is because if we have an even number of numbers and we divide the numbers into two groups with equal cardinality (number in each), the minimum sum will be $\leq$ half the total.

The minimum weight perfect matching found from the complete graph having vertices (1 to 4) will by definition have to be $\leq$ the minimum weighted matching found from the TSP. Therefore, the weights of the edges added to the MST

$$L_{\text{matching}} \leq \frac{L_o}{2}$$

Therefore,
$$L_h \leq L_o + \frac{L_o}{2}$$

and
$$\frac{L_h}{L_o} \leq 1.5$$

This heuristic will give a solution that is within 1.5 times the optimal always.

9.4 SEARCH ALGORITHMS

Over the last twenty years several search algorithms have been developed, which provide superior solutions to the problem specific heuristics that we have seen. These search algorithms called **metaheuristics**, are generic in nature and can be applied to a variety of combinatorial optimization problems. Some of these that have been applied successfully to solve TSPs are:

1. Simulated annealing
2. Genetic algorithms
3. Tabu search
4. Ant colony optimization

All the algorithms have a starting solution that can be a randomly generated solution or taken from a heuristic algorithm. Some of these have more than one starting solution. In simulated annealing, we generate a neighbour solution using an interchange procedure. The neighbour is accepted if it is superior. It is also accepted with a certain probability if it is inferior. The probability of accepting an inferior solution decreases as the search continues.

In genetic algorithms, we take two feasible solutions and create offspring through crossover, mutation and inversion. These have to be feasible. It is found that by accepting superior offspring into the mating pool, we can generate good solutions to TSP.

In tabu search, we generate neighbours and accept superior neighbours. Once accepted, the move is set tabu and the interchange is not effected for a fixed number of iterations. In ant colony optimization, the procedure mimics the way ants search food by moving in different directions and quickly converging to the target. A similar procedure is followed in solving combinatorial optimization problems.

Among these metaheuristics, simulated annealing and ant colony optimization are found to work well for TSP. All these algorithms search a large number of solutions till they converge to the best possible solution. These are still heuristics and do not guarantee optimal solutions.

9.5 CHINESE POSTMAN PROBLEM

The chinese postman problem is as follows:

A postman has to visit a set of roads, deliver mail and return to the starting point. The roads are represented as the arcs of a network. The postman has to visit every arc at least once and return to the starting point travelling minimum total distance. The problem is called a *Chinese Postman problem* because the first modern work appeared in a Chinese Journal (Minieka, 1979).

Let us consider an example network with 8 nodes and 13 arcs given in Figure 9.15.

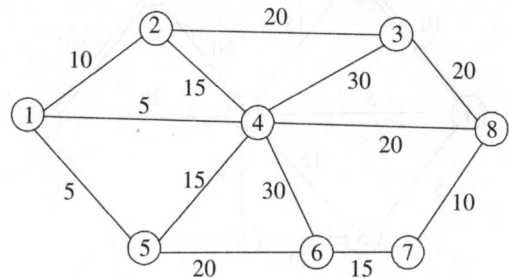

Figure 9.15 Network for Chinese postman problem.

If the given graph has an Eulerian circuit then it is optimal and the postman can travel minimum distance (equal to the some of the distances of all the arcs) which is the length of the Eulerian. If the given graph is not Eulerian then some edges have to be travelled again and this is to be minimized. The problem then reduces to adding minimum distance into the network so that the resultant network is Eulerian. If a network has vertices of odd degree then it is not Eulerian.

ILLUSTRATION 9.9

Our example of Figure 9.15, has vertices 1, 2, 3, 5, 6, and 8 having odd degree and hence is not Eulerian. Let us start with a feasible solution 1-2-3-8-7-6-4-6-5-4-5-1-4-2-4-3-4-8-4-1 with a total distance of 330. Here, edges 1-4, 2-4, 3-4, 4-5, 4-6, 4-8 are repeated twice incurring an additional distance of 115 to the edge distances of 215 to result in a total distance of 330.

Knowing that the given graph is not Eulerian, the problem now is to find the minimum additional distance. One way of doing this is to make these repeated edges have a negative value and to identify negative length cycles. The network with negative values for repeated edges is shown in Figure 9.16.

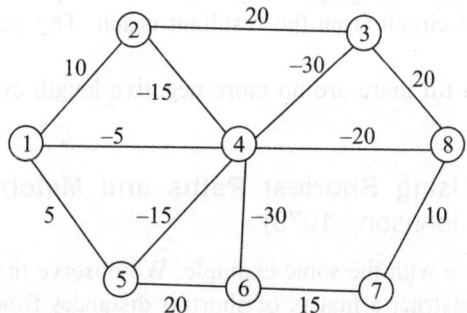

Figure 9.16 Repeated edges have negative lengths.

There are four negative cycles 1–2–4–1, 2–3–4–2, 3–4–8–3 and 4–5–6–4 with values –10, –25, –30 and –25, respectively. The cycle 1–2–4–2 is changed such that arcs 1–4 and 2–4 appear once and arc 1–2 is repeated. Similarly, the cycle 3–4–8–3 would have 3–4 and 4–8 appearing once and 3–8 repeating. The cycle 4–5–6–4 would have arcs 4–5 and 4–6 appearing once and arc 5–6 repeating. Now, the 2–3–4–2 is not a negative length cycle. The graph now looks as shown in Figure 9.17.

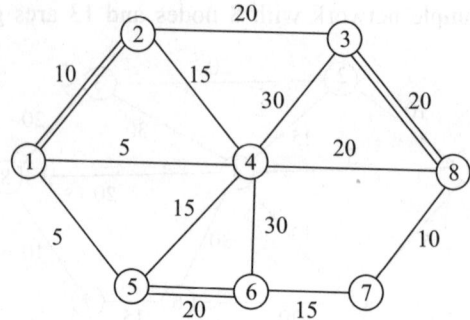

Figure 9.17 Final solution to Chinese postman problem with repeated edges shown.

We can identify an Eulerian circuit from the graph given by 1–2–3–8–3–4–8–7–6–5–6–4–5–1–4–2–1 with a total weight of 265. The repeated edges have a weight of 50 which when added to the original graph distance of 215 gives us 265. Through the negative cycles we saved a distance of 65, which when subtracted from the feasible solution of 330 gives us 265.

We now repeat the algorithm and try to identify negative length cycles in the feasible solution after replacing the repeating edges with a negative value. We observe that there are no negative length cycles and the solution is optimal with an additional minimum distance of 50.

The algorithm

1. Verify whether the given graph is Eulerian. If so then the Eulerian circuit is optimal to the Chinese postman problem.
2. If the given graph is not Eulerian, obtain a feasible solution to the Chinese postman problem with some edges repeating.
3. Replace the repeated edges with a negative sign and identify if there is negative length cycle. If so, replace the negative lengths by the positive lengths. The positive length edges are repeated once while the negative length cycles are repeated one less.
4. Construct an Eulerian circuit from the resultant graph. This represents a better feasible solution.
5. Repeat Steps 3 and 4 till there are no more negative length cycles. The best solution is the optimal solution.

9.5.1 An Algorithm Using Shortest Paths and Matching
(Edmonds and Johnson, 1973)

Let us explain this algorithm with the same example. We observe that vertices 1, 2, 3, 5, 6, and 8 have odd degree. We construct a matrix of shortest distances from each node to every other node in the graph. This matrix is given in Table 9.21.

ILLUSTRATION 9.10

Table 9.21 Shortest Distances

	1	2	3	5	6	8
1	–	10	30	5	25	25
2		–	20	15	35	35
3			–	35	45	20
5				–	20	35
6					–	25
8						–

From this table, we have to find a perfect matching with minimum total weight. For example, a feasible matching 1–2, 3–5, 6–8 has a total weight of 10 + 25 + 35 = 70. Many algorithms are available for getting the optimal matching. We observe that the solution with matchings 1–2, 5–6, 3–8 with weight 50 is optimal.

We also realize that the distances represent the direct arcs from 1–2, 5–6 and 3–8 and we, therefore, add these to the given graph. If the distances involved a shortest path with multiple arcs then we add all the arcs in the shortest path. The new graph is Eulerian and has a weight of 265, which is optimal.

The algorithm

1. Identify the odd degree vertices in the given graph.
2. Construct a matrix of shortest distances from every vertex to every other vertex. Each distance is computed by the shortest path between the vertices.
3. Identify the minimum weight matching from this matrix.
4. Add the matching to the given graph to obtain an Eulerian graph.
5. The length of the Eulerian is the optimal solution to the Chinese postman problem.

9.6 VEHICLE ROUTING PROBLEMS

These form an important class of optimization problems that are well researched and have immense practical application. One of the early research in this problem is by Dantzig and Ramser (1959). The simplest vehicle routeing problem (VRP) is stated as:

Given a single depot and a certain number of vehicles, the problem is to meet the requirements of n number of customers. Each customer requires a certain quantity that is to be delivered from the depot. There are a fixed number of vehicles available and the capacity of the vehicles are known. The distance among the customer locations as well as from the depot to the locations are known. The vehicles start from the depot and return to the depot after meeting customer requirements. The problem is to deliver the quantities to the customers such that the vehicles used travel minimum total distance.

The above problem is called the **single depot vehicle routing problem**. There are multiple depot vehicle routing problems where the customer can be served from any vehicle (from any depot). In this chapter we will consider only the single depot vehicle routing problem. There are three types of problems:

1. All the vehicles have to be used [It is assumed that every vehicle will have at least one city (customer) attached to it].
2. Using the minimum number of vehicles.
3. Using enough number of vehicles such that the total distance travelled is minimum.

Let us explain the algorithms and the various problems using an example.

9.6.1 Optimal Solutions

ILLUSTRATION **9.11**

We consider a 6 customer (city) VRP. The depot is denoted by 0 (zero) and the distance matrix is given in Table 9.22.

(The depot and cities are numbered in bold). The requirement in the six cities are [4 6 3 2 3 2] respectively and the vehicle capacity is 10.

Let us find the optimal solution to some problem instances. Let us assume that the vehicle capacity is sufficiently large to hold the requirements of any number of customers. The problem of finding the minimum distance VRP for a given number of vehicles (say 4 vehicles) is given by solving a TSP created as follows:

Table 9.22 Distance Matrix

	0	1	2	3	4	5	6
0	–	20	18	14	16	12	19
1	20	–	22	18	30	26	28
2	18	22	–	32	20	22	21
3	14	18	32	–	20	22	21
4	16	30	20	20	–	30	32
5	12	26	22	22	30	–	26
6	19	28	21	21	32	26	–

1. Add as many rows and columns as the number of vehicles (in this case we get a 10 × 10 TSP). Rows 1 to 6 represent the cities and rows 7 to 10 represent the vehicles (depot).
2. Distance between cities and distance between depot and city is taken from the given table.
3. Distance between any entity and itself is infinity.
4. Distance between any two depots is infinity.

The resultant 10-city TSP is given in Table 9.23.

Table 9.23 10-City TSP

	1	2	3	4	5	6	D7	D8	D9	D10
1	–	22	18	30	26	28	20	20	20	20
2	22	–	32	20	22	21	18	18	18	18
3	18	32	–	20	22	21	14	14	14	14
4	30	20	20	–	30	32	16	16	16	16
5	26	22	22	30	–	26	12	12	12	12
6	28	21	21	32	26	–	19	19	19	19
D7	20	18	14	16	12	19	–	–	–	–
D8	20	18	14	16	12	19	–	–	–	–
D9	20	18	14	16	12	19	–	–	–	–
D10	20	18	14	16	12	19	–	–	–	–

A feasible solution to the TSP is *D–2–1–3–D–4–D–5–D–6–D* with $Z = 166$.

We solve this TSP optimally by applying Little's algorithm. The sum of row minimum is 18 + 18 + 14 + 16 + 12 + 19 + 12 + 12 + 12 + 12 = 145. We also observe that some columns do not have zeros and subtracting column minimum gives us a lower bound of 164.

The maximum penalty is for 1–2 with a value of 2. Branching on this variable we get the branch and bound tree shown in Figure 9.18.

The branch $X_{12} = 0$ has $LB = 164 + 2 = 166$ and fathomed because we have a feasible solution with $Z = 166$. The branch $X_{12} = 1$ creates a new table with one of the columns not having a zero. The minimum number is that column (value = 2) is subtracted from every element. The lower bound increases to 166. This node is also fathomed by feasibility and the feasible solution D–2–1–3–D–4–5–D–6–D with $Z = 166$ is optimal.

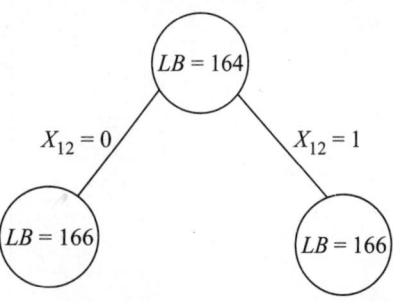

Figure 9.18 Solving the VRP as TSP.

Vehicle visits cities 2–1–3 in that order, vehicle 2 visits 4, vehicle 3 visits 5 and vehicle 4 visits city 6.

Here we assume that a vehicle has enough capacity to meet the requirements of 2, 1, 3 and has a capacity of 13 or more. If capacity constraints are to be rigidly considered, the branch and bound algorithm should be modified to handle capacity constraints.

Consider the capacity constraint of 10 per vehicle, a minimum of 2 vehicles are needed and the solution is D–5–1–3–D, D–4–2–6–D with $Z = 146$. If we ignore the capacity constraint and solve for 2 vehicles we get the optimal solution D–4–2–1–3–6–D–5–D with $Z = 140$.

For 3 vehicles without capacity restrictions we have the optimal solution D–3–1–2–6–D–4–D–5–D with $Z = 150$.

9.6.2 Heuristic Solutions

One of the most popular heuristics is the savings based algorithm of Clarke and Wright (1964). The method is based on the possible gain by combining cities i and j. If a vehicle has to go separately to City i and City j from the origin, the total distance covered will be $2[d_{0i} + d_{0j}]$. If a vehicle leaves the depot goes to i and then j and returns to the depot, the distance covered will be $(d_{0i} + d_{0j} + d_{ij})$. The saving will be the difference between them. The saving S_{ij} is given by

$$S_{ij} = (d_{0i} + d_{0j} - d_{ij})$$

If the distances satisfy triangle inequality, the savings will be non-negative. There will always be a non-negative saving by combining cities. The feasibility in terms of vehicle capacity has to be ascertained when routes (cities) are combined together.

ILLUSTRATION 9.12

The savings for our example (in descending order) are given in Table 9.24. The requirements are assumed to be [4 6 3 5 3 6] and the vehicle capacity is 15.

Table 9.24 Savings in Descending Order

i–j	S_{ij}	i–j	S_{ij}
1–2	16	1–4	6
1–3	16	1–5	6
2–6	16	5–6	5
2–4	14	3–5	4
3–6	12	4–6	3
1–6	11	2–3	0
3–4	10	4–5	–2
2–5	8		

The negative savings indicates that the distances do not satisfy triangle inequality. We start assigning cities to vehicles. Cities 1 and 2 are allotted to Vehicle 1. Since 1–3 has the next best saving, City 3 is added since it does not violate the capacity constraint. Pair 3–6 has the next highest saving. City 6 cannot be added because it violates the capacity constraint. The next feasible pair is 5–6 with a saving of 5. After that the feasible pair is 4–6 with a saving of 3. This is added to the second vehicle to result in a feasible solution D–2–1–3–D, D–5–6–4–D with a total distance of 72 + 86 = 158.

If a vehicle goes to every city from the depot and comes back, the total distance would be equal to DIS = $2[d_{01} + d_{02} + d_{03} + d_{04} + d_{05} + d_{06}]$ = 2(20 + 18 + 14 + 16 + 12 + 19) = 198. The savings based on the assignment is 16 + 16 + 5 + 3 = 40. The total distance is 198 – 40 = 158.

The Clarke and Wright method is a heuristic algorithm and need not guarantee the optimal solution. It is also a single pass algorithm where cities once allocated cannot be reallocated to other vehicles. We also explain the refinement by Holmes and Parker (1976).

ILLUSTRATION 9.13

9.6.3 Holmes and Parker Refinement

We explain this algorithm using the distance matrix in Table 9.22. The requirement in the six cities are [4 6 3 5 3 6] respectively and the vehicle capacity is 15. The Clarke and Wright solution is first obtained with a total saving of 40. The first allocation 1–2 is permanently labelled at zero, and the savings algorithm is now applied to result in a saving of 50 (the allocations are D–1–3–4–D and D–6–2–5–D). This is a better solution than the first solution. Since this is the best solution, the first fixed allocation 1–3 is disabled and the savings algorithm results in a savings of 40 (D–6–2–4–D and D–1–5–3–D). The best incumbent solution with a savings of 50 is branched further by fixing 2–6 to zero. This process of branching from a solution by setting its first saving arc to zero is continued. The branching tree is shown in Figure 9.19. The algorithm can be terminated when good solutions are found or after a certain number of solutions can be evaluated. The algorithm by itself will terminate only when all possible solutions have been evaluated.

The two best solutions obtained from the Holmes and parker refinement are as follows: The solution D–1–3–D and D–5–2–4–D with a total distance of 198 − 50 = 148 and the solution D–1–3–4–D and D–6–2–5–D with a distance of 148. Both the solutions satisfy the vehicle constraint capacity of 15. These are better than the Clark Wright solution with a total distance of 158. We observe that the Holmes and Parker extension can result in better solutions (savings) than the Clarke Wright savings algorithm.

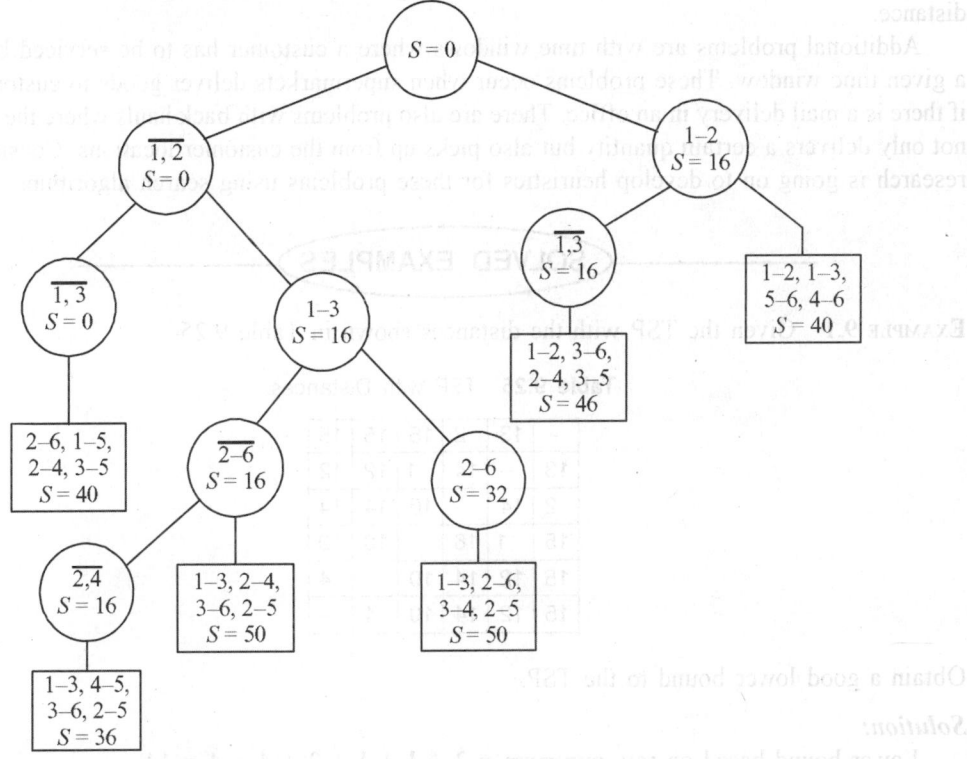

Figure 9.19 Holmes and Parker refinement solution to VRP.

In the above figure, we have taken into account feasibility of the allocation. For example, we cannot allocate 1, 2 and 6 to the same vehicle.

9.6.4 Other Forms of Savings Based Method

Instead of defining $S_{ij} = (d_{0i} + d_{0j} - d_{ij})$, we can define

$$S_{ij} = (d_{0i} + d_{0j} - \gamma d_{ij}).$$

By defining γ suitably, we can get different feasible solutions to the VRP.
For example $\gamma = 0.15$ gives us a solution D–1–4–6–D, D–2–3–5–D with a savings of 27. The original Clarke and Wright method with $\gamma = 1$ gives a better value in this case.

9.7 OTHER FORMS OF VEHICLE ROUTEING PROBLEMS

Vehicle routing problems have a wide range of application in supply chain management, distribution problems and in school pickup problems. When we want all the people to arrive at the same time at work or in a school, we use more vehicles so that the maximum time spent by a vehicle is minimized. In disribution problems, when vehicles have to be hired, we use minimum number of vehicles. When we do not have any additional constraints, we try to minimize total distance.

Additional problems are with time windows where a customer has to be serviced between a given time window. These problems occur when supermarkets deliver goods to customers or if there is a mail delivery in an office. There are also problems with back hauls where the vehicle not only delivers a certain quantity but also picks up from the customer locations. Considerable research is going on to develop heuristics for these problems using search algorithms.

SOLVED EXAMPLES

EXAMPLE 9.1 Given the TSP with the distances shown in Table 9.25.

Table 9.25 TSP with Distances

-	13	2	15	15	15
13	-	14	1	12	12
2	14	-	16	14	14
15	1	16	-	10	10
15	12	14	10	-	4
15	12	14	10	4	-

Obtain a good lower bound to the TSP.

Solution:

    Lower bound based on row minimum = 2 + 1 + 1 + 2 + 4 + 4 = 14

    Lower bound based on column minimum = 2 + 1 + 1 + 2 + 4 + 4 = 14

    LB based on assignment problem = 14 (since row minima gives a feasible solution to the assignment problem)

    LB based on MST = 30 (MST has edges 1-3, 2-4, 5-6, 1-2, 4-5)

Assignment problem gives 3 subtours 1-3-1, 2-4-2 and 5-6-5 with cost = 14

    The reduced matrix after row and column subtraction is given in Table 9.26.

Table 9.26 Reduced Matrix after Row and Column Subtraction

-	11	0	13	13	13
12	-	13	0	11	11
0	12	-	14	12	12
14	0	16	-	9	9
11	8	10	6	-	0
11	8	10	6	0	-

From this reduced matrix, we construct another matrix that captures the distances among the subtours in the reduced matrix. This is given in Table 9.27.

The solution to this assignment problem gives us a cost of 11 + 9 + 10 = 30. The lower bound using the assignment algorithm is 14 + 30 = 44.

Table 9.27 Matrix of Subtours

Subtours	1–3	2–4	5–6
1–3	–	11	12
2–4	12	–	9
5–6	8	6	–

EXAMPLE 9.2 Solve the TSP in Table 9.25 using nearest neighbourhood search and twice around the tree and comment on the goodness of these solutions.

Solution: Nearest neighbourhood search gives the following solutions:

$$1\text{–}3\text{–}5\text{–}6\text{–}4\text{–}2\text{–}1 \text{ with } Z = 44$$
$$2\text{–}4\text{–}5\text{–}6\text{–}3\text{–}1\text{–}2 \text{ with } Z = 44$$
$$3\text{–}1\text{–}2\text{–}4\text{–}5\text{–}6\text{–}3 \text{ with } Z = 44$$
$$4\text{–}2\text{–}5\text{–}6\text{–}3\text{–}1\text{–}4 \text{ with } Z = 48$$
$$5\text{–}6\text{–}4\text{–}2\text{–}1\text{–}3\text{–}5 \text{ with } Z = 44$$
$$6\text{–}5\text{–}4\text{–}2\text{–}1\text{–}3\text{–}6 \text{ with } Z = 46$$

Twice around the MST gives us the Eulerian circuit 1–3–1–2–4–5–6–5–4–2–1, from which many TSP solutions can be obtained. Eliminating some of them by symmetry, a few solutions with distinctly different values of the objective function are:

$$1\text{–}3\text{–}2\text{–}4\text{–}5\text{–}6\text{–}1 \text{ with } Z = 46$$
$$1\text{–}2\text{–}4\text{–}5\text{–}6\text{–}3\text{–}1 \text{ with } Z = 44$$
$$1\text{–}4\text{–}5\text{–}6\text{–}2\text{–}3\text{–}1 \text{ with } Z = 57$$

There is a feasible solution with $Z = 44$. The best solution has $Z = 44$ and the lower bound is 44. Hence the solution is optimal.

EXAMPLE 9.3 The data in Table 9.28 pertains to a network for a AGV system for a FMS.

Table 9.28 Arc-Distance Matrix

Arc	Distance
1–2	10
2–1	10
2–3	8
3–2	8
1–4	12
2–4	14
3–4	16

The AGV starts from point 1 goes through all arcs and comes back to the starting point. What is the minimum distance it covers before it reaches the starting point?

Solution: The given problem is a Chinese postman problem and the network for the problem is shown in Figure 9.20.

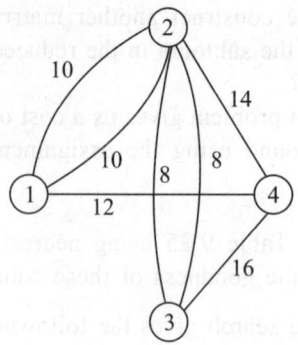

Figure 9.20 Network for Example 9.3.

It is observed that the degree of the vertices are 3, 5, 3, 3, respectively. All vertices have odd degree. A matrix of shortest distances among the vertices is created (Table 9.29).

The minimum weighted matching is 1–4 and 2–3 with weight = 20. Adding these to the graph gives us the Eulerian 1–2–1–4–2–3–2–3–4–1 with length = 98.

Table 9.29 Shortest Distance Matrix

–	10	18	12
10	–	8	14
18	8	–	16
12	14	1	–

EXAMPLE 9.4 Consider the single depot VRP with six cities. The distances from the depot are 10, 7, 9, 7, 7, 6, respectively. Assume the intercity distances as in Example 9.1 (Table 9.25). Each city requires 1 tonne of resource and each vehicle can carry 4 tonnes. Solve the VRP to find the number of vehicles with which the distance is minimized and for the minimum number of vehicles.

Solution: The minimum number of vehicles needed is 2 because a vehicle can handle 4 customers. Solving a TSP with 6 cities (2 vehicles), we get a solution 1–2–4–d–5–6–d–3–1 with distance = 49. Solving a TSP with 9 cities (3 vehicles) gives us a solution 1–3–d–2–4–d–5–6–d–1 with distance = 53. We use 2-city solution which has minimum distance and uses minimum number of vehicles.

Clarke and Wright savings algorithm also gives us the same solution because 1–3 has maximum saving of 17 followed by 2–4 with a saving of 13 and 5–6 with a saving of 9. We can have cities 1, 2, 3 and 4 covered by the same vehicle.

EXAMPLE 9.5 Solve the TSP given in Table 9.30 using the branch and bound algorithm of Little et al (1963). How does the twice around the tree heuristic solve the same problem?

Table 9.30 Distance Matrix

–	10	25	25	10
1	–	10	15	2
8	9	–	20	10
14	10	24	–	15
10	8	25	27	–

Travelling Salesman and Distribution Problems **381**

Solution: Subtracting row minima and column minima gives us $LB = 37 + 9 + 12 = \mathbf{58}$. Reduced matrix is shown in Table 9.31.

Table 9.31 Reduced Matrix

-	0	6	3	0
0	-	0	2	1
0	1	-	0	2
4	0	5	-	5
2	0	8	7	-

In Table 9.31 every row and every column has a zero. The penalties are calculated and the maximum penalty is for $X_{23} = 5$. We branch on this node. The entire tree is shown in Figure 9.21.

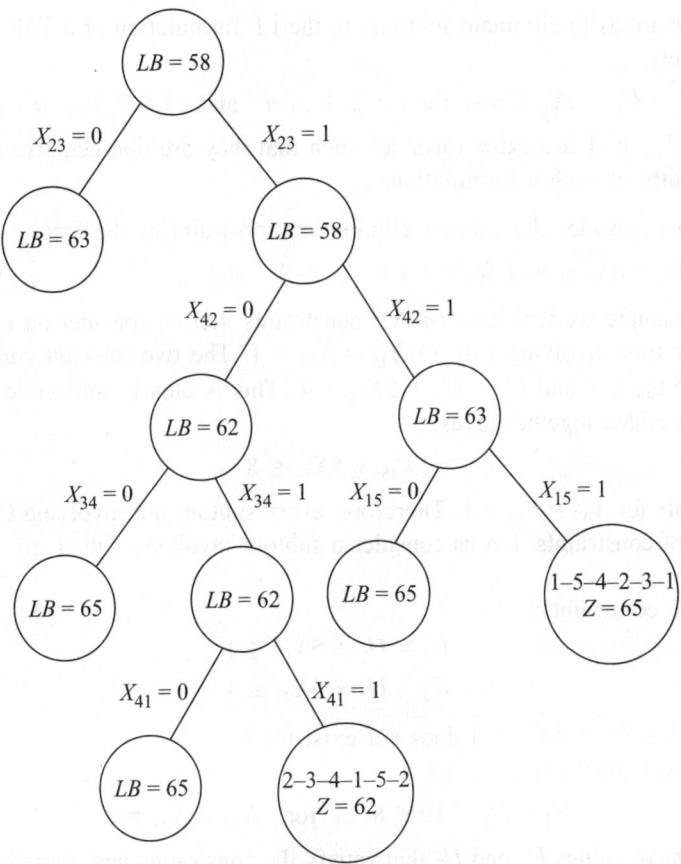

Figure 9.21 Branch and bound tree for Example 9.5.

Optimum 2–3–4–1–5–2 with Z = 62: We start by branching on variable X_{23} (penalty = 5) (Nodes 2 and 3). We branch further on variable X_{42} (penalty = 5) (Nodes 4 and 5) (LB = 63). We branch further on variable X_{15} (penalty = 2) (Nodes 6 and 7). We evaluate a feasible solution 1–5–4–2–3–1 at Node 6 with Z = 65. We fathom Node 7 and branch from Node 5 on variable

X_{34} (penalty = 3) (Nodes 8 and 9). We fathom Node 9 (LB = 65). We branch from Node 8 on variable X_{41} (penalty = 3) and create Nodes 10 and 11. Node 11 with LB = 65 is fathomed. Node 10 has a feasible solution 2–3–4–1–5–2 with Z = 62. This is updated. Node 3 is fathomed by LB. The solution 2–3–4–1–5–2 with Z = 62 is optimal.

The given matrix is not symmetric and hence MST has to be carefully defined. The worst case performance bound may not hold. Nevertheless we can obtain heuristic solutions using this approach. We create MST with edges 1–2, 2–4, 4–3, 1–5. Duplicating the edges, we get the Eulerian 1–2–4–3–4–2–1–5–1.

We get several Hamiltonians and for each we can evaluate the reverse path (non-symmetric matrix). The best solution is 1–5–2–4–3–1 with Z = 65. The worst case upper bound of 2 is not applicable because the matrix is not symmetric and does not satisfy triangle inequality.

EXAMPLE 9.6 How many constraints and variables does the LP formulation to a 5-city TSP have?

One of the methods to eliminate subtours in the LP formulation of a TSP is by introducing a set of constraints:

$$U_i - U_j + nX_{ij} \leq n-1 \text{ for } i = 2,3,\ldots, n \quad \text{and} \quad j = 2,3,\ldots,n \; i \neq j$$

where U_i i = 1, 2,...,n–1 are extra variables such that they are non-negative integers for all i. Discuss the validity of such a formulation.

Solution: Let us consider the subtour elimination constraint of the form:

$$U_i - U_j + nX_{ij} \leq n-1 \text{ for } i = 1,2,\ldots, n-1 \quad \text{and} \quad j = 2, 3, \ldots, n, \; U_j \geq 0$$

For our 5-city example we will have $(n-1)^2$ constraints. Let us consider an infeasible solution having a subtour (not involving City 1) $X_{45} = X_{54} = 1$. The two relevant constraints are:

$U_4 - U_5 + 5X_{45} \leq 4$ and $U_5 - U_4 + 5X_{54} \leq 4$. This is clearly infeasible because the two constraints when added together gives

$$5X_{45} + 5X_{54} \leq 8$$

which is infeasible for $X_{45} = X_{54} = 1$. Therefore, every subtour not involving City 1 will violate the relevant set of constraints. Let us consider a subtour involving City 1 given by $X_{12} = X_{23} = X_{31} = 1$.

We have two constraints:

$$U_1 - U_2 + 5X_{12} \leq 4$$
$$U_2 - U_3 + 5X_{23} \leq 4$$

The constraint $U_3 - U_1 + 5X_{31} \leq 4$ does not exist for U_j = 1.

Adding the two constraints, we get

$$U_1 - U_3 + 10 \leq 8 \quad \text{for} \quad X_{12} = X_{23} = 1$$

It is possible to have values U_1 and U_3 that satisfy the constraints and, therefore, the constraint $U_i - U_j + nX_{ij} \leq n-1$ is unable to prevent subtours involving City 1 from occurring. However, we realize that for every subtour involving City 1 there has to be a subtour that does not involve City 1 (the subtour $X_{45} = X_{54} = 1$ in our example) and the constraints are able to prevent them from happening. Therefore, the constraints eliminate all subtours. The only requirement is that we define $d_{jj} = \infty$ (or M) so that the singleton subtours are indirectly eliminated.

Let us consider a feasible solution $X_{12} = X_{24} = X_{45} = X_{53} = X_{31}$. The relevant constraints are:

$$U_1 - U_2 + 5X_{12} \leq 4$$
$$U_2 - U_4 + 5X_{24} \leq 4$$
$$U_4 - U_5 + 5X_{45} \leq 4$$
$$U_5 - U_3 + 5X_{53} \leq 4$$

The constraint $U_3 - U_1 + 5X_{31} \leq 4$ does not exist for $U_j = 1$.

Adding the constraints, we get $U_1 - U_3 + 20 \leq 16$ for the given feasible solution. Clearly, we can define values for U_1 and U_3 to satisfy the constraint. Therefore, the constraint does not eliminate any feasible solution. This can effectively replace the earlier set of constraints.

EXAMPLE 9.7 Kumar wants to pick up four friends – Ajit, Arun, Akhil and Anuj on his way to college. The distance matrix is the same as in Table 9.25 assuming that point 1 is Kumar's house and point 6 is the college, find a good solution to Kumar's problem.

Solution: The problem that we are addressing here is called the **Travelling salesman path problem** or **Hamiltonian path problem**. Here we wish to find the shortest Hamiltonian path from a given start node to a given destination node. Some points related to the Hamiltonian path problem are:

1. This has only five edges for a six vertex problem unlike the TSP that has six edges.
2. The optimal solution is a spanning tree.
3. It is a minimum spanning tree with the added restrictions that the start and destination nodes have a degree of one while every other node has a degree of two.
4. It is related to the TSP (circuit problem). Every TSP can be solved as a suitably defined path problem and the path problem is reducible to the TSP, the optimal solution to the path problem cannot always be read from the optimal solution to the TSP.

The Hamiltonian path problem is a hard problem and we attempt to modify known heuristics of the TSP to suit the path problem.

The nearest neighbourhood search solutions starting from 1 with an additional restriction that 6 has to be final destination are 1–3–5–4–2–6 with distance = 39 and 1–3–2–5–4–6 with distance = 31.

The minimum spanning tree provides a lower bound to the optimal solution to the path problem because the Hamiltonian path is a spanning tree. We, therefore, have a lower bound of 30. The twice around the tree method can give us feasible solutions to the path problem. The Eulerian from the twice around the tree algorithm is 1–3–1–2–4–5–6–5–4–2–1 from which a feasible solution to the path problem 1–3–2–4–5–6 with distance 31.

The Kruskal's (or Prim's) algorithm can be modified suitably to provide a Hamiltonian path. We construct the minimum spanning tree using Kruskal's algorithm. The first three edges are 2–4, 1–3 and 5–6. The fourth edge to be included is 4–5 (even though 4–6 has distance of 10, it is not included because it cannot result in a Hamiltonian path between 1 and 6). The edge 1–2 is also not included for the same reason. We include edge 2–3 to complete the spanning tree that is a Hamiltonian path from 1 to 6. This gives us a solution 1–3–2–4–5–6 with distance = 31.

The optimal solution to the path problem can be obtained by a branch and bound algorithm where every node is a minimum spanning tree and we branch in such a way to ensure the intermediate nodes in the MST have a degree of exactly two.

It is also to be observed that a feasible solution to the given path problem may not be available from the optimal solution to the TSP unless the edge connecting the start and destination nodes is in the optimal solution to the TSP. It is also to be noted that the spanning tree obtained by deleting the edge with maximum distance from the optimal TSP is the optimal solution to the corresponding path problem (if it is not so, then the optimal solution to the TSP has to be different).

For our example, there are two MSTs and both have a value of 30 and are infeasible to the path problem. Since we have integer values of distances and since we have a feasible solution to the path problem with distance 31, the solution has to be optimal.

EXAMPLE 9.8 Solve the 4-city TSP whose distance matrix is given in Table 9.32.

Table 9.32 Distance Matrix

City	1	2	3	4
1	–	12	10	14
2	12	–	13	8
3	10	13	–	12
4	14	8	12	–

Solution: Starting with City 1, the nearest neighbourhood search solution is 1–3–4–2–1 with $Z = 42$.

If we subtract the row minimum from every row, we get a lower bound of $10 + 8 + 10 + 8 = 36$. The assignment solution is $X_{13} = X_{24} = X_{31} = X_{42} = 1$ with $Z = 36$. This has two subtours and the minimum that can be added to tighten the lower bound is 6. This results in a lower bound of 42. Since we have a feasible solution with $Z = 42$, the solution 1–3–4–2–1 is optimal.

If we had started with a lower bound of 36 and found the penalty, the maximum penalty is 6 for variable X_{24}. Creating two nodes by branching on this variable ($X_{24} = 0$ and $X_{24} = 1$), we would get the lower bound to be 42 in both the nodes (the reader should compute and verify). This also leads to the same conclusion that the solution 1–3–4–2–1 is optimal.

(We have computed a quick feasible solution and used it in a branch and bound algorithm to fathom nodes. This need not give us the optimum always in the first iteration as in this example. It is still a very popular method applied in solving large TSPs. Otherwise the branch and bound algorithm may evaluate many nodes before it finds a feasible solution. This difficulty could be avoided with this method of initializing an upper bound using a feasible solution).

EXAMPLE 9.9 Consider the distance matrix shown in Table 9.33. Start with a feasible solution 1–4–2–5–3–6–1 and apply an iteration of the three-opt heuristic to the solution.

Table 9.33 Distance Matrix

–	12	10	14	8	9
12	–	13	8	9	10
10	13	–	12	8	9
14	8	12	–	11	10
8	9	8	11	–	12
9	10	9	10	12	–

Solution: We start with the solution 1–4–2–5–3–6–1 with $Z = 57$. We set 1–4 as a–b, 2–5 as p–q and 3–6 as u–v. The seven other possible solutions using a three-opt heuristic are:

a–b, p–u, q–v gives 1–4–2–3–5–6–1 with $Z = 64$
a–p, b–q, u–v gives 1–2–4–5–3–6–1 with $Z = 57$
a–p, b–u, q–v gives 1–2–4–3–5–6–1 with $Z = 61$
a–q, u–b, p–v gives 1–5–3–4–2–6–1 with $Z = 55$
a–q, u–p, b–v gives 1–5–3–2–4–6–1 with $Z = 56$
a–u, q–b, p–v gives 1–3–5–4–2–6–1 with $Z = 56$
a–u, q–p, b–v gives 1–3–5–2–4–6–1 with $Z = 54$

The best solution found using the three-opt search has $Z = 54$. The reader can solve the problem optimally using any of the exact methods and verify that this solution is optimal.

The three-opt is a very effective search method by itself and can also be used to provide feasible solutions to the branch and bound algorithm to fathom nodes.

EXAMPLE 9.10 Srikanth and Sriram have to start from their house to invite six friends in person for a function. The time taken to travel from their house to the six houses is 10, 7, 9, 7, 7, 6 minutes, respectively. The travel time matrix among the six houses is given in Table 9.34. They have to meet the friends before 10, 30, 20, 30, 20, 10 minutes, respectively. They wish to minimize the time taken to travel and return to their house. Provide a good solution to their problem. What happens if the due times are 10, 20, 20, 30, 20, 10, respectively?

Table 9.34 Travel Time Matrix

–	13	2	15	15	15
13	–	14	1	12	12
2	14	–	16	14	14
15	1	16	–	10	10
15	12	14	10	–	4
15	12	14	10	4	–

Solution: If they decide to go together, they will not be able to meet the friends before the due times. They have to go separately. This results in a single depot vehicle routeing problem. Assuming that their house is the depot, one solution to the problem (from Example 9.4) is d–3–1–4–2–d–5–6–d with time = 49. The times at Srikanth reaches the houses are 9, 11, 24, 25 and reaches home at time = 32 minutes. This is infeasible because he meets friend 1 at 11 minutes when he has to meet the person before 10 minutes. A feasible solution for Srikanth could be d–1–3–4–2–d with times 10, 12, 28, 29 minutes but he returns home at time = 36 minutes.

If Sriram takes the route d–5–6–d, the times he meets the friends are 7 and 11 and can return home at time = 17 minutes. This is infeasible because he is unable to meet friend 6 before 10 minutes. He can however change the route to d–6–5–d which meets the due times. He returns home at time = 17 minutes.

If the due times are 10, 20, 20, 30, 20, 20, we can easily verify that it is not possible for the two of them to meet all the friends within the due times, even if they choose to meet three friends each. In VRP terminology, a 2-vehicle solution is infeasible. It is necessary to use 3 vehicles. The solution d–1–3–d, d–2–4–d and d–5–6–d is feasible. The three vehicles can return at times 21, 15 and 17 minutes, respectively.

(The problem that we have attempted to solve is called **VRP with time windows**. This is a further constrained VRP and is a "difficult" or "hard" problem to solve. Heuristics such as savings based methods or exact algorithms using TSP cannot be directly applied to solve this problem. They have to be suitably modified to solve this problem. It can also happen that the introduction of time windows can increase the number of vehicles).

CASE STUDY 9.1: The Wafer Electronics Company

The Wafer Electronics Company is in the business of making different PCBs. The process involves fixing several components into the PCB using a single flexible machine. The machine can hold a maximum of K components. Different PCB types have to be assembled using different components. It can be assumed that the maximum number of components required for any PCB assembly is not more than the capacity of the machine in terms of number of components.

Mr. Bhaskar, the planning manager has the task of scheduling nine PCBs that require ten components each from a set of thirty components. Sample data are shown in Table 9.35.

Table 9.35 Component Product Matrix

Component	\multicolumn{9}{c}{Product}
	1	2	3	4	5	6	7	8	9
1	0	0	0	1	0	0	0	0	0
2	0	0	1	1	0	0	0	0	0
3	1	0	1	1	0	0	0	1	1
4	0	1	1	1	0	0	0	1	0
5	1	0	1	0	0	0	0	0	1
6	0	0	0	0	0	0	0	0	1
7	0	1	0	0	0	1	1	0	0
8	1	0	0	0	0	0	0	0	0
9	0	0	0	1	0	0	0	0	1
10	1	1	0	0	0	0	1	0	0
11	0	1	0	0	0	1	0	0	1
12	1	0	1	0	0	0	1	1	0
13	1	0	1	1	0	0	0	0	0
14	0	0	0	0	0	0	0	0	1
15	0	0	0	0	1	1	0	0	0
16	1	0	0	0	0	0	1	0	1
17	0	1	0	0	0	1	0	0	0
18	1	0	0	0	0	0	0	1	0
19	1	1	0	0	0	0	0	0	0
20	1	0	0	0	0	0	0	0	1
21	0	0	0	0	0	1	0	0	0
22	0	1	1	0	0	0	0	1	0
23	1	0	0	0	0	0	0	1	0
24	1	0	1	0	0	0	1	0	0
25	0	0	0	1	0	0	1	1	0
26	0	1	0	0	0	0	1	1	0
27	1	0	1	0	0	1	1	1	0
28	1	0	0	0	1	1	1	0	0
29	0	0	1	0	1	0	1	0	0
30	0	0	0	0	1	1	0	1	0

Bhaskar assesses that the changeover time from PCB A to B depends on the number of components that have to be removed and those to be added. Bhaskar makes a changeover matrix that captures the number of components that have to be added and removed for every pair of PCBs.

Bhaskar thinks that it is sufficient to solve a travelling salesman problem using the changeover matrix. This assumes that the company will start with some PCB (say A) manufacture all the PCBs in some order and return to the starting PCB.

Bhaskar is also aware that the next set of orders need not start with A and therefore believes that is enough to complete all the PCBs in the present order and not worry about changing back to A. He also knows that among the orders for the nine PCBs that have to be produced, the sixth PCB has the maximum due date.

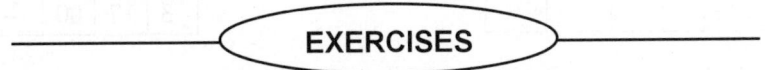

EXERCISES

9.1 You are given a 10-city TSP with the distance matrix given in Table 9.36.

Table 9.36 Distance Matrix

–	11	8	18	13	20	26	30	33	34
11	–	7	10	9	7	8	13	15	14
8	7	–	10	10	15	19	20	25	23
18	18	10	–	21	11	15	11	27	20
13	9	10	21	–	13	9	20	17	18
26	7	15	11	13	–	6	12	15	9
22	8	19	15	9	6	–	12	8	7
30	13	20	11	20	12	12	–	15	7
33	15	25	27	17	15	8	15	–	10
34	14	23	20	18	9	7	7	10	–

What is your solution to the TSP? If you are giving an approximate solution, what is the % deviation from your lower bound?

9.2 Show that in a symmetric TSP, any three distinct cost elements $C(i,j)$, $C(j,k)$, $C(k,i)$ can be set to infinity without eliminating all minimum length tours.

9.3 Given the distance matrix in Table 9.37.

Table 9.37 Distance Matrix

–	160	120	74	40	95	122	131
	–	168	191	137	85	71	166
		–	107	84	80	143	240
			–	54	115	150	214
				–	61	95	178
					–	62	156
						–	94
							–

Obtain a good lower bound to the TSP. If City 1 is the depot find the solution to the VRP with $Q = 20$ and $q_i = [7\ 6\ 7\ 6\ 5\ 9\ 8]$. If one of the cities is the depot, which city will you choose? Why?

9.4 There are four sites with the following symmetric distance matrix (Table 9.38) and non-symmetric requirement matrix (Table 9.39):

Table 9.38 Symmetric Distance Matrix

–	65	104	53
	–	77	101
		–	98
			–

Table 9.39 Requirement Matrix

–	30	3	11
4	–	14	24
12	7	–	6
3	17	00	–

Two vehicles with capacity 20 tonnes are available in each site.

(a) Provide a solution to the VRP problem that minimizes total distance travelled if each vehicle can visit more than two sites and only drops items and does not pick up.

(b) Provide a feasible solution VRP that minimizes total distance travelled if each vehicle can visit more than two sites and can pick up for other sites if capacity is available.

9.5 A person starting from City 1 wants to visit each of the n cities once and only once and return to the starting point in as short a time as possible. In addition he has to reach city ($k = 2$ to n) during the time interval (a_k, b_k). Formulate this TSP with time windows as an integer-programming problem. Compute the number of variables and constraints.

9.6 You are given a 10-city TSP shown in Table 9.40.

Table 9.40 10-City TSP

–	99	275	142	400	475	600	250	135	270
99	–	400	250	500	575	500	350	36	300
275	400	–	135	160	260	350	600	436	550
142	250	135	–	300	400	450	500	350	500
400	500	160	300	–	89	144	800	525	675
475	575	260	400	89	–	87	889	614	659
600	500	350	450	144	87	–	802	543	589
250	350	600	500	800	889	802	–	386	345
135	36	436	350	525	614	543	386	–	312
270	300	550	500	675	659	589	345	312	–

(a) Find the minimum spanning tree and obtain a lower bound to TSP.
(b) Find a solution using twice around the tree algorithm.
(c) Find a solution using the method of perfect matching.
(d) Find a better lower bound than in (a).
(e) Generate a solution using nearest neighbour and improve it using a single three-opt search.

9.7 You are given a Chinese postman problem on a network given in Table 9.41.

Table 9.41 Arc Weights

Arc	Weight	Arc	Weight	Arc	Weight
1–2	10	2–5	6	4–5	10
1–3	9	3–5	5	4–6	7
1–4	8				

Find the minimum additional distance the postman has to travel.

9.8 Consider a 6-city TSP with the data in Table 9.42.

Table 9.42 Distance Matrix

–	10	7	8	9	6
	–	7	8	10	12
		–	8	7	9
			–	10	5
				–	9
					–

(a) Provide a lower bound to the optimum distance.
(b) Provide a good heuristic solution to the problem and evaluate the gap.

9.9 Consider a single depot VRP with six cities. If the distance from the depot d_{0i} is the same for all the cities and if all the demands are equal to 15 units and if the vehicle capacity is 30, use Clark-Wright heuristic to get a solution to the VRP. Use the data in Table 9.42.

9.10 Solve the 5-city TSP given in Table 9.43 where the data represents the time taken to travel from i–j

Table 9.43 Time Taken to Travel

–	10	12	14	8
10	–	13	8	9
12	13	–	12	8
14	8	12	–	11
8	9	8	11	–

9.11 Naveen has to start from his house to invite four friends in person for a function. The travel time matrix among the five houses is given in Table 9.42, where point 1 is Naveen's house. He can meet the friends after 10, 20, 30, 40 and 40 minutes, respectively. Provide a feasible solution to determine when Naveen can return home at the earliest.

9.12 Starting with a feasible solution 1–2–3–4–5–1, apply an iteration of the three-opt procedure to improve the solution. (Since there are only five vertices, it is not possible to identify distinct vertices for a,b,p,q,u,v. You may have to repeat one variable. For example, use 1–2 for a–b, 3–4 for p–q and 4–5 for u–v. You may not have seven distinct solutions, but fewer distinct solutions).

9.13 Formulate a single depot vehicle routeing problem as an integer programming problem considering five cities and two vehicles.

9.14 Five jobs have to be processed on a machine. There is a processing time on the machine and the changeover time from job i to job j in minutes. This is given in Table 9.44.

Assume that the machine has just finished processing Job #2. What is the order in which the other jobs have to be taken up such that the sum of changeover times is minimized? (Assume that you need not changeover to Job #2 after the remaining jobs are processed.)

Table 9.44 Distance Matrix

–	9	12	14	10
9	–	13	8	9
12	13	–	13	8
14	8	13	–	11
10	9	8	11	–

9.15 Consider a 6-city single depot VRP with the distance data among cities shown in Table 9.45. The distances of the six cities from the depot are 12, 8, 10, 11, 10 and 9 units, respectively. There are three vehicles and each visits two cities. Provide a solution using Clarke-Wright savings algorithm. Provide a better solution than the one from the savings based method using Holmes-Parker refinement or otherwise.

Table 9.45 Distance among Cities

–	12	8	10	7	10
	–	7	9	11	14
		–	12	10	8
			–	7	9
				–	6
					–

10

Dynamic Programming

Dynamic programming is used when the problem can be solved in *'stages'*. Here the decisions made in a stage will affect the decisions at the subsequent stages but are dependent on each other. We usually follow a backward recursive approach where we make decisions from the end stages rather than from the beginning stages.

We illustrate the concepts of dynamic programming, the idea of recursion approach and the terminology using an example called the **stage coach problem**.

10.1 STAGE COACH PROBLEM

ILLUSTRATION 10.1

A person wants to go from City 1 to City 10. The various possibilities and the distances are given in Table 10.1. The network is shown in Figure 10.1.

Table 10.1 Arc Distances

Arc	Distance	Arc	Distance	Arc	Distance	Arc	Distance
1–2	5	2–7	8	4–6	5	6–9	7
1–3	5	3–5	8	4–7	7	7–8	5
1–4	6	3–6	10	5–8	6	7–9	7
2–5	4	3–7	5	5–9	8	8–10	8
2–6	7	4–5	4	6–8	9	9–10	9

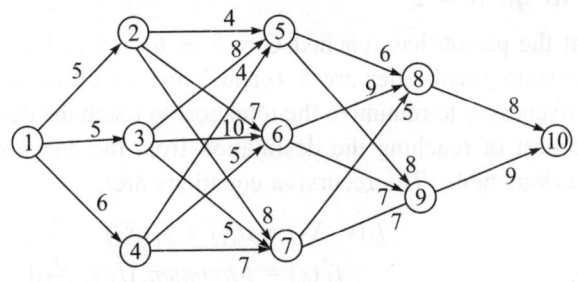

Figure 10.1 Network for STAGE Coach problem.

391

Let us apply the backward recursion approach. We assume that in order to reach the destination (City 10), the person should start from City 8 or 9. We now find the best (or least cost way) to reach City 10, if we were at City 8 or 9. Since the decisions as to where to go next depends on the stage of decision making, we have to make a decision when we have one more stage to go.

We define four parameters for every dynamic programming problem:

1. *Stage:* Each stage indicates a decision point. The number of stages indicates the number of decisions made.
2. *State:* This represents the state of the system or the resource available at that point. In this example, the state is the city from which the person can go.
3. *Decision variable:* This represents the decision alternatives the person has. In this example, it is the set of possible destinations from the given state of the system.
4. *Criterion of effectiveness or objective function:* This represents the objective of the problem. In this example, it is to minimize total distance travelled.

Stage (n to go): Stage
State (s) : City from which the person is travelling
Decision variable (X): Next destination
Criterion of effectiveness [f(s, X)]: Minimizing total distance travelled

In backward recursion, when the person has one more stage to complete, the states are 8 and 9. There is only one decision, to go to City 10. We indicate this in Table 10.2

One more stage to go n = 1

$$f_1(s, X) = d_{sX}$$
$$f_1^*(s) = Minimum \ [f_1(s, X)]$$

The above equations are the recursive equations and represent that the objective function is the distance travelled. Table 10.2 shows the calculations when the person has one more stage to complete.

Table 10.2 One More Stage to Go

s	X	$f_1^*(s)$	X^*
8	10	8	10
9	10	9	10

Two more stages to go n = 2

Here, we assume that the person has reached City 5 or 6 or 7 and decides to move to either City 8 or 9. The three state possibilities are 5, 6 and 7 and the decision is to go to City 8 or 9. The criterion of effectiveness is to minimize the total cost to reach the destination and, therefore, include the minimum cost of reaching the destination from the decision made, which can be obtained from the previous table. The recursive equations are:

$$f_2(s, X_2) = d_{sX_2} + f_1^*(X_2)$$
$$f_2^*(s) = Minimum \ [f_2(s, X_2)]$$

Table 10.3 shows the computations.

Table 10.3 Two More Stages to Go

s	$f_2(s, X_2) = d_{sX2} + f_1^*(X_2)$		$f_2^*(s)$	X_2^*
	$X_2 = 8$	$X_2 = 9$		
5	6 + 8 = 14	8 + 9 = 17	14	8
6	9 + 8 = 17	7 + 9 = 16	16	9
7	5 + 8 = 13	7 + 9 = 16	13	8

If the person is in City 5, the next destination is 8 and from then the person reaches 10 and so on.

Three more stages to go n = 3

The person has three more stages to go before reaching the destination and is in either City 2 or 3 or 4. The next destination is either 5 or 6 or 7. The criterion of effectiveness is to minimize total distance travelled and includes the time to reach the next destination and the minimum distance from that to City 10, which can be obtained from the previous table. The recursive equations are:

$$f_3(s, X_3) = d_{sX3} + f_1^*(X_3)$$
$$f_3^*(s) = Minimum \ [f_3(s, X_3)]$$

Table 10.4 shows the computations.

Table 10.4 Three More Stages to Go

s	$f_3(s, X_3) = d_{sX3} + f_2^*(X_3)$			$f_3^*(s)$	X_3^*
	$X_3 = 5$	$X_3 = 6$	$X_3 = 7$		
2	4 + 14 = 18	7 + 16 = 23	8 + 13 = 21	18	5
3	8 + 14 = 22	10 + 16 = 26	5 + 13 = 18	18	7
4	4 + 14 = 18	5 + 16 = 21	7 + 13 = 20	18	5

Four more stages to go n = 4

Here the decision maker has four more stages to go and is at present at the beginning of the journey at City 1. The decisions are to go to either 2 or 3 or 4. The criterion of effectiveness is the distance between the starting point and the next destination and the distance from this to City 10, obtained from the previous table. The recursive equations are:

$$f_4(s, X_4) = d_{sX4} + f_1^*(X_4)$$
$$f_4^*(s) = Minimum \ [f_4(s, X_4)]$$

Table 10.5 shows the computations.

Table 10.5 Four More Stages to Go

s	$f_4(s, X_4) = d_{sX4} + f_1^*(X_4)$			$f_4^*(s)$	X_4^*
	$X_4 = 2$	$X_4 = 3$	$X_4 = 4$		
1	5 + 18 = 23	5 + 18 = 23	6 + 18 = 24	2,3	23

From this we observe that the minimum distance from 1 to 10 is 23. There are two paths. These are 1–2–5–8–10 and 1–3–7–8–10. From Table 6.5, we realize that the next destination could be 2 or 3 giving us two alternate paths. From Table 6.4, we know that the person has to travel from 2 to 5 and from 3 to 7. Table 6.3 tells us that the next destination is 8 from either 5 or 7, from which the person reaches 10. This is a case of alternate optima.

The above example is a case of using dynamic programming to solve a problem where the decision variables take discrete values. Here we use the tables to show the computations and write the recursive equations explicitly for every table (every stage). We have also discussed the definitions of stage, state, decision variable and criterion of effectiveness for every problem.

10.2 RELIABILITY PROBLEM

ILLUSTRATION 10.2

Let us consider an equipment that functions using four components connected in series. Each component has a certain reliability and the reliability of the equipment is the product of the individual reliabilities. In order to increase the reliability of the equipment, we can have some additional components in standby. The reliabilities and cost for standby units for the four components are shown in Table 10.6.

Table 10.6 Reliabilities and Cost for Standby Units

Number of units	Component A Reliability	Cost	Component B Reliability	Cost	Component C Reliability	Cost	Component D Reliability	Cost
1	0.6	6	0.4	10	0.7	5	0.5	8
2	0.75	11	0.65	14	0.9	10	0.6	13
3	0.85	15	0.8	17	0.95	14	0.8	16

We assume that Rs. 40 is available. How many units of each component (including the standby) should we have that maximizes the total reliability of the system?

We follow the backward recursive approach to solve the problem. We define the problem parameters as follows:

Stage: Each component (A to D)
State: Amount of money available for allocation
Decision variable: Number of units of each component to buy
Criterion of effectiveness: Maximize reliability

One more stage to go n = 1

The minimum amount needed here is Rs. 8, sufficient to buy at least one unit of D, otherwise the reliability will become zero. The maximum amount that we can have for buying D is Rs. 19. This will be the maximum money that we will have for D, if we buy one each of A, B and C. The state variable is between 8 and 19. Table 10.7 shows the computations. The recursive equations are:

$$f_1(s_1, X_4) = R_4(X_4)$$
$$f_1^*(s_1) = \text{Maximum } f_1(s_1, X_4) \text{ subject to } C_4(X_4) \leq s_1$$

Table 10.7 One More Stages to Go

s	X_4	$f_1^*(s)$	X_4^*
8–12	1	0.5	1
13–15	2	0.6	2
16–19	3	0.8	3

Two more stages to go n = 2

Here, we make decision for component C. The minimum amount that we will have is to buy at least one of C and D, i.e., Rs. 13 and the maximum of Rs. 24 if we had bought 1 of A and B and spent Rs. 16. Out of the state (amount available) whatever amount spent on C is subtracted from s and carried as state variable to buy D. The recursive equations are:

$$f_2(s_2, X_3) = R_3(X_3) + f_1^*[s_3 - C_3(X_3)]$$
$$f_2^*(s_2) = \text{Maximum } f_2(s_2, X_3) \text{ subject to } C_3(X_3) \leq s_2$$

The computations are shown in Table 10.8.

Table 10.8 Two More Stages to Go

s_2	$f_2(s_2, X_3) = R_3(X_3) + f_1^*(s_2 - C_3(X_3))$			$f_2^*(s)$	X_3^*
	$X_3 = 1$	$X_3 = 2$	$X_3 = 3$		
13–17	0.7 * 0.5 = 0.35	—	—	0.35	1
18–20	0.7 * 0.6 = 0.42	0.9 * 0.5 = 0.45	—	0.45	2
21	0.7 * 0.8 = 0.56	0.9 * 0.5 = 0.45	—	0.56	1
22	0.7 * 0.8 = 0.56	0.9 * 0.5 = 0.45	0.95 * 0.5 = 0.475	0.56	1
23–24	0.7 * 0.8 = 0.56	0.9 * 0.6 = 0.54	0.95 * 0.5 = 0.475	0.56	1

Three more stages to go n = 3

Here, we make decision for component B. The minimum amount that we will have is to buy at least one of B, C and D, i.e. Rs. 23 and the maximum of Rs. 34 if we had bought 1 of A and spent Rs. 6. Out of the state (amount available) whatever amount spent on B is subtracted from s and carried as state variable to buy C and D. The recursive equations are:

$$f_3(s_3, X_2) = R_2(X_2) + f_2^*[s_3 - C_3(X_3)]$$
$$f_3^*(s_3) = \text{Maximum } f_2(s_3, X_2) \text{ subject to } C_2(X_2) \leq s_3$$

The computations are shown in Table 10.9.

Table 10.9 Three More Stages to Go

s_3	$f_3(s_3, X_2) = R_2(X_2) + f_2^*(s_3 - C_2(X_2))$			$f_3^*(s)$	X_2^*
	$X_3 = 1$	$X_3 = 2$	$X_3 = 3$		
23–26	0.4 * 0.35 = 0.14	—	—	0.14	1
27	0.4 * 0.35 = 0.14	0.65 * 0.35 = 0.2275	—	0.2275	2
28–29	0.4 * 0.45 = 0.18	0.65 * 0.35 = 0.2275	—	0.2275	2
30	0.4 * 0.45 = 0.18	0.65 * 0.35 = 0.2275	0.8 * 0.35 = 0.28	0.28	3
31	0.4 * 0.56 = 0.224	0.65 * 0.35 = 0.2275	0.8 * 0.35 = 0.28	0.28	3
32–34	0.4 * 0.56 = 0.224	0.65 * 0.45 = 0.2925	0.8 * 0.35 = 0.28	0.2925	2

Four more stages to go n = 4

Here, we make decision for component A. The amount that we have is Rs. 400. Out of the state (amount available) whatever amount spent on A is subtracted from s and carried as state variable to buy B, C and D. The recursive equations are:

$$f_4(400, X_1) = R_1(X_1) + f_3^*[400 - C_1(X_1)]$$

$$f_4^*(400) = \text{Maximum } f_4(400, X_1) \text{ subject to } C_1(X_1) \leq 400$$

The calculations are shown in Table 10.10. The decision variable X_1 can take values 1 to 4.

Table 10.10 Four More Stages to Go

S	$f_4(400, X_1) = R_1(X_1) + f_3^*(400 - C_1(X_1))$			$f_4^*(s)$	X_1^*
	$X_1 = 1$	$X_1 = 2$	$X_1 = 3$		
40	0.6 * 0.2925 = 0.1755	0.75 * 0.2275 = 0.170625	0.85 * 0.14 = 0.119	0.1755	1

The optimal solution is given by

$X_1^* = 1$ (spend Rs 6 on Component A) and carry Rs 34

$X_2^* = 2$ (spend Rs 14 on Component B) and carry Rs 20

$X_3^* = 2$ (spend Rs 10 on component C) and carry Rs 10

$X_4^* = 1$ (spend Rs 8 on Component D) and keep Rs 2 unspent to have an overall reliability of 0.1755.

10.3 EQUIPMENT REPLACEMENT PROBLEM

ILLUSTRATION 10.3

Here, we consider the equipment replacement problem where decisions are made once a year whether to retain the machine for one more year or to replace it. The relevant parameters are the maintenance cost, salvage value and profit associated with running the machine. All these vary with the age of the machine. The cost of a new machine is constant. The problem parameters are:

Stage: Number of years to go (in the planning period)
State: Present age of the machine
Decision variable: Keep (K) or Replace (R)
Criterion of effectiveness: Maximize profit

The recursive equations are:

$$f_n(i, K) = p(i) - m(i) + f_{n-1}^*(i + 1)$$
$$f_n(i, R) = p(0) - m(0) - s(0) + s(i) + f_{n-1}^*(1)$$

Relevant data is given in Table 10.11. If we decide to retain a machine i years old, we make a profit of $p(i)$ and incur a maintenance cost of $m(i)$. To this we add the profit from the next stage. The age of the machine at the end of the year becomes $i + 1$. If we decide to replace, we get a salvage value of $s(i)$ and spend on the new machine [C or $s(0)$]. The age of the machine at the end of the year is 1. The computations are shown in Table 10.12.

Table 10.11 Data for Equipment Replacement Problem

Age (i)	0	1	2	3	4	5	6	7	8
p (i)	200	180	160	150	130	120	100	90	80
m (i)	10	15	20	27	35	45	55	65	75
s (i)	800	700	650	600	550	500	500	400	400

Table 10.12 Computations Using Dynamic Programming

		i = 0	i = 1	i = 2	i = 3	i = 4	i = 5	i = 6	i = 7	i = 8
n = 1	K	190	165	140	123	95	75	45	25	5
	R	190	90	40	−10	−60	−110	−110	−210	−210
n = 2	K	190 + 165 = 355	165 + 140 = 305	140 + 123 =263	123 + 95 =218	95 + 75 = 170	75 + 45 = 120	45 + 25 = 70	25 + 5 =30	
	R	190 + 190 = 380	90 + 165 = 255	40 + 165 = 205	−10 + 165 = 155	−60 + 165 = 105	−110 + 165 = 55	−110 + 165 = 55	−210 +165 = −45	
n = 3	K	190 + 305 = 495	165 + 263 = 428	140 + 218 = 358	123 + 170 = 293	95 + 120 = 215	75 + 70 = 145	45 + 30 = 75		
	R	190 + 305 = 495	90 + 305 = 395	40 + 305 = 345	−10 + 305 = 295	−60 + 305 = 245	−110 + 305 = 195	−110 + 305 = 195		
n = 4	K	190 + 428 = 618	165 + 358 = 523	140 + 295 = 435	123 + 245 = 368	95 + 195 = 290	75 + 195 = 270			
	R	190 + 428 = 618	90 + 428 = 518	40 + 428 = 468	−10 + 428 = 418	−60 + 428 = 368	−110 + 428 = 318			

n = 5 K	190 + 523 = 713	165 + 468 = 633	140 + 418 = 558	123 + 368 = 491	95 + 318 = 413				
R	190 + 523 = 713	90 + 523 = 613	40 + 523 = 563	−10 + 523 = 513	−60 + 523 = 463				
n = 6 K	190 + 633 = 823	165 + 563 = 728	140 + 513 = 653	123 + 463 = 586					
R	190 + 633 = 823	90 + 633 = 723	40 + 633 = 673	−10 + 633 = 623					
n = 7 K	190 + 728 = 918	165 + 673 = 838	140 + 623 = 763						
R	190 + 728 = 918	90 + 728 = 818	40 + 728 = 768						
n = 8 K	190 + 838 = 1028	165 + 768 = 933							
R	190 + 838 = 1028	90 + 838 = 928							

From this table, we can compute the cost and strategy to adopt when we are given the number of years to go and the age of the equipment. For example, if we have $n = 3$ and $i = 1$, the decisions would be K, K and R, i.e., to keep it for one more year, move to $n = 2$, $i = 2$ and keep and move to $n = 1$, $i = 3$ which is to replace.

If we have $n = 7$ and $i = 2$, the decisions would be to R, K, R, K, K, K and K. Whenever we keep, we should look at $i + 1$ in the next year (previous row) and when we replace we should look at $i = 1$ in the previous row.

10.4 CONTINUOUS VARIABLES

ILLUSTRATION 10.4

In this example we introduce problems that involve variables that take continuous values (non-integer values).

Minimize $X_1 + X_2 + X_3$

Subject to

$$X_1 X_2 X_3 = 27$$

$$X_1, X_2, X_3 \geq 0$$

Stage: Each variable
State: Resource available for allocation
Decision variable: Values of X_1, X_2 and X_3
Criterion of effectiveness: Maximize Z

One more stage to go n = 1

$$f_1(s_1, X_3) = X_3$$
$$f_1^*(s_1) = \text{Maximize } X_3$$

Subject to $\quad 0 \le X_3 = s_1$

$$= s_1 \text{ at } X_3^* = s_1$$

(Here s_1 represents the state variable, which is the resource available. X_3^* is the optimum value of X_3).

Two more stages to go n = 2

$$f_2(s_2, X_2) = X_2 + f_1^*(s_1) \text{ where } s_2 = X_2 * s_1$$
$$f_1^*(s_2) = \text{Maximize } X_2 + f_1^*\left(\frac{s_2}{X_2}\right)$$
Subject to $0 \le X_2$
$$= \text{Maximize } X_2 + \frac{s_2}{X_2}$$
Subject to $0 \le X_2$

Differentiating w.r.t. X_2 and equating to zero, we get

$$1 - s_2 X_2^{-1/2} = 0$$

from which $\quad X_2^* = +\sqrt{s_2} \quad$ and $\quad f_2^*(s_2) = 2\sqrt{s_2}$

The second derivative is positive for $X_2 \ge 0$, indicating minimum.

Three more stages to go n = 3

$$f_3(27, X_1) = X_1 + f_1^*(s_2) \text{ where } s_2 = \frac{27}{X_1}$$
$$f_1^*(s_2) = \text{Maximize } X_1 + f_1^*\left(\frac{27}{X_1}\right)$$
Subject to $0 \le X_1$
$$= \text{Maximize } X_1 + 2\sqrt{\left(\frac{27}{X_1}\right)}$$
Subject to $0 \le X_1$

Differentiating w.r.t. X_1 and equating to zero, we get

$$1 + 2 \times \left(\frac{-1}{2}\right)\sqrt{27} \times X_1^{-3/2} = 0$$

from which $X_1^* = +3\sqrt{27} = 3$ and $f_1^*(27) = 3\sqrt[3]{27} = 9$

We have $X_1^* = X_2^* = X_3^* = 3$ with $Z = 9$.

(In this example we have a single constraint leading us to a single state variable at every stage. Since the constraint is an equation we allocate all the available resource to the variable when we have one more stage to go so that we satisfy the equation. We optimize in the subsequent stages).

10.5 CONTINUOUS VARIABLES—HIGHER DEGREE

ILLUSTRATION 10.5

Minimize $X_1^3 - 5X_1^2 + 8X_1 + X_2^3 - 2X_2^2 - 10X_2 + 10$
Subject to
$$X_1 + X_2 \le 4$$
$$X_1, X_2 \ge 0$$

Stage: Each variable
State: Resource available for allocation
Decision variable: Values of X_1 and X_2
Criterion of effectiveness: Minimize Z

In this problem we first solve for variable X_1 and then for variable X_2. The objective function is rewritten as:

Minimize $X_2^3 - 2X_2^2 - 10X_2 + X_1^3 - 5X_1^2 + 8X_1 + 10$

One more stage to go n = 1

$$f_1(s_1, X_1) = X_1^3 - 5X_1^2 + 8X_1 + 10$$
$$f_1^*(s_1) = \text{Minimize } X_1^3 - 5X_1^2 + 8X_1 + 10$$
$$0 \le X_1 \le s_1$$

Differentiating with respect to X_1 and equating to zero, we get

$$3X_1^2 - 10X_1 + 8 = 0$$

or $$X_1 = 2 \text{ or } X_1 = \frac{4}{3}$$

Second derivative is $6X_1 - 10$ and takes positive value for $X_1 = 2$ indicating minimum. Therefore, $X_1^* = 2$ if $s_1 \ge 2$ and $X_1^* = s_1$ if $s_1 < 2$.

$$f_1^*(s_1) = 8 - 20 + 16 + 10 = 14 \text{ if } s_1 \ge 2$$
$$= s_1^3 - 5s_1^2 + 8s_1 + 10 \text{ if } 0 = s_1 < 2$$

Since the function is cubic, we also verify the value of the function at $X_1 = 0$. At $X_1 = 0$, the value of $f_1(s_1) = 10$ which is less than 14 and since s_1 can take only non-negative values we have $X_1^* = 0$ and $f_1^*(s_1) = 10$.

Figure 10.2 shows the graph for the function and the optimum.

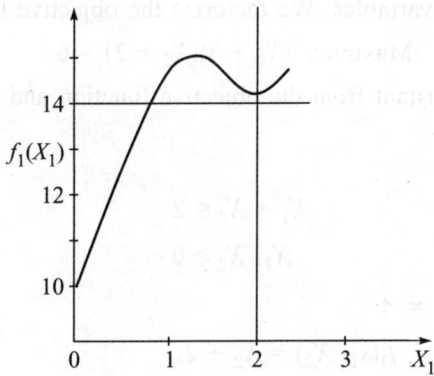

Figure 10.2 Graph for the function.

Two more stages to go n = 2

$$f_2(4, X_2) = X_2^3 - 2X_2^2 - 10X_2 + f_1^*(4 - X_2)$$
$$f_2^*(4) = \text{Minimize } X_2^3 - 2X_2^2 - 10X_2 + 10$$
$$0 \leq X_2 \leq 4$$

Considering each objective function in the given range and differentiating with respect to X_2 and equating to zero, we get

$$3X_2^2 - 4X_2 - 10 = 0$$
$$X_2 = \frac{4 + \sqrt{136}}{6}$$
$$X_2 = 2.61$$

At $X_2^* = 2.6$ $f_2^*(4)$ is -11.944
The optimum solution is $X_2^* = 2.61$, $s_1 = 1.4$ and $Z = -11.944$.
(In this example, we decided to choose that variable whose first derivative is factorable as the first variable to solve the problem so that the first stage is solved easily).

ILLUSTRATION 10.6

10.6 FACTORIZING THE TERMS

Maximize $2X_1 + 3X_2 + X_1X_2$
Subject to
$$X_1 + X_2 \leq 2$$
$$X_1, X_2 \geq 0$$

Stage: Each variable
State: Resource available for allocation
Decision variable: Values of X_1 and X_2
Criterion of effectiveness: Maximize Z

In this example the term X_1X_2 makes it difficult to separate the objective function in terms of separable functions of the variables. We factorize the objective function as:

$$\text{Maximize } (X_1 + 3)(X_2 + 2) - 6$$

We can leave out the constant from the objective function and write the problem as:

Maximize $(X_1 + 3)(X_2 + 2)$

Subject to

$$X_1 + X_2 \leq 2$$
$$X_1, X_2 \geq 0$$

One more stage to go n = 1

$$f_1(s_1, X_2) = X_2 + 2$$
$$f_1^*(s_1) = \text{Maximize } X_2 + 2$$
$$\text{Subject to } 0 \leq X_2 \leq s_1$$

Here, the maximum value is at $X_2^* = s_1$ and $f_1^*(s_1) = s_1 + 2$

Two more stages to go n = 2

$$f_2(2, X_1) = (X_1 + 3)f_1^*(2 - X_1)$$
$$f_2^*(s_1) = \text{Maximize } (X_1 + 3)(2 - X_1 + 2)$$
$$\text{Subject to } 0 \leq X_1 \leq 2$$

Maximize $(X_1 + 3)(4 - X_1)$
Subject to $0 \leq X_1 \leq 2$
Maximize $-X_1^2 + X_1 + 12$

Differentiating with respect to X_1 and equating to zero, we get $X_1 = \frac{1}{2}$. The second derivative is negative indicating maximum. We have $X_1^* = 1/2$, $s_1 = 3/2$ and $X_2^* = 3/2$ with $Z = 49/4 - 6 = 25/4$ (for the original problem).

10.7 MANPOWER PLANNING PROBLEM

ILLUSTRATION 10.7

The manpower requirements for a company for the next four months are 90, 120, 80 and 100, respectively. They can employ more than the requirement but incur a cost of underutilization of $10X$, where X is the excess number of employees. They cannot employ fewer than the requirement. There is a cost of changeover given by Y^2, where Y is the amount of decrease/increase of employees. Initially 100 employees are available. Let us determine the least cost solution to employ people in the four months.

Stage: Each month
State: Number of employees available (employed last month)
Decision variable: Number of people to employ this month (X_1 to X_4 for months 1 to 4)
Criterion of effectiveness: Minimize the sum of changeover cost and underutilization cost

We use backward recursion.

One more stage to go n = 1

$$f_1(s_1, X_4) = 10(X_4 - 100) + (s_1 - X_4)^2$$
$$f_1^*(s_1) = \text{Minimize } 10(X_4 - 100) + (s_1 - X_4)^2$$
$$\text{Subject to } X_4 \geq 100$$

Differentiating with respect to X_4 and equating to zero, we get

$$10 - 2(s_1 - X_4) = 0$$

from which
$$X_4^* = s_1 - 5$$

Since $X_4 \geq 100$, we have

$$X_4^* = s_1 - 5 \quad \text{when} \quad s_1 \geq 105 \quad \text{and} \quad f_1^*(s_1) = 10(s_1 - 105) + 25$$
$$X_4^* = 100 \quad \text{when} \quad s_1 < 105 \quad \text{and} \quad f_1^*(s_1) = (s_1 - 100)^2$$

Two more stages to go n = 2

$$f_2(s_2, X_3) = 10(X_3 - 80) + (s_2 - X_3)^2 + f_1^*(X_3)$$
$$f_2^*(s_2) = \text{Minimize } 10(X_3 - 80) + (s_2 - X_3)^2 + f_1^*(X_3)$$
$$\text{Subject to } X_3 \geq 80$$

In this problem, the maximum requirement is for the second month and having $X_2^* > 120$ would only increase the cost further. We will have $X_2^* = 120$ and $s_2 = 120$.
We substitute the expressions for $f_1^*(X_3)$ in the defined range to get

$$f_2^*(s_2) = \text{Minimize } 10(X_3 - 80) + (120 - X_3)^2 + 10(X_3 - 105) + 25$$
$$\text{Subject to } 105 \leq X_3 \leq 120$$
$$f_2^*(s_2) = \text{Minimize } 10(X_3 - 80) + (120 - X_3)^2 + (X_3 - 100)^2$$
$$\text{Subject to } 80 \leq X_3 \leq 105$$

Differentiating the first expression with respect to X_3 and equating to zero, we get

$$10 - 2(120 - X_3) + 10 = 0$$

from which $X_3^* = 110$. Second derivative is positive at $X_3 = 110$ and hence is a minimum. This is also within the range and $f_2^*(120) = 475$.

Differentiating the second expression with respect to X_3 and equating to zero, we get

$$10 - 2(120 - X_3) + 2(X_3 - 100) = 0$$

from which $X_3^* = 107.5$. Second derivative is positive and hence is a minimum. This is outside the range ($80 \leq X_3 \leq 105$) and, therefore, the minimum is at $X_3 = 105$. $f_2^*(120) = 275 + 156.25 + 56.25 = 487.5$
The optimum value of $X_3^* = 110$ and $f_2^*(120) = 475$.

Three more stages to go n = 3

$$f_3(s_3, X_2) = 10(X_2 - 120) + (s_3 - X_2)^2 + f_2^*(X_2)$$
$$f_3^*(s_3) = \text{Minimize } 10(X_2 - 120) + (s_3 - X_2)^2 + f_2^*(X_2)$$
$$\text{Subject to } X_2 \geq 120$$

In this problem, the maximum value that X_2 can take is 120 beyond which we incur unnecessary additional cost. We, therefore, have $X_2^* = 120$ and $f_3^*(s_3) = (s_3 - 120)^2 + 475$

Four more stages to go n = 4

$$f_4(100, X_1) = 10(X_1 - 90) + (100 - X_1)^2 + f_3^*(X_1)$$
$$f_4^*(100) = \text{Minimize } 10(X_1 - 90) + (100 - X_1)^2 + (X_1 - 120)^2 + 475$$
$$\text{Subject to } X_1 \geq 90$$

Differentiating the expression with respect to X_1 and equating to zero, we get
$10 - 2(100 - X_1) + 2(X_1 - 120) = 0$, from which $X_1^* = 107.5$. Second derivative is positive at $X_3 = 110$ and hence is a minimum. This is also within the range and $f_4^*(100) = 175 + 56.25 + 156.25 + 475 = 862.5$.

The optimum solution is $X_1^* = 107.5$, $X_2^* = 120$, $X_3^* = 110$, $X_4^* = 105$ and $Z = 862.5$.

In this problem, we realize that X_1^* is not an integer though it represents the number of people employed. This integer restriction has not been stated explicitly in the problem and has not been considered in the solution. However, due to the quadratic nature of the objective function we can evaluate $X_1^* = 107$ and $X_1^* = 108$ and find out that both give the same value of the objective function. We can choose either.

Also in this problem the fact that the maximum demand occurs the second period making $X_2^* = 120$, considerably decreases the computational effort. This has been used to our advantage while solving the problem.

10.8 OIL EXPLORATION PROBLEM

ILLUSTRATION 10.8

A company has found that oil is available for the next three years in two of its sites (A and B). For every Rs. 100 invested in Site A, the yield is expected to be 2 barrel and Rs. 200 as backup (from other minerals and oil that are taken) at the end of that year and every succeeding year. For Site B, the figures are 1½ barrel of oil and Rs. 300 as backup capital at the end of that year and every succeeding year for every Rs. 100 invested. The company has Rs. K available (in multiple of 100). How should the allocation be made so as to maximize the oil available at the end of the third year?

Stage: Each year

State: Money available at the beginning of the year

Decision variable: Money allotted to Site A. (The profits are such that the balance gets allotted to B. So there is effectively one decision variable)

Criterion of effectiveness: Maximize the oil

One more year to go n = 1

$$f_1(s_1, X_3) = 2X_3 + 1\tfrac{1}{2}(s_1 - X_3)$$
$$f_1^*(s_1) = \text{Maximize } 2X_3 + 1\tfrac{1}{2}(s_1 - X_3)$$
$$\text{Subject to } 0 \leq X_3 \leq s_1$$

The objective function is linear and we evaluate the function at the end points to reach the maximum at $X_3^* = s_1$ and $f_1^*(s_1) = 2s_1$.

Two more years to go n = 2

$$f_2(s_2, X_2) = 4X_2 + 1\frac{1}{2} \, 2(s_2 - X_2) + f_1^*[2X_2 + 3(s_2 - X_2) + s_2]$$

For every Rs. 100 invested in A, we get a barrel at the end of that year and also at the end of the third year. Therefore, we have $4X_1$ and $3(s_2 - X_2)$, respectively. The amount of money generated by the investment is $2X_2 + 3(s_2 - X_2)$. In addition we would get some money out of the investment made in the previous year (three more years to go). The returns are such that all the money would have been invested and no money would be carried to the next year without investing. The investment in the previous year (three more years to go) has resulted in the s_2 years available at the beginning now. The same s_2 will be additionally available in the beginning of the next year also.

$$f_2^*(s_1) = \text{Maximize } 4X_2 + 3(s_2 - X_2) + f_1^*(2X_2 + 3(s_2 - X_2) + s_2)$$
$$\text{Subject to } 0 \leq X_2 \leq s_2$$

$$f_2^*(s_1) = \text{Maximize } 4X_2 + 3(s_2 - X_2) + 4X_2 + 6(s_2 - X_2) + 2s_2$$
$$\text{Subject to } 0 \leq X_2 \leq s_2$$

$$f_2^*(s_1) = \text{Maximize } 11s_2 - X_2$$
$$\text{Subject to } 0 \leq X_2 \leq s_2$$

The objective function is linear and we evaluate the function at the end points to reach the maximum at $X_2^* = 0$ and $f_2^*(s_2) = 11s_2$.

Three more years to go n = 3

$$f_3(K, X_1) = 6X_3 + 1\frac{1}{2} \, 3(K - X_1) + f_2^*[2X_1 + 3(K - X_1)]$$

$$f_3^*(K) = \text{Maximize } 6X_1 + 1\frac{1}{2} \, 3(K - X_1) + 11[2X_1 + 3(K - X_1)]$$

$$= \text{Maximize } \frac{75}{2}K - \frac{19}{2}X_3$$

The maximum happens at $X_3^* = 0$ and $Z = 75/2K$.

10.9 INTEGER PROGRAMMING (KNAPSACK PROBLEM)

ILLUSTRATION 10.9

Maximize $7Y_1 + 8Y_2 + 4Y_3 + 9Y_4$
Subject to
$$3Y_1 + 2Y_2 + Y_3 + 2Y_4 \leq 15$$
$$Y_j \geq 0 \text{ and integer}$$

While solving these problems we have to simplify (modify the problem) in such a way that there is at least one variable with a coefficient of 1 in the constraint. Variable Y_3 satisfies the condition and we solve for this variable first always. The problem is rewritten as:

Maximize $7X_1 + 8X_2 + 9X_3 + 4X_4$

Subject to

$$3X_1 + 2X_2 + 2X_3 + X_4 \le 15$$

$$X_j \ge 0 \text{ and integer}$$

Stage: Each variable
State: Amount of resource available
Decision variable: Values of X_1 to X_4
Criterion of effectiveness: Maximize Z

One more stage to go n = 1

$$f_1(s_1, X_4) = 4X_4$$

$$f_1^*(s_1) = \text{Maximize } 4X_4$$

Subject to $X_4 \le s_1$ and X_4 integer

Assuming that s_1 is a non-negative integer, $X_4^* = s_1$ and $f_1^*(s_1) = 4s_1$

Two more stages to go n = 2

$$f_2(s_2, X_3) = 9X_3 + f_1^*(s_1)$$

$$f_2^*(s_2) = \text{Maximize } 9X_3 + f_1^*(s_2 - 2X_3)$$

Subject to $2X_3 \le s_2$ and X_3 integer

$$f_2^*(s_2) = \text{Maximize } 9X_3 + 4(s_2 - 2X_3) = \text{Maximize } 4s_2 + X_3$$

Assuming that s_2 is a non-negative integer, $X_3^* = \lfloor s_2/2 \rfloor$ and $f_2^*(s_2) = 4s_2 + \lfloor s_2/2 \rfloor$ where $\lfloor \ \rfloor$ is used to denote lower integer value of a mixed number.

Three more stages to go n = 3

$$f_3(s_3, X_2) = 8X_2 + f_2^*(s_2)$$

$$f_3^*(s_3) = \text{Maximize } 8X_2 + f_2^*(s_3 - 2X_2)$$

Subject to $2X_2 \le s_3$ and X_2 integer

$$f_3^*(s_3) = \text{Maximize } 8X_2 + 4(s_3 - 2X_2) + \lfloor (s_3 - 2X_2)/2 \rfloor$$

$$= \text{Maximize } 4s_3 + \lfloor (s_3 - 2X_2)/2 \rfloor$$

Assuming that s_3 is a non-negative integer the maximum occurs at $X_2^* = 0$ and $f_3^*(s_3) = 4s_3 + \lfloor s_3/2 \rfloor$

Four more stages to go n = 4

$$f_4(15, X_1) = 7X_1 + f_3^*(s_3)$$
$$f_4^*(15) = \text{Maximize } 7X_1 + f_3^*(15 - 3X_1)$$
Subject to $3X_1 \leq 15$ and X_2 integer
$$f_4^*(15) = \text{Maximize } 7X_1 + 4(15 - 3X_1) + \lfloor(15 - 3X_1)/2\rfloor$$

X_1 can take values 0, 1, 2, 3, 4 or 5. We evaluate $f_4^*(15)$ for each of these values.

At $X_1 = 0$, $f_4^*(15) = 0 + 60 + 7 = 67$
At $X_1 = 1$, $f_4^*(15) = 7 + 48 + 6 = 61$
At $X_1 = 2$, $f_4^*(15) = 14 + 36 + 4 = 54$
At $X_1 = 3$, $f_4^*(15) = 21 + 24 + 3 = 48$
At $X_1 = 4$, $f_4^*(15) = 28 + 12 + 1 = 41$
At $X_1 = 5$, $f_4^*(15) = 35 + 0 + 0 = 35$

The optimum values are $X_1^* = 0$, $s_3 = 15$, $X_2^* = 0$, $s_2 = 15$, $X_3^* = 7$, $s_1 = 1$, $X_4^* = 1$ with $Z = 67$. The solution to the original problem is $Y_1^* = 0$, $Y_2^* = 0$, $Y_3^* = 1$, $Y_4^* = 7$ with $Z = 67$.

10.10 LINEAR PROGRAMMING

ILLUSTRATION 10.10

Let us solve a linear programming problem using dynamic programming.
Maximize $Z = 6X_1 + 5X_2$
Subject to
$$X_1 + X_2 \leq 5$$
$$3X_1 + 2X_2 \leq 12$$
$$X_1, X_2 \geq 0$$

Here there are two resources and hence we have two state variables. We call them u and v, respectively.

Stage: Each variable
State: Amount of resource available (u and v)
Decision variable: Values of X_1 and X_2
Criterion of effectiveness: Maximize Z

One more stage to go n = 1

$$f_1(u_1, v_1, X_2) = 5X_2$$
$$f_1^*(u_1, v_1) = \text{Maximize } 5X_2$$
Subject to $0 \leq X_2 \leq u_1$, $0 \leq 2X_2 \leq v_1$

We have
$$X_2^* = \text{Minimum}\left(u_1, \frac{v_1}{2}\right) \text{ and } f_1^*(u_1, v_1) = 5 \text{ Minimum}\left(u_1, \frac{v_1}{2}\right)$$

Two more stages to go n = 2

$$f_2(5, 12, X_1) = 6X_1 + f_1^*(5 - X_1, 12 - 3X_1)$$

$$f_2^*(5, 12) = \text{Maximize } 6X_1 + 5 \text{ Minimum}\left[5 - X_1, \frac{(12 - 3X_1)}{2}\right]$$

Subject to $0 \le X_1 \le 5$, $0 \le 3X_1 \le 12$

At $X_1 = 2$, we have

$$5 - X_1 = \frac{(12 - 3X_1)}{2}$$

$$f_2^*(5, 12) = \text{Maximize } 6X_1 + 5(5 - X_1) \quad 0 \le X_1 \le 2$$

$$f_2^*(5, 12) = \text{Maximize } 6X_1 + 5\frac{(12 - 3X_1)}{2} \quad 2 \le X_1 \le 4$$

At $X_1 = 0$, $Z = 25$, at $X_1 = 2$, $Z = 27$, at $X_1 = 4$, $Z = 24$.
The optimum solution is $X_1^* = 2$, $u_1 = 3$, $v_1 = 6$, $X_2^* = \text{Minimum } (u_1, v_1/2) = 3$, $Z = 27$.

10.11 SOME ADDITIONAL COMMENTS

1. Dynamic programming can be used to solve problems where we can do stage wise optimization. Usually we solve for one variable at every stage. It is preferable and easy to have only one state variable.
2. The state variable represents the effect of the optimized variables at earlier stages and the optimum found up to the earlier stage is unaffected by the solution at the current stage.
3. In all these problems, we had constraints of the $\le$ type. These types of constraints can be handled well by the DP algorithm. It is usually more difficult to interpret the $\ge$ type of constraint.
4. In linear programming problems, when we have more than three constraints or more than two variables, it becomes difficult to solve by DP. This is called **curse of dimensionality** where the dimensions (state variables) increase with increase in resources.
5. Most of the examples that we have used were of the single constraint type indicating a single resource and a single state variable.
6. In the integer programming application, we were able to solve a four-variable problem because one variable took zero value. Normally we can solve three variable single constraint problems using the approach that we used.
7. We need not write the recursive equations separately for the continuous variables problems as we did for the cases where the variable took discrete values.
8. The integer programming problem could also have been solved by the tabular method but the tabular method becomes cumbersome as the right hand side value increases.
9. It is always advisable to use the tabular method whenever the variable takes discrete integer values.

SOLVED EXAMPLES

EXAMPLE 10.1 A person contesting in an election has nine more days left for campaign and has to visit three towns in his constituency for campaign. He chooses to spend at least one day in each town. The expected number of votes (in tens of thousands) that the candidate gets if he spends j days in town i is given in Table 10.13. Use dynamic programming to allocate the days available to the towns so that the expected votes are maximized.

Table 10.13 Expected Number of Votes

Town	Expected votes per day spent				
	1	2	3	4	5
1	2	3	6	12	20
2	4	7	13	24	30
3	6	11	20	36	40

Solution: We use the backward recursive approach to solve the problem. Variables X_1, X_2 and X_3 are used to denote the number of days allotted to the three towns. Since a maximum of five days can be allotted to a town, the maximum value of the state variable when we have one more stage to go is 5 days.

Stage = Town
State = Number of days available
Decision variable = No. of days alloted
Cef = Maximize total expected

The recursive equations are:

$$f_n(s, X_n) = P_{xn} + f_{n-1}^*(s - X_n)$$
$$f_n^*(s) = \text{Maximum } f_n(s, X_n)$$
at $X = X_n^*$

One more stage to go n = 1

Table 10.14 shows the calculations.

When we have two more stages to go, the state variable can take a maximum of eight days and the decision variable X_2 can take values 1 to 5. If the state variable is 6 days and he allots three days to town 2 the expected number of votes is $13 + 20 = 33$ votes. The thirteen votes are from allotting three to town 2 and the remaining three to town 1 would fetch him an expected 20 votes (Table 10.15). Table 10.15 shows the calculations for $n = 2$.

Table 10.14 One More Stages to Go

s_1	$f_1(X_3)$	X_3^*
1	6	1
2	11	2
3	20	3
4	36	4
5	40	5

Table 10.15 Two More Stages to Go

s_2	$X_2 = 1$	$X_2 = 2$	$X_2 = 3$	$X_2 = 4$	$X_2 = 5$	$f_2(s, X_2)$	X_2^*
2	4 + 6	–	–	–	–	10	1
3	4 + 11	7 + 6	–	–	–	15	1
4	4 + 20	7 + 11	13 + 0	–	–	24	1
5	4 + 36	7 + 20	13 + 11	24 + 6	–	40	1
6	4 + 40	7 + 36	13 + 20	24 + 11	30 + 6	44	1
7	4 + 40	7 + 40	13 + 36	24 + 20	30 + 11	49	3
8	4 + 40	7 + 40	13 + 40	24 + 36	30 + 20	60	4

We now move to $n = 3$, three more stages to go. We have all the nine people available and the decision variable takes value 1 to 5. Table 10.16 shows the calculations.

Table 10.16 Three More Stages to Go

s	$X_4 = 1$	$X_1 = 2$	$X_1 = 3$	$X_1 = 4$	$X_1 = 5$	$F_3(X_1)$	X_1^*
9	2 + 60	3 + 49	6 + 44	12 + 40	20 + 24	62	1

$X_1^* = 1$ gives us eight days available as s_2. From Table 10.15 we know that the best value of X_2 for a state variable of 8 days is 4 days. This gives us 4 days available for town 3 and from Table 10.14 we allot all 4 days to town 3.

EXAMPLE 10.2 Consider an equipment whose replacement decisions have to be made over a period of N years. A new equipment costs C rupees and has a salvage value $S(T) = N - 1/2\ T$ for an equipment which is T years old when $T \leq N$ and $S(T) = 0$ when $T > N$. The annual profit for a T-year old equipment is: $P(T) = N^2 - 2T$ for $T \leq N$; $P(T) = 0$ for $T > N$. Formulate this as a dynamic problem and solve for an equipment which is 2 years old and has $N = 3$ and $C = 8$.

Solution: *Stage:* Year
State: Age of equipment
Decision variable: Replace or keep
Objective: Maximize profit
Recursive relation: $f_n(i,K) = (N^2 - 2i) + f_{n-1}^*(i + 1)\ i \leq N$
$\qquad\qquad\qquad\quad = f_{n-1}^*\ (i + 1)\ i > N$
$\qquad f_n(i,R) = -c + N - 1/2\ i + N^2\ i \leq N$
$\qquad\qquad\quad = -c + N^2\ i > N$

Table 10.17 shows the calculations for the recursive equations.

When we have a 2 years old equipment and we have $N = 3$. We have $i = 2$ and $N = 3$. For these values, from Table 10.17, the best strategy is to Replace. We move to $i = 1, N = 2$ for which the strategy is to keep. This takes us to $N = 1, i = 2$ for which the strategy is to keep. The optimal policy is:
R, K, K with profits equal to 15

Table 10.17 Calculations Using DP

i		0	1	2	3	4
N = 1	K	9	7	5	3	0
	R	4	3.5	3	2.5	1
N = 2	K	9 + 7	7 + 5	5 + 3	3 + 0	
	R	4 + 7	3.5 + 7	3 + 7	2.5 + 7	
N = 3	K	9 + 12	7 + 10	5 + 9.5		
	R	4 + 12	3.5 + 12	3 + 12		

EXAMPLE 10.3 Maximize $Z = 12X_1 - 4X_1^2 - X_1^3 + 6X_2 - X_2^2$

Subject to

$$X_1 + X_2 \leq 1$$
$$X_1, X_2 \geq 0$$

Solution: *Stage:* Variable
State: Remaining amount of each variable
Decision variable: X_1, X_2
Objective: Maximize Z

One more stage to go n = 1

$$f_1(s_1, X_2) = 6X_2 - X_2^2$$
$$f_1^*(s_1) = \text{Maximize } 6X_2 - X_2^2$$
$$X_2 \leq s_1 \quad X_2 = 0$$

df_1/X_2 gives

$$6 - 2X_2 = 0$$
$$X_2 = 3 \text{ violates } X_2 \leq 1$$

The function takes value zero at $X_2 = 0$ and increases as X_2 increases. Therefore,

$$X_2^* = s_1; f_1^*(s_1) = 6s_1 - s_1^2$$

Two more stages to go n = 2

$$f_2(1, X_1) = 12X_1 - 4X_1^2 - X_1^3 + f_1^*(1 - X_1) \quad 0 \leq X_1 \leq 1$$
$$f_2^*(1) = \text{Maximize } 12X_1 - 4X_1^2 - X_1^3 + 6(1 - X_1) - (1 - X_1)^2$$
$$0 \leq X_1 \leq 1$$

First derivative: $12 - 8X_1 - 3X_1^2 - 6 + 2(1 - X_1) = 0$

$-3X_1^2 - 10X_1 + 8 = 0$ gives $X_1 = -4$ or $2/3$

Second derivative: $-6 - 6X_1 < 0$ at $X_1 = 2/3$. Hence maximum.

$$X_1^* = \frac{2}{3}; s_1 = \frac{1}{3}, X_2^* = \frac{1}{3} \text{ and } Z = \frac{211}{27}$$

Since the function takes value 5 at $X_1 = 0$ and value 3 at $X_1 = 1$, the optimum solution is:

$$X_1^* = \frac{2}{3}, \; s_1 = \frac{1}{3}, \; X_2^* = \frac{1}{3} \text{ and } Z = \frac{211}{27}$$

EXAMPLE 10.4 Consider the problem:
Minimize $Z = X_1^2 + 3X_2^2 + 5X_3^2$
Subject to

$$X_1 \, X_2 \, X_3 = 10$$

$$X_i \geq 0 \text{ for } i = 1, 2, 3$$

Formulate as a dynamic programming problem, give the recursive relationship and solve.

Solution: *Stage:* Variables
State: Remaining amount of each resource available
Objective: Minimize $3X_1^2 + 4X_2^2 + X_3^2$
Decision variable: $X_i \geq 0$

One more stage to go n = 1

$$f_1(s_1, X_3) = 5X_3^2$$
$$f_1^*(s_1) = \text{Minimize } 5X_3^2 \text{ at } X_3^* = s_1 \text{ and } f_1^*(s_1) = 5s_1^2$$

Two more stages to go n = 2

$$f_2(s_2, X_2) = 3X_2^2 + f_1^*\left(\frac{s_2}{X_2}\right)$$

$$= 3X_2^2 + 5\left(\frac{s_2}{X_2}\right)^2$$

First derivative: $\quad 6X_2 - 10\left(\dfrac{s_2^2}{X_2^3}\right) = 0$

$$6X_2 = 10\left(\frac{s_2^2}{X_2^3}\right)$$

$$X_2^4 = \frac{5}{3} s_2^2$$

$$X_2^* = 1.136 \sqrt{s_2}$$

Second derivative: $\quad 6 + 30\left(\dfrac{s_2^2}{X_2^4}\right) > 0$ at $X_2^* = 1.136 \sqrt{s_2}$

$$f_2^*(S_2) = 3X_2^2 + 5\left(\frac{s_2}{X_2}\right)^2 = 7.746 s_2$$

Three more stages to go n = 3

$$f_3(10, X_1) = X_1^2 + f_2^*\left(\frac{10}{X_1}\right)$$

$$= X_1^2 + 7.746\left(\frac{10}{X_1}\right)$$

$$f_3^*(10) = \text{Minimize } X_1^2 + \frac{77.46}{X_1}$$

First derivative: $\quad 2X_1 - \dfrac{77.46}{X_1^2} = 0$ gives $X_1^3 = 38.73$

or $\quad X_1 = 3.383$

Second derivative > 0 indicating minimum at $X_1^* = 3.383$

Therefore, $\quad s_2 = \dfrac{10}{3.383} = 2.956$

and $\quad X_2^* = 1.136\sqrt{s_2} = 1.953 s_1 = \dfrac{2.956}{1.953} = 1.513$

$$X_1^* = 1.513 \text{ with } Z = 34.333$$

EXAMPLE 10.5 The Estate Manager of Messrs Dry View Nuts Plantation, has had a yield of B kg of nuts this year. He has to decide the quantity to be sold and quantity to be used as seeds for cultivation each year for the next years. If X_n kg are sold in the nth year, the returns are ad_n where $a > 0$. If Y_n kg are used for cultivation in the nth year, the yield is bY_n at the end of year ($b > 1$). If the objective of the manager is to maximize the total earnings over the next ten years, determine using dynamic programming, the quantities of nuts to be sold and to be used for cultivation each year.
Clearly define the stage, state and develop the recursive relationship.

Solution:

Stage: Year
State: Amount of nuts available
Decision variable: X_n quantity to be sold in nth year.
c.e.f: Maximize earnings

$$f_n(X_n, S_n) = aX_n + f_{n-1}^*[b(s - X_n)]$$
$$f_n^*(s) = \text{Maximize } aX_n + f_{n-1}^*[b(S - X_n)]$$

EXAMPLE 10.6 The Macrohard software company has n people available to do two jobs, say A and B. If P out of these n people do Job A, they produce profit worth $4P$. If P out of these n machines do Job B, they produce profit worth $3P$. After doing Job A, only $2/3P$ out of P remain available for further work and for Job B, only $¾P$ remain available for further work. The process is repeated with the remaining people for two more stages. Find the number of people to be allocated to each job at each stage in order to maximize the value of the total profit earned, using dynamic programming (Assume that any non-negative real number of people can be assigned at each stage).

Solution:

Stage: Month

Decision variable: No. of people allotted to Job A (X_n) (The rest are allotted to B)

State: Number of people available

c.e.f: Maximize total profit produced

$$f_n(s, X_n) = 4X_n + 3(s - X_n) + f_{n-1}^*\left[\frac{2X_n}{3} + \frac{\{3(s - X_n)\}}{4}\right]$$

$$f_n^*(s) = \text{Max } f_n(X_n, s)$$

EXAMPLE 10.7 Maximize $Z = 8X_1 + 7X_2$
Subject to

$$2X_1 + X_2 \le 8$$
$$5X_1 + 2X_2 \le 15$$
$$X_1, X_2 \ge 0$$

Solution:

Stage: Each variable

State(s): Resources available

Decision variable: X_1, X_2

c.e.f: Maximize Z

One more stage to go n = 1

$$f_1(U_1, V_1, X_2) = 7X_2$$

$$f_1^*(U_1, V_1) = \text{Max }\{7X_2\}$$

$$X_2 \ge 0, X_2 \le U_1, 2X_2 \le V_1$$

$$f_1^*(U_1, V_1) = 7 \text{ Min}\left(\frac{U_1, V_1}{2}\right)$$

Two more stages to go n = 2

$$f_2^*(8, 15) = \text{Max}\left\{8X_1 + 7 \text{ Min}\left(8 - 2X_1, \frac{(15 - 5X_1)}{2}\right)\right\}$$

$$X_1 \ge 0 \ \ 2X_1 \le 8, 5X_1 \le 15$$

$$= \text{Max}\left\{8X_1 + 7 \text{ Min}\left(8 - 2X_1, \frac{(15 - 5X_1)}{2}\right)\right\}$$

$$f_2^*(8, 15) = \text{Max}\left\{8X_1 + 7\frac{(15 - 5X_1)}{2}\right\}$$

$$= \text{Max}\left\{8X_1 + \frac{105}{2} - \frac{35X_1}{2}\right\}$$

$$X_1 \geq 0,\ X_1 \leq 4,\ X_1 \leq 3$$

The maximum is at $X_1^* = 0$. This gives

$$X_2^* = \frac{15}{2},\ Z = \frac{105}{2}$$

EXAMPLE 10.8 Anand has eight hours to prepare for the O R exam. He has three books to read and estimates the expected marks to be $10 + 3X_1$, $6 + 4X_2$ and $3 + 6X_3$, respectively if X_1, X_2 and X_3 hours are allotted to the three books. He wants to allot the time in such a way to maximize the minimum among the three marks that can be got. Solve this problem using dynamic programming.

Solution:

Stage: Book
State: Hours available
Decision variable: Hours allotted
Objective function: Maximize the minimum marks

One more stage to go n = 1

$$f_1(s_1, X_3) = 3 + 6X_3$$
$$f_1^*(s_1) = \text{Max Min}(3 + 6X_3)$$
$$0 = X_3 = s_1$$

This happens at $X_3^* = s_1$ and $f_1^*(s_1) = 3 + 6s_1$

Two more stages to go n = 2

$$f_2(s_2, X_2) = 6 + 4X_2$$
$$f_2^*(s_2) = \text{Max Min}\ [6 + 4X_2,\ 3 + 6(s_2 - X_2)]$$
$$0 = X_2 = s_2$$

This happens when

$$6 + 4X_2 = 3 + 6(s_2 - X_2)$$
$$6 + 4X_2 = 3 + 6s_2 - 6X_2$$

$$X_2^* = \frac{(6s_2 - 3)}{10}$$

and

$$f_2^*(s_2) = 6 + 4\,\frac{(6s_2 - 3)}{10}$$
$$= \frac{(24s_2 + 48)}{10}$$

Three more stages to go n = 3

$$f_3(8, X_1) = 10 + 3X_1$$

$$f_3^*(8) = \text{Max Min}\left\{10 + 3X_1, \frac{[24(8 - X_1) + 48]}{10}\right\}$$

$$0 \leq X_1 \leq 8$$

This happens when

$$10 + 3X_1 = \frac{(192 + 48 - 24X_1)}{10}$$

$$X_1^* = 2.592$$

and $f_3^*(8) = 10 + 3 * 2.592 = 17.78$

$s_2 = 5.408$, $X_2^* = 2.945$, $s_1 = 2.463$, $X_3^* = 2.463$

EXAMPLE 10.9 Solve the following problem by dynamic programming.

Minimize $X_1^2 + 2X_2^2 + 3X_3^2 + 4X_4^2$

Subject to

$$X_1 + X_2 + X_3 + X_4 = 10$$
$$X_1, X_2, X_3, X_4 = 0$$

Solution: Stage: Each variable
State: Resource available
Decision variable: X_j
Objective function: $\Sigma j X_j^2$

One more stage to go n = 1

$$f_1(s_1, X_4) = 4X_4^2$$
$$f_1^*(s_1) = \text{Minimize } 4X_4^2$$
$$\text{Subject to } X_4 = s_1$$

(This is because the constraint is an equation. When the constraint is an equation, we have to allocate all the available resource to the variable in this stage)

$$X_4^* = s_1 \text{ and } f_1^*(s_1) = 4s_1^2$$

Two more stages to go n = 2

$$f_2(s_2, X_3) = 3X_3^2 + f_1^*(s_2 - X_3)$$
$$f_2^*(s_2) = \text{Minimize } 3X_3^2 + 4(s_2 - X_3)^2$$
$$\text{Subject to } X_3 \leq s_2$$

First derivative equal to zero gives us $6X_3 - 8(s_2 - X_3) = 0$ from which $X_3 = 4/7s_2$. The second derivative is positive at $X_3 = 4/7s_2$ and hence is a minimum. The value of $f_2^*(s_2)$ is:

$$\frac{3*16}{49}s_2^2 + \frac{4*9}{49}s_2^2 = \frac{12}{7}s_2^2$$

Three more stages to go n = 3

$$f_3(s_3, X_2) = 2X_2^2 + f_2^*(s_3 - X_2)$$

$$f_3^*(s_3) = \text{Minimize } 2X_2^2 + \frac{12}{7}(s_3 - X_2)^2$$

Subject to $X_2 \leq s_3$

First derivative equal to zero gives us:

$$4X_2 - \frac{24}{7}(s_3 - X_2) = 0$$

from which

$$X_2 = \frac{6}{13}s_3$$

The second derivative is positive at $X_2 = 6/13\ s_3$ and hence is a minimum.

$$f_3^*(s_3) = \frac{2*36}{169}s_3^2 + \frac{84}{169}s_3^2 = \frac{12}{13}s_3^2$$

Four more stages to go n = 4

$$f_4(10, X_1) = X_1^2 + f_3^*(10 - X_1)$$

$$f_4^*(10) = \text{Minimize } X_1^2 + \frac{12}{13}*(10 - X_1)^2$$

Subject to $X_1 \leq 10$

First derivative equal to zero gives us:

$$2X_1 - \frac{24}{13}(10 - X_1) = 0$$

from which $X_1 = 4.8$

The second derivative is positive at $X_1 = 4.8$ and hence is a minimum.
$X_1^* = 4.8$, $s_3 = 5.2$, $X_2^* = 2.4$, $s_2 = 2.8$, $X_3^* = 1.6$, $s_1 = 1.2$ and $X_4^* = 1.2$ and $f_4^*(10) = 32.8$

EXAMPLE 10.10   Solve the following problem by dynamic programming:
Minimize $8X_1 + 6X_2$
Subject to
$$X_1 + X_2 \geq 2$$
$$X_1, X_2 \geq 0$$

Solution: We add a slack variable to convert the inequality to an equation and get
Minimize $8X_1 + 6X_2$
Subject to
$$X_1 + X_2 - X_3 = 2$$
$$X_1, X_2, X_3 = 0$$

Stage: Variable
State: Resource available
Decision variable: X_1 to X_3
Objective function: Minimize $8X_1 + 6X_2$

One more stage to go n = 1
$$f_1(s_1, X_3) = 0$$
$$-X_3 = s_1, X_3 = 0$$
we should have $s_1 \leq 0$ and $f_1^*(s_1) = 0$.

Two more stages to go n = 2
$$f_2(s_2, X_2) = 6X_2 + f_1^*(s_1)$$
$$f_2^*(s_2) = \text{Minimize } 6X_2$$
$$X_2 \geq s_2, X_2 = 0 \text{ (The condition } X_2 \geq s_2 \text{ would make } s_1 \leq 0)$$
$$f_2^*(s_2) = 6s_2 \text{ at } X_2^* = s_2$$

Three more stages to go n = 3
$$f_3(2, X_1) = 8X_1 + f_2^*(2 - X_1)$$
$$f_3^*(2) = \text{Minimize } 8X_1 + 6(2 - X_1)$$
$$X_1 \leq 2, X_1 \geq 0$$

The minimum happens at $X_1^* = 0$ and $f_3^*(2) = 12$. $X_1^* = 0$ means $s_2 = 2$ and $X_2^* = 2$, $s_1 = 0$ and $X_3^* = 0$ with $Z = 12$.

EXAMPLE 10.11 Solve the following problem by dynamic programming:
Minimize $8X_1 + 4X_2$
Subject to
$$3X_1 + X_2 \geq 7$$
$$X_1, X_2 \geq 0 \text{ and integer}$$

Solution: We add a slack variable to convert the inequality to an equation and get
Minimize $8X_1 + 4X_2$
Subject to
$$3X_1 + X_2 - X_3 = 7$$
$$X_1, X_2, X_3 \geq 0 \text{ and integer}$$

Stage: Variable
State: Resource available
Decision variable: X_1 to X_3
Objective function: Minimize $8X_1 + 4X_2$

One more stage to go n = 1

$$f_1(s_1, X_3) = 0$$
$$-X_3 = s_1, X_3 = 0 \text{ and integer}$$

We should have $s_1 \leq 0$ and $f_1^*(s_1) = 0$.

Two more stages to go n = 2

$$f_2(s_2, X_2) = 4X_2 + f_1^*(s_1)$$
$$f_2^*(s_2) = \text{Minimize } 4X_2$$
$$X_2 \geq s_2, X_2 = 0 \quad \text{(The condition } X_2 \geq s_2 \text{ would make } s_1 \leq 0\text{) and integer}$$
$$f_2^*(s_2) = 4s_2 \text{ at } X_2^* = s_2$$

Three more stages to go n = 3

$$f_3(7, X_1) = 8X_1 + f_2^*(7 - 3X_1)$$
$$f_3^*(7) = \text{Minimize } 8X_1 + 4(7 - X_1)$$
$$X_1 \leq 2, X_1 \geq 0 \text{ and integer}$$

The minimum happens at $X_1^* = 2$ and $f_3^*(7) = 20$. $X_1^* = 2$ means $s_2 = 1$ and $X_2^* = 1$, $s_1 = 0$ and $X_3^* = 0$ with $Z = 20$.

EXAMPLE 10.12 A person has 80 sheep with him and considers a three-year period to sell them for profit. The cost of maintaining the sheep in year n is $120n$. If he can sell X sheep at the end of year n, the value is nX^2. If X sheep are maintained, they multiply and become $1.5X$ at the end of the year. Solve by dynamic programming, the amount of sheep to be sold at the end of each year.

Solution: We assume that decisions are made at the end of the year and if we start the year with X sheep (after the sale has been made), we have $1.5X$ sheep at the end of the year and the maintenance cost is for X sheep.

Stage: Each year
State: Number of sheep available at the beginning of the year
Decision variable: Number of sheep sold at the end of year j (X_1 to X_3 for end of years 1 to 3)
Criterion of effectiveness: Maximize the profit (difference between the value and the cost of maintenance)

One more year to go n = 1

$$f_1(s_1, X_3) = 3X_3^2 - 360s_1$$

$$f_1^*(s_1) = \text{Maximize } 3X_3^2 - 360s_1$$

Subject to $0 \leq X_3 \leq 1.5s_1$

(This is because the s_1 sheep available at the beginning of year 3 multiply to $1.5s_1$ and are available for sale at the end of the third year).

Differentiating the expression with respect to X_3 and equating to zero, we get $X_3 = 0$. The second derivative is positive indicating minimum but we are interested in maximizing the return function. Due to the quadratic nature of the objective function, we evaluate at the extreme points of the range and have

$$X_3^* = 1.5s_1 \quad \text{and} \quad f_1^*(s_1) = 6.75s_1^2 - 360s_1$$

(This is also obvious because at the end of the planning period, we would sell off all the available sheep and make maximum profit).

Two more years to go n = 2

$$f_2(s_2, X_2) = 2X_2^2 - 240s_2 + f_1^*(1.5s_2 - X_2)$$

$$f_2^*(s_2) = \text{Maximize } 2X_2^2 - 240s_2 + 6.75(1.5s_2 - X_2)^2 - 360(1.5s_2 - X_2)$$

Subject to $0 \leq X_2 \leq 1.5s_2$

The differentiation would give us a minimum and since we are maximizing, we evaluate the function at the two extreme points $X_2 = 0$ and $X_2 = 1.5s_2$.

At $X_2 = 0$, $f_2^*(s_2) = -240s_2 + 6.75(1.5s_2)^2 - 360(1.5s_2) = 15.1875s_2^2 - 780s_2$

At $X_2 = 1.5s_2$, $f_2^*(s_2) = 4.5s_2^2 - 240s_2$

At $s_2 = 0$ and $s_2 = 50.53$, the values of $15.1875s_2^2 - 780s_2$ and $4.5s_2^2 - 240s_2$ are equal.

We conclude that for $s_2 \geq 50.53$, $f_2^*(s_2) = 15.1875s_2^2 - 780s_2$ is maximum at $X_2^* = 0$ and for $s_2 < 50.53$, $f_2^*(s_2) = 4.5s_2^2 - 240s_2$ is maximum at $X_2^* = 1.5s_2$.

Three more years to go n = 3

$$f_3(80, X_1) = X_1^2 - 120 * 80 + f_2^*(120 - X_1)$$

$$f_3^*(80) = \text{Maximize } X_1^2 - 12000 + f_2^*(120 - X_1)$$

Subject to $0 \leq X_1 \leq 120$

We have two functions for $f_2^*(120 - X_1)$ and we express $f_3^*(80)$ as:

$$f_3^*(80) = \text{Maximize } X_1^2 - 9600 + 15.1875(120 - X_1)^2 - 780(120 - X_1) \text{ for } (120 - X_1) > 50.53; X_1 \leq 69.47$$

and $f_3^*(80) = \text{Maximize } X_1^2 - 9600 + 4.5(120 - X_1)^2 - 240(160 - X_1) \text{ for } (160 - X_1) \leq 50.53; X_1 \geq 69.47$

The differentiation would give us a minimum and since we are maximizing, we evaluate the function at the extreme points $X_1 = 0$, $X_1 = 69.47$ and $X_1 = 120$. At $X_1 = 0$, $Z = 115500$. At $X_1 = 69.47$, $Z = -5411.35$ and at $X_1 = 120$, $Z = 4800$.

The function is maximum at $X_1^* = 0$, $s_1 = 120$, $X_2^* = 0$, $s_2 = 180$, $X_3^* = 1.5*180 = 270$ and $Z = 115500$.

CASE STUDY 10.1: Nalabagam Foods

Nalabagam foods have recently entered the packed food industry. They make three varieties of prepared ready food that can be served as side dishes to *rotis* and *naans*. They make one variety at a time in their factory at Thanjavur. The food preparation is a three-stage process involving mixing, cooking and packing. The packed food has a shelf life of two months for each of the three varieties. They would like to produce all the three varieties every week and meet the weekly demand but since the changeover times are high, they would not mind producing in large batches that may also meet the demand of subsequent weeks. The product life is such that they can even produce the demand of their fourth week, store it and sell it. They would not like to store their products for more than three weeks.

Mr. Subramanian, the production manager has to make production decisions for their fast moving item, aloo gravy. The data for the next four weeks are shown in Table 10.18.

Table 10.18 Demand Data

Week	Demand	Set-up Cost	Inventory Cost	Production Cost
1	2000	3600	1.00	50
2	3000	4000	1.25	50
3	3000	4200	1.00	50
4	2500	3900	1.25	50

Mr. Subramanian incurs a set-up cost every week the item is produced. All the production per week is carried out as a single batch. He does not face capacity constraints in his plant and can produce as much as he can in any week.

Mr. Subramanian wants the production quantities in such a way that the demands can be met. His principal dealer has built up inventory and therefore can accept late orders by a week. Mr. Subramanian would not ideally like to use this option but would like to see whether backordering can provide a cost advantage. He estimates his backorder cost to be Rs 2/kg/week.

EXERCISES

10.1 An expensive machine in a factory has to be replaced periodically as it wears out. An optimal replacement plan for a machine newly acquired has to be drawn up for the next four years, after which the machine is no longer needed. The relevant data are given in Table 10.19.

Table 10.19 Data for Machine Replacement Problem

Time (years)	Cost of machine Rs. × 1000	Scrap value Rs. × 1000	Operating cost Rs. × 1000
1	200	80	50
2	210	60	80
3	225	40	100
4	240	20	140

Assume that the scrap value and operating cost depend strictly on the age of the machine and not on the rising cost of the machine. Determine the optimum replacement plan for the machine using dynamic programming.

10.2 Solve the following problem by dynamic programming clearly indicating the stage, state, etc.

Minimize $7X_1^2 - 4X_1 + 3X_2 - X_2^2$

Subject to

$$X_1 + X_2 \leq 3$$

$$X_1, X_2 \geq 0$$

10.3 Solve the following problem by DP:

Maximize $X_1 X_2^2 X_3^3$

Subject to

$$X_1 + X_2 + X_3 = 11$$

$$X_i \geq 1 \text{ and integer}$$

10.4 Ms. Mannur Foundries Ltd. has to plan the production of a casting using the data shown in Table 10.20.

Table 10.20 Production Data

Period I	Demand D_i	Set up cost S_i	Carrying cost
1	4	4	1
2	2	7	2
3	3	6	2

Demand is assumed to be known and deterministic. The company enters Period 1 with an inventory of 1 unit. The production cost is given by

$$C_i(X_i) = 10X_i \quad \text{for} \quad 0 \leq X_i \leq 3$$

and

$$C_i(X_i) = 30 + 20(X_i - 3) \quad \text{for} \quad X_i \geq 4$$

Shortages are not allowed. Inventory at the end of Period 3 should be zero. The objective is to determine the value of X_i that minimizes the sum of set up costs, carrying costs and production costs. Determine the optimum production plan using dynamic programming.

10.5 Solve using dynamic programming:
Maximize $\quad 8x_1^2 + 5x_1 + 6x_2^2$
Subject to
$$x_1 + 2x_2 \leq 9$$
$$x_1 + 3x_2 \leq 10$$
$$x_1, x_2 \geq 0$$

10.6 Ten lakh litres of a chemical has to be produced and sent at the end of the next three weeks. If X_n is the lakh of litres produced in the nth week prior to the date of despatch, the cost is nX_n. The total cost of production over the next three weeks is to be minimized, subject to the condition that exactly 1 lakh litres is to be produced. Assuming X_n to be continuous, use dynamic programming to determine the optimum production quantities for the next three weeks.

10.7 A factory has 50 machines, each can produce two products A and B. A machine when allotted to a product produces that product during the entire period while the product can be changed in the next period. The factory gains Rs. 5000 per period per machine by producing A and Rs. 7000 per period per machine when it produces B. However, 20% machines breakdown when they make A and 25% when they make B per period and they are not available for further use. Solve by DP, the number of machines allotted to products for 3 periods to maximize profit.

10.8 Solve using DP.
Maximize $\quad 6x_1 + 7x_2 + 4x_3$
Subject to
$$4x_1 + 6x_2 + 3x_3 \leq 30$$
$$x_i \geq 0 \text{ and integer}$$

10.9 Given $f_1(X_1) = 5X_1 + 4, f_2(X_2) = 3X_2 + 6, f_3(X_3) = 7X_3 + 2$ and $X_1 + X_2 + X_3 = 10$, find using DP the values of $X_1, X_2,$ and X_3 that maximizes the minimum of the three functions.

10.10 The Poisse and Gass Chemical company must destroy 1000 litres of a toxic effluent. Four sites are available for this purpose at different locations in the city. If X litres of pollutant are destroyed at site n, the cost to the company is $nx^2 - 4x$. Using DP, determine how much of pollutant should be destroyed at each site so that the total cost is minimized.

10.11 Ms Spoilda Soil Fertilizer company has undertaken a contract to supply 50 tons of fertilizer at the end of the first month, 60 tons at the end of second month and 70 tons at the end of third month. Cost of producing X tons of fertilizer in any month is $2500X + 10X^2$. The inventory carrying cost is Rs. 100 per ton per month. Assuming initial and final inventory to be zero, solve the problem using DP.

10.12 Solve the following non-linear problem using dynamic programming:
Maximize $\quad Z = X_1 X_2 + 3X_1 - 2X_2$
Subject to
$$2X_1 + X_2 = 17, X_1, X_2 \geq 0$$

10.13 Consider a DP problem of alloting workers to meet monthly demand. The requirements are 90, 80, 85 and 60 and the initial availability is 100. The cost of changeover is X^2 where X is the quantity changed and the cost of underutilization is $10X$. Find a least cost solution.

10.14 Solve using DP.
Maximize $6X_1^2 + 7X_2 + 8X_3$
Subject to
$$2X_1 + 2X_2 + 3X_3 \le 8$$
$$X_1, X_2 \ge 0 \text{ and integer}$$

10.15 Solve using DP.
Maximize $X_1(1 - X_2)X_3$
Subject to
$$X_1 - X_2 + X_3 \le 10$$
$$X_1, X_2, X_3 \ge 0$$

10.16 The Poise & West Company has to process 9000 litres of effluents every week at three of its treatment plants. If X_n litres of effluent is destroyed at plant n, the cost incurred by the company is nX_n^2. Assuming X_n to be continuous, determine the optimal quantities of effluent to be treated at each plant using dynamic programming.

10.17 Solve the following non-linear problem using dynamic programming:
Maximize $Z = X_1X_2 + 2X_1 + X_2$
Subject to
$$X_1 + 2X_2 \le 6$$
$$X_1, X_2 \ge 0 \text{ and integer}$$

10.18 Mani has 10 days to prepare before the exams. He has three exams and estimated his expected marks (out of 100) in exams j (j = 1, 2, 3) if he prepares for i days (i = 1, 2, 3, 4) is given in Table 10.21. Use dynamic programming to determine Mani's time allocation problem to maximize the total marks in the three exams.

Table 10.21 Expected Marks

Days	Exam 1	Exam 2	Exam 3
1	60	70	60
2	80	80	70
3	90	90	80
4	100	100	90

Basic Queueing Models

In this Chapter, we introduce the reader to the basics of queueing models and queueing theory. No course on Operations Research is complete without an understanding of queueing models. In this book we keep the material on queueing theory to the minimum for two reasons. The main focus of the book being linear optimization, the material on queueing models is kept to a minimum since they show non-linear behaviour. Also the book primarily deals with deterministic models and queueing models are different in the sense that they attempt to model probabilistic behaviour of systems.

We find queueing systems quite frequently in real life situations. A bank teller, an ATM machine, the reservation counters and a gas station are all examples of queueing systems. The important entities in the queueing systems are:

1. Arrivals
2. Servers
3. Service
4. Queue length
5. Population

The arrivals are the reason for the existence of queueing systems. They are the ones who require the service. The people coming to a doctor or a barber shop represent the arrivals. Arrivals are not deterministic but are assumed to follow certain probability distributions. The common assumption is that arrivals follow a Poisson distribution.

The servers are the service providers. The doctor, the ATM machine, the reservation counter persons are examples of servers. Queueing systems are classified as:

1. Single server queueing models
2. Multiple server queueing models

The service determines the order in which arrivals into the system access the servers. Ordinarily the queue discipline is First Come First Served (FCFS). However, it may be necessary sometimes to follow Last In First Out queue discipline. The service times are usually not deterministic but follow a service distribution. The most commonly used distribution for service times is the exponential distribution.

The population determines the theoretical maximum number who could join the queue. Most queueing systems assume infinite population, while finite population models exist. If we are modelling the maintenance of machinery in a shop with M machines as a queueing system, the arrivals are the breakdowns and the servers are the maintenance people. Here it is a finite population model because a maximum of M breakdowns can only happen. In this chapter, we will be considering infinite population models.

The queue length can also be infinite or finite. If we consider doctor as a server and infinite population, we can also have infinite queue length. On the other hand, if we are considering a car service station that has space for a maximum of N cars, the queue length is finite and can go up to N. Here it is assumed that if the garage is full, the arrival does not join the queue and go away. We consider both infinite queue length and finite queue length models in this chapter.

Three other situations happen in real-life queueing systems. An arrival chooses not to join the queue even if there is space to join. This phenomenon is called **balking**. Sometimes balking is forced in finite queueing models where the arrival cannot join the queue if the maximum queue length is reached. Sometimes the arrival leaves the queue after staying in the queue for some time. This phenomenon is called **reneging**. The third situation is when there are multiple lines and the arrival moves from one line to another. This is called **jockeying** and takes place during the initial period in the queue. Since the person has to join as the last person in the new line, jockeying reduces as the person advances in the line towards the server.

It is possible to analyze both the steady state behaviour and the transient behaviour of queueing systems. In this chapter, we restrict ourselves to the steady state behaviour of queueing systems. We restrict ourselves to single server and multiple server models with finite and infinite queue length. We assume Poisson arrivals and exponential service times due to their Markovian (memory less) property. We have slightly modified the notation used in Taha (2003) to describe the basic queueing models.

11.1 SINGLE SERVER INFINITE QUEUE LENGTH MODEL ($M/M/1/\infty/\infty$ MODEL)

In the notation given above, the first M stands for Poisson arrivals (Markovian) and the second M stands for exponential service. The number of servers is one. The two infinity indicate infinite queue length and infinite population. The memory less property ensures that during a small interval h a maximum of only one event takes place. The arrivals follow a Poisson distribution with mean λ and service is exponential with mean μ.

Let $p_n(t)$ be the probability that there are n people in the system at time t.

Probability that there are n people at time $t + h$

= Probability that there are n people at time t and there is no arrival or service completed during h

+ Probability that there are $n - 1$ people at time t and there is one arrival and no service

+ Probability that there are $n + 1$ people at time t and there is no arrival and one service during the period h

This equation assumes that only one event (either an arrival or service) can happen during a small interval h and both cannot happen during the small interval h.

The probability of one arrival happening is given by λh and the probability of one service completed is μh. Probability of no arrival during h is $(1 - \lambda h)$ and probability of no service completed is $(1 - \mu h)$. We have

$p_n(t+h) = p_n(t)$ * Probability of no arrival and no service + $p_{n+1}(t)$ * Probability of no arrival and one service + $p_{n-1}(t)$ * Probability of one arrival and no service

$$p_n(t+h) = p_n(t)(1-\lambda h)(1-\mu h) + p_{n+1}(t)(1-\lambda h)\mu h + p_{n-1}(t)\lambda h(1-\mu h)$$

At steady state, we have

$$p_n = p_n(1-\lambda h)(1-\mu h) + p_{n+1}(1-\lambda h)\mu h + p_{n-1}\lambda h(1-\mu h) \qquad (11.1)$$

Neglecting higher order terms, we have

$$(\lambda + \mu)p_n = \lambda p_{n-1} + \mu p_{n+1}$$

However, when we consider p_0 (probability that there is none in the system), we have the following relationship:

$p_0(t+h) = p_0(t)$ * Probability of no arrival + $p_1(t)$ * Probability of no arrival and one service

At steady state,

$$p_0 = p_0(1-\lambda h) + p_1(1-\lambda h)\mu h \qquad (11.2)$$

Neglecting higher order terms and simplifying, we get

$$\lambda p_0 = \mu p_1$$

$$p_1 = \left(\frac{\lambda}{\mu}\right) p_0 \qquad (11.3)$$

Substituting this in Eq. (11.1) for $n = 1$, we get

$$p_1(\lambda + \mu) = \lambda p_0 + \mu p_2$$

Substituting from Eq. (11.3), we get

$$p_2 = \left(\frac{\lambda}{\mu}\right) p_1 = \left(\frac{\lambda}{\mu}\right)^2 p_0 \qquad (11.4)$$

Generalizing, we get

$$p_n = \left(\frac{\lambda}{\mu}\right) p_{n-1} = \left(\frac{\lambda}{\mu}\right)^n p_0 \qquad (11.5)$$

If we had used λ_n and μ_n to represent the arrival and service rate when there are n people in the system, Eqs. (11.3) and (11.5) become

$$p_1 = \left(\frac{\lambda_0}{\mu_1}\right) p_0$$

$$p_n = \left(\frac{\lambda_{n-1}}{\mu_n}\right) p_{n-1} = \left(\frac{\lambda_0 \lambda_1 \ldots \lambda_{n-1}}{\mu_1 \mu_2 \ldots \mu_n}\right) p_0 \qquad (11.6)$$

To get the value of p_0, we use the condition:

$$\sum_{j=0}^{\infty} p_j = 1$$

Substituting from Eq. (11.5) to the above equation, we get an infinite geometric progression with 1 as the first term and λ/μ as common difference. We get

$$p_0 = 1 - \left(\frac{\lambda}{\mu}\right) = 1 - \rho \qquad (11.7)$$

where $\rho = \lambda/\mu$. To use the expression for summation of an infinite geometric progression, it is necessary to have $\lambda/\mu < 1$. This is true because if the arrival rate is greater than service rate, and if we consider infinite queue length, the person arriving can never get served. It is, therefore, necessary that $\lambda/\mu < 1$ for infinite queue length situations.

We evaluate the performance of a queueing system based on four parameters, L_s, L_q, W_s and W_q. L_s represents the expected length of the system, which means the expected number of people in the system. This is defined as follows:

$$L_s = \sum_{j=0}^{\infty} jp_j = p_1 + 2p_2 + 3p_3 + \ldots$$

$$L_s = \sum_{j=0}^{\infty} jp_j = \sum_{j=0}^{\infty} j\rho^j p_0 = \rho p_0 \sum_{j=0}^{\infty} j \rho^{j-1}$$

$$L_s = \rho p_0 \sum_{j=0}^{\infty} j\rho^{j-1} = \rho p_0 \sum_{j=0}^{\infty} \frac{d}{d\rho}\rho^j = \rho p_0 \frac{d}{d\rho} \sum_{j=0}^{\infty} \rho^j$$

$$= \rho p_0 \frac{d}{d\rho} \sum_{j=0}^{\infty} \rho^j = \rho p_0 \frac{d}{d\rho}\left(\frac{1}{1-\rho}\right)$$

$$L_s = \rho p_0 \frac{d}{d\rho}\left(\frac{1}{1-\rho}\right) = \frac{\rho p_0}{(1-\rho)^2} = \frac{\rho}{1-\rho} = \frac{\lambda}{\mu - \lambda} \qquad (11.8)$$

L_q, the number of people in the queue is given by

$$L_q = \sum_{j=2}^{\infty} (j-1) p_j = p_2 + 2p_3 + 3p_4 + \ldots$$

Adding $(1 - p_0)$ to both sides, we get

$$L_q + 1 - p_0 = p_1 + 2p_2 + \ldots = L_s$$

From which

$$L_q = L_s - (1 - p_0) = L_s - \rho \qquad (11.9)$$

Little's (1961) equation gives us the relationship between the queue lengths and the waiting times. We have

$$L_s = \lambda W_s \quad \text{and} \quad L_q = \lambda W_q \qquad (11.10)$$

Also, we have
Expected waiting time in the system = Expected waiting time in the queue + Expected service time

$$W_s = W_q + \frac{1}{\mu} \qquad (11.11)$$

From Eqs. (11.9) and (11.10), we have

$$L_s = L_q + \frac{\lambda}{\mu} \qquad (11.12)$$

11.2 SINGLE SERVER FINITE QUEUE LENGTH MODEL (*M/M/*1*/N/*∞ MODEL)

In this model we assume that the maximum number in the system is N and when there are N people in the system, the $N + 1$th person will not join the queue. Therefore, the number in the system can be from zero to N. Equations (11.3) and (11.5) will hold and $\sum_{n=0}^{N} p_n = 1$ gives

$$p_0 + p_1 + p_2 + \ldots + p_N = 1$$

From which

$$p_0 + \rho\, p_0 + \rho^2\, p_0 + \ldots + \rho^N\, p_0 = 1$$

$$p_0 = \frac{1-\rho}{1-\rho^{N+1}} \quad \text{when } \rho \neq 1 \qquad (11.13)$$

$$p_0 = \frac{1}{N+1} \quad \text{when } \rho = 1 \qquad (11.14)$$

Here ρ can take a value greater than 1. The expected number of customers (people excluding the server) is given by

$$L_s = \sum_{n=0}^{N} n p_N = p_0 \sum_{n=0}^{N} n\rho^n = \rho\, p_0 \sum_{n=0}^{N} \frac{d}{d\rho}\rho^n = \rho\, p_0 \frac{d}{d\rho} \sum_{n=0}^{N} \rho^n$$

$$L_s = \rho\, p_0 \frac{d}{d\rho}\left(\frac{1-\rho^{N+1}}{1-\rho}\right) = \frac{\rho\,[1-(N+1)\rho^N + N\rho^{N+1}]}{(1-\rho)(1-\rho^{N+1})}; \quad \rho \neq 1 \qquad (11.15)$$

When $\rho = 1$, $N_s = N/2$

In this model, some customers arriving are forced to leave if there are N people in the system. The probability of a customer forced to leave is p_N. The expected number of arrivals not joining the line is λp_N and the effective arrival into the system is given by

$$\lambda_e = \lambda - \lambda p_N = \lambda(1 - p_N) \qquad (11.16)$$

We can obtain expressions for L_q, W_s and W_q using Eqs. (11.10) to (11.12) and replacing λ by λ_e.

11.3 MULTIPLE SERVER INFINITE QUEUE LENGTH MODEL (M/M/C/∞/∞ MODEL)

Let the number of servers be c. There is a single line and as soon as a server is free, the first person in the line will get the service from the free server. All servers are assumed to be similar and have a service rate μ per hour. Customers arrive at the rate of λ per hour and since we have infinite queue length, we require that $\lambda/c\mu < 1$.

Here we have to define the arrival rate and service rate using the state of the system because when we have fewer than c ($n < c$) people in the system, the service rate is $n\mu$. We have

$$\lambda_n = \lambda \quad \mu_n = n\mu(n < c) \text{ and } \mu_n = c\mu(n \geq c)$$

Substituting these in Eq. (11.6), we get

$$p_n = \frac{\lambda^n}{\mu(2\mu)(3\mu)\ldots(n\mu)} p_0 = \frac{\lambda^n}{n!\mu^n} p_0 = \frac{\rho^n}{n!} p_0 \text{ when } n < c$$

$$p_n = \frac{\lambda^n}{\mu(2\mu)(3\mu)\ldots(c\mu)(c\mu)^{n-c}} p_0 = \frac{\lambda^n}{c!c^{n-c}\mu^n} p_0 = \frac{\rho^n}{c!c^{n-c}} p_0 \text{ when } n \geq c \quad (11.17)$$

From $\Sigma p_n = 1$, we get

$$p_0 \sum_{n=0}^{c-1} \frac{\rho^n}{n!} + \sum_{n=c}^{\infty} \frac{\rho^n}{c!c^{n-c}} p_0 = 1$$

$$p_0 \left[\sum_{n=0}^{c-1} \frac{\rho^n}{n!} + \frac{\rho^c}{c!} \sum_{n=c}^{\infty} \frac{\rho^{n-c}}{c^{n-c}} \right] = 1$$

$$p_0 \left[\sum_{n=0}^{c-1} \frac{\rho^n}{n!} + \frac{\rho^c}{c!} \left(\frac{1}{1-\frac{\rho}{c}} \right) \right] = 1 \text{ where } \rho/c < 1 \quad (11.18)$$

We derive an expression for L_q as follows:

$$L_q = \sum_{n=c}^{\infty} (n-c) p_n = \sum_{j=0}^{\infty} j p_{j+c} = \sum_{j=0}^{\infty} j \frac{\rho^{j+c}}{c^j c!} p_0$$

$$L_q = \sum_{j=0}^{\infty} j \frac{\rho^{j+c}}{c^j c!} p_0 = \frac{\rho^{c+1}}{c!c} p_0 \sum_{j=0}^{\infty} j \left(\frac{\rho}{c}\right)^{j-1} = \frac{\rho^{c+1}}{c!c} p_0 \sum_{j=0}^{\infty} \frac{d}{d\left(\frac{\rho}{c}\right)} \left(\frac{\rho}{c}\right)^j$$

$$L_q = \frac{\rho^{c+1}}{c!c} p_0 \frac{d}{d\left(\frac{\rho}{c}\right)} \sum_{j=0}^{\infty} \left(\frac{\rho}{c}\right)^j = \frac{\rho^{c+1}}{c!c} p_0 \frac{d}{d\left(\frac{\rho}{c}\right)} \left(\frac{1}{1-\frac{\rho}{c}}\right)$$

$$L_q = \frac{\rho^{c+1}}{c!c\left(1-\frac{\rho}{c}\right)^2} p_0 = \frac{\rho^{c+1}}{(c-1)!(c-\rho)^2} p_0$$

The values of L_s, W_s and W_q are calculated using Eqs. (11.10) to (11.12).

11.4 MULTIPLE SERVER FINITE QUEUE LENGTH MODEL (*M/M/C/N/∞* MODEL)

Here the queue length is restricted to N and customers leave the system without joining it if the number in the system equals N. The corresponding equations are:

$$\lambda_n = \lambda \text{ for } 0 \le n < N$$
$$\lambda_n = 0 \text{ for } n \ge N$$
$$\mu_n = n\mu \text{ for } 0 \le n < c$$
$$\mu_n = c\mu \text{ for } n \ge c$$

Substituting these values in Eq. (11.6), we get

$$p_0 = \left\{ \sum_{n=0}^{c-1} \frac{\rho^n}{n!} + \frac{\rho^c \left(1 - \left(\frac{\rho}{c}\right)^{N-c+1}\right)}{c!\left(1 - \frac{\rho}{c}\right)} \right\}^{-1} \text{ for } \rho/c \ne 1$$

$$p_0 = \left\{ \sum_{n=0}^{c-1} \frac{\rho^n}{n!} + \frac{\rho^c}{c!}(N-c+1) \right\}^{-1} \text{ for } \rho/c = 1$$

We compute L_q using the relationship:

$$L_q = \sum_{n=c}^{N}(n-c)p_n = \sum_{j=0}^{N-c} jp_{j+c} = \frac{\rho^c \rho\, p_0}{c!c} \sum_{j=0}^{N-c} j\left(\frac{\rho}{c}\right)^{j-1} = \frac{\rho^{c+1} p_0}{c!c} \frac{d}{d\left(\frac{\rho}{c}\right)} \sum_{j=0}^{N-c} \left(\frac{\rho}{c}\right)^j$$

which on simplification yields

$$L_q = \frac{\rho^{c+1}}{(c+1)!(c-\rho)^2} \left\{ 1 - \left(\frac{\rho}{c}\right)^{N-c+1} - (N-c+1)\left(1 - \frac{\rho}{c}\right)\left(\frac{\rho}{c}\right)^{N-c} \right\} p_0$$

Since we have a finite queue length, some of the arrivals do not join the line and leave.

$$\lambda_e = (1 - p_N)\lambda$$

We calculate L_s, W_s and W_q using λ_e and Eqs. (11.10) to (11.12).

SOLVED EXAMPLES

EXAMPLE 11.1 Customers arrive at a clinic at the rate of 8/hour (Poisson arrival) and the doctor can serve at the rate of 9/hour (exponential).
 (a) What is the probability that a customer does not join the queue and walks into the doctor's room?
 (b) What is the probability that there is no queue?

(c) What is the probability that there are 10 customers in the system?
(d) What is the expected number in the system?
(e) What is the expected waiting time in the queue?

Solution: (a) Given $\lambda = 8$/hour, $\mu = 9$/hour

Then
$$\rho = \frac{\rho}{\lambda} = \frac{8}{9}$$

(a) The customer goes directly to the doctor when there is no one in the system. The probability is:

$$p_0 = 1 - \rho = 1 - \frac{8}{9} = 0.111$$

(b) There is no queue when there is either no one in the system or there is one person in the system. The probability is:

Probability $= p_0 + p_1$

$$= 0.111 + 0.111 \times \frac{8}{9} = 0.2098$$

(c) The probability that there are 10 customers in the system is:

$$p_{10} = \rho^{10} p_0$$

$$= \left(\frac{8}{9}\right)^{10} \times 0.111 = 0.0341$$

(d) Expected number in the system $L_s = \dfrac{\lambda}{\mu - \lambda} = 8$

(e) Expected waiting time in the queue

$$W_q = \frac{L_q}{\lambda} = \frac{L_s - \rho}{\lambda}$$

$$= \frac{8 - 8/9}{8} = 0.88 \text{ hours} = 53.33 \text{ minutes}$$

EXAMPLE 11.2 Suppose in Example 11.1 we have a restriction of 10 people in the system, find:

(a) The probability that the server is free.
(b) The probability that a person entering does not see a queue.
(c) The probability of an entering person forced to leave the queue without joining it.
(d) The expected number in the system.
(e) The expected waiting time in the queue.

Solution: (a) Given $\lambda = 8$/hour, $\mu = 9$/hour

Then
$$\rho = \frac{\lambda}{\mu} = \frac{8}{9} \quad N = 10$$

The customer goes to the doctor directly when there is no one in the system. The probability is:

$$p_0 = \frac{(1-\rho)}{(1-\rho^{N+1})} = \frac{(1-8/9)}{(1-(8/9)^{11})} = \frac{0.1111}{0.7262} = 0.153$$

(b) There is no queue when there is either no one in the system or there is one person in the system. The probability is:

$$\text{Probability} = p_0 + p_1$$

$$= 0.153 + 0.153 \times \frac{8}{9} = 0.3031$$

(c) The probability that there are 10 customers in the system is:

$$p_{10} = \rho^{10} p_0$$

$$= \left(\frac{8}{9}\right)^{10} \times 0.153 = 0.047$$

(d) Expected number in the system:

$$L_s = \frac{\rho[1-(N+1)\rho^N + N\rho^{N+1}]}{(1-\rho)(1-\rho^{N+1})}$$

$$= \frac{0.888[1 - 11 \times 0.3079 + 10 \times 0.2737]}{0.111 \times (1 - 0.2737)} = 3.856$$

(e) Effective arrival $\lambda_e = \lambda(1 - p_N)$

$$= 8 \times (1 - 0.0494) = 7.6048/\text{hour}$$

$$W_s = \frac{L_s}{\lambda_e}$$

$$= \frac{3.856}{7.6048} = 0.5070 \text{ hour}$$

$$W_q = W_s - \frac{1}{\mu}$$

$$= 0.5070 - 0.1111 = 0.3959 \text{ hour} = 23.75 \text{ minutes}$$

EXAMPLE 11.3 People arrive at a web browsing centre at the rate of 10/hour (Poisson arrival). There are two computers used for browsing and the expected time taken by a person is 10 minutes (exponentially distributed). Find:
  (a) The probability that both the computers are free when a person arrives.
  (b) The probability that the person can use a computer immediately on arrival.
  (c) The probability that there is no queue on arrival.
  (d) The expected number in the system.
  (e) Waiting time in the queue.
  (f) How many computers should be made available if the expected waiting time in the queue is to be less than 10 minutes?

Solution: (a) Probability that both computers are free is given by

$$p_0 = \left[\sum_{n=0}^{c-1} \frac{\rho^n}{n!} + \frac{\rho^c}{c!}\left(\frac{1}{1-\frac{\rho}{c}}\right)\right]^{-1} = \left[1 + \rho + \frac{\rho^2}{2\left(1-\frac{\rho}{c}\right)}\right]^{-1}$$

$$= \left[1 + 1.666 + \frac{2.777}{2 \times 0.1666}\right]^{-1} = 0.0909$$

(b) A computer is free for browsing when there are no people in the system or when there is one person in the system.

$$\text{Probability} = p_0 + p_1 = p_0 + \rho p_0$$

$$= 0.0909 + \frac{10}{6} \times 0.0909 = 0.2424$$

(c) Probability that there is no queue on arrival is the probability of having no person or one person or two persons in the system.

$$\text{Probability} = p_0 + p_1 + p_2 = p_0 + \rho p_0 + \frac{\rho^2}{2}p_0$$

$$= 0.0909 + 0.1515 + 0.1263 = 0.3687$$

(d) Expected number in the system $L_s = L_q + \rho$

$$L_q = \frac{\rho^{c+1}}{(c-1)!(c-\rho)^2} p_0$$

$$\frac{\left(\frac{5}{3}\right)^3}{\left(2 - \frac{5}{3}\right)^2} \times 0.0909 = 3.7878$$

$$L_s = 3.7878 + 1.6666 = 5.4544$$

(e) Expected waiting time in the queue $W_q = \frac{L_q}{\lambda}$

$$= \frac{3.788}{10} = 0.3788 \text{ hour} = 22.73 \text{ minutes}$$

(f) The solution found in (e) exceeds the waiting time requirement of 10 minutes. Let us consider $c = 3$ (three computers).

$$p_0 = \left[\sum_{n=0}^{c-1} \frac{\rho^n}{n!} + \frac{\rho^c}{c!}\left(\frac{1}{1-\frac{\rho}{c}}\right)\right]^{-1} = \left[1 + \rho + \frac{\rho^2}{2} + \frac{\rho^3}{6\left(1-\frac{\rho}{c}\right)}\right]^{-1}$$

$$= [1 + 1.666 + 1.39 + 1.736]^{-1} = 0.1726$$

$$L_q = \frac{\rho^{c+1}}{(c-1)!(c-\rho)^2} p_0$$

$$= \frac{\left(\frac{5}{3}\right)^4}{2\left(3-\frac{5}{3}\right)^2} \times 0.1726 = 0.3746$$

$$W_q = \frac{L_q}{\lambda}$$

$$= \frac{0.3745}{10} = 0.0374 \text{ hour} = 2.247 \text{ minutes}$$

It is enough to have three servers for an expected waiting time in the queue for less than 10 minutes.

EXAMPLE 11.4 Assume that in Example 11.3, there are two computers and that there are five additional chairs for waiting people to sit and that people do not join the line if these chairs are full.
  1. Find:
     (a) The probability that both the computers are free when a person arrives.
     (b) The probability that the person can use a computer immediately on arrival.
     (c) The probability that there is no queue on arrival.
     (d) The expected number in the system.
     (e) Waiting time in the system.
     (f) The number of computers that should be made available if the expected waiting time in the queue is to be less than 10 minutes.
  2. The centre can rent additional space to add five more chairs at a rent of Rs. 150 per month. Assume that the centre works for 30 days in a month and for 12 hours a day. Should they rent the space?

Solution: **1.** (a) Probability that both the computers are free is given by

$$p_0 = \left\{ \sum_{n=0}^{c-1} \frac{\rho^n}{n!} + \frac{\rho^c \left(1-\left(\frac{\rho}{c}\right)^{N-c+1}\right)}{c!\left(1-\frac{\rho}{c}\right)} \right\}^{-1} = \left\{ 1 + \rho + \frac{\rho^2 \left(1-\left(\frac{\rho}{c}\right)^8\right)}{c!\left(1-\frac{\rho}{c}\right)} \right\}^{-1}$$

$$= [1 + 1.666 + 5.5425]^{-1} = 0.1218$$

  (b) A computer is free for browsing when there are no people in the system or when there is one person in the system.

$$\text{Probability} = p_0 + p_1 + p_0 + \rho p_0$$

$$= 0.1218 + \frac{10}{6} \times 0.1218 = 0.3248$$

(c) Probability that there is no queue on arrival is the probability of having no person or one person or two persons in the system.

$$\text{Probability} = p_0 + p_1 + p_2 = p_0 + \rho p_0 + \frac{\rho^2}{2} p_0$$

$$= 0.1218 + 0.203 + 0.1692 = 0.4939$$

(d) Expected number in the system $L_s = L_q + \dfrac{\lambda_e}{\mu}$

or $\quad L_q = \dfrac{\rho^{c+1}}{(c-1)!(c-\rho)^2} \left\{ 1 - \left(\dfrac{\rho}{c}\right)^{N-c+1} - (N-c+1)\left(1-\dfrac{\rho}{c}\right)\left(\dfrac{\rho}{c}\right)^{N-c} \right\} p_0$

$$= \dfrac{1.666^3}{2 \times (2 - 1.666)^2} \left\{ 1 - \left(\dfrac{5}{6}\right)^6 - 6 \times \left(1-\dfrac{5}{6}\right)\left(\dfrac{5}{6}\right)^5 \right\} \times 0.1218 = 0.5409$$

Then $\quad p_N = p_7 = \dfrac{\lambda_0 \lambda_1 \ldots \lambda_6}{\mu_1 \mu_2 \ldots \mu_7} p_0$

$$= \dfrac{10^7}{6 \times 12^6} \times 0.1218 = 0.068$$

$$\lambda_e = (1 - p_N)\lambda$$

$$= (1 - 0.068) \times 10 = 9.32$$

$$L_s = L_q + \dfrac{\lambda_e}{\mu}$$

$$= 0.5409 + \dfrac{9.32}{6} = 2.094$$

(e) Waiting time in the system $W_s = \dfrac{L_s}{\lambda_e}$

$$= \dfrac{2.094}{9.32} = 0.2247 \text{ hour} = 13.48 \text{ minutes}$$

(f) $W_q = \dfrac{L_q}{\lambda_e}$

$$= \dfrac{0.5409}{9.32} = 0.058 \text{ hours} = 3.48 \text{ minutes}$$

The given two computers are enough.

2. $N = 12$

$$p_0 = \left\{ \sum_{n=0}^{c-1} \frac{\rho^n}{n!} + \frac{\rho^c \left[1 - \left(\frac{\rho}{c}\right)^{N-c+1}\right]}{c!\left(1 - \frac{\rho}{c}\right)} \right\}^{-1} = \left\{1 + \rho + \frac{\rho^2 \left[1 - \left(\frac{\rho}{c}\right)^{11}\right]}{c!\left(1 - \frac{\rho}{c}\right)} \right\}^{-1}$$

$$= [1 + 1.666 + 14.42]^{-1} = 0.058$$

$$p_N = p_{12} = \frac{\lambda_0 \lambda_1 \ldots \lambda_{11}}{\mu_1 \mu_2 \ldots \mu_{12}} p_0$$

$$= \frac{10^{12}}{6 \times 12^{11}} \times 0.058 = 0.013$$

Assuming that the centre works for 30 days and for 12 hours per day, the additional customers served per month would be

$$(0.068 - 0.013) * 12 * 30/\text{month} = 19.8 \text{ customers.}$$

The earning associated would be Rs. 198 per month. Since the rent is Rs. 150 per month, it is advisable to rent the space.

EXAMPLE 11.5 Patients visit a dentist at the rate of 8/hour (Poisson) and the service times are 11/hour (exponentially distributed). Find the expected waiting time in the system. If the dentist wishes to have a finite queue length model, find N for which time in the system is less than 15 minutes.

Solution: The first model is a single server infinite population model with $\lambda = 8$/hour and $\mu = 11$/hour. Then

$$L_s = \lambda W_s = \frac{\lambda}{\mu - \lambda}$$

$$= \frac{8}{11 - 8} = \frac{8}{3} \text{ hour}$$

and

$$W_s = \frac{1}{3} \text{ hour}$$

For a finite population model,

$$L_s = \frac{\rho[1 - (N+1)\rho^N + N\rho^{N+1}]}{(1 - \rho)(1 - \rho^{N+1})} = W_s \lambda (1 - p_N) \text{ and } p_N = \frac{\rho^N (1 - \rho)}{1 - \rho^N}$$

We have to find N such that $W_s = 0.25$ hour. Table 11.1 shows the computations.

Table 11.1 Queuing Computations

N	p_N	L_s	W_s
10	0.0116	2.347	0.297
9	0.016	2.252	0.286
7	0.0317	2.00	0.2582
6	0.045	1.8335	0.24

From Table 11.1, we conclude that for $N \leq 6$ we have $W_s = 15$ minutes.

EXAMPLE 11.6 Compare the performance of a single server infinite population model with $\lambda = 5$/hour and $\mu = 8$/hour with a two server model with $\lambda = 10$/hour and $\mu = 8$/hour under the assumption that the second model has one queue and people join whichever server becomes free. (Assume infinite queue length models).

Solution: Single server model

Given $\qquad \lambda = 5$/hour, $\mu = 8$/hour

Then $\qquad \rho = \dfrac{\lambda}{\mu} = 0.625$ and $p_0 = 1 - \rho = 0.375$

$$L_s = \lambda/(\mu - \lambda) = \frac{5}{3} = 1.666$$

$$L_q = L_s - \rho = 1.0417$$

$$W_s = L_s/\lambda = 0.33 \text{ hour}$$

$$W_q = L_q/\lambda = 0.2083 \text{ hour}$$

Multiple server model

$\qquad \lambda = 10$/hour, $\mu = 8$/hour, $\rho = \lambda/\mu = 1.25$, $c = 2$. Then

$$p_0 \left[\sum_{n=0}^{c-1} \frac{\rho^n}{n!} \frac{\rho^c}{c!} \left(\frac{1}{1 - \dfrac{\rho}{c}} \right) \right] = 1$$

From which $p_0 = 0.3$.

Now,
$$L_q = \frac{\rho^{c+1}}{(c-1)!(c-\rho)^2} p_0$$

From which $L_q = 1.0416$, $W_q = 0.104$ hours, $L_s = 2.29$ and $W_s = 0.229$ hours.
On comparison the following observations are made:
1. The server utilization is higher in the second model.
2. The number in the system is higher for the second model.
3. The time in the system is lesser because of multiple servers.

CASE STUDY 11.1: The Railway Reservation System

The Rampur Railway Station has a reservation counter with five terminals at present. These counters work for twelve hours a day from 8 a.m. to 8 p.m. Different categories of customers at present book their tickets using the counters. These are:

1. Regular booking that would take about 2 minutes per ticket booked.
2. Bulk booking that would take about 5 minutes per ticket booked.
3. Cancellations that would take 3 minutes per ticket cancelled.
4. Booking using a Credit card that takes 3 minutes.

At present there are five terminals and the following procedure is followed:

1. A separate counter for bulk booking and credit card booking. The average service time is about 4 minutes per ticket and people arrive at the rate of 12/hour. In the present system, a person can book a maximum of one ticket.
2. The remaining four counters where regular booking and cancellation happen. Here the average service is 2.5 minutes. People arrive at the rate of 80/hour.

Mrs. Sandhya Prabhu, the newly appointed manager of the facility would like to reorganize the counters if the waiting time in the system was more than 20 minutes for the bulk booking or if it exceeded 10 minutes in the regular booking counters.

Customer feedback suggests that cancellation need not be clubbed with regular booking because the time spent on cancellation could be used in reservation. This is significant considering the overall demand for advance reservation in railways and the several booking officers from where customers can reserve their tickets. The railways are also considering introducing an automated booking machine where booking can be made only using debit/credit cards. Since it is a self-help facility, the service time to book increases to 5 minutes. The railways can buy more than one machine of this type but has to face the risk of an arriving person booking more than one ticket.

Ms. Prabhu would like to consider the following alternatives:

1. Self-booking for credit cards, separate counter for cancellation alone and combining bulk booking with regular booking. Here the arrival rates are 8/hour for credit card booking, 8/hour for cancellation and 84/hour for regular and bulk booking. Regular and bulk booking put together, average service times are 2.5 minutes per ticket.
2. Self-booking for credit cards, one exclusive counter for bulk booking and cancellation and four for regular booking. The arrival rates are 12/hour for cancellation and bulk booking put together and 80/hour for regular booking. The average service times when bulk booking and cancellation are together is 4 minutes.

When cancellation is combined with bulk booking, the customers waiting for bulk booking would be disappointed with the loss of time spent in cancellation.

EXERCISES

11.1 Derive the expression $L_s = L_q + \rho$ for a $M/M/1/\infty/\infty$ model.

11.2 Derive from the first principle the expressions for p_0 and L_q for a $M/M/1/\infty/\infty$ model.

11.3 Customers arrive at the rate of 5/hour (Poisson) and are served by a dentist at the rate of 6/hour (exponential).

(a) Find the probability that the dentist is idle.

(b) Assume that the maximum allowed in the system is 10, what is the expected length of the system?

(c) Assume that the arrival rate is increased to 8/hour and another dentist who serves at 6/hour is introduced. Compare the length of the queue if there is a common queue and if there are separate queues.

(d) Do (c) if the maximum number in the system is 8.

(e) In (d), what is the probability that a person quits the system without joining the common queue?

11.4 A bank has a single window clearance system and two teller counters. Customers arrive at the rate of 12/hour (Poisson) and are served at the rate of 8/hour (exponential). Calculate the waiting time in the queue and the expected number in the system. How many tellers should they have if the waiting time in the queue is less than 10 minutes?

11.5 Customers arrive at an ATM machine at the rate of 20/hour (Poisson) and are served at the rate of 20/hour (exponential). Assuming a finite queue length model, find N such that the ATM has a utilization of 80%. Find the expected number in the system.

11.6 Customers arrive at a video game centre at the rate of 5/hour (Poisson) and spend on an average 30 minutes (exponential). How many terminals should the shop have such that the expected number in the queue is less than or equal to 1. Compute the probability that a person enters immediately gets a terminal to play.

11.7 A car garage has a single mechanic and has parking space for 12 cars (including the one that is being attended to). Customers arrive at the rate of 6/hour (Poisson) and are served at the rate of 8/hour (exponential). What is the probability that a person does not find a parking space for his car on arrival (Assume that people go away if there is no parking space)? What happens to this probability if the service rate is increased to 8/hour? What is the utilization of the server in both the cases?

11.8 Customers visit an astrologer at the rate of 4/hour (Poisson) and take an average of 12 minutes (exponential). Compute the probability that

(a) there are three or less people in the system.

(b) there are 5 or more people in the system.

(c) the astrologer is free.

11.9 A railway booking office has five counters for booking. One of these is dedicated to bulk booking while the other four are for regular booking. Arrivals to the bulk counter are 18/hour and service is 3 minutes on an average. Find the expected number of people in the system. If forced balking occurs if more than 10 people are in the system and the office loses Rs. 10 per person turned away find the expected loss. Assume that the office works 12 hours a day and for 330 days in a year. The railways have estimated that it costs Rs. 1,00,000 to create facilities and space such that the system can accommodate 15 people. What would be your suggestion?

The regular booking counters have arrivals at the rate of 80/hour and each counter takes 3 minutes on an average. Estimate the loss under the same circumstances. Also it costs Rs. 40,000 for a computer and Rs. 60,000 to add a person. Would you recommend this?

11.10 Mithun is the student secretary of his hostel and is organizing a hostel day celebrations. He wants to have juice served as people arrive for the event. Assume that people arrive at the rate of 10/hour. He has a single counter that can serve at 5 minutes per person. Assume Poisson arrivals, exponential service and infinite population.

(a) Find the utilization of the server.
(b) Find the average number of people served per hour. Derive an expression for the above.
(c) If we assume that an arrival does not join the line if more than 10 people are in the system, find the probability that a person coming does not join the line. Find also the expected number of people who leave without joining the queue in three hours.
(d) What is the expected waiting time in the system for the situation in (c)?

11.11 Mithun next plans the food counters. He wishes to have as many servers so that the average waiting time in the system does not exceed 10 minutes. People arrive at the rate of 20/hour and are serviced at the rate of 5 minutes per person. Assume Poisson arrivals, exponential service and infinite population. Determine the number of service counters that Mithun should plan. Derive the expression for the number in the queue.

What is the gain between having a single queue and the situation where we had individual dedicated lines in front of each of the servers? Assume that the arrival rate is equally divided among the individual servers and that there is no jockeying.

What happens to the number in the queue if people don't join the queue if the number in the system is 10?

12

Non-linear Programming

In this chapter we address the following aspects of non-linear optimization:
1. Unconstrained extremum points
2. Constrained problems with equality constraints—Lagrangean method
3. Constrained problems with inequalities—Kuhn Tucker conditions
4. Quadratic programming

12.1 UNCONSTRAINED EXTREMUM POINTS

The necessary condition for X_0 to be an extreme point of $f(X)$ is that $\nabla f(X_0) = 0$. A sufficient condition for a stationary point X_0 to be extremum is that the Hessian matrix evaluated at X_0 is:

(a) Positive definite when X_0 is a minimum point.
(b) Negative definite when X_0 is a maximum point.

Here, $\nabla f(X_0)$ represents the first derivative evaluated at $X = X_0$.

ILLUSTRATION 12.1

Consider the function $f(x_1, x_2, x_3) = x_1 + x_1 x_2 + 2x_2 + 3x_3 - x_1^2 - 2x_2^2 - x_3^2$
The necessary condition $\nabla f(X_0) = 0$ gives

$$\frac{\partial f}{\partial x_1} = 1 + x_2 - 2x_1 = 0$$

$$\frac{\partial f}{\partial x_2} = x_1 + 2 - 4x_2 = 0$$

$$\frac{\partial f}{\partial x_3} = 3 - 2x_3 = 0$$

The solution is given by

$$x_0 = \{6/7, 5/7, 3/2\}$$

For sufficiency, we evaluate

$$H = \begin{bmatrix} \dfrac{\partial^2 f}{\partial x_1^2} & \dfrac{\partial^2 f}{\partial x_1 \partial x_2} & \dfrac{\partial^2 f}{\partial x_1 \partial x_3} \\ \dfrac{\partial^2 f}{\partial x_2 \partial x_1} & \dfrac{\partial^2 f}{\partial^2 x_2^2} & \dfrac{\partial^2 f}{\partial x_2 \partial x_3} \\ \dfrac{\partial^2 f}{\partial x_3 \partial x_1} & \dfrac{\partial^2 f}{\partial x_3 \partial x_1} & \dfrac{\partial^2 f}{\partial^2 x_3^2} \end{bmatrix}$$

$$= \begin{bmatrix} -2 & 1 & 0 \\ +1 & -4 & 0 \\ 0 & 0 & -2 \end{bmatrix}$$

The principal minor determinants of H have values -2, 7 and -18, respectively indicating that $\{6/7, 5/7, 3/2\}$ represents a maximum point.

12.2 CONSTRAINED OPTIMIZATION PROBLEMS—LAGRANGEAN METHOD FOR EQUALITY CONSTRAINTS

Consider the problem:
Minimize $Z = f(X)$
Subject to
$$g(X) = 0$$

Where $X = (x_1, x_2, \ldots, x_n)$ and $g = (g_1, g_2, \ldots, g_m)^T$. The functions $f(X)$ and $g_i(X_i)$ are assumed to be twice differentiable.

In the Lagrangean method, we bring the constraints into the objective function by creating the Lagrangean function of the form:

$$L(X, \lambda) = f(X) - \lambda g(X)$$

The equations $\partial L / \partial X = 0$ and $\partial L / \partial \lambda = 0$ are the necessary conditions for a point to be a minimum or maximum.

Given the stationery point (X_0, λ_0) for the Lagrangean function $L(X, \lambda)$ and the bordered Hessian matrix H^B evaluated at (X_0, λ_0) then X_0 is:

1. A maximum point if starting with the principal major determinant of order $(2m + 1)$, the last $(n - m)$ principal minor determinants of H^B form an alternating sign pair starting with $(-1)^{m+1}$.
2. A minimum point if starting with the principal major determinant of order $(2m + 1)$, the last $(n - m)$ principal minor determinants of H^B form an alternating sign pair starting with $(-1)^m$.

Here $$H^B = \begin{bmatrix} 0 & P \\ P^T & Q \end{bmatrix}_{m+n X m+n}$$

where $P = [\nabla g(X)]$ and $Q = \partial^2 L(x, \lambda) / \partial x_i \, \partial x_j$.

Illustration 12.2

Maximize $X_1^2 + 2X_2^2 + 2X_3^2$

Subject to

$$X_1 + X_2 + X_3 = 5$$
$$X_1 + 3X_2 + 2X_3 = 9$$

The Lagrangean function is given by

$$L = X_1^2 + 2X_2^2 + 2X_3^2 - \lambda_1(X_1 + X_2 + X_3 - 5) - \lambda_2(X_1 + 3X_2 + 2X_3 - 9)$$

$\partial L/\partial x_1 = 0$ gives $2X_1 - \lambda_1 - \lambda_2 = 0$

$\partial L/\partial x_2 = 0$ gives $4X_2 - \lambda_1 - 3\lambda_2 = 0$

$\partial L/\partial x_3 = 0$ gives $4X_3 - \lambda_1 - 2\lambda_2 = 0$

$\partial L/\partial \lambda_1 = 0$ gives $-(X_1 + X_2 + X_3 - 5) = 0$

$\partial L/\partial \lambda_2 = 0$ gives $-(X_1 + 3X_2 + 2X_3 - 9) = 0$

Solving, we get

$$X_0 = (x_1, x_2, x_3) = (2.365, 1.362, 1.272)$$

and

$$\lambda = (\lambda_1, \lambda_2) = (4.37, 0.36)$$

Computing the bordered Hessian matrix, we get

$$H^B = \begin{bmatrix} 0 & 0 & 1 & 1 & 1 \\ 0 & 0 & 1 & 3 & 2 \\ 1 & 1 & 2 & 0 & 0 \\ 1 & 3 & 0 & 4 & 0 \\ 1 & 2 & 0 & 0 & 4 \end{bmatrix}$$

We have $n = 3$ and $m = 2$. We need to verify that the sign of determinant of H^B is $(-1)^2$. The value of determinant of H^B is $+17$, the point is a maximum.

12.3 CONSTRAINED OPTIMIZATION PROBLEMS—KUHN TUCKER CONDITIONS FOR INEQUALITY CONSTRAINTS

When we have inequality constraints, we can convert them into equations and use the Lagrangean method. The problem is of the form:

Maximize $Z = f(X)$

Subject to

$$g(X) \leq 0$$

Where $X = (x_1, x_2, \ldots x_n)$ and $g = (g_1, g_2, \ldots g_m)^T$. The functions $f(X)$ and $g_i(X_i)$ are assumed to be twice differentiable.

Let S_i^2 be the slack quantity added to the ith quantity. (The slack variable need not be strictly non-negative as the decision variable in non-linear programming problems. In LP problems, we have $X_j \geq 0$, whereas in NLPs, this is not necessary. If a variable is of the form $X_j \geq 0$, we have to include it as a constraint).

The Lagrangean function is of the form:

$$L(X, \lambda) = f(X) - \lambda[g(X) + S^2]$$

The equations $\partial L/\partial X = 0$, $\partial L/\partial S = 0$ and $\partial L/\partial \lambda = 0$ are the necessary conditions for a point to be a minimum or maximum.

$$\frac{\partial L}{\partial X} = \nabla f(X) - \lambda \nabla g(X) = 0$$

$$\frac{\partial L}{\partial S_i} = -2\lambda_i S_i = 0$$

$$\frac{\partial L}{\partial \lambda} = -[g(X) + S^2] = 0$$

The Kuhn Tucker conditions necessary for X and λ to be stationary point for a maximization problem is as follows:

$$\lambda \geq 0$$
$$\nabla f(X) - \lambda \nabla g(X) = 0$$
$$\lambda_i g_i(X) = 0$$
$$g(X) \leq 0$$

(The same conditions apply to minimization as well with the difference being that λ must be non-positive. When we have equations, for both maximization and minimization the Lagrangean multipliers are unrestricted in sign).

The Kuhn Tucker conditions are also sufficient if the objective function and constraints satisfy conditions regarding convexity. For maximization, the objective function should be concave and the solution space is a convex set. For minimization, the objective function should be convex and the solution space is a convex set.

ILLUSTRATION 12.3

Minimize $X_1^2 + 2X_2^2 + 3X_3^2$

Subject to
$$X_2 + X_3 \geq 6$$
$$X_1 \geq 2, X_2 \geq 1$$

Since it is a minimization problem, the KT conditions are:

$$\lambda_1, \lambda_2, \lambda_3 \leq 0$$
$$2X_1 + \lambda_2 = 0$$
$$4X_2 + \lambda_1 + \lambda_3 = 0$$
$$6X_3 + \lambda_1 = 0$$
$$\lambda_1(6 - X_2 - X_3) = 0$$
$$\lambda_2(2 - X_1) = 0$$
$$\lambda_3(1 - X_2) = 0$$

$$X_2 + X_3 \geq 6$$
$$X_1 \geq 2$$
$$X_2 \geq 1$$

(We have $\lambda_1, \lambda_2, \lambda_3 \leq 0$ because we have a minimization problem and we have used $L(X, \lambda) = f(X) - \lambda[g(X) + S^2]$

Solving, we get

$X_1 = 2, X_2 = 3.6, X_3 = 2.4, \lambda_1 = -14.4, \lambda_2 = -4, \lambda_3 = 0$ with $Z = 47.2$

It may be observed that it may be difficult to solve the resultant system, particularly when the terms are non-linear. The resultant system is easy to solve when the objective function is quadratic and the constraints are linear. We illustrate such an application to a quadratic programming problem next.

12.4 QUADRATIC PROGRAMMING (WOLFE 1959)

Consider the problem:

Maximize (or Minimize) $Z = CX + X^T DX$

Subject to

$$AX \leq b$$
$$X \geq 0$$

This problem with a quadratic objective function, linear constraints and an explicit non-negativity restriction on the decision variables is a Quadratic Programming Problem (QPP).

When we apply Kuhn Tucker conditions, we have to consider the non-negativity restrictions on the decision variables as explicit constraints.

The problem becomes

Maximize $Z = CX + X^T DX$

Subject to

$$G(X) = \begin{pmatrix} AX \\ -I \end{pmatrix} - \begin{pmatrix} b \\ 0 \end{pmatrix} \leq 0$$

Let λ be the set of Lagrangean multipliers corresponding to the problem constraints and $U = (\mu_1, \mu_2 ...)$ represent the multipliers corresponding to the decision variables. The Kuhn Tucker conditions are:

$$\lambda, U \geq 0$$
$$\nabla Z - (\lambda^T, U^T) \nabla g(X) = 0$$
$$\lambda_i(b_i - \Sigma a_{ij} X_j) = 0$$
$$\mu_j X_j = 0$$
$$AX \leq b$$
$$-X \leq 0$$

Let $S = b - AX \geq 0$ represent the slack variables of the constraints. We also have
$$\nabla Z = C + 2X^T D$$
$$\nabla G(X) = \begin{pmatrix} A \\ -I \end{pmatrix}$$

The Kuhn Tucker conditions reduce to
$$-2X^T D + \lambda^T A - U^T = C$$
$$AX + S = b$$
$$\lambda_i S_i = \mu_j X_j = 0$$
$$\lambda, U, X, S \geq 0$$

It may be observed that except for the condition $\lambda_i S_i = m_j X_j = 0$, the rest of the system is linear and boils down to solving linear equations. A feasible solution satisfying all these conditions is also optimal.

We can separate the non-linear constraints and solve the linear system using simplex algorithm. We will need artificial variables (with objective function of 1) to start the basic feasible solution and we minimize the sum of the artificial variables as the objective function. A feasible solution (not having artificial variables in the basis) is optimal.

ILLUSTRATION 12.4

Minimize $X_1^2 + \dfrac{3}{2} X_2^2 - X_1 - X_2$

Subject to
$$X_1 + X_2 \geq 6$$
$$X_1, X_2 \geq 0$$

The objective function is rewritten as:

Maximize $-X_1^2 - \dfrac{3}{2} X_2^2 + X_1 + X_2$

We have $A = (-1\ -1)$ and
$$D = \begin{bmatrix} -1 & 0 \\ 0 & -3/2 \end{bmatrix}$$

The Kuhn Tucker conditions reduce to
$$2X_1 - \lambda_1 - \mu_1 = 1$$
$$3X_2 - \lambda_1 - \mu_2 = 1$$
$$-X_1 - X_2 + S_1 = -6$$

$X_1, X_2, \lambda_1, \mu_1, \mu_2, S_1 \geq 0$ along with $\lambda_1 S_1 = \mu_1 X_1 = \mu_2 X_2 = 0$

We set up the simplex table with three artificial variables a_1, a_2 and a_3 each having an objective function coefficient of 1. We minimize $a_1 + a_2 + a_3$. The simplex iterations are shown in Table 12.1.

Table 12.1 Simplex Iterations

C_B	X_B	X_1	X_2	λ_1	μ_1	μ_2	S_1	1 A_1	1 A_2	1 A_3	RHS	θ
1	A_1	2	0	−1	−1	0	0	1	0	0	1	
1	A_2	0	3	−1	0	−1	0	0	1	0	1	1/3
1	A_3	1	1	0	0	0	−1	0	0	1	6	6
	$C_j - Z_j$	−3	−4	0	0	0	1	0	0	0	8	
1	A_1	2	0	−1	−1	0	0	1	0	0	1	1/2
0	X_2	0	1	−1/3	0	−1/3	0	0	1/3	0	1/3	
1	A_3	1	0	1/3	0	1/3	−1	0	−1/3	1	17/3	17/3
		−3	0	2/3	1	−1/3	1	0	4/3	0	20/3	
0	X_1	1	0	−1/2	−1/2	0	0	1/2	0	0	1/2	
0	X_2	0	1	−1/3	0	−1/3	0	0	1/3	0	1/3	
1	A_3	0	0	5/6	1/2	1/3	−1	−1/2	−1/3	1	31/6	31/5
		0	0	−5/6	−1/2	−1/3	1	3/2	4/3	0	31/6	
0	X_1	1	0	0	1/10	1/5	−3/5	−1/10	−1/5	0	18/5	
0	X_2	0	1	0	1/5	−1/5	−2/5	−1/5	1/5	2/5	12/5	
0	λ_1	0	0	1	3/5	2/5	−6/5	−3/5	−2/5	6/5	31/5	
		0	0	0	0	0	0	1	1	1	0	

In the first iteration X_2 enters (and can enter because μ_2 is non-basic). In the next iteration X_1 enters (μ_1 is non-basic) and in the third iteration λ_1 enters and S_1 is non-basic. We ensure that the conditions $\lambda_1 S_1 = \mu_1 X_1 = \mu_2 X_2 = 0$ are satisfied when we choose the entering variables. The solution $X_1 = 18/5$, $X_2 = 12/5$ is optimal.

SOLVED EXAMPLES

EXAMPLE 12.1 Minimize $X_1^2 + 3X_2^2 - 2X_1 X_2 - 6X_1 - 8X_2$

Solution: The necessary condition $\nabla f(X_0) = 0$ gives

$$\frac{\partial f}{\partial X_1} = 2X_1 - 2X_2 - 6 = 0$$

$$\frac{\partial f}{\partial X_2} = -2X_1 + 6X_2 - 8 = 0$$

The solution is given by $X = \{13/2, 7/2\}$. For sufficiency, we evaluate

$$H = \begin{bmatrix} \dfrac{\partial^2 f}{\partial X_1^2} & \dfrac{\partial^2 f}{\partial X_1 \partial X_2} \\ \dfrac{\partial^2 f}{\partial X_2 \partial X_1} & \dfrac{\partial^2 f}{\partial X_2^2} \end{bmatrix} = \begin{bmatrix} 2 & -2 \\ -2 & 6 \end{bmatrix}$$

The principal minor determinants of H have values 2 and 8, respectively indicating that the matrix is positive semidefinite. The point is a minimum point.

EXAMPLE 12.2 Minimize $3X_1^2 + 5X_2^2$

Subject to $X_1 + 2X_2 = 8$

Solution: The Lagrangean function is given by

$$L = 3X_1^2 + 5X_2^2 - \lambda_1(X_1 + 2X_2 - 8)$$

$\partial L/\partial X_1 = 0$ gives $6X_1 - \lambda = 0$

$\partial L/\partial X_2 = 0$ gives $10X_2 - 2\lambda = 0$

$\partial L/\partial \lambda = 0$ gives $-(X_1 + 2X_2 - 8) = 0$

Solving, we get

$$X_0 = (x_1, x_2) = (2.353, 2.823), \lambda = 14.12$$

Computing the bordered Hessian matrix, we get

$$H^B = \begin{bmatrix} 0 & 1 & 2 \\ 1 & 6 & 0 \\ 2 & 0 & 10 \end{bmatrix}$$

We have $n = 2$ and $m = 1$. We need to verify that the sign of determinant of H^B is $(-1)^1$. The value of determinant of H^B is -34, the point is a minimum.

EXAMPLE 12.3 Maximize $2X_1 - X_1^2 + 3X_2 - 2X_2^2$

Subject to

$$X_1 + X_2 \leq 3$$

Solution: Since it is a maximization problem, the KT conditions are:

$$\lambda \geq 0$$
$$2 - 2X_1 - \lambda = 0$$
$$3 - 4X_2 - \lambda = 0$$
$$\lambda(X_1 + X_2 - 3) = 0$$
$$X_1 + X_2 \leq 3$$

Solving, we get

$$X_1 = 1, X_2 = 0.75, \lambda = 0 \text{ with } Z = 2.125$$

EXAMPLE 12.4 Solve the Example 12.3 with the additional restriction that $X_1, X_2 \geq 0$.

Maximize $2X_1 - X_1^2 + 3X_2 - 2X_2^2$

Subject to

$$X_1 + X_2 \leq 3$$
$$X_1, X_2 \geq 0$$

Solution: The problem is a quadratic programming problem. We have

$$A = (1\ 1),\quad C = \begin{bmatrix} 2 \\ 3 \end{bmatrix} \quad \text{and} \quad D = \begin{bmatrix} -1 & 2 \\ 0 & -2 \end{bmatrix}$$

The Kuhn Tucker conditions reduce to

$$2X_1 + \lambda_1 - \mu_1 = 2$$
$$4X_2 + \lambda_1 - \mu_2 = 3$$
$$X_1 + X_2 + s_1 = 3$$

$X_1, X_2, \lambda_1, \mu_1, \mu_2, s_1 \geq 0$ along with $\lambda_1 s_1 = \mu_1 X_1 = \mu_2 X_2 = 0$

We set up the simplex table with three artificial variables a_1 and a_2 each having an objective function coefficient of 1. We minimize $a_1 + a_2$. The simplex iterations are shown in Table 12.2.

Table 12.2 Simplex Iterations

C_B	X_B	X_1	X_2	λ_1	μ_1	μ_2	s_1	a_1 (1)	a_2 (1)	RHS	θ
1	a_1	2	0	1	−1	0	0	1	0	2	
1	a_2	0	4	1	0	−1	0	0	1	3	3/4
0	s_1	1	1	0	0	0	1	0	0	3	3
	$C_j - Z_j$	−2	−4	−2	1	1	0	0	0	6	
1	a_1	2	0	−1	−1	0	0	1	0	2	1
0	X_2	0	1	1/4	0	−1/4	0	0	1/4	3/4	
0	s_1	1	0	−1/4	0	1/4	1	0	−1/4	9/4	9/4
		−2	0	−1	1	0	0	0	0	2	
0	X_1	1	0	1/2	−1/2	0	0	1	0	1	
0	X_2	0	1	1/4	0	−1/4	0	0	1/4	3/4	
0	s_1	0	0	−3/4	1/2	1/4	1	0	−1/4	5/4	
		0	0	0	0	0	0	1	1	0	

In the first iteration X_2 enters (and can enter because μ_2 is non-basic). In the next iteration X_1 enters (μ_1 is non-basic). We ensure that the conditions $\lambda_1 S_1 = \mu_1 X_1 = \mu_2 X_2 = 0$ are satisfied when we choose the entering variables. The solution $X_1 = 1$, $X_2 = 3/4$ is optimal.

(We get the same solution as in Example 12.3 because the optimal solution to 12.3 satisfies the additional constraint $X_1, X_2 \geq 0$. Only when the constraint $X_1, X_2 \geq 0$ is added, the problem becomes a quadratic programming problem).

CASE STUDY 12.1: An Investment and Gain Company

An investment and gain company manages portfolio of investments for its clients. The clients choose the shares in which they wish to invest and the company helps them in identifying the proportion of investment in each of the chosen shares. The company wishes to guarantee a certain expected return based on the shares chosen by the customer while claiming to minimize the risk associated with the investments. The company encourages customers to choose shares of companies in different industry segments so that the risk is minimized.

One of the customers has chosen to invest in a cement company (A) and in a software company (B). Shrey Ginoria, the portfolio manager has calculated the expected return on both the securities for the last six years. Table 12.3 provides the return distribution for the two shares.

Table 12.3 Return Distribution

Year	A	B
1	21.43	17.66
2	14.56	14.29
3	18.29	19.14
4	21.14	18.8
5	20.06	15.5
6	18.61	16.12

Shrey computes the total risk as the covariance of the distribution while the expected return is the expected value of the distribution of earnings. Shrey wishes to solve a quadratic programming problem that minimizes the risk subject to a certain desired return.

EXERCISES

12.1 Minimize $3X_1^2 + 4X_2^2 - 3X_1X_2 - 7X_1 - 9X_2$

12.2 Maximize $9X_1 + 7X_2 - 2X_1^2 + 3X_2^2 + 3X_1X_2$

12.3 Minimize $7X_1^2 + 6X_2^2$
Subject to $3X_1 + 2X_2 = 8$

12.4 Maximize $7X_1 + 6X_2 - X_1^2 - 5X_2^2$
Subject to $X_1 + 2X_2 + 3X_3 = 9$

12.5 Maximize $3X_1 - 4X_1^2 + 3X_2 - X_2^2$
Subject to $X_1 + X_2 \leq 3,\ 2X_1 + 3X_2 \leq 7$

12.6 Minimize $5X_1^2 + 7X_2^2 - 2X_1 - 4X_2$
Subject to $X_1 + X_2 = 9$

12.7 Minimize $Z = 121X_1^2 + 62.7X_1X_2 + 78X_2^2 + 43.4X_2X_3 + 148X_3^2 + 87.1X_2X_3$
Subject to $18.2X_1 + 17.6X_2 + 20.3X_3 \geq 19$
$$X_1 + X_2 + X_3 = 1$$
$$X_1, X_2, X_3 \geq 0$$

(a) Write the Kuhn Tucker conditions for the problem.
(b) Set up the QPP table for the problem with a basic feasible solution.
(c) Outline the procedure to obtain the optimum solution (Don't solve the problem).
(d) What happens to the optimum solution if the RHS value of the first constraint is changed to 22?

12.8 Consider the problem:

Minimize $Z = 2X_1^2 + 2X_1X_2 + 2X_2^2 + 2X_2X_3 + 3X_3^2 + X_1 - 3X_2 - 5X_3$

Subject to $3X_1 + 2X_2 + X_3 \leq 6,\ X_1 + X_2 + X_3 \geq 1$

$$X_1, X_2, X_3 \geq 0$$

Set up the initial table to solve a QPP. What are the modifications required to solve this as a LPP?

12.9 Minimize $X_1^2 + \dfrac{3}{2}X_2^2 - X_1 - X_2$

Subject to $X_1 + X_2 \geq 6$

$$X_1, X_2 \geq 0$$

(a) Set up the initial simplex table corresponding to the above QPP.
(b) Find the initial leaving and entering variables.
(c) Solve the QPP.

13
Deterministic Inventory Models

Inventory control deals with ordering and stocking policies for items used in the manufacture of industrial products. In every manufacturing environment about 80% of the items are bought from outside and the rest enter as raw material, are manufactured and assembled into the final product.

Items bought from vendors have the following costs associated with the purchase:

1. Cost of the product
2. Ordering cost per order
3. Carrying cost for holding the items
4. Shortage cost (backorder costs)

We consider deterministic multiperiod inventory models in this chapter. The annual demand and the various costs listed earlier are known with certainty. We consider single item and multiitem models. The important decision in inventory problems is "How much to order"? The order quantity is denoted by Q. Let us consider the costs associated with the inventory system in detail.

Cost of the product C

This is represented as C Rs. /unit. Since the annual demand for the item is known and has to be met, this cost does not play a part in determining the order quantity. The only effect of the unit price C in the order quantity is when there is a discount by which the unit price reduces by a known fraction.

Order cost C_o

This is represented as Rs. /order. The essential costs that contribute to this cost are:

1. Cost of people
2. Cost of stationery
3. Cost of communication—fax
4. Cost of follow up—travel, fax
5. Cost of transportation

6. Cost of inspection and counting
7. Cost of rework, rejects

Carrying cost/Holding cost C_c

This is represented as Rs./unit/year. The costs that contribute to carrying the items are:
1. Cost of capital
2. Cost of people
3. Cost of space
4. Cost of power
5. Cost of special facilities—air conditioners, chillers, dust free environment
6. Cost of pilferage
7. Cost of obsolescence

Sometimes when the cost of capital i, dominates the rest of the costs, carrying cost is expressed as $C_c = iC$, where C is the unit price in Rs. and i, the interest rate (cost of capital) in %/year.

Shortage cost C_s

This is represented as Rs./unit/year. Here we mean backordering indicating that any unfulfilled demand is met subsequently. The necessary costs that contribute to shortage cost are:
1. Loss of customer goodwill
2. Cost of losing a customer
3. Loss of profit associated with not delivering the product

The components of the shortage cost are not easy to measure. Usually shortage cost is given a large value to minimize the occurrence of shortage in planning stage of the inventory. Let us consider the deterministic inventory models.

13.1 CONTINUOUS DEMAND INSTANTANEOUS REPLENISHMENT MODEL

The inventory-time behaviour is given in Figure 13.1.

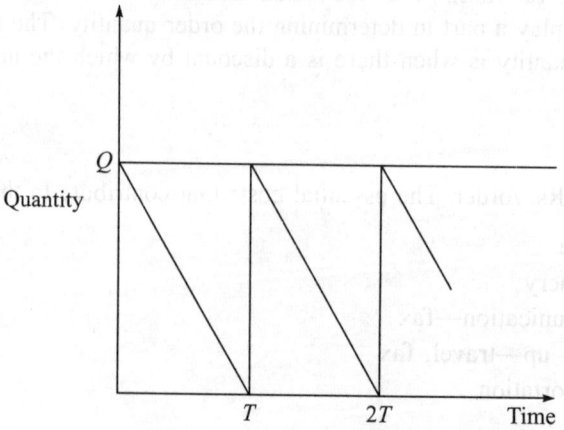

Figure 13.1 Inventory vs. time.

The coefficients are:

Annual demand = D/year

Order cost = C_o

Carrying cost = C_c

Order quantity = Q

Number of orders/year = $\dfrac{D}{Q}$

Annual order cost = $\dfrac{DC_o}{Q}$

Average inventory in the system = $\dfrac{Q}{2}$

Annual inventory carrying cost = $\dfrac{QC_c}{2}$

Total cost $(TC) = \dfrac{DC_o}{Q} + \dfrac{QC_c}{2}$

The value of Q that minimizes the total cost is obtained by setting the first derivative to zero. We get

$$\dfrac{-DC_o}{Q^2} + \dfrac{C_c}{2} = 0$$

from which

$$Q^* = \sqrt{\dfrac{2DC_o}{C_c}}$$

and substituting Q^* in TC, we get

$$TC^* = \sqrt{2DC_o C_c}$$

ILLUSTRATION 13.1

D = 10000/year, C_o = Rs. 300/order and C_c = Rs. 4/unit/year

Then
$$Q^* = \sqrt{\dfrac{2DC_o}{C_c}}$$

$$= \sqrt{\dfrac{2 \times 10000 \times 300}{4}} = 1224.74$$

and
$$TC^* = \sqrt{2DC_o C_c}$$

$$= \sqrt{2 \times 10000 \times 300 \times 4} = 4898.98$$

(This total cost does not include the cost of the item). Q^* is called the **Economic Order Quantity** or **EOQ**. (Harris 1913, Wilson 1934).

$$\text{Number of orders/year } (N) = \frac{D}{Q}$$

$$= \frac{10000}{1224.74} = 8.17 \text{ orders/year}$$

If we increase the order quantity by 15% and round it off to 1500, the total cost becomes

$$TC = 10000 \times \frac{300}{1500} + 1500 \times \frac{4}{2} = 2000 + 3000 = 5000$$

which is approximately a 2% increase from the optimum cost. This is because the total cost curve is very flat near the optimum and gives the decision maker the flexibility to suitably define the actual order quantity (nearer the optimum or economic order quantity). This is seen in Figure 13.2.

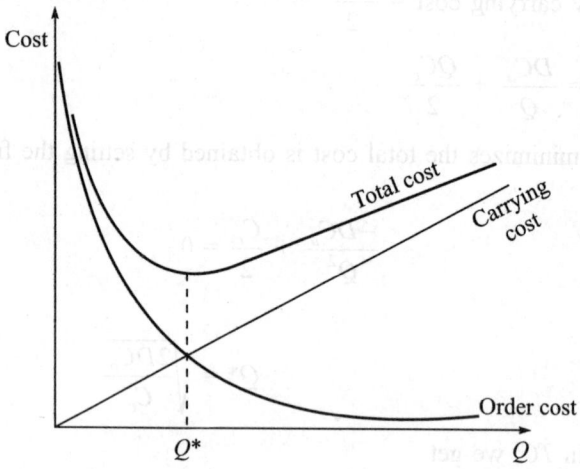

Figure 13.2 Cost vs. inventory.

In the above model we assume that there is instantaneous replenishment. The lead time (time taken between placing an order and getting the item) is assumed to be zero. If there is a lead time then the time to place the order, given by the reorder level (ROL) is equal to the product of the lead time (days) and daily demand. When the stock position is equal to the reorder level, the order for Q^* is placed.

13.2 CONSIDERING BACKORDERING

In this model, we allow a backorder of s units every cycle and as soon as the order quantity Q arrives, we issue the backordered quantity. Figure 13.3 shows the model. The maximum inventory held is $I_m = Q - s$. There is an inventory period of T_1 per cycle and a backorder period of T_2 per cycle.

Deterministic Inventory Models

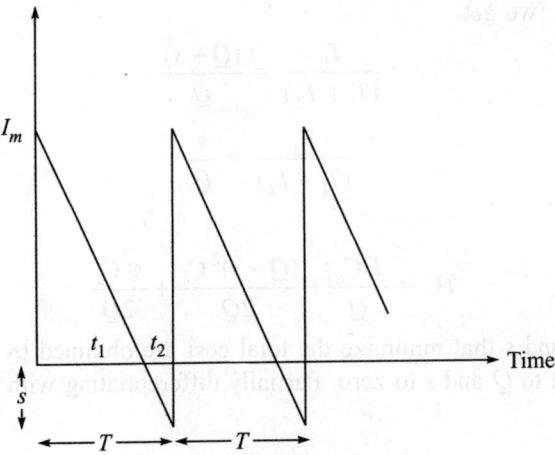

Figure 13.3 Inventory vs. time.

The coefficients are:
- Annual demand = D/year
- Order cost = C_o
- Carrying cost = C_c
- Shortage (backorder) cost = C_s
- Order quantity = Q
- Backorder quantity = s
- Maximum inventory in a cycle = I_m
- Number of orders/year = $\dfrac{D}{Q}$
- Annual order cost = $\dfrac{DC_o}{Q}$
- Average inventory in the system = $\dfrac{I_m}{2}$
- Annual inventory carrying cost = $\dfrac{I_m C_c}{2}$
- Average shortage in the system = $\dfrac{s}{2}$
- Annual shortage cost = $\dfrac{sC_s}{2}$
- Total cost $TC = \dfrac{DC_o}{Q} + \dfrac{I_m C_c}{2} \times \dfrac{T_1}{(T_1+T_2)} + \dfrac{sC_s}{2} \times \dfrac{T_2}{(T_1+T_2)}$

From similar triangles, we get

$$\frac{T_1}{(T_1 + T_2)} = \frac{(Q-s)}{Q}$$

and

$$\frac{T_2}{(T_1 + T_2)} = \frac{s}{Q}$$

Substituting, we get

$$TC = \frac{DC_o}{Q} + \frac{(Q-s)^2 C_c}{2Q} + \frac{s^2 C_s}{2Q}$$

The values of Q and s that minimize the total cost are obtained by setting the first partial derivative with respect to Q and s to zero. Partially differentiating with respect to s and setting to zero, we get

$$s = \frac{QC_c}{(C_c + C_s)}$$

Partially differentiating with respect to Q and substituting for s, we get

$$Q^* = \sqrt{\frac{2DC_o (C_c + C_s)}{C_c C_s}}$$

ILLUSTRATION 13.2

Considering the same data as in Example 13.1 with an additional C_s = Rs. 25 per unit/year, we get

$$Q^* = \sqrt{\frac{2DC_o (C_c + C_s)}{C_c C_s}}$$

$$= \sqrt{\frac{2 \times 10000 \times 300 \times (4+25)}{4 \times 25}} = 1319.09$$

$$s = \frac{QC_c}{(C_c + C_s)}$$

$$= \frac{1319.09}{(4+25)} = 181.9435$$

We order 1319.09 but also build a backorder of 181.9435 units. The maximum inventory held in a cycle is now $I_m = Q^* - s^* = 1137.147$ only.

Number of orders/year $N = D/Q = 7.58$

Each cycle is for 0.1319 years out of which the inventory cycle is 0.1137 years and the shortage cycle is 0.0181 years. Then

$$TC = \frac{DC_o}{Q} + \frac{(Q-s)^2 C_c}{2Q} + \frac{s^2 C_s}{2Q} = 4548.59$$

When compared to the previous model, we observe that the order quantity increases but the maximum inventory decreases. There is a gain in order cost and carrying cost but there is an additional backorder cost. There is a net decrease in the total cost and this model would suggest that backordering would be advantageous.

We also observe that if $C_s = \infty$, the order quantities are the same. For all other values of C_s, however large it may be, the second model would yield a lesser total cost than the first. The learning from this model is that we should keep C_s to infinity and eliminate backordering rather than encourage it by a wrong value of C_s. It is necessary that shortages can happen only due to uncertainty in demand. The value of C_s should be large enough to have a very small quantity backordered.

13.3 PRODUCTION CONSUMPTION MODEL

In this model, we produce and consume the item when it is produced. The production rate is P per year ($P > D$). The production is for a period t_1 and the item is consumed for a period t_2. The cycle time is $t_1 + t_2$. Figure 13.4 shows the model.

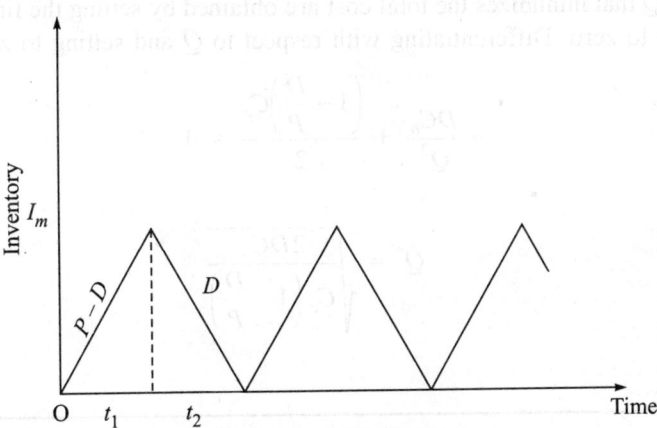

Figure 13.4 Inventory vs. time.

The coefficients are:

Annual demand = D/year

Production rate = P/year

Order cost = C_o

Carrying cost = C_c

Order quantity = Q

Maximum inventory in a cycle = I_m

Number of orders/year = $\dfrac{D}{Q}$

Annual order cost = $\dfrac{DC_o}{Q}$

Average inventory in the system = $\dfrac{I_m}{2}$

Annual inventory carrying cost = $\dfrac{I_m C_c}{2}$

Total cost $TC = \dfrac{DC_o}{Q} + \dfrac{I_m C_c}{2}$

We also have $Q = Pt_1$ and $I_m = (P - D)t_1$ from which $I_m = Q(1 - D/P)$. Substituting, we get

$$TC = \dfrac{DC_o}{Q} + \dfrac{Q\left(1 - \dfrac{D}{P}\right)C_c}{2}$$

The values of Q that minimizes the total cost are obtained by setting the first derivative with respect to Q and s to zero. Differentiating with respect to Q and setting to zero, we get

$$-\dfrac{DC_o}{Q^2} + \dfrac{\left(1 - \dfrac{D}{P}\right)C_c}{2} = 0$$

from which

$$Q^* = \sqrt{\dfrac{2DC_o}{C_c\left(1 - \dfrac{D}{P}\right)}}$$

ILLUSTRATION 13.3

Considering the same data as in Example 13.1 with an additional $P = 20000$ units/year, we have

$$Q^* = \sqrt{\dfrac{2DC_o}{C_c\left(1 - \dfrac{D}{P}\right)}}$$

$$\sqrt{\dfrac{2 \times 10000 \times 300}{4\left(1 - \dfrac{10000}{20000}\right)}} = 1732.05$$

$$I_m = Q\left(1 - \dfrac{D}{P}\right) = 866.03$$

$$t_1 = \dfrac{Q}{P} \text{ years} = 0.08666 \text{ years}$$

$$T = \frac{Q}{D} = 0.173205 \text{ years}$$

$$t_2 = 0.08666 \text{ years}$$

$$TC = \frac{DC_o}{Q} + \frac{Q\left(1 - \frac{D}{P}\right)C_c}{2} = 3464.10$$

13.4 PRODUCTION CONSUMPTION MODEL 3 WITH BACKORDERING

Here, we allow a backordering and build a quantity of s, which is delivered as the items are produced in the next cycle. Figure 13.5 explains the model.

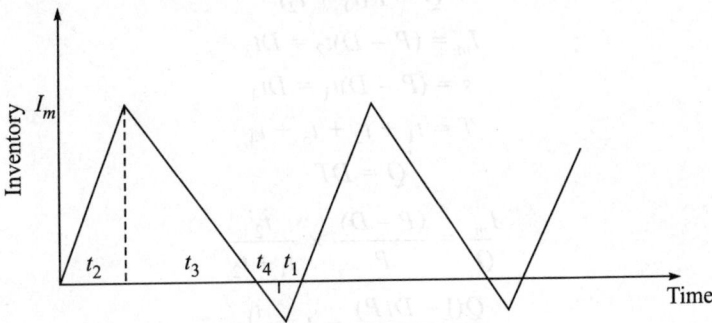

Figure 13.5 Inventory vs. time.

The coefficients are:

Annual demand = D/year

Production rate = P/year

Order cost = C_o

Carrying cost = C_c

Shortage (Backorder) cost = C_s

Order quantity = Q

Backorder allowed = s

Maximum inventory in a cycle = I_m

Number of orders/year = $\dfrac{D}{Q}$

Annual order cost = $\dfrac{DC_o}{Q}$

Average inventory in the system = $\dfrac{I_m}{2}$

This is held for $(t_2 + t_3)$ time out of a cycle of T.

$$\text{Annual inventory carrying cost} = \frac{I_m C_c}{2} \times \frac{(t_2 + t_3)}{T}$$

$$\text{Average quantity backordered} = \frac{s}{2}$$

This is held for a period $(t_1 + t_4)$ out of a cycle of T.

$$\text{Annual backorder cost} = \frac{sC_s}{2} \times \frac{(t_1 + t_4)}{T}$$

Then
$$TC = \frac{DC_o}{Q} + \frac{I_m C_c}{2} \frac{(t_2 + t_3)}{T} + \frac{sC_s}{2} \frac{(t_1 + t_4)}{T}$$

We also have
$$Q = P(t_1 + t_2)$$
$$I_m = (P - D)t_2 = Dt_3$$
$$s = (P - D)t_1 = Dt_4$$
$$T = t_1 + t_2 + t_3 + t_4$$
$$Q = DT$$
$$\frac{I_m}{Q} = \frac{(P - D)}{P} \times \frac{t_2}{t_1 + t_2}$$
$$\frac{Q(1 - D/P)}{I_m} = 1 + \frac{t_1}{t_2}$$

From similar triangles $\dfrac{t_1}{t_2} = \dfrac{s}{I_m}$

Substituting, we get
$$I_m = Q\left(1 - \frac{D}{P}\right) - s$$

Also
$$\frac{Pt_2}{T} = \frac{D(t_2 + t_3)}{T}$$

$$\frac{(t_2 + t_3)}{T} = \frac{Pt_2}{DT} = \frac{PI_m}{Q(P - D)}$$

and
$$\frac{(t_1 + t_4)}{T} = \frac{s}{Q(1 - D/P)}$$

Substituting in TC, we get
$$TC = \frac{DC_o}{Q} + \left[Q\left(1 - \frac{D}{P}\right) - s\right]^2 \frac{C_c}{2} \frac{1}{Q(1 - D/P)} + \frac{s^2 C_2}{2Q(1 - D/P)}$$

The values of Q and s that minimizes the total cost are obtained by setting the first derivative with respect to Q and s to zero. The expression for s in terms of Q is given by

$$s = \frac{QC_c\left(1 - \frac{D}{P}\right)}{(C_c + C_s)}$$

The final expression for Q^* on differentiation, substitution and simplification is:

$$Q^* = \sqrt{\frac{2DC_o\,(C_c + C_s)}{C_c\,(1 - D/P)\,C_s}}$$

ILLUSTRATION 13.4

Let us consider the same data as in Example 13.3 with the additional C_s = Rs. 25/unit/year.

$$Q^* = \sqrt{\frac{2DC_o\,(C_c + C_s)}{C_c\,(1 - D/P)\,C_s}}$$

$$= \sqrt{\frac{2 \times 10000 \times 300 \times 29}{4 \times 25 \times \left(1 - \frac{1}{2}\right)}} = 1865.48$$

$$s = \frac{QC_c\left(1 - \frac{D}{P}\right)}{(C_c + C_s)}$$

$$= \frac{1865.48 \times 4 \times \frac{1}{2}}{29} = 128.65$$

$$I_m = Q(1 - D/P) - s$$
$$= 1865.48 * 0.5 - 128.65 = 804.09$$

$$\therefore \quad TC = \frac{DC_o}{Q} + \left[Q\left(1 - \frac{D}{P}\right) - s\right]^2 \frac{C_c}{2\,Q(1 - D/P)} + \frac{s^2 C_2}{2Q\,(1 - D/P)} = 3216.338$$

We observe that the total cost comes down when backordering is considered. The maximum inventory in the system comes down though the order quantity is more.

13.5 INVENTORY MODEL WITH DISCOUNT

ILLUSTRATION 13.5

Let us consider inventory models with discount. Consider Example 13.1, whose data is as follows:

Annual demand $D = 10000$
Order cost C_o = Rs. 300
Unit price C = Rs. 20
Interest rate = 20% per annum

Here the economic order quantity is:

$$Q^* = \sqrt{\frac{2DC_o}{C_c}} = 1224.74$$

and
$$TC = 4898.98$$

Let us assume that the vendor is willing to give a 2% discount on unit price if the order quantity were 2000 or more and is willing to give a 4% discount if the order quantity were 5000 or more. The total cost including the item cost at EOQ is:

$$4898.98 + 10000 * 20 = 204898.98$$

If the order quantity is 2000 then

$$TC = \frac{10000}{2000} \times 300 + 2000 \times 0.2 \times 20 \times \frac{0.98}{2} + 10000 \times 20 \times 0.98 = 201420$$

If the order quantity is 5000 then

$$TC = \frac{10000}{5000} \times 300 + 5000 \times 0.2 \times 20 \times \frac{0.96}{2} + 10000 \times 20 \times 0.96 = 202200$$

The total cost (including the item cost) is minimum when we avail a 2% discount at an order quantity of 2000 units.

In all discount problems, we have to include the item cost because the unit price depends on the order quantity. It is enough to evaluate only at the price break because for order quantities other than those at price break, the cost will be higher. It is also assumed that all price breaks will be for order quantities higher than the economic order quantity. If there is a price break at a quantity less than the EOQ then it is accepted and evaluated at the EOQ for comparison with other price break options. The discount that gives minimum TC is always chosen.

13.6 MULTIPLE ITEMS INVENTORY (CONSTRAINT ON TOTAL NUMBER OF ORDERS)

ILLUSTRATION 13.6

Let us consider two items with the data shown in Table 13.1.

Table 13.1 Data for Two Items

	Item 1	Item 2
Annual demand D	10000	20000
Order cost C_o	300	300
Unit price C	20	25
Interest rate	20%	20%

Considering the first item, we have

$$Q_1^* = \sqrt{\frac{2D_1C_o}{iC_1}} = 1224.74$$

and
$$TC_1 = 4898.98$$

$$\text{Number of orders/year } N_1 = \frac{D_1}{Q_1} = 8.16$$

Considering the second item, we have

$$Q_2^* = \sqrt{\frac{2D_2C_o}{iC_2}} = 1549.19$$

and
$$TC_2 = 7745.97$$

$$\text{Number of orders/year } N_2 = \frac{D_2}{Q_2} = 12.91$$

Together, we have $8.16 + 12.91 = 21.07$ orders/year.

In practice, we have more than thousand items in a factory and each has a unique order cycle resulting in a very large number of orders. The organization might want to reduce the total number of orders to lessen the burden though it may be uneconomical. Let us assume that we would restrict to 15 orders for the above two items together. The problem formulation would be to

Minimize $\sum_{j=1}^{n} \frac{D_j C_o}{Q_j} + \frac{iQ_j C_j}{2}$

Subject to

$$\sum_{j=1}^{n} \frac{D_j}{Q_j} \leq N$$

$$Q_j \geq 0$$

The objective function is the sum of the total ordering costs and carrying costs for all the items. The constraint ensures that the total number of orders is restricted to a fixed number N. We assume that the constraint is violated by the individual economic order quantities and attempt to solve the problem. If the constraint is satisfied by the individual EOQs then they are optimal to the problem.

When the constraint is violated by the individual EOQs, we can show that the constraint will be satisfied as an equation (and not as an inequality). Therefore, the constraint becomes

$$\sum_{j=1}^{n} \frac{D_j}{Q_j} = N$$

The problem has a non-linear objective function with a single constraint, which is a linear equation. We use Lagrangean multiplier technique, introduce λ (Lagrangean multiplier) and write the Lagrangean function as:

$$L = \sum_{j=1}^{n} \frac{D_j C_o}{Q_j} + \sum_{j=1}^{n} \frac{iQ_j C_j}{2} + \sum_{j=1}^{n} \lambda \left(\frac{D_j}{Q_j} - N \right)$$

The optimum values of Q_j and λ can be obtained by equating the partial derivatives $\partial L/\partial Q_j$ and $\partial L/\partial \lambda$ to zero. $\partial L/\partial Q_j = 0$ gives

$$\frac{-C_o D_j}{Q_j^2} + \frac{iC_j}{2} - \frac{\lambda D_j}{Q_j^2} = 0$$

from which

$$Q_j = \sqrt{\frac{2D_j (C_o + \lambda)}{iC_j}}$$

$\partial L/\partial \lambda = 0$ gives $\Sigma D_j/Q_j = N$. To get the optimum value of λ, we substitute for Q_j^* in $\Sigma D_j/Q_j = N$.

$$\sum_{j=1}^{n} \frac{D_j \sqrt{iC_j}}{\sqrt{2D_j (C_o + \lambda)}} = N$$

This on simplification gives

$$\lambda = \frac{i \left(\sum_{j=1}^{n} \sqrt{D_j C_j} \right)^2}{2N^2} - C_o$$

For the two item example with $N = 15$, we have

$$\lambda = 292.20$$

$$Q_1 = \sqrt{\frac{2D_1 (C_o + \lambda)}{iC_1}} = 1720.76$$

$$Q_2 = \sqrt{\frac{2D_2 (C_o + \lambda)}{iC_2}} = 2176.607$$

$$N_1 + N_2 = \frac{10000}{1720.76} + \frac{20000}{2176.607} = 15$$

$$TC = \Sigma C_o \frac{D_j}{Q_j} + \Sigma iQ_j \frac{C_j}{2}$$

$$= \frac{10000}{1720.76} \times 300 + \frac{1720.76}{2} \times 4 + \frac{20000}{2176.607} \times 300 + \frac{2176.607}{2} \times 5 = 13383.04$$

We observe that because of the restriction on the number of orders, the individual order quantities increase and the total cost increases. We can also prove that

$$\frac{Q_1^*}{Q_1} = \frac{1720.76}{1224.74} = 1.405$$

$$\frac{Q_2^*}{Q_2} = \frac{2176.607}{1549.19} = 1.405$$

$$\frac{(N_1 + N_2)}{N} = \frac{21.07}{15} = 1.405$$

(The reader may refer to Exercises Problem 13.12 where the proof is given as an exercise)

When the constraint is violated by the EOQs, we observe that λ is strictly positive and roughly of the order of C_o. The strictly positive value indicates that the constraint is violated by the EOQs. This method should be used only when the constraint is violated by the EOQs. For example, if we had directly used the equation to find λ for $N = 25$, we will get a negative value of λ indicating that the constraint is satisfied by the EOQs. This is because in the Lagrangean method we are forcing the constraint to be an equation. When the constraint is satisfied by the EOQs, the optimal order quantities remain unchanged but this method will force the Q_j to satisfy the constraint as an equation and give a negative value for λ.

Constrained inventory problem

1. Solve the unconstrained problem and get the values of Q^*.
2. If the constraint is satisfied, the existing value of Q^* (EOQ) are optimal.
3. Use the Lagrangean multiplier method **only when the constraint is violated**.

13.7 MULTIPLE ITEMS INVENTORY (CONSTRAINT ON INVENTORY VALUE)

ILLUSTRATION 13.7

Let us consider two items with the data shown in Table 13.2.

Table 13.2 Data for Two Items

	Item 1	Item 2
Annual demand D	10000	20000
Order cost C_O	300	300
Unit price C	20	25
Interest rate	20%	20%

Considering the first item, we have

$$Q_1^* = \sqrt{\frac{2D_1 C_o}{iC_1}} = 1224.74$$

and
$$TC_1 = 4898.98$$

$$\text{Average inventory value} = \frac{Q_1 C_1}{2} = 12247.50$$

Considering the second item, we have

$$Q_2^* = \sqrt{\frac{2D_2 C_o}{iC_2}} = 1549.19$$

and
$$TC_2 = 7745.97$$

$$\text{Average inventory value} = \frac{Q_2 C_2}{2} = 19364.88$$

Total value of the inventory (average) = 31612.38

In practice, we have more than thousand items in a factory and each has a certain inventory resulting in a very large amount of money stocked in goods. The organization might want to reduce the total money value of inventory to lessen the burden. Let us assume that we would restrict to Rs. 25000 worth of inventory for the above two items together. The problem formulation would be to

Minimize $\sum_{j=1}^{n} \frac{D_j C_o}{Q_j} + \frac{iQ_j C_j}{2}$

Subject to

$$\sum_{j=1}^{n} \frac{Q_j C_j}{2} \leq B$$

$$Q_j \geq 0$$

The objective function is the sum of the total ordering costs and carrying costs for all the items. The constraint ensures that the money value of the average inventory is restricted to a fixed amount B. We assume that the constraint is violated by the individual economic order quantities and attempt to solve the problem. If the constraint is satisfied by the individual EOQs then they are optimal to the problem.

When the constraint is violated by the individual EOQs, we can show that the constraint will be satisfied as an equation (and not as an inequality). Therefore, the constraint becomes

$$\sum_{j=1}^{n} \frac{Q_j C_j}{2} = B$$

The problem has a non-linear objective function with a single constraint, which is a linear equation. We use Lagrangean multiplier technique, introduce λ (Lagrangean multiplier) and write the Lagrangean function as:

$$L = \sum_{j=1}^{n} \frac{D_j C_o}{Q_j} + \sum_{j=1}^{n} \frac{iQ_j C_j}{2} + \sum_{j=1}^{n} \lambda \left(\frac{Q_j C_j}{2} - B \right)$$

The optimum values of Q_j and λ can be obtained by equating the partial derivatives $\partial L/\partial Q_j$ and $\partial L/\partial \lambda$ to zero. $\partial L/\partial Q_j = 0$ gives $\dfrac{-C_o D_j}{Q_j^2} + \dfrac{iC_j}{2} + \dfrac{\lambda C_j}{2} = 0$

from which

$$Q_j = \sqrt{\dfrac{2D_j C_o}{(i+\lambda)C_j}}$$

and $\partial L/\partial Q_j = 0$ gives

$$\Sigma Q_j \dfrac{C_j}{2} = B$$

To get the optimum value of λ, we substitute for Q_j^* in $\Sigma Q_j C_j / 2 = B$.

$$\sum_{j=1}^{n} \sqrt{\dfrac{2D_j C_o}{(i+\lambda)C_j}} \dfrac{C_j}{2} = B$$

This on simplification gives

$$\lambda = \dfrac{C_o}{2B^2}\left(\sum_{j=1}^{n}\sqrt{D_j C_j}\right)^2 - i$$

For the two-item example with $B = 25000$, we have

$$\lambda = 0.12$$

$$Q_1^* = \sqrt{\dfrac{2D_1 C_o}{(i+\lambda)C_1}} = 968.5647$$

$$Q_2^* = \sqrt{\dfrac{2D_2 C_o}{iC_2}} = 1225.148$$

$$\dfrac{Q_1^* C_1 + Q_2 C_2}{2} = \dfrac{968.5647 \times 20 + 1225.148 \times 25}{2} = 25000$$

$$TC = \Sigma C_o \dfrac{D_j}{Q_j} + \Sigma i Q_j \dfrac{C_j}{2}$$

$$= \dfrac{10000}{968.5647} \times 300 + \dfrac{968.5647}{2} \times 4 + \dfrac{20000}{1225.148} \times 300 + \dfrac{1225.148}{2} \times 5$$

$$= 12994.73$$

We observe that because of the restriction on the inventory, the individual order quantities decrease and the total cost increases. We can also prove that

$$\dfrac{Q_1^*}{Q_1} = \dfrac{968.5647}{1224.74} = 0.7908$$

$$\frac{Q_2^*}{Q_2} = \frac{1225.148}{1549.19} = 0.7908$$

$$\frac{B}{(Q_1C_1/2 + Q_2C_2/2)} = \frac{25000}{31612.38} = 0/7908$$

(The reader should refer to Example 13.9 for the proof of the above result)

When the constraint is violated by the EOQs, we observe that λ is strictly positive and roughly of the order of i. The strictly positive value indicates that the constraint is violated by the EOQs. This method should be used only when the constraint is violated by the EOQs. For example, if we had directly used the equation to find λ for $B = 35000$, we will get a negative value of λ indicating that the constraint is satisfied by the EOQs. This is because in the Lagrangean method we are forcing the constraint to be an equation. When the constraint is satisfied by the EOQs, the optimal order quantities remain unchanged but this method will force the Q_j to satisfy the constraint as an equation and give a negative value for λ.

Constrained inventory problem
1. Solve the unconstrained problem and get the values of Q^*.
2. If the constraint is satisfied, the existing value of Q^* (EOQ) are optimal.
3. Use the Lagrangean multiplier method *only when the constraint is violated*.

13.8 MULTIPLE ITEMS INVENTORY (CONSTRAINT ON SPACE)

ILLUSTRATION 13.8

Let us consider two items with the data shown in Table 13.3.

Table 13.3 Data for Two Items

	Item 1	Item 2
Annual demand D	10,000	20,000
Order cost C_o	300	300
Unit price C	20	25
Storage space (S)	20%	20%
Storage space (S) required (cuft/unit)	3	4

Considering the first item, we have

$$Q_1^* = \sqrt{\frac{2D_1C_o}{iC_1}} = 1224.74$$

and
$$TC_1 = 4898.98$$

$$\text{Average space needed} = \frac{Q_1 S_1}{2} = 1837.125$$

Considering the second item, we have

$$Q_2^* = \sqrt{\frac{2D_2C_o}{iC_2}} = 1549.19$$

and

$$TC_2 = 7745.97$$

$$\text{Average space required} = \frac{Q_2S_2}{2} = 3098.38$$

$$\text{Total space required (average)} = 4935.505$$

In practice, we have more than thousand items in a factory and each has a certain inventory resulting in a very large amount of space required. The organization might want to reduce the space of inventory to lessen the burden. Let us assume that we would restrict to 4000 cu feet of space for the above two items together. The problem formulation would be to

Minimize $\sum_{j=1}^{n} \frac{D_j C_o}{Q_j} + \frac{iQ_j C_j}{2}$

Subject to

$$\sum_{j=1}^{n} \frac{Q_j S_j}{2} \leq S$$

$$Q_j \geq 0$$

The objective function is the sum of the total ordering costs and carrying costs for all the items. The constraint ensures that the space required for the average inventory is restricted to a fixed volume S. We assume that the constraint is violated by the individual economic order quantities and attempt to solve the problem. If the constraint is satisfied by the individual EOQs then they are optimal to the problem.

When the constraint is violated by the individual EOQs, we can show that the constraint will be satisfied as an equation (and not as an inequality). Therefore, the constraint becomes

$$\sum_{j=1}^{n} \frac{Q_j S_j}{2} = S$$

The problem has a non-linear objective function with a single constraint, which is a linear equation. We use Lagrangean multiplier technique, introduce λ (Lagrangean multiplier) and write the Lagrangean function as:

$$L = \sum_{j=1}^{n} \frac{D_j C_o}{Q_j} + \sum_{j=1}^{n} \frac{iQ_j C_j}{2} + \sum_{j=1}^{n} \lambda \left(\frac{Q_j S_j}{2} - S \right)$$

The optimum values of Q_j and λ can be obtained by equating the partial derivatives $\partial L/\partial Q_j$ and $\partial L/\partial \lambda$ to zero.

$\partial L/\partial Q_j = 0$ gives

$$\frac{-C_o D_j}{Q_j^2} + \frac{iC_j}{2} + \frac{\lambda S_j}{2} = 0$$

from which

$$Q_j = \sqrt{\frac{2D_j C_o}{(iC_j + \lambda S_j)}}$$

and $\partial L/\partial Q_j = 0$ gives

$$\sum_{j=1}^{n} \frac{Q_j S_j}{2} = S$$

To get the optimum value of λ, we have to use a trial and error approach for various values of λ. The value of the space requirement $\Sigma Q_j S_j/2$ for various values of λ are given in Table 13.4.

Table 13.4 Computing λ

λ	$\Sigma Q_j S_j/2$
0.4	4308.06
0.6	4072.501
0.66	4009.04
0.669	3999.77

The best value of λ is taken as 0.669 which has a space requirement of 3999.77.

$$Q_1 = \sqrt{\frac{2D_1 C_o}{(iC_1 + \lambda S_1)}} = 999.4172$$

$$Q_2 = \sqrt{\frac{2D_2 C_o}{(iC_2 + \lambda S_2)}} = 1250.326$$

$$Q_1^* S_1 + \frac{Q_2^* S_2}{2} = 3999.77$$

$$TC = \frac{10000}{999.4172} \times 300 + \frac{999.4172}{2} \times 4 + \frac{20000}{1250.326} \times 300 + \frac{1250.326}{2} \times 5 = 12925.15$$

We observe that because of the restriction on space, the individual order quantities decrease and the total cost increases.

We can also observe that

$$\frac{Q_1^*}{Q_1} = \frac{999.4172}{1224.75} = 0.816$$

$$\frac{Q_2^*}{Q_2} = \frac{1250.326}{1549.19} = 0.807$$

$$\frac{S}{(Q_1 S_1/2 + Q_2 S_2/2)} = \frac{4000}{4935.505} = 0.81$$

(The above relationships may also be used as an approximation to get the values of Q_j^*)

When the constraint is violated by the EOQs, we observe that λ is strictly positive. The strictly positive value indicates that the constraint is violated by the EOQs. This method should be used only when the constraint is violated by the EOQs. For example, if we had directly used the equation to find λ for $S = 5000$, we will get a negative value of λ indicating that the constraint is satisfied by the EOQs. This is because in the Lagrangean method we are forcing the constraint to be an equation. When the constraint is satisfied by the EOQs, the optimal order quantities remain unchanged but this method will force the Q_j to satisfy the constraint as an equation and give a negative value for λ.

Constrained inventory problem

1. Solve the unconstrained problem and get the values of Q^*.
2. If the constraint is satisfied, the existing values of Q^* (EOQ) are optimal.
3. Use the Lagrangean multiplier method *only when the constraint is violated*.

13.9 MULTIPLE ITEMS INVENTORY AND MULTIPLE CONSTRAINTS

Let us consider situations where we have multiple constraints.

Case 1 Number of orders + Inventory

Let us assume that we have restriction on both these constraints and that the EOQs of the multiple items violate both these constraints. In this case we will have an infeasible solution. This is because the number of orders restriction tries to increase the order quantity while the inventory restriction tries to reduce the order quantity. We can handle only one of the two and not both.

Case 2 Number of orders + Space

Suppose we have restriction on both these and the EOQs of the multiple items violate both these constraints. In this case, the solution is infeasible. This is because the number of orders restriction tries to increase the order quantity while the space restriction tries to reduce the order quantity. We can handle only one of the two and not both.

Case 3 Inventory + Space

ILLUSTRATION 13.9

Let us assume that we have restriction on both of these and the EOQs of the multiple items violate both these constraints. In this case one of them will be binding eventually. For example,

$$B = 25000 \text{ and } S = 4000$$

Considering only the inventory restriction, we have

$$Q_1 = \sqrt{\frac{2D_1C_o}{(i+\lambda)C_1}} = 968.5647$$

$$Q_2 = \sqrt{\frac{2D_2C_o}{(i+\lambda)C_2}} = 1225.148$$

Total space requirement is:

$$\frac{Q_1 S_1}{2} + \frac{Q_2 S_2}{2} = 3903.144$$

This satisfies the space constraint and is optimal. We need not solve a Lagrangean considering two constraints because only one of them will be optimal. Usually we solve the inventory restriction first cause it is easier and verify whether the space constraint is satisfied. If so, the solution is optimal. If not, we solve the space constraint and this will be optimal.

We can handle two constraints only when both try to shift the order quantity in the same direction. In this case, both the inventory constraint and the space constraint try to reduce the order quantity.

If for the same problem we had $B = 30000$ and $S = 4000$, solving for inventory we would have got $Q_1^* = 1162.278$, $Q_2^* = 1470.178$ with average space requirement $= Q_1 S_1/2 + Q_2 S_2/2 = 4683.772$. This violates the space constraint.

We solve for $S = 4000$ and get $Q_1^* = 999.4172$ and $Q_2^* = 1250.326$. The inventory value for this solution is $(Q_1^* C_1 + Q_2^* C_2)/2 = 25623.24$ which satisfies the inventory restriction.

The solution is $Q_1^* = 999.4172$ and $Q_2^* = 1250.326$ with inventory value $= 25623.24$ and space requirement of 4000 cu ft.

SOLVED EXAMPLES

EXAMPLE 13.1 Let Q^* be the optimal order quantity in the simple ECQ model (Constant rate of demand, instantaneous supply, no shortages). Let the actual order quantity be Q given by

$$Q = K Q^* \qquad K > 0$$

(a) Derive an expression for the ratio of the actual total cost/unit time to the optimal cost.
(b) If the holding cost/unit/unit time is overestimated by 20%, what is the percentage increase in the total cost over the optimal cost?

Solution: (a)

$$Q^* = \sqrt{\frac{2DC_o}{C_c}}$$

$$TC = \frac{DC_o}{kQ^*} + \frac{kQ^* C_c}{2}$$

$$TC = \frac{DC_o \sqrt{C_c}}{k\sqrt{2DC_o}} + \frac{kC_c \sqrt{2DC_o}}{2\sqrt{C_c}}$$

$$TC = \frac{1}{2k}\sqrt{2DC_o C_c} + \frac{k}{2}\sqrt{2DC_o C_c}$$

$$TC = \frac{1}{2}\left(k + \frac{1}{k}\right) TC^*$$

(b) If new $C_c = 1.2C_c$,

$$TC = \sqrt{2DC_o}\sqrt{1.2C_c} = \sqrt{1.2}\,TC^* = 1.095 TC^*$$

There is a 9.5% increase in the total cost.

EXAMPLE 13.2 M/s Shah and Company is an old firm where scientific inventory management is totally unknown. For a certain raw material that they buy, it is estimated that each purchase order would cost Rs. 200. The cost of the raw material is Rs. 30/kg. The annual inventory cost is 14% of the cost per kg. The monthly requirement is 100 kg. The ordering quantity has been arbitrarily fixed at 440 kg. If this ordering quantity is to be optimum, what should be the shortage cost assuming that shortages are allowed?

Solution: Given C_o = Rs. 200, C = Rs. 30, i = 14% per year, D = 100 kg/Month = 1200 kg/year Q = 440, C_S = ?

Then

$$Q^* = \sqrt{\frac{2DC_o\,(C_c + C_s)}{C_c C_s}}$$

or

$$440 = \sqrt{\frac{2 \times 1200 \times 200}{4.2}}\sqrt{1 + \frac{4.2}{C_s}}$$

∴ $C_s = 6.052$

EXAMPLE 13.3 Readychand fabrics run a huge showroom for readymade garments. The showroom is famous for garments made of a certain variety of cotton. The firm has quarterly requirements of 2000 metres length of this variety of cloth, which costs Rs. 19 per metre.

The proprietors have made a precise estimate of their ordering cost—32 rupees 30 paise per order. The carrying cost per year is estimated to be 17% of the cost per metre.

Mr. Lalit Chand, who has recently joined the business after completing his MBA, insists that they should procure the cloth in economic order quantities. However, their supplier is not willing to sell less than 2000 metres of the cloth per order.

What discount percentage on the cost per metre should Mr. Lalit Chand claim to give up his insistence on EOQ?

Solution: Given Demand = 2000 m/quarter D = 8000 per year C = Rs. 38 C_o = Rs. 32.30 i = 8.5% C_c = 38 * 8.5/100 = 3.23

Then

$$Q^* = \sqrt{\frac{2DC_o}{C_c}}$$

$$= \sqrt{\frac{2 \times 8000 \times 32.30}{3.23}} = 400$$

$$TC = \sqrt{2DC_o C_c} + 8000 \times 38 = 305292 \text{ (including the cost of the item)}$$

Let discount be d% then

$$C_c = 38 * 8.5\frac{(1-d)}{100}$$

$$= \text{Rs. } 3.23(1 - d)$$

$$TC = \frac{8000 \times 32.3}{2000} + \frac{2000 \times 3.23\,(1-d)}{2} + 8000 \times 38 \times (1-d)$$

Equating, we have $129.2 + 307230(1-d) = 305292$

$$1 - d = 0.9937$$
$$d = 0.0063$$

i.e. 0.63% discount

EXAMPLE 13.4 The Hostel Management of a college is considering quotations from three vendors to whom it has to place orders for rice. Nellore provision stores quotes Rs. 120 per bag irrespective of the quantity ordered. Green & Company will accept orders only for 800 or more bags but quotes a price of Rs. 108 per bag. Ponni Trading Company will accept orders only for 1000 or more bags at Rs. 100 per bag. Chamba and Company will accept orders for 400 bags or more for a cost of Rs. 112 per bag. The total requirement of the 12 hostels for which the management buys is 3000 bags per semester (six months). Inventory carrying costs are 20% of the unit cost and the ordering cost is Rs. 400 per order. Which vendor would you recommend for placing the orders and for what quantity per order?

Solution: Given $D = 3000$ per semester = 6000 per year, $C_o =$ Rs. 400, $i = 20\% = 0.2$

Vendor 1

$C =$ Rs. 120

Then
$$Q^* = \sqrt{\frac{2DC_o}{C_c}}$$
$$= \sqrt{\frac{2 \times 6000 \times 400}{24}} = 447.21$$

and
$$TC = \sqrt{2DC_oC_c}$$
$$= \sqrt{2 \times 6000 \times 400 \times 24} = 10733.126$$

Total cost including the price of the item = $10733.126 + 6000 \times 120 = 730733.13$

Vendor 2

$C =$ Rs. 108
$Q = 800$ or more

Then
$$Q^* = \sqrt{\frac{2DC_o}{C_c}}$$
$$= \sqrt{\frac{2 \times 6000 \times 400}{21.6}} = 471.4$$

Since EOQ is less than 800, we evaluate the cost at an order quantity of 800.

$$TC = \frac{6000 \times 400}{800} + \frac{800 \times 21.6}{2} = 11640$$

Total cost including the price of the item = 11640 + 6000 × 108 = 659640

Vendor 3

C = Rs. 100
Q = 1000

Then
$$Q^* = \sqrt{\frac{2DC_o}{C_c}}$$

$$= \sqrt{\frac{2 \times 6000 \times 400}{20}} = 489.9$$

Since the EOQ is less than 1000, we evaluate the cost at an order quantity of 1000. At Q = 1000,

$$TC = \frac{6000 \times 400}{1000} + \frac{1000 \times 20}{2} = 12400$$

Total cost including the price of the item = 12400 + 6000 × 100 = 612400

Vendor 4

C = Rs. 112
Q = 400 or more

Then
$$Q^* = \sqrt{\frac{2DC_o}{C_c}}$$

$$= \sqrt{\frac{2 \times 6000 \times 400}{22.4}} = 462.91$$

Since the EOQ is less than 400, we evaluate the cost at EOQ.

$$TC = \sqrt{2 \times D \times C_o \times C_c} = 10369.19$$

Total cost including the price of the item = 10369.19 + 6000 × 112 = 682369.19
Vendor 3 is chosen with an order quantity of 1000 bags since the annual cost is the least.

EXAMPLE 13.5 Consider a two-item inventory problem with the data given in Table 13.5.

Table 13.5 Data for Two-Item Problem

	Item 1	Item 2
Annual demand	10,000	15,000
Ordering cost	Rs. 200/order	Rs. 250/order
Carrying cost	Rs. 4/unit/year	Rs. 5/unit/year
Item cost	Rs. 10/unit	Rs. 20/unit

(a) Find the economic order quantity for each product separately.
(b) Owing to a liquidity problem, the company requires that the average yearly investment in the inventory for the two products taken together be less than or equal to Rs. 15000. Is the answer found in part (a) consistent with this added constraint?

Solution: (a) Given $D_1 = 10000$, $D_2 = 15000$, $C_1 = $ Rs. 10, $C_2 = $ Rs. 20, $C_{C1} = $ Rs. 4, $C_{C2} = $ Rs. 5, $C_{O1} = $ Rs. 200, $C_{O2} = $ Rs. 250

Then
$$Q_1^* = \sqrt{\frac{2D_1 C_{o1}}{C_{c1}}} = 1000$$

Average investment in inventory $= \dfrac{Q_1 C_1}{2} = $ Rs. 5000

$$Q_2^* = \sqrt{\frac{2D_2 C_{o2}}{C_{c2}}} = 1224.74$$

Average investment in inventory $= \dfrac{Q_2 C_2}{2} = $ Rs. 12274.40

(b) Amount invested in inventory (average) $= \dfrac{Q_1 C_1}{2} + \dfrac{Q_2 C_2}{2}$

$$= 17274.40 > 15000$$

We setup the Lagrangean function:

$$L = \sum_{j=1}^{2} \frac{D_j C_{oj}}{Q_j} + \sum_{j=1}^{2} \frac{Q_j C_{cj}}{2} + \sum_{j=1}^{2} \frac{\lambda C_j}{2}$$

which is to be minimized.
$\partial L / \partial Q_j = 0$ gives

$$Q_j = \sqrt{\frac{2D_j C_{oj}}{(C_{cj} + \lambda C_j)}}$$

Substituting in $Q_1 C_1/2 + Q_2 C_2/2 = 15000$, we get

$$\frac{10000}{\sqrt{(4+\lambda)}} + \frac{27386.1}{\sqrt{(5+\lambda)}} = 15000$$

We calculate the LHS for various values of λ and get the value of λ for which the LHS is closest to 15000.

For $\lambda = 1$, LHS = 15652.46
For $\lambda = 1.5$, LHS = 15005.72
For $\lambda = 1.505$, LHS = 14999.66

We approximate the value of λ to 1.505, using which we get $Q_1 = 852.42$ and $Q_2 = 1073.76$, respectively.

(In this example, we cannot use the expression for λ derived earlier because the inventory ordering costs are different for the two items. The expressions for λ can be used only when the inventory carrying cost is represented as a fraction of the unit cost and the fraction has to be the same for both the items.)

EXAMPLE 13.6 A shop orders two products that it periodically orders from one supplier. The demand rates for both products are predictable and constant. Demand rates and inventory costs are given in Table 13.6.

Table 13.6 Demand Rates and Inventory Costs

Product	Demand rate units/month	Order cost Rs./Order	Holding cost Rs./unit/month
A	200	60	2
B	300	60	4

(a) Find the optimum values of the inventory cost per month and the length of both inventory cycles under the assumption that both inventory processes are managed separately.

(b) The shop finds that they could save on the order cost of B if both the products were ordered together. This course of action can be evaluated by finding the minimum total inventory cost per month subject to the constraint that the two inventory periods are equal.

Solution: (a) **Product A**

Given $D_1 = 200$ per month, $C_{01} = $ Rs. 60, $C_{c1} = 2$

Then
$$Q_1^* = \sqrt{\frac{2D_1 C_{01}}{C_{c1}}}$$

$$= \sqrt{\frac{2 \times 200 \times 60}{2}} = 109.54$$

and
$$TC_1 = \sqrt{2 D_1 C_{01} C_{c1}}$$

$$= \sqrt{2 \times 200 \times 60 \times 2} = 219.08$$

Number of cycles per month $= \dfrac{200}{109.54} = 1.826$

Product B

Given $D_2 = 300$, $C_{02} = $ Rs. 60, $C_{c2} = 4.0$

Then
$$Q_2^* = \sqrt{\frac{2D_2 C_{02}}{C_{c2}}}$$

$$= \sqrt{\frac{2 \times 300 \times 60}{4}} = 94.86$$

480   Operations Research: Principles and Applications

and
$$TC_2 = \sqrt{2D_2C_{02}C_{c2}}$$
$$= \sqrt{2 \times 300 \times 60 \times 4} = 379.47$$

$$\text{Number of cycles per month} = \frac{300}{94.86} = 3.162$$

The order cycles are different for the two items.

(b) We save an order cost if they are ordered together. The periods have to be equal $D_1/Q_1 = D_2/Q_2 = n$ (say)

Then
$$TC = nC_0 + \frac{D_1 C_{c1}}{2n} + \frac{D_2 C_{c2}}{2n}$$

Differentiating the total cost with respect to n, we get

$$n = \sqrt{\frac{D_1 C_{c1} + D_2 C_{c2}}{4C_0}} = 3.65$$

$$Q_1 = \frac{D_1}{n} = 54.79$$

$$Q_2 = \frac{D_2}{n} = 82.19 \quad TC = 438$$

EXAMPLE 13.7 Messrs Millennium Chemicals Private Ltd own a plant that processes three chemicals in liquid form for consumption within the factory itself. The particulars relating to the three items are given in Table 13.7.

Table 13.7 Particulars Relating to the Three Items

Item	Annual consumption (Litres)	Cost per litre	Processing time for 100 litres
1	36000	20	2 hrs 13 1/3 min
2	30000	40	3 hrs 20 min
3	50000	20	1 hr 36 min

Setting up the plant to start production of any of the three products takes 8 hours for every setup. However, during setup, the plant is not productively engaged, the estimated cost of the idleness of the plant due to setup is Rs. 100 per hour.

The company works on a two-shift-5-day week basis for 50 weeks, the remaining 2 weeks being the annual shut down period for maintenance work. Each shift is of eight hours duration.

The inventory carrying charges per year are 10% of the cost per litre for each chemical.

The chemicals are stored in 20 litre cans. On an average how many such cans should be available to store if the items are produced according to their economic batch quantities? If there is a restriction of 500 cans, what happens to the production batch quantities of the three items?

Solution:
Item A
Given $D = 36000$, $C_o =$ Rs. 100 per hour *8 hrs = Rs. 800, $C = 20$, $i = 10\%$, $C_c =$ Rs. 2
$P = 100 \times 4000 \times 60 \times 3/400 = 180000$ litres

Then
$$Q^* = \sqrt{\frac{2DC_o}{C_c\left(1-\dfrac{D}{P}\right)}}$$

$$= \sqrt{\frac{2 \times 36000 \times 800}{2\left(1-\dfrac{36}{180}\right)}} = 6000 \text{ litres}$$

$$I_{max} = Q\left(1-\frac{D}{P}\right)$$

$$= 6000\left(1-\frac{1}{5}\right) = 4800$$

$$\text{No. of cans} = \frac{I_{max}}{20} = 240 \text{ cans}$$

Item B
Given $D = 30000$, $C_o =$ Rs. 800, $C = 40$, $i = 10\%$, $C_c =$ Rs. 4/unit/year, $P = 100 \times 4000 \times 60/200 = 120000$ litres/year

Then
$$Q^* = \sqrt{\frac{2DC_o}{C_c\left(1-\dfrac{D}{P}\right)}}$$

$$= \sqrt{\frac{2 \times 30000 \times 800}{4\left(1-\dfrac{30}{120}\right)}} = 4000 \text{ litres}$$

and
$$I_{max} = Q\left(1-\frac{D}{P}\right)$$

$$= 4000\left(1-\frac{30}{120}\right) = 3000$$

$$\text{No. of cans} = \frac{3000}{20} = 150 \text{ cans}$$

Item C

$D = 50000$, C_o = Rs. 100 per hour × 8 hrs = Rs. 800, $C = 20$, C_c = Rs. 2, $P = 100 \times 4000 \times 60/96 = 250000$ litres

Then
$$Q^* = \sqrt{\frac{2DC_o}{C_c\left(1-\frac{D}{P}\right)}}$$

$$= \sqrt{\frac{2 \times 50000 \times 800}{2\left(1-\frac{50}{250}\right)}} = 7071.067 \text{ litres}$$

and
$$I_{max} = Q\left(1-\frac{D}{P}\right)$$

$$= 7071.067\left(1-\frac{50}{250}\right) = 5656.85$$

$$\text{No. of cans} = \frac{5656.85}{20} = 282.84 \text{ cans}$$

Total cans required = 240 + 150 + 282.84 = 672.84 cans

An average of 672.84 cans is required. Only 500 cans are available. We wish to

Minimize $\sum_{j=1}^{n} \frac{D_j C_o}{Q_j} + \sum_{j=1}^{n} Q_j i C_j \left(1-\frac{D_j}{P_j}\right)/2$

Subject to

$$\frac{\sum_{j=1}^{n} Q_j\left(1-\frac{D_j}{P_j}\right)S_j}{2} \leq S$$

Here S_j is the number of cans per litre which is 1/10 and S is the total number of cans available. We have used I_m instead of Q because the backordered quantity s is supplied instantaneously and the average quantity $I_m/2$ is to be stored. We have not subtracted setup time component of the available time to compute P_j because we know the number of setups after solving the problem. The Lagrangean function is:

$$\sum_{j=1}^{n} \frac{D_j C_o}{Q_j} + \sum_{j=1}^{n} Q_j i C_j \left(1-\frac{D_j}{P_j}\right)/2 + \lambda \left(\frac{\sum_{j=1}^{n} Q_j\left(1-\frac{D_j}{P_j}\right)S_j}{2} - S\right)$$

Differentiating with respect to Q_j, we get

$$\frac{-D_j C_o}{Q_j^2} + \frac{\left(1-\frac{D_j}{P_j}\right)iC_j}{2} + \frac{\left(1-\frac{D_j}{P_j}\right)\lambda S_j}{2} = 0$$

from which
$$Q_j = \sqrt{\frac{2D_j C_o}{\left(1 - \frac{D_j}{P_j}\right)(iC_j + \lambda S_j)}}$$

Substituting, we get
$$Q_1 = \frac{8485.28}{\sqrt{2 + \frac{\lambda}{10}}}$$

$$Q_2 = \frac{8000}{\sqrt{4 + \frac{\lambda}{10}}}$$

$$Q_3 = \frac{10000}{\sqrt{2 + \frac{\lambda}{10}}}$$

We also have
$$\frac{Q_1\left(1 - \frac{D_1}{P_1}\right)}{20} + \frac{Q_2\left(1 - \frac{D_2}{P_2}\right)}{20} + \frac{Q_3\left(1 - \frac{D_3}{P_3}\right)}{20} = 500$$

Substituting, we have
$$\frac{338.33}{\sqrt{2 + \frac{\lambda}{10}}} + \frac{300}{\sqrt{4 + \frac{\lambda}{10}}} + \frac{400}{\sqrt{2 + \frac{\lambda}{10}}} = 500$$

We calculate the LHS for various values of λ and get the value of λ for which the LHS is closest to 500.

For $\lambda = 10$, LHS = 560.44
For $\lambda = 18$, LHS = 503.32
For $\lambda = 18.5$, LHS = 500.32

We can take $\lambda = 18.5$ from which $Q_1 = 4324.5$, $Q_2 = 3307.6$ and $Q_3 = 5096.47$.

EXAMPLE 13.8 M/s Kanjivellam Enterprises Pvt. Limited own a medium-sized factory divided into 3 manufacturing shops. The factory makes three products A, B and C. Manufacturing one unit of A requires 2 hours at Shop I, 1 hour at Shop II and 2 hours at Shop III. Manufacturing one unit of B requires 3 hours at Shop II and 2 hours at Shop III. Manufacturing one unit of C requires 1 hour at Shop I and 2 hours at Shop III. The available capacities for Shops, I, II, and III are 90 machine-hours, 120 machine-hours and 220 machine-hours, respectively. The profits per unit of A, B and C are Rs. 5, Rs. 5 and Rs. 3, respectively. What is the optimal weekly product-mix that maximizes the total profit of M/s Kanjivellam Enterprises Pvt. Ltd?

Some of the components required for the products A, B and C are bought from outside sources and assembled at the factory. The following particulars are available from the design specifications of the product. Each Unit of A requires 2 units of component P Each Unit of B requires 3 units of component Q. Each Unit of C requires 2 units of P and 3 units of R. The cost per unit of the components P, Q and R given as Rs. 5 and Rs. 4.20 and Rs. 3, in that order.

The factory works 50 weeks in a year. Given that the cost of placing an order is Rs. 50 and the inventory carrying cost is 20 per cent of the unit cost, find the optimal ordering quantity for the components P, Q, and R subject to the restriction that the total average inventory does not exceed Rs. 5000.

Solution: Let $X_1 X_2 X_3$ be the quantities of A, B, and C, respectively produced per week. The objective function is to maximize weekly profit and the three constraints are for the weekly capacity of the machines. The LP formulation is:

Maximize $5X_1 + 5X_2 + 3X_3$

$$2X_1 + 2X_2 + 2X_3 \le 220$$
$$2X_1 + X_3 \le 90$$
$$X_1 + 3X_2 \le 120$$
$$X_1, X_2, X_3 \ge 0$$

The optimal solution to the LP is $X_1 = 15$, $X_2 = 35$ and $X_3 = 60$.

Quantity of P required = $2X_1 + 2X_3 = 150$/week

Q required = $3X_2 = 105$/week

R required = $3X_3 = 180$/week

Item P

$D = 150 \times 50 = 7500$

$C_o = 50$

$i = 20\%$ of Rs. 5 = Re. 1

Then

$$Q^* = \sqrt{\frac{2DC_o}{C_c}}$$

$$= \sqrt{\frac{2 \times 7500 \times 50}{1}} = 866.02$$

$$\frac{QC}{2} = 2165.06$$

Item Q

$D = 150 \times 50 = 5250$

$C_o = 50$

$i = 20\%$ of Rs. 4.2 = Re. 0.84

Then
$$Q^* = \sqrt{\frac{2DC_o}{C_c}}$$
$$= \sqrt{\frac{2 \times 5250 \times 50}{0.84}} = 790.56$$
$$\frac{QC}{2} = 1660.20$$

Item R

$D = 180 \times 50 = 9000$
$C_o = 50$
$C_c = 20\%$ of Rs. 3 = Re. 0.60

Then
$$Q^* = \sqrt{\frac{2DC_o}{C_c}}$$
$$= \sqrt{\frac{2 \times 9000 \times 50}{0.6}} = 1224.74$$
$$\frac{QC}{2} = 1837.117$$

Money value of average inventory = 2165.06 + 1660.20 + 1837.12 = 5662.38
This violates budget restriction of Rs. 5000. We set up the Lagrangean function.

$$L = \sum_{j=1}^{n} \frac{D_j C_o}{Q_j} + \sum_{j=1}^{n} \frac{iQ_j C_j}{2} + \sum_{j=1}^{n} \lambda \left(\frac{Q_j C_j}{2} - B \right)$$

from which we have

$$Q_j = \sqrt{\frac{2D_j C_o}{(i + \lambda) C_j}}$$

The expression for λ is:

$$\lambda = \frac{C_o}{2B^2} \left(\sum_{j=1}^{n} \sqrt{D_j C_j} \right)^2 - i$$

Substituting, we get $\lambda = 0.0565$. Thus,
The order quantity for:
  Item P = 764.71
  Item Q = 698.09
  Item R = 1081.48

EXAMPLE 13.9 Given n items ($j = 1,...,n$) where D_j represents the annual demand and C_j represents the unit price. Let C_o be the order cost for each item and i be the percentage of unit price representing the carrying cost. Let Q_j^* be the economic order quantity. If there is an additional restriction on the average inventory given by $\Sigma Q_j C_j/2 \le B$ and the values of Q_j^* are such that the constraint is violated, prove that

$$\frac{Q_j}{Q_j^*} = \frac{2B}{\sum_{j=1}^{n} Q_j^* C_j}$$

where Q_j is the order quantity obtained using the Lagrangean multipliers.

Solution: We have

$$Q_j^* = \sqrt{\frac{2D_j C_o}{iC_j}}$$

$$Q_j = \sqrt{\frac{2D_j C_o}{(i+\lambda)C_j}}$$

$$\frac{Q_j}{Q_j^*} = \frac{\sqrt{i}}{\sqrt{(i+\lambda)}}$$

From the Lagrangean multiplier formula for constrained inventory problem, we have

$$i+\lambda = \frac{C_o}{2B^2}\left(\sum_{j=1}^{n}\sqrt{D_j C_j}\right)^2$$

Substituting for $\sqrt{(i+\lambda)}$, we get

$$\frac{Q_j}{Q_j^*} = \frac{\sqrt{i}\sqrt{2B}}{\sqrt{C_o}\left(\sum_{j=1}^{n}\sqrt{D_j C_j}\right)^2}$$

From $Q_j^* = \sqrt{\frac{2D_j C_o}{iC_j}}$ we have

$$\frac{Q_j^* C_j}{2} = \frac{\sqrt{2D_j C_o} C_j}{2\sqrt{iC_j}} = \frac{\sqrt{C_o}\sqrt{D_j C_j}}{\sqrt{2}\sqrt{i}}$$

Substituting, we get

$$\frac{Q_j}{Q_j^*} = \frac{2B}{\sum_{j=1}^{n} Q_j^* C_j}$$

EXAMPLE 13.10 Consider the production-consumption inventory model with backorders. The data are $D = 10000$/year, $P = 16000$/year, $C_o = $ Rs. 350/set up, $C_c = $ Rs. 3.6/unit/year and $C_s = $ Rs. 100/unit/year. Find the batch quantity Q and the total cost. Find the time in a cycle, where there is production and consumption, consumption of existing inventory, and build up of backorder.

Solution:

$$Q^* = \sqrt{\frac{2DC_o(C_c + C_s)}{C_c\left(1 - \frac{D}{P}\right)C_s}}$$

$$= \sqrt{\frac{2 \times 10000 \times 350 \times 103.6}{3.6 \times 0.375 \times 100}} = 2317.73$$

$$s = \frac{QC_c\left(1 - \frac{D}{P}\right)}{(C_c + C_s)}$$

$$= \frac{2317.73 \times 3.6 \times 0.375}{103.6} = 30.2$$

$$I_m = Q\left(1 - \frac{D}{P}\right) - s$$

$$= 2317.73 \times 0.375 - 30.2 = 838.95$$

$$T = \frac{Q}{D} = 0.2318$$

$$t_3 = \frac{I_m}{D} = 0.0839$$

$$t_2 = I_m/(P - D) = 0.1398$$

$$t_4 = s/D = 0.0030$$

$$t_3 = s/(P - D) = 0.0053$$

Then

$$TC = \frac{DC_o}{Q} + \frac{I_m C_c}{2}\frac{(t_2 + t_3)}{T} + \frac{sC_s}{2}\frac{(t_1 + t_4)}{T} = 3020.20$$

Time of production and consumption = $t_1 + t_2 = 0.1451$ year
Consumption of existing inventory = $t_3 = 0.0839$ year
Backorder period = $t_4 = 0.0030$ year.

CASE STUDY 13.1: XYZ Limited

XYZ Ltd. has been facing problems with inventory for some time. They decide to do an ABC classification and have decided to look at the inventory policy for the top two items. The data for the two items are given in Table 13.8.

Table 13.8 Data for Two Items

	Item 1	Item 2
Annual demand	25000	40000
Ordering cost	1000	1000
Carrying cost percentage	20%	20%
Unit cost	Rs 50	Rs 75

The company places orders for both the items with the same supplier. Sumit, the materials manager computed the EOQ using the basic model for both the items and discussed the implications with the top management and the purchasing department. Vikas, the purchasing manager, felt that there were too many orders and wanted a limit of a total of 20 orders for both the items. Arjun, the finance manager felt that too much money was locked up in inventory and wanted a limit of Rs 100,000 in average inventory for the two items together.

In reaction to Arjun's observation, Vikas argued that a limit on the number of orders would increase the inventory which would help XYZ in planning uncertainties in lead time demand by having a higher buffer. He supported his argument further by adding that the supplier Gurunath is willing to give a 1% discount on price if the order quantity exceeded 3000 units for either item. XYZ also realizes that by ordering the items together they can save on transportation cost and the order cost comes down to Rs 1500 for the two items together.

The items require special storage facilities including dust proof and air-conditioned environment. Each unit of A requires 2 cubic feet of space and each unit of B requires 3 cubic feet. The space available is 4000 cubic units but the company can increase it by even 50%, if required.

EXERCISES

13.1 A painting company makes two types of paints, Renolac and Nickson. They have a single mixer that mixes the chemicals to make the two types of paints. The data pertaining to Renolac is given in Table 13.9.

Table 13.9 Data Pertaining to Inventory

Annual demand (D)	25000
Production rate (if they produce only Renolac) (P)	40000/year
Set up cost	Rs. 1000 set up
Inventory holding cost	Rs. 20/unit/year
Shortage cost	Rs. 200/unit/year

The company decides to have a production system such that the demand for the item is met both from production and from stock. It also allows shortages to be built and backordered. Compute the production batch quantity Q, the maximum inventory I_{max} and the maximum shortage s. Derive an expression for I_{max} in terms of D, P, Q and s. Find the production cycle for Renolac indicating the actual production time. Determine the time availabe for the company to produce Nickson during Renolac's production cycle.

13.2 The hostel management of a college has decided to place orders for rice and wheat from a nearby grocery chain store. The data pertaining to these items are given in Table 13.10.

Compute the economic order quantities and the associated costs when shortage is not allowed. Find the economic order quantities and the associated costs when shortages are allowed.

Table 13.10 Data for Two Items

	Rice	Wheat
Demand	30000 kg/year	25000 kg/year
Order cost	Rs. 300	Rs. 300
Carrying cost %	18%	18%
Unit price	Rs. 20/kg	Rs. 12 per kg
Shortage cost	Rs. 10/kg/year	Rs. 8/kg/year

The management understands that by ordering the items together they can save one order cost, that is, if both items are ordered together the total order cost is Rs. 300 only. Determine the order quantities under this assumption. The management wants to reduce the total orders in (a) by 10%. Compute the new order quantities and the increase in cost. The grocery shop is willing to give a 1% discount if the total order quantity (when both items are ordered together) exceeds 20,000. Is it profitable to use the discount?

13.3 Consider two items A and B with the data shown in Table 13.11.

Table 13.11 Data for Two Items

Item	Demand	Order cost	Unit cost	Carrying cost %
A	1000/year	Rs. 100	Rs. 20	18%
B	2000/year	Rs. 100	Rs. 10	18%

Find the EOQ for items A and B and the associated costs. If $(C_A Q_A^* + C_B Q_B^*)/2 = P$ and the budget restrictions are of the form $(C_A Q_A + C_B Q_B)/2 \leq P/2$, find the new order quantities and the associated costs. What is the percentage increase in the cost?

13.4 The Mekkit and Yoose Company produces four types of components that are used in the factory itself in the assembly of the final products. The company wishes to produce these items in economic batch quantities and optimize its work-in-progress inventory. The data is given in Table 13.12.

Table 13.12 Data for Four Products

Product	Annual usage	Unit cost (Rs.)	Manufacturing time per unit
A	20000	10	1
B	18000	16	2
C	15000	12.5	2.4
D	22000	12	1.2

Setting up the machines to produce any item takes 5 hours. The company works 8 hours a day, 5 days a week for 50 weeks in a year, the remaining 2 weeks are used for annual maintenance. The setting up of the machine is done by skilled setters whose wage is Rs. 24 per hour. The inventory carrying cost is 18% of the unit cost.

(a) If all items are produced in economic batch quantities, how many hours of overtime will be required?

(b) If overtime is not permitted, set up a Lagrangean formulation for the problem of finding the optimal batch quantities.

(c) Show how this problem can be approached using dynamic programming.

13.5 An item of inventory has an annual demand of 2500 units and costs Rs. 48 per unit. The order cost is Rs. 110 and carrying cost is 50/3% of the unit cost. Shortage cost is Rs. 80 per unit per year. Determine the duration for which shortage occurs in every cycle when the order quantity as well as the permitted shortage is optimal.

13.6 Shankar has to supply 10,000 bearings per day to an automobile manufacturer. He begins a production run every 10.5 days. The carrying cost is 2 paise per bearing per year and the set up cost is Rs. 18. What should be his optimal production rate to meet the demand?

13.7 The production process of M/s Kutti Chemicals results in the continuous build up of a toxic waste at the rate of W kg/year. The pile of waste is chemically destroyed at regular intervals at the rate of T kg/year ($T > W$). Waste emitted during the period is also destroyed as it comes out. The cost of holding up the piled up waste under controlled conditions is Rs. h per kg/year and the cost of destroying the pile is Rs. k irrespective of the quantity destroyed. Determine the optimal levels of waste build up at which destruction must be arranged and hence determine the optimal periodicity of destruction.

13.8 A chemical company blends and processes a certain raw material to obtain a substance for its own consumption throughout the year. The following data are available:

Annual consumption = 36000 litres

Cost per litre = Rs. 20

Processing time for 100 litres = 2 hours 13 1/3 minutes

Set up cost = Rs. 800 per set up

The company works for 8 hours per shift for 2 shifts, 5 days a week for 50 weeks in a year. The inventory carrying charges are 10% of the cost per year. The company is willing to let shortages to occur since the shortage cost is only Rs. 25 per unit per year. Determine besides the optimal manufacturing quantity and shortage level, the following duration per cycle under optimal conditions:

(a) Production during which only the backlogged shortages are cleared.
(b) Production when the inventory is above zero level.
(c) Demands met as they occur.
(d) Shortages occur, production yet to commence.

13.9 Shlok, the manager of a chemical plant faces the problem of effluent disposal at one of the plants. The production process results in a continuous build up of an effluent at the rate of W kg per year. This is to be destroyed periodically and each destruction takes a certain amount of time. The rate of destruction (U kg/year) is much higher than the effluent build up rate. The factory needs to maintain a minimum level of effluent to retain the wetness of the ground and this is called **zero level**. Unfortunately, the treatment process destroys the effluent completely and it costs the company b rupees per kg per year to restore it to zero level. The cost of keeping the untreated effluent above zero level is h rupees per kg per year while the cost of destroying the effluent each time is k rupees per setting, irrespective of the quantity destroyed. Determine the optimal level up to which the effluent should be allowed to build up and the permissible erosion below zero level at each setting for destruction of the effluent. How often should the destruction occur under optimal conditions? What will be the duration of destruction of each cycle? How much time would it take in each cycle to restore the zero level of the effluent from the dry floor condition after each destruction?

13.10 Consider a single item inventory model with **backordering** with the following data (in the usual notation):

$$D = 30000/\text{year}, \ C_o = \text{Rs. } 500/\text{order}, \ C_c = 10\% \text{ of Rs. } 60/\text{unit/year}$$

(a) Find the value of C_s for which $Q^* = 2500$.
(b) For the C_s in (a) find the quantity backordered and the total cost at the optimum.
(c) The supplier is willing to give a 1% discount if the order quantity exceeds 3000 units. Is it advantageous to accept the discount?
(d) Each unit requires a storage space of 2 sq. ft. There is a space restriction of 2000 sq. ft. for this item and an inventory restriction of Rs. 54000. What happens to the ordering quantity?
(e) What should be the value of s for the chosen order quantity under (d) such that there is minimum increase in the total cost when compared to (b)? What is the corresponding % increase?

13.11 Consider the data for a two item inventory model given in Table 13.13.
The company initially does not want to consider shortage cost but realizes that a 1% discount can be got if the order quantity is 100 units more than the EOQ for each item. It is willing to try and experiment with backorders. Verify if the discount can be accepted.

Table 13.13 Data for Two Items

	Item A	Item B
Annual demand	10000	15000
Order cost	300	300
Carrying cost	20% of Rs. 30	20% of Rs. 50
Shortage cost	80	150

13.12 Given n items ($j = 1,...,n$) where D_j represents the annual demand and C_j represents the unit price. Let C_o be the order cost for each item and i be the percentage of unit price representing the carrying cost. Let Q_j^* be the economic order quantity and N_j represent the number of orders/year for item j. If there is an additional restriction that $\Sigma N_j \leq N$ and the values of N_j are such that the constraint is violated, prove that

$$\frac{Q_j}{Q_j^*} = \frac{\sum_{j=1}^{n} N_j}{N}$$

where Q_j is the order quantity obtained using the Lagrangean multipliers.

Appendix

SOLUTIONS TO SELECTED EXERCISE PROBLEMS

Chapter 1

1.1 Let X_j be the distance covered by person i using the bicycle. Person covers the distance $d - X_i$ by walk.

Time taken by person i is $t_i = \dfrac{X_i}{b_i} + \dfrac{(d-X)}{a_i}$

The objective is to find the time when all three reach at the earliest. This is to minimize the maximum of the three t_i values. The formulation is
Minimize u

$$u \geq \frac{X_i}{b_i} + \frac{(d-X)}{a_i} \quad \text{for } i = 1, 2, 3$$

$X_i, u \geq 0$

1.2 Let X_1 be the number of large refrigerator produced and X_2 be the number of small refrigerator produced. We assume that each refrigerator requires one compressor and one body.

Let P be the time available in the compressor shop. The time to produce one large compressor is $P/1200$ and the time to produce a small compressor is $P/3000$. If we make X_1 large and X_2 small compressors, time required is $\dfrac{PX_1}{1200} + \dfrac{PX_2}{3000}$. The constraint becomes

$$\frac{PX_1}{1200} + \frac{PX_2}{3000} \leq P \quad \text{which reduces to}$$

$$5X_1 + 2X_2 \leq 6000$$

Similarly, the capacity constraint on the body reduces to

$$5X_1 + 3X_2 \leq 7500$$

We also have $X_1 \geq 2000$ and $X_2 \geq 1000$.
The objective function is maximize $1500X_1 + 1000X_2 - 1500000$
The non-negativity constraints are $X_1, X_2 \geq 0$

1.4 Let X_j and Y_j be the number of type A and type B shirts sent to retailer j. The constraints are

$$\sum_j X_j \leq P$$

$$\sum_j Y_j \leq Q$$

$X_j + Y_j + u_j \geq D_j$ where u_j is the unfulfilled demand for retailer j.

$$\frac{0.9 D_j}{\sum_j D_j} \leq \frac{X_j}{\sum_j X_j} \leq \frac{1.1 D_j}{\sum_j D_j}$$

The objective function minimizes the cost of production of two types and the cost of unfulfilled demand

Minimize $R \sum_j X_j + S \sum_j Y_j + \sum_j c_j u_j$

The non-negativity restrictions are $X_j, Y_j, u_j \geq 0$

1.6 Let X_1, X_2, X_3 be the number of employees who are on leave on Tuesday, Wednesday and Thursday, respectively. Since employees work for four days and for three consecutive days, all have to work on Monday and Friday.
The constraints are $X_1 + X_2 + X_3 \geq 6$

$$X_1 + X_2 + X_3 \geq 6$$
$$X_2 + X_3 \geq 4$$
$$X_1 + X_3 \geq 5$$
$$X_1 + X_2 \geq 3$$
$$X_1 + X_2 + X_3 \geq 7$$
$$X_1, X_2, X_3 \geq 0$$

Since we want maximum people to go on leave, we wish to
Minimize $X_1 + X_2 + X_3$

The constraint $X_1 + X_2 + X_3 \geq 6$ may be left out because it is dominated by the constraint $X_1 + X_2 + X_3 \geq 7$.

1.8 Let X_{ij} be the number of parts i produced in department j. The capacity constraints are

$$\frac{X_{11}}{8} + \frac{X_{21}}{5} + \frac{X_{31}}{10} \leq 100$$

$$\frac{X_{12}}{6} + \frac{X_{22}}{12} + \frac{X_{32}}{4} \leq 80$$

We have produced $X_{11} + X_{12}$ of part 1, $X_{21} + X_{22}$ of part 2 and $X_{31} + X_{32}$ of part 3. The total products made is the minimum of the three that we would like to maximize. The formulation is
Maximize u

$$u \leq X_{11} + X_{12}$$
$$u \leq X_{21} + X_{22}$$
$$u \leq X_{31} + X_{32}$$
$$\frac{X_{11}}{8} + \frac{X_{21}}{5} + \frac{X_{31}}{10} \leq 100$$
$$\frac{X_{12}}{6} + \frac{X_{22}}{12} + \frac{X_{32}}{4} \leq 80$$
$$X_{ij} \geq 0$$

1.11 Let X_1, X_2 and X_3 be the number of answer scripts corrected by the three teachers, respectively. Each teacher works for a maximum of four hours. We have constrains

$$X_1 \leq 40$$
$$X_2 \leq 32$$
$$X_3 \leq 36$$

The expected number of reevaluation would be 5%, 3% and 2% of the sheets, respectively. This gives us an objective function
Minimize $5X_1 + 2X_2 + 3X_3$
and $X_1, X_2, X_3 \geq 0$

1.12 Let X_{ijk} be the number of cartons of fruit k transported from grower j to plant i.
The requirement constraint at plant i is $\sum_j X_{ijk} \geq b_{ik}$

The availability constraint at the grower is $\sum_i X_{ijk} \geq a_{jk}$

The objective function is to minimize the sum of purchase and transportation costs. This is given by
Minimize $\sum_j \sum_k C_{jk} \sum_i X_{ijk} + \sum_i \sum_j \sum_k C_{ijk} X_{ijk}$
Since it is an LP formulation $X_{ijk} \geq 0$.

Chapter 2

2.1 The unrestricted variable X_3 is written as $X_5 - X_6$ where $X_5, X_6 \geq 0$. Simplex gives the optimal solution in one iteration with $X_6 = 2$ and $Z = 4$. The problem does not have an alternate optimum.

2.2 The unrestricted variable X_1 is written as $X_3 - X_4$ where $X_3, X_4 \geq 0$. Simplex gives the optimum $X_3 = 3, Z = 6$ which result in the solution $X_1 = 3$.
The graph considering X_1 unrestricted has an unbounded region with corner points (3, 0), (0, 3/2) and (–7, 5). The objective function maximize $2X_1 + X_2$ gives the optimal solution $X_1 = 3, X_2 = 0, Z = 6$.

2.3 (a) $b, d \leq 0$ and one of them is zero. If $b = 0$, either e or $f > 0$. If $d = 0, c > 0$
(b) Either $A < 0$ or X_5 is an artificial variable and $A > 0$
(c) $b > 0$ and $e = f$ and both $e, f > 0$
(d) $d > 0$ c $\leq 0, A \geq 0$
(e) $b > 0, f > e$ and $e, f > 0$. The increase in the objective function is $100b/f$.

2.4 $X_1 = 5.4, X_2 = 1.2, X_3 = 0. Z = 12$. Simplex will have three artificial variables and after three iterations will give the optimum solution. Here, there is no alternate optimum because there is only one feasible point which is optimal.

2.7 We can solve this by the graphical method. The corner pints are (0, –8), (0, 4) and (24/7, 16/7). The optimal solution is $X_1 = 24/7, X_2 = 16/7$ with $Z = 272/7$.

2.8 $X_1 = 0, X_4 = 0$ $X_2 = 4, X_3 = 16/3$
$X_2 = 0, X_3 = 0$ $X_1 = 12, X_4 = 16$
$X_2 = 0, X_4 = 0$ $X_1 = 4, X_3 = 8/3$

2.9 The simplex algorithm would require three artificial variables to obtain an initial basic feasible solution. Depending on the tie breaking rule to enter a variable, it can terminate with the solution $X_2 = 20/6, a_1 = 52/6, a_2 = 46/6$.

2.10 The optimum solution by simplex algorithm is $X_3 = 12, Z = 0$. If this problem represents a practical product mix problem, we need to find the contribution of X_3 to the objective. It may also be necessary to verify the sign of the inequalities.

2.11 To find whether the system $\Sigma a_{ij} X_j \leq 0, i = 1, m, \Sigma b_j X_j > 0, X_j \geq 0$ has a solution, we can formulate an LP which maximizes $\Sigma b_j X_j$ subject to the constraints $\Sigma a_{ij} X_j \leq 0$, $i = 1, m, X_j \geq 0$. If the objective function value at the optimum is positive, the given system has a solution.

2.13 The corner points are (1, 0), (0, 2), (–1, 0) and (0, –2). When we maximize $X_1 + X_2$ subject to non-negativity restrictions on X_1 and X_2, the optimum solution is $X_1 = 0, X_2 = 2$ with $Z = 2$.
When X_1 and X_2 are unrestricted in sign and we minimize $X_1 + 10X_2$, the optimum solution is $X_1 = 0, X_2 = -2$ with $Z = -20$.

2.14 The variable with the largest c_i/a_i is the basic variable at the optimum with value b/a_i and $Z = bc_i/a_i$.

2.17 The solution $X_1 = X_2 = X_3 = X_4 = X_5 = 1$ is feasible but not basic feasible. The basic solution $X_2 = 3, X_1 = 0$ is basic feasible.

2.18 The problem has alternate optima. Any non corner point solution that is feasible and has objective function value = 13 is a non basic optimal solution. The solution $X_1 = 1$, $X_2 = 5/63$ is a non basic optimal solution.

2.21 The graph will show that the problem is infeasible.

Chapter 3

3.1 The solution is $X_1 = X_2 = 3$. The value of the dual is $y = [5\ 1]$.
$X_1 = 15/2$, $X_4 = 3/2$ with $Z = 105/2$.

3.2 Maximize $8Y_1 + 10Y_2 + 12Y_3$
subject to
$$4Y_1 + 5Y_2 + 6Y_3 \geq 5$$
$$-7Y_1 + 6Y_2 + -9Y_3 = -9$$
$$6Y_1 + 4Y_2 + 8Y_3 \leq 6$$
$$7Y_1 - 5Y_2 + 7Y_3 \leq -5$$

$Y_1 \leq 0$, Y_2 unrestricted in sign and $Y_3 \geq 0$

3.3 Unique optimum with $y_7 = 7$, $y_5 = 4$ with $Z = 0$.

3.4 The dual is solved using the graphical method. The solution is (1, 0) with $Z = 13$.
$X_1 = 13/5$, $X_5 = 19/8$ with $Z = 13$.

3.5 $X_1 = 1/5$, $X_2 = 19/10$. This is feasible to the primal.
$Y_1 = 7/10$, $Y_2 = 24/10$ with $w = 187/10$. This is feasible to the dual and hence optimal.

3.8 (a) The dual solution is $Y_1 = 8$, $Y_2 = 0$ with $W = 64$.
(b) $Y_2 = 0$, which means that resource is not fully utilized. It is not profitable to buy an additional resource at Re 1.
(c) The present solution is optimal with $Z = 48$.
(d) $X_1 = 8$, $X_3 = 4$ with $Z = 64$.
(e) $X_1 = 4$

3.10 (b) $Y_2 = 3/2$, $Y_3 = 1$, $Z = 72$, $X_1 = 0$, $X_2 = 12$.
(c) $Y_1 = 3$ and $Z = 54$, $X_2 = 9$ and $Z = 54$.
(d) There is no change to the primal and dual optimal solutions.
(e) Alternate optima. One more simplex iteration can be carried out.

3.11 (a) $Y_1 = 3/2$, $Y_3 = 1$, $W = 17/2$
(b) $Y_3 = 1$, $Y_2 = 3$ with $W = 13$. There is an alternate optimum.
(c) It is not profitable to use the new raw material.
(d) $y_1 = 3$ and $W = 12$.

3.12 (a) $X_1 = X_2 = 5$ with $Z = 30$.
(b) When $a \leq 1$, variable X_3 will enter the basis.
(c) The present optimal solution satisfies the additional constraint. Therefore, it will remain optimal.

3.14 (a) $X_1 = 6$, $X_2 = 9$, $Z = 102$.
(b) $Z = 132 + 5/3 = 401/3$.
(c) The present solution remains optimal. The objective function value is 138.

3.17 (a) $X_1 = 20/7$, $X_2 = 2/7$, $Z = -18/7$.
(b) Variable X_1 leaves the basis (dual simplex iteration) and there is no entering variable. The problem has infeasible solution.

Chapter 4

4.1 Venus gets extra 2 units and Mercury gets extra 1 unit. The total cost is 160. The problem has alternate optima.

4.4 $X_{12} = 15, X_{21} = 25, X_{31} = 5, X_{34} = 25, X_{43} = 25, X_{45} = 20$ with Profit = 570. There are multiple optimal solutions. The additional 25 units left after allocating 30 to A and 15 to B is given to C. B and D do not get the extra amount.

4.5 The optimal solution is $X_{11} = 25, X_{21} = 15, X_{22} = 10, X_{32} = 5, X_{32} = 40, X_{43} = 25$ and $X_{44} = 95$ with profit = –5. There is a bank loan of 25 for 1 month.

4.6 The present degenerate basic feasible solution is optimal with cost = 482.

4.7 The $X_{13} = 50, X_{11} = 22, X_{23} = 43$. We allot $X_{12} = 39, X_{22} = 39$ and $X_{32} = 22$. The cost of this allocation is 2776. The optimal solution has $Z = 2732$.

4.8 (a) The given feasible solution has a loop that is broken. The revised allocations are $X_{12} = 35, X_{14} = 5, X_{24} = 35, X_{25} = 15, X_{33} = 30, X_{41} = 45$ and $X_{45} = 15$. The cost reduces from 1805 to 1745.
(b) $C_{11} \leq 15$.

4.10 The given solution has a loop. This is broken but the cost remains the same. The cost is 482. This solution is optimal with cost = 482. The given feasible solution is not basic feasible but is optimal.

4.11 $X_{31} = 62, X_{23} = 53, X_{12} = 61, X_{22} = 29$ and $X_{32} = 10$. The cost is 2688. The solution from VAM with cost = 2688 is found to be optimal. The problem has alternate optima.

4.12 The present solution is not basic feasible because it has a loop. The basic feasible solution will be degenerate $X_{21} = 40, X_{21} = 40, X_{23} = 10, X_{33} = 22$. The cost is 432.

4.14 $\beta = 3, \alpha \geq 8$. If $\alpha = \beta = M, X_{11} = 30, X_{13} = 20, X_{22} = 30, X_{23} = 30$.

4.16 $X_{31} = X_{22} = X_{13} = 40$ with 1200 hours. There are multiple optimal solutions. The optimal solution indicates that an entire class gets allotted to a new elective. When we have an equal number of supply and demand points and the same supply and demand, the transportation problem becomes an assignment problem which is the problem of allotting batches to electives.

4.17 Solving a maximization transportation problem, the optimal allocation indicates that the first professor takes students 2 and 5, second professor takes students 1 and 3 and the fourth student goes to professor 3. The total preference is 33. There are alternate optimum solutions.

Chapter 5

5.1 $X_{11} = X_{22} = X_{33} = X_{44} = X_{55} = 1$ with profit = 194.

5.2 $X_{13} = X_{24} = X_{31} = X_{45} = X_{52} = 1$ with $Z = 37$. We can form two groups $\{1, 3\}$ and $\{2, 4, 5\}$ from this solution, We formulate a 6×6 assignment problem with each row repeated three times. The solution is $X_{14} = X_{25} = X_{36} = X_{41} = X_{52} = X_{63} = 1$. Ram gets cities 4 and 5, while Shyam gets cities 1, 2 and 3.

Appendix   499

5.4 $X_{15} = X_{23} = X_{31} = X_{42} = X_{54} = 1$ with $Z = 220$. Delete all costs less than or equal to 40 (replace them with M) and solve. $X_{14} = X_{22} = X_{35} = X_{43} = X_{51} = 1$ with $Z = 320$.

5.5 We have a 5×5 assignment problem where the profits are calculated when wine planted in year i is used in year j. The optimum solution is $X_{11} = X_{22} = X_{33} = X_{44} = X_{55} = 1$ with profit = 217.

5.8 Starting with $X_{22} = 1$, we get the other assignments as X_{11} and X_{33}. We get four lines as the minimum lines to cover all zeros. This means that 4 assignments are possible. We assign $X_{23} = 1$ in the unassigned column and get other assignments as $X_{32} = X_{44} = 1$. This along with $X_{11} = 1$ completes the optimum solution. This example tells us that starting with an arbitrary assignment can give us less than optimum number of assignments.

5.10 Create a 8×8 assignment problem by duplicating each row twice. The optimum solution (minimization) is $X_{14} = X_{25} = X_{32} = X_{48} = X_{56} = X_{67} = X_{73} = X_{81} = 1$ with $Z = 55$.

5.12 We cannot assign the fifth classroom to the fifth course. We have a cost of M here. The optimum solution to the assignment problem (minimization) is $X_{11} = X_{25} = X_{34} = X_{43} = X_{52} = 1$ with $Z = 57$.

5.13 Create a balanced assignment problem by adding two dummy rows. The optimum solution to the minimization assignment problem is $X_{16} = X_{27} = X_{33} = X_{41} = X_{55} = X_{64} = X_{72} = 1$ with $Z = 50$.

The present solution has two experienced operators assigned. If all experienced operators have to be assigned, put M in the dummy columns involving all experienced operators. The optimal solution becomes $X_{12} = X_{26} = X_{33} = X_{41} = X_{57} = X_{64} = X_{75} = 1$ with $Z = 60$.

5.15 $X_{15} = X_{21} = X_{33} = X_{42} = X_{54} = 1$ with $Z = 33$.

Chapter 6

6.2 The leaving variable is r such that r is Minimum $\{\max (\theta_r, \alpha_r), U_r\}$. If a_j is positive, $\theta_j = (U_j - b_j)/a_j$. If a_j is negative, $\alpha_j = b_j/a_j$. The leaving variable is r such that r is Minimum $\{\max (\theta_r, \alpha_r), U_r\}$.

6.3 $X_1 = 6, X_2 = 1, Z = 34$.

6.4 $X_2 = 3, X_3 = 9, Z = 54$.

6.5 (a) $X_2 = 15/13$ and $X_3 = 33/13$ with $Z = 159/13$. $y_1 = 7/13, y_2 = 5/13$ and $W = 159/13$.
(b) $X_2 = 5/2, X_3 = 2$ and $Z = 16$.

6.6 The dual to the given problem is Minimize $5Y_1 + 12Y_2$ subject to $Y_1 + 2Y_2 \geq 6, -Y_1 + 3Y_2 \geq 4, Y_1, Y_2 \geq 0$. The required system of inequalities is
$X_1 - X_2 \leq 5, 2X_1 + 3X_2 \leq 12, Y_1 + 2Y_2 \geq 6, -Y_1 + 3Y_2 \geq 4, 6X_1 + 4X_2 \geq 5Y_1 + 12Y_2, X_1, X_2, Y_1, Y_2 \geq 0$.

6.7 $X_2 = 2$ and $X_4 = 4$. This means that out of the corner points for the first problem only $(0, 0)$ and $(0, 8/3)$ qualify. Similarly from the corner points of the second sub problem only $(0, 0)$ and $(0, 6)$ qualify. The three corner points are $(0\ 0\ 0\ 6), (0\ 8/3\ 0\ 0)$ and $(0\ 8/3\ 0\ 6)$. If they have weights λ_1, λ_2 and λ_3, respectively, we have $8/3(\lambda_2 + \lambda_3) = 2, 6 (\lambda_1 + \lambda_3) = 9$ and $\lambda_1, \lambda_2, \lambda_3 \geq 0$. This gives us $\lambda_1 = 3/4$ and $\lambda_3 = 3/4$.

6.8 From the constraint $Y_1 + Y_2 \leq 4$ is left out because it is dominated by the constraint $4Y_1 + 4Y_2 \leq 3$. Subproblem $S1$ has the constraint $4Y_1 + 4Y_2 \leq 3$. $S2$ has the constraints $Y_3 + 2Y_4 \leq 6, 2Y_3 - Y_4 \leq 1$. The corner points for $S1$ are $(0, 0)$, $(3/4, 0)$ and $(0, 3/4)$. The corner points for $S2$ are $(0, -1), (0, 3)$ and $(8/5, 11/5)$. We start with an artificial variable. The solution $(3/4, 0, 0, 3)$ is optimal with $W = 69/2$.

6.10 $S1$ constraints are $5X_1 + X_2 \leq 12$. The corner points are $(0, 0), (12/5, 0)$ and $(0, 12)$. The second sub problem $S2$ has constraints $X_3 + X_4 \geq 5$ and $X_3 + 5X_4 \leq 50$. The corner points are $(5, 0), (0, 5), (50, 0)$ and $(0, 10)$. The point $(0, 0, 0, 0)$ is not feasible and we start with an artificial variable.

The corner points in the optimum basis are $(0, 12, 5, 0)$ with weight $22/45$ and $(0, 12, 50, 0)$ with weight $23/45$. The optimal solution is $X_2 = 12, X_3 = 28$ with $Z = 88$.

6.11 The total number of cuts $= 268.625$. Objective function of the dual is $y_b = 268.625$. Hence, optimal. The entering pattern [4 0 0] cannot reduce the number of cuts. It provides an alternate optimum.

6.12 Let X_j be the number of sheets of pattern j cut from 16" sheets and Y_j be the number of sheets from 18" sheets.
Minimize $\sum X_j + \sum Y_j$
$$\sum a_{ij} X_j + \sum a_{ij} Y_j = b_i$$
$$X_j, Y_j \geq 0$$

We can start with a basic feasible set. We need to solve two knapsack problems to verify whether there is an entering pattern.

6.16 Let X_{ij} be the hours spent on topic i from book j. The constraints are
$$\sum_i X_{ij} + \eta_{1j} - \rho_{1j} = a_j$$
$$\sum_i \sum_j m_{ij} X_{ij} + \eta_2 - \rho_2 = 50$$
$$\sum_j m_{ij} X_{ij} - b_i + \eta_{3i} - \rho_{3i} = 0$$

The objective is to Minimize $\left[\sum_j \eta_{1j} + \rho_{1j}, \eta_2, \sum_i \eta_{3i} + \rho_{3i} \right]$
$$X_{ij}, \eta, \rho \geq 0$$

6.17 $X_1 = 3, X_3 = 5$ with $= 35$.

6.18 Based on smallest subscript rule X_1 enters. There is a tie for the leaving variable. Based on smallest subscript rule variable X_3 leaves. The optimal solution is found in one iteration. It is $X_1 = 4, Z = 40$.

6.19 $X_{11} = 10, X_{12} = 30, X_{21} = 20, X_{23} = 40$ with $Z = 600$.

Chapter 7

7.2 There are several formulations. There are n jobs and m machines. The machines are numbered according to the order of the visits. We define S_{ij} to be the start time of job i on machine j. The completion time for job I on machine j is $S_{ij} + p_{ij}$, where p_{ij} is the known processing time.

For each job, it has to immediately start on its next machine. This is given by $S_{i,j+1} = S_{i,j} + p_{i,j} \forall j = 1, m - 1$ and $i = 1, \ldots n$.

Each machine can process only one job at a time. For any two jobs i and k either $S_{i,j} \geq S_{k,j} + p_{k,j}$ or $S_{k,j} \geq S_{i,j} + p_{i,j}$. This is modeled as two constraints $S_{k,j} + p_{k,j} - S_{i,j} \leq M\delta_{ijk}$, $S_{i,j} + p_{i,j} - S_{k,j} \leq M(1 - \delta_{ijk})$ for every pair i, k on every machine j.

The objective is to minimize u such that $u \geq S_{i,m} + p_{i,m} \forall i$. Also $S_{ij} \geq 0$ and $\delta_{ijk} = 0,1$. The order of S_{i1} would give us the order of sequence of the jobs.

7.4 The sum of the reference times is 23 assuming that he reads one book at a time, completes the book and takes the next. The maximum due date is 16. The lower bound is $23 - 16 = 7$.
The optimal sequence is 2-1-3-4 with a total delay of 12.

7.5 $X_1 = 11/2$, $Z = 165/2$. The IP optimal solution is $X_1 = 4$, $X_3 = 1$ with $Z = 76$.

7.6 The optimum solution is $X_3 = X_4 = 1$ with $Z = 900$.

7.7 The optimal solution is $X_1 = X_2 = 0$, $X_3 = 1$, $Z = 13$.

7.10 The LP optimum is $X_1 = 10/3$, $Z = 200$. The optimum solution is $Z = 190$. $X_4 = X_7 = 1$ with $Z = 60 + 60 + 10 + 3 = 133$ as the optimal solution.

7.12 Solution is $Y_1 = Y_4 = 1$ which is choose projects 2, 3, 5 with $Z = 5$.

7.14 $X_1 = X_3 = 1$, $Z = 12$.

7.15 Unbounded Solution.

7.16 LP optimum is $X_2 = 10/3$, $X_4 = 2/3$, $Z = 50/3$. The tighter LB is $50/3 + 1/3*2/3 \div 2/3 = 17$. The IP optimum is $X_1 = 1$, $X_2 = 3$, $Z = 19$.

7.19 The given LP has an unbounded solution. Therefore, the IP also has an unbounded solution.

7.20 Let $X_j = 1$ if song j is chosen. The constraints are $\Sigma t_j X_j \leq 60$, and $X_2 + X_4 + X_6 + X_8 \geq 2$. $X_j = 0,1$. The objective is Maximize $\Sigma d_j X_j$.

7.21 Let $X_1 = Y_1 + 2Y_2 + 4Y_3$ and $X_2 = Y_4 + 2Y_5 + 4Y_6$. The objective function is Maximize $4Y_1 + 8Y_2 + 16Y_3 + 3Y_4 + 6Y_5 + 12Y_6$. The constraints are $3Y_1 + 6Y_2 + 12Y_3 + Y_4 + 2Y_5 + 4Y_6 \leq 12$. $Y_1 + 2Y_2 + 4Y_3 + 4Y_4 + 8Y_5 + 16Y_6 \leq 8$, $Y_1 + Y_2 + Y_3 = 1$, $Y_4 + Y_5 + Y_6 = 1$, $Y_j = 0,1$.

7.23 We start with X_3 and X_4 as basic variables. The starting solution is both primal and dual infeasible. We start by entering X_2 into the basis. Variable X_4 leaves the basis. We have a leaving variable and are unable to find an entering variable since all elements in the row have positive coefficients. The problem is infeasible.

Chapter 8

8.2 $X_{15} = 4$, $X_{24} = 3$, $X_{35} = 5$, $X_{56} = 5$, $X_{46} = 1$. $Z = 52$.

8.3 The shortest path is 1-3-7-9-11 distance = 125.
The shortest distance from 1 to 11 passing through 4 is 156. The third shortest path is 1-3-6-9-11 with $Z = 145$. We have three solutions with $Z = 145$.

8.4 The solution is 4-3, 3-3, 2-1, 1-1, 2-3 and 1-3 with $Z = 47$.

8.7 The maximum spanning tree for the above matrix is as follows: 1-5 (9), 1-10 (9), 3-10 (9), 2-8 (9), 4-7 (9), 1-9 (8), 2-6 (8), 1-2 (6) and 1-4 (6). Four groups are obtained by deleting the four last edges that were added. The groups are {1, 5, 10, 3, 9}, {2, 8}, {4, 7} and {6}.

8.10 The node labels are 0, 9, 6, 17, 14 and 23 for the six nodes. The longest distance is 23 and the path is 1-2-4-6.

8.11 $X_{14} = 3$, $X_{16} = 2$, $X_{23} = 4$, $X_{35} = 2$, $X_{45} = 1$ with $Z = 25$.

8.12 The shortest distance between 1 and 5 using Dijkstra's algorithm is 20 and the path is 1-4-5.

8.13 There are two shortest paths from 1 to 9. These are 1-3-6-8-9 and 1-2-6-8-9 with distance = 30. One of them qualifies to be the second shortest path. The path 1-3-5-8-9 with $Z = 31$ is the third shortest path.

8.14 There are four flow augmenting paths 1-2-4-6 with flow = 20. 1-3-6 with flow = 30, 1-5-6 with flow = 10 and 1-3-5-6 with flow = 20. The maximum flow = 80.

8.15 The minimum spanning tree has the following arcs 1-6, 1-4, 1-5, 2-5, 1-3 with distance = 23. The degree of vertex 1 is 4, which is higher than the allowable 3. A heuristic solution would be to use another arc instead of 1-3. If we use arc 2-3 (or 2-6) we have a heuristic solution with distance = 24.

Chapter 9

9.1 The optimal solution to the given TSP is 1-3-4-8-10-9-7-6-2-5-1 with distance = 89. Nearest neighbourhood search solution starting with 5 is 5-2-3-1-4-6-7-10-8-9-5 with $Z = 105$. Solving it is an assignment problem, we get a lower bound of 86 with the assignment solution $X_{13} = X_{25} = X_{31} = X_{46} = X_{52} = X_{64} = X_{79} = X_{8,10} = X_{97} = X_{10,8} = 1$.

9.3 The lower bound to the TSP using an assignment solution is 652, with the assignments $X_{15} = X_{26} = X_{34} = X_{43} = X_{51} = X_{62} = X_{78} = X_{87} = 1$.

If city 1 is the depot, the three routes are d-2-7-d, d-4-3-6-d and d-5-8-d with used capacity = 16, 18 and 14, respectively. It would be a good idea to choose the city with least total distance as the depot. In our example, City 8 with total distance of 1179 can be the depot.

9.6 The minimum spanning tree has the edges 1-2, 1-4, 1-8, 1-10, 2-9, 3-5, 4-3, 5-6, 6-7 with total weight = 1268. This is a lower bound to the TSP. An assignment problem gives LB = 1527. The twice around the tree heuristic gives 1-8-10-9-2-4-3-5-7-6-1 with distance = 2194. The matching based method gives 1-10-8-4-3-5-6-7-9-2-1 with distance = 2264. 3-opt gives 1-2-9-8-10-7-6-5-3-4-1 with distance = 1068.

9.7 Edges 1-3, 3-5 and 4-6 have to be duplicated. Extra distance = 21.

9.8 An assignment = 42. A nearest neighbourhood search gives 1-6-4-2-3-5-1 with $Z = 42$. Hence, the value 42 is optimal.

9.9 Minimum distance is maximum savings. The Clarke Wright solution is d-4-6-d, d-2-3-d and d-1-5-d.

9.10 The assignment solution is $X_{13} = X_{24} = X_{35} = X_{42} = X_{51} = 1$ with $Z = 44$. The solution 1-2-4-3-5-1 with $Z = 46$ is optimal.

9.12 The feasible solution 1-2-3-4-5-1 has $Z = 54$. Taking a-b as 1-2, p-q as 3-4 and u-v as 4-5, we get 1-4-2-3-5-1 with $Z = 46$.

9.14 A nearest neighbourhood search algorithm starting from 2 gives 2-4-5-3-1 with total changeover time = 39 units. This is not optimal.

9.15 The Clarke and Wright solution is 1-5, 3-6 and 2-4 with saving = 36. A better solution could be 1-3, 5-6 and 2-4 with savings = 37.

Chapter 10

10.2 The solution is $X_1^* = 2/7$, $X_2^* = 0$, $Z = -4/7$.

10.3 $X_1 = 2$ giving us $X_2 = 3$ and $X_3 = 5$, $Z = 1250$.

10.4 The optimal solution is to produce each month's demand in the same month. The minimum cost is 99.

10.5 The given function is quadratic and differentiation gives minimum. The maximum is obtained at the extreme points in each stage. The best solution is $X_1 = 9$ with $Z = 693$.

10.6 $X_1 = 10$, $X_2 = X_3 = 0$ with $Z = 10$.

10.7 The answer is to allot everything to B in all the three periods. The units produced is 809375 units.

10.8 The constraint is written as $4/3 X_1 + 2X_2 + X_3 \leq 10$. The maximum is at $X_1 = 6$, $X_2 = 0$, $X_3 = 2$ with $Z = 44$.

10.9 $X_1 = 3.07$, $X_2 = 4.45$, $X_3 = 2.48$, $Z = 19.36$. The maximum value of the minimum is when the values are equal.

10.10 $X_1 = 480$, $X_2 = 240$, $X_3 = 160$, $X_4 = 120$ with $Z = 476000$.

10.11 The solution is $X_1 = 55$, $X_2 = 60$, $X_3 = 65$ with $Z = 111500$.

10.12 The objective function becomes maximize $(X_1 - 2) * (X_2 + 3) - 6$. The solution is $X_1 = 6$, $X_2 = 5$ with $Z = 32$.

10.13 The solution is $X_1 = 90$, $X_2 = 90$, $X_3 = 85$, $X_4 = 80$ with $Z = 350$.

10.14 Divide the constraint by 2. The solution is $X_1 = 4$, $X_2 = X_3 = 0$ with $Z = 96$.

10.15 Use $(1 - X_2) = X_4$. The solution is $X_1 = X_4 = X_3 = 11/3$ with $Z = 1331/27 = 49.296$. We get $X_2 = 8/3$.

10.16 $X_1 = X_2 = X_3 = 3000$ with $Z = 27000000$.

10.18 The problem has several optima with $Z = 270$. The solutions are (2, 4, 4), (3, 3, 4), (3, 4, 3), (4, 2, 4), (4, 3, 3) and (4, 4, 2).

Chapter 11

11.3 Probability that the dentist is idle $p_0 = 0.1666$.
$N = 10$, $L_s = 3.29$.
If we consider two separate lines, We have $\lambda = 4$/hour and $\mu = 6$/hour. $L_q = 1.333$.
If we consider a single line with $\lambda = 8$/hour and $\mu = 6$/hour and $c = 2$. $L_q = 1.066$.
When $N = 8$ and we have two lines each with $\lambda = 4$/hour. $L_q = 0.6257$.
When $N = 8$ and we have one line with $\lambda = 8$/hour. $L_q = 0.809$.

11.4 $W_q = 0.1606$ hours and $L_s = 3.4278$. Two tellers are enough.

11.5 $p_0 = 0.2$, $N = 4$.

11.6 $L_q = 0.7022$. Therefore, three servers are enough. Probability that an entering person does not wait $= p_0 + p_1 + p_2 = 0.2974$.

11.7 $p_{12} = 0.0081$. If $\mu = 10$/hour and $N = 12$. $p_{12} = 0.0087$.

11.8 $p_0 + p_1 + p_2 + p_3 = 0.9875$. $1 - p_0 - p_1 - p_2 - p_3 - p_4 = 0000418$. Server utilization is 0.333.

11.9 Bulk booking counter: $L_s = 9$. If $N = 10$, $p_{10} = 0.05$. If $N = 15$, $p_{15} = 0.025$. Gain per year Rs. 1782. Regular Booking: $p_{40} = 0.0256$. If $N = 60$, $p_{60} = 0.0168$. Gain = Rs. 348.48 per year. If $N = 40$ and $c = 5$, $p_{40} = 0.0002$ and Gain = Rs. 1013/year.

11.10 Server utilization = 0.83333. Average people served/hour = 8.333. If $N = 10$, $p_{10} = 0.0311$ and 0.933 people leave the line without joining in three hours. $W_s = 0.338$ hours.

11.11 $W_s = 0.1021$ which is less than 10 minutes. If we consider three individual lines, we have $\lambda = 20/3$ per hour $\mu = 12$/hour and $W_s = 0.12$ hour. If $N = 10$ and $c = 3$ (common line) we have $L_q = 0.3505$.

Chapter 12

12.1 $X_1 = 166/78$, $X_2 = 25/13$, $Z = -16.5225$. The principal determinants of the H matrix are 6 and 39 indicating minimum.

12.2 $X_1 = 5$, $X_2 = 11/3$, $Z = 35.333$. The principal determinants of the H matrix are -4 and 13 indicating maximum.

12.3 $X_1 = 1.76$, $X_2 = 1.36$, $\lambda = 8.195$, $Z = 32.78$. The principal determinants of the H matrix indicate minimum.

12.4 $X_1 = 3.5$, $X_2 = 0.6$, $X_3 = 1.433$, $\lambda = 0$, $Z = 14.05$. The principal determinants of the H matrix indicate minimum.

12.5 $X_1 = 3/8$, $X_2 = 3/2$ with $Z = 2.8125$. We can verify that it is a maximum.

12.6 $X_1 = 5.166$, $X_2 = 3.833$ with $Z = 210.617$. We can verify that it is a minimum.

12.9 The solution $X_1 = 3.6$, $X_2 = 2.4$ is optimal.

Chapter 13

13.1 $Q = 2708.01$, $s = 92.31$ and $I_m = 923.19$. $T = 0.1083$ year = 1.299 months. $t_1 + t_4 = Q/P$ = 0.812 months. The remaining time of 0.4878 months is available for Nickson. We have not included the set-up time for Renolac in this calculation.

13.2 Model 1 – without shortages For rice $Q = 2236.07$, $TC = 8049.84$. For wheat, $Q = 2635.23$, $TC = 5692.1$. With shortage – For rice $Q = 2607.68$, $s = 690.27$, $TC = 6902.69$.

For wheat $Q = 2969.75$, $s = 605.16$, $TC = 5050.93$. When items are ordered together, $n = 16.43$. $TC = 9859.51$. If we reduce the orders by 10%, Q for rice = 2485.5 with $TC = 8094.90$ (no shortage) and for wheat $Q = 2928.08$ with $TC = 5723.73$. There is an increase of Rs. 76.69 in the total cost. If we consider equal number of orders and a total ordering quantity of 20000, $n = 2.75$, this gives $TC = 920460$ (including cost of item). TC at EOQ = 913741.94 (including cost of items). It is not advisable to accept the discount.

13.3 For item 1, $Q = 235.70$, $TC = 848.53$, $QC/2 = 2537$.
For item 2, $Q = 471.40$, $TC = 848.53$, $QC/2 = 2537$.
If we have budget 50% of 5074 = 2537, the order quantities reduce by 50%.
Now, for item 1, $Q = 117.85$, $TC = 1060.66$ and for item 2, $Q = 235.70$ and $TC = 1060.66$. There is an increase of 424.27 which is 25% compared to the situation without budget restriction.

13.4 The batch quantities are 1788.85, 1463.85, 1511.85 and 1770.28, respectively. The number of batches/year for each are 11.18, 12.29, 9.92 and 12.43 with a total of 45.82 batches/year with a set-up time of 229 hours. The time taken to produce the annual demand is 1973.33 hours and there is a total requirement of 2202.33 hours. There is an overtime requirement of 202.33 hours.

If overtime is not allowed, the batch quantities increase proportionately.

13.5 $Q = 275$ and $s = 25$. Duration of shortage $t_2 = 0.12$ months.

13.6 $D = 3650000$, $Q = 105000$ from which $1-D/P = 0.6$. This gives us $P = 9125000$/year.

13.7 The model is the same as Model 3, the production-consumption model. We have

$$Q^* = \sqrt{\frac{2Wk}{h[1-(W/T)]}}$$ and the periodicity $T = W/Q$.

13.8 $Q = 6235.38$, $s = 369.5$ from which $t_4 = 0.00433$, $t_1 = 0.03207$, $t_2 = 0.1283$ and $t_3 = 0.01026$.

13.10 $Q = 1.25$ from which $C_s = 24$, $s = 500$, $TC = $ Rs. 12000. It is advantageous to use the discount. Total cost (including item cost) at $EOQ = $ Rs. 1812000. At discount (for the same s) $TC = 1794250$.

13.11 At EOQ, $Q_1 = 1000$, $TC_1 = 6000$, $Q_2 = 948.68$, $TC_2 = 9486.83$. Total annual cost for two items including item cost = 1065486.83.

Using shortages, $Q_1 = 1036$, $TC_1 = 5786.91$, $Q_2 = 979.8$, $TC_2 = 9185.58$. Total annual cost for two items including item cost = 1064972.49.

We get a 1% discount if $Q_1 = 1100$ and $Q_2 = 1043.5$. $TC = 1054454.95$. It is advisable to avail the discount. (Assumption: s is calculated for a given Q).

Bibliography

(Some of the references cited are very old and are available as cross references from other sources that are provided here. The original references are provided to familiarize the reader with the historical development of the various topics/algorithms)

Ahuja, R.K., T.L. Magnanti, and J.B. Orlin, 1991, Some Recent Advances in Network Flows, *SIAM Review*, 33, 175–219

Ahuja, R.K., T.L. Magnanti, and J.B. Orlin, 1993, *Network Flows*, Prentice Hall, Englewood Cliffs, New Jersey.

Avis, D., and V. Chvatal, 1978, Notes on Bland's Pivoting Rule, *Mathematical Programming Study*, 8, 24–34.

Balas, E., 1965, An Additive Algorithm for Solving Linear Programs with Zero-One Variables, *Operations Research*, 13, 517–546.

Balinski, M.L., 1961, Fixed Cost Transportation Problems, *Naval Research Logistics Quarterly*, 8.

Balinski, M.L., and R.E. Gomory, 1964, A Primal Method for the Assignment and Transportation Problems, *Management Science*, 10, 578–593.

Bazaara, M.S., J.J. Jarvis, and H.D. Sherali, 1990, *Linear Programming and Network Flows*, 2nd ed., Wiley, New York.

Beale, E.M.L., 1955, Cycling in the Dual Simplex Algorithm, *Naval Research Logistics Quarterly*, 2, 269–276.

Beightler, C., D. Phillips, and D. Wilde, 1979, *Foundations of Optimization*, 2nd ed., Prentice Hall, New Jersey.

Bellmore, M. and G.L. Nemhauser, 1968, The Travelling Salesman Problem: A Survey, *Operations Research*, 16, 538–558.

Benders, J.F., 1962, Partitioning Procedures for Solving Mixed-Variables Programming Problems, *Numerische Mathematic*, 4, 238–252.

Bertsimas, D., and J.N. Tsitsiklis, 1997, *Introduction to Linear Optimization*, Athena Scientific, Belmont, Massachusetts.

Bertsekas, D.P., 1990, The Auction Algorithm for Assignment and Other Network Flow Problems: A Tutorial, *Interfaces*, 20, 133–149.

Bland, R.G., 1977, New Finite Pivoting Rules for the Simplex Method, *Mathematics of Operations Research*, 2, 103–107.

Boffey, T.B., 1982, *Graph Theory in Operations Research*, Macmillan Press, London.

Bradley, S.P., A.C. Hax, and T.L. Magnanti, 1977, *Applied Mathematical Programming*, Addison-Wesley, Reading, Massachusetts.

Charnes, A. and W.W. Cooper, 1954, The Stepping Stone Method for Explaining Linear Programming Calculations in Transportation Problems, *Management Science*, 1, 49–69.

Charnes, A., W.W. Cooper, J.K. DeVoe and D.B. Reinecke, 1968, A Goal Programming Model for Media Planning, *Management Science*, 14, B423–B430.

Charnes, A., W.W. Cooper, and E. Rhodes, 1981, Evaluating Program and Managerial Efficiency: An Application of Data Envelopment Analysis to Program Follow Through, *Management Science*, 27, 668–697.

Christofides, N., 1972, Bounds for the Travelling Salesman Problem, *Operations Research*, 20, 1044–1056.

Chvatal, V., 1983, *Linear Programming*, W.H. Freeman, New York.

Clarke, G., and J.W. Wright, 1964, Scheduling of Vehicles from a Central Depot to a Number of Delivery Points, *Operations Research*, 4, 568–581.

Dakin, R.J., 1965, A Tree Search Algorithm for Mixed Integer Problems, *Comput. Journal*, 8, 250–255.

Dantzig, G.B., 1963, *Linear Programming and Extensions*, Princeton University Press, New Jersey.

Dantzig, G.B., 1982, Reminiscences about the Origins of Linear Programming, *Operations Research Letters*, 1, 43–48.

Dantzig, G.B., and J.H. Ramser, 1959, The Truck Dispatching Problem, *Management Science*, 6, 80–91.

Dantzig, G.B., and P. Wolfe, 1960, The Decomposition Principle for Linear Programs, *Operations Research*, 8, 101–111.

Dijkstra, E., 1959, A Note on Two Problems in Connexion with Graphs, *Numerische Mathematik*, 1, 269–271.

Eastman, W.L., 1958, Linear Programming with Pattern Constraints, *Ph.D. Thesis*, Harvard University.

Edmonds, J., and E. Johnson, 1973, Matching, Euler Tours and the Chinese Postman, *Mathematical Programming*, 5, 88–124.

Edmonds, J., and R.M. Karp, 1972, Theoretical Improvements in Algorithmic Efficiency for Network Flow Problems, *Journal of the ACM*, 19, 248–264.

Erlenkolter, D., 1990, Ford Wtitman Harris and the Economic Order Quantity Model, *Operations Research*, 38, 937–946.

Fisher, M.L., 1981, The Lagrangean Relaxation Method for Solving Integer Programming Problems, *Management Science*, 27, 1–18.

Flood, M.M., 1956, The Travelling Salesman Problem, *Operations Research*, 4, 61–75.

Floyd, R.W., 1962, Algorithm:97 Shortest Path, *Communications of the ACM*, 5, 345.

Ford, L.R., and D.R. Fulkerson, 1962, *Flows in Networks*, Princeton University Press, New Jersey.

Garey, M.R., and D.S. Johnson, 1979, *Computers and Intractability: A Guide to the Theory of NP-Completeness*. W.H. Freeman, New York.

Garfinkel, R.S., and G.L. Nemhauser, 1972, *Integer Programming*, John Wiley & Sons, New York.

Gilmore, P.C., and R.E. Gomory, 1961, A Linear Programming Approach to the Cutting Stock Problem, *Operations Research*, 9, 849–859.

Gilmore, P.C., and R.E. Gomory, 1963, A Linear Programming Approach to the Cutting Stock Problem—Part II, *Operations Research*, 11, 863–888.

Golden, B., L. Bodin, T. Doyle, and W. Stewart Jr, 1980, Approximate Travelling Salesman Algorithms, *Operations Research*, 28, 694–721.

Gomory, R.E., 1963, All-integer Integer Programming Algorithm in J.F. Muth and G.L. Thompson (Eds.), *Industrial Scheduling*, Prentice-Hall, Englewood Cliffs, New Jersey.

Gomory, R.E., 2002, Early Integer Programming, *Operations Research*, 50, 78–81.

Hadley, G., 1962, *Linear Programming*, Addison-Wesley, Reading, Massachusetts.

Harris, F.W., 1913, How Many Parts To Make at Once, Factory, *The Magazine of Management*, 10, 135–136.

Held, M., and R.M. Karp, 1970, The Travelling Salesman Problem and Minimum Spanning Trees, *Operations Research*, 18, 1138–1162.

Hitchcock, F.L., 1941, The Distribution of a Product from Several Sources to Numerous Locations, *Journal of Mathematics and Physics*, 20, 224–230.

Holmes, R.A., and R.G. Parker, 1976, A Vehicle Scheduling Procedure based upon Savings and a Solution Perturbation Scheme, *Operational Research Quarterly*, 27, 83–92.

Hu, T.C., 1969, *Integer Programming and Network Flows*, Addison-Wesley, Reading, Massachusetts.

Karmarkar, N., 1984, A New Polynomial-time Algorithm for Linear Programming, *Combinatorica*, 4, 373–395.

Khachian, L.G., 1979, A Polynomial Algorithm in Linear Programming, *Soviet Mathematics Doklady*, 20, 191–194.

Klee, V., and G.J. Minty, 1972, How Good is the Simplex Algorithm? In O. Shinka (Editor), *Inequalities*, III, 159–175, Academic Press, New York.

Kolesar, P.J., 1966, A Branch and Bound Algorithm for the Knapsack Problem, *Management Science*, 13, 723–735.

Kotiah, T.C.T., and D.I. Steinburg, 1978, On the Possibility of Cycling with the Simplex Method. *Operations Research*, 26, 374–376.

Kruskal, J.B., 1956, On the Shortest Spanning Subtree of a Graph and the Travelling Salesman Problem, *Proceedings of the American Math. Society*, 7, 48–50.

Kuhn, H.W., 1955, The Hungarian Method for the Assignment Problem, *Naval Research Logistics Quarterly*, 2, 83–97.

Land, A.H., and A.G. Doig, 1960, An Automatic Method of Solving Discrete Programming Problems, *Econometrica*, 28, 497–520.

Lin, S., 1965, A Computer Solution of the Travelling Salesman Problem, *Bell Systems Tech. Journal*, 44, 2245–69.

Little, J.D.C., 1961, A Proof of the Queueing Formula L-λW, *Operations Research*, 9, 383–387.

Little, J.D.C., K.G. Murty, D.W. Sweeney, and C. Karel, An Algorithm for the Traveling Salesman Problem, *Operations Research*, 11, 972–989.

Marshall, K.T., and J.W. Suurballe, 1969, A Note on Cycling in the Simplex Method, *Naval Research Logistics Quarterly*, 16, 121–137.

Mathirajan, M., and B. Meenakshi, 2004, Experimental Analysis of Some Variants of Vogel's Approximation Method, *Asia Pacific Journal of Operations Research*, 21, 447–462.

Minieka, E., 1979, The Chinese Postman Problem for Mixed Networks, *Management Science*, 25.

Murty, K.G., 1983, *Linear Programming*, Wiley, New York.

Nemhauser, G.L., and L.A. Wolsey, 1988, *Integer and Combinatorial Optimization*, Wiley, New York.

Papadimitriou, C.H., and K. Steiglitz, 1982, *Combinatorial Optimization: Algorithms and Complexity*, Prentice Hall, Englewood Cliffs, New Jersey.

Prim, R.C., 1957, Shortest Connection Networks and Some Generalizations, *Bell Systems Technical Journal*, 36, 1389–1401.

Ravindran, A., D.T. Phillips, and J. Solberg, 1976, *Operations Research: Principles and Practice*, Wiley, New York.

Reinfeld and Vogel, 1958, *Mathematical Programming*, Prentice-Hall, Englewood Cliffs, New Jersey.

Taha, H.A., 2003, *Operations Research: An Introduction*, Prentice-Hall of India, New Delhi.

Wagner, H.M., 1959, On a Class of Capacitated Transportation Problems, *Management Science*, 5, 304–318.

Wagner, H.M., 1969, *Principles of Operations Research with Application to Managerial Decisions*, Prentice Hall, Englewood Cliffs, New Jersey.

Wilf, H.S., 1975, *Algorithms and Complexity*, Prentice Hall, Englewood Cliffs, New Jersey.

Wilson, R.H., 1934, A Scientific Routine for Stock Constant, *Harvard Business Review*, 13, 116–128.

Wolfe, 1959, The Simplex Method for Quadratic Programming, *Econometrica*, 27.

Yaspan, A., 1966, On Finding a Maximal Assignment, *Operations Research*, 14, 646–651.

Yen, J.Y., 1971, Finding the k-shortest Loopless Paths in a Network, *Management Science*, 17, 712–715.

Index

3-opt heuristic, 366

Additive algorithm, 249
Algebraic method, 23
All integer dual algorithm, 268
All integer primal algorithm, 271
Alternate optimum, 37
Artificial variable, 34
Assignment problem, 145
Auction algorithm, 154

Backordering, 456, 461
Balking, 426
Basic feasible solution, 23
Basic solution, 23
Basic variable, 23
Bender's partitioning algorithm, 279
Big M method, 32
Bland's rule, 41, 210
Bounded variables (Simplex algorithm), 180
Branch and Bound algorithm, 259, 266, 328, 355, 362, 363

Caterer problem, 15, 136
Chinese postman problem, 305, 371
Clarke-wright heuristic, 375
Column generation, 186
Complementary slackness, 66

Corner point, 22
Cutting plane algorithm, 253
Cutting stock problem, 186
Cycling, 39

Dantzig-Wolfe decomposition algorithm, 193
Decision variable, 2
Degeneracy, 35
Dijkstra's algorithm, 310
Dual, 61
Dual simplex algorithm, 71
Dynamic programming, 391

Economic order quantity, 456
Economic interpretation of the dual, 68
Either or constraint, 244
Eta matrix, 175
Eulerian (Graph), 305, 371

Fixed charge problem, 242
Floyd's algorithm, 316
Flow augmenting path, 320
Fundamental theorem of linear programming, 66

Gaussian elimination, 173
Gauss-Jordan method, 78
Goal programming, 202

Index

Gomory, 253
Graph theory, 301
Graphical method, 21

Hamiltonian, 305, 382, 383
Heuristics, 365
Heuristic using perfect matching, 368
Holmes-Parker method, 376
Hungarian algorithm, 151

Infeasibility, 38, 39
Integer programming, 238
Initialization, 30
Inventory models, 453
Inverse matrix, 172
Iteration, 35

Job shop scheduling problem, 243
Jockeying, 426

Kachian's algorithm, 213
Karmarkar's algorithm, 214
Klee and Minty problems, 211
K-Median problem, 241
Knapsack problem, 188, 405
Kruskal's algorithm, 309
Kuhn-Tucker conditions, 441

Lexicographic pivoting rule, 41
Lexicographic method of goal programming, 202
Lagrangeian multiplier, 466
Lagrangean relaxation, 318, 337
Little's algorithm, 365
Little's equation, 429

Main duality theorem, 66
Marginal value, 69
Matrix inversion, 172,
Max flow-Min cut theorem, 325
Maximum flow problem, 318

Minimization problem, 30
Minimum cost flow problem, 330
Minimum cost method, 107
Minimum spanning trees, 308, 367, 368
Minimum weighted matching, 373
Mixed integer programming, 276
Modified distribution method, 116
Multiple objectives, 202
Multicommodity flow problem, 342

Nearest neihgbourhood search, 365
Network problems, 301
Network simplex algorithm, 333
Nonbasic variable, 23
Nonlinear programming, 442
Northwest corner rule, 106
NP-completeness, 353

Objective function, 2
Optimality criterion theorem, 65
Optimal solution, 22

Pairwise interchange heuristic, 366
Penalty cost method, 108
Pivot column, 27
Pivot element, 27
Pivot row, 27
Primal, 61
Primal dual relationships, 63
Primal dual algorithm, 199,
Prim's algorithm, 308

Quadratic programming, 446
Queueing models, 425

Revised simplex algorithm, 171

Search algorithms, 370
Sensitivity analysis, 79
Shadow price, 92

Index

Shortest augmenting path algorithm, 326
Shortest path problem, 309
Simplex algorithm, 24
Slack variable, 23
Successive shortest paths, 316
Stage coach problem, 391
Stepping stone method, 112

Transportation problem, 104
Transshipment problem, 307, 335
Travelling salesman problem, 239, 350
Twice around the tree heuristic, 367
Two phase method, 32

Unboundedness, 36, 37

Vehicle routing problem, 373
Vogel's approximation method, 108

Weak duality theorem, 64

Yen's algorithm, 317

Zero-one problems, 246